ACTING
WORDS ON

An Integrated Rhetoric, Research Guide, Reader, and Handbook

THIRD EDITION

DAVID BRUNDAGE
Athabasca University

MICHAEL LAHEY
University of Alberta

Associate Contributors

Joyce Miller
Athabasca University, Yellowhead Tribal College

Adien Dubbelboer
Athabasca University

Pearson Canada
Toronto

Library and Archives Canada Cataloguing in Publication

Brundage, David
    Acting on words : an integrated rhetoric, research guide, reader, and handbook / David Brundage, Michael Lahey. —3rd ed.

Includes bibliographical references and index.
ISBN 978-0-13-212544-4

    1. Exposition (Rhetoric).   2. English language—Rhetoric—Textbooks.
3. College readers.   I. Lahey, Michael, 1954–   II. Title.

PE1408.B78 2011   808'.042   C2010-906310-4

ISBN 978-0-13-212544-4

Vice-President, Editorial Director: Gary Bennett
Editor-in-Chief: Ky Pruesse
Acquisitions Editor: David S. Le Gallais
Marketing Manager: Loula March
Developmental Editor: Rema Celio
Project Manager: Marissa Lok
Production Editor: Avivah Wargon
Copy Editor: Lisa Berland
Proofreaders: Cheryl Cohen, Kathryn J. Dean
Compositor: Aptara®, Inc.
Permissions Research: The Editing Company
Art Director: Julia Hall
Cover Designer: Miguel Angel Acevedo
Interior Designer: Geoff Agnew
Cover Image: Getty Images

4 5   15 14 13

Printed and bound in the United States of America.

For Professors Faith Guildenhuys, Tom Henighan, Robert Lovejoy, Robin MacDonald, and the entire English Faculty of Carleton University, 1969 to 1975. Their commitment to student-centred learning predated the term.
David Brundage

For Rosemary and Catherine Lahey, who know a thing or two about a thing or two.
Michael Lahey

Brief Contents

Contents

PART 2 THE RESEARCH
GUIDE 255

PART 3 THE READER 355

Section 2 Exploring Subjects 270

Section 3 Problems, Proposals, and Opinions 417

PART 4 THE HANDBOOK 449

Section 1 Forms (Including Nine Parts of Speech) 451

Preface

TO THE INSTRUCTOR

Since the first edition of this book was published seven years ago, we have been able to gather suggestions from dozens of instructors and, through them, thousands of students. We also received evaluations from hundreds more of our own students. Combined with numerous publisher-administered reviews and our own teaching experiences with the first and second editions, this process helped us to confirm and refine our vision for the third edition. We dedicated many hours of research and writing to the enrichments, not least of all a concerted effort to identify new student work that illustrates or responds to important parts of the text and the needs of our student reader. We revised most sections of the book, smoothing readability, inserting many new insights and references that followed publication of the previous editions, and generally striving to refresh this resource for us all. We believe the result should be a text that firmly preserves the strengths of the first and second editions while sharpening, expanding, and updating methods and content.

As we know, many students enter college and university programs needing to develop their reading, research, critical thinking, and analytical writing skills. None of these skills can be entirely separated from the others. Each plays a crucial role in academic success. Adding support to your encouragement of those skills, we have provided more basic classical theory (especially logos, pathos, and ethos) and illustration of persuasive appeal; more coverage of critical analysis and argument, with increased models of how the two combine in academic writing; more sample essays and essay outlines; more illustrations of MLA and APA documentation methods; more student research essays; and more consistent demonstration of academic documentation throughout all parts of the text. Many of you may wish to combine this text with Pearson's MyCanadianCompLab, which contains excellent guidance to reinforce the Research Guide as well as the Handbook of this text.

While increasing the focus on critical skills and styles, we have nevertheless retained and, in fact, enhanced our attention to more personal and journalistic forms. Over the years we have come increasingly to believe that for many students, academic writing is best learned through recognizing its location in the family of writing and through exploring personal voice and the basic issues inherent in all writing occasions. We do still address the personal essay and various forms influenced by the creative non-fiction of our time, but we do so with the clear intent of encouraging students to draw from their experiences, as critical writers.

We like to say that if writing is breathing out, then reading is breathing in. You will find even more expanded attention to effective reading in this edition of the text. We believe the updated Reader continues to offer a valuable range of issues to interest and challenge today's Canadian students. Many of the pieces, we think you will agree, represent achieved levels of literary craft. Others present accomplished student work within reach of diligent, motivated undergrads. Still others invite analysis of media purpose, style, and effect. The range of related concerns and styles throughout the Reader should offer much to serve your particular classroom interests and approaches.

We have continued to focus on the needs of Canadian students. However, we have aimed equally to serve those students who come from other countries or who will go on to other countries. Not least, we hope this text serves *you*, the most important resource of all in the mystery of learning—the constantly developing instructor.

Supplement

The following instructor supplement is available for download from the instructor section of Pearson Education Canada's online catalogue (vig.pearsoned.ca). See your local sales representative for details and access.

Instructor's Manual: The Instructor's Manual is an extensive in-depth guide to teaching with *Acting on Words*, Third Edition. It provides practical guidance on such important concerns as approaches to teaching; creating an effective syllabus; marking and student evaluation; dealing with grammar and mechanics; and English as a foreign language. It offers instructors examples of how to enhance the topics addressed in the text; sample summaries, a rhetorical table of contents for the Reader; and a comprehensive set of overheads, which can be used in the classroom in multiple ways.

TO THE STUDENT

Welcome to *Acting on Words*, a set of guidelines and sample readings aimed at easing and inspiring your ability to handle the challenges before you as an evolving scholar. The central goal of this book is to increase your success in all courses that require critical reading, research, and writing—which is to say, most if not all of the courses you will take at university.

Over many years of working with student writers—some of whom initially believe, often incorrectly, that they cannot write and do not like writing—we have heard many of the same concerns and questions. What does my instructor mean by "critical thinking"? I don't want to be critical of everything. What does my instructor mean by "employ rhetoric"? I don't want to sound like some phony politician. Why does your book tell us to place our thesis sentence at the end of the first paragraph when not that many readings in the Reader of this book seem to do that? What's wrong with using Wikipedia? It's the first source I find through Google. And what's "academic documentation style," anyway? I never learned any grammar terms or how to parse a sentence—how am I going to deliver the correct sentences and punctuation my program says it requires? Suggesting brief answers to these questions may be the best way to introduce you to this book and the potential it has to enrich your academic career and, we hope, your life in general.

Let's start with the first question about "critical thinking." Helping you to understand and apply critical thinking within the academy is the central purpose of your first-year writing, communications, or English course. It is therefore the main purpose of this text. As we explain in more detail in Chapter 16, the word "critical" in university usage does *not* mean fault-finding or hostile censure. In their trenchant book *They Say, You Say: The Moves That Matter in Academic Writing*, Gerald Graff and Cathy Birkenstein summarize the essence of critical thinking at university: it is a matter of recognizing what is being said on a particular issue of importance and then adding something useful of your own to the discussion. They say . . . and then you say . . . . This basic operation sums up a majority of work at the university. Thinking critically requires command of the methods covered in this text—how to summarize, how to analyze the language of a text when its main assertions do not appear obvious, how to evaluate the assertions of a text, how to find and evaluate sources of further information on the topic, how to reach your own position—what *you* say—and, finally, how to organize and write an effective, persuasive essay that contributes your views. The various parts of this book, then, all serve this central need to understand and practise critical thinking and writing.

"Rhetoric" in its original, classical sense—as we use it here—does not mean dishonest language but rather *the art of language*. This art functions at the level of words, sentences, paragraphs, and complete structures. If you decide to explain a point by using a comparison, you are applying rhetoric. If you recognize that an essay assignment calls for the third person point of view and a general or even formal level of diction, you are employing rhetorical awareness. While this book and the course it serves aim ultimately to strengthen your critical thinking and writing, attention to the basic dynamics of writing—covered in Chapters 1 to 7—and attention to the various patterns of writing—covered in Chapters 10 to 14—should help you sharpen the rhetorical tools you need to inform your analytical (i.e., critical) writing. Increasing your command of rhetoric, therefore, does not shanghai you onto a ship of "phony politicians." It simply awakens and intensifies your awareness of the nature and effects of language. It helps you to use words for things that matter to you—something that should continue to enrich your life in the long term.

In the short term, by illuminating the art of rhetoric, this text should help you to write effective essays for course purposes. To do that means considering that your instructor, who is most likely overworked, hopes your paper will quickly demonstrate that it has a central point to make and will go on to make it. In Chapter 6 we discuss the parts of a complete thesis statement, and we recommend placing that statement at the end of your opening paragraph. This formula helps you to ensure your paper is on track and remains on track. This positioning of your thesis reassures your instructor that you have come to a clear, interesting, critical position, one that will focus your entire essay. Our advice to you concerning thesis elements and location has to do with the situation you are in as an undergraduate writer. It is a matter of adapting to the occasion, to your reader, and to your purpose. It doesn't mean that everything you go on to write for all readers on all occasions will need a thesis at the end of the first paragraph (though that technique is surprisingly versatile!).

Nor will you be expected to limit your reading—your search for further sources of information—to other undergraduate essays. While we recommend that you hone complete, precise thesis statements in your own essays, you will surely encounter written and spoken material that does not always present an explicit thesis statement at the end of the first paragraph. You will need to develop your ability to find the main ideas in many different styles of writing. You may well go on to explore philosophers, anthropologists, psychologists, physicists, literary theorists, linguists, and so on. Our Reader therefore reflects a wide range of styles, from classical and highly academic to personal, evocative and journalistic. Much of the sample writing in the Reader (as opposed to that in the Rhetoric) is not purely or even highly academic, and much of it lacks the formal approach to thesis placement that we recommend in Chapter 6 and demonstrate in sample student essays throughout the book. Your awareness of academic style, however, is increased by recognizing its distinctions from other forms. The Reader represents not only a taste of academic style, but a taste of broader writing styles, from personal to highly analytical and argumentative. Accordingly, Chapters 15, 16, and 17 are specially designed to increase your "higher-level" reading skills. The same degree of questioning that we encourage in those chapters on reading should guide your thinking as you search for additional information on assigned topics.

This, of course, brings us to the subject of research. Is a given source of information written by someone who really understands the subject? Has the information been reviewed and edited by other experts? Has it been properly tested? Wikipedia, for example, is a reader-generated source: its entries are not approved by editors expert in the many fields in question. While studies suggest that Wikipedia may—surprisingly—be more accurate and comprehensive than some critics imagine, Wikipedia still has no guarantee of reliability. Anyone can add to its contents—how do we know that the contributors are experts and have taken care to be completely accurate? As part of your critical thinking at university, you will increase your ability to find and evaluate useful, reliable sources of further information. Various parts of this text, particularly the Research Guide, present the reasoning behind research methods and how those methods work. It takes time, patience, and practice to gain full confidence in handling "academic documentation style"—in other words, *to acknowledge your sources*—but the basics are much simpler than you may think. Much success comes by setting aside your initial doubts and uncertainties and simply plunging into the basics. Cite a valuable source or two in your first essay and you are already on your way.

We can also reassure you that while taking control of grammar and punctuation does, in many cases, demand effort and patience, the task can usually be accomplished by the end of your course through careful, systematic use of the Handbook. Our Fifteen Common Errors approach allows you and your instructor to find the main points of grammar that may be most in need of attention in your work. Perhaps just three or four of the common errors will apply in your case. After diagnosing your current knowledge and skills, you can pursue the recommended background information and upgrading for each specific common correction.

If you are like many students (and if we are honest, we are all students), a crucial step forward is to work on becoming an *active* participant in your own learning by defining for yourself what university scholarship really entails: thinking and participating actively in your learning, finding small important details, understanding processes, and seeing connections to a bigger picture. Your course and this book may be considered analogous to a surfboard: it takes much basic understanding and repeated effort to climb aboard in the right stance, but once you have done that, the experience truly begins.

ACKNOWLEDGMENTS

Many talented and dedicated people have contributed their time and efforts to *Acting on Words*. We would like to thank them all.

Writing instructor Karen Overbye of Mount Royal College wrote material on logos, pathos, and ethos and portions of Chapter 17, "Rhetorical Analysis." ESL coordinator Veronica Baig of Athabasca University contributed Appendix A, "Twelve Verb Tenses," and Appendix B, "Irregular Verbs," to the Handbook. Professor Rebecca Cameron of DePaul University in Chicago wrote major portions of "how-to" instructions in Chapter 13 as well as research and documentation material that has been integrated throughout the Research Guide. Professor Jolene Armstrong, Athabasca University, provided several introductions to selections in the Reader. John Ollerenshaw, Managing Editor, Centre for Learning Design and Development, Athabasca University, reviewed our earlier version of Documentation (now part of the Research Guide). A number of valuable Reader contributions, retained from the first two editions, were made by Lisa Cameron, also with support of the Centre for Language and Literature, Athabasca University. Contributing as well to the Reader, first edition, was Robbie Chernish.

Shamim Datoo, formerly with the Department of English at the University of Alberta, gave generously of her time in the preparation of parts of the first edition manuscript. Joyce Miller worked extensively on permissions for the first edition and made important contributions to the Reader on all editions. Adien Dubbelboer also made significant contributions to this edition. Shari Mitchell contributed manuscript assistance.

We thank the fine tutorial staff of Athabasca University's English 255 Introductory Composition as well. Their numerous suggestions have made a significant contribution. William Aguiar, Blue Quills First Nations College, offered particularly helpful recommendations for Chapter 16, "Critical Analysis and Evaluation." Sharren Patterson of Mount Royal College and Donald McMann of Grant MacEwan University similarly provided valuable manuscript advice.

Kelly Torrance made this book possible with essential support and understanding in the formative stages. It was further propelled along by editor Lisa Berland, who has returned, to our delight, on this edition. Former Acquisitions Editor Marianne Minaker enabled the next step by establishing the book with Pearson. We are grateful for the ongoing professional support of Developmental Editor Rema Celio, Supervising Editor Avivah Wargon, and Acquisitions Editor David S. Le Gallais.

On a personal note, Michael Lahey wishes to add his thanks to the following instructors for their past support, scholarly guidance, and professional inspiration: Professors Lynn Penrod and Mark Simpson of the University of Alberta; Professors Stanley Cowan, John Fraser, Lisa Bugden, Bruce Greenfield, Ron Huebert, and Victoria Rosenberg of Dalhousie University; Professors Ann J. Abadie, Donald Kartiganer, and Jay Watson of the Center for Southern Culture, University of Mississippi; Prof. Martin Kriezwirth of McGill University; and Dr. Barney Edwards of Manawagonush Institute.

Finally, we are greatly indebted to our many reviewers, who offered wonderful advice and suggestions at various stages of the manuscript's development: Brent Cotton, Georgian College; Deborah Delorme-D'Ulisse, Seneca College; Colleen Mahy, George Brown College; Jennifer Payson, The University of British Columbia, Okanagan Campus; Jennifer Read, Capilano University, and Trisha Yeo, George Brown College.

Part 1

THE RHETORIC

INTRODUCTION

RHETORIC, in the classic sense, refers to the art of using language: it is the craft of shaping spoken and written persuasions. By "persuasions" we mean to suggest the classical idea that all successful speeches and essays affect us as the writer intended: the works deepen our knowledge and understanding, motivate us to action, and possibly even exert some nurturing magic within. Accomplished rhetoric persuades us that the author knows the subject well and has something interesting to add to it. The writer combines knowledge of the subject with logic, feeling, and ethical awareness in proper proportion relative to the purpose and intended audience of the essay or speech.

Successful writers, amateur and professional alike, invariably work through three basic stages: outlining, drafting, and revising. We have therefore organized our Rhetoric to suggest those three stages.

Before starting the applied process itself, which begins with Section 2, "Starting the Journey," you may first review the basic concepts and terms in Section 1, "Reviewing the Basics." In Chapter 1 we invite you to enter into the state of mind of a writer and consider what writing *is.* Remembering the communicative purpose and special demands of writing is often all you need to do to make the best strategic decisions on your own. In light of that preliminary reflection, we move on to explain the purpose of basic matters of tone, logic, paragraph skills, standard essay structure, thesis statements, and introductions and conclusions. This part of the Rhetoric serves as preliminary review, reference, and guidance according to individual need.

Section 2, by contrast, is more applied and active: it presents you with the reality of starting an essay of your own. How do you find your ideas on the topic and manoeuvre your way as efficiently and effectively as you can from pre-writing activities to drafting? We stress the value of outlining, in accordance with a sound knowledge of basic essay structure and thesis statements (reviewed in detail in Section 1), and the value of drafting according to one or more of the patterns described in Section 3, "Forms to Draft By." Like Section 1, Section 3 can be used according to individual need.

Section 4, "Oral Presentations," deals with the concerns of that special form of communication, while Section 5, "Completing the Journey: Revision," reinforces the fact that successful writing depends on revision. Section 5 offers a practical, three-step model to guide that final stage of your process. The model refers you strategically to various pertinent chapters of the Rhetoric as well as to other parts of the text.

For clarity of presentation, we cover research and citation skills in a separate part of this text, the Research Guide. Unless you are already a whiz at summarizing what you read, you should study Chapter 15 of the Rhetoric, "The Summary," in conjunction with your use of the Research Guide. Getting a good start on any research required for your essay occurs at the pre-writing stage, so you will often use the Research Guide in conjunction with the Rhetoric.

Underscoring the importance of researching topics, Chapter 8, "Ways of Starting," and Chapter 9, "Outlining," provide reminders to begin your search for information right away as you explore any new topic. The key to meaningful research is how you evaluate (think critically) about what you find. Indeed, post-secondary work in general rests on critical thinking, a matter covered in Chapter 3, "More about Logic," and Chapter 16, "Critical Analysis and Evaluation," and, we hope, demonstrated throughout all parts of the Rhetoric.

In the following pages, then, from basic concepts and terms to applied process and standard patterns, you should find all you need to craft thoughtful, effective essays and oral presentations.

Section 1

Reviewing
the Basics

INTRODUCTION

Consider how, when someone talks to you in person, a lot of the communication may depend on facial features, body language, and tone of voice. Furthermore, when somebody tells you something in person, you can ask questions and receive feedback. None of this happens in the case of a written communication. The reader sees no facial features, hears no voice, receives no further answers to questions—unless the writer, through method, art, and magic, provides those otherwise missing ingredients.

When you consider this basic reality, you can appreciate why writing effectively requires special care and expertise. The following review of the basics of writing is intended to provide you with the techniques, the artistry, and, yes, the magic needed to transform marks on a page into meaningful conversation for your reader. You will be able to consider crucial terms and concepts such as reader awareness, purpose, tone, logic, paragraph craft, standard essay structure, and thesis statements—basics that should serve you well in the practical journey of writing an effective academic essay.

With these basics refreshed and perhaps deepened in your mind, you should be ready to choose a topic and plunge into the practical steps laid out in the opening chapter of Section 2, "Ways of Starting."

Chapter 1
What Is Writing?

Writing is both the act of putting thoughts on pages for the purpose of communication and the resulting text that intends to communicate ideas. The key words here are "communication" and "communicate." For writing to be effective, the writer needs to be thoroughly aware of the topic or issue under discussion as well as being aware of the intended reader(s) and, by implication, of the reason for the communication.

READER AWARENESS

Effective writers form a strong sense of their intended readers: What do the intended readers know about the subject already? What more should they know? What methods of expressing that information will be most comprehensible for them? Writing instructors teach "reader awareness" because unless you consider your intended readers, you may not engage, inform, or persuade them, even though what you have written seems clear and successful to you. What words mean to you may not be what they mean to readers.

Your Reader

A good person for you to consider as the primary intended reader for many of your university papers is another course student, one who is keenly interested and active in the process of learning. This may simply be an imagined, idealized student, not necessarily one actual person. Let's hope that most or even all of your peers in the course are, like you, interested and active.

However, you and your instructor may wish to set up different writing "occasions" for some of your assignments: that is, you may wish to imagine that you are writing to a particular audience (perhaps outside the university) for a particular purpose. This increased or specialized attention to reader awareness can be an excellent means of growing as a writer.

Word Connotations

The problem of words meaning different things to different people can be best appreciated in the case of certain words that tend to be loaded with strong emotional connotations. The *Nelson Canadian Dictionary* defines *connotation* as "[a]n idea or meaning suggested by or associated with a word." This association, however, need not be the meaning given by the dictionary. To test out this idea, try the following exercise.

PRACTICE
Word Connotations

Draw a line across a piece of paper and mark the left end of the line as minus 5. Mark the right end of the line as plus 5. Place a zero at the middle point of the line. Your line now represents a spectrum, from −5 to +5. Now read the following list of eight words and rate each along the spectrum, according to how you feel about each word. If the word has extremely good connotations for you, give it plus 5. If it has extremely bad connotations for you, give it minus 5. Be as precise as you can in placing each word on the spectrum, but trust your initial emotional response to tell you where the word should be. Here are the exercise words:

Lawyer
Politics

Marriage
Alcohol
College
Tradition
Peacekeepers
Banks

With classmates and your instructor, explore the range of negative to positive responses that may occur through this exercise. Consider and discuss different writing situations that might present a writer with readers who harbour strong connotative meanings of words that vary from the denotative meanings. Consider and discuss various strategies a writer might adopt to avoid distancing and possibly losing such readers.

Since we have been discussing reader awareness, and rhetoric as a response to that awareness, now is a good time to consider more formal (and classical) theory on how language and writing work.

PERSUASIVE APPEALS: LOGOS, PATHOS, AND ETHOS

As you will see from exploring the different sections of our Rhetoric and Reader, writing falls into a wide range of categories—and often one piece of writing stretches across the borders of two or more categories, incorporating certain characteristics of each—but all effective writing shares the characteristic of being somehow *persuasive*. **Personal and evocative writing** persuades the reader that the writer really lived these experiences, really understands the events, characters, and places described, really feels the emotions and insights expressed. **Expository writing** persuades the reader through detailed explaining that there is a valuable way to understand the topic; effective exposition convinces the reader that the writer truly knows the topic and that the topic is significant. Successful **argumentative writing** persuades the reader, while recognizing opposing views, to consider the merits of the author's proposed way of dealing with a certain issue or controversy. In short, all effective writing, in its own ways according to its own special purposes and audiences, *persuades* a reader of its value.

Classical rhetoric (the art of composition) refers to persuasive attributes as *appeals*: that is, the writing, *in some sense,* reaches out and contacts the reader. Understanding these appeals and how they are used—sometimes in combination—can benefit both your own writing and your ability to recognize the strengths and weaknesses in the written persuasions of others. To help you consider the logical, emotional, and ethical dynamics that operate when we read or write, the following sections give these dynamics a little more traditional, theoretical context.

Logos

Logos literally means "word" in Greek and refers to the authority of the word, or logic. All logical arguments depend on the writer's (or speaker's) judicious use of logos, or logical appeal. This means the development of your argument must be logical, and you must provide evidence for your points. For two basic forms of reasoning, see "Induction" and "Deduction" as well as "Premises and Conclusions" (Chapter 3, pp. 24, 25). Stephen Toulmin's argument model (discussed in Chapters 3, 15 and 18) provides a "modern" approach to detecting and applying forms of reasoning. All the methods of essay development that you may look at in Chapters 11 to 14, especially comparison-contrast and cause-effect, can serve as logical and rhetorical strategies to help you convince your readers of the strength of your argument. Note that it is important to examine any personal examples with logic, because personal examples may be emotionally compelling but not always logically sound, as you will be reminded in Chapter 3 (in reference to various logical fallacies) and in Chapter 4 in a discussion of "warm" and "cool" appeals.

Your evidence must be sound; it must be accessible to testing and verification. Evidence may take the form of facts, statistics (bearing in mind that statistics involve varying levels of interpretation in their presentation), primary sources (eye-witness testimony, legal transcripts, ledgers, and other original pieces of evidence), and secondary sources (such as analysis by experts). Refer to the Research Guide's section on primary and secondary sources (Section 1), and especially to Section 2 on evaluating sources.

We have discussed logos first because as a college or university student, you will be expected, above all, to handle the logical demands of your assignments. As we explain below, careful attention to logos also helps you gain an increased degree of personal credibility—or ethos—on a topic that may be still relatively new to you.

Pathos

Pathos literally means "suffering" in Greek, but in the more modern sense, it refers to appeals that may trigger a variety of emotions: sympathy or empathy, fear, sense of loss or grief, and even anger, to name the most common. An argument that relies mostly on emotional appeal may be compelling in the short term, but any genuine persuasion demands logical evidence as well. Ideally, pathos can add to logos so that the audience is "touched" by an argument. For example, an argument for Canada to send more aid to countries in need might begin with a sad story of a needy family. When that argument is then backed up with logical appeals—to equality, ethics, and justice—it will garner greater creditability from the readers. Pathos by itself, however, is a weak hand to draw upon for the long term.

Certain writers may deliberately give pathos free rein to manipulate readers without giving them recourse to complex, balanced thought. Indeed, pathos is a key device in propaganda techniques: methods intended to sway an audience by escaping the demands of logos. See the discussion of logical fallacies in Chapter 3, especially fallacies 7 to 10, for problems that occur from the misuse of pathos. Significantly, one reason that academic writing has traditionally favoured the third-person viewpoint is that by removing the "I" from your text, you are encouraged to shift your perception from personal focus and emotions to the more broadening logos that your topic requires.

Used moderately, emotional appeal is powerful, representing what we describe in Chapter 4, "Paragraph Skills," as *warm appeals*. The main rhetorical methods you will use to create emotional appeal are description (particularly figurative language) and narration, methods that draw the reader to your topic. These are discussed in Chapter 10 (starting on p. 97) and Chapter 12 (starting from the top of p. 114). Description and narration need not be confined to personal writing or fictional forms but can contribute in significant ways to analytical and formal argumentative forms.

Nonetheless, as mentioned in the previous discussion of word connotations, you need to be sensitive to the "trigger" potential of many emotionally loaded words and descriptions. These can result in undesired emotional distraction. The tone recommended for most university analysis and formal argumentation is *moderate*, meaning that any pathos has to be careful and controlled.

Ethos

Ethos means, literally, "character" in Greek. Some texts explain ethos as *ethical appeal*, meaning that the writer must have a demonstrated right to speak on the topic. Often this means finding a credible angle from which to view the topic, an angle that does not claim more authority than the writer really has, yet one that also brings something informative to the subject. On certain subjects, we simply lack sufficient knowledge and credibility; in such instances, we are best to hold silent, at least until we have a little further learning. Writers sometimes speak of the need to "earn" their material. A creator of virtual-reality technology has probably earned more right to author a book called *You Are Not a Gadget* than has an English professor with no hands-on computing science experience. Indeed, most discussions—whether evaluating technology, running a successful business, or travelling on a shoestring—pose immediate demands for credibility. We need to anticipate those expectations.

Many students worry, understandably, that because they are taking introductory subjects, they are only junior researchers, not "experts." They fear that they therefore have no ethos. You can, however, establish your authority by showing effective use of logos and by showing that you have consulted a variety of sound sources of evidence, especially those of experts, those who have established ethos. In most respects as a student writer, your use of logos and pathos (developed through research) will establish your ethos. You can become knowledgeable. You also must be seen as trustworthy; the audience should not feel manipulated or lied to. Be aware of the attitude toward your audience, your subject, and even yourself that comes across in your argument. Carelessness, for example, reveals your indifference to your work, your reader, and your grade.

You can build and maintain strong ethos through correctness. You need to be fair and careful in your use of language and acknowledgment of source material. For example, presenting the ideas of others as your own (i.e., plagiarism) immediately discredits you and therefore your argument. See the Research Guide on evaluating, integrating, and documenting sources. Choose valid sources and use them correctly: summarize, paraphrase, and quote accurately.

ORAL TRADITION AND MYTHOS

Oral cultures practise different ways of knowing from those of Western colleges and universities. For some, it is not necessarily "true" to say that you must provide empirical evidence and apply a logically demonstrated hypothesis. Oral cultures often view scientific method not as an infallible or superior system but as a *story,* one that reveals the presumptions of those who practise it. And maybe this view has a point. As UBC professor William Rees observes, "The assertion that ours is a myth-free culture may actually be one of our most important cultural myths" (9). The oral way of mind, while often in greater command of logos than some realize, subordinates the pragmatic, scientific mode of being to **mythos,** a Greek word meaning "story" or "legend." The story happened but continues to happen. Mythos is not meant to be historical in a sense of literal accuracy. As Karen Armstrong observes, this word derived from the verb *muein,* "to close the eyes or the mouth" (720). It is thus related to mystery, mysticism, darkness, and silence, a manner of knowing through unknowing, a mode of transmitting values through art and imaginative narrative. While oral tradition and mythos lie mainly outside the concerns of this book, they are worth remembering. Chapter 10 on the personal essay discusses narration and description, staples of storytelling and therefore techniques that can be used to appeal to mythos as well as to pathos and logos.

PRACTICE

Write a one-paragraph summary of some of the main ideas you find expressed by this chapter in reply to the question "What is writing?" You may wish to look over Chapter 15, "The Summary," before you start.

Works Cited

Armstrong, Karen. *The Case for God.* Detroit: Gale, 2009. Print.

Rees, William. "Science, Cognition, and Public Policy." *Academic Matters.* Apr.–May 2008: 9-12. Print.

Chapter 2

Characteristics of Writing Tones

Purpose is *why* you are writing and audience is *to whom* you are writing. Tone is *how* you handle your writing. More specifically, tone is the attitude you take to your purpose, topic, and reader—to your interweaving of logos, pathos, and ethos.

A RANGE OF TONES ADAPTED TO AUDIENCE AND PURPOSE

Depending on your audience and purpose, your tone may range widely from informal to formal: from blue jeans to a business suit to a scholar's hat.

Individual words, sentences, paragraphs, and overall construction of these building blocks all contribute to your tone. This may surprise you, since we often think of tone as primarily auditory, something we hear. When you write, however, you translate the emotion and content of your spoken voice, expressed through sound, into the same values expressed visually in marks and patterns on a page. If you do this well, you approximate (insofar as possible) the strengths of face-to-face communication in your text.

Three Main Levels of Tone Related to Occasion

Notwithstanding infinite variations of tone, three broad categories deserve our recognition: **informal, general,** and **formal.** None of these is "suitable" or "unsuitable," "sincere" or "dishonest" in isolation. The key is whether tone respects the reader and the needs of the writing occasion while also demonstrating a true connection to the writer.

Three Main Levels of Tone Related to Purpose

Personal or "creative" writing tends to use an informal approach. The tone of such writing is generally considered **evocative** or **expressive.** Its purpose is to connect emotionally with the reader, to effect some change, to stimulate an imaginative experience, perhaps at the unconscious as well as conscious level. Writing that seeks to inform or raise awareness, in the manner of textbooks, for example, uses an **expository** tone. Its purpose is to *inform*. Writing that seeks to alter thinking and even incite a call to action is **persuasive** in tone. The purpose of such writing is to *change* how the reader thinks or acts in relation to a certain issue.

On pages 18 to 21 of this chapter, we illustrate four somewhat differently shaded writing tones, each resulting from a specific academic occasion and purpose.

TONES CHART—A CRUCIAL REFERENCE

Refer to the following Characteristics of Writing Tones chart with frequency and care: it may well be one of the most useful resources in this text. It will guide you to the characteristics of writing tone suitable to your reader and purpose for everything you write. For handy future reference, this chart is also reproduced on the inside back cover of this book.

Characteristics of Writing Tones

Elements	Informal	General	Formal
Diction	Everyday, plain, concrete, colloquial, slang, casual, contractions, shorter words	Assumes a high school education, mixes concrete and abstract, mixes shorter and longer words	Assumes a higher level of education or training, abstract, technical jargon, longer words
Sentences	Short, simple, some fragments, some comma splices, frequent dashes	Nearly all complete, fragments very carefully controlled, somewhat longer, balances simple and combined structures, fewer dashes, and few (if any) sentence fragments or comma splices	Mostly longer and combined structures, no fragments, few dashes, no comma splices
Paragraphs	Mostly short, casual, no rigorous use of topic sentences, implied rather than explicitly stated transitions	Some longer, more fully developed, more deliberate use of topic sentences and explicit transitions within and between paragraphs	Mostly long, fully developed, consistent use of explicit transitions, complex content organized by clear patterns, firm topic sentences
Supporting details	"Warm"—anecdotes, personal descriptions, more appeal to emotion than to logic (see Chapter 4)	Includes some "cooler" proofs—data, studies, logical formulations (see Chapter 4)	"Cool"—empirical data and structured logical formulations, academic authorities and references

(continued)

Organization (or Structure)	Casual, spontaneous, loose, lacking explicit connectors, mainly based on emotion	Deliberate, tighter, using some explicit connectors, reflecting one or more methods, blending emotion and logic, cause and effect	Highly controlled, explicitly connected throughout, tight application of patterns, mostly intellectual
Purposes	More often personal, blending of purposes but often not sustained	Some personal, expository, and argumentative, combined and somewhat controlled	Expository—often analytical, argumentative
Typical uses	Personal letters, diaries, journals, some fiction, much advertising, some newspapers	Many newspapers and magazines, business writing, many expository books and articles, fiction	Academic writing, most textbooks, scientific writing, legal documents

WORDS: CONTEXTS AND ORIGINS

Levels of diction are related to cultural contexts, whether the speaker is addressing friends or strangers, one group of people or another, and so on. Where a word comes from in the long, complex history of English also affects tone.

Recognizing Colloquial Language and Jargon

In capturing the best tone for each writing occasion, you may need to treat two types of diction with particular care: **colloquial language** and **jargon.** *Colloquial* means "spoken together." Language at this level comprises the informal words we use when speaking or writing to friends or colleagues. In a more formal piece directed at an audience that you do not know well, you will find your readers take you less seriously if you use such language. This impression increases if you use slang (nonstandard "in" talk). Hollywood film noir classics have frozen in time the American slang of certain eras—words such as *heater* for "gun" or *dame* for "woman." Colloquial language and slang can convey vitality but also tend to date quickly, and they may puzzle certain readers unfamiliar with the culture involved. Such terms serve various writing purposes, but are not suitable for academic writing.

Adding to the problems of colloquial language, some novice essay writers tend to spell words in the way that they hear them. They may think that the instructor has said "I am not bias," but what she really said, according to standard grammar, is "I am not bias**ed**." For scholarly audiences, you should also avoid contractions (*can't* instead of *cannot* and so on). While overly informal words create problems for academic purposes, so do words that sound needlessly formal (jargon).

Jargon is trendy specialized language (professional catchphrases) used by and for a narrow audience of readers who share a great deal of common technical knowledge. When used with discretion, jargon effectively communicates complex knowledge within specialized fields. It has an important purpose, but often is used simply because of elitism. As an example of needless jargon, suppose that as writing-text authors we referred to linking words (such as *and, so, but*) as "linguistic coherence devices." We might sound much more elevated than a plain writer if we did, but alas our editors would not allow it. Resisting the tendency to show off in this way will gain you considerable respect and gratitude from those readers more interested in the value of what you write than in taking stock of how important and sophisticated you may appear. Since the academy—college or university—is not a perfect place, it already contains a good deal of needless jargon.

Sifting through opaque shoptalk in pursuit of constructive critical analysis can be frustrating. If a technical phrase seems crucial in your communication to a general audience, then define it for your reader. But ask yourself seriously if a certain word or phrase of jargon (yours or that of another writer) is necessary. Would a plain, everyday word express the thought more clearly and simply? Often it would.

For an amusing look at how academic pretension may be manipulated to create an appearance of importance in place of clarity, see Daniel Kies's web page on "Grammatical Manipulation of the Audience."

Consider Word Origins: Consult Your Dictionary

Origin is another important aspect of words: What are the linguistic roots of the word and what associations do these create? Words of Germanic, Latin, Greek, Norse, and French origin have different tones and connotations, in part because of the differing roles played by the various root languages in British history.

Your dictionary, if you have chosen it carefully for college and university purposes, will tell you the etymology (history) of most words. Some reference books, like the 1998 *Nelson Canadian Dictionary,* provide valuable expanded histories for many entries. English has incorporated words from hundreds of other languages, adding the textures and tones of those cultures. In today's age of information, globalization, and specialist languages, this multilingual nature of English continues to increase—yet its mixed heritage can be traced back to its earliest years. Gaining a sense of this history will help you recognize associations that contribute to the stylistic effects of diction.

SENTENCES AND TONE

Sentence length may indicate a writer's sense of the reader's available time as much as it does the complexity of the writer's ideas. Short sentences imply that the reader wants the information in as brief a time as possible. Magazine articles use sentences that are a little longer than those in bus advertisements, because a magazine article can usually be read at a more leisurely pace. Sentences in academic articles are even longer because the audience is expected to think hard about the information and construct a reasoned and layered response. Sentence length is therefore often a prime indicator of what you expect your reader to do with your information.

It is important to recognize that tone and its resultant meanings are heavily influenced by patterns—rhythms, repetitions, variations—and these are embodied in the types of sentences you use. Whether we call patterns and rhythms *paralinguistic* or *visceral* or some other term, the important idea to recognize is that style helps to express meaning, and style is much more than the denotative dimension of your words.

Impact Points in Sentences

To reflect a little further on the important contribution of craft to style and tone, consider the shape of the simplest standard sentence in English.

The standard English sentence moves from subject to verb.

In this typical sentence, the subject "sentence" (preceded by two descriptive words) is immediately followed by the verb "moves." The sentence both states and demonstrates a basic fact of English sentence structure. With this pattern in mind, consider the following rhetorical principle: **Words at the beginning and end of the sentence tend to draw the most attention and thus have the most impact.** In their workshops on communication, Eric McLuhan and Roger Davies refer to a "Bermuda Triangle" of sentences (based on the popular idea that somewhere over Bermuda is a portal into another dimension, swallowing up passing aircraft and the like).

As you can see in Figure 2.1, the underlined words at the beginning and end are the ones that stand out and prove memorable. Guided by this principle, experienced playwrights tend to make sure that important ideas occur at the beginnings and ends of speeches, even if some manipulation of usual speaking style is needed to achieve this effect. The same words will have greater or lesser impact depending on where they are placed in your sentences (and paragraphs). Remember to use the impact points of sentences and overall structure to maximum effect.

End Terms Qualify Previous Ones: Word Order Is Meaning

A closely related principle of word placement is that **final terms qualify or define previous ones.** As an example, the phrase "beggars and kings" suggests that

Figure 2.1
The "Bermuda
Triangle" of
Sentences

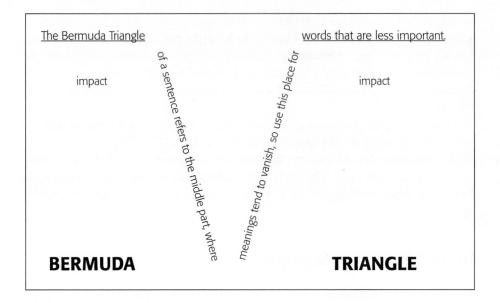

The Bermuda Triangle   words that are less important.

impact   impact

of a sentence refers to the middle part, where

meanings tend to vanish, so use this place for

BERMUDA   **TRIANGLE**

we may be dealing with literal beggars who are somehow metaphorical kings. The last word describes the inner quality of the former word. Reverse the phrase to "kings and beggars" and you reverse the implication: now you appear to be dealing with literal kings who are, at heart, beggars. Word order creates a range of other effects as well, particularly as part of entire sentences and sequences of sentences.

Types of Sentences

Although the most basic sentence pattern in English moves from subject to verb to object or indirect object, numerous variations and combinations exist. Your sentence lengths, structures, and patterns all contribute to tone and style. Academic style, for instance, favours longer sentences, considerable sentence variation, and a liberal number of complex and compound structures.

The wide range of sentence patterns in English means that writers can play with rich formal and rhythmical possibilities. You can have fun manipulating sentence patterns in order to achieve various effects that further your meaning. Sometimes these are best discovered by you in your writing adventures (and pointed out by your instructor), rather than adopted exclusively from a book of guidelines. Even the most thorough rhetoric book is merely a prompt to get you started; furthermore, the ability to shape sentence patterns resides within you, intuitively. Nevertheless, to inspire your innate ability with sentence lengths and patterns, try your hand at the following activity.

PRACTICE
Sentence Patterns, Rhythm, and Tone

Make up a paragraph in which you use the following six sentence patterns at least once:

1. Simple declarative sentence (subject to verb), e.g., "Love takes time" ("The Pleasures of Love," Reader, p. 420)
2. Compound sentence (two or more independent clauses linked by a coordinating conjunction), e.g., "The crowd cheered and booed and raged, and Bill and I celebrated the new heavyweight champion of the world" ("Lemon Pie with Muhammad Ali," Reader, p. 359)
3. Complex sentence (independent clause + dependent clause), e.g., "I remember the dread I would feel every Christmas when my mama would send a huge box filled with fluorescent coloured pants and shirts with "Kelvin Cloin" proudly displayed on the front" ("My Father the Hero," Reader, p. 366)
4. Imperative sentence (gives a command; the subject "you" is understood or elliptical), e.g., "Just run away" ("Confessions of the World's Worst Parent," Reader, p. 425)
5. Interrogative sentence (a question, often placing the subject between the auxiliary and the root of the verb), e.g., "How can we say that about our governments?" ("A Solution to the Climate Problem," Reader, p. 434)
6. Sentence beginning with a "dummy" subject (also referred to as an "expletive"), e.g., "Now it was Britain's time to pursue its strategy in shaping a British North America" ("British North America—Whose Creation?" Research Guide, p. 331)

Now try another paragraph in which you favour just one or two of these patterns. You might even try a third paragraph in which you play with alternating or symmetrical arrangements of the different sentence types. Show your paragraph(s) to your classmates and your instructor and discuss the effects of using the sentence patterns this way.

The length of paragraphs—like that of sentences—expresses tone, indicating the pace at which you expect your reader to consider your writing. Tabloid newspapers prefer single-sentence paragraphs. Such writing provides information quickly but does not encourage the reader to process the information at any complex level. In your academic writing, aim for focused, well-developed paragraphs directed by concise, explicit topic sentences, as discussed in Chapter 4. A typical first-year essay employs paragraphs composed of 5 to 10 sentences.

DEFINING ACADEMIC TONE

Throughout this chapter, we have referred to academic tone as tending toward the formal. Although we cautioned against striving too hard for an elevated level of diction and thereby appearing pretentious, adapting to a suitably formal level for your scholarly writing is not in itself pretentious or artificial. It is simply respectful of the occasion and reader needs. Certain carefully chosen abstract terms will be necessary. Also keep in mind that formal scholarly tone derives from much more than diction: it is influenced by kinds of sentences and by developed paragraphs of at least 5 to 10 sentences. Most university courses require mastery of third-person expositional, analytical, and argumentative tones. Furthermore, academic tone partly derives from the disciplined integration and documentation of research. Within this fairly broad definition of academic tone, you will find numerous shadings and variations. You gain as a writer by recognizing the distinctions of various tones.

Here, then, are samples of common academic styles integrating and documenting sources.

Sample Writing   Academic Expository Tone—Illustration

A Pace of Their Own

1   The speed of speech in various parts of Canada reveals a significant range of difference. Parts of Newfoundland and Montreal present two examples of rapid speech. In her essay "Newfoundlandese, If You Please," Diane Mooney observes that "[a]ll Newfoundlanders talk fast; this is just a given" (415). Mooney suggests that certain Irish roots are partly the reason for this. Visitors to Montreal hear a similar quickness of spoken English. This may be due partly to the influence of French, dominant in the city;[1] as well, Yiddish and Mediterranean communities, described by linguist Charles Boberg, have had an influence on the English spoken in the city (Haldane). No doubt the fast city pace of Montreal also influences the speed of speech and vice versa.

2   In contrast to the speech of Newfoundland and Montreal, much slower patterns occur in other parts of the country, for example, in much of Prince Edward Island (PEI), as well as on the prairies. Robert Deal, owner of a small bed and breakfast on the south shore of PEI, says, "On the Island, things are more relaxed: we don't drive so fast as people from away, and we don't rush our conversation." A similar observation is offered by Brenda Mitchell of Carstairs, Alberta, after a holiday in Montreal. "I couldn't get over how much faster people talk in this city," she says. Are ethnic roots as well as lifestyles responsible for the slower pace of speech in these parts of the country? The answer is probably yes.[2] As Boberg states to Maeve Haldane of the *McGill Reporter,* language variation across Canada is a last bastion of cultural separation from the United States.

Notes

1. In his essay "Politics and the English Language," George Orwell deplores the influence upon English of foreign words. However, University of Montreal linguist Professor Blake T. Hanna argues the opposite view in his article "Is French Corrupting Montreal English?"According to Hanna, French in Montreal has reinvigorated English to a degree that has not occurred since the eleventh century.

2. In Spring 2006, at the University of New Hampshire course website for English 790, "Language Variations in Canada," Professor Naomi Nagy stated the following: "Canada is a rich environment for socio-linguistic investigation, because there is every possible type of language contact situation imaginable."

Works Cited

Deal, Robert. Personal interview. 10 Aug. 2003.

Haldane, Maeve. "Speaking of Montreal." *McGill Reporter*. McGill University, 21 Nov. 2002. Web. 16 Aug. 2003.

Hanna, Blake T. "Is French Corrupting Montreal English?" *Circuit*. N.p., Mar. 1990. Web. 20 Nov. 2006.

Mitchell, Brenda. Personal interview. 13 June 2003.

Mooney, Diane. "Newfoundlandese, If You Please." *Acting on Words: An Integrated Rhetoric, Research Guide, Reader, and Handbook*. 3rd ed. By David Brundage and Michael Lahey. Toronto: Pearson Prentice Hall, 2012. 385–87. Print.

Nagy, Naomi. "Language Variations in Canada." Eng. Dept. and Ling. Prog., College of Liberal Arts, University of New Hampshire, 2006. Web. 20 Nov. 2006.

Orwell, George. "Politics and the English Language." 1946. *Project Gutenberg Australia*. Web. 12 Oct. 2010.

Sample Writing   Academic Analytical Tone—Illustration

Tony and the Bard

1 *The Sopranos*—now entering its final season on HBO—has all the features of a Shakespearean history play, as defined by Norrie Epstein: battlefield heroics, familial relationships, feisty characters, power politics, and covert scheming (151). Like Prince Harry overcoming Hotspur in *Henry IV, Part 2,* Tony prevails over an attempted assassination (season 1, episode 12) as does Chris (season 1, episode 21). Shakespeare's use of domestic scenes is paralleled in *The Sopranos* by similar scenes of family relationships involving Tony, Carmela, Meadow, Anthony Junior, and various other members of the extended crime "family." Feisty Shakespearean characters such as Hotspur, Falstaff, and Mistress Quickly find their modern counterparts in *Sopranos* early-season regulars like Chris, Uncle Junior, and Janice. In particular, Tony resembles Henry IV in his concealing of private anguish beneath a mask of political action. On the matter of power politics, Shakespeare's histories begin with the question of who will succeed to power, who will prevail in the bitter feud between the houses of Lancaster and York. Similarly, *The Sopranos* begins with the death of the local crime boss, Jackie Aprile, Sr., a consequential power vacuum, and problems of how to gain control according to the old code of honour, which means less to certain characters than it does to Tony. Uniting all of these similarities is the strong appeal that both the histories and *The Sopranos* have for their audiences: we envy the rich and the powerful, we experience the vicarious thrill of sin and danger, and we recognize in the ruthless main characters the same moral compromises that sometimes govern our own lives.

Work Cited

Epstein, Norrie. *The Friendly Shakespeare: A Thoroughly Painless Guide to the Best of the Bard.* New York: Penguin, 1993. Print.

Sample Writing   Academic Analytical Tone with Argumentative Edge

Publish or Perish

1   In 1990, historian Page Smith published an indictment of higher education in America, condemning, among other things, the publish-or-perish culture. Now 20 years later, publish-or-perish at Canadian universities is, if anything, worse than ever. No longer is the aspiring academic rightly encouraged to research and publish; he or she must publish as many separate titles a year as possible. A recent faculty advertisement for a posting in *University Affairs* reflects this disturbing reality: "Relative to research funding . . . only Harvard's faculty publish more than UBC's" ("Let's Talk Excellence"). Nothing is said about the quality or value of these publications, or of the teaching compromises made to attain this "distinction." While the UBC ad writer would no doubt reply that quality is assumed, nevertheless, the ad strongly implies that quantity is priority one. Examples abound of how this emphasis on quantity discourages devotion to farsighted works in favour of feeding the KPI mill.[1] Perhaps more disturbingly, this demand for endless short publications may undermine teaching. It is generally acknowledged on large university campuses that teaching excellence does not play a sufficient part in advancement. Surely the university's ideal of seeking and teaching truth suffers when the seeking consists mostly of rapid-fire publications and the teaching garners diminishing respect.

Note

1. "KPI" stands for "key performance indicators," a type of accountability criteria used in business but, according to various critics, unsuitable to the university. See Bruneau and Savage.

Works Cited

Bruneau, William, and Donald C. Savage. *Counting Out the Scholars: The Case against Performance Indicators in Higher Education*. Toronto: Lorimer, 2002. Print.
"Let's Talk Excellence." *University Affairs* June–July 2003: 24. Print.
Smith, Page. *Higher Education in America: Killing the Spirit*. New York: Viking, 1990. Print.

Sample Writing   Concession-Refutation: Persuasive Tone

Eating Your Cake Before the Icing: Is It True What They Say?

Our last sample of academic tone for this chapter arose from the following fictional scenario. A former business school graduate was asked to write two paragraphs of advice to a graduating class at his alma mater. Here is what he wrote.

1   Five years ago, as I approached my last year of university, my parents and older relatives— with one exception—all advised me to make as much money as I could first, so that I

could do what I really wanted to do later, after looking after financial concerns. My parents are practical people; I knew they wanted the best for me. They reminded me that eating the icing after the cake would still be the best plan, even now that I was grown up. The one person who disagreed was my grandmother. Her sister's husband had made his family wait to do the things they wanted—moving to the country—and the year that he finally paid off the mortgage and said, "Let's move," he died of a heart attack. This story prompted me to do some research.

2   I happened upon an interesting study reported in *Natural Life* magazine, November/ December 2002. The study tracked the careers of 1500 business school graduates from 1960 to 1980. From the beginning, the graduates were grouped into Category A and Category B. Category A was people who wanted to make money first and do what they wanted to do later. Category B pursued their true interests right away, confident that money would follow eventually. Eighty-three percent of the graduates were in Category A. Doing our math, we know that only 17 percent were in Category B. Probably you are in Category A, right? After 20 years, there were 101 millionaires overall. Just one of those came from Category A. So am I a millionaire now, five years after graduating? No, I'm not even close. But I'm in no financial stress, my young family is happy, and if I died of a heart attack tomorrow, my wife could honestly say that our time together was joyful and rich.

Work Cited

"Designing a Livelihood: Do What You Love & Love What You Do." *Natural Life Magazine.*
    Life Media, Nov.–Dec. 2002. Web. 10 Dec. 2006.

 PRACTICE

See if you can find the differing features of diction, sentence style, point of view, and structure in the above sample writings that result in different tones and reflect the purposes connected to those tones. Consider such features as diction, sentences, use of topic sentences, organization, and types of supporting detail (see Chapter 4 for more tips on these aspects). Also consider what the samples have in common from the point of view of purpose and tone. Discuss your findings with your classmates and your instructor.

VOICE

You may hear the term *voice* in discussions of tone. The idea of voice is very close to that of tone, with one useful distinction. As we have seen, tone is an overall attitude expressed by the writer toward himself or herself, the specific subject, and the audience. Your tone may well change quite radically from one piece of writing to another, while your voice will not change, or at least not very much, unless the form requires suppression of it. **Voice** may be closely identified with the character and personality of the writer, with his or her individuality. Some writers and instructors distinguish voice from style and tone as the expression of self, whereas style and tone are expressions of strategy.

 PRACTICE

Read the three following essays: "Introversion: The Dreaded Other" by student writer Colleen McCaffery, Research Guide, p. 322; "Elementary Observations: The Special Skill of Sherlock Holmes" by Doctor Robert Penner, Reader, p. 392; and "Multiple Embryo Transfer: At What Cost?" p. 282. Describe the tone and the voice of each essay. Discuss your findings with your classmates and your instructor.

Now think of one author whose writings you particularly enjoy or admire and a good number of whose works you have read. Pick two works by this writer that differ in tone. Try to define what is consistent in the writing style and values of both works. You can choose a fiction writer or a poet, but essay writers, politicians, or newspaper columnists are also useful for this exercise. Remember, you are examining the abiding voice in one given writer (or speaker) beneath different stylistic choices and various forms.

Imagine the sort of voice you might expect from a seasoned oil-rig worker and the one you would expect from a career banker. At the risk of stereotyping, we might consider that the oil-rig worker and banker could vary in tone based on attitudes to the world. Both would always retain the essence of their individual voices, however, even when each person was adapting to situations in which expected formality or informality and form would vary. That part of your expression that remains in touch with the values, distinctiveness, and quirks of your own identity is your voice. Voice is one of the most difficult qualities of writing to define, yet one of the most indisputable and influential presences on the page. It subtly characterizes both the shape and the content of everything you write.

Works Cited

Kies, Daniel. "Grammatical Manipulation of the Audience." Hypertextbooks. Dept. of English, College of DuPage, 6 June 2006. Web. 6 Apr. 2010.

McLuhan & Davies Communications, Inc. *Excellence in Thinking and Writing: A Two-Day Workshop Manual.* Toronto. 1988. Print.

 PRACTICE

Review the paragraph that you wrote as the final practice activity at the end of Chapter 1. With the main points of Chapter 2 now in your mind, what would you add to your original paragraph?

Chapter 3

More about Logic

Chapter 1 introduced the classical idea of a writer's **logos,** or logic. Scholarly experience fundamentally involves the use of logic as you gain, analyze, and contribute to knowledge. When you write a formal paper presenting your analysis and evaluation, you need to provide more than first thoughts, which are sometimes in the category of "knee-jerk" responses. You need to use logic.

THE MAIN CULPRIT IS HASTY THINKING

This chapter will go on to describe logical operations and to identify a number of common logical fallacies. But the basic advice that runs through this discussion is simple: *stop and think.*

Really think.

Our first responses to anything we see or read are invariably emotional. When you find yourself wanting to make initial emotional reactions the basis of your next paper, count to 10 (for the 10 logical fallacies described later in this chapter). Consider whether you are confusing facts and opinions, relying on narrow inductive thinking, or muddling premises as conclusions in deduction. To use Stephen Toulmin's terms (see p. 31), are you assuming, without sufficient investigation, that a proposed element of argument—such as warrant or grounds—is valid? The main unintended logical shortcoming is almost always *hasty thinking.*

Consider the following statement:

> Proper education includes developing and applying skills in citing sources according to the Modern Language Association (MLA), American Psychological Association (APA), or some other approved academic style guide.

Has the writer of this sentence stopped to think that the word "education" in its broadest, most open sense simply means *learning?* The word does not designate where or how one learns. There is so-called informal education—the proverbial university of life—as well as formal education based on institutionalized mechanisms, as well as different cultural forms of institutionalized learning, not all of which practise Western-style citation techniques. Adding the word "post-secondary" in the above statement to describe the word "education" would remove an apparent assumption that all good education occurs only in college or university. Before allowing your assumptions to see the light of day and be seen by other readers, be sure your choices of words and the thinking behind your choices have not been too hasty.

FACT AND OPINION: A MATTER OF FACT . . . OR IS IT?

All writing essentially involves articulating an *opinion* on a topic and then providing support based on evidence—various facts and forms of reasoning—to persuade readers that the stated (or sometimes implied) opinion is true or, at least, useful in some important respect. This sounds straightforward enough, so let's move on to the next point—but wait a minute. We just considered the dangers of hasty thinking. Before accepting the previous statement, we should ask, what is an opinion and what is a fact? Try the following quiz, and let's see just how many of us do—or perhaps do not—agree on the answers to these questions.

 PRACTICE

Discuss with your classmates and instructor whether the following statements are facts or opinions.

1. Christopher Columbus was the first person to discover North America.
2. Women are physically weaker than men.
3. Alberta has refused to support the Kyoto agreement due to self-interest.
4. Canada's national sport is hockey.
5. The birthplace of hockey was Victoria Rink, Montreal, March 3, 1875.
6. In 1763, under terms of the Treaty of Paris, almost all of New France was ceded to Britain.
7. *Buffy the Vampire Slayer* was the best series on TV during its seven-year run and should have been continued.
8. Oil, a fossil fuel, is a non-renewable resource.

The integrity of facts and opinions, together with careful calculating from premise to conclusion, determines the truth and validity of arguments.

PREMISES AND CONCLUSIONS

Lying at the heart of logic is a basic structure consisting of one or more premises from which a conclusion naturally follows.

Premise: John is shorter than Bob.
Conclusion: Therefore Bob is taller than John.

In this first example the premise is a fact. A premise might also be an opinion.

Premise: John is kinder than Bob.
Conclusion: Therefore Bob is meaner than John.

If the fact is accurate and the opinion is convincingly derived, then the premises are considered *true*. As long as the reasoning that flows to the conclusion makes sense, then the conclusion is both *valid* (correctly reasoned in the sense that an algebra equation is correctly traced to its answer) and true (drawn from true premises).

INDUCTIVE AND DEDUCTIVE FORMS OF REASONING

In the Middle Ages, scholarship, closely tied to the church, was dominated by a type of intellectual reasoning responding to hypotheses (tentative explanations inviting testing) that tended to be general principles and doctrinal presumptions. A premise in those days was often some assertion about the nature of God, which certain other times and traditions would consider ineffable and unknowable. This situation prevailed until the Renaissance in Europe, which flourished in the sixteenth century. The study and evolution of empiricism followed: the scientific method of setting up experiments and basing conclusions on rigorous analysis through observation of phenomena and the collection and measurement of data. This "modern" method of reasoning emphasizes **induction**, the use of concrete particulars to derive some larger principles. The much older method of reasoning tends to emphasize **deduction,** which posits (theorizes) a large assumption and then looks for supporting examples.

Induction

Inductive conclusions flow from experience and observation. For example, a child touches a red-hot burner. The next time she sees a red-hot burner, she will probably not touch it, because she has formed a conclusion, based on experience. Inductive reasoning moves outward from the individual experience; that is, it moves from particular instances to general conclusions.

Deduction

Deductive reasoning, by contrast, moves inward, from the concept to the cases. Deduction starts with general principles and applies analysis in order to reach specific conclusions. In the 1941 film *The Maltese Falcon,* the police suspect Sam Spade (Humphrey Bogart) of having murdered his partner Miles Archer (Jerome Cowan). Miles has been shot from the front and must have seen someone approaching him before the gunshot. His overcoat is still buttoned up and his gun still in its holster. The police reason that the victim therefore knew (in the sense of knew and trusted) his assailant. This reasoning may be expressed in the form of the **syllogism.**

The deductive construction of all syllogisms consists of three steps: a major premise, a minor premise, and a conclusion. A "premise" may be defined as a statement of accepted truth, such as "People generally don't prepare to defend themselves physically when approached by people they know" and "Miles did not appear to have taken action to defend himself when he died." The first of these statements expresses a general principle about all humans, so this may be considered a major premise. The second statement offers an accepted truth concerning a specific case, so it may be considered a minor premise. Considering the minor premise in relation to the established major premise, we can derive a conclusion:

Major premise: People generally don't prepare to defend themselves physically when approached by people they know.

Minor premise: Miles did not appear to have been defending himself against suspected danger when he died.

Conclusion: Miles was killed by someone he knew.

Be aware, however, that while the technical reasoning behind a syllogism can sometimes lead to a formally correct (valid) result, it can still prove untrue. Consider the following example of this caution:

Major premise: Serious study requires personal discipline.

Minor premise: Andrew is disciplined.

Conclusion: Andrew studies seriously.

If Andrew is disciplined in other ways (in exercise, diet, money management, confidentiality, dental care, punctuality, and so on) but not in studying, the conclusion does not hold, though the formal logic in the syllogism may seem structurally sound. A review of Andrew's personal history as a student might reveal that he has never been able to transfer his disciplined behaviour in other areas to his studies. So be prepared for the possibility that a syllogism may seem convincing, yet the conclusion may be wrong when tested against the reality of the specific case.

In short, the premises must be perfectly reliable for the conclusion to be reliable. A classic example of a reliable syllogism goes as follows: "All humans are mortal; Socrates is human; therefore Socrates is mortal." The major premise that all humans are mortal is harder to dispute than the previous major premise that people generally don't expect to be murdered when approached by people they know. There may well be exceptions to that major premise. More significantly, the minor premise given above in connection with *The Maltese Falcon* (Miles did not appear to have been defending himself when he died) posits an opinion, whereas the classic syllogism about Socrates posits a fact (Socrates is human). The minor premise concerning Miles is simply an inference (an informed guess) drawn from investigation, since the murder was not witnessed. The following alternative explanations might also be considered as explaining the state of Miles's body after the murder: "Assassins disguised as nuns are often trusted" or "Assassins may rearrange a body so that it appears the victim attempted no defence."

In other words, the syllogism the police use in *The Maltese Falcon* to identify a category of suspected killers results not in a certainty but rather in a theory, one that demands further investigation and testing of specifics. Further thinking and investigating is exactly what Sam Spade does. Mindful of the police syllogism, he instead narrows to one that deals more specifically with the sort of man Miles appears to have been. (Readers of this "enlightened" era will have to excuse the element of misogyny that seemingly underlies the film noir femme fatale convention.)

Major premise:	Conventional-minded men of limited intelligence are particularly susceptible to being fooled by attractive, scheming females.
Minor premise:	Miles is a conventional-minded man of limited intelligence (unaware that his wife is having an affair with Sam) and has recently taken a shine to Brigid O'Shaugnessy (Mary Astor).
Conclusion:	Brigid killed Miles.

Again, this reasoning simply suggests a possible suspect. Alternative syllogisms might be built to identify other suspects in the category of people Miles knew, such as his wife or, as the police had postulated, Sam himself. (As it turns out, Sam uncovers the motives that explain why Brigid did indeed kill the unsuspecting Miles.)

Modern inquiry tends to proceed with a similar understanding that few if any premises result in dependable truth until their conclusions are rigorously investigated. And even after rigorous testing, researchers have an understandable reluctance to declare absolute truth, just as *film noir* shows a reluctance to provide clear answers of right and wrong. Remember that most deductive conclusions need to be carefully qualified (*may be true, often appears to be so,* etc).

The Interplay of Induction and Deduction

Most everyday thinking, as well as scholarly work (and detective work!), combines both forms of reasoning, inductive and deductive. Modern scientific method, for example, tends to look closely at specific cases (an inductive prompt), then speculates on possible explanations for what is observed and thus forms a tentative general principle (a theory or hypothesis) for testing. Even the main premise of the classic Socrates syllogism, however, derives from induction. When we say that all humans die, it is because we have witnessed deaths, have heard of numerous cases, and have not witnessed or heard of any exceptions. But we have not observed the story of every individual human to be sure of our belief. Induction results in generalizations based on a limited range of observations, and as we know, various laws of science may sooner or later prove inadequate. Since deduction so often begins and operates on partial induction—on generalizations derived from imperfect methods—(not to mention other prompts such as hearsay, intuition, and other forms of received belief) it must be considered an informed estimate rather than a beautifully reliable, self-contained, mathematical derivation, despite what Sherlock Holmes, *Star Trek's* Mr. Spock, and late-night television detectives would try to lead us to believe. Despite best efforts—and sometimes through an absence of effort or will—logic may fail or at least require reconsidering.

LOGICAL FALLACIES

Most of us pride ourselves on our command of reason, yet in daily life we frequently stray into illogical conclusions. Acknowledging our biases, seeing issues from unfamiliar points of view, and properly applying the tools of reason may be the greatest tasks we face in college or university, as well as in life. Below, we discuss 10 common forms of logical fallacies. As you will see, the first six of these clearly come from hasty thinking resulting in **oversimplification**: a reduction of complex situations to easy descriptions and one-dimensional conclusions. The last four, while they, too, might be addressed by taking more time for complex analysis, are generally considered **fallacies of distortion** in that writers and speakers purposely use them to appeal unfairly to our emotions or prejudices—or even to cut down on the time required to complete a last-minute essay assignment.

1. Overgeneralization

If you argue that all British people are understated, you make a hasty generalization (in this case producing a **stereotype**) that can be easily invalidated. All it takes is one counter-example—Mick Jagger, for example, is British *and* flamboyant—to undermine your claim. As our discussion of induction and deduction illustrates, generalizing is an inevitable part of moving from specifics to presumptions, of exploring broader possibilities. But generalize with caution, knowing that your presumption is simply a device in the cause of experimentation, not an absolute certainty.

2. Either/Or Assumptions

There are many authentic either/or situations. These cases of contrasting choices and fairly certain outcomes are pressing and sometimes dramatic: "Bill Gates had to either limit Microsoft as a monopolistic company or face further legal penalties." But in many cases, so-called either/or situations are instances of oversimplification: for example, "Our hockey coach said that if we lose these high school playoffs, we'll never accomplish anything worthwhile in our lives."

Try to think past either/or false opposites toward a range of available, workable alternatives more appropriate to our multi-layered world of complex situations and challenges.

3. False Analogy

Just because two things are alike in some respects, and just because one may illuminate the other on certain points, they will not be alike in all respects. At some point all analogies break down.

A false analogy is a comparison with a faulty basis that detracts from, rather than contributing to, your point. Consider the following: "Accountants are artists: both are important observers of details." In this analogy, the writer presumes that because both accountants and artists analyze diverse, detailed information, they are essentially the same. This overlooks the fundamental distinction that artists—by definition—must use their imaginative powers to create original works of art, whereas accountants use their analytical skills to interpret existing numbers. In another example, technological expert Jaron Lanier argues that comparing a machine's computation to human intelligence or vice versa "obscures more than it illuminates" (36). To refute the idea that digital information is alive and has its own ambitions, Lanier applies an analogy of his own: stored information is like a brick resting on a ledge. It has potential energy, but that energy will not be released until prodded by something—in which case, the brick falls (28). Lanier's conclusion is that bits of information can mean something only if they are experienced. Is his analogy more compelling than the one he criticizes as too misfitting? Why or why not?

4. Slippery Slope Assumptions

Your car gets chipped; you dream that night that it is covered in rust. Such overwrought emotions conspire to remind you that you should coat the chipped area. However, if you were truly to believe that your chipped car would soon be covered in rust, you would be committing the fallacy of slippery slope: asserting urgently that a certain event will lead to another event (often an extreme event) along an understood continuum, without considering how. A mother finds alcohol in her daughter's knapsack and concludes that the girl will soon be hooked on heroin. The mother has overlooked that a number of significant events along the continuum (or slope) need to occur before the imagined dire outcome.

With slippery slopes, clear boundaries between steps along the continuum are indeterminate or "slippery" in that they are hard to define, their cause-effect connections uncertain. A conclusion opposite to the mother's above but equally hasty would be to assume that because borders and transitions along the continuum are "slippery," therefore no possible connection or relationship could even exist between one end and the other. Complex study would be needed to appraise the odds for or against the girl's proceeding to addiction.

5. False Correlations

College tuition fees triple, and six months later, fraud by college students also triples. You conclude that the one event caused the other. Maybe it did, at least to some extent, but without further study, you have committed the presumption that because A precedes B, A must therefore be the cause of B. The traditional Latin term for this fallacy is *post hoc, ergo propter hoc* (after this, therefore because of this). This is the fallacy of correlation, assuming that two things associated in time (and often space) share a causal or reciprocal relationship. If you always have a headache after drinking coffee and conclude that caffeine (rather than, say, the heat or sugar) causes your ailment, you may also have committed a wrong assumption. The same basic fallacy applies if you assume that two events occurring simultaneously share a causal relationship (*cum hoc, ergo propter hoc*—with this, therefore because of this).

6. Disconnected and Circular Statements

"After O'Driscoll's arrest, neighbours found it difficult to believe he was a cigarette smuggler. They say he was always friendly, hard-working, and punctual." But isn't smuggling itself hard work? Wouldn't it *help* a smuggler to be punctual and friendly? Such statements that do not follow logically are sometimes known by their classical Latin label, *non sequiturs* (things that do not follow). Another *non sequitur* is the notion that "the more you buy, the more you save."

A similar lapse of logic, known as circular reasoning, occurs when premises are stated as conclusions, thereby presuming that what has *yet* to be proven can be treated as a self-evident fact or conclusion. Circular reasoning is sometimes not too hard to spot: "The comedian is humorous because he is so funny." The terms "humorous" and "funny" have virtually the same meaning here, and neither states a supporting reason, such as, "With impeccable timing and hangdog expressions, the comedian makes everyone laugh, so it's hard to deny that he is funny."

7. Red Herring

The red herring uses any number of false appeals—usually highly emotional ones—to lead us away from the real issue or scent. A typical red herring occurs in the following rhetorical question: "Of course Native people were promised certain lands and payments, but wouldn't they like to stand on their own feet?" The writer intends to sweep aside a whole array of complex ethical and legal considerations by this emotional appeal to self-reliance, which draws on a racist stereotype of Native people as dependent and which is irrelevant to the historical and legal matter in question. The following fallacies of bandwagon appeal, *ad populum*, and character attack all function as forms of red herring, techniques intended to run counter to the spirit of genuine, even-handed argumentation. When used deliberately for political purposes, as they often are, such logical fallacies are sometimes called **propaganda techniques**.

8. Bandwagon Appeal

Bandwagon appeal is groupthink, calling upon urges toward inclusion but also on fears of exclusion. If we were all honest with ourselves, we might see that we ride various bandwagons at various times in our lives. Bandwagon appeal is the principle upon which so much designer clothing is sold: "Tilo has a pair of Nikes, Mom, so I have to have a pair, too." Here, preference is not really personal expression, only mindless conformity. According to this fallacy, a desire—often a selfish one for a questionable goal—is misrepresented as a need. Like conventional *ad populum* appeals, which we deal with below, this fallacy preys on an aspect of our emotional nature: the urge to fit in, to join the crowd, to be accepted. At its worst, bandwagon appeal becomes mob mentality.

9. *Ad Populum* Appeals

The Latin term *argumentum ad populum* means "appeal to the people." Such appeals speak to traditional community values and seek to manipulate emotional responses to popular symbols or ideas. Such appeals make careless use of *glittering generalities*: words such as "country," "family values," "prosperity," "decency," and "freedom," terms that traditionally have positive but vague associations. "This community believes in family values, and so we don't follow the stampede to legalize gay marriage." The alarmist note of warning is intended to imply that gays don't live in families and will somehow threaten conventional family life. No definitions are offered, no complexities acknowledged. Fear, not discussion and analysis, is the statement's only foundation.

Ad populum appeals draw upon other propagandistic strategies such as "plain folks," whereby politicians dress and speak falsely like the "ordinary" people they imagine will support them. Underlying these appeals is the circular argument that we should be (or remain) what we are because this is what we are.

10. Character Attacks

Also known as *ad hominem,* Latin for "to the man," character attacks include name-calling, mudslinging, and innuendo. *Ad hominem* attacks zero in on the person rather than his or her argument or policy. Such attacks serve as a form of red herring (deflecting attention from real issues), and sometimes they include the *straw-man* strategy of deliberately inflating a perceived threat from a certain opponent in order to focus on a supposedly justified counterattack.

PRACTICE

Try to find at least one instance of each of the above 10 fallacies in various essays in the Reader. Compare your findings with those of your classmates and your instructor.

TOULMIN'S ARGUMENT MODEL

Modern rhetorician Stephen Toulmin believed that the classical syllogism does not lend itself particularly well to analyzing modern arguments. He advanced his own model, which is described and illustrated in greater detail in Chapter 18, "Argumentation."

Toulmin's model breaks arguments down to a main claim, such as "City Council should enact a bylaw to prevent cats from roaming." Then his model looks for the claim's grounds, consisting of data or other forms of evidence: "Over 500 citizens have signed a petition objecting to roaming cats using neighbourhood gardens as litter boxes." Finally, there must be a "warrant" expressing common support for the claim and the evidence. In this example, the warrant would be that "citizens in this society don't like their private property to be violated." Toulmin stresses the importance of sufficient backing for the warrant—evidence that the warrant is true.

PRACTICE

Read "College Girl to Call Girl" (p. 388) and "The Pleasures of Love" (p. 420). For each essay see if you can identify the claim, the grounds (evidence/support), and the warrant (assumed public attitude). Then look at the summaries of these essays in Chapter 15 ("Summary of 'The Pleasures of Love,'" p. 165) and Chapter 20 ("Outline Summary of 'College Girl,'" p. 224). Discuss your answers and questions with your classmates and your instructor.

CULTURAL CONSIDERATIONS

Certain cultures neither engage in nor admire the oppositional, sometimes intensive adversarial approach we discuss in Chapter 18, an approach vigorously taught in North American colleges and universities. For instance, the idea of challenging appeals to social tradition is considered generally unacceptable in many Indigenous communities.

Furthermore, some teachers and writers in mainstream Western culture also regret what they consider the unnecessarily combative spirit our society endorses in critical thinking. In an essay entitled "Burying the Hatchet in Language," McGill University professor David Smith observes how frequently our culture uses military metaphors to discuss academic work or verbal engagements—metaphors such as "defend your claims" or hit the "target" (540–44). He refers to linguistic research suggesting that the sort of language we accept can influence our perceptions and therefore our behaviour. He then offers a creative challenge: "Suppose instead of thinking about argument in terms of war, we were to think of critical argument as a pleasing, graceful dance" (544).

Works Cited

Lanier, Jaron. *You Are Not a Gadget.* New York: Alfred A. Knopf, 2010. Print.

Smith, David. "Burying the Hatchet in Language." *Reader's Choice.* 3rd. ed. Ed. Kim Flachmann, Michael Flachmann, and Alexandra MacLennan. Scarborough: Prentice Hall, 2000. 540–44. Print.

Chapter 4

Paragraph Skills: The "4-F Test"

Just as sentences represent completed thoughts in pieces of writing, paragraphs represent completed ideas. Here we are using the word "idea" in the sense of an opinion, conviction, or claim specifically attached to a certain topic. You may say, "I am going to the lake" and convey a complete thought but not an idea; you simply impart awareness of an action or state of being—a **fact** (see Chapter 3 for more on facts and opinions). If you say, however, "I am going to the lake because it helps me to experience inner peace," then you express what we mean here by an idea. This expression of a meaningful idea would also occur if you said, "I am going to the life-giving lake." Your discussion would then go on to illustrate the life-giving aspects. The core "idea" emerges here through one word or phrase of intensification. This idea—opinion, interpretation, understanding, or claim—then needs further discussion to become complete.

WHAT IS A PARAGRAPH?

A paragraph is a block of writing, generally of 5 to 10 sentences in academic settings, that expresses a complete idea. *The Canadian Writer's Workplace*—an excellent workbook—defines a paragraph as follows:

> A paragraph is a group of sentences that develops one main idea. A paragraph may stand by itself as a complete piece of writing, or it may be a section of a longer piece of writing, such as an essay. (Lipschutz et al. 157)

Remembering this guideline is an important aspect of shaping your academic essays. You do not want your paragraphs to be too short or too long.

For most of your academic writing, especially in the first years of your program, a good rule of thumb is to use paragraphs ranging between 5 and 10 sentences.

INDENTATION

A new paragraph is signalled by indentation of the first word of the opening sentence. This "small" matter of mechanics makes a *major* contribution to readability. Remember to indent five spaces when you begin a new paragraph. Your reader can thus easily ascertain the pattern of building blocks with a mere glance at your page.

The 4-F Test

Here is a mnemonic device to help you test your paragraphs:

The 4-F Test.

Make sure every paragraph you write meets the following requirements: **f**ocus, **f**ine points, **f**low, and **f**inality.

FOCUS

The most effective way to focus paragraphs is through the topic sentence. This sentence expresses the controlling idea of the paragraph. A unified purpose for your paragraph emerges: the goal of explaining and supporting the topic sentence's central assertion. Like the thesis of an essay, the topic sentence sets a track for the elaborating discussion to follow. Thus **focus** refers to unity of idea. Focus, however, also means consistency and purpose of tone, created by point of view, choice of words, and types of details (fine points). Fine points, flow, and finality, in effect, harmonize your paragraph: they work together in fulfillment of one purpose—asserting the controlling idea of each paragraph and, thereby, of the essay.

More about Topic Sentences

As we said, you control paragraph focus with each paragraph's topic sentence, usually the first sentence of the paragraph. In fairly rare cases, some paragraphs can work without an explicit topic sentence. The main idea comes across as a result of careful organization and implicit clues. However, to ensure clarity and control, especially in your first-year academic writing, it is a good idea to shape a topic sentence for every paragraph you write. Placing this sentence first in the paragraph usually serves you well.

The Canadian Writer's Workplace uses an engaging cinematic metaphor to describe the relationship of one paragraph to others: an individual paragraph in a longer piece of writing should be a "sequel to a movie" (158). The authors mean that every paragraph should stand on its own, even though it may flow from and toward other paragraphs.

What the topic sentence says and how it says it establish a clear sense of where the paragraph is going and why.

Examples of a Topic Sentence

- There is indeed an insistent rhythm to the routine of London.
  —Peter Ackroyd, *London*, 457
- Surprisingly, the 1990s grunge movement owes as much to David Bowie's strange vocal modulations as to Neil Young's style and attitude.
- Mary Shelley's *Frankenstein* questions the ethical responsibility of inventors.

What are the "controlling ideas" in the topic sentences above?

In Peter Ackroyd's sentence from his book *London*, the main idea makes a statement about the routine of London: it proceeds with an *insistent rhythm*. Topic sentences do not simply point to their subject: they point to it with a *specific view*—they have something to *say*. The topic sentence states more than a fact; it states a *claim*, a position, an important point of view. But as you can see, these sentences also have carefully designed limits. On a small scale, and often without explicitly including its reasons, a topic sentence is like the thesis of an essay.

✒ PRACTICE

Read the four writing samples in Chapter 2, pp. 18 to 21, entitled "A Pace of Their Own," "Tony and the Bard," "Publish or Perish," and "Eating Your Cake Before the Icing: Is It True What They Say?" For each paragraph, decide which sentence serves as the topic sentence. For each topic sentence, identify the main topic and the controlling idea. Discuss your answers with your classmates and instructor.

Watch Your Point of View: Avoid *Confusing* Shift in Person (Pronouns)

Point of view refers to the writer's voice and address when referring to the topic. First-person voice (*I, me, we, us*) openly refers to the writer(s) as well as to the topic of the writing. When writers use the first person, some attention remains directed to them as well as to the topic. This point of view suits informal, personal, expressive, evocative purposes, and often works well for certain types of instruction or persuasion. Second-person voice (*you*) places unusual emphasis on the reader. The reader is directly addressed. This point of view also tends to be informal and works well for how-to (directional process) writing or certain forms of creative writing. As we know, the second person is the staple of advertising, which wishes to make the reader or listener feel central. Third-person point of view (*he, she, him, her, it, they, them*) reduces attention to the writer and suits most academic purposes, such as expository and analytical reports, essays, and discussions. This point of view increases detached, impersonal, or impartial attention to the subject.

It is almost always jarring to come upon shifting points of view within a single paragraph. Since point of view has a major determining effect on how writing is received, such sudden shifts will confuse and irritate any reader.

Occasionally, however, changing points of view within paragraphs can be warranted, a natural way to serve certain situations. Look for examples where we change point of view between the second and third person in this text. Are those shifts disruptive? In any case, the point we are making here is a caution that changing points of view in the middle of a paragraph can cause disruption, ambiguity of purpose, and confused angle of reference.

Post-secondary academic essays almost *always* use third-person point of view.

 PRACTICE
Focusing Point of View

Read the following paragraph. Determine whether it has lapses in point of view. If you are having trouble recognizing the unwarranted shifts of person, see Common Error 4 in section 3 of the Handbook—Pronoun Problem—and then try solving the shifts in this paragraph again.

> Are you a college student who finds it hard to find time to study? Are you falling behind in your courses? Never fear! We at Learning A–Z for Youth have the answer for you. To use our exciting new product, one has only to plug it in, place it under your pillow, and learn while one is sleeping. Yes—it's that easy. We recommend that customers read our online pamphlet before purchasing our product: a machine that reads CDs of school material to them in a gentle, soothing voice while you sleep. Learning A–Z for Youth guarantees you will get higher grades, or it will gladly refund the customer's money. Try our QuickLearn today—and get that A tomorrow.

Discuss your answers with your classmates and instructor.

FINE POINTS

How do fine points affect tone and content? In any expository or analytical paragraph, the fine points uphold the topic sentence, develop the paragraph's point, and advance the overall purpose of the essay.

Types of Fine Details

Fine points are various sorts of evidence offered to support the claim stated in the topic sentence. These include summaries, paraphrases, and quotations from sources. More specifically, supporting proof may include facts, descriptions, statistics, and data from first-hand observation or published studies (secondary sources), as well as various forms of logical reasoning, such as analogies. Without the topic sentence, the paragraph would not be focused. Without the supporting details, the topic sentence would not be sufficiently sustained.

> ## Fine Details Support the Topic Sentence
>
> All paragraph writing, in essence, is a proper balancing of claims and supports, positions and proofs. This balance results from the clarity and commitment of the topic sentence and the validity of the detailed support through the rest of the paragraph.

Fine Details Express Tone: Warm, Neutral, and Cool Appeals

Different types of supporting detail express different tones as a result of presenting different appeals. First-person point of view, personal stories, human subjects, and evocative language tend to appeal to pathos or emotion; these and related techniques create "warm" tones. "Neutral" tones emerge from writing that appeals more directly to logos (logic) than to personal examples but that does not enter fully into numbers and statistical assessments. "Cool" appeals speak primarily to logos, at considerable distance from pathos. Using (and often combining) these three appeals is an important part of rhetorical strategy.

 **PRACTICE**
Fine Details Creating Tone

Read the following three sample paragraphs. For each one, decide what you think is the dominant form of supporting detail and dominant tone (warm, neutral, cool). Explain why you believe the details express the tone you have suggested. The topic sentence of each paragraph has been italicized.

Sample paragraph A: Find the dominant tone

By the encouragement of self-confidence, self-worth and a feeling of pride in their ethnic origin, multiculturalism has helped the immigrants succeed in their social and economic life and has made them feel at home. There is no better indication of how self-image determines the future of the country than when I visited the northern Alberta Arab community of Lac La Biche in the late summer of 1996. "I love it here! In this town we prospered and here we have established our roots." Khalil Abughoush, owner of the IGA supermarket in Lac La Biche, was full of enthusiasm

when talking about his small northern city. Like his fellow countrymen—
20 percent of the town's 3,000 inhabitants are of Arab-Lebanese origin—he had
come to seek his fortune in this northern Alberta resort. In Canada's multicultural
society, Abughoush, like the majority of immigrants and their descendants, felt at
home. As he prospered he felt no coercion to fit in, no pressure to leave his
culture behind.

—Habeeb Salloum, "The Other Canadians and Canada's Future,"
from *Contemporary Review*, March 1997

Sample paragraph B: Find the dominant tone

Fundamentally, an understanding of the sacred helps us to acknowledge that there are
bounds of balance, order, and harmony in the natural world which set limits to our
ambitions and define the parameters of sustainable development. In some cases
Nature's limits are well understood at the rational, scientific level. As a simple
example, we know that trying to graze too many sheep on a hillside will, sooner
or later, be counterproductive for the sheep, the hillside, or both. More wisely, we
understand that the overuse of insecticides or antibiotics leads to problems of
resistance. And we are beginning to comprehend the full, awful consequences of
pumping too much carbon dioxide into the Earth's atmosphere.

—HRH Charles, Prince of Wales, the Reith Lecture broadcast, 17 May 2000

Sample paragraph C: Find the dominant tone

One of the sad consequences of the push towards a hyper-masculine image is that it can
rarely be obtained without the use of potentially harmful drugs. A 1993 study conducted
for the Canadian Centre for Ethics in Sport concluded that four per cent of males
aged 11 to 18—as many as 83,000 young Canadians—used anabolic steroids in
1992 and 1993. In the study, which involved 16,169 high-school and elementary
students, one in five reported that they knew someone who was taking anabolic
steroids. Among the reasons given for their use, nearly half said it was to change
their physical appearance. That contrasted starkly with previously held notions that
steroids were used mostly to increase athletic performance, says Paul Melia, the
Centre's director of education. "The reality is for most of these young men, even if
they do get on a regimen of weight training, they are not going to look like these
picture boys," said Melia. "And sustaining that look is a full-time job."

—Susan McClelland, "The Lure of the Body Image," *Maclean's,* 22 February 1999

Discuss your findings with your classmates and your instructor.

Combining Warm and Cool Supporting Detail: Weaving Tones for Added Strength

Any single paragraph in your essay tends to emphasize one form of support over
others, which is how paragraphs maintain consistency of tone and purpose. Usually,
an academic essay would use neutral or cool proofs.

Sometimes, however, essayists interweave warm, neutral, and cool proofs in order to add more dynamic to their persuasions. The following paragraph comes from a persuasive essay by student Marylou Orchison in favour of banning smoking in public places. Notice her effective combination of warm, neutral, and cool details, even within the single paragraph.

Sample student paragraph combining warm and cool supporting detail

Up front, I admit it: I used to be one of the many people who indulge everyday in the pleasures of a cigarette. I would light up in public places, without any regard to the fact that over 33,000 Albertans die every year as a result of smoking-related diseases (Health Canada 1997). I was as aware as the next smoker of the arguments against public control: "My dad lived to be 104, and *he* smoked" and "I have my rights—I thought this was supposed to be a free country." I frequently used these very arguments to defend my habit. Then in 1996 my mother became seriously ill. Despite her dry hacking cough, she continued to smoke. She seemed to be suffocating. When she died, I had to face the consequences of smoking, not only for myself but for those around me.

Commentary on Sample Student Paragraph

Orchison's style is relatively informal. This paragraph could almost be the text of a public address, a text intended for the ear. The first-person perspective gives the paragraph considerable emotional weight, a potential persuasive power. At the same time, too much sentimentality on this topic could have the reverse effect to the one desired, and might seem manipulative. Notice that Orchison guards against the use of loaded adjectives or adverbs (*horrifying, terrible,* etc.). She speaks personally yet simply, concisely, and declaratively—she states the precise personal facts and leaves the emotional reaction to us. This control of tone (keeping the personal aspect constrained) allows her to blend a cool proof (the statistics) into her discussion without creating a jarring sense that emotional focus has radically altered.

After stating the statistic, Orchison refers to public attitudes, looking outside herself and the personal. This represents a cooler or at least a neutral approach to her analysis. But she expresses those attitudes as representative dialogue, an evocative technique, which draws us closer to the personal. Next Orchison says, "I frequently used these very arguments." In other words, she brings the focus back to herself. From there she concludes with the strong emotional appeal related to her mother. The power of the provincial statistic remains, however, and the essay will return from the convincing personal case to its broader relevance. Orchison implies that the personal realm of knowledge supports and is supported by the empirical realm of studies and analysis. She has managed to combine warm, neutral, and cool proofs into one paragraph without compromising consistent tone.

Beware of Misuse of Facts and Figures

Use of neutral and "cool" appeals is the distinguishing method of most academic research. But remember that statistics and data may be manipulated to reach various faulty conclusions. They may be used emotionally and politically, that is, as warm appeals. Here's an example: "Unemployment claims for this year exceed those of 15 years ago by 10 percent. Clearly, abuse is on the increase." This could be a **faulty comparison,** since—for one thing—the number of workers may have significantly increased over 15 years. Other factors could be involved as well, such as a national or global recession. Another misuse of numbers is the following: "Salaries in our company are excellent, averaging over $70,000 per year." This could be a faulty conclusion based on the **myth of the mean.** Perhaps executives make $350,000 each, and a majority of other employees earn less than $25,000.

FLOW

Flow refers to the way thoughts proceed coherently and purposefully. Within paragraphs, this quality results from two main attributes: (1) purposeful arrangement of supporting ideas (fine points), and (2) transitional words.

Purposeful Order of Points within a Paragraph

Here is an example from student Lenny Halfe's expository essay "My Dream Home":

> The internal layout of my dream home is very specific. The east side of the main floor contains a large master bedroom with a walk-in closet, a smaller second bedroom, and a large bathroom. The living room/den is located in the southwest corner, while the kitchen sits in the northwest corner. A large closet greets people as they enter through the back door along with a doorway that leads to the stairs to the basement.

Halfe imagines guiding us in a natural spatial progression. Other principles of coherent order include time, cause-effect relationships, contrasts, and intensification (climactic order). Once you have organized your points, you need to consider firming up the natural flow by use of appropriate transitional words.

Transitional Words and Repetitions

Transitional words organize, guide, and intensify the flow of thought. Here is a sample paragraph by Jacqueline O'Rourke, a writing instructor, in the Athabasca University *English 155 Study Guide: Developing Reading and Writing Skills* (1990). Transitional words are in bold.

> A home usually reflects the owner's personality. **First of all,** the furniture one chooses can tell us a lot about that person. **If one chooses** modern, colourful furniture, then

we can assume that the person is a modernist, one who appreciates the present. **If one chooses** antiques, then we assume one has a sense of nostalgia for times gone by. The way one decorates the walls and floors **also** tells us a lot. **If** walls are left bare, the person may be a minimalist, **one who** prefers the simple. **If** walls are cluttered, the person may be disorganized and indecisive. **Finally, if** floors match furniture, the person may be organized and may strive to see the patterns in life. **On the other hand,** if floors are in bold contrast to walls and furniture, the person may be slightly eccentric, preferring the unpredictable and chaotic. **Therefore,** by observing someone's choice in home decoration, you can get to know that person without an actual meeting.

We can see two main types of linking devices at work in this paragraph, **transitional terms** and **repetitions.** The transitional phrases include "first of all," "on the other hand," "also," "finally," and "therefore." They reinforce a sense of logical order, reminding the reader that information is presented in a certain patterned manner. The repetition of certain key words may work as a coherence device, or the repetition may use a particular sentence pattern. In this case, the sentence pattern of dependent/independent clauses is repeated through the structure "If . . . then. . . ." As well, there is the repetition of relative clauses: "one who appreciates the present," "one who prefers the simple." In your reading of the selections in this text as well as your reading in general, pay close attention to how writers use coherence devices—transitional terms and repetitions—to glue their passages together.

Here is a partial table of **transitional terms** commonly used in connection with the organizing principles outlined earlier in this section. These terms are used within or between sentences and paragraphs.

Standard Transitional Terms

Time:	first, next, then, later, afterwards, presently, by and by, after a while, soon, as soon as, at first
Space:	on, over, under, around, beside, by, from, next, after, across, farther, toward, at, there
Comparison:	like, unlike, in contrast, similarly, on the other hand, conversely
Features:	first, second, third (etc.), another, the last, the final, also, as well, in addition, above all, especially, indeed, more important, particularly, unquestionably
Causes/Effects:	as a result, because, consequently, so, for, therefore, thus, hence

Inserting the Right Transitional Terms

The following paragraph has a clear topic sentence that provides focus at the start, supporting details that elaborate on the topic sentence in a logical, consistent manner, and a concluding sentence that clinches the discussion. But is there a shortcoming in this writing?

Reading is a difficult act. As a writer you should make this act as easy as possible by previewing your points, linking them in logical progression with appropriate transitional terms, and adhering to standard punctuation. There is good reason to preview your points. Doing so is like providing a roadmap to a traveller. The path will be clearer. You should be sure that the path you have charted on the map is efficient, that it leads as logically as it can from point to point. Your points should be in effective order, flowing purposefully one to the other. You should use linking words. This will remove any possible uncertainty about where you are going next and why. Punctuation needs to be considered because lack of correct mechanics can cause readers to wonder where one thought ends and the next begins. An opening overview of points followed by a logical flow of ideas clarified by suitable transitional terms and correct punctuation will earn you grateful readers.

You have probably observed that this paragraph is choppy. Your task is therefore to insert linking terms, as appropriate, to guide the discussion. Discuss your answers with your classmates and instructor.

Transitional Paragraphs

In addition to transitional words, **transitional paragraphs** (often just two or three sentences long) are sometimes used in essays to mark major shifts. Typically, such paragraphs summarize the discussion so far and preview the remaining points. As short paragraphs among longer ones, transitional paragraphs stand out as effective markers of division. This effect is lost, however, if they are overused.

FINALITY

Finality reminds you of the principle of clinching or cinching your paragraph: ending with a strong signal that your paragraph is now "wrapping up." Concluding your paragraphs with an appropriate final sentence fully articulates, or emphasizes, the main point and controlling idea of the paragraph. It synthesizes the thought.

The following paragraph from an essay by a university student, Jessica Serene Walker, builds to a decisive concluding sentence. This paragraph comes from an essay called "Los Niños de Nicaragua," which describes the author's 1999 trip to Managua with the non-profit organization Change for Children Association. In a previous paragraph, she has described how in certain marketplaces "projects" have been set up to offer children a place to meet and play: "Some of the projects are located in small corners of the market, blocked off from the chaos by a few boards nailed together."

Sample paragraph (note the final sentence)

One of the most difficult things to face in the projects is the hardship in these children's lives. Most come from large families and are expected to sell goods in the market by day and then come home. I met a girl who attended one of the projects for only a couple of hours in the morning because her parents wanted her to resume her sales in the market. She told me she has 10 brothers and sisters, and that after she has sold enough in the market, she must hurry home to start supper for her younger siblings, clean the house, and do laundry. She seemed so much older than she really was. She drew me a colourful picture of a house with a walkway and an abundance of flowers in the front garden—a picture so similar to the ones I used to draw when I was a little girl. She lives in one of the many homes put together with garbage-bag walls and a hard-packed dirt floor. The home in her picture is a dream.

   For the kids who live on their own in the market, life is harder still. . . . [Paragraph continues.]

Walker's terse final sentence in the first paragraph above—"The home in her picture is a dream"—sums up the details she has provided and drives home the position of her topic sentence. It also prepares us for a transition from children like this young girl to another category of children who are even more unfortunate, the homeless. This worse-off category becomes the focus of the ensuing topic sentence ("For the kids who live on their own in the market, life is harder still"). This transition also demonstrates the effect of climactic organization (building to increasingly powerful points).

   Remember that paragraph conclusions, like paragraph topic sentences, frequently assist the important process of linking ideas.

SHOULD YOU END PARAGRAPHS WITH A FACT OR A QUOTATION?

The safest answer to this question is no. Do not end with a statement of fact, because a fact does not explicitly explain the idea of the paragraph. Similarly, a quotation taken from a source is not *your* explanation. Although a fact can "speak volumes" in and of itself, and someone else's words certainly can be understood as saying what you believe, your own words best underscore the meaning of your preceding discussion.

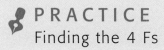
PRACTICE
Finding the 4 Fs

Look at the sample research paper in the Research Guide, Section 7 (p. 322). Critique one paragraph in the paper according to the 4-F test.

   Repeat this for one paragraph from a selection in the Reader.

Discuss your critiques with classmates and your instructor.

FINAL WORD

You have now considered the four major attributes of successful paragraphs: focus, fine points, flow, and finality. Certain paragraphs call for additional special awareness. To learn more about these special paragraphs—notably essay introductions and conclusions—and their particular strategies, see Chapter 7, "Introductions and Conclusions."

A paragraph needs to be complete in itself and offer proper support for the larger controlling idea expressed by the thesis statement of the essay. Your formal organization of these complete ideas, or paragraphs, will provide a staircase for your reader, a logical progression to a new level of awareness and relationship to the topic.

Works Cited

Ackroyd, Peter. *London: The Biography*. London: Vintage, 2001. Print.

Lipschutz, Gary, John Roberts, John Scarry, and Sandra Scarry. *The Canadian Writer's Workplace*. 5th ed. Toronto: Thomson Nelson, 2004. Print.

O'Rourke, Jacqueline, and David Brundage. *English 155 Study Guide: Developing Reading and Writing Skills*. Athabasca: Athabasca U, 1990. Print.

Chapter 5

Standard Essay Structure

As you have no doubt heard many times, all essays have a basic three-part structure.

1. OPENING

As Chapter 7 discusses in more detail, the opening introduces the topic by drawing the reader into it. Introductions briskly offer essential background information and quickly narrow to the main concern or question to be examined and explained. Most instructors of undergraduate courses expect the introduction to end with an assertion of the writer's main idea and supporting reasons, which we call the thesis statement (more on this in Chapter 6).

2. BODY

The body of the essay demonstrates the validity and truth of the thesis through argument and logical explanations based on evidence. The body needs to be substantial enough to provide and explain supporting points. The body should be organized in a way that regularly yet progressively refers back to the main idea of the essay (i.e., to advance the main idea). In a typical 750-word essay, the body will likely have three paragraphs, each dealing with a different point in support of the thesis.

3. CONCLUSION

As discussed in Chapter 7, the conclusion reinforces the main idea and points to any interesting further implications. A good conclusion closes your argument but also compels a reader to think beyond the last paragraph.

PUTTING IT ALL TOGETHER: INTRODUCTION, BODY, AND CONCLUSION

Read the following sample essay and consider how the student, Jayne Schuyler, has applied her opening, body, and conclusion. If you were to describe this essay in a short outline, how would you structure your outline, and what main points would you write down for each section? Remember to use quotation marks around any words that are those of the writer rather than your own words of summary or paraphrase. Once you have read the essay and worked out your brief outline, read our commentary, which appears right after the essay.

Sample Standard Essay Structure

Should Cats Be Allowed to Roam?
Jayne Schuyler

Topic introduced with concession to wishful thinking	1 Many people believe that because of cats' independent nature, they should be allowed to roam free. This allows them to satisfy their hunting instincts and to function within cat society, one that has its own rules and structure. Some people assert that free-roaming cats are happier cats, living a life closer to that intended by Nature. This is all true, but it is	Opening
Main idea and three reasons	not compatible with modern life in suburban North America. <u>Roaming cats are susceptible to attack</u> by <u>other animals,</u> to <u>trapping</u> by angry neighbours, and most of all, to <u>traffic accidents</u>.	
First reason	2 Despite leash laws in most communities, <u>mauled cats</u> often turn up in veterinarians' offices and city pounds. A cat raised with dogs may not recognize a dangerous dog quickly enough. Also, coyotes are a concern in most parts of Canada, including suburban areas, as most domestic cats have lost the degree of wariness they need to protect themselves	Body
Supporting details	against wild predators. For the first four months of 2006, as disclosed by Andrea Jensky of the Edmonton SPCA, there were 17 reported coyote attacks on cats living near that city's ravine. Jensky suggests that the risk may be even larger this year with higher numbers of coyotes and shortages of their usual prey. On January 4, 2006, the Vancouver *Province* reported a Vancouver woman suing the city and the B.C. government for allegedly failing to keep the streets safe after her pet cat was killed by two coyotes (Williams A-7). With all respect for the emotional state of the woman concerned, it isn't	
Reminder of the main idea	realistic to expect Canadian cities to prevent wandering coyotes or ensure that dogs never slip loose with a notion to chase the nearest roaming pet cat.	
Second reason	3 A cat is also unequipped to protect itself against <u>traps</u> set out by angry neighbours. As recorded in the *Humane Society of Canada Year-End Report for 2003,* on March 31 of that year, Edmonton City Council approved a live-capture trapping by law to apply	
Supporting details	from April to September. Citizens may obtain live-capture traps from the city to	

catch roaming cats on their properties and deliver the animals to Animal Control. Owners must pay a $100 fine and kennel fees (Humane Society of Canada). In most other municipalities whose city halls may be less willing to assist, the traps can be rented from private firms. The welfare of the cat is then in the hands of the person who was angry enough to trap it. Cats in the suburbs have to live with other people, not just with other cats, and they cannot be expected to understand the human notion of territory. Do pet owners have the right to make neighbours "share" their animals involuntarily, especially when cats exercise their feline rights to spray, dig in gardens, and fight? *Reminder of the main idea*

4   According to Dr. Ellen Talbot of the Edmonton South-east Veterinary Clinic, studies confirm that the serious <u>cat injuries</u> seen most frequently by veterinarians are those <u>caused by cars</u> (next are injuries from falls). Edmonton SPCA officer Andrea Jensky reinforces this awareness by describing numerous cases of traffic-injured cats that came to her attention in the final months of 2006. Her descriptions should make all cat owners think twice about allowing their feline pet to roam. According to the veterinarian Nicholas Dodman, free-roaming cats live, on average, four years less than do indoor cats. Car accidents are a major contributor to this shorter life expectancy of outdoor cats. Cars are not part of the natural world, but they are an unavoidable part of ours. *Third reason* *Supporting details* *Reminder of the main idea*

Conclusion 5   People in Edmonton, such as the cast of a new Stewart Lemoine play about cat ladies and computer-game addicts, certainly talk about attempts in that city to pass "zany cat laws" that would restrict the free movement of cats. People from elsewhere say the same thing. But these laws recognize a large contingent of the public. Perhaps in an ideal world cats should be allowed to roam and live their mysterious, separate lives; our world, however, is not ideal. So we need to recognize that and prevent our cat pets from becoming victims of our wishful thinking. It doesn't have to be all that bad for our pets as a consequence. We can do our best to accommodate their needs with outdoor enclosures and opportunities for friendship both human and feline (two young, compatible cats will play and sleep together as well as groom each other). For most city dwellers, <u>the dream of the free-ranging cat must be surrendered</u> as a pastoral myth. *Reprises respect for the other view* *Reminds reader that this other view is wishful thinking* *Reinforces main idea: in an unnatural place, compromises are inevitable*

Works Cited

Dodman, Nicholas. "The Great Debate: Indoor versus Outdoor Cats." *PetPlace.com*. Intelligent Content Corp., n.d. Web. 12 Oct. 2010.

Humane Society of Canada. *Humane Society of Canada Year-end Report*. Humane Society of Canada, 2003. Web. 24 Jan. 2007.

Jensky, Andrea. Personal interview. 13 Jan. 2007.

Talbot, Ellen. Personal interview. 17 Jan. 2007.

Williams, Joan. "Woman Sues over Eaten Tabby." *Province* [Vancouver] 4 Jan. 2006: A-4+. Print.

Commentary on Sample Essay

We now offer the following comments on what the student accomplishes with each section of her essay and how she has tied the separate parts together.

Opening

Schuyler draws her reader into the debate over city cats by stating arguments in favour of allowing them to roam free. She concedes that the arguments make good points—it is *natural* for cats to roam—but cities are *unnatural*. She thus states her main idea that roaming cats are "susceptible" to excessive risks (and, as her conclusion makes explicit, should be confined). She includes three reasons in support of her idea: (1) other animals, (2) angry neighbours, and (3) traffic accidents.

Body

The body of Schuyler's discussion deals with each reason one topic at a time, *in the same order* given at the end of paragraph 1. Each paragraph of the body begins with a topic sentence that includes *clear contact* with one of the three reasons given in the introduction. For instance, Paragraph 2 talks about "mauled cats," a clear suggestion of harm from "other animals." Paragraph 3 includes reference to "traps," obviously set by angry neighbours. Paragraph 4 includes the words "cat injuries . . . caused by cars." The paragraphs are sufficiently developed to provide solid supporting detail. They begin and end by reinforcing the main idea flowing from one of the three reasons given.

Conclusion

The conclusion, paragraph 5, reflects on implications of the argument that has been made.

Summing Up

As you can see, Schuyler has given herself a clear, interconnected structure so that her ideas flow in support of one main assertion. The clear points of contact between the introduction and the topic sentence of each paragraph create unity and development of purpose. Increasing this effect of unity is consistency of the points discussed: all three are *effects* of roaming.

✏ PRACTICE

Read the following essay and annotate it as we have done for the essay on roaming cats. Indicate the opening, body, and conclusion. Use different-coloured pens or different underlining styles to show the main idea and any reasons that have been included in the opening.

In the body, at contact points, match colours or underlining to the reasons previewed in the opening. Finally, suggest how additional unity may be created. When you are done, compare your thoughts with those of your classmates and instructor.

Sample Essay   Standard Essay Structure

Beginning Riders: The Untold Story

Joyce Miller

When a beginning rider mounts a horse for the first time, the rider feels awkward, unbalanced, and unsure of what to do. The horse feels exactly the same way. As a result, a horse develops one of three attitudes to beginning riders: playing dead, taking control, and taking off.

The first attitude is that of a middle-aged family pet who belongs to the new rider's neighbour, best friend, or relative. This horse spends its time dreaming in the field, the carefree succession of days broken only for the odd pleasure ride. The horse doesn't much care what gets on its back, so long as the mounted thing doesn't expect much expenditure of energy. While the new rider tries several times to swing a leg high enough to get on without dislocating a hip, the horse catches a few winks. At an uncertain tap from the rider's heels, the horse ambles a couple of metres, then lowers its head to graze. This process is repeated several times. Thirty minutes later, the ride ends six metres from where it began. The rider is a little frustrated, but no mishaps have occurred and the horse's state of Zen remains undisturbed.

A higher level of energy and more experience with beginning riders creates a horse with the second attitude: a foreman mentality. This is usually a lesson or trail horse. The horse knows what needs to be done, quickly senses that the rider doesn't know what needs to be done, and sets out to do it as efficiently as possible. Intelligent new riders realize this and, with great relief, hand over control to the most competent member of the team. This works great until the horse decides it is time to (a) return to its stall, (b) visit with friends, or (c) clear the one-metre jump in the centre of the ring. The rider may come out of this ride embarrassed, but the worst injury is usually to the ego.

The third attitude belongs to the horse no beginner should ride, and few do for long. This horse may be the "really calm cutting horse" on Uncle Fred's ranch; the "excellent young prospect" being sold cheap by a dealer; or the high-octane, under-used acreage horse whose owner is sure he's safe to ride, although she's never been on him, because the previous owner was a 13-year-old (never mind that she was a 13-year-old provincial barrel racing champ). Such a horse has lots of energy, a lively imagination, and complete inexperience with beginning riders. The sensation of 100 to 200 pounds of yanking, wobbling weight on his back brings to life a race memory of killer cougars. He makes an instant, life-saving decision which would win him a berth in the Kentucky Derby if only anyone were there with a stopwatch, and if only he still had a rider on his back. This is definitely the most painful introduction to riding, but strangely enough, there are some riders who don't give up.

Despite frustration, terror, and/or pain (or perhaps because of them), the stubborn novice rider persists until he or she no longer flops on the horse like a sack of ill-sorted potatoes. The magic day arrives when balance and technique come together. Riding becomes almost effortless; the horse seems to respond to the thought of the rider. Best of all, it is clear that the horse enjoys the experience, no longer feeling the need to play dead, take control, or flee.

FINAL WORD

In Chapter 4 we reviewed how paragraphs work. Here we have seen how three paragraphs in the body of an essay and a final concluding paragraph are linked to the introductory paragraph through the core and spine of the larger structure: the thesis statement. To alter metaphors, the topic sentences of each of the paragraphs might be thought of as rivers feeding into and sustaining that main idea. The essay has a consistent, logical shape and flow.

Both sample essays in this chapter list three reasons in support of the main idea and reinforce unity by examining effects in the first essay and by examining effects and causes in the second. Other essays may create unity by developing an extended definition, by pursuing a formal comparison, by explaining three different varieties of one subject, by looking entirely at causes, or by examining some other pattern as laid out in Section 3, "Forms to Draft By." While an essay patterned on three reasons (or points) is commonly taught in secondary levels and often occurs in the first year of college or university, it is by no means a template to suit all needs. All thesis statements contain a main idea, but not all thesis statements are shaped exactly like those we have seen in this chapter. Different types of thesis statements—suited to various purposes—will affect certain specifics of the essay structure. But the basic idea we have illustrated here is constant: successful scholarly essays are unified by a firm main idea, a thesis. More on this essential ingredient follows in Chapter 6.

Chapter 6
Thesis Statements

A **thesis statement** is the one crucial sentence in an essay that focuses you and your readers on your chosen attitude to your topic. You will be most sure of success if your thesis statement, when it first appears, does the following three things:

- occurs as the last sentence of your introduction
- expresses a strong position (a controlling idea)
- expresses the reason(s) for this position and your methods of examination

Making Your Thesis the Last Sentence of Your Introduction

Do all different types of essays use or require a clear, complete thesis statement at the end of the first paragraph? As you will see from the variety of essays in our Reader, they do not. The structure of a piece of writing depends upon the purpose of that writing. This chapter provides guidance to you *as a writer of academic undergraduate essays*. For those types of essays, the following advice is especially appropriate.

Sample Design Opening Paragraph of Short Essay

Xxxxxxxxxxxxxxxxxxxxxxxxxxxxxxxxxxxxxxxxxxx. Xxxxxxxxxxxxxxxxxxxxxxxxxxxxxxxxxxxxx xxxxxxxxxxxxxxxxxxxxxxxxxxxxxxxxxxxxxxxxxxxxxxxxxxxxxxxxxxxxxxxxxxxxxxxxxxxxxxxx xxx. Xxxxxxxxxxxxxxxxxxxxxxxxxxxxxxxxxxxxxxxxxxxxxxxxxxxxxxxxxxxxxxxxxxxxxxxxxxx xxxxxxxxxxxxxxxxxxxxxxxxxxxxxxxxx. Xxxxxxxxxxxxxxxxxxxxxxxxxxxxxxxxxxxxxxxxxxxxx. Xxxxxxxxxxxxxxxxxxxxxxxxxxxxxxxxxxxxxxxxxxxxxxxxx. Your thesis sentence goes here, concluding your introductory paragraph.

In longer, often upper-level essays, with introductions of sometimes more than one paragraph, the thesis statement appears a bit later.

Providing your thesis statement as the *last* sentence of the first paragraph makes use of a natural impact location to help ensure that your reader will recognize the importance of this statement and remember it during and after reading the essay. Here, just before launching into the journey proper, your thesis statement clearly notifies the reader of the course you have charted. Both you and your reader should be properly oriented, secure in the direction you intend to pursue as you now begin the first leg of your exploration. Although you will not see this pattern in many of the readings in the Reader, or in many writings apart from those found in academic scholarship, you will find it the most practical pattern to employ for your student papers.

Expressing a Strong Position

The first step in constructing your thesis is to work out your own **opinion** about the topic.

 PRACTICE

Which of the following statements do you think could serve as a potential thesis? Which could not, and why?

a.   According to Health Canada, in 1996–1997, 20 746 male Albertans and 12 602 female Albertans died of smoking-related illnesses.

b.   Today's universities are moving further into ill-advised collaborations with private corporations, threatening scientific neutrality and pure research.

c.   The percentage of female students attending universities since 1965 has steadily risen to the point that women now outnumber men.

Only statement b above expresses a value judgment and could therefore serve as a thesis. Statements a and c set out facts (see Chapter 3, p. 24, for more on distinguishing between fact and opinion). Your thesis should express *pathos*—a strong conviction about your topic, an attitude that you will go on to demonstrate using logos and ethos (Chapter 1 discusses the basic elements of logos, pathos, and ethos). The pathos of a solid thesis sentence is tested and supported by logos and ethos and adapted to its intended reader.

To shape an effective thesis, you first need to discover and then express a *strong position*, also known as the **controlling idea**. Remember that even the most objectively presented expository essay is never completely detached from the writer; it has focused pathos, a core of opinion. For example, on the topic of learning to play guitar, the following thesis statement might be used: "Practising one hour a day, six days of the week, is an excellent way to progress." The words "excellent" and "progress" express a strong position on the approach being recommended—the controlling idea. The essayist would also be implicitly arguing that learning music is a worthwhile endeavour in contrast to, say, watching *CSI: Miami* reruns.

Including Reasons for Your Position

You need to produce *reasons* for your position and clarify your way of presenting and explaining them. You don't want your thesis to be purely opinion, because then your readers can dismiss your position as only one person's view; someone else could have an entirely different position on the subject. Without reasons, the thesis will merely focus on you as a person. With reasons, your thesis will focus on your ideas as a reasoned argument. Most post-secondary papers require the third person, so the following examples use that voice. We have included a hypothetical "I think" in parentheses to remind you that even though you may be using the third person to focus more on the topic than on you, the fact that this is your opinion based on your reasoning is implied.

Thesis statements with reasons

(I think that) tattoos may represent, at least in part, attainment of warrior status, because that was so for traditional Polynesians.

(I think that) Alice Munro's stories demonstrate a complex view of humanity because her central characters are ordinary and flawed, her settings contain good and bad aspects, and her endings often feel unresolved.

In the first example, the reason is the point that follows the word "because." The essay introduced by this thesis appears to be a hybrid of expositional writing: reporting on research into Polynesian history and culture and analyzing the modern tattoo. In the second example, the reasons are those three items that follow the word "because." Both thesis statements present a complete map of the essay, which will discuss the stated reasons in the same order as laid out in the thesis statement. Both the reasons and their order of discussion are presented. We refer to this type of complete thesis statement as a **direct list**, because all the reasons for the position are listed directly. After reading a direct-list thesis statement, your audience will have no questions about the content and scope of your essay.

Reasons Connected to the Controlling Idea

The previous sample thesis statements use the word "because," thereby establishing that a position on the topic (a *conclusion* in logic) results from, is caused by, certain reasons. But writers often express their causes in different ways. Each of the following three thesis statements conveys reasons.

Roaming cats are susceptible to attack by other animals, to trapping by angry neighbours, and, most of all, to traffic accidents.

I begin to realize that my procrastination is caused by distractions, mounting hopelessness, and despair.

One of *The Sopranos'* meaningful motifs seems relatively overlooked thus far: food and its relationship to culture, gender, and the violence underlying the world of the characters.

These three thesis statements might be rephrased as follows:

Roaming cats invite danger because they may fall victim to predators, trapping, or vehicles.

I begin to realize that I procrastinate because I am distracted and increasingly affected by consequent hopelessness and despair.

The overlooked motif of food is extremely meaningful in *The Sopranos* because it relates to culture, gender, and the violence that underlies the characters.

As you can see, with or without the word "because," complete thesis sentences include the *idea* of "because"; that is, they include reasons for the writer's position.

Thesis as Formal Argument

As we have been suggesting, the thesis statement of a formally shaped essay asserts your reasons for a premise or premises leading to a conclusion. Think of the controlling idea of an essay as the conclusion that the body paragraphs will then prove.

When the conclusion is presented as *following* the premises, the linking word "therefore" or some similar term often leads to it. When the conclusion is stated *before* the premises, the word linking them tends to be "because" or some similar term. The introduction of your essay explicitly states the position that you have already reached—it previews your conclusion on the topic. The essay body then works through your premises, leading your reader logically and convincingly to a re-statement of that controlling idea in your essay's last paragraph.

Including Words That Express Your Method

As you discover your controlling idea and reasons and thus begin to sharpen a sense of how you might outline your essay, it is time to think ahead to the information in Section 3 of the Rhetoric, "Forms to Draft By." According to the idea and reasons you have developed, you are likely to sense a certain pull toward a particular pattern of organization.

Chapters 10 to 14 as well as 16, 17, and 18 illustrate various patterns of organization that writers use to suit their particular expositions and arguments according to purpose and intended reader. These approaches may be conveyed concisely, often with a single word, for example, "types," "ways," "examples," "kinds," "contrast," "causes," "effects," "process," "define," "analyze," and "argue." Be alert to variations of these core method words and synonyms for them. A writer may say "examine" or "explore" for "analyze," for instance, or "question" for "rebut" or "argue." By using such signal words—words keyed to the proposed *form* of discussion—writers provide valuable focus on method. You will find signal words illustrated in further detail in the above-mentioned chapters dealing with forms.

Keeping these words in mind can help you significantly, especially if you are still gaining assurance as a writer of analytical and persuasive essays.

FURTHER COMMENTS ON THESIS STATEMENTS

So far this chapter has dealt only with the direct-list thesis statement. That is for practical reasons: this approach is best for many students, especially for essays in the early stages of post-secondary work. But there is more about thesis statements that you might find interesting and helpful, if not right away, then for future reference. We conclude with this additional information.

How *Not* to Phrase Your Thesis Statements

Students sometimes have learned, or conclude on their own, that they should state their written thesis in the style of an oral explanation. Here is a typical statement using a style that is often discouraged in university writing:

> In this essay I will argue that *The Sopranos* features the motif of food, and I will show that it relates to culture, to gender, and to the violence that underlies the show and our society.

This sentence *does* express a controlling idea, reasons, and a planned method (organization) of discussion. However, its oral style sounds too informal for much university writing. Since the purpose of the essay that this sentence introduces is analysis, the first-person voice is likely not needed for any part of the paper, including the thesis. During pre-writing it would be fine for the writer to produce the above sentence as a way to connect with the topic and to ensure that he or she finds a controlling idea. But by the final draft, the writer should revise the thesis to something like this:

> One of *The Sopranos'* meaningful motifs seems relatively overlooked thus far: food and its relationship to culture, gender, and the violence that underlies the world of the characters (and by extension, our society).

There is no need to announce to your reader what you intend to get around to saying in your essay—simply say it. This advice applies even when you are using the first person.

> **Do not say** "In this essay I will argue that there are three causes of my procrastination."

> **Simply say** "I procrastinate because I am distracted and increasingly affected by consequent hopelessness and despair."

This advice, however, does not apply to all courses or situations. It is culturally relative. In Aboriginal cultures, not to mention in several post-secondary fields and programs, speaking clearly in the first person—as a person, an individual—is considered an important act of empirical experience and transparency. You must consider individual instructor expectations and program practices.

General Thesis Statements

A disadvantage of the direct-list thesis statement is that it sometimes leaves very little to the reader's imagination. Some writers therefore prefer their thesis statements to refer briefly to several reasons for their position without listing each of these reasons separately. Such thesis statements simply refer to all the reasons in a general way. A direct-list thesis statement might say the following:

> Roch Carrier's narrator in "The Hockey Sweater" is significantly expressed through two settings: the family home and the hockey rink.

A different version, cutting to just the controlling idea, might read as follows:

> Roch Carrier uses setting effectively to develop the character of his narrator.

A statement of this type might be referred to as a **general thesis** whose reasons will unfold through the essay's paragraphs.

Restating Your Thesis toward the End of Your Essay

Restating your thesis toward the end of your essay will sum up where the journey has taken us, writer and reader, and reinforce your main message in preparation for a concluding thought or challenge. Such restatement of your thesis emphasizes your focus on a controlling idea, as well as on essay structure.

Deductive Thesis Placement

Thesis statements appearing in the opening are called "deductive." The term "deductive" in this context refers primarily to location within a piece of writing (at the start) rather than to the nature of argument, though like deduction, this approach states the general principle at the start—as the final sentence of the opening paragraph. We have already discussed such a thesis location, which is the standard for the academic essay.

Inductive Placement

Delayed thesis statements appearing at the conclusion are called "inductive." The term "inductive" in this context refers primarily to location within a piece of writing (at the end) rather than to the nature of argument, though like induction, this approach carefully explores details before stating the most general principle at the end. In an essay called "British North America—Whose Creation?" (Research Guide, p. 331), student Isaac Paonessa does not state his thesis until the end:

> All these forces teamed up and laid the corner stones for a pluralistic Canada, but British North America grew into a hybrid creature of metropolitan and frontier character, with metropolitanism playing the dominant role.

This thesis location—at the end of the essay—is inductive. At the opening of his paper, Paonessa observes that following the British Conquest of New France on 8 September 1760, "it was Britain's turn to pursue its strategy in shaping British North America." He continues:

> Britain did not always get its way, for the forces within the new colonies also moulded the colonists and their governments—but when the mother country did get its way, it was through metropolitanism.

Paonessa goes on to define and illustrate metropolitanism as the main mechanism by which Britain attempted to shape its new possession. Then Paonessa defines and illustrates "frontierism," a counter-force arising from the settled populace no longer identifying as strongly or at all with the mother country. This discussion, while building toward an answer to the question posed in the title, still does not provide an explicit reply to the topic question. Only in the final paragraph does Paonessa prepare for his answer: both metropolitanism and frontierism fed British North America. At this point in his conclusion, he has expressed his position in reply to the question in his title, but his final sentence—stated above—serves to leave the reader with his most complete and firm answer, thus, his thesis.

After you have read "British North America—Whose Creation?" consider the effectiveness of this method in both focusing attention on a central topic question and piquing our curiosity to read on in search of the author's answer, which will be stated at last as the thesis. Please be aware, however, that such a delayed thesis statement is far less common than an up-front, explicit assertion in your introduction.

Using a Question to Anticipate Your Inductive Thesis

If you decide to use inductive structure, placing your thesis at the end, it is a very good idea to focus your discussion with a carefully worded question. Isaac Paonessa embeds a question in the title of his essay. Another common location for the topic question is at the end of the introductory paragraph(s). A question here will alert the reader to the central issue you intend to consider and to the specific understanding you are seeking. This focus helps to keep your essay clearly structured and motivated throughout. If Paonessa had placed his question at the end of his opening paragraph, he might have worded that paragraph something as follows:

> The British Conquest of New France on 8 September 1760 ushered in a new era. Now it was Britain's time to pursue its strategy in shaping a British North America. Britain did not always get its way—for frontierism, the forces within the new colonies, also moulded the colonists and their governments—but when the mother country did get its way, it was through metropolitanism. Only though an examination of these two counter-forces of metropolitanism and frontierism can we begin to answer the overriding question: What created British North America?

Finding an Implicit Thesis

The last type of thesis placement (or, in a sense, non-placement) is **implicit thesis placement**. This type is the most challenging for both you and your readers. It creates an air of mystery, and so invites your readers to participate more in your essay because they have to decipher the position you only suggest. Writing and shaping this kind of thesis statement takes time and thought. Creative writing essays, which tend toward informality, sometimes leave their theses unstated.

FINAL WORD

One of the smartest moves a first-year undergraduate can make in pursuit of academic success is to understand how to shape an effective thesis. Shaping an effective thesis means that you can manage applied reading skills, analysis, in many cases research skills, and understanding of persuasive tone and style.

In Section 2 we will look at how to develop an essay and, specifically, at the importance of using your evolving thesis statement to shape a careful outline prior to serious drafting. Outlining—which draws upon sound knowledge of standard essay structure and thesis statements—is an essential strategy.

Chapter 7
Introductions and Conclusions

Chapter 4 discussed qualities common to all good paragraphs. The present chapter looks at two special forms of paragraphs occurring at major impact locations: introductions and conclusions.

Openings of academic essays articulate your approach to your topic and assert a thesis statement. Closings assert finality by discussing a last idea in support of the thesis, or alternatively, summarizing the prior evidence and implications.

PARAGRAPHS USED TO INTRODUCE ESSAYS

The introduction of an essay—usually one paragraph—is where you inform readers of your chosen topic. The introduction also allows you to demonstrate that you are serious, informed, and prepared to discuss your topic with insight.

There are many types of essay introductions, but all of them achieve the following:

- announce the topic
- focus the discussion
- limit the scope of the topic to be examined in the body of the essay

Your commitment to clarity and organization in the introduction will go a long way toward earning your audience's attention and good faith for the discussion that unfolds. Introductions frequently **funnel** your readers into your topic. The first sentence addresses the topic in broad terms: "Homelessness is an intolerable situation in a prosperous society." The second sentence begins to narrow the focus of this large topic: "Government subsidies continue to provide inadequate support for Canadian homeless people and for those on the verge of homelessness." A third and perhaps fourth sentence will continue to narrow the introduction's focus on the subject while adding particular information: "Despite the annual increase in national homelessness, politicians' recent proposals to cut taxes for social aid (and 'reward taxpayers') can only signal the continued neglect of society's most helpless citizens." Finally, after setting out and narrowing your field of inquiry, you can announce your **main assertion** about your selected topic in your thesis statement. The thesis statement provides the **main claim** (or controlling idea) that you will establish, explain, and/or argue in the essay's body paragraphs. The funnel model is a helpful (and widely used) visual concept that captures the dynamic of the steady narrowing and focusing that a good introduction requires. From the first broad sentence to the specific thesis statement that you will examine in detail, the structure of your introduction should reflect this picture in your mind:

Figure 7.1
The Funnel
Introduction

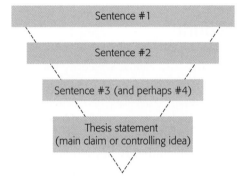

Sentence #1

Sentence #2

Sentence #3 (and perhaps #4)

Thesis statement
(main claim or controlling idea)

Sample Funnel Introduction to Essay (Showing Linking Devices)

Female action movies appear more **frequently** now since Sigourney Weaver's portrayal of the smart, tough, courageous Ripley in *Alien* and its sequel, *Aliens*. Directors realize audiences are prepared to reject the stereotype of the action movie as an **exclusively** male genre. **In particular**, James Cameron's *Terminator II: Judgment Day*, Ridley Scott's *Thelma & Louise*, and Luc Besson's *La Femme Nikita* attempt to redefine the male action genre by depicting independent women capable of defending and asserting themselves **successfully** in moments of danger and crisis. <u>The **significance** of this recent genre is its examination of everyday social presumptions about female independence, especially under extreme conditions.</u>

In this sample, the bolded linking devices serve as transitions between statements while also effectively narrowing the scope of discussion until it eventually culminates in the thesis statement (underlined).

There are several other types of introductions that can work within (or even separate from) the funnel model. As an essayist you should be prepared to work confidently with all of them in order to allow yourself the most flexibility possible in dealing with different types of essays and writing situations over your student years—and after. The method that will work best for you in a given circumstance will depend on your audience and your purpose and so will require your best judgment as an evolving writer.

> ## Seven Types of Commonly Used Introductions
>
> - The head-on account
> - The opening definition
> - The gesture to authority
> - The counter-argument
> - The anecdote
> - The question
> - The unusual or unexpected fact

The Head-on Account

The head-on account relies on crisp declarative sentences that simply establish the topic and narrow the focus to the thesis statement. Our example of introduction-building on the topic of homelessness employs this head-on method: you declare your subject and intently press forward with clear, increasingly narrowing statements. You ask no rhetorical questions, present no provisional counter-views (alternative claims), and do not have to (but can) cite authority beyond your own writer's voice. The head-on account sets a candid, certain tone for the entire essay.

We strongly recommend this no-nonsense style of introduction for your first essay in a first-year course, unless the instructor has stipulated differently in the assignment.

Open with assertions that are short and to the point—assertions that move your reader as briskly as possible to your main concern, to your thesis statement.

> ## Sample Head-on Account
>
> The Vampire in the Modern Era
>
> Norman Plummer
>
> The vampire in literature and film represents a fantasy of immortality and power. It used to be a figure of repulsion, however, a creature alone and damned. Since Bram Stoker's Victorian novel, the modern vampire has taken on new and more appealing assets: wisdom, rebel status, tragic stature, and even sexual allure. This recent appeal of vampires probably speaks to the modern age's willingness to embrace all manner of self-flattering yet grue-some fantasies, including Facebook, credit card debt, and plastic surgery—all fictions of self-transformation.

The Opening Definition

The **opening definition** specifies the objective meaning of a term or concept. This tech-nique establishes your sense of fairness and of valid questioning, since you appear to be seeking some neutral middle ground with your audience. Usually the opening-definition method signals that you will carefully and reflectively add to, qualify, or refute this accepted definition in the course of your essay. This type of introduction works best with ambiguous, contested, or emotional terms and concepts, such as "community," "family," "education," "justice," "success," and so on. Always use the opening-definition method sincerely, and not as a convenient way to chew up space.

The Gesture to Authority

The **gesture to authority** is a technique of establishing the importance of your topic beyond the bounds of the essay itself. This method creates initial momentum through your introduction and possibly creates grounds too for debate in your discussion: "Lisa Bugden, a Halifax philosopher, argues that time is a slippery concept, not an empirical fact" or "A recent Canadian survey indicates that more than 75 percent of young adults approve of multiculturalism." By citing an authority or a published credible reference, you show that you have marshalled some pertinent facts to support your views. You should make sure, however, that your introduction integrates this reference within your own position. Also remember that you may cite an authority or reference in order to contend with that view. For instance, "The Manitoban historian Patricia Murphy hastily concludes that Louis Riel was 'an outlaw capable only of reckless decisions.' The facts and purpose of Riel's defiant uprising invite a far different interpretation, however."

The Counter-Argument

The introduction as **counter-argument** sets a debate in motion. You may cite an authority or reference as in the above example or simply state a commonly held view. This is how George Orwell begins his essay "Politics and the English Language":

> Most people who bother with the matter at all would admit that the English language is in a bad way, but it is generally assumed that we cannot by conscious action do anything about it.

Orwell elaborates on this typical view in his opening paragraph and then, in his second paragraph, he opposes it by asserting that "the process is reversible."

By starting with a counter-argument, you pit your essay's thesis against the assertion of an authority or the commonly held view. This strategy generates a reader's interest immediately because you have energetically engaged in a clearly defined debate—presumably with something important at stake. The counter-argument introduction also confers some solid credit on you as a contentious essayist—a resolved and independent thinker, who is willing to question and redefine accepted notions. Both the opening definition and gesture to authority may adopt the counter-argument strategy of debate and contention.

The Anecdote

The **anecdote** introduction illustrates a point with a "language sketch": a brief episode to tell by showing. Since this type of introduction draws upon the personal, be sure your audience will appreciate a slightly informal essay opener like this one:

> Two of my Vancouver friends who listen almost entirely to American music tell me that Canadian music no longer exists as a distinct cultural expression. I always quickly remind them of the Tragically Hip's continued references to Canadian history, people, places, habits, and events. I also remind them of the Guess Who's song "American Woman," a 1970s rock 'n' roll expression of the importance of Canadian cultural resistance to Americanization.

The anecdote introduction sets a conversational tone, since it strives to share between writer and reader a vivid personal experience or private observation. Some instructors may prefer that you choose the more formal, traditional approach of beginning your paper with direct exposition or analysis.

The Question

Students often overuse the **question** introduction, often because they have not thought of any real assertions. If you quickly reel off as many as four consecutive questions in your introduction—not necessarily in logical sequence—in the hope that some focus will magically appear on the page, you undermine the potential benefits of this strategy. Try to resist this tempting late-night writing strategy for your introduction.

You should usually limit your question introduction to a maximum of two carefully considered, genuine inquiries that trigger the reader's immediate interest in the forthcoming discussion. The questions should be sufficiently complex and/or significant to arouse and sustain the reader's interest: "If, as many people claim, capital punishment is legally just in extreme crimes, can anyone ensure that a system of judgment that places people on death row is itself socially just? Why, for instance, are there mostly poor people on death row?"

The Unusual or Unexpected Fact

It was not unusual for media reports on amateur hockey in Alberta in the 1990s to open along the following lines:

> The Calgary Cougars bantam hockey team continues to record wins, holding its own in full-contact competition after moving up from the non-contact division where it dominated. By all accounts the best 14-year-old player in Alberta can be found on the Cougars. Like everyone else on the team, she's a girl. Chances are, you'll be hearing a lot more about her—so remember the name Hayley Wickenheiser.

The same technique sometimes serves for critical analysis, where it can be just as effective at making information interesting.

Example of the unusual or unexpected fact applied to critical analysis

Betraying the Spirit of Punk? The Clash's "The Card Cheat"

Mark Simpson

"The Card Cheat," track 14 on the Clash's 1979 masterpiece *London Calling,* is on first listen the album's most improbable song. Combining plaintive piano, surging horns, keening vocals, and cinematic narrative, it recollects a species of pop-rock anthem—Elton John's "Rocket Man," Billy Joel's "The Piano Man," Kenny Rogers' "The Gambler," even Meat Loaf's "Paradise by the Dashboard Light"—that, epitomizing the bloated excess of popular music in the 1970s, was anathema to punk's buzz-saw sensibility and a ready target for its vitriolic assault. Yet to conclude from this irony in musical style that "The Card Cheat" betrays the spirit of punk would be a mistake. The song's force comes from its ability to transform what punk means.

Simpson's argument, employing the unexpected "fact," is that "The Card Cheat" sounds like anything *but* a punk song, yet on further exploration, it reveals itself to be not only a punk song but one that stretches the genre. Starting with the unusual challenges the reader to continue, to see if the unusual claim has merit.

The following is the application of this surprise technique used for literary analysis:

Literary critics generally agree that *The Mystery of Edwin Drood,* Charles Dickens's unfinished final work, maintains his high standards and, in some cases, even surpasses them. These critics are wrong, not because *Edwin Drood* lacks merit, but because it isn't Dickens's last *unfinished* work. It was simply his last work. Three months ago, I discovered the remainder of the work in an old trunk at my uncle's cottage in Portsmouth. Complete scientific tests have now confirmed the authenticity of this claim.

Of course, if this were true, the writer would not need to go on developing her writing skills—at least not for purposes of financial security, since she would be able to profit vastly from her discovery.

PARAGRAPHS USED TO COMPLETE ESSAYS

An essay conclusion offers you the final chance to reinforce your ideas and persuade your readers. This is where you want to compress your discussion into one lasting expository or analytical package. This package should

- reinforce main ideas

- clinch your discussion
- raise implications for further consideration

For academic analyses of 750 to 1500 words or so, instructors often prefer short, concise conclusions. As a weary, overworked professor once said, "When your final proof has been explained, just end!" In her critical analysis "'College Girl to Call Girl': Defining the Writer's Stance" (in Chapter 17, pp. 191–193), student Valerie Desjardins pushes the short, concise conclusion to its limit by compressing it into a final, stand-alone sentence. To appreciate this conclusion, let us consider how the preceding parts of her analysis lead up to it.

Desjardins was asked to reply analytically to a topic question asking whether writer Sarah Schmidt, in her magazine article on prostitution, hides behind a stance of journalistic detachment but really sympathizes with students who engage in prostitution to pay their staggering tuition fees. Desjardins observes that Schmidt never explicitly supports or condemns the student prostitutes, so the reader must infer her intention and attitude. Desjardins examines all of Schmidt's sources and what they say and represent. She next observes that Schmidt's structure, in various ways, draws attention to a theme of middle-class rationalization and hypocrisy. She concludes by examining the effects of notable words. In her eighth and final full (or regular) paragraph, Desjardins notes that the article ends with "a resonating repetition of the word 'job'" to provide "a closing sense of what *is* against what is *seen as*." The last part of her final full paragraph and her stand-alone concluding sentence are as follows:

Sample concluding paragraph

. . . This ironic poetry of job repetition takes us through the labourer's grind of punishing physical work and tedium to the prostitute's detached ministrations to the dream job that one must "land," suggesting through this progression that in essence the jobs define each other; in essence they are one and the same.

Schmidt's tone lacks any note of serious moral accusation, but that's quite a different matter from describing the wonky world of this story as innocent.

As this example suggests, in order to convey maximum power, **final sentences** of paragraphs and especially of essays are often aphoristic reflections on the thesis. A paper on corporate greed and environmental abuse, for example, might end with the saying of the Cree elder Lone Wolf: "Only when the last tree has died and the last river has been poisoned and the last fish has been caught will we realize we cannot eat money." As illustrated here, in some cases, simply one or two final sentences of this nature at the end of the last body paragraph or standing alone as a brief, separate paragraph will be sufficient for a conclusion. Check with your instructor, however, to see if this technique will be acceptable.

Exhaustive Conclusions

Beginner essayists are often encouraged in their conclusions to repeat their thesis statement as well as the main points of the preceding discussion. This approach, known as the **exhaustive conclusion**, resembles checking off a grocery list (tell 'em what you just told 'em). The following sample exhaustive conclusion ends a paper that has examined the controversy over the Nike company's use of Third World labour to make expensive running shoes.

Sample exhaustive conclusion

Corporate good will cannot be measured directly on a profit sheet. The long-term benefits of the public's perception of corporate responsibility have become a fact in the modern market. The controversy over the continuing claims that Nike exploits Third World workers for the construction of a recreational item that promotes the health, appearance, and perhaps hollow vanity of First World joggers may impede the conscientious consumer's willingness to purchase Nike products. Nike should work more on developing a graceful long-season strategy rather than continuing to grasp for the quick, questionable win, especially as young consumers become more politically aware on the global level.

Such a conclusion summarizes the essay's previous discussion. The first three sentences do not add anything new; they consolidate the content of the paper, repeating points in the same order as before, but in language slightly different from that used in the discussion itself. The final sentence may also be repeating a point made in the body, or alternatively it might be a considered recommendation of the essayist that has not been previously mentioned (a "suggestive" strategy). An important part of this final sentence's rhetorical strategy is its use of a sports metaphor (the "long season" as opposed to the "questionable win") to drive home both an ethical and a profitable distinction. Your conclusion should represent the completion of the main strategies of your paper.

A weakness of the exhaustive conclusion is that it can seem predictable and tedious; it may also lull you into using too much of your earlier wording. Like a canoe, an essay usually works best when it's in constant motion. Even in the conclusion, where you must engage in a certain amount of backward reflection, you need to keep moving forward as well.

Suggestive Conclusions

In contrast to the exhaustive approach, the **suggestive conclusion** spends little time revisiting past ground and gives attention to implications for the reader's further consideration. This strategy assumes that if your discussion has been vigorous, then your main points have already been made; it simply remains to gather them briefly together for parting resonance and future consideration. The following suggestive conclusion completes an essay that has discussed three of Wayne Gretzky's contributions to the sport of hockey (as opposed to the business of hockey).

Sample suggestive conclusion

Gretzky's presence in hockey not only introduced more complicated and unpredictable passing strategies, and intensified team play directly in front of the net, but it also reconceptualized the offensive player as a trickster rather than as only a power-skater and power-shooter. His curious habit of suddenly stopping behind the opposing net to survey the scene also proved to be more than a crowd-pleasing showboat gesture. Gretzky in his "office" (behind the opposing net) gave his teammates a sudden wealth of opportunities to evade defenders and position themselves for a pass in front of the net. This recurrent positioning strategy momentarily allowed Gretzky, as a lone player, to set the pace of the entire action at will. Most importantly, Gretzky in his office also demonstrated that hockey can be strategically and psychologically closer to chess than anyone before his appearance was probably willing to believe.

The conclusion's first sentence—its topic sentence—summarizes the three main points of the previous discussion. Now that the entire essay has been cinched, the writer goes on to probe further into those points, thus introducing a fourth point: that Gretzky revolutionized the game with a previously unimagined cerebral style of play. The claim that Gretzky transformed an entire sport is certainly large enough in its suggestive implications to close the whole discussion. The last sentence—asserting large psychological implications to Gretzky's style of play—will probably continue to resonate with the reader after she or he has finished the essay.

In most cases, your conclusions will draw upon both the exhaustive and the suggestive models. Some instructors prefer very brief conclusions of simply three sentences. Others may expect a full exhaustive recapitulation. Ask your instructor about his or her expectations for what a conclusion should or should not attempt.

FINAL WORD

Introductions and conclusions are "specialty" paragraphs that respect the same principles of craft required of all effective paragraphs, but with the additional need to serve your reader's first and last senses of understanding. Remember that all openings and closings—whether of sentences, paragraphs, or essays—convey heightened impact. Novelist Brian Moore has said that he rewrites his opening pages over a dozen times. If your opening does not work, you risk losing your reader or at least failing to achieve your purpose. If your ending is weak, you dilute your thesis. Take extra care with opening and closing paragraphs, and—the other parts of your essay holding constant—you should see a difference in your essay grades.

Work Cited

Orwell, George. "Politics and the English Language." *The Collected Essays, Journalism and Letters of George Orwell*. Ed. Sonia Orwell and Ian Angus. Vol. 4, *In Front of Your Nose: 1945–1950*. Harmondsworth, UK: Penguin, 1970. 156-70. Print.

THE
RHETORIC

Section 2 Starting
the Journey

INTRODUCTION

You have read Section 1, "Reviewing the Basics," or know that material already, so you are ready to begin your journey. In the two crucial chapters that follow, we turn from the concepts and terms (the review material) of the previous section to an active, applied process: you start your writing. (You can always refer back to parts of Section 1 as you go.)

Chapter 8, "Ways of Starting," describes various types of activities that may help to spark and develop ideas. Too often this stage of writing, like the final stage of revision, is marginalized. Such pre-writing may seem unproductive because you are not yet turning out essay pages, but you need to settle on an interesting idea and approach in order for your essay to have meaning. Some relaxed contemplation and often a little background research and reading are ideal ways for that interesting idea to emerge. Pick a topic and give at least one or two of the recommended pre-writing methods a try—you may be pleasantly surprised by the discoveries that follow.

Some writers like to plunge into an early draft without pre-writing activities or outlining. If this works for you as a way to discover and clarify your ideas, then fine, but consider it your own form of pre-writing. The draft you produce in this rather unguided, spontaneous manner (an activity akin to extended *inkshedding*, defined on p. 76) will almost always need considerable reassembling and sharpening before it is usable. So after producing this very rough draft, break it down and develop an outline from your analysis of it, an outline that will guide your next, more formal draft.

We strongly recommend building a good outline between pre-writing activities and serious drafting. As you begin to develop your outline, you may find it helpful not only to review previous information (on standard essay structure and thesis statements, for instance), but also to consult relevant chapters of Section 3, "Forms to Draft By." Your assignment description may explicitly steer you to suitable organizational patterns. If you have doubts, however, consult your classmates and instructor. Writing is very much a collegial process, relying on good editorial thoughts from others as well as your own ultimate decisions.

You should see a notable improvement in your essays and the results they garner after applying the following practical tips on getting started and outlining.

Chapter 8
Ways of Starting

The prospect of trying to write an effective essay sometimes feels daunting. How does one begin? Some students, anxious to take up the challenge, dive right into a first draft. If that is your preference, then consider your draft as a pre-writing activity rather than a formal first draft—what we call inkshedding below. Before working on your formal first draft, ease into the topic by exploring it intuitively through pre-writing activities and contemplation. Different pre-writing activities suit different people. In this chapter we present seven choices that you may wish to try and perhaps adapt with others. Spending up to a quarter of your time on your essay with pre-writing and outlining (see Chapter 9) is entirely reasonable. This is especially so when you need to do some preliminary research (often the case for post-secondary assignments).

SEVEN PRE-WRITING STRATEGIES

At the pre-writing stage you are encouraged to indulge in conceptual play. Pre-writing is a helpful way of talking to yourself that creates some chain of associations that will eventually take shape as the essay's first draft. Here are some common strategies you can use at this pre-writing stage:

- making a collage
- freewriting
- brainstorming
- diagramming
- building a topic-sentence tree
- inkshedding
- keeping a journal

Making a Collage

Collages can be a good way to explore your feelings and ideas about some topic for personal writing (such as your community) or about an artistic subject, such as a novel, film, or piece of music. The images in your collage need not be "realistically representational," but instead could be abstract lines, patterns, word concepts, shapes, or colours. The real point is that these images speak to you as coming from the meaning and heart of the topic. Developing this playful, intuitive, tactile, even physical relationship may help you grasp your own connections to the topic from unconscious, non-verbal sources.

Imagine that your assignment is to discuss some aspect of Mary Shelley's nineteenth-century novel, *Frankenstein.* You could find images in magazines and elsewhere or produce drawings that express important elements of the narrative for you. What images would you choose to portray Dr. Frankenstein and the creature (whom Victor Frankenstein has created from various remains of corpses)? How would these images relate to others expressing ideas raised by the novel, such as the direction of Western science, the notion of progress, the pain of losing a loved one? Assemble these images in whatever spatial relationship feels appealing and meaningful to you. A sample collage on *Frankenstein* is provided here by Canadian artist Randy Tripp (Figure 8.1).

Figure 8.1
Sample Collage for
Mary Shelley's
Frankenstein, by
Randy Tripp

Occupying the entire right side, the creature dominates the collage—as he does the novel. Here he is portrayed without an arm, suggesting the sense of incompleteness that always besets him. In the left foreground, the figure representing the fictional Dr. Frankenstein also suggests a real-life twentieth-century physicist. Breakthroughs in physics enabled the early 1940s work of the Manhattan Project under Dr. J. Robert Oppenheimer, sometimes called "the father of the atomic bomb." Above the physician/physicist figure, a mushroom cloud speaks to the dark outcomes of science. Reportedly the co-pilot of the B-29 that dropped "Little Boy" on Hiroshima on 6 August 1945 wrote in the plane's log, "My God, what have we done?" The bombings of Hiroshima and Nagasaki happened over 100 years after Mary Shelley wrote her novel, and yet her depiction of Dr. Frankenstein wildly misusing the new scientific wonder of his age—electricity—foreshadows such "wonders" to come as the splitting of the atom. Dr. Oppenheimer himself, after watching the atomic bomb's test on July 16, 1945, quoted Hindu scripture: "I am become Death, the shatterer of worlds." These sorts of thoughts could inform a preliminary outline. Analyzing and discussing your collage with others is a good transitional step from free-form thinking to translating your ideas into words.

 PRACTICE

Make your own collage to express your preliminary responses to one of the seven narrative pieces in the Reader, Section 1. You may also try a collage or two based on a film, song, or current event.

Freewriting

Freewriting means picking up pen or pencil or sitting at the keyboard and simply letting yourself go. You write whatever comes into your head, without stopping, for a designated short period. The continuous nature of freewriting allows for no self-doubting, paralyzing hesitations in your thinking, diction, syntax, or editing: no second-guessing in any way of your thoughts in that moment. The experimental U.S. writers called "The Beats," including Jack Kerouac, who famously wrote *On the Road,* believed in freewriting to access genuine content. Some or even much of your freewriting may not even directly address your topic. The point is not direction or polished content here—only writing in uninterrupted motion, only unfettered thinking as highly personal expression. After all, freewriting is for *you only,* not for any other audience.

The following sample of freewriting comes from an essay by internationally renowned writing teacher Peter Elbow. He notes that this is "a fairly coherent" sample. Yours may be just as coherent or less so.

Freewriting

I think I'll write what's on my mind, but the only thing on my mind right now is what to write for ten minutes. I've never done this before and I'm not prepared in any way—the sky is cloudy today, how's that? Now I'm afraid I won't be able to think of what to write when I get to the end of the sentence—well, here I am at the end of the sentence . . . I forgot what I was leading into. This is kind of fun oh don't stop writing—cars and trucks speeding by somewhere out the window, pens clittering across people's papers.

—Peter Elbow, "Freewriting," in *Exploring Language*, 7th ed., ed. Gary Ghoshgarian (New York: HarperCollins, 1995), 19–21.

It may help you to think of this raw prose as a type of play, like making a collage or brainstorming. Freewriting sidesteps your inner critic and releases you from the pressures of grammar, vocabulary, and structure. As a result, you can contemplate the more associative, mysterious dimensions from which you may later draw ideas of more potential analytical value.

 PRACTICE

Freewrite for one page on one or more of the following topics: an ideal vacation, why you do or do not vote, some good memories, a favourite song.

Brainstorming

When you brainstorm, you think about, talk about, and/or jot down spontaneous thoughts, feelings, associations, and notions evoked by your topic. As with freewriting, this activity is intuitive and open. But whereas freewriting flows *continuously* and inkshedding (discussed later in this chapter) makes more *considered connections* between sentences, brainstorming is more intermittent: a scattering of only possibly related points. It allows you to try out particular hunches, to let your ideas churn. Here, you still conjure rather than edit, writing down single words, phrases, or brief sentences. You may make lists and draw pictures to represent your conceptualizing. You may lie on the couch listening to music, asking yourself what part of your topic interests you. Trust that answers will come, if you take the activity of reflection seriously. You may wish to try out your initial ideas on a friend or classmate. Some teachers encourage group brainstorming as a creative search in which the participants' ideas stimulate further ideas in one another. We often simply call this "group work" in the classroom context.

Brainstorming poses questions for mental stimulation. What is my sense of this? Why do I have this impression? Can I link two of my observations? If I sense some contradictions, can I account for this tension or disjunction?

Centuries of suddenly revealed solutions, definitions, and intuitions indicate that the results of productive brainstorming often emerge under the influence of other activities. Take a bath, listen to music, clean the kitchen, write a letter, or go for a walk—just keep trying out parts of your ideas.

Brainstorming on the topic of buying a car

Graduation! Time to buy a car??? Cost/features/insurance? Really need a new one or how about second-hand? Student loan still large! One debt after another—just normal life or becoming a consumer drone? What if . . . real life = consumer drone? But a car creates a great private space to and from work: music, thoughts. But car necessary purchase? Perhaps bus not so bad but lots of eccentric commuters who want to talk about the CIA and X-Files. Car looking good.

 **PRACTICE**

Brainstorm on one of the following topics: living with a difficult roommate, achieving an interesting look on $30 or less, recognizing four types of customer or music fan.

Diagramming

Diagramming draws (brilliant pun intended) on the strong link between picturing your ideas and writing about them. Once you have formed some ideas through various intuitive techniques, you can visualize, explore, and develop relationships among these ideas through diagramming. The following figure represents diagramming used to identify and organize ideas in response to essay topics. Diagramming will help you to both develop a thesis—your specific position to be supported—and consider counter-arguments against your thesis.

Figure 8.2
Diagramming on the Topic of the Ethics of Cloning

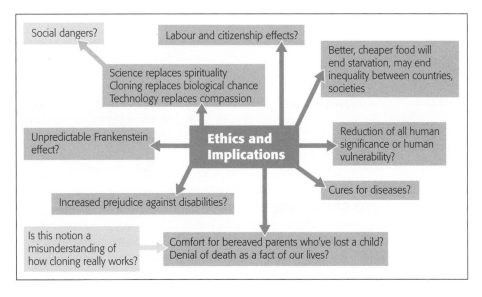

Using this last example for ideas, try the following exercises.

 PRACTICE

Diagram ideas on two or more of the following topics:

- a comparison of old-car and new-car ownership
- the benefits and/or disadvantages of home learning
- the benefits and/or disadvantages of the Internet

- an argument for or against reducing carbon emissions to 350 parts per million within the next 80 years
- a how-to essay sharing your enthusiasm for a favourite activity, such as playing pool

Building a Topic-Sentence Tree

Collaging, freewriting, brainstorming, and diagramming will lead you to ideas about your topic. A topic-sentence tree develops that sense further, so that you can shape a tentative thesis and overall discussion. Like diagramming, a topic-sentence tree visually represents relationship, examples, assertions, and counterpoints. However, it is a more advanced form of diagramming in that the statements you place in your "tree" may, with a little further consideration and refinement, stand as topic sentences in your essay. You are still at the exploratory stage, still testing—but now with an eye to evolving fully articulated topic sentences in effective relation to the thesis (main tree trunk) of the whole. You do not yet know what precise order they will take.

See Figure 8.3 for an example of a topic-sentence tree for an essay on the 2004 film *The Bourne Supremacy*.

All writing is a form of rewriting, so as you develop your essay from the topic-sentence tree you will probably revise the wording of some topic sentences, cut certain ones, and add new ones. You may wish to explore two or three versions of a topic-sentence tree for your essay.

 PRACTICE

Build topic-sentence trees for a discussion of one of the following subjects:
- a plan for improving some procedure at your college or place of work

- an analysis of a film or short story or poem
- a position for or against mandatory musical education until Grade 12

Inkshedding

Inkshedding is a focused form of freewriting that expresses a view or analysis, and the rules of grammar apply. You take more time with your diction and syntax and

Figure 8.3
Topic-Sentence
Tree: *The Bourne
Supremacy*

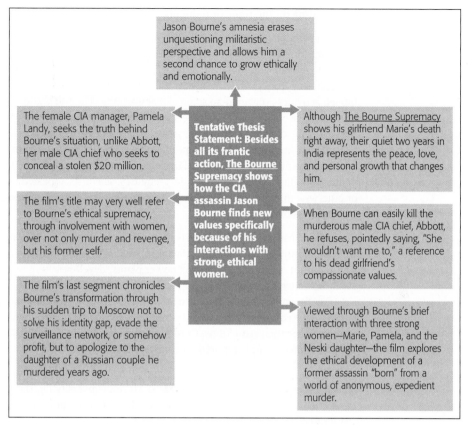

Jason Bourne's amnesia erases unquestioning militaristic perspective and allows him a second chance to grow ethically and emotionally.

The female CIA manager, Pamela Landy, seeks the truth behind Bourne's situation, unlike Abbott, her male CIA chief who seeks to conceal a stolen $20 million.

The film's title may very well refer to Bourne's ethical supremacy, through involvement with women, over not only murder and revenge, but his former self.

The film's last segment chronicles Bourne's transformation through his sudden trip to Moscow not to solve his identity gap, evade the surveillance network, or somehow profit, but to apologize to the daughter of a Russian couple he murdered years ago.

Tentative Thesis Statement: Besides all its frantic action, The Bourne Supremacy shows how the CIA assassin Jason Bourne finds new values specifically because of his interactions with strong, ethical women.

Although The Bourne Supremacy shows his girlfriend Marie's death right away, their quiet two years in India represents the peace, love, and personal growth that changes him.

When Bourne can easily kill the murderous male CIA chief, Abbott, he refuses, pointedly saying, "She wouldn't want me to," a reference to his dead girlfriend's compassionate values.

Viewed through Bourne's brief interaction with three strong women—Marie, Pamela, and the Neski daughter—the film explores the ethical development of a former assassin "born" from a world of anonymous, expedient murder.

will probably reread your piece of writing to make little adjustments. Though no grade is assigned, the instructor or classmates may read and comment on this writing, which is never the case with freewriting. Inkshedding is spontaneous writing but not necessarily a continuous motion activity. In some forms of inkshedding, one student can even write after another, as a chain of composition. For one inkshedding exercise, an instructor can give students approximately 15 minutes to produce half a page of relatively unified commentary on an assigned topic. Many non-fiction prose classes, introductory English classes, and communications classes use inkshedding as a writing activity that allows students quick feedback on their writing skills.

See the next page for an inkshedding sample. The exercise focuses a student's efforts on taking responsibility for a view that he or she expresses in writing. Inkshedding's spontaneous nature and short duration also encourage students to learn to feel confident in their own writing voices.

Inkshedding on the topic of reducing carbon emissions to 350 parts per million

Should governments seriously pursue a reduction in carbon (greenhouse gas) emissions to 350 parts per million? Some people brought the fear of global warming caused by humans to public attention in the 1980s. Very few people then took the idea seriously. Today, while there are still some skeptics, most scientists agree that human activities contribute to some global warming. The International Panel on Climate Control (IPCC) believes we should cut carbon emissions to 350 ppm by the end of the century. It's true that some IPCC scientists were suspected of having shaped their findings to some extent to conform to current views of human influence, but scientists are human, and these would not be the first to be influenced by politics. We might also point out how many U.S. scientists appeared to be muzzled or otherwise influenced to agree with the party line that there is nothing to fear with carbon emissions.

The IPCC consists of many scientists from many countries. They recommend that we exploit only the most readily available oil and gas. Some further recommend a moratorium on building coal-fired power plants, development of unconventional fossil-fuels such as tar sands, leasing of public lands and remote areas for oil and gas exploration, and hydraulic fracturing. Some experts believe a carbon tax is needed, rather than Kyoto-type accords that result in political and financial wheeling and dealing rather than reductions. Certainly little changed in Canada under Kyoto— the government simply ignored its commitments.

I rely on my doctor to interpret X-rays and recommend treatment, so why not rely on earth scientists? In a speech last year at McGill University Dr. David Suzuki suggested that some of our political leaders could be put in jail for having neglected our written agreements.

 PRACTICE

Produce a half-page of inkshedding on one of the following topics: cellphone use, rock concert experiences, standard English versus slang, non-smoking legislation, an essay of your choice from the Reader, violence in sports or in film, tattooing and/or body piercing, true love in the modern world, an enlightening moment.

Keeping a Writer's Journal

Journals are notebooks in which writers record thoughts, ideas, pictures, descriptions, summaries, quotations, dreams, responses to readings, social and political events, and just about anything else of substance or fleeting impression.

A journal can prove a valuable reference source. Keeping it encourages the writer to look intently, to think seriously, to stretch awareness, to keep writing every day (*jour* is French for "day"). From this brief daily exercise, new inspiration and skills will flow.

The journal provides an excellent forum for thinking before and after classes. Before lectures or workshops you can write down your ideas on the approaching topic. After the class, while the content is still fresh in your mind, you can review your preliminary ideas and contrast them with what you have learned. You can note any points that may remain unclear to you. Dating your entries allows you to look back on the unfolding logic of your various subjects.

Remember that you are writing for yourself in order to produce expressions that help you think through class texts, discussions, or indirectly related issues. With an academic journal, your instructor may wish to examine your entries and may have some format requests, but otherwise entries can take whatever form works best for you. Many writing instructors find that students produce their best writing in journal entries. This may be because students feel less inhibited when writing for themselves. You can be direct, natural, and honest. These are fundamentals of good writing and connect you with your own voice, one of the greatest breakthroughs in the growth of any writer.

Here is a brief example of what a journal entry might look like:

Journal entry

– Was given an interesting assignment in my writing class last week (finally!)

– Had to pick a news story from a recent newspaper and look for any social biases in it—in language, the photograph accompanying the article, or the headline. The teacher asked, "<u>How</u> is a meaning or interpretation created?" Weird!!!

– Don't know yet what exactly I'll write my analysis on, but started reading the newspaper a little bit every day now—amazed at how the photos and headlines work as interpretation <u>before</u> I even read the news story.

– Also noticed how different newspapers treat the <u>same</u> story a little differently. (The teacher asked us, "Who is the target audience of different newspapers? And for each news story?")

– Now I'll have to pick a particular story and start a rough draft of my analysis soon.

Example from a Professional Writer

Many professional writers keep journals. Following is a sample from the journal of Canadian writer Thomas Wharton, author of two internationally acclaimed novels,

Icefields (1995) and *Salamander* (2001); one collection of short fiction, *The Logogryph* (2004); and works for children.

> Sitting here, nothing by me, rock, and the flutter of the paper in the wind. The barest elements for writing.
>
> I haven't really tried to describe the mountains themselves yet, though. How to do it without lapsing into the easy clichés about their very palpable majesty and fearfulness? Maybe try to think of them as a quantum extrapolation of the ground-up pebbles at my feet. Pick up a single rock and describe it. The cool, pitted, unpretentious, ancient, trustworthy, secretive, implacable feel of a rock in my hand. The delicate, minute surface striations and scoring etchings. Whorls of veins of colour. The globular, unplannable asymmetry that gets recreated in the vast peaks above.
>
> Next try a boulder. Well, it's more an obelisk easily six feet taller than me. That D.H. Lawrence poem about a boy and a horse standing next to each other. The poet says they are in another world. That's what it feels like standing next to this massive rock. We are together, somehow, in another world, where no one speaks.
>
> —Excerpt from journal of Thomas Wharton, spring 1990

In a personal communication for our first edition of *Acting on Words,* Wharton reflects on keeping a journal and using it to work out the problem of how to describe the Rocky Mountains in *Icefields*:

> Early on, I realized that it was healthy to think of what I was doing as a kind of translation. That this place I was trying to write about had a language, so to speak, all its own, a non-verbal language. And that if I was going to go beyond mere post-card clichés about the majesty of the peaks, the pristine beauty, etc., I was going to have to try to carry across to the reader something of that non-verbal world. And that, as I carried my impressions across into words, something of that non-verbal world would be lost.
>
> As I wrote, I kept notebooks of my thoughts, ideas, dreams, alternative story-lines, etc. I saw this series of notebooks as a kind of "dream-version" of the book I was writing, where I allowed myself to write all the immediate, unedited, silly things that might not necessarily be allowed into the novel.
>
> And I find this dream-book fascinating to read through now because it is a raw record of process, in a way that the finished book isn't. I can see the processes of translation at work in my journals. Taking material from my own experiences and memories, from history and literature, from the sheer seductive power of words.
>
> —Commentary by Thomas Wharton, 2002

Remember, you don't have to be writing a novel to apply the journal-writing process. Passages from your journal may, in part, make their way into your essays or exam answers, or into questions and answers in class.

PRACTICE

Look in bookstores for a style of blank notebook that suits you. It should be durable and portable, yet large enough to allow fluid writing. Many writers like a notebook that lies open without pressure.

Remember to date your entries.

YOUR TOPIC NARROWED

Having explored a topic or topics through one or more creative pre-writing activities, you will likely have found an angle of interest and some specific points of relevance. You are now ready to move on to the next stage of more formal drafting, which we will deal with in the next chapter.

Chapter 9
Outlining

Your instructor hands out topic choices for an essay of around 750 words. You choose a topic and begin to think about it and to explore one or two methods of pre-writing. Depending on your personality, you may jump right into a rough draft without worrying about its organization. This can be energy- and time-intensive, but for some it serves as an extended form of inkshedding. The result is a disorderly but potentially useful source of initial thoughts and ideas. However, *the time comes when you should work from an outline.*

Some writers, in contrast to the above example, feel ready to build an outline without much or any pre-writing activity aside from contemplation of the topic—it depends on the individual. In any case, starting to outline marks a transition from brainstorming and preliminary rough explorations *toward serious drafting.*

THE FIRST OF THREE IMPORTANT STEPS

Some instructors may ask you to recognize the essay writing journey formally by submitting papers in three stages:

1. outline and source information,
2. first draft, and
3. final draft incorporating revisions based on instructor and peer feedback.

Whether or not this is a formal requirement of your course, we strongly recommend proceeding to the final draft according to these three steps (when you have done some pre-writing). Step one is developing an outline around a solid thesis statement and related topic sentences. As we discussed in Chapter 5, "Standard Essay Structure," and Chapter 6, "Thesis Statements," an effective thesis sentence is critical. *Outlining is how you sharpen your thesis while organizing your discussion around it.*

Furthermore, outlining helps you consider the sorts of appeals you should make to your reader. It also draws to your attention important steps you still need to take—whether gathering more information on your topic, learning about a particular pattern of organization that suits your purpose, applying special rhetorical techniques, such as an opening strategy, and so on. Finally, outlining reminds you of the key impact points in standard essay structure (introductions, thesis, topic sentences, conclusions) and how to make them work for your particular topic.

DEVELOPING YOUR OUTLINE

Ideas, Standard Essay Structure, and Thesis Statement Shaping One Another

Remember Standard Essay Structure and Thesis Statements

As we showed in Chapter 5, all essays have defined openings, bodies, and conclusions. We also showed that each paragraph has a topic sentence (see p. 48). As we explained in Chapter 5 and Chapter 6, essay structure relates to the controlling idea and its supporting reasons given. The topic sentences of the body paragraphs connect to the reasons of the thesis. Outlines establish this interconnected relationship between main ideas and content.

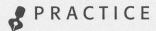 PRACTICE

Read Jayne Schuyler's essay "Should Cats Be Allowed to Roam?" in Chapter 5 (p. 46). Without looking at what follows, outline the main parts of that essay. Observe any key rhetorical appeals or techniques as well as sorts of support for main points.

Now that you have outlined "Should Cats Be Allowed to Roam?" compare your outline with the following suggestion.

Outline for "Should Cats Be Allowed to Roam?" by Jayne Schuyler

Opening

Intro paragraph: Uses concession-refutation to establish argumentation tone—ends with the thesis statement.

Thesis: Roaming cats are susceptible (1) to attack by other animals, (2) to trapping by angry neighbours, and (3) to traffic accidents.

Body

Topic sentence 1: Mauled cats often turn up in veterinarians' offices [demonstrating a high incidence of attacks by predators]. Examples of animals that could attack cats are given. SPCA statistics reinforce this problem, and an SPCA worker speculates that the risk of attacks by wild animals may be increasing. A newspaper story reports an attack in Vancouver. The paragraph ends by saying that cities cannot prevent these attacks. Thus the topic of animal attacks is intensified.

Topic sentence 2: A cat is also unequipped to protect itself against traps. Referring to documentation in a Humane Society report, the author discusses a live-capture bylaw and the problems this raises. The paragraph ends asking rhetorically if it is reasonable to expect neighbours to tolerate the impact of cats on neighbours' properties. Thus the inevitability of trapping is reinforced.

Topic sentence 3: The serious injuries seen most often by veterinarians are those caused by cars. SPCA statistics and information from a veterinarian and an SPCA worker present an impression of numerous seriously injured cats. The paragraph concludes by stressing that cars are not natural whereas cats are: the latter cannot mix with the former.

Conclusion

The concluding paragraph begins with reference to an Edmonton play on cat ladies, leading to a concession that confining cats may seem "zany," but the laws reflect a large segment of citizens in a less-than-ideal world. Topic sentence: Although in an ideal world cats should be allowed to roam, our urban world is not ideal, and so— for their own good—it is best to keep cats confined.

Commentary on the Suggested Outline for "Should Cats Be Allowed to Roam?"

This is a "descriptive" outline, one that simply *observes* the essay. It is a rhetorical process description. Writing descriptive outlines of essays you read will sharpen your sense of how to outline your own essays.

The list on the next page gives you 10 steps you can follow to outline an essay on any topic, including your hypothetical essay on the Internet. In contrast to the descriptive outline on roaming cats we have just illustrated, the outline to writing your own essay will be "prescriptive"; that is, it will tell you not only what to say but also what research to pursue and what rhetorical strategies might serve you best.

Outlining an Essay: 10 Steps to Success

Here are 10 steps you can follow in an outline on an essay on the benefits and detractions of the Internet.

1. Adapt for length. An essay of five paragraphs is like a small suitcase; you cannot jam it full of too many things, so find a way to narrow. For example, discuss the benefits of the Internet *in education.*
2. Consider your audience. If you are to read or present your paper to a classroom of students belonging to a group that boycotts social software because of perceived ulterior corporate motives, acknowledge those concerns.
3. Strategically position in your outline main ideas from experts and thinkers that reflect your awareness of those critical of your position as well as those favouring it.
4. Work through various versions of the outline until you feel satisfied with your direct-list thesis statement, for example, "Although the Internet raises various serious questions, we should embrace its potential for good because technology itself is not harmful and because we find valuable contributions of the Internet in many important fields, such as education."
5. Work through the outline until you find a suitable number of promising topic sentences (usually four or five), one for each important point you intend to discuss.
6. Reflect on the form of organization that your discussion seems best suited to. Consult Section 3 of the Rhetoric, "Forms to Draft By," for illustrations of organizational structures that could suit your emerging purpose.
7. With a suitable organizational strategy in mind, revisit your ideas for topic sentences and decide where they best fit in your sequence. Consider revising their wording to help reflect your main idea.
8. Include notes to yourself—reminders and tips—for example, "Open with the quotation from Lanier," "Check for data on numbers of Internet users," "See Chapter 14 on Comparison-Contrast structures," "See Chapter 18 on concession-refutation approaches and ways to frame the message."
9. Consider discussing your draft outline with classmates and your instructor.
10. Set your outline aside for a time. "Sleep on it" for at least one or two nights. Then look at it again and try to imagine how it will affect someone else. Does it seem to offer a clear and convincing path that supports your main idea? Are there any confusing or possibly illogical transitions?

FORMAL GUIDELINES FROM YOUR INSTRUCTOR

In some cases, your instructor may require you to fill in a pre-set outline form, perhaps for a portion of the overall assignment mark. This can help you to sharpen your outline. Here is a typical outline assignment form from an instructor.

Assignment: Essay Outline

With your chosen topic in mind, provide answers to the following seven categories:

1. Topic: _____

2. Intended audience for my essay: _____

3. Purpose of my essay: _____

4. Working title of my essay: _____

5. Tentative thesis statement (controlling idea and reasons):

    _____

6. Five or six sources I am considering and why. List your sources in the format used for Works Cited. In a few sentences for each source, explain why you think it will be useful. You may put your source information on the back of this form or attach it as a separate page.

7. Detailed prescriptive outline. This portion must be at least 350 words long and should include your thesis statement and topic sentences for your paragraphs. Include self-directed instructions referring to rhetorical appeals you need to accomplish, further information you need to find, and any additional writing techniques you think may serve in various places. Please attach your outline to this form as a separate page.

Answering Your Instructor's Initial Six Questions Related to Developing Your Outline

The seventh question in the instructor's outline assignment form deals with the main concern of this chapter: shaping a detailed prescriptive outline. But the first six questions are valuable to consider as you complete that important self-guide. Before we deal with the detailed outline itself, here are suggestions to help you fill in the first six categories of the instructor's form. These first six points help to contextualize and sharpen your outline. Let us stay with the Internet topic.

1. **Topic.** For 750 words, the topic of the Internet is huge, especially if you are to reflect on both problems and potential. However, being asked to reflect on "big"

questions—such as whether the world is getting better or worse—immediately forces you to summarize effectively. Taking on such large, complex issues in a short essay will work only if you adapt a tone of offering ideas for further thinking rather than stating absolutes. Most importantly, narrow your topic.

2. **Intended audience.** For many post-secondary essays, the audience may simply be "other interested students and instructors." But it helps to develop a more specific sense of your imagined readers. For instance, let's imagine that you are to present your essay to another section of your English or Communications course, one that is known to be concerned with elite domination of the Internet (certain corporations exercising too much control and deriving dispro-portionate gains) and inadequate privacy protections. You would name that section as your audience, for example, "Communications 1030 (B)."

3. **Purpose.** For the purpose of your essay, using the Internet topic example, you would say something like this: "To motivate Communications 1030 (B) to consider that while certain problems definitely exist and need attention, the Internet has much potential, as is notably illustrated in education."

4. **Working title.** A working title, like a working thesis, can and usually will develop and sharpen as you go along. For the Internet topic, for now you might write "The Internet: The Bad and the Good." You could include a note saying that your title will somehow change to incorporate the idea of learning, for example, "The Internet: The Bad and the Educational," but you don't think that sounds quite right. By placing "good" after "bad" in your first essay title, you at least suggest that your essay will concede the bad but emphasize the good. You keep thinking about your final version of your title.

5. **Tentative thesis statement.** Your tentative or working thesis statement should include your controlling idea and your reasons. Early drafts of your outline may have a fairly vague controlling idea and simply a general sense of reasons. For example, your early outline might say, "The Internet should be accepted, because it is part of a technological wave that will not stop." After further thinking and development, you might settle on the following working thesis for your outline: "Although the Internet raises problems that demand suitable responses, it is inherently neutral, simply a tool that can be used for bad or, as the field of education demonstrates, for good." The revised version for your improved outline results in a thesis that points to the overall strategy of your essay (concession-refutation) as well as to your main reason (demonstrated contributions in education). You may still make the point that the Internet is part of an irreversible wave, but this point alone is not much of a justification. As well as being a stronger argument, the new version of the thesis avoids an overly simple and perhaps dogmatic-sounding response to a large, complex topic that you cannot reasonably "solve" in 750 words. This new version provides an explicit reason to which you will clearly connect what follows.

6. **Planned sources.** Your instructor has asked for five or six sources. The ones you finally decide to use for your citations need to be the best you can find in fulfilling the expectations for good sources: up-to-date, authoritative, interesting,

and somewhat complex. Complexity arises from sources that demonstrate concession-refutation, as well as from sources that do not all agree with each other. It is up to you to explain to your reader how to reconcile the different views suggested by the contending sources.

Filling Out the Instructor's Outline Assignment Form

Assignment: Essay Outline

With your chosen topic in mind, provide answers to the following seven categories:

1. Topic: _____

The Internet—problems and potential, with particular attention to education

2. Intended audience for my essay: _____

Communications 1030 (B)—who are boycotters of social software

3. Purpose of my essay: _____

To motivate Communications 1030 (B) to consider that while certain problems definitely exist and need attention, the Internet has much potential, as notably illustrated in education.

4. Working title of my essay: _____

The Internet: The Bad and the Educational

5. Tentative thesis statement: (controlling idea and reasons)

_____

Although the Internet raises problems that demand suitable responses, it is inherently neutral— simply a tool that can be used for bad or, as the field of education demonstrates, for good.

6. Five or six sources I am considering and why. List your sources in the format used for Works Cited. In a few sentences for each source, explain why you think it will be useful. You may put your source information on the back of this form or attach it as a separate page.

Bodain, Yan, and Jean-Marc Robert. "Investigating Distance Learning on the Internet." *Proceedings of the INET Conference 2000*. 18–21 July 2000. Japan: Internet Society. *Internet Society*. Web. 14 Apr. 2010.

　　Although sponsored by spanky IT companies, the INET Conference uses peer review. Bodain works for a research centre, Robert for a polytechnic. Their paper identifies as many disadvantages as advantages of Internet-delivered education. Information from 2010, 10 years after this paper was published, shows a big growth in Internet users and capabilities. Quite a contrast between online education 10 years ago and views of today.

Duffy, Thomas, and Jamie R. Kirkley. *Learner-centered Theory and Practice in Distance Education: Cases from Higher Education*. Mahwah, NJ: Erlbaum, 2004. Print.

> My interest is Part II, "Community Building" In their 2000 paper, Bodain and Robert refer to the "lack of inter-action" with other students in online learning. Articles in the Duffy and Kirkley anthology show that only four years later, much had happened to build student communi-ties within courses or at least to make the scholarly com-munities more aware of online community building.

Lanier, Jaron. *You Are Not a Gadget: A Manifesto*. New York: Knopf, 2010. Print.

> *Publishers Weekly* says this recent publication is a "fascinating . . . exploration of the internet's problems and potential." I agree. A Silicon Valley web designer since 1980, Lanier coined the term "virtual reality" and has worked on the interface between computer science and medicine, physics, and neuroscience. Despite being a strong critic of certain directions of the Internet today, he still sees its potential. Lanier's book is very informative and sees the pros and cons. He doesn't say too much about the Internet in education, though.

Miniwatts Marketing Group. "Internet Usage Statistics." *Internet World Statistics*. Miniwatts Marketing Group, 2010. Web. 14 Apr. 2010.

> The latest statistics from this site confirm claims of "rapid and unrelenting technological change" over the decade from 2000 to 2010 (see Ruhe below). Seventy-two percent of Canadians and 78% of North Americans are reportedly Internet users. Growth rates over the past 10 years have been sky-high, e.g., 1675% in the Middle East. There are currently an estimated 764 million users in China. This growth has included all types of online groups using forums and conferencing tools. The uncertainty expressed by Bodain and Robert in 2000 over whether the Internet can provide ways to create communities of interactive learning is surely fading.

Ruhe, Valerie, and Bruno D. Zumbo. *Evaluation in Distance Education and E-learning: The Unfolding Model*. New York: Guilford, 2009. Print.

> This recent scholarly publication says that there has been a "recent expansion of distance and e-learning

courses" arising from "rapid and unrelenting technological change." This supports the idea that the Internet is not only gaining a greater base but moving forward in solving educational needs. Some of these needs arise from social change, and some relate to long-standing lack of access.

7. Detailed prescriptive outline. This portion must be at least 350 words long and should include your thesis statement and topic sentences for your paragraphs. Include self-directed instructions referring to rhetorical appeals you need to accomplish, further information you need to find, and any additional writing techniques you think may serve in various places. Please attach your outline to this form as a separate page.

See the draft answer below.

An Outline of Your Hypothetical Essay on the Internet

Observing the 10 steps to success on page 85, here is how your outline for your hypothetical essay on the Internet might look. Of course, many other structures are possible.

Sample Outline

The Internet: The Bad and the Good (the Educational)

Opening

1. Start with personal experience with online education as someone who was home-schooled in the North and whose younger sister is now learning from home by Internet. Summarize how swiftly the Internet has infiltrated and transformed modern life since its origins with U.S. military research in the 1960s. Concede to a number of problems: online predators; loss of personal connections; addictive behaviours—escapist games, trivial pursuits, and pornography; threats to personal information and freedoms; concerns that corporate control by a limited number of parties may be skewing benefits to an elite, contributing to the widening gap between rich and poor; concerns that "creative" applications tend to be third-rate,

anemic, and derivative; concerns that for all its so-called newness, it reflects a retro world. Refer to critics such as the coiner of "virtual reality" Jaron Lanier. If those who were in on Web 2.0 now raise concerns, surely these are real. Thesis: "We should recognize the Internet's potential for good, because despite many serious concerns, technology itself is not harmful, as shown by valuable contributions of the Internet in many important fields, such as education."

Body

2. Topic sentence: "Serious critics have certainly alerted us to an array of problems with the Internet." Expand briefly on the problems stated in the intro; cite Lanier on social and economic concerns, the question of the relationship between computers and the human being, and the importance of the individual human being. Paragraph conclusion: "It is always helpful to have our eyes open."

3. Topic sentence: "When fully considered, the problems of the Internet are largely a continuation in the latest modern form of problems that have hounded people for centuries, problems that arise from human nature, not inanimate technologies." Perhaps open the paragraph with a rhetorical question, "Do these problems mean we should somehow attempt to dismiss the Internet?" Work through discussion to the topic sentence, making it inductive. Perhaps add one last reflection after the thesis sentence: Western society has rarely been able to curb a technology once it was released, yet technology need not be a threat to the individual human being but even, in some cases, an empowerment.

4. Topic sentence: "In contrast to the bad stories concerning the Internet are just as many or more good ones." Summarize valuable contributions in science and arts, but focus on examples in education. Stress beneficial effects. Focus on extending learning to populations formerly denied; overcoming various learning disabilities; creating communities of learning and thus breaking down expanding knowledge of other cultures; mounting resistance through exposing wrongdoing when necessary; providing ever-improving research access.

> **Conclusion**
>
> 5. Return to my personal experience and how much the Internet has made possible for my sister. Topic sentence: "The future of online education offers much promise." Provide some of the latest examples from personal observation and the literature. Consider that out of military research came a tool that has vastly broadened and deepened educational initiatives worldwide, a fine example of pounding swords into ploughshares. This redirecting of efforts could intensify. Explain and illustrate. Wouldn't a focus on what the Internet can do for human societies be the best use of our energies?

This sample outline for an essay on the Internet is called "prescriptive" or "directive" as opposed to "descriptive." That is, the Internet essay outline gives directions for an essay not yet written. It says what should be there and includes self-directives on what to do to meet the desired goals. On the other hand, a "descriptive" outline, as reflected earlier in this chapter, observes the main parts of an existing essay. Writing descriptive outlines is an excellent exercise in rhetorical observation, one that helps you to build better "prescriptive" outlines for your own essays in development.

PRACTICE
Outlining

Write a detailed descriptive outline for one of the following essays: "Beginning Riders: The Untold Story" by Joyce Miller, Chapter 5, p. 49; "'College Girl to Call Girl': Defining the Writer's Stance," by Valerie Desjardins, Chapter 17, p. 191; "Multiple Embryo Transfer: At What Cost?" by Amanda Harrison, Research Guide, p. 282; or "Elementary Observations: The Special Skill of Sherlock Holmes," by Robert Penner, Reader, p. 392.

When you have created an outline that seems to capture the key parts of the essay, discuss your results with your classmates and instructor.

Section 3   Forms to
Draft By

INTRODUCTION

Many of us know someone who can "play by ear," who can compose or perform songs and other musical compositions without being able to read or write music. If you do not know such persons, a little research will uncover dozens. Their example should remind us that forms can be produced and reproduced without reference to written instructions. Furthermore, it's unlikely that the first music composer found a score and thereby "invented" harmonics, or that the first writer found some equivalent of *Acting on Words* and thereby wrote the world's first essay of argumentation. Documentation of the forms used in composition, musical or literary, comes *after* the appearance of those forms. Information on forms, such as that in the following section of this book, simply records what has already been discovered or created naturally.

This may be well worth remembering as an antidote to the fearful notion that there is a "right" form and that it is highly unnatural but can be produced by finding the necessary set of instructions. Forms are simply tools we use to give our content impact. We use them as much or as little as we need to serve our particular purpose. If we trust our instincts and use our wits, we will "invent" the forms anew for ourselves. They exist because they are natural and because they make sense—at least, within the culture to which they belong.

A highly deliberate "forms approach" to teaching first-year essay writing was not nearly as common in Canada 30 or more years ago as it is today. Teachers stressed thesis statements and basic essay outlines but did not generally use the fully detailed breakdown of patterns that you will find in the following pages and in numerous other texts on the market. It was assumed that students had absorbed a strong sense of forms from much active reading. Teaching methods, however, follow trends, like the fashion industry, and some would say that the forms approach arose in part because young people read less today than they used to and therefore need more prompting to recognize basic patterns of thought in writing. Whether this is an unfair stereotype (as it may well be) or whether it really explains the predominance of the forms approach in first-year teaching, we suggest that the forms approach has some not-so-good possible side effects along with some important benefits.

Let's take a moment to consider the not-so-good side effects, since any method is best applied with your eyes open. The main risk in relying on forms is that your writing could fall into the condition that cultural historian Johan Huizinga believes afflicted literature in the waning Middle Ages. In his view, that literature was "almost exclusively concerned with giving a finished and ornate form to a system of ideas which had long since ceased to grow" (253). According to Huizinga, forms had become "the servants of an expiring mode of thought" (253). Anachronistically speaking, writers of that age were, to Huizinga, on autopilot. They were painting by numbers. This can happen if you are too engrossed by the idea of reproducing a conventional pattern.

Many suggest that we today are overly absorbed with materialism, with things rather than content, with forms rather than ideas. Are we, as a result, turning out the same proportion of "empty rhetoric" that Huizinga finds in the waning Middle Ages?

Without taking on that huge question here, we *can* point to small examples of how institutionalized attention to form may, however unintentionally, limit our reasoning. A certain essay-writing text, for instance, will classify a model essay as an example of comparison-contrast; a "rival" text will classify the same essay as an example of definition. By letting the idea of form rule us, we can end up believing that an essay must be only comparison-contrast or only definition (or worse still, one form for one professor, another for another professor, and good luck guessing which is which). We can end up concluding that the writer of this "puzzling" essay set out to write a comparison or definition (rather than to take a position). So we wish to make a strong point here, even at the risk of belabouring it: you should remember that consulting forms is not an invitation to produce form only for form's sake.

Accomplished writing, however, invariably results in effective form. The notion of individual voice opposing form, and having to choose one or the other, can be an example of false opposites. There is a Hindu story, for example, of an acolyte whose master taught him that God is not apart from us—God is within. Thus, in a sense, we are God. The acolyte liked this idea. Soon after his lesson, he was on a jungle trail, feeling godly, when a rogue elephant appeared, rampaging toward the acolyte. The master happened to be present. Noticing the elephant bearing down on the young man, the master suggested that the acolyte move aside. "But I am God," the young man protested. "Ah," said the master, "that is true. But so is the elephant."

An essay assignment bearing down on you can be something of a rogue elephant. You must grant the elephant its measure of reality. Look the assignment over carefully. What form or forms is the assignment directing you to follow, whether implicitly or explicitly? As we suggest in various parts of this text, form is an expression of purpose. If your assignment is to explain something, then exposition is your purpose, as discussed in Chapter 11. If your assignment is to analyze, then see Chapter 16. If your assignment is to argue, then see Chapter 18.

In addition, Chapter 11 presents seven common patterns of organization (see page 109). These choices (illustrated in further detail from Chapter 12 to Chapter 14) offer further ways for you to refine your approach.

Remember, however, that although these seven patterns are introduced under exposition, they may serve many different intentions. Comparison, for example, may stress a difference in value between two things or establish a point shared in common. Comparison may serve personal, expository, or analytical goals, and it underlies the concession-refutation structure of argumentation.

Summarization, covered in Chapter 15, is another form that you will apply in almost everything you write as you re-state ideas from other sources before further explaining or critiquing them. Knowing how forms work, in short, does not mean reproducing forms for forms' sake but rather mastering technique to fulfill your chosen intentions.

The following section can assist you in a wealth of future writing. We wish you much satisfaction and many rewards as you negotiate the mysterious relationship between your writing voice and the storehouse of existing forms from which to choose.

Work Cited

Huizinga, Johan. *The Waning of the Middle Ages.* London: Edward Arnold, 1924. Print.

Chapter 10
The Personal Essay

Depending on your field of study, your academic assignments will likely require a *non-*personal style. So why study the personal essay? There are at least three good reasons for giving some attention to first-person voice and reflection on your life as you prepare for your career.

1. Most work on the job entails effective informal communication. The ability to speak and write purposefully in your own natural voice could prove as valuable to your employer as the ability to write a formal report. Well over half of important work-related communication is oral, and much of that is informal.

2. Mastering the personal essay takes you a step closer to becoming a well-rounded writer. Versatility counts as much in writing as it does in other disciplines. We learn and think a great deal through comparisons. To better apply impersonal styles of writing, we benefit from having some experience with personal ones. Furthermore, many writing occasions call upon a combination of approaches, including in some cases a blending of personal and impersonal techniques. "Fusion" occurs as much in writing as it does in music, and we know that musicians playing in fusion groups simply must be adept in the different styles required for the new combination.

3. The personal essay can be an excellent starting point in developing the habit of critical thinking. George Orwell's classic personal essay "Shooting an Elephant," for example, brings author and reader to grips with colonialism. All of the personal essays in this text contain a certain component of critical thinking, after all. Indeed, there is an old Sufi belief that until you are able to tell the story of your life simply and concisely, you are not ready to progress further in any knowledge and understanding. This view holds that life is holistic; therefore, the academic and personal sides of existence cannot and should not be totally severed any more than the mind and the body should be. Accordingly, fields such as anthropology, ethology, and women's studies often use the first person as a vehicle for academic and critical expression, although vigorous debate continues over the value of employing this personal perspective. Almost all business memos also

use the first-person voice to some extent. In any case, we suggest that becoming comfortable with your own voice grounds you as a writer and connects you with yourself and your relationship to purpose. You can then modify that natural voice to suit the demands of various different writing projects.

DEFINING THE PERSONAL ESSAY

In the personal essay, the thesis, whether explicit or implicit, expresses a point of view on a matter of life experience important to the writer. Usually the personal essay employs *narration* and *description,* methods shared with fiction (novels, short stories, and oral stories). Like other forms of artistic storytelling, fiction—at least, effective fiction—engages and somehow changes the perception of the reader. This "change" may involve a purge, some form of healing, or some form of vicarious understanding. In the classical terms discussed in Chapters 1 and 2, fiction and, to some extent, personal writing emphasize pathos, connecting with the reader on emotional and psychological levels. Personal writing therefore appeals to its readers and "persuades" them in ways that may not appeal as explicitly to logic as standard academic analytical writing. This is not to say that logic is absent from personal writing; logic underlies personal writing, but does not always have as direct an influence over its tone.

A wide spectrum of styles can be found in the personal essay, with moods ranging from light and humorous to profoundly solemn. The writer does not necessarily focus directly or at length on the self. A personal essay often concerns something observed, with someone other than the writer as the main subject. Usually, however, personal writing expresses an empathetic, close connection between the writer and the subject. The writer narrates or describes something that he or she has either witnessed or experienced.

The personal essay has **three major impulses:**

- narration
- description
- reflection

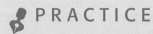 PRACTICE

Arrange with two or more classmates to read and discuss at least two pieces of personal writing from the Reader, Section 1.

For each piece, discuss the dominant style. Identify examples of organization, paragraphing, sentence structure, and literary technique that convey voice and tone.

NARRATION

Narration simply means telling a story, recounting events, typically in chronological order. There are two important things to consider when telling a story. The first is that narration is a fundamental impulse and need of human beings, so primal and important that many scholars, as well as elders in traditional societies, regard storytelling as a basic aspect of being human. Some argue that storytelling is as essential to human existence as food and shelter. When you tell a story, you enter into a natural, life-giving process; you enter into a state as basic and mysterious as sleep.

The second important point to consider is that storytelling arises from and constantly draws upon oral traditions. First Nations author Daniel David Moses says that "the three functions of all stories prehistorically seem to have been: (1) to entertain, (2) to instruct, and (3) to heal" (91).

 PRACTICE

Explore oral stories from any of the world's ancient traditions, insofar as we are able to revisit those stories today. Think about old stories you have been told. Talk with family, friends, and classmates to learn about stories they have been told and can share with you. Do you agree that these stories entertain, instruct, and heal? Do you find any common patterns or elements in their structure?

To further your explorations of personal narrative forms, you might wish to consider the following oral-style pattern, which was introduced to us by writing instructor Jannie Edwards.

Short oral story pattern using five steps

Many traditional oral stories reflect the following five steps:

Subject
Background
Problem (conflict or issue)
Climax and resolution
Moral (or thesis)

 PRACTICE

Form a story circle within your class. If you have a large class, consider dividing into smaller circles of perhaps seven or eight members each. Try to limit your story to no more than two minutes (using a relaxed, natural pace). Be sure to *tell* the story, using notes or simply memory. If you really wish to read it, use an oral style. Consider following the above five-step pattern to shape your story. In many traditional societies, storytelling reflects the time of year. Certain stories are to be told only at certain times, for certain purposes connected to that time. In addition, certain stories belong to certain people and must not be re-told without their permission. If you choose a story that you have been told by an elder or someone in the role of guide or teacher, check with that person to see if she or he approves your re-telling it for the purposes of the story circle. If you choose a traditional story that has been handed down in a book, try to determine if the story was published with permission of the person or people to whom the story belongs. Determine to what degree the editor of the story understands and respects the culture to which the story belongs. If you aren't sure that a certain story should be re-told, you can do as student John Roberts did (below) and tell one of your own. The subject might be something that happened to you or to someone who would not mind having the experience re-told. If your instructor agrees, you might invent part or all of your story.

Sample Personal Narrative

The Time I Nearly Burned Down Northern Quebec
John Roberts

1   This is about the time I nearly burned down northern Quebec.

2   I was a young counsellor in the Laurentians. Camp Napawingue[1] prided itself on being the best boys' camp in Canada, if not the world. Camp Napawingue combined a British boarding school with an RCMP boot camp. Visitors to the white-birch shore of Lake Napawingue breathed in the fresh scent of pine and wood smoke—but we campers breathed in competition. I had to show that I was the best counsellor among the best staff in the best camp.

3   I was assigned to lead a canoe trip through La Vérendrye Park, named for the celebrated explorer. It was important to instill good morale on a canoe trip. The students would write a report afterwards for the canoe trip director, and he must note my impressive teambuilding. I learned how to build team morale from old-time counsellors over an evening beer at Napawingue Hotel (which turned a certain blind eye, Quebec style, to minors). The most impressive counsellor in recent history had been photographed with his campers beside a towering bonfire on a La Vérendrye lake. Everyone referred approvingly to this photo. It was tucked away somewhere in the Administration Building. This added somehow to its mythic power.

4   The canoe trip approached. We packed and packed—and then we set off. After a long truck ride to La Vérendrye Park, we loaded our canoes and paddled: we paddled, portaged, and paddled. The hours slipped by like water alongside our canoes. At last came the first evening. We pitched our tent on a sandy beach, under the nodding tops of pine trees. It was time for the Big Event. We leaned the tallest logs we could into a teepee, which we gleefully ignited. We had ourselves a merry inferno, crackling and flaming against the night sky. Then one of the campers started to look anxious. That seemed hardly surprising, since the rest of us considered him a sort of Piglet from the Pooh

Title conveys subject and tone; implies goal and thesis.

Step 1: Tell what the story is about.

Step 2: Give enough background to set up the issue, tension, concern, or conflict to follow.

Step 3: Establish the main character's challenge, goal, concern, or issue. In traditional Western terms, this may be the conflict.

Brief narrative summary.

A definite plan unfolds, leading to . . .

Step 4: Climax. A final new element in the plot raises the stakes and hastens the conclusion.

[1]The name has been fictionalized.

stories: timid, hesitant, forever anxious. He pointed behind us. "Those sparks are getting kind of close to the trees." Sure enough: a hail of fiery embers was cascading onto the boughs.

5   Did I remember to mention that it had not rained in over a week?

6   I shouted for everyone to grab pots, pans, boots, anything that could hold water. We doused every side of the roaring teepee, and every ember we could find in the bush. But sparks continued to rain from above as if the sky itself were on fire. Then came the distant roar of a motor boat. Everyone knew where it was headed and why. Its mournful motor grew louder and closer. After the park ranger arrested us, I would be fired. I would be as big a disgrace as the famous counsellor was a hero. That is, if the forest didn't burn us to ashes first.

7   The last embers were still hissing when the motor backed off and then began to fade into the distance.

Step 5:
Resolution. Flowing from the climax, the resolution answers the plot question: Will John burn down northern Quebec?

8   When I returned to the best camp in the world, with the best staff anywhere, I found a discreet moment to sneak into the Administration Building. There, in a dusty binder, I came upon the famous photo of the heroic counsellor posed with his proud and admiring campers beside their blazing bonfire. It wasn't easy to see who was the famous counsellor and who were the admiring campers. Their eyes were masked by the hoods of their rain slicks. The downpour between camera and subject made it difficult, in fact, to see anything at all.

9   And the moral of the story is . . .

Focus Questions

1. Can you think of stories you might tell that would benefit from a little more mingling of the five steps? For instance, what might happen to the reader's interest if the storyteller takes too long with step 2? What other reasons can you think of to alter the steps?
2. What do you think is the moral (thesis) of this story? What, then, is its underlying subject?
3. Can you think of a possible connection between the teaching of this story and the Research Guide of this text?
4. In what ways does this story entertain?
5. In what ways does this story heal?

Three Features of Effective Narration

You need not be a professional novelist to benefit from the skills of a storyteller. For example, you may need these skills to begin a speech, an essay, or an article. Narrative techniques are also required in occurrence reports, though often the author uses a detached third-person point of view in such cases. Regardless of the viewpoint used to tell a story, good narration relies on three characteristics:

- defining and organizing parts
- proportioning and linking parts
- expressing a sense of causality

Defining and Organizing Parts

Your story should consist of a *manageable* number of discrete sections. These may be expository subtopics; descriptions; summaries of stages, people, and events; or scenes of action and dialogue (reported speech enclosed within quotation marks). You need to define for yourself exactly what these parts are before you produce a final draft of your essay.

 PREPARATION

Read Roch Carrier's "The Hockey Sweater" (Reader, p. 364). Define the separate sections of this fictional memoir and the types of writing techniques used in each section. What principle of organization has been used to structure these sections?

Roch Carrier has clearly conceptualized three main sections for his memoir: (1) an introductory section of background information to "set the stage"; (2) the first half of his story; and (3) the second half and conclusion of his story. These broad sections can in turn be broken down into finer parts.

Part one comprises three paragraphs. The first paragraph tells, in an expository manner, about the Quebec "winters of my childhood." They were "long," and they consisted of life at school, the church, and the skating rink. The first two places merely served the third "real" place—the rink. The rink was important above all because that was where the children became Maurice Richard. The second introductory paragraph carries on with the subject of Maurice Richard, supplying details of how the boys emulated their hockey hero. The third paragraph narrows the subject further to describe how the boys pursued this emulation on the rink. Part one, then, works like a funnel, moving from a broad, general orientation to increasingly specific concerns. But even in paragraph 3, Carrier still refers to the way things were in general, not to one particular day.

He takes us into the second part of his memoir with the opening of paragraph 4: "One day." Now we enter the story proper, a story based entirely on the Toronto Maple Leafs sweater. Everything in the narration will describe either why the sweater appeared in his life or what happened as a result. First, he deals with the *whys*. In paragraph 4, he tells us that his Montreal Canadiens sweater was becoming too small and wearing out, and he summarizes the character of his mother. Much humour arises from the discord between the boy's objectives and those of his mother. All he wants is that his old Canadiens sweater last forever. She doesn't want her son to look poor, so she orders a new one through the fashionable department store, Eaton's.

Carrier now moves his story along by chronological cause and effect. Because his mother writes to the store, the store, in paragraph 5, responds by sending a sweater. This creates the great crisis of the memoir: the mother, for her own practical reasons, expects her boy to wear the new sweater, even though it bears the notorious Maple Leaf. At this most intense moment, Carrier uses scene, action, and dialogue—a good way to convey crucial material. Not too much speech is recorded, so the lines of dialogue that are reported are very important. In the confrontation with her son, for example, the mother says, "You aren't Maurice Richard." This one line resonates deeply because the story is concerned with boyhood fantasy and illusion. This scene, bringing part two of the memoir to a climax, concludes with the boy forced to wear the Maple Leafs sweater.

Part three is signalled by the transitional word "so": "So I was obliged to wear the Maple Leafs sweater. When I arrived on the rink . . ." Thus the author leads us into the final extended scene of his memoir. The boy's captain, clearly biased against the detested Toronto sweater, keeps the boy from playing. When the young narrator at last jumps onto the ice, he is penalized for being one player too many on the ice. He breaks his stick in frustration, and ironically the vicar assumes the boy has acted out of the pride of non-conformity. The memoir ends with the amusing tale of the boy sent to church to pray for forgiveness; his actual prayer is for moths to destroy the alien sweater.

In sum, the memoir consists of a three-paragraph introduction, another long paragraph describing the decline of the Canadiens sweater, the character of the mother and her consequent decision (the inciting incident), some 10 paragraphs of action and dialogue when the Leafs sweater arrives, two paragraphs when the boy wears his new sweater to the rink, and a final scene in which he prays for moths to arrive. In each of the two major scenes, the boy's objectives are clear. In the first scene, his objective is to avoid wearing the Leafs sweater. In the second scene, his objective is to get on the ice. Focusing on one main character with one clear objective is a good way to make scenes powerful. Through Carrier's control of specific scenes, we gain a touching portrait of a child's relative powerlessness before culture, change, and adults.

Proportioning and Linking Parts

The charm that this memoir holds for so many readers rises in large measure from the author's craft. Carrier knows how long to spend sketching in the background, what to say, and what to leave out. He is careful not to pack in more information than three pages can contain, not to wander into tempting but digressive subplots. For a writer, choosing whether to summarize information or to show it directly through scene and action is a major decision. Balance and variation are key principles. The writer needs to "stay ahead" of the reader—to maintain suspense, yet not to take so long to propel the story forward that the reader loses interest. Like all good narratives, Carrier's memoir consists of a certain amount of summary and a certain amount of direct action. Two scenes, one right after the other, are probably as much direct action as he would present before returning to further summary and exposition.

Links between the sections are simple yet essential—words such as "so," "when," and "one day." In the opening expository section, the image of Maurice Richard ends one paragraph and, logically, becomes the main topic of the next two. Once the story proper begins, the sections are organized according to chronology, one condition occurring *as a result of* a previous action.

Expressing a Sense of Causality

We have already noted how material in "The Hockey Sweater" has been organized according to logical cause-and-effect relationships. The mother orders a new sweater *because* the old one is worn out and *because* she cares what people think. The boy resists wearing the new sweater *because* all the boys idolize the Montreal Canadiens. He feels shame and persecution *because* his mother wins the disagreement over his wearing the sweater. He is treated unfairly by the team captain *because* of bias against the sweater, and so on. The narrative plot's emphasis on causes and effects compels readers to ponder the deeper meaning of the story. Why do certain things happen? What possible social, political, economic, psychological, or spiritual factors are at play? Carrier offers no explicit answers to such questions in his memoir, yet he provokes us to think beyond the issues of one boyhood to the history of Quebec and its unresolved future with English Canada.

DESCRIPTION

Description in all writing concerns the organized observation of significant details. In expressive or evocative writing, such detail has two main features:

- appeal to the five senses
- service of a dominant impression

Appeal to the Five Senses

Visual images abound in Carrier's memoir. The blue-and-white Maple Leafs and the red-and-white Canadiens sweaters appeal to sight. Sound comes in for the first time with reference to the "tranquility of God," the silence of the church. It occurs again when the referee blows his whistle. Smell and touch are both evoked, if indirectly, by the image of the hair glue. Touch enters again with the detail of the mother smoothing down the creases in the new sweater. Taste is not especially present in this memoir, though we might imagine the enjoyable taste of the blue-and-white sweater for moths, as a sweater at that time likely contained a good portion of wool. Note that all these sensuous details are *precise*. Student writers sometimes think that descriptive writing calls for stock, general phrases such as "a beautiful blanket of snow." But notice how such phrases are not used by Carrier or by any of the descriptive models in this book. Good description puts emphasis on the close observation of distinct characteristics. Contrary to common belief, nouns and verbs matter more than adjectives and adverbs. We see this demonstrated in the following example of dominant impression.

 PRACTICE

- Does Carrier appeal to all five senses in his descriptions? Find five examples of language that evoke sight, sound, smell, taste, and touch.

- Write a brief story about a personal experience. Use all five senses in your details.

Service of a Dominant Impression

Dominant impression refers to the central quality or characteristic created by a particular passage of description, or indeed, by an entire work. Here, for example, is a passage from Charles Dickens's *The Mystery of Edwin Drood*:

> Not only is the day waning, but the year. The low sun is fiery and yet cold behind the monastery ruin, and the Virginia creeper on the Cathedral wall has showered half its deep-red leaves down on the pavement. There has been rain this afternoon, and a wintry shudder goes among the little pools on the cracked uneven flagstones, and through the giant elm trees as they shed a gust of tears. Their fallen leaves lie strewn thickly about. Some of these leaves, in a timid rush, seek sanctuary within the low arched Cathedral door; but two men coming out resist them and cast them forth again with their feet; this done, one of the two locks the door with a goodly key, and the other flits away with a folio music book.

At this point in his story, Dickens wishes to convey the suspicion of a murder. The waning of the day and season, the fallen leaves, the reds, the "cracked" flagstones, the ruined monastery, the association of one of the men with a bird (Dickens is continuing a reference to rooks—carrion birds), the rain and the cold gusts of wind that affect the "little" pools as well as the "giant" trees all contribute to a mood that is not only melancholic but, in this context, also suggestive of death—the dominant impression that comes through. There are no more than 15 adjectives here, to some 30 nouns. The accuracy and precision of the nouns convey much of the impression:

not just a vine but a "Virginia creeper" (with a nuance of sinister activity implied in "creeping"); not just a book but a "folio music book." The verb "flits" describes a birdlike action with no need for adjectives or adverbs.

Regarding structure, we may note how logically organized the description is. Dickens begins with a "wide angle," taking in the full scene of the cathedral, ruined monastery, and horizon. He then moves in to the creepers on the walls and follows these down, echoing the movement of the falling leaves, to the pavement. With the "shudder," he returns us to a wider awareness, encompassing the elms, yet keeps the focus downward, on the fallen leaves. The wind carries some of these leaves toward the opening door of the cathedral, thus connecting his dominant impression with the two men who emerge, one of whom, we suspect, in ironic contrast to the religious setting, is the murderer. Not all of us can animate descriptions with the magic and symbolism of Dickens, yet we can learn from such descriptions the effect of careful order, movement, and attention to specific, telling detail.

What might we suggest is the dominant impression of "The Hockey Sweater"? As captured so well in the National Film Board's animated film of this memoir, the dominant impression is one of humorous conformity—all the boys dressing, acting, and thinking the same way, all aspiring to be their idol, Maurice Richard.

As you can see, description and narration are hardly separable. Rarely do we have description without some sense of story or vice versa.

REFLECTION

Just as description and narration are intertwined, we cannot read a narration or a description without sensing that through these words the writer is reflecting on some larger theme, issue, or concern. Your personal essay, however implicit its meaning, should have a thesis. When the personal essay addresses thematic ideas explicitly, the work becomes more overtly reflective. Here is the opening paragraph of student Mark Radford's personal reflection "Different Worlds":

> The world is changing rapidly. When I think about the way my father grew up, compared to the way I grew up and the way my son is growing up now, I'm amazed by the differences. Changes are all around us every day, some seemingly significant and some not, but it isn't until you consciously compare certain things over a number of years that the significance is truly revealed. The differences between my childhood and my son's are not as fundamental as the differences between my father's and mine, but they are still significant.

Radford clearly announces that he will be comparing his three subjects in order to reach a new understanding of the fundamental distinctions between their respective generations. He will be reflecting quite consciously on implications of the differences he examines.

FINAL WORD

Personal writing may not be the dominant form you pursue in your academic studies, but gaining confidence with this form will not only be personally rewarding, it will ground your writing approach in general.

Works Cited

Edwards, Jannie. Personal interview. 3 Oct. 1992.

Moses, Daniel David. *Pursued by a Bear: Talks, Monologues, and Tales.* Toronto: Exile, 2005. Print.

Orwell, George. "Shooting an Elephant." *The Collected Essays, Journalism and Letters of George Orwell.* Ed. Sonia Orwell and Ian Angus. Vol. 1, *An Age Like This: 1920–1940.* Harmondsworth, UK: Penguin, 1970. 265-72. Print.

Chapter 11
Exposition and Expository Patterns

Chances are that most of your writing at the secondary level called for **exposition**. You will find that many of your university course textbooks, like those in high school, are expository—that is, they inform you on some topic. While your writing at college or university will increasingly focus on analysis, persuasive discussion, and interpretation of various critical questions, you may well also be called upon by some university assignments to provide expository essays, reports, and oral presentations. Furthermore, the seven patterns presented below as "expository patterns" are, in fact, patterns that writers adapt to many major purposes—analytical, argumentative, and even personal—as well as expository. They are expository, then, in the broadest sense of helping to communicate—to expose—information and ideas.

Exposition explains and clarifies—a process that goes on, fundamentally, in *all* writing. This chapter should assist you, then, both by reviewing the nature of expository purpose and tone and by introducing the idea of seven distinctive patterns of organization, which the following three chapters (Chapters 12 to 14) define and illustrate in further detail.

EXPOSITION DEFINED

"Expository" writing informs. Its *primary* purpose is to clarify a subject rather than express the voice of the writer or build an argument. Traditionally, exposition has been defined as a "neutral," "impartial," or "objective" stance, with emphasis on accurate facts and unbiased observation or an exploration of how those facts relate to each other and an overall meaning. Traditionally, exposition uses the third person, especially in academic writing, as a way to place emphasis on the subject.

VARIATIONS AND MIXTURES

On the other hand, expository essays *may* use a personal approach by directly discussing the writer's relationship to the subject. Within non-academic forums, such as newspapers and specialty magazines, a personal approach can help interest the reader in the subject. For instance, travel writing, sometimes viewed as its own genre, reflects a balance of personal and expository writing. Traditionally, though, post-secondary institutions have discouraged first-person approaches as unscientific and uncritical.

This attitude has been changing, although academics do not agree to what extent or whether the change is good. Some first-year assignments permit students, or even encourage them, to integrate personal voice within expository style. "Introversion: The Dreaded Other," Colleen McCaffery's essay in section 7 of the Research Guide, includes strategic use of personal voice within a quasi-journalistic style that employs exposition (definitions, explanations, and examples) to argue her thesis. Amanda Harrison's research paper in Section 3 of the Research Guide provides another example of judicious moments of the first person within expository writing that is predominantly in the third person.

Whether you explore exposition in part through the personal essay or entirely through the more traditional third-person academic approach will be up to you and your instructor. If you do mix first-person and third-person voice within the same paper, then at some stage before completing the writing you will need to think carefully about where and how to do so. Considerable care is needed for smooth transitions to and from the first person. For more on the problem of shifting pronouns, see "Watch Your Point of View: Avoid *Confusing* Shift in Person (Pronouns)" in Chapter 4, "Paragraph Skills."

FEATURES OF EXPOSITION

In Chapter 15 we provide instruction on writing the summary, an exercise in observation, accuracy, and concision. Several important features of the summary apply to traditional academic expository writing:

- third-person point of view
- impartial tone
- accuracy
- thorough knowledge of the topic
- conciseness
- use of your own words, aside from key technical labels
- attention to a main issue and meaningful connections

Supporting Details as Paramount

Unlike the summary, the expository essay *does* include details; it is imperative, in fact, that all important points or aspects be established through appropriate details, whether data from first- and second-hand studies, statements by reputable sources, or analogies and other necessary descriptive techniques. The type of supporting detail required, the organization of that detail, and your style will depend on the precise nature of your essay, including your purpose and intended readers. As with any essay, you will shape a standard opening and thesis statement, a body elaborating upon the thesis, and a conclusion.

METHODS OF EXPOSITION

Within the body you will expand on your thesis according to one or more of seven patterns of organization:

- classification-division
- example
- cause-effect
- directional process (how-to instructions)
- process description (process analysis)
- definition
- comparison-contrast

Chapters 12 to 14 provide illustrations and definitions of these seven common patterns of support. Learning to recognize these patterns will improve your awareness as a reader as well as your organizational and explicative skills as a writer. We have presented comparison-contrast as its own chapter, with special attention, because learning to master comparison-contrast pays major dividends to academic writers. As we noted earlier, these patterns, and the strengths of expository tone, can easily be adapted to serving the complete range of purposes.

Give Your Expository Writing Life

A common problem with expository writing is the writer's failure to imbue the discussion with energy and a sense of purpose. To overcome this problem, you, the writer, must make and express a meaningful connection with your topic. This requires having a solid ethos, which you can build through research. But this ethos should also consist of a true interest in the topic. Ideally, you should participate in some aspect of the topic to some extent. You must also ensure that your reader can find a meaningful connection with it. While the subject must matter to you, you should shape your discussion with your readers in mind and consider how that group of people will be influenced by what you say. Consider the questions they are likely to ask and how best to provide answers in terms they will understand. Above all, ensure that you have a vigorous thesis statement with a committed controlling idea (see Chapter 6, "Thesis Statements," for the importance of a controlling idea).

Expository Writing and Research Sources

Remember that quantity is not quality, and it may even work against quality. You get no extra marks for how *many* sources you list. The important thing is whether your sources are reliable, important, and current. Have they helped to shed new light on the topic? Although you should do enough research to be aware of important voices on your topic, more significant than how many sources you list is how meaningfully you connect to the sources and how effectively you present them for your reader. The controlling idea of your essay should be strongly shaded by your ethos, pathos, and logos—not simply a re-statement of what someone else says.

Think "Suitcase" and Remember to Outline

As we suggested in our introduction to this section on forms, you can effectively compare your assigned essay to a suitcase. Its required length represents volume or capacity. You can put just so many clothes and other items in there. If you don't pack enough of the right things, on the other hand, the contents will rattle around. Your goal is to judge how much content you need for the assigned length. You must narrow sufficiently, but not so much that you have content for just two paragraphs, instead of the typical five or six. To make these "packing" decisions before your final draft for submission, remember to use an outline. Chapter 9, "Outlining," provides you with the tools to write effective outlines.

Sample Expository Writing

From "The Scientific State of Mind"
Jane Jacobs

1 Science is distinguished from other pursuits by the precise and limited intellectual means that it employs and the integrity with which it uses its limited means. The standard description of the scientific state of mind outlines four steps or stages, beginning with a fruitful question. . . .

2   Equipped with a fruitful question, the scientist frames a hypothetical answer, accounting as elegantly and economically as possible—"parsimoniously" is the word favored—for the truth that he or she suspects is hiding behind the question. The question, and the hypothetical answer, together constitute two closely linked stages that require insight, imagination, and courage, qualities possessed by all creative scientists, and in high degree by scientific geniuses.

3   In the third stage, the hypothesis is tested, by . . . [After discussing this stage, Jacobs starts a new paragraph to discuss the fourth stage.]

Commentary

The complete book chapter "The Scientific State of Mind" starts on page 398 of the Reader. Jane Jacobs's purpose in the above excerpt is to define her subject: What *is* the scientific state of mind? She makes the interesting point that along with certain values, a *process* comprising four stages defines this state. These four steps organize her discussion. Characterizing her style are use of the third person and an elegantly economical manner to match the one she attributes to science at its ideal. Note that in the first 112 words of this sample, Jacobs uses only 18 modifying words (adjectives or adverbs). Every one of these modifiers contributes by narrowing her topic and driving home her controlling idea—for example, "four steps," a "fruitful question," "precise and limited intellectual means," and "two closely linked stages." Despite her firm focus on the topic, she imparts an emotional attitude: admiration, respect, and even wonder. Science requires insight, imagination, courage, and integrity, values imbuing the subject described—the four stages—with their dominant impression.

Jacobs contributes to the energy and brisk pace of these sentences by using strong verbs and the active voice. Rather than saying "A fruitful question and hypothetical answer are put forward," she says, "the scientist [equipped with a fruitful question] frames a hypothetical answer." The linking verb "is," which can drain energy, appears just once, in the first sentence. Along with "frames," two other strong verbs, "outlines" and "constitute," add energy to her writing.

You will improve all your expository writing by emulating the vigorous, economical, and informative style of Jacobs's example. For her complete chapter, see Section 2 of the Reader.

Sample Expository Writing

From "Multiple Embryo Transfer: At What Cost?"

Amanda Harrison

1   Since the birth of the first "test-tube" baby, Louise Brown, in 1978, artificial reproductive therapy (ART) has become a controversial topic with personal, financial, ethical, and religious implications (Pence 152). One specific form of ART is in vitro fertilization (IVF), defined as the "procedure in which an egg is removed from a follicle and fertilized by a sperm cell (outside of the human body) in the laboratory" (IVF Canada). The reasons for using such a procedure in order to conceive are multifaceted and may include blocked fallopian tubes, poor sperm quality, or the use of donor eggs by aging potential mothers. However, one much-debated topic, regardless of why IVF is used, is the *number* of embryos created by IVF and transferred to the uterus for implantation. This specific issue has been debated in the medical community for some time, but in light of a California woman's recent giving birth to an octuplet "litter" in January 2009, embryo transfer has become a current public issue as well (Saul). In the complex debate surrounding reproductive technology, "going too far" includes the transfer of too many embryos.

Works Cited

IVF Canada. "IVF Canada & the Life Program." *Our Services: IVF (In Vitro Fertilization)*. IVF Canada, 2009. Web. 30 Dec. 2009.

Pence, Gregory E. *Classic Cases in Medical Ethics*. 4th ed. New York: McGraw-Hill, 2004. Print.

Saul, Stephanie. "Birth of Octuplets Puts Focus on Fertility Clinics." *New York Times* 12 Feb. 2009: A1. Print.

Commentary

Whereas Jane Jacobs's paragraphs defining the scientific state of mind address the general public as part of a book analyzing current societal problems, Amanda Harrison's research paper on the multiple-embryo-transfer controversy represents academic style intended for scholarly purposes. She therefore incorporates citations (using APA form) and achieves a suitably formal tone. Harrison makes effective use of the funnel introduction (see Chapter 7, "Introductions and Conclusions"). Her first sentence addresses the topic in broad terms with reference to ART (a large, general category), its relatively brief history, and its various implications. From this broad start, the writer briskly narrows to "one specific form" (her topic for the paper), IVF. She sketches in what this procedure entails and the reasons for its appeal. Then she narrows the discussion even more to the "specific issue" that she will go on to describe and assess: "the *number* of embryos created by IVF." Her strategic italicizing of the key word helps to ensure that her readers recognize the point of the funnel. The final sentence of her opening clearly implies the main question of her paper: What are the different opinions concerning "too many" embryos, and what does the writer think?

You can read Harrison's complete paper in the Research Guide (p. 282). It illustrates an effective transition from exposition of an issue to an increasingly analytical and argumentative treatment of the topic. In addition, this paper illustrates effective selection and integration of source material.

Sample Expository Writing

From "Finding His Style"
Katherine Gibson

1   If drawing class was a disaster, painting class was just as dismal. "I learned to paint academically—my mountains sort of looked like mountains, a head sort of like a head. We copied Degas and Cézanne, even using the same size brushes they had used. It was really something to see our results, which were nothing more than poor imitations of those great painters." An oil-on-canvas self-portrait Ted painted during that time was just

such an imitation. The painting replicates Cézanne's self-portrait of 1875. In both, we see subjects dressed in sombre-coloured clothing, positioned on the diagonal, eyes averted, with stern, serious expressions. "I was shut in," remembers Ted. "I didn't know how to express anything and just did as I was told." Copying, copying, copying but never disturbing the surface to see what beauty might lie beneath. Honest work, but unemotional. The essence—the spark—in a subject was stamped out in the rendering of subjects made stale by the brush of others.

Commentary

In her biography of artist Ted Harrison, from which this paragraph is taken, Katherine Gibson addresses general readers interested especially in a personal angle on the subject. She therefore uses considerable amounts of narration and description, methods prevalent in personal, evocative forms (sometimes called creative non-fiction). Note that her use of quoted dialogue marks her style as considerably less formal than Jacobs's style, which addresses general readers interested in rigorous analysis of societal problems. Gibson also uses creative repetition of one word along with two sentence fragments: "Copying, copying, copying but never disturbing the surface to see what beauty might lie beneath. Honest work, but unemotional." The style suggests sympathetic proximity to her subject's thoughts and feelings during the difficult time described. Finally, she refers to her subject by first name. Surnames rather than first names are expected in the tones established by Jane Jacobs and Amanda Harrison in the preceding two writing samples. Note that while all three of the expository style writing samples in this chapter use the third person, other aspects of style result in considerable variations of tone from one to the other.

In the Reader (p. 411) you can read the longer selection from which Gibson's biographical paragraph comes.

 **PRACTICE**

Think of three topics that interest you. In the style of the three samples of expository writing presented in this chapter, write one paragraph on each topic. Shape one paragraph according to the general expository style used by Jane Jacobs. Shape another of the paragraphs according to the formal research paper style of Amanda Harrison (cite at least two sources). In the third paragraph, use the relatively informal expository style of Katherine Gibson. As she has done, integrate at least two choice quotations by your subject (whom you have interviewed for the purpose).

Chapter 12

Classification-Division, Example, and Cause-Effect

When writing instructors refer to "forms of writing" or "patterns of exposition," they are signalling how the writing has been organized. Is the material organized according to *time,* as it is in narration, or *space,* as it is in description, or some combination of the two, as in a close reading and interpretation of a song or poem? Other patterns are common as well.

This chapter provides definitions and examples of three such patterns:

Classification-division
Example
Cause-effect

CLASSIFICATION-DIVISION: YOUR BASIC OPERATING SYSTEM

Classification-division affects your writing any time you take pen in hand or turn on the computer to compose. We present classification-division as the first of the expository patterns because, in a sense, it is the operating system needed to enable basic shapes and separations to appear. Things must be categorized according to their fundamental identities before we can think further about their relationships and meanings. Through classification-division, we realize the possibility of deciding how, effectively, to group things together. From tables of elements to orders of life forms or other schematic overviews of relationships, classification-division underlies the basic content of most academic disciplines. It is, in a sense, the operating system you must have before going any further in your field.

All fields of science depend upon classifications. For example, biology groups plants or animals according to a "family tree" (taxonomy). This hierarchy descends from class to order to family to subfamily to genus and finally to species and even subspecies. Behind such divisions into subordinate groupings stands the idea of identifying meaningful shared elements in order to enable our understanding more about the nature of things. All of the items being subdivided share the same fundamental characteristics as every other member of the overall (or highest) category. At the level of the largest class, the fundamental characteristics are very basic and broad—communication by vocal signs in language studies, for example, or warm-bloodedness in the study of animals. Various members are then subdivided further into their own subordinate groupings according to shared differences, such as grammatical patterns or four legs.

Critics of Western thinking—for example, Albert Borgman in his book *Crossing the Postmodern Divide*—maintain that this "pigeonhole" outlook has become too rigid and, in fact, has enslaved us. Whatever you may decide about that critical opinion (after reading his book, of course), recognizing our reliance on specific tools does offer us an increased opportunity to control them.

Example of Classification

The following partial paragraph about Canada's Aboriginal peoples at the time of European contact is taken from Olive Dickason's *Canada's First Nations*:

> These people spoke about fifty languages that have been classified into twelve families, of which six were exclusive to present-day British Columbia. By far the most widespread geographically were those within the Algonkian group, spread from the Rocky Mountains to the Atlantic and along the coast of the Arctic to Cape Fear; Cree and Inuktitut had the widest geographical ranges. This accords with Roger's hypothesis, that by the proto-historical period areas that were once glaciated (most of Canada and a portion of the northern United States) had fewer languages than areas that had been unglaciated. While Canada was completely covered with ice during the last glaciation, except for parts of the Yukon and some adjacent regions, the strip along the Pacific coast was freed very early. According to Roger's calculations, once-glaciated areas averaged eighteen languages per million square miles, and unglaciated regions 52.4 languages per million square miles (2,590,000 square kilometres). . . . (64–66)

 **PRACTICE**

In what ways has this paragraph been organized according to a sense of classifying? Discuss your findings with others.

Terms of Classification

An essay may be organized according to divisions of time or space. It may be organized according to types, attitudes, methods, reasons, or to many other features or attributes occurring within a shared category. You will certainly find examples of classification in other parts of this text. In the Reader (p. 442), Martin Luther King, Jr.'s "The Ways of Meeting Oppression" is organized around three attitudes. Note that in King's essay, the pattern serves argumentation. Here are some other examples:

"Should Cats Be Allowed to Roam?" Ch. 5, page 46 (classifies three effects)
"Beginning Riders: The Untold Story," Ch. 5, page 49 (classifies three attitudes)
"Saskatchewan's Indian People—Five Generations," Reader, page 379

In "Saskatchewan's Indian People—Five Generations," the terms of classification are process divisions (stages) of history. This classification is analogous to the chronological stages used in personal narration.

 PRACTICE

Review the Reader for further examples of classification-division. Find at least three paragraphs, passages, or complete selections in which this pattern dominates. Describe the pattern in each as precisely as you can. *How* do the examples you have chosen apply this pattern?

Share your findings with your classmates and your instructor to see whether you agree with each other's findings. Ask your instructor to clarify any uncertainties and differing interpretations.

An Aid to Direct-List Thesis Outlining

Classification-division underlies the presentation of a controlling idea followed by a carefully controlled number of reasons (often three). The reasons may be thought of as a division of the more general position expressed by the controlling idea. For example, a writer might express the idea that blood clotting, intended by nature as a healthy response to cuts, can have dire consequences, as illustrated by certain problems in the brain, heart, and lungs. In this example, the three areas of the body (divisions of the common organism) will provide specific illustrations of the shared controlling idea. You may think of your three reasons, commonly stated in your thesis statement at the end of your opening paragraph, as establishing three subtopics (divisions of the main idea), to be covered in the body paragraphs. Whether spatial, temporal, or other order, classification is the simplest and surest approach to take in your expository essays. But to make this method work, you must be able to identify terms (values, functions, features) that truly share a clear common denominator.

Tips for Using Classification Effectively

1. For an essay of five to seven paragraphs, restrict your categories to three. If you try to cover more categories, you may not have sufficient space to support each properly. Furthermore, you may be over-complicating your organization.

Consider whether certain terms in a lengthy list may in fact be sub-points of other terms in the list. Often a list of six, seven, or even more terms proposed in a rough draft outline can be effectively compressed into only three terms.

2. Be sure your classified terms or sections are properly matching—that they are genuine subdivisions of a common source or ancestor. Remember that if you choose terms that are not commonly considered to fit within the same broad category of phenomena (things of the same family, things of the same subject, things sharing the same function or application), many readers will find your paper or speech somehow illogical or unbalanced. Consider the following draft thesis statement, which presents unmatched terms as though they are matched:

> Every food server knows the four classes of obnoxious customer: the commander, the mumbler, the sweet talker, and the vanisher.

The problem, not at first apparent, with this scheme is that only the first three are distinguished by speaking style. Presumably the vanisher—who ducks out before paying the bill—could be any of the previous three. Consider the following more careful way of signalling this relationship to your reader:

> Every food server knows the three obnoxious customer types according to speaking styles and, of course, knows the worst of all customers: the one with no speaking style when it comes to paying the bill.

The same need to sharpen and clarify your categories occurs if you try to demonstrate the danger of blood clots by organizing a discussion of the veins, brain, heart, and lungs as four completely parallel terms. In this example, blood clots that occur in the veins in various regions of the body could travel to specific critical organs. Such a paper may really be viewing the process in the veins as a cause and that in the organs as an effect. It would thus make better sense for your reader if you introduced your discussion as dealing with a process that begins in the veins and then affects three key organs in specific ways. The paper would emphasize a process description starting in the veins, then move to a classification of three impacted organs. In other words, classification would serve in an important way and yet be suitably subordinated to the main concern with process, in this case one involved with causes and serious effects.

3. Remember the principle of building to a climax. To continue using the blood clot example, if you know from research that serious harm from blood clots occurs most often in one of the three regions and least often in another, you would likely build to the area of most serious impact. This pattern would intensify your controlling idea that blood clots can be serious. Your order does not always need to build to the most intense point, but there should be a strategic connection between your order of classified items and your underlying purpose.

Final Word on Classification-Division

As we said, classification-division is your basic operating system. It places basic content in logical order. *How* you explore that basic content—whether through carefully observed and extended examples, comparisons, discussion of causes and/or effects, or complex definitions—leads us naturally to consider the remaining patterns of organization.

EXAMPLE: YOUR KEY TO BEING VIVID

Perhaps the most familiar comment writing instructors place on first-year students' essays is, "Interesting point, but now give an effective example." Examples are the bedrock of achieved, sound prose. Sometimes examples enter so significantly into an essay that they may be considered the dominant organizational pattern. A classic example is George Orwell's essay "Politics and the English Language," easily accessible online. Orwell argues that "English is full of bad habits which spread by imitation and which can be avoided if one is willing to take the necessary trouble." He provides five prose passages from the writing of his time. He then analyzes these five examples, identifies categories and forms of faults common to them all, then gives further examples of the categories and forms. His examples are so extensive and his analysis so precise that he makes his case by satisfying "the burden of proof." All convincing writing must make its case through compelling examples that are shown to be genuinely representative.

 PRACTICE

Read James Hoggan's "Put It on Ice?" (Reader, p. 428) and Ross McKitrick's "The Environmental Crisis: The Devil Is in the Generalities" (Reader, p. 430).   Document the use of examples in each. What purpose do they serve?

Selecting and Explaining Examples

As discussed in Chapter 4, "Paragraph Skills," the sorts of supporting details you select and how you discuss them will affect the tone of your writing. Select examples that serve your purpose.

The general purpose of most scholarly writing is to convey a sound and thorough knowledge of the topic, which cannot be conveyed merely by one or even more extended examples. Drawing a conclusion from isolated examples, as you are reminded in Chapter 3, "More about Logic," often results in overgeneralization.

Examples gain effect, however, when logically connected to a base of studies by authorities and investigators on the topic. Using examples to "put a face" on the implications of data helps to drive points home. In "Canada's 'Genocide'" (Reader, p. 445), Michael Downey's opening personal example uses the narrative and descriptive techniques of creative non-fiction; he goes on to explain the relationship of his example to formal research and historical documentation. His example adds power for the purposes of a journalistic article. For scholarly purposes, however, he would likely adopt a different tone by concentrating more on information sources and treating any specific personal illustrations less dramatically. Amanda Harrison's essay "Multiple Embryo Transfer: At What Cost?" (Research Guide, Section 3) sets up her topic and issues through brief reference to specific cases (examples); however, she then concentrates on the issues raised, which is an illustration of scholarly method.

 PRACTICE

Read Robert Penner's essay "Elementary Observations: The Special Skill of Sherlock Holmes" (Reader, p. 392).

Explain how he uses example to represent the pertinent character attributes of Holmes as well as to expound the thesis that Holmes possesses a physician's "special skill."

Example as Symbol

Symbol and metaphor are staples of literature. In some forms of writing, extended examples are meant to function as parables or allegories, serving figuratively or symbolically to explain and comment on deeper or larger conditions, which the example merely represents. Plato (428–348 BCE), who as a founder of Greek philosophy departed from oral tradition by expressing his ideas in writing, uses the allegorical method at various times throughout his collected dialogues, often at points when the meaning he wishes to convey challenges or even defies rational understanding. For an example of Plato's use of symbolic examples, search online for Plato's "Allegory of the Cave" taken from Book VII of *The Republic*.

 PRACTICE

In a suitable reference source, look up definitions for the words "metaphor" and "symbol." A glossary of literary terms or a text on literary analysis—especially one providing examples—would be ideal. Then look through Section 1 of the Reader for at least one piece of writing that you think uses example with such resonance that a metaphoric or symbolic effect clearly emerges.

Discuss your specific findings with your classmates and your instructor.

Final Word on Example

Remember, example is the bedrock of your writing. With no examples to connect and explain your points, your essays will be deemed insufficient, no matter how promising their ideas may be.

CAUSE-EFFECT: TOWARD CRITICAL ANALYSIS AND EVALUATION

What makes the world around us the way it is? The pursuit of knowledge triggered by this question involves careful examination of causes and effects. A focus on causes and/or effects usually marks where and how expository tools begin to serve the purposes of analysis, evaluation, and argumentation—the most common forms of thinking and writing at college and university. Cause-effect thinking also underscores narration (focusing attention on motivation and responses) and process description (e.g., explaining how photosynthesis takes place).

Cause-Effect as a Pattern

Cause-effect writing simply refers to text that is organized according to a concern with causes, effects, or both. When just a few effects or causes are highlighted, the discussion will draw almost equally upon classification. Here are two examples of cause-effect statements taken from an article entitled "The Lure of the Body Image" by Susan McClelland (*Maclean's,* 22 February 1999):

> Statistics on steroid use show an alarming number of male teenagers across the country are using the substance illegally simply to put on muscle.

> One of the sad consequences of the push towards a hyper-masculine image is that it can rarely be obtained without the use of potentially harmful drugs.

The first statement gives a *cause*—the desire to look like a beefcake. The second statement gives an *effect*—the harm for the steroid user.

Focusing for one or more paragraphs on the causes of something, on the effects of something, or—as so naturally occurs—on an alternating relationship of cause and effect, can help to provide information or pursue analysis in a clear, meaningful way. Two sample essays in Chapter 5, "Standard Essay Structure," demonstrate the pattern. "Should Cats Be Allowed to Roam?" organizes around three effects on cats of roaming. "Beginning Riders: The Untold Story" refers initially to three effects that may occur when a horse experiences a beginning rider. Those effects, however, are related to one of three particular horse attitudes. The writer spends the rest of the essay discussing the various causes of those three attitudes.

Following are three more samples of cause-effect.

Sample Writing   Causes

The following paragraphs are adapted from "Homework: A Continuing Question in Education" by Yanina Vihovska. Note that she uses APA style for documentation.

1   Various obstacles, including parental circumstances, prevent optimal learning through homework. Parents report feeling uncomfortable as tutors. They may have trouble understanding their children's assignments and may lack access to needed resources (Reach & Cooper, 2004, p. 234). Socioeconomic status can intensify the difficulty. Children whose parents are absent working overtime or night shifts must cook family meals and babysit, activities not easily reconciled with completing homework (Lacina-Gifford & Gifford, 2004). Children facing social disadvantages, such as poor family cohesion and absence of resources, may develop behaviour problems that further complicate their chances of academic success (Ellefsen & Beran, 2007, p. 168). In the 1950s, on limited evidence, some optimists claimed that homework tightens a bond between children and parents (Gill & Schlossman, 2004). Most critics today believe that homework is more likely to frustrate parents, to the point that some even do the work for their child simply to get it out of the way.

2   While some children lack computers and other technical resources, a great many are preoccupied with keeping up in the "technology age," acquiring and using the latest computers, cell phones, PDAs, Xboxes, Wiis, PSPs, etc. Since the thrust of this technology for young people is toward entertainment and communication, it is not surprising that much time is spent after school "chilling" on games, talk, and text messaging. Some critics suggest that the superficial experience promoted by this technology has ill-prepared young people to cope with real-life situations that demand decisiveness and responsibility.

3   As the last comment suggests, a lack of conclusive findings and considerable speculation surround the problems associated with homework. One thing that appears clear, however, is the pressure on students and parents of too many demands and not enough time. A student spends somewhere around six to eight hours a day in school, then is expected to spend up to three hours doing homework (Ellefsen & Beran, 2007). The desire to "chill," seen in this light, may be understandable. According to Cooper (2003, p. 8), the typical heavy and hectic student schedule "leads to general physical and emotional fatigue." She recommends "shorter" assignments, while Lacina-Gifford and Gifford suggest that rather than present homework as a "task," educators should reshape it as an invitation to create, to interact socially, and to apply technology for learning-related quests. For the most part, this type of innovative thinking has yet to be applied.

References

Cooper, H. (2003). Homework. In J. W. Guthrie, J. M. Braxton, & S.P. Heyneman (Eds.),
     Encyclopedia of education (2nd ed., Vol. 3, pp. 1063–1065). New York, NY:
     Thomson Gale.

Ellefsen, G., & Beran, T. N. (2007). Individuals, families, and achievement: A comprehensive
     model in a Canadian context. *Canadian Journal of School Psychology, 22,* 167–181.
     doi:10.1177/0829573507304875

Gill, B. P., & Schlossman, S. L. (2004). Villain or savior? The American discourse on homework,
     1850–2003. *Theory into Practice, 43,* 174–181. doi:10.1207/s15430421tip4303_2

Lacina-Gifford, L. J., & Gifford, R. B. (2004). Putting an end to the battle over homework.
     Education, 125, 279–281.

Reach, K., & Cooper, H. (2004). Homework hotlines: Recommendations for successful
     practice. *Theory into Practice, 43,* 234–241. doi:10.1207/s15430421tip4303_10

Commentary

Vihovska focuses her reader on three broad factors believed by some researchers to compromise the efficacy of homework: parental circumstances, technology distractions, and time pressures. Because time pressures intensify the first two, placing it last makes sense. The writer's awareness of causes as her controlling rhetorical principle helps her to stay focused, cover points thoroughly, and use suitable transitions to reinforce essay coherence and purpose. Yet she is not bound to speak only of the causes of homework problems at all times. She ends, for example, with three recommendations of ways to offset the homework difficulties that have been discussed.

Sample Writing Effects

The following excerpt is taken from a personal essay titled "El Salvador" by writing student Savina Kelly.

1   The war in this country is officially over. The UN-initiated talks between the government and FMLN (Frente Farabundo Marti para la Liberación Nacional) finally concluded with a peace agreement in 1992. Now the people are left to fight their own personal wars: against fear, poverty, violence, and crack cocaine.

2   The turbulence is evident in La Libertad. Stories of people being held up at gunpoint by petty thieves are common. The owner of a once-popular beachside restaurant reminisces about the good old days when business was booming; the good old days of war when money was being poured into the country by the Reagan administration to support government action against the guerrillas.

3   We have been tense since arriving in El Salvador, worse in the evening when night falls. Our sleep is light, and we wake frequently disturbed by noises. We end up spending several nights camped within a hotel compound in La Libertad, the owner more than willing to let us park our van for a few extra dollars. A rusted iron fence wraps the perimeter of the hotel, with a feral-looking pit bull chained in the courtyard. These are measures taken for guest security, but they feel like imprisonment. The owner warns us several times to keep our distance from the wild beast as he is likely to devour human flesh if given the chance.

4   There is a transvestite in the room adjacent to us. She spends the night pacing in and out of the doorway to her room. She looks wretched and emaciated. She is high on crack, and her thoughts pour out of her mouth mumbled and delirious. I struggle not to make eye contact, but her madness has me captivated.

Commentary

Kelly's personal narrative, like all good evocative writing, conveys a dominant impression: the mood of El Salvador after the war. This mood is presented as an effect of the war; these paragraphs represent a concentration on effect. The narrative is both expository and creative.

The first paragraph names the effects specifically. The second paragraph provides a brief moment of comparison-contrast as the restaurant owner reminisces about "the good old days." Thus, a secondary rhetorical method is called upon to serve the dominant one of cause-effect. Kelly handles this moment of comparison-contrast in a way that maintains and intensifies her main point: effects of the war. Rather than deal with the named effects in sequence, one by one, as a writer might choose to do in an academic style of writing, Kelly applies the imaginative method of moving scenically from the general to the specific. She paints in the streets and local businesses, narrows to her partner and her being surrounded by the "imprisoning" hotel, then narrows further to end with the image of the solitary decrepit transvestite, a final embodiment of all the effects she originally named. This figure would not suffice to support a conclusion about El Salvador in a scholarly argument, but in imaginative writing and taken after the previous descriptions, she is a powerful reinforcement of the dominant impression of squalor.

Sample Writing Causes and Effects

Note that the writer, working within the discipline of history, uses Chicago *style.*

From "British North America—Whose Creation?"

Isaac Paonessa

1   Near the end of this migrational period, another war of both frontier and metropolitan character shaped the British colonies unexpectedly—the War of 1812. A jingoistic common enemy united many in a patriotic defence of British North America, which included radical evangelical churches and conservative Anglican elements.[1] Britain seized this opportunity by establishing the British Wesleyan Methodist Society. The Society encouraged acceptance of traditionalism while still holding to many evangelical precepts, thus fostering a passive spirit in the evangelicals. The War of 1812 enabled Britain to rein in some of the republicanism that was sweeping across its colonies and furthered its goal of moulding a loyal ruling class. Moreover, the issues that led to conflict, military strategy during the war, and the war's resolution were handled by British authorities in England.[2] So, the abovementioned wars were actually mother-country influences with a veneer of frontierism.

Notes

1. Nancy Christie, "In These Times of Democratic Rage and Delusion: Popular Religion and the Challenge to the Established Order, 1760–1815," in *The Invention of Canada: Readings in Pre-Confederation History*, ed. Chad Gaffield (Toronto: Copp Clark Longman,1994), 268.
2. Margaret Conrad and Alvin Finkel, *Beginnings to 1867,* Vol. 1 of *History of the Canadian Peoples* (Toronto: Pearson Longman, 2009), 170.

Commentary

Paonessa's opening sentence firmly announces his intention to examine the effects caused ("shaped") by the War of 1812. The sense of a common enemy brought people together, including churches that would normally remain distant. Recognizing an opportunity to increase influence, Britain created the Wesleyan Methodist Society to promote traditionalism in the face of the republicanism that had been on the rise. So although this paragraph traces what happened because of the war (effects), the main specific interest is in how the war incited Britain to intensify its hold under a veneer of frontier independence. The phrase "Britain seized this opportunity" mingles effect and cause. How Britain reacted was prompted by certain conditions, but that effect allowed Britain to take an assertive action, turning an effect into a cause. Historical writing often uses process description (discussed further in the next chapter) to look at how one event or condition is caused by a previous one and then goes on to cause the next one. Causes and effects may alternate in a chain-reaction sequence. (See Research Guide, Section 8, for the full Paonessa essay.)

 PRACTICE

- Find at least one cause-effect statement from each of the three sections of the Reader. Do you find cause-effect writing equally prevalent in personal, expository, and argumentative forms? In response to this question, discuss your impressions and ideas with your classmates.
- Find at least one selection from the Reader that uses a cause-effect pattern as its primary method of organization. Compare your answer with those of your classmates.
- Provide your class discussion group with one example of cause-effect writing taken from a source other than the Reader in this text.

Signal Words

Certain words help to signal an author's use of cause-effect structure. A complete list of words and phrasing used in this structure would fill many pages; the following is a small sample taken from the above three student writing samples.

Signal words and phrases showing causes

various obstacles prevent
the thrust of this is toward
the experience has prompted
there is pressure on
a conflict shaped
the society encouraged
issues that led to
seized the opportunity
metropolitanism took advantage of . . . to . . .

Signal words and phrases showing effects

now the people are left to
the [resulting] turbulence is evident
we have been tense since
the war enabled
a [resulting] common enemy
this opportunity

PRACTICE

Look over the cause-effect passages and essays you have already identified as part of previous practice work in this chapter. Underline or highlight those words and phrases you feel signal the writers' cause-effect rhetorical patterns and purposes. Discuss your answers with your classmates and your instructor.

Organizing Cause-Effect Essays

For less experienced writers of university essays, we recommend organizing your cause-effect writing through a deductive, direct-list thesis statement at the end of your opening paragraph—of the kind represented by the following two sample thesis statements. The first sample focuses on causes, the second on effects.

> I have followed all the steps recommended to begin my essay, but I cannot seem to start. I begin to realize that my procrastination is caused by distractions, mounting anxiety, and *Dancing with the Stars*.

> When a beginning rider mounts a horse for the first time, the rider feels awkward, unbalanced, and unsure of what to do. The horse feels exactly the same way. As a result, a horse develops one of three attitudes to beginning riders: playing dead, taking control, and taking off.

The first thesis presents the controlling idea that starting an essay can be hard for three specific reasons. The second thesis presents the controlling idea that a beginning rider can disturb a horse, with three specific results.

Striving for Sound Conclusions (or Three Parts Superstition, One Part Science)

Those of us with experience as parents or guardians of young children know only too well their questionable sense of causes and effects. "Take your sweater to the picnic," we say, knowing that the warm day will turn into a chilly evening. Unless the child is remarkably obedient, he or she will ignore our suggestion; six hours later we will be treated to bemused observations about the cold. Yet, in our writing, we too can neglect relevant cause-effect considerations. We may have heard the caution that our ancestors based decisions on three parts religion to one part superstition whereas we base decisions on three parts superstition to one part science—but have we considered what that wry comment is trying to suggest? Review our discussion of logical fallacies, and the problems of oversimplification and distortion, in Chapter 3, "More about Logic." People take great pride in their ability to reason, yet careful analysis of hasty reasoning, of the tendency to ignore or warp major causal considerations, to bend even the most carefully collected empirical facts and statistics, and to discount personal and cultural bias should remind us that careful thinking—when it does occur—does so only with major effort.

Final Word

Cause-effect thinking underlies critical analysis and evaluation, which comprises the heart of scholarship. Almost all of your university papers should contain ample amounts of solid cause-effect organization.

Works Cited

Borgman, Albert. *Crossing the Postmodern Divide.* Chicago: U of Chicago P, 1992. Print.

Dickason, Olive. *Canada's First Nations: A History of Founding Peoples from Earliest Times.* Toronto: McClelland & Stewart, 1992. Print.

Chapter 13

How-to Instructions, Process Description, and Definition

This chapter provides brief definitions and examples of three expository patterns:

Directional process (how-to instructions)
Process description (process analysis)
Definition

DIRECTIONAL PROCESS: HOW-TO GUIDELINES

Rarely do we come across a piece of writing that can move its readers to tears, rage, or profanity. Instructions have this power. Although they can have a more direct impact on the reader than almost any other form of communication, instructions are often overlooked, underestimated, or poorly written.

Instructions are a form of process explanation that assumes that the reader will participate in the process. Instructions aim to teach the reader to replicate a process. Assembly instructions for furniture, operating manuals for cars, the Help function on a word processor, and a college registration pamphlet are all examples of instructive writing. One of the most common texts on the market is a form of directional process: the cookbook—but be aware that it uses note form, not the sentences required of a scholarly essay.

PRACTICE

- Think of an activity that you know well enough to describe to a specified reader. Imagine how you would go about describing that activity.

- Find a set of instructions that you believe are *not* well written. Why not?

Steps to Writing Directional Process (How-to) Guidelines

Process instructions follow a pattern of organization very similar to a process description. The main difference is that instructions address the reader or user directly, usually in the form of short commands.

1. State the goal of the process and its importance (if not obvious from the goal). List any equipment the reader will need to perform the procedure. Is any other preparation necessary or recommended? For complex procedures, you may want to provide an overview of the major steps or tasks involved. Include in your introduction the time, money, and effort that will be required of the reader (when relevant). Establish a tone that encourages your reader. Use of the second person—"you"—helps create this friendly, assuring tone.
2. Break the process into ordered steps. You may want to begin with these steps laid out as a series of numbered statements or paragraphs with headings.

For a complex process, divide the instructions into major tasks and subtasks, stating the overall goal as well as the goal of each major task.

REMEMBER YOUR READER AND FOCUS ON THE INSTRUCTIONS

In many ways, this form of writing is one of the world's most thankless. The writer is much less present than in a persuasive essay or a personal narrative. A good set of instructions simply allows the reader to accomplish the task at hand effectively and to dismiss the author forever, whether the task is assembling a bookshelf, setting up a VCR, or operating a piece of machinery. Well-written instructions tend not to call attention to themselves except through their absolute clarity, their transparency as pure, practical information. We could say that their aim is the opposite of what we would call establishing or asserting voice in other forms of writing. Although the art of writing instructions is often unappreciated, readers immediately notice poorly written instructions. Of course, poor instructions can cause the reader frustration, despair, or even injury.

Good instructions, like good process descriptions, guide the reader through a process one step at a time, leaving no room for confusion or misunderstanding. The only test of a set of instructions is that a reader can actually follow them. Writing good instructions, however, is not as easy as it may seem. Some instructors like to begin a class on the subject by asking students to write instructions for a seemingly simple task such as tying their shoelaces. Students soon see that this task that they perform automatically on a daily basis is much more complex than they would have thought. Writers find that they know a process so well that they omit important information and stages. Unfortunately, this is often the case with far more crucial instructions, which are usually written by people with expert knowledge of the process they describe. One of the greatest challenges in writing instructions is *putting yourself in the place of the people who will need to follow the instructions* and trying to imagine what they need—and do not need—to know.

Instructive writing can be more than a straightforward sequence of steps. Sometimes you will have to combine descriptive modes (process description) with attention to causes and effects in order to explain a process clearly and effectively. For instance, if your purpose is to explain to a reader how to use a variety of Internet search engines for different purposes, you might want to describe generally how each search engine works behind the scenes before you move to step-by-step instructions from a user's perspective.

Consider the following strategies in writing effective instructions:

- Address the reader directly in the form of a command. Avoid the passive voice. (See p. 455 of the Handbook on active and passive voices, and also Common Error 14, "Overuse of Passive Voice," p. 497.)

  Poor: Once the coin is inserted, the knob should be turned.
  Better: Insert the coin and turn the knob.

- Use strong, precise verbs to describe the doer's actions: "grasp," "pull," "turn," "stab," "twist," and so on. Stay away from vague terms such as "proper," "correct," "ready," "right," and so forth. If your readers already know what you mean by "ready" or "correct," chances are they do not need your instructions.

  Poor: Bake the ingredients for 30 minutes, or until they are ready.
  Better: Bake the ingredients for 30 minutes, or until they are golden brown.

- Avoid ambiguous language that could lead to potential misunderstandings.

  Poor: Place the bookshelf on the floor.
  Better: Lay the bookshelf on the floor so that the back faces the ceiling.

- Do not over-instruct. Sometimes you will have to tell your reader exactly how to stand, or which finger to place where, but often this level of detail is unnecessary. Don't make your instructions into a game of Twister for readers trying to follow them.

- State conditions before actions.

  Poor: Press Ctrl-X if you have highlighted the text you want to delete.
  Better: If you have highlighted the text you want to delete, press Ctrl-X.

- State the goal of a particular step before the action.

  Poor: Rub the lens with three or four drops of solution for about 20 seconds to clean it.
  Better: To clean the lens, rub it with three or four drops of solution for about 20 seconds.

- Place warnings and cautions *before* the step to which they apply. There is no use telling your readers the step they've just completed was actually quite dangerous, especially if they're already bruised or bleeding!

- Use illustrations to assist the text by identifying parts and equipment or by demonstrating what specific steps should look like.

Directional Process and Persuasion

Persuasion plays a subtle role in many types of instructions. For instance, a pamphlet in a doctor's office instructing women how to examine themselves for breast cancer also aims to persuade its audience of the importance of stopping breast cancer in its early stages. Self-help and how-to books not only teach their readers about a particular approach to weight loss, relationships, or sales, but also persuade them that the particular method or system described is better than others. Instructions on some commercial products are primarily intended to persuade. For example, one Australian shampoo bottle includes the following instructions under the heading "Salon Directions": "Saturate hair with water. Massage shampoo deeply into scalp and roots. Drench with water to rinse. Repeat." These instructions are clearly not intended to teach the novice user how to use shampoo, but to persuade him or her to believe in this particular shampoo's luxurious or sensuous effect.

Now here is a sample directional process essay by student Gisela Becker. Notice that while she does use the first person to introduce her topic and engage interest, she then switches to the more typical second person ("you"), appropriate for speaking directly in a friendly, informal manner to an involved reader. Note her use of MLA citation style.

Sample How-to Essay

Scuba Diving
Gisela Becker

1   It feels strange the first time. The mask. The awkward gear, a bit heavy. You ease into the water and your face slips below the surface. Inhale; the air comes with a reassuring hiss, and for the first time you breathe underwater. In moments, you forget the mask. The equipment transforms itself into something light and agile, and you're free as you've never been before. With that first underwater breath, the door opens to a different world. Not a world apart, but different nonetheless. Go through that door. Your life will never be the same. (International Professional Association of Diving Instructors 1)

The writer quotes from a suitable source, with present tense description and second person to draw us in.

2 I had decided that I wanted to learn how to scuba dive. First I read through the *Open Water Diver Manual,* I watched several diving videos, and I received further useful information from my dive instructor. Then I went through several "confined water dives" in the pool. Finally I was ready and prepared for my first open water dive. I had it all in

She suggests ways to become informed.

my head about buoyancy and pressure, volume and density underwater, hand signals and emergency procedures. Yes, I was ready for the underwater excitement!

She summarizes what will be involved.

3   Before I could go for my very first sea dive under the watchful eye of my instructor, several preparatory steps had to be completed: finding the right diving location, reviewing and assembling the scuba equipment, gearing up, entering the water, and finally scuba diving.

Having previewed the steps, she elaborates on each in order.

4   Finding the right dive location is not as easy as it sounds, but do not worry. During your dive course your dive instructor will choose the dive site for you. As you gain more experience in scuba diving, you will also acquire confidence in deciding on an appropriate dive spot. Depths of water, water movement, low or high tide, and easy accessibility are all considerations when choosing the right location. Do not forget about the weather, because changing weather conditions affect the water conditions.

5   Now that you have found a nice dive location, you need to get the scuba equipment ready for the dive. First let me say a sentence or two about whether it is better to buy or to rent scuba equipment. Scuba equipment is very expensive! It is probably best to rent your equipment for a starter, until you know how much diving you are going to do. Most dive centres rent the necessary equipment at a reasonable price.

6   Before assembling your scuba equipment, you need to gather all your gear to ensure that nothing is missing. If you thought that you could just jump into the water and enjoy the underwater world, you are wrong there!

Notice her use of effective transitional words ("First," "then," "until," "next," etc.) to guide us from step to step.

7   First you need a mask that covers your eyes and nose, then a snorkel for surface swimming until you reach the dive site, and certainly you need scuba fins to increase your foot power. Your next piece of equipment is a weight belt. If you are like most people, you naturally float in the water. An extra weight system in the form of a belt will help you to sink.

8   Finally your scuba unit consists of three basic components: the buoyancy control device (BCD), the scuba tank, and the regulator.

9   By now you probably think this is pretty complicated stuff, but I can reassure you that between now and a few dives you will have mastered the equipment with no problems at all. Until that mastery becomes second nature, you have your dive instructor at your side for assistance.

10   The BCD is most commonly a jacket style that you inflate or deflate to regulate your buoyancy. "You can do this orally, using air from your lungs, though most of the times you'll use a low pressure inflator, which inflates the BCD with air directly from your tank" (IPADI 38).

11   Your BCD integrates a backpack to hold the scuba tank on your back. The scuba tank itself is a metal container filled with high-pressure oxygen, which allows you to breathe underwater. With your regulator attached to the tank you are able to use the

air from your scuba tank. The regulator has two main pieces: the first stage, which connects to the tank valve, and the second stage, which integrates the mouthpiece. The two stages reduce high-pressure air from the scuba tank; this allows comfortable breathing underwater. You may want to consider wearing a wetsuit depending on the water temperature and the climate you are diving in, but this is also a question of personal choice and preference.

12   You must be getting tired from all these explanations about scuba equipment! No? Maybe because you dream of that underwater world, where time seems endless and stress does not exist. You will not be that one inexperienced diver who is trying to remain neutrally buoyant, breathing frantically into his/her mouthpiece. Let me reassure you that with every moment you are getting closer to this extraordinary experience: your first underwater dive.

She remembers to reassure and motivate her reader.

13   Now that you have had a chance to look at your gear, you want to get ready to assemble your scuba equipment. First you have to put together your tank, regulator, and BCD. You start with sliding the BCD over the standing scuba tank from the top. Then you secure the tank band tightly. You want to avoid a loose tank on your back while you are underwater. As a next step you attach the regulator on the tank valve and also connect the low-pressure hose from the regulator to the BCD low-pressure inflator. Finally turn on the air and confirm that the whole unit is working properly. Take a few breaths from the regulator. Your equipment is ready for your dive.

She maintains her "you" approach from the reader's perspective.

14   Remember I told you that I was about to go for my first sea dive. Take a moment and picture me in all my gear: I put on my mask and snorkel. My instructor had to help me to put on the BCD jacket and the heavy scuba tank filled with air. I still remember wondering why air would be so heavy.

As in her opening, she appeals to the senses, to the reader's imagination.

15   I have a 12-pound heavy weight belt around my hips and smaller weights around each of my ankles, because my feet kept floating on the surface during the training sessions in the pool. As a final step I put on my scuba fins.

She balances opening description of the activity with a concluding image of the activity about to begin.

16   In all my heavy gear I stand at the edge of the pier. My instructor asks me to enter the water with a giant stride entry. "Simply step out with one foot," I hear him say with an encouraging tone. When I finally decide that I have the courage to do it, I enter the water with one big splash. And there I am underwater, breathing and experiencing the freedom of "weightlessness" with the most beautiful sights of corals, ferns, and underwater creatures.

Her closing shows that this is really about us, not her.

17   Now it is your turn to get ready for your first underwater adventure.

Work Cited

International Professional Association of Diving Instructors. *Open Water Diver Manual.*
    Santa Margarita, CA: IPADI, 1999. Print.

PROCESS DESCRIPTION: EXPLAINING HOW SOMETHING HAPPENS

Process description explains how a particular process works, but unlike directional process does not expect the reader to perform that process. This form is sometimes also known as "process analysis" or "descriptive analysis."

Process descriptions can be used in a wide variety of circumstances, whether you are describing how language develops in a child from gurgles to full sentences, explaining how a pulp-and-paper mill operates, or demonstrating the means by which a piece of writing builds meaning and appeals to its reader. In process description, you present and clarify for your reader a certain operation within a certain system, natural or human made. Writers who report on the unfolding events in the history of a certain place or people do so in the manner of a process description. Many of your textbooks, including this one, contain descriptions of a variety of processes. The following brief example represents the spirit of this mode:

> There is no such thing as new water. The Earth is a closed system and the water that quenched the thirst of dinosaurs is the same recycled water we're drinking today. In fact, it's been estimated that eight people before you have consumed every glass of water you drink, so the same molecules of H_2O that passed over the lips of Napoleon, Columbus, Joan of Arc, or Shakespeare could be snaking their way through an underground labyrinth of pipes to a faucet in your home or office.
>
> —Kim Green, "Water, Water Everywhere . . .," *New Trail,* Spring 2007, 15.

Scientific and Technical Writing

Process descriptions are especially common in scientific and technical writing, where they often describe mechanical or natural processes such as combustion, cell division, or oxidation.

Chronological Order

Process descriptions are organized chronologically most often, moving in sequence from the first stage in a process to the last. We can organize cyclical processes, such as respiration or photosynthesis, in chronological steps, but we have to choose where to begin and end our descriptions.

 PRACTICE

Find examples of descriptive process among the selections in the Reader. Compare your findings with those of your classmates.

Reading and Writing Are Processes

You may gain considerable insight and skill as a reader and writer if you realize that these activities are processes, with cause-effect steps along the way. Chapter 17, "Rhetorical Analysis," describes various ways to understand a piece of writing as a process of interacting components. The use of the word "process" in this case refers to the text in relationship to the reader, not to the creative process of composition that created the text (also a process, but a relatively separate one). A heightened understanding of rhetoric as a process informs both your reading and your writing.

For examples of texts analyzed as processes, see Chapter 17.

Steps to Organizing Process Description

Not every process description will be subjected to intense scrutiny, but you should imagine your readers will all be skeptics anyway and will be looking for holes in your methods. In describing a process, you should find that the following organizational pattern works whether you are providing a brief description of a process within a longer paper or writing a lengthy report describing a more complex process:

1. Explain the purpose of the process by stating its main goal or its final result. You may want to give a general overview of the process by itemizing its main steps in the order in which you have written them. Besides defining the objective, consider defining how you will measure the results of stages in the process and how you will mark the passage of time.

2. Divide the process into stages or steps, and explain them one at a time. In a process description of several paragraphs, begin each major step with a new paragraph. Steps are often—but not always—arranged in chronological order. A flow-chart diagram may help both you and your reader understand the overall process in its steps. For instance, if you are describing the writing process, the following flow chart may prove useful:

   collage ➡ brainstorm ➡ topic sentence tree ➡ research ➡ revised topic sentence tree ➡ draft ➡ peer edit ➡ draft ➡ peer edit ➡ revision ➡ submission

3. Bring the steps back together. How do all the stages you have described work together? Is the whole as you have outlined it a cyclical process? Is it linear? Is there a predictable or variable final result? You may also want to re-state the purpose of the process.

For a note-form process description of methods used in the essay "College Girl to Call Girl" (Reader, p. 388), see "Outline—Process Description of 'College Girl,'" Chapter 20, page 223.

History—A Form of Process Description

Process description is a staple of technical and scientific writing. Another field that uses process description, however, is history. Think about the history texts and essays you have read—do they not concentrate, primarily, on describing how various historical forces unfold or *proceed*? See Isaac Paonessa's paragraph in Chapter 12, page 124, as well as his research paper "British North America—Whose Creation?" in the Research Guide (p. 331). Another example is "Saskatchewan's Indian People—Five Generations," Reader (p. 379).

Describing Complex Processes

To describe a complex process, such as building a bridge or staging a play, you may have to divide the process into several sub-processes, each of which involves several steps. In these cases, the introduction and conclusion are especially important. You can use them to help the reader understand how you have broken down the major process into smaller processes, and how these processes work in combination with one another. If you are describing a process unfamiliar to your reader, you may find definitions, comparisons, and analogies helpful.

Process Description Combined with Other Strategies

As we have already seen in this chapter, process description is often used in combination with other rhetorical strategies. For instance, your process description could be one part of a persuasive or analytical essay, report, or letter. To analyze a public relations campaign, write a critical paper on a theory of psychological development, or recommend environmentally friendly changes for a production process, you might provide a brief description of the process before you go on to analyze it or argue for or against it.

DEFINITION: DRAWING ON OTHER PATTERNS TO EXPLAIN COMPLEX TERMS

In the opening of an essay, "Global Warming and Population" (an excerpt from which appears below), student Brenda Platt asks two central questions: "Does population growth contribute to global warming? Should population control be a central strategy in stabilizing global environmental change?" Then she says, "In order to answer these questions it is necessary to introduce key concepts . . ."

Definition Used Widely in Introductions

Platt's opening represents a typical start to many academic papers dealing with complex issues: the need to establish the meaning of key terms. One of the terms she goes on to describe is global warming:

Global warming is the increase in the mean average temperature of the earth's atmosphere. It occurs when the so-called greenhouse gases (carbon dioxide, methane, nitrous oxide, tropospheric ozone) absorb infrared radiation from the planet's surface that would otherwise escape into space. This absorbed radiation is converted to heat, and the atmosphere becomes warmer. The predicted consequences include a decline in agricultural productivity, desertification, changes in forestation patterns, more and stronger storms, and flooding of low-lying coastal regions.

Drawing on Other Expository Patterns

Notice that Platt's explanation features descriptive-process writing that serves the larger purpose of definition.

 PRACTICE

1. Search online for Wayne C. Booth's essay "The Rhetorical Stance," an extended attempt to define the ideal position for a writer in any writing occasion. How many different patterns does Booth call on to serve his central purpose in that essay?

2. Select any essay from the Reader or the Research Guide and identify the dominant and supporting expository patterns that it uses. Discuss your findings with your classmates and instructor.

Sample Student Writing Definition

From "In the Words of Stompin' Tom"
Gustavo Miranda

2 On a variety of forums and websites, Canadians are asking themselves and others, "What does it mean to be Canadian?" As we progress deeper into the 21st century it is becoming clearer that definitions of Canadian identity need to be reconsidered and reworked to better reflect the realities of the demographic and cultural reality of the country. For too many decades, Canadians have relied on 19th-century definitions and institutions as foundations for the creation of a new identity. As communications and information technology expanded in the latter half of the 20th century, coupled with a dramatic increase in non-British immigration into the country, definitions of what it meant to be Canadian were eventually drawn from negative relationships. That is, Canadians defined themselves in terms of what they were not, rather than what they were. It was simple enough to define oneself as "not American," since, given the multicultural makeup of post-Trudeau Canada, what a Canadian truly was differed greatly between individuals. In the last quarter of the 20th century, the Trudeau-era policy of multiculturalism took root, and the previous stereotypes of English or French Canadians no longer applied. As the 21st century dawned, multiculturalism and demographic diversity seemed to be the driving force behind the construction of a new Canadian identity.

Commentary

Miranda's paragraph reflects the complex issues people consider when attempting to define Canadian identity. He surveys past points and says: "For too many decades, Canadians have relied on 19th-century definitions." In their place he proposes a definition based on "multiculturalism and demographic diversity."

Sample Student Writing Definition

From "Canadian Equals Canada"
Brad Henderson

6 Currently, there seems to be a gap between what Canadians feel they are, and how they may be seen around the world. Canadians have allowed their reputation as a peaceful, helpful and fair country to fade away and are now living on past accomplishments in their current conception of themselves. Canadians should express themselves honestly and consider the world's view of them. It may be attractive for Canadians to believe they are something other than who they are, but it can make achieving their inner goal of being genuinely appreciated difficult and prolonged. Being Canadian means taking on the responsibility to contribute inner thoughts, feelings, and beliefs toward the positive and honest goal of building a nation that supports its citizens literally and metaphorically. Being a Canadian means assuming that the image one has of oneself will be interpreted accurately around the globe, that the world will see Canadians for who they'd like to be. Being Canadian means believing in Canada's ability to present its citizens' self-image to the rest of the world. If Canadians are going to have a country represent their inner thoughts and feelings, they should expect their country to get it right. The feedback they receive internationally and within their own country should complement their struggle to be good, attractive human beings, capable of improving the Canadian ideal and the environment in which Canadians live. Although the image Canadians have of themselves may be inaccurate, it is positive. Perhaps it is enough to help Canadians' self-image improve the way Canada should be seen through the eyes of its neighbours.

Commentary

Henderson's paragraph, the final one of a six-paragraph essay, concludes a discussion in which he surveys various attributes Canadians commonly present in defining themselves: "environmentally responsible," "caring for the poor," and "kind toward others." One by one, he refutes those claims with evidence suggesting the contrary to be true. His controlling idea emerges: the definition of *Canadian* is self-delusion.

Henderson concludes that the common definition of Canadian suffers from received assumptions rather than recognition of how others may see us.

The paragraphs by Miranda and Henderson represent the range of ideas and critical perspectives that may figure in definitions. On the question of defining Canadian identity, cultural critic John Ralston Saul would agree with both Miranda and Henderson but would add that each has overlooked an essential ingredient. For Saul's thoughts on this complex topic, see "The Roots of Continuous Negotiation: In Praise of the Courts" in the Reader (p. 407).

Chapter 14
Comparison-Contrast

Classification-division is the operating system beneath many expository patterns, because it establishes items and catalogues of items organized in relation to each other. Comparison-contrast, in turn, is surely the conceptual tool we use most commonly to make sense of the world around us. Comparison-contrast makes sense of those things that we recognize to be distinct from each other, yet through classification to share kinship in some categories. Through comparison-contrast, one thing in a certain category is placed side by side with another thing in the same category. Suppose you wish to indicate how much your nephew has grown in the past year—you might say, "He comes up to my hip." The equation of your nephew's new height to the height of your hip gives a basic understanding. The extent to which we rely on comparison can be found at the heart of our language, specifically in our use of metaphor. Someone asks you how your hockey team did last night. You reply, "We were on fire." You compare the degree of your performance to the intensity of a fire, even though the comparison was not directly stated by words such as "like" or "as." This natural way of thinking is reflected in our frequent use of analogy. For example, bad timing might be compared to someone's being caught on the highway in a passing lane when the line of cars behind the driver has filled in and suddenly an oncoming car appears. With this analogy, the individual's bad timing creates choices (to speed up or slow down) that now appear limited. (You should remember, as we said in Chapter 3, that any analogy will break down eventually!)

COMPARISON DEFINED

To **compare** means to place two things side by side in order to reach a better understanding of each, and usually, of some third thing. This could result in stressing similarity or difference, advantage or disadvantage. The two things being compared normally share some sort of generic category: two cars, two athletes, two friends, two cities, the country and the city, etc. A dog is not generally compared to a computer, except for comic purposes. Some people feel that the phrase "compare with" signals the general act of comparing, whereas the phrase "compare to" indicates that contrast will be emphasized. "Her records are not yet impressive compared to Wickenheiser's." Reference books do not agree on this fine point of distinction, however.

CONTRAST DEFINED

To **contrast** means to deal only with the difference between two things being compared. The study of difference could lead to upholding one thing over the other, or it could simply point out distinctions between them.

Remember, if you are asked to *compare* two things, you are free to decide whether to stress similarity *or* difference. If you are asked to *contrast* two things, you must attend to differences.

WIDESPREAD USES OF COMPARE AND CONTRAST

As we said in our opening comments, comparison is the most common and fundamental form of human reasoning. Consider that the binary code (a basic division of two) underlies the complex functions of the computer. Comparison-contrast serves *all* writing purposes—evocative, analytical, and argumentative as well as expository. (See Chapter 18, "Argumentation," on the crucial importance of comparison in fair and effective debate.) Comparison-contrast is used across all academic disciplines. Students in literature might compare or contrast two characters in a play, two novels, or two poems. Students in political science might compare two political parties or electoral systems. Students in mechanical engineering might contrast gasoline and electric car engines, concentrating on technical processes and specifications. Ecologists might compare these two while concentrating on environmental effects. Instructors consider comparison-contrast topics an excellent way to test your knowledge and thinking.

TWO MAIN PURPOSES

Dealing with comparison-contrast in an essay involves deft control of breadth and structure; the demands can sometimes make your head spin. To ward off this kind of vertigo, consider that, fundamentally, comparison-contrast writing has just two possible *purposes*:

1. To show that one thing is (on specified grounds) to be preferred over another, thus guiding our thinking about value
2. To demonstrate how both things, in some way, share an important common cause and/or effect or state of being, which points to an interesting broader implication

Comparison-contrast writing places an emphasis on one or the other of these two basic purposes.

TWO WAYS TO STRUCTURE COMPARISONS

Another consideration to help organize comparison-contrasts is to realize there are *two main ways* for such essays to unfold:

- subject by subject (sometimes called "block") because each subject gets a paragraph or "block"
- point by point (alternating between subjects within one paragraph)

Sample Comparison 1 Purpose and Structure

From Prison to Paradise
John Roberts

Subject A
-Location
-How obtained
-Rent
-Landlord
-Space
Transition words

During my first year of university I took a basement apartment in the suburb of Montreal West, many kilometres from campus. Student housing was going fast around Concordia in downtown, and the rent on the basement seemed okay. On the very first evening, however, the landlord dropped in with a list of repressive rules. The place was cramped with low ceilings and a worm's-eye view out the half windows. I could hear the family upstairs constantly, even though they had rules against hearing me.

Subject B
-Location
-How obtained

-Rent
-Landlord

-Space

On the other hand, I transferred the following year to University of Alberta in Edmonton and found an old two-storey cottage-style house in McKernan, a five-minute walk from campus. I had had lots of time to search the new city over the summer; some friends put me onto this remarkable find. Unbelievably, the rent was the same as I had been paying in Montreal West; the landlord, who lived across the city and never bothered me, was evidently a philanthropist. I had three rooms downstairs, two upstairs, and even a cellar for storage. I had windows galore, with multiple views. I realize that for a different person, the basement apartment in Montreal would have had advantages, but it just didn't suit my personality. In the old house in McKernan, I spent much time between studies giving thanks for my amazing reversal of fortune.

Commentary

In Sample Comparison 1, student John Roberts structures his two paragraphs according to the subject-by-subject (block) approach. He writes in order to assert the value of one subject over the other (Purpose 1 as explained on p. 141). His overall topic is his personal experience with student housing. Subject A, the *basement apartment,* in his experience is awful. Subject B, the *old cottage-style house,* is excellent. Notice that he arranges his points in precisely the same order on both sides of the comparison, and that he uses the signal words"on the other hand" to guide his reader from one side of the discussion to the other.

Sample Comparison 2 Purpose and Structure

A Tale of Two Happy Homes

John Roberts

In my first year of university I lived in a basement apartment many kilometres from campus, whereas in my second I was a five-minute walk from classes. Since I was in Montreal my first year, I got to hear French on the long bus ride as well as to sightsee and prepare for class. In my second year I had transferred to a program in Edmonton. By then it was nice just to walk out my door and reach class so quickly. Rents were the same, so no problems there. Landlords were quite the contrast, but again, no problems. The Montreal one came on a little heavy, but when I commented sympathetically on his prison-camp tattoo, he invited me upstairs, and I had access to the whole house from then on. The Edmonton landlord was absent though willing to pay for inexpensive, essential repairs, provided I did the work. As it happens, I enjoy fixing things up. The surroundings were different but interesting and appealing in both cases. The Montreal house contained war-years photos and documents that were priceless, and I loved working evenings in the great Jewish delicatessens a fifteen-minute walk to the north. As for second year in Edmonton, who wouldn't enjoy having an old house to wander around in, without the responsibilities, and then to step outside and smell the stately trees of McKernan. A student's life may well be one of no fixed address, but as Thoreau once said, life's goal should be to spend each night "everywhere at home."

> Subject A and Subject B
>
> -Location A
>
> -Location B
>
> -Rents A & B
>
> -Landlord A
>
> -Landlord B
>
> -Space A
>
> -Space B

Commentary

In Sample Comparison 2, John Roberts structures his paragraph point by point, alternating points within the same paragraph. He writes in order to assert the underlying value of both subjects (Purpose 2 as explained on p. 141). His common topic is his personal experience with student housing. Subject A, the *basement apartment,* in his experience is great, and so is Subject B, the old *cottage-style house.* Notice that under each point—location, discovery, rent, landlord, and space—he explains A first and B second, maintaining a consistent pattern. His discussion exposes considerable contrast between Subject A and Subject B, yet he maintains his controlling idea that beneath the differences (because of them, in fact), both places were rewarding.

Effects of These Two Main Methods of Organization

Both methods of comparison, subject by subject (block) and point by point, have at least one main advantage in common: both patterns help the writer, and therefore the reader, to maintain an *even-handed* attention to both sides of the topic. This can be particularly helpful to ensure complete and fair consideration in, for instance, the case of two opposed critical theories, especially if you (the writer) have an immediate bias toward one side over the other. The concession-refutation pattern, described in Chapter 18, "Argumentation," represents a specific application of comparison-contrast, one that reminds you to give both sides of a debate a fair hearing.

In addition, each method of comparison, point by point and subject by subject, has at least one specific advantage and one specific disadvantage.

Advantage of Subject by Subject (or Block)

This method allows the reader to process one side of the subject at a time, sometimes a good way to establish and hold interest. If you write an essay that tends to jump around, moving to second and third aspects before revealing much of the first, there is a risk that some readers will not have time to build up enough interest in the first subject to be curious about the second. The subject-by-subject method allows room and therefore time to develop the reader's interest in one half of the comparison before moving to the second. It also clearly foreshadows the scheme or pattern to be used for the ensuing "block" dealing with the second subject, the second half of the comparison. Subject by subject uses a more gradual and in some ways, for some readers, a more calmly methodical approach than does point by point.

Disadvantage of Subject by Subject (or Block)

By devoting more room and therefore more time to one side of the comparison, the writer risks forgetting the essential comparative purpose of the discussion. In the first block of discussion, most subject-by-subject essays tend not to refer much to the other subject examined in the second block. Then, in the second block, for each point in the scheme, the writer inserts reminders of the previous half of the discussion, for instance, "Like Toronto's public transit system, New York's suffers from serious age and overload." We can imagine that in the first block, the writer discussed three points about Toronto—perhaps size, parks, and transportation. Linking language, such as that we have just illustrated, is most common in the second block, reminding the reader of connections on the same point of discussion to the first block. Despite this use of connecting language, especially in the second block, the subject-by-subject approach can seem looser than the point by point one and less clearly motivated by comparative intention.

Advantage of Point by Point

This method keeps the comparison tight; you maintain awareness of both subjects and how each participates, through comparison, in deepening understanding. Point by point, however, requires strong paragraph control.

Disadvantage of Point by Point

Because this method involves referring back and forth to both subjects, writing and reading point-by-point essays can begin to feel like following a ping-pong match. The writer is called upon to sprinkle in frequent linking terms suitable for comparison—for example, "on the other hand," "when we look at the other side," "in contrast to this impression," "in the same manner," and so on. This almost constant back-and-forth, while it keeps the discussion balanced and clear, usually needs some work to ensure smooth, natural flow.

Choosing What Works—Hybrid Patterns

To maximize the strengths of both basic patterns of organization while minimizing their weaknesses, writers often adapt from point by point and subject by subject to shape a hybrid pattern. In fact, we seldom find "pure" examples of subject by subject (that is, essays that use that approach from start to finish). Essay introductions often use point-by-point organization to clarify for the reader that the discussion will equally concern Subject A and Subject B. If there is too much initial attention to Subject A and no mention of Subject B, the essay may not announce itself as a comparison. So most subject-by-subject comparisons apply the block pattern only after the introduction. Writers naturally shape hybrids in respect of fundamental principles of clear communication.

 PRACTICE

Read the following two essays, taking precise note of their organizational strategies. See where they use subject by subject and where they use point by point. What is the purpose of the first essay? What is the purpose of the second essay? Compare your findings with those of your classmates and instructor.

Sample Comparison-Contrast Essay Find the Purpose and Structure

Venus Meets the Devil
Joyce Miller

1 I recently saw two movies in which an older, flawed mentor initiates a young apprentice into the secrets of his or her respective art in a manner close to hazing. In *The Devil Wears Prada* (2006), Anne Hathaway plays Andrea (Andy), a recent graduate of journalism school. Her dream is to write for *The New Yorker* and other magazines of that ilk. However, she ends up instead as a personal assistant to Miranda Priestly (Meryl Streep), chief editor of *Runway,* a top fashion magazine. A terrifying bully, Miranda sends Andy on a series of abusive challenges, representing a far harsher and more confusing "initiation" into art and life than she had ever imagined. In *Venus* (2007), Jodie Whittaker plays Jessie, a jaded, dispirited young woman vaguely interested in an old stage and film star, Maurice (pronounced "Morris"), played by Peter O'Toole. She is interested simply because he was

once famous. Maurice makes it his mission to teach Miranda that there is more to art and acting than celebrity. Similar in choosing initiation plots, the films otherwise differ remarkably, the one unbelievable and clichéd, the other painfully honest. We see this gap in how the two stories handle character and the respective arts in question.

2   Andy, protagonist of *Prada,* comes from nowhere and, not surprisingly, goes there. She manages to be well informed about *The New Yorker* and other magazines, yet has never even heard of *Runway*. She also manages to write well, we are told, without ever looking at or referring to a book or magazine. A young woman in her group of apparently casual friends announces that she has known Andy for 16 years. Nothing in Andy's characterization suggests any such connection. There is no explanation of how she met her boyfriend, an aspiring chef, or any hint within her characterization of why the two remain a couple. Andy doesn't seem the type to cross social-class borders so easily. She goes through the expected adventure of almost selling her soul to the fashion industry, but at the last moment (we aren't sure why), she recovers her senses and returns to her true calling.

3   On the other hand, Jessie, protagonist of *Venus*, seems painfully real, consistent, and complex. While her young, lost soul draws on some common enough devices (among them a mother who resents her existence), the sheer unlikeableness of her character renders these devices believable. Jessie truly resembles those surly "real-life" people who, convinced they are too horrid to be loved, make that belief come true, not in a cute "for-the-movies" way, but in a real, "I'll sit over here across the room as far from you as possible" way. The only person, at first, who perceives any beauty in Jessie is the equally repugnant Maurice. Unlike the innocent (and unreal) Andy, Jessie prevents a possible melodrama or sex farce of naive girl and lecherous old man by being as hard-bitten and disappointed by life as he, as well as equally manipulative. And yet she has traces of lingering vulnerability and a developing if unconscious desire to understand what it is Maurice has to teach—again, all believable.

4   The flawed mentor figures also demonstrate the major gap between the two films. While there is no denying Meryl Streep's talent and ability to pull off a complex role, here she has no such opportunity. For the most part, her character in *Prada* incarnates over-the-top evil. In a gesture toward giving Miranda a human, vulnerable side, the story shows her in tears after her latest husband has left. But the only glimpse we have of Miranda's relationship with that husband is one previous scene of them arguing in a heavy foreshadowing of the departure. With no sense of the relationship, we are asked to react emotionally to a gesture. In contrast, the flawed mentor Maurice of *Venus* is as real, complex, and disturbing as his "protegé" Jessie. Spoiled by having been once a heartthrob of the British stage, Maurice has become an ugly embodiment of the lustful old man. In one particularly pathetic incident, he gets Jessie work as a figure model, then ogles her naked body from hiding until crashing down from his precarious perch, an unforgettable pratfall of the spirit. O'Toole looks older than his age, and his character

disintegrates before our eyes. He, too, has a former spouse, Valerie (Vanessa Redgrave). But their scene together, far from telling us next to nothing like the Miranda and husband scene in *Prada,* reveals a great deal: Maurice still metes out long-overdue support payments to his ex-spouse, but only, it seems, when he literally needs a shoulder to cry on. His ex-wife's ongoing affectionate and tolerant attitude toward him is positively saint-like in contrast to his childish attitude toward her. Nevertheless, there is a point to the lesson he wishes to teach Jessie. As the story unfolds, we realize that Maurice recognizes an artist in Jessie, presumably because he knows that his own inner artist is now hidden by the shell of an unpleasant old man.

5   How the two films handle their respective arts reinforces the major gap of believability and depth between them. Miranda, chief editor of *Runway,* for some reason interviews a recent journalism grad, with no executive administrative experience, for a top-level position as her personal assistant. The story does not explain the mysterious power that sent Miranda Andy's resumé, but even if she did mistakenly receive it, why would she give it a second look? *Prada* is loaded with product placement, celebrity cameos, and people wheeling racks of clothing around, but without these, the setting could be any high-pressured business. There is one nod to fashion as art you live in, but one line doesn't last long under the ongoing ogling of product and celebrity for ogling's sake. The very behaviour that *Venus* invites us to pity in Maurice, *Prada* asks us to embrace. *Venus,* on the other hand, presents the admirable as well as the tawdry side of art. The British stage appears as both a gift to cherish and a dull waste of time. Maurice's old actor friends are petty and silly, but Jessie's great uncle Ian (Maurice's uncelebrated acting crony, played by character actor Leslie Phillips) *was* a great actor whose art gave much to others, something we suspect Jessie will one day come to appreciate.

6   Driving home the difference between the two films and their ideas of art are two climactic scenes. In *Prada,* when Andy discovers Miranda crying over the loss of her husband, Streep plays the scene without makeup. In the counterpart scene from *Venus,* Maurice takes Jessie to the set where he has a cameo in a cheesy period piece. He has an attack—perhaps a fake, we aren't sure because of his quality acting—and he then looks directly into the camera, knowing Jessie is at the viewfinder. "Do you see?" he seems to be asking. At this point she still does not see. She prefers the actress who conjures up crocodile tears while delivering hackneyed dialogue. But the viewer connects this scene of a flattened Maurice to an earlier one in the hospital after he had surgery for prostate cancer. In that scene as he basked in his celebrity, he hid his colostomy bag from everyone else but insisted that Jessie see it. Whereas *Prada* conceives of spiritual nakedness as a weeping star without makeup, *Venus* seeks that expression through a much higher and more courageous level of imagination.

7   At the end of Jessie's journey in the film, rather than making a grand change in her life, like Andy, she simply walks with confidence into a room full of artists, drops her robe, and assumes the pose of *Venus* for a female painter. What the one film attacks head-on

with hammers forged of formula, the other sees in the only manner possible given the theme: from the corner of the eye.

Works Cited

The Devil Wears Prada. Screenplay by Aline Brosh McKenna, based on a novel by Lauren Weisberger. Dir. David Frankel. 20th Century Fox, 2006. Film.

Venus. Screenplay by Hanif Kureishi. Dir. Roger Michell. Miramax, 2007. Film.

Sample Comparison-Contrast Essay Find the Purpose and Structure

Possibilities of Redemption

Stephen Kuntz

1   The theme of seeking redemption is an almost clichéd motif in cinema. However, the films *The Machinist* (2003) and *Levity* (2003) approach this issue in fresh ways, generally avoiding the traps of Hollywood. Both films' central characters have done something in the past that they regret and feel guilty about. To be sure, the paths to peace and redemption the films offer are different: one presents an individual struggle left incomplete, the other a communal, transcendent experience. This richness of difference, however, leaves the viewer with a heightened, enriched appreciation of the power and scope of redemption, the one film, as it were, completing the other.

2   In *The Machinist,* Trevor Reznik (Christian Bale) is an emaciated figure who has not slept in a year. Initially, the source of his turmoil is unknown, but it is causing him, literally and figuratively, to be wasting away—something is gnawing at his insides. And it is Trevor's inside, externally manifested, that becomes the focus of the film. The viewer follows Trevor from his drone-like job at a menacingly portrayed machine factory (thus the title) to his equally threatening apartment. Along the way, Trevor's life becomes increasingly narrow and internal; paranoia, confusion, hallucinations, and alienation become the mainstay of Trevor's tortured existence. His response to what emerges only at the end of the film as repressed memory is a growing alienation from those around him and reality itself: his co-workers ostracize him, his boss (Robert Long) fires him, and his one friend, a prostitute (Jennifer Jason Leigh), wants nothing to do with him.

4   Where that journey might take him next is suggested by *Levity*. In this film, Manuel Jordan (Billy Bob Thornton) begins where Trevor ends: in a prison. Manuel has spent the last 22 years in prison for accidentally killing a store clerk during a botched robbery. Similar to Trevor, Manuel is wasting away because of his guilt, but it is his spirit, not his body or mind, that is suffering. The viewer knows immediately the source of Manuel's guilt and that he neither expects nor wants forgiveness. It seems he would rather stay in prison, continually and passively paying for his crimes, than face society and the individuals he has hurt.

Manuel, literally and figuratively, wants to stay inside, but the parole board forces him out and the film focuses on his outward journey toward a redemption that he had not thought was available to him. His movements and responses upon release from prison are almost ghost-like. As he stands in the crowded subway going in the opposite direction of all the other passengers, his realness becomes certain to him and us only when, in the now empty subway, someone bumps into him, stops, stares, and offers a "sorry."

5   In contrast to Trevor's existence, Manuel's life becomes increasingly complex and interrelated as he enters into relationships, seemingly with little choice, with an inner-city preacher (Morgan Freeman), the sister of his victim (Holly Hunter), her son (Geoffrey Wigdor), a young self-destructive woman (Claire Mellinger), and others. In the midst and because of these relationships, Manuel unknowingly and perhaps unwillingly embraces the forgiveness he felt unworthy of and thought non-existent.

6   In *Levity,* unlike *The Machinist,* guilt and redemption are not private issues to be struggled with by oneself. We see both the personal and public nature of Manuel's crime affecting even the next generation. While the individual has responsibility and must embrace his own responsibility, guilt and redemption require the involvement of others, sometimes many others and perhaps, the film hints, something beyond ourselves and the laws of this dimension. While the belief in a transcendent being is uncertain for those in the film, the preacher "believe[s] in the lie" and tells Manuel to "never underestimate its power." Redemption, then, is presented as not only possible but maybe inevitable. In the end, Manuel does not get the girl and must move on, away from this place of his guilt and forgiveness; now with the crowd, facing in the same direction, Manuel, now solid and real, disappears onto the subway, becoming one of the many forgiven and redeemed.

7   These films offer us two characters seemingly headed in different directions and two perspectives on the possibilities of redemption. In *The Machinist* Trevor has blocked out the moment of his guilt, and privately, personally and physically relives it in a distorted, confused, unrecognizable psychotic manner until he can face the truth. In *Levity,* from the moment he kills, Manuel personally embraces his guilt and pain and chooses to spend his life passively paying for his action, but he is forced to live his guilt out in public and thus be open to the possibility of forgiveness and redemption. *The Machinist* is certainly a memorable film: its dark, despairing, cold steel version of personal guilt seems to offer little rest or hope for those who need forgiveness. But is this a final state or simply an expression of a stage, a dark night of the soul when everything feels hopeless but may not really be so? *Levity,* as its title suggests and in opposition to the gravity of individual responsibility and guilt, suggests that after the dark night of the soul comes a lighter path to redemption through engagement beyond ourselves with others.

Works Cited

Levity. Dir. and Screenplay by Ed Solomon. Studio Canal, 2003. Film.
The Machinist. Screenplay by Scott Kosar. Dir. Brad Anderson. Filmax, 2004. Film.

Finding Your Focus in Comparison-Contrast Writing

When you are assigned a comparison-contrast topic (assuming it is still fairly general), how do you narrow to a controlling idea? You know that you may find a controlling idea that expresses some main reason to favour one subject over the other, or you may find a controlling idea that asserts some common function of the two subjects. You also know that once you find your controlling idea and supporting evidence, you may arrange your discussion according to subject by subject, point by point, or a hybrid of the two. But that still leaves you without the specifics you need. At this brainstorming stage, it can be helpful to apply two "tests" of the subjects: the differences and similarities test and/or the disadvantages and advantages (or weaknesses and strengths) test.

Differences and Similarities Test

Thinking about differences and similarities helps you to narrow to emerging points of interest. Draw a line down the middle of a page and on the left-hand side write down all the ways in which you think Subject A and Subject B of your topic are different. On the right-hand side of the page, write down all the ways in which you think Subject A and Subject B are similar. Then review your results and decide if the differences outweigh the similarities or vice versa, and consider why. If there appears to be a near-equal balance, consider what meaning may emerge from that discovery.

This test of meaning might just as well be called "Similarities and Differences," because the priority you assign to one or the other should be decided only after you explore your topic according to these criteria. If this test leads you to Purpose 1 (p. 141), then it morphs into the advantages-disadvantages test (see the next section) and helps you determine which subject may be more suitable for a specific application or may better satisfy certain critical criteria. Used for Purpose 2 (p. 141), the differences-similarities test helps you recognize underlying common meaning despite (even because of) differences.

Disadvantages and Advantages Test (Weaknesses and Strengths Test)

This test is a refinement of the previous one, in service of Purpose 1 (p. 141). With only minor modification, it becomes the weaknesses and strengths test. In basically the same manner used to test for the broader differences and similarities approach, draw a line down the middle of a page. Use this page to test Subject A. On the left side of the page, write down all the possible disadvantages (or weaknesses) of Subject A. On the right side of the page, write down all the possible advantages (or strengths) of Subject A. Repeat this process for Subject B. On one side of a second page, write down all the disadvantages (or weaknesses) of Subject B. On the other side of the page, write down all the advantages (or strengths) of Subject B. Then review your results and decide if, for each subject, the disadvantages outweigh the advantages or vice versa, and consider why. If there appears to be a near-equal balance, consider what meaning may emerge from that discovery. Then compare your results for Subject A and your results for Subject B and do a further test to see which has more advantages (or strengths) of which type. Consider what that means.

For a short essay, you would select no more than three points for each subject, preferably ones dealing with the same issues. For two restaurants, for example, you might choose food quality and selection, atmosphere and service, and prices. A smaller-scale approach is to apply the disadvantages-advantages test to just *one* subject (e.g., one restaurant), thereby treating advantages as Subject A and disadvantages as Subject B. An important part of your thinking here will be in determining which criteria to privilege and why.

Disadvantages and Advantages and Similarities and Differences as Blocks

Some writing instructors suggest using disadvantages and advantages or similarities and differences in block format as a way to organize a comparison. In other words, you might brainstorm all the advantages of a certain topic and all the disadvantages. You would then select what you consider the three outstanding advantages and discuss them in the first half of your essay body, followed by the three outstanding disadvantages in the second half. Your opening and conclusion would make clear your final opinion and reasons. This essay would serve Purpose 1 (p. 141).

As an example of this approach, a student was asked on an essay exam to compare the advantages and disadvantages of TV and argue which category outweighed the other. The student decided that the disadvantages of TV outweighed the advantages. She therefore discussed disadvantages second, a good way to add emphasis to her position. Here is a brief outline of her essay, with advantages and disadvantages arranged in two blocks:

Title—The Good, the Bad, and the Unplugged

Thesis controlling idea: Although TV does present a number of advantages, after close consideration, the disadvantages outweigh the advantages.

Topic sentence of first body paragraph: TV offers a number of advantages: news and information, some quality programs, and jobs. Discuss each advantage. [This may run into two paragraphs]

Topic sentence of second body paragraph: These advantages pale, however, when weighed against the disadvantages: household disruption and alienation, media addiction, and manipulation of children. [This may run into two paragraphs]

Short conclusion: Recommend that after sampling the good and anticipating the bad, one's best move is to unplug (which also eliminates a drain on energy).

An essay asking you to compare Vancouver and Seattle, Calgary and Edmonton, or Ottawa and Quebec City might work well with one half of the body dealing with similarity and the second with difference (or vice versa, depending on your controlling idea and purpose). This essay would likely serve Purpose 2 (p. 141), or else you would rephrase similarities and differences to advantages and disadvantages. There does not have to be an absolute division between the two purposes, but failing to be strict about your purpose and controlling idea can result in an essay that includes lots of information but that lacks a central point.

 P R A C T I C E

If you were to compare two cities with an intention of showing that the two are fundamentally more similar than different, would you place similarities first or second? Why?

If you were to compare the same two cities with an intention of showing that fundamentally the two are more different than similar, would you place similarities first or second? Why?

To help you to think further about these questions, here are some choices for comparison: Halifax and Ottawa, Toronto and New York, Montreal and Winnipeg, Regina and Edmonton, Edmonton and Calgary, Vancouver and Victoria, Victoria and Seattle.

Remember Reader Awareness and Writing Intention

What if you realize that some aspect of a certain city could be seen as an advantage *or* a disadvantage (e.g., nightlife as exciting versus nightlife as noisy)? Recognizing complexity is always a good thing, but how to harness it? Remember why you are writing the essay and for whom. If you are writing advice to potential tourists or visitors, then you can frame your assessments not as absolutes but as comments related to two or three main personality types. If that leads to an overly long essay, then be much more specific about the sort of reader you are addressing (Montreal for the young and urban, etc.) This sort of "consumer advice" stance can result in a natural blend of Purpose 1 (advantages and disadvantages) and Purpose 2 (recognizing shared merit). You recognize that the two subjects (cities, for example) have equal overall value but that each has specific appeals representing certain advantages to certain visitors.

Avoiding Problems in Comparison-Contrast

Comparison-contrast is one of the most challenging patterns to use effectively. In the preceding discussion, we referred to a number of potential problems. To help you ensure that none of these has slipped into your essay, the following checklist may be of use. Try to avoid these problems:

- failing to balance the discussion, so that one subject predominates
- creating a ping-pong effect by using too much point-by-point structure without due care

- dwelling on one subject for so long that the reader begins to forget the essay's underlying comparative purpose
- applying a structure that revisits rather than advances the main points of discussion
- forgetting that comparison-contrast is a tool for focusing on a controlling idea, not an end in itself

The final problem is especially common. You may be tempted to cover all parts of your plan, noting, for example, similarities and differences, but then fail to conclude your essay with any useful meaning or insight that flows from this comparison. Simply observing that subjects are equally weighted in their similarities and differences or advantages and disadvantages can lead to an essay that lacks any point or clear value. Your comparisons will have a stronger edge if your thesis sentences suggest strong subordination and emphasis, or assign specific value.

 PRACTICE

Outline an essay of 1000 to 1500 words in which you compare two films that you have seen recently or recall well. Decide on which purpose to argue. Apply point by point, subject by subject, or a hybrid of the two.

FINAL WORD

Concentration and sustained thinking are needed to craft a successful comparison-contrast essay. But the rewards exceed the investment. Skills honed through comparison writing will make all your other writing easier and more effective than it used to be. Choose comparison topics, when you can, as an ideal way to stretch your thinking and compositional abilities. If you follow the advice in this chapter, you should have the precise guidelines you need to succeed with each new effort.

Chapter 15
The Summary

The ability to write a summary confirms that you are a good reader. This ability is of considerable importance, since reading skills contribute to writing skills in general. More specifically, you will often be called upon to apply the skills of summary in your academic and professional writing.

SUMMARIZATION AND ACADEMIC WORK

In your studies, you will be expected to report to your instructor and classmates on the contents of various books, articles, studies, and so on. Since the goal of research is not simply to repeat what has already been said but to add to that work, you will need to identify the main points of existing work as briefly as you can, leaving time and space for your own critical response to it.

A **summary** concisely re-states the central ideas of a reading, using different words to express the writer's meaning accurately and neutrally. Some summaries also mention the kinds of rhetorical methods used in the material being summarized. Dwelling on *how* a piece is written, however, can result in process description, a combination of summary and overt critical judgment. Summaries avoid such overt judgment.

WRITING THE SUMMARY

Writing a summary calls upon active reading. To do this well, you must exercise *two* main skills:

1. *First, identify the thesis (controlling idea + reason[s]) and any other support-ing ideas. Separate these ideas from the details used to explain them.*

    You may adapt this guideline somewhat on different occasions. Some instructors may want you to include supporting details, depending on the nature of the assignment. Some may request more or less attention to the rhetorical mechanics of the writing. However, for the purposes of learning to separate ideas from details, it is good practice to learn to write summaries that omit any detail that is not crucial to expressing a central point.

How long should a summary be? Again, you will want to satisfy different expectations for different assignments. Since good writing expresses one main idea per paragraph (i.e., a unit of 5–10 sentences), try to follow the rule of thumb of using no more than one or two sentences for each paragraph of the original. In most cases, your summary should be less than one-quarter the length of the source. Later in this chapter we provide a terse sample summary that is 15 percent of the length of the source.

2. ***The second main skill required for a summary is to express the writer's ideas in your own words without altering the original meaning.***

Finding your own words to re-present the writer's ideas—paraphrasing— helps you to understand those ideas. It also develops your ability to *avoid* stating other people's words as your own, which is plagiarism.

You may quote one or two key words or phrases to convey the essence of an idea, but use quotation sparingly. In longer essays, summarizing supplements analysis, critical response, and other types of writing. Yet the summary itself should not express your personal responses to what you are summarizing. Whether you strongly approve or reject what a writer says, your summary should simply paraphrase the writer's ideas accurately and impartially. Using the third-person voice for your summaries helps to keep you from stating your own response.

FINDING THE CONTROLLING IDEAS AND SUPPORTING REASONS (THE THESIS)

Bear in mind that almost all writing aims to persuade us of something. As rhetoricians like Stephen Toulmin remind us, most persuasions involve a central claim or assertion (controlling idea), grounds to support that idea (various reasons, proofs, evidence), and awareness of a general attitude or attitudes toward the topic among the intended readers (what Toulmin and others call *warrants*).

Three Tips for Finding the Thesis

Here are three tips to help you identify the controlling idea and supporting reasons in an essay:

1. Determine who the author is and where the reading was published, which may help you to imagine the intended audience. In the case of anthologies, you can find where an item was originally published by looking under the literary credits, often at the back of the book. Knowing the background of the author and his or her intended audience may help you to infer what public attitudes and assumptions preceded and perhaps precipitated the essay you are to summarize.

2. Scan and skim, concentrating on the title, the opening and closing paragraphs, and the topic and closing sentences of each paragraph. From these

key locations, you should be able to infer the main topic (and probably much more). Turn the title[1] of the essay into a question in your mind and read the text seeking an answer to that question: What is this and why is it important? Titles may convey the topic and controlling idea or just one or the other. Some titles prefer to pose riddles, not making perfect sense until the essay is completed. For example, some titles state metaphors or allusions; some state the reason for the controlling idea or a warrant (a belief likely held by the social group addressed) but not the controlling idea itself. Your goal is to gather clues from various key locations. As you seek answers, ask yourself what the main assertion (claim) and evidence (grounds) are (see Chapter 18, p. 205).

3. Skim through paragraphs looking for rhetorical methods: stylistic features of the point of view, language that contributes to a dominant tone, and patterns of organization—a purposeful structure that helps you understand the relationship between ideas and language.

Would you have difficulty identifying the thesis (controlling idea + reason[s]) in the following opening paragraph from Jayne Schuyler's essay in Chapter 5?

Opening paragraph of "Should Cats Be Allowed to Roam?"

Many people believe that because of cats' independent nature, they should be allowed to roam free. This allows them to satisfy their hunting instincts and to function within cat society, one that has its own rules and structure. Some people assert that free-roaming cats are happier cats, living a life closer to that intended by Nature. This is all true, but it is not compatible with modern life in suburban North America. Roaming cats are susceptible to attack by other animals, to trapping by angry neighbours, and most of all, to traffic accidents.

Prompted by the title, you infer that the controlling idea will be an answer to the question. At the end of the opening paragraph you encounter "[r]oaming cats are susceptible." The author is clearly answering, "no, (city) cats should not be allowed to roam." You recognize here the style of a student essay using standard structure. According to this style and its intended readers, the reason(s) will follow the controlling idea in the thesis statement: other hostile animals, angry neighbours, and traffic dangers. Finding the thesis of a carefully written academic paper using standard structure is not difficult because the form stresses a code of explicit clarity. But as a sample of readings in our Reader demonstrates, different essay forms are not so explicit or predictable in stating their controlling ideas and reasons. Sometimes you must infer the controlling idea from the overall essay.

---

[1] Use the title tip with caution when summarizing from a newspaper or magazine. Titles of media articles are usually decided upon by an editor (headline writer) working hastily and sometimes with more interest in sensational effect than in accurate reflection of the article's main ideas.

PRACTICE
Finding the Controlling Idea and Reasons

Read Robertson Davies' essay "The Pleasures of Love" (Reader, p. 420). Find his controlling idea and supporting reason(s). Use a combination of highlighting or underlining along with marginal notes to apply the above tips. Then look at our notations on Davies' essay. We provide a follow-up re-statement of what we take to be his controlling idea and reasons. Compare your answer to ours. Then read our commentary on how we applied the above reading tips to construct our summary of his basic argument.

Reminder—Finding the Controlling Idea Is Not a Personal or Critical Response

One of the greatest obstacles to successful reading is an emotional resistance to finding and "giving time" to ideas that we oppose or don't initially understand. We all have a tendency to shape discussions on a topic into ideas we have already received or formed, and even to dismiss a complex discussion before completing it. Whether or not you agree with what Robertson Davies says in his essay, your goal as summarizer is to capture his ideas impartially. Once you have done that, once you have recognized his claim and his reasons, you are in a stronger position to develop a critique of his position.

Sample Active Reading Seeking the Controlling Idea and Reason(s)

The Pleasures of Love
Robertson Davies

1   Let us understand one another at once: I have been asked to discuss the pleasures of love, not its epiphanies, its ecstasies, its disillusionments, its duties, its burdens or its martyrdom—and therefore the sexual aspect of it will get scant attention here. So if you have begun this piece in hope of fanning the flames of your lubricity, be warned in time.

2   Nor is it my intention to be psychological. I am heartily sick of most of the psychologizing about love that has been going on for the past six hundred years. Everybody wants to say something clever, or profound, about it, and almost everybody has done so. Only look under "Love" in any book of quotations to see how various the opinions are.

3   Alas, most of this comment is wide of the mark; love, like music and painting, resists analysis in words. It may be described, and some poets and novelists have described it movingly and well; but it does not yield to the theorist. Love is the personal experience of lovers. It <u>must be felt directly</u>.

What main point will emerge about them?

"Discuss" may signal exposition, maybe definition.

First person suggests he will be shaping a personal view—an element of argument.

Something one can't express with logic but can only feel

"Opinion" could
be controlling
idea.
Love takes time—
but why?

4   My own <u>opinion</u> is that it is felt most completely in marriage, or some comparable <u>attachment of long duration</u>. Love <u>takes time</u>. What are called "love affairs" may
afford a wide, and in retrospect, illuminating variety of emotions; not only fierce satisfactions and swooning delights, but the horrors of jealousy and the desperation of
parting attend them; the hangover from one of these emotional riots may be long and
dreadful.

Long-term-
commitment

5   But rarely have the pleasures of love an opportunity to manifest themselves in
such riots of passion. Love affairs are for emotional sprinters; the pleasures of love are
<u>for the emotional marathoners</u>.

"Then" means
"therefore" here—
as result of previ-
ous point

6   Clearly,<u> then</u>, the pleasures of love are <u>not for the very young</u>. Romeo and Juliet
are the accepted pattern of youthful passion. Our hearts go out to their furious abandonment; we are moved to pity by their early death. We do not, unless we are of a
saturnine disposition, give a thought to what might have happened if they had been
spared for fifty or sixty years together.

7   Would Juliet have become a worldly nonentity, like her mother? Or would she,
egged on by that intolerable old bawd, her Nurse, have planted a thicket of horns on
the brow of her Romeo?

8   And he—well, so much would have depended on whether Mercutio had lived;
quarrelsome, dashing and detrimental, Mercutio was a man destined to outlive his wit
and spend his old age as the Club Bore. No, no; all that Verona crowd were much
better off to die young and beautiful.

9   Passion, so splendid in the young, wants watching as the years wear on. Othello
had it, and in middle life he married a young and beautiful girl. What happened? He
believed the first scoundrel who hinted that she was unfaithful, and never once took
the elementary step of asking her a direct question about the matter.

Concession-
refutation form

10   <u>Passion is</u> a <u>noble</u> thing; I have no use for a man or woman who lacks it; <u>but</u> if we
seek the pleasures of love, <u>passion should be occasional</u>, and common sense continual.

11   Let us get away from Shakespeare. He is the wrong guide in the exploration we
have begun. If we talk of the pleasures of love, the best marriage he affords is that of
Macbeth and his Lady. Theirs is not the prettiest, nor the highest-hearted, nor the wittiest match in Shakespeare, but unquestionably they knew the pleasures of love.

12   "My dearest partner of greatness," writes the Thane of Cawdor to his spouse.
That is the clue to their relationship. That explains why Macbeth's noblest and most
desolate speech follows the news that his Queen is dead.

A moral aspect;
rejects the worldly

13   But <u>who wants to live</u> a modern equivalent of the life of the Macbeths—continuous
<u>scheming to reach the Executive Suite</u> enlivened, one presumes, by an occasional Burns
Nicht dinner-party, with the ghosts of discredited vice-presidents as uninvited guests.

Spiritual note—
greater than the
individual

14   The pleasures of love are certainly not for the very young, who find a bittersweet
pleasure in trying to reconcile two flowering <u>egotisms</u>, nor yet for those who find satisfaction in "affairs." Not that I say a word against young love, or the questings of

uncommitted middle-age; but these notions of love correspond to brandy, and we are concerned with something much <u>more like wine</u>.

15 The pleasures of love are for those who are <u>hopelessly addicted</u> to another living creature. The <u>reasons</u> for such addiction <u>are so many</u> that I suspect they are never the same in any two cases.

Again a metaphor

16 It <u>includes passion</u> but does not survive by passion; it has its whiffs of the agreeable vertigo of young love, but it is stable more often than dizzy; it is a growing, changing thing, and it is tactful enough to give the addicted parties occasional rests from strong and exhausting feeling of any kind.

Love includes passion but is something more.

17 "Perfect love sometimes <u>does not come until the first grandchild</u>," says a <u>Welsh proverb</u>. <u>Better</u> [by] far <u>if perfect love</u> does not come at all, but <u>hovers just out of reach</u>. Happy are those who never experience the all-dressed-up-and-no-place-to-go sensation of perfection in love.

Like a marathon—ongoing work. Aspiration—but what is the value?

18 What do we seek in love? From my own observation among a group of friends and acquaintances that includes a high proportion of happy marriages, most people are <u>seeking a completion of themselves</u>. Each party to the match has several qualities the other cherishes; the marriage as a whole is decidedly more than the sum of its parts.

Value is to complete the self

19 Nor are these cherished qualities simply the obvious ones; the reclusive man who marries the gregarious woman, the timid woman who marries the courageous man, the idealist who marries the realist—we can all see these unions: the marriages in which tenderness meets loyalty, where generosity sweetens moroseness, where a sense of beauty eases some aridity of the spirit, are not so easy for outsiders to recognize; the parties themselves may not be fully aware of such elements in a good match.

Love is emotional balancing.

20 Often, in choosing a mate, people are <u>unconsciously wise</u> and apprehend what they need <u>to make them greater than they are</u>.

Instinct; inner self seeking completion

21 Of course the original disposition of the partners to the marriage points the direction it will take. When Robert Browning married Elizabeth Barrett, the odds were strongly on the side of optimism, in spite of superficial difficulties; when Macbeth and his Lady stepped to the altar, surely some second-sighted Highlander must have shuddered.

22 If the parties to a marriage have chosen one another unconsciously, knowing only that they will be <u>happier united than apart</u>, they had better <u>set to work as soon as possible</u> to discover why they have married, and to <u>nourish the feeling which has drawn them together</u>.

Work to "nourish" the attraction to each other.

23 I am constantly astonished by the people, otherwise intelligent, who think that anything so complex and delicate as a marriage can be left to take care of itself. One sees them fussing about all sorts of lesser concerns, apparently unaware that side by side with them—often in the same bed—a human creature is perishing from lack of affection, of emotional malnutrition.

Comparison to unwedded seeks essence, not surface	24	Such people are living in sin far more truly than the <u>loving but unwedded</u> couples whose unions they sometimes scorn. What pleasures are there in these neglected marriages? What pleasure can there be in ramshackle, jerrybuilt, uncultivated love?
Not a matter of form or surface	25	A <u>great part of all the pleasure</u> of love begins, continues and sometimes ends with <u>conversation</u>. A real, enduring love-affair, in marriage and out of it, is an extremely exclusive club of which the entire membership is two <u>co-equal</u> Perpetual Presidents.
Talking a key part of the work—and it's fun		
Talking to each other, not shrinks	26	In French drama there used to be a character, usually a man, who was the intimate friend of husband and wife, capable of resolving quarrels and keeping the union in repair. I do not believe in such a creature anywhere except behind the footlights. <u>Lovers who need a third party</u> to discuss matters with are <u>in a bad way</u>.
	27	Of course there are marriages that are kept in some sort of rickety shape by a psychiatrist—occasionally by two psychiatrists. But I question if pleasure of the sort I am writing about can exist in such circumstances. The club has become too big.
Authenticity as love	28	I do not insist on a union of chatter-boxes, but as you can see I do not believe that still waters run deep; too often I have found that still waters are foul and have mud bottoms. People who love each other should talk to each other; they should confide their <u>real thoughts</u>, their <u>honest emotions</u>, their <u>deepest wishes</u>. How else are they to keep their union in repair?
	29	How else, indeed, are they to discover that they are <u>growing older and enjoying it</u>, which is a very great discovery indeed? How else are they to discover that their union is stronger and richer, not simply because they have shared experience (couples who are professionally at odds, like a Prime Minister and a Leader of the Opposition, also share experience, but they are not lovers) but because they are waxing in spirit?
Mutual opportunism wears out.	30	During the last war a cruel epigram was current that Ottawa was full of brilliant men, and the women they had married when they were very young. If the brilliant men had talked more to those women, and the women had replied, the joint impression they made in middle-age might not have been so dismal. It is often asserted that sexual compatibility is the foundation of a good marriage, but this pleasure is doomed to wane, whereas a daily affectionate awareness and a ready tongue last as long as life itself.
	31	It always surprises me, when Prayer Book revision is discussed, that something is not put into the marriage service along these lines—"for the mutual society, help, comfort and unrestricted conversation that one ought to have of the other, both in prosperity and adversity."
Talk a "subtle" pleasure	32	Am I then advocating marriages founded on talk? I can hear the puritans, who mistrust conversation as they mistrust all <u>subtle pleasures</u>, tutting their disapproving tuts.
	33	Do I assert that the pleasures of love are no more than the pleasures of conversation? Not at all: I am saying that <u>where the talk is good</u> and copious, <u>love is less</u>

<u>likely to wither</u>, or to get out of repair, or to be outgrown, than among the uncommunicative.

Not the only pleasure but the nourishing one

34   For, after all, even lovers live alone much more than we are ready to admit. To keep in constant, sensitive rapport with those we love most, we must open our hearts and our minds. Do this, and the rarest, most delicate pleasures of love will reveal themselves.

35   Finally, <u>it promotes longevity</u>. Nobody quits a club where the conversation is fascinating, revealing, amusing, various and unexpected until the last possible minute. Love may be snubbed to death: talked to death, never!

Controlling Idea and Reason Drawn from the Above Notations

Having been asked in 1961, by *Maclean's* magazine, to write about "the pleasures of love," Robertson Davies responded with his "opinion" that these enjoyments are most likely to thrive through time only with communication: a long-lasting relationship of equals dedicated to open and intimate discussion. He believes this private talking is necessary because the rewards of maturing love flow from the combining of two matching if different portions of a greater whole, an investment demanding ongoing work and adjustments.

The above underlining and marginal notes reflect an effort to apply the three tips for finding the thesis. Here is how you might think further about this essay and other information that you have gathered.

1.   *Determine who the author is and where the reading was published.*

   You'll find this information in the Reader on page 420, as an introduction to the article. Place of publication also appears in the Literary Credits at the end of the book. Knowing that Davies has an interest in mystery and the unconscious suggests that he will likely imagine love as something that can be only felt, not expressed in words. In addition, knowing where a piece of writing was published alerts you to the intended readers. This in turn suggests the assumed "warrants" underlying the subject. A warrant is a belief that a social group generally holds on a particular topic. The belief against premarital or "promiscuous" sex at the time Davies wrote this essay was not animated by the medical threat of HIV, which did not come to wide public awareness until the early 1980s, but by social, moral, and religious injunctions. There had been another warrant as well—the very practical concern about unwanted pregnancy. In the year before this essay, however, Canada had approved the recently invented birth control pill for the Canadian market. By 1964, CBC reported 80 million women were using this new effective form of contraception world wide. Society became preoccupied with "the pill" and its perceived impact on changing attitudes to love and relationships. The warrant that you shouldn't have premarital sex because it would lead to pregnancy was crumbling. For some members of the changing society, this new freedom from consequences seemed to open the door to unrestricted sexual activity ("passion" was still the preferred term for "sex" in 1961). For some this was liberating, for others repugnant. Considering this cultural context, we may approach Davies' essay with an increased sense of pressing concerns of the time and possible responses to them. Knowing the context surrounding the topic increases active reading, the ability to frame educated guesses concerning the ideas and beliefs to which the writer is responding.

2. *Scan and skim, concentrating on the title, the opening and closing paragraphs, and the topic and closing sentences of each paragraph.*

The title suggests that the essay will deal with "the pleasures of love," but does not indicate how. Consulting the opening and closing sections of the essay offers guidance, but here it is important to consider the news magazine format in which Davies' essay appeared. Newspapers and magazines, using multiple columns, tend to break text into new paragraphs after two or three sentences, and sometimes even after one. This is to maintain sufficient amounts of white space. The chunks of writing created by this practice, however, are usually pseudo-paragraphs, because the writer may still be addressing a particular unifying idea when the break occurs. To find meaning and purpose in magazine articles, look past the paragraph breaks on the page to determine where an actual paragraph may end. As a very approximate rule of thumb, three magazine-break paragraphs may represent one "regular" paragraph in the sense of a number of related sentences all expanding upon and supporting a subtopic. So when we refer to the opening and closing paragraphs of this essay, we mean something like the first three or four at either end of the complete text.

Paragraphs 1 to 3 seem to work together to introduce the topic and purpose, with attention to narrowing scope. Davies tells us what he will *not* be discussing, including psychology and sex. He says he will not try to define love in words, something he says cannot be done. This restriction prompts us to anticipate that he will be looking, then, at something practical rather than theoretical, perhaps at how or where to find the pleasures his title alludes to. Then we come to the sentence that starts paragraph 4: "My own opinion is . . ." To convert Davies' essay into standard essay format for academic purposes, we could combine the first three paragraphs with the first sentence of paragraph 4, placing this sentence at the end of paragraph 3. This re-formatting would place the writer's first iteration of his thesis at the end of his opening paragraph, a standard location for academic essays. His preamble tells us what he won't do, tells us that love must be simply felt, then offers an opinion on where it is to be best felt (in an "attachment of long duration"). This opinion signals his controlling idea.

This idea makes us curious to learn his reason(s) and leads us to anticipate that there must be special conditions about this form of relationship that encourage the "pleasures." We examine the closing paragraphs 32 to 35 and find that they begin with a rhetorical question announcing the writer's intention to offer his final word on a main point. We find that his topic here is the importance of conversation to the health of a love relationship, allowing for its continuation and the emergence thereby of "the rarest, most delicate" or "subtle" pleasures. These statements together with his opening opinion that "[l]ove takes time" inclines us to the hypothesis that Davies is saying something about the importance of time and communication in tandem and how they lead to refined joys connected with the deepened awareness of advancing age. This suggests that passion and/or sex will not be critical to these pleasures, but we aren't sure yet where the more ardent side of love fits in Davies' view. We also aren't sure yet of the reason(s) behind Davies' apparent main assertion: why is time plus communication the path to rewards? We may assume that it has something to do with the benefits of teamwork or something like that. We read on to refine and correct our guesses.

We scan and skim the middle of the essay, recognizing that the choppy paragraphs could be assembled into larger units or chunks based on topic ideas in the various parts. In paragraph 6 we find further answer to the question of youth and passion. Davies reminds us that the story of Romeo and Juliet ends with no assurances they would have cared for each other into later life. Paragraph 9 uses the example of Othello to show the problem of ungoverned passion in midlife, as Shakespeare's tragic hero falls into the clutches of quick jealousy. In paragraph 13 we gain a sense of something more philosophical than worldly about the sort of love Davies has in mind as he distances it from climbing social ladders or playing political games.

Returning to passion in paragraph 16, he allows that love includes this condition but "does not survive" by it. These statements help to answer the questions we formed by reading the opening and closing, but we still need a statement of reason—*why* is passion a possible start to love but not the key to nurturing it?

Paragraph 18 provides the all important answer: "most people are seeking a completion of themselves." Paragraph 20 adds that people are "unconsciously wise" in feeling drawn to a mate who will be able "to make them greater than they are," so the process begins by something mysterious and intuitive but then, as paragraph 22 makes clear, the conscious work must start. Paragraph 24 adds that some people in wedlock are in effect "living in [the] sin" of not treating their relationship with respect, not nourishing it. Davies signals that he is not concerned with outward social signs of a love union but with authentic, active love.

Helping to fill in the answers to how all the ingredients of the discussion fit together, paragraph 25 says that a "great part" of love's enjoyment is conversation, and that the talk is between equals, a reminder of the idea that love is a uniting over time of complementary beings. Davies goes on to reinforce the work demanded by expressing distrust of others (e.g., therapists) brought into the union to help with the talk and understanding. In paragraph 28, he suggests that if the couple share "real," "honest," and "deepest" thoughts and feelings, they will grow and realize true fulfillment. The result, as paragraph 29 repeats, will be "growing older [together] and enjoying it."

3. *Look for rhetorical methods, a purposeful structure that helps you understand the relationship between ideas and sections of the reading.*

Davies' essay takes the form of a personal opinion piece, a blend of personal reflection and exposition drawing liberally on argumentation to drive home points. His purpose is to define the "pleasures of love," but with priority given to process description: to *how* these enjoyments are to be realized, in a practical sense. Davies' use of images and metaphors as well as examples from Shakespeare is a notable feature of his literary method. It seems to fit with his basic view that love is not something one can describe or understand in prosaic words, even though the use of words to reveal deep feelings and ideas is critical in nourishing what one finds through feeling. His structure, as we have found, does reveal a logical argument, but rather than being formally laid out in clearly reasoned steps, it is relaxed and informal, with a number of repetitions of previous ideas before the thread resumes. His main point deals with the importance of a personal, intuitive dimension, and the style or writing would seem to express that.

From Controlling Idea and Reason(s) to Completed Summary

Now that we have identified the writer's thesis—or made our best attempt to capture it— our work as summarizer is well underway. Without the controlling idea and reasons (thesis), we cannot provide a summary of value. With it, we are ready to move on to the next stage to complete our assignment. To do so, we apply the following 10 steps.

Ten Steps to a Successful Summary

1. Begin by identifying the author and title of the reading.
2. In your first sentence or short paragraph, re-state the complete thesis (controlling idea and supporting reasons).
3. Include all significant points (ideas) and only inseparable details (e.g., an analogy that forms the basis of the main argument).
4. Re-present content in the same order that the author does (but place the thesis at the start, no matter where it occurs).
5. Make each part of your summary directly proportional to the part it summarizes (e.g., three sentences to compress three paragraphs).
6. Use a neutral (impartial/objective) tone—third-person point of view. Avoid using your own metaphors or other literary figures of speech, which convey personal voice and a possible tone of critical evaluation.
7. Exclude any of your own critical response.
8. Be brief—try to summarize each paragraph or comparable section in no more than a sentence.
9. Use almost entirely your own language—select only key words for quotation.
10. Enclose any of the author's words in quotation marks.

PRACTICE

Applying the previous 10 steps, and making any revisions you think necessary to your re-statement of Davies' thesis, write a short summary of his essay. Compare your result to our sample summary below and read our final remarks.

Following is our summary constructed from the above reading analysis:

Summary of "The Pleasures of Love"

Having been asked in 1961, by *Maclean's* magazine, to write about "the pleasures of love," Robertson Davies responded with his "opinion" that these enjoyments are most likely to thrive through time and communication: a long-lasting relationship of equals dedicated to open and intimate discussion. He believes this is necessary because the rewards of maturing love flow from the combining of two matching if different portions of a greater whole, an investment demanding ongoing work and adjustment.

Davies opens by saying he will not discuss sex or psychology or try to define love itself, which according to him cannot be verbalized as cerebral philosophy but "felt only directly." By virtue of its time of life, the passionate love of youth may lack the integrity to endure. Passion in middle age may betray good judgment.

Davies suggests that those seeking the enjoyment of truly fulfilling love should set aside excessively worldly and egotistic preoccupations. He allows that the enjoyments he speaks of are for those "addicted" to another being, adding that it may be best if the craving never quite achieves a sense of perfection attained but continues to motivate the lovers to reach further.

Adding to his earlier thought that genuine love is "felt," Davies suggests that people are guided by an inner knowing to the partner who can best complete them. He believes their completion is best pursued, without third-party therapists, through respecting each other as equals sharing intimate, open, and honest discussion of personal thoughts and feelings. This commitment will be more than repaid by the "subtle" joys of talking and aging together.

Commentary

- It is 15 percent of the essay's length but (we hope) includes all the main points.
- It applies the 10 steps to a successful summary.
- It includes a few points that were not highlighted on the essay pages because the highlighting searched for just the central argument. Some assertions, although not parts of the core argument, are useful to positioning the argument.
- It maintains reminders that the statements given are those of the writer, but attempts to do so without mechanical repetition of "he says" and the like.
- It omits supporting details, examples, imagery, and figurative devices (e.g., the Shakespeare examples, the Welsh proverb, the images of "marathon" versus "sprinter" and "wine" versus "brandy").

It is sometimes difficult to understand the distinction between a point (an idea, an opinion, an assertion, or a claim) and a supporting detail. Supporting details can include any of the following:

- authorities cited or quoted
- data and other research findings
- examples, whether brief or extended (including anecdotes)
- logical illustrations such as analogies (except when the argument depends on one)
- literary devices such as metaphors and imagery.

 PRACTICE

Write as many summaries as you can until you have internalized these skills. To get started, try to summarize the following: "Elementary Observations: The Special Skill of Sherlock Holmes" (Reader, p. 392); "The Scientific State of Mind" (Reader, p. 398); "Murderous Martyrdom: Religion or Politics?" (Reader, p. 404): and "Enough Already, It's Time We Decriminalize Prostitution" (Reader, p. 436).

Which of these four readings seems to most closely follow the standard essay format explained in Chapter 5, "Standard Essay Structure"? Explain. Discuss with others your sense of controlling idea and reasons in the readings you examine. Also discuss the rhetorical nature of each reading and how it appears shaped to the writer's apparent purpose and intended readers.

FINAL WORD

In a postscript to a friend, the French mathematician and philosopher Blaise Pascal (1623–1662) once apologized for sending a long letter, saying he didn't have time to write a short one. No magic formula or list of steps can remove the fact that achieving brevity is demanding. Writing a summary—compressing a longer text into a shorter one without losing anything essential, and furthermore converting it into your own words—can be complex, tiring work. As Davies says of love's fulfillment, it takes time and communication skills. In the case of active reading, those skills involve asking the right questions and listening alertly for the answers. As Davies also says of love's pleasures, however, the effort brings great rewards, including the desire to continue and deepen the relationship.

Summary writing is not an absolute science; no two summaries will be exactly alike. As we have noted, different writing requirements affect the final form of any summary. Nevertheless, the tips, examples, and explanations in this chapter should serve you well.

Chapter

Critical Analysis and Evaluation

Critical analysis may refer both to the activity of analyzing and evaluating and to the subsequent written report, essay, or oral presentation that argues a point of view based upon the results of that process. Chapter 15 looked at how to summarize ideas by others. This chapter looks at ways to develop your own critical views of the ideas you have summarized.

CRITICAL ANALYSIS FURTHER DEFINED

The word "critical" in scholarly usage does not have the commonly assumed meaning of belabouring faults. A critical essay may support and expand on the ideas of others as well as find shortcomings. Furthermore, critical thinking (which assesses) and creative thinking (which originates) are interwoven: neither can be truly separated from the other. Your response to critical questions should contain a strong measure of creative thinking as you imagine new lines of exploration and synthesize from the analysis you have performed.

You must, however, employ appropriate logic, research methods, and due impartiality. You should remember to account for the appeals of pathos and ethos, and distinguish ethics (consideration for others) from other prescribed systems (e.g., theology, social conventions, or law). "Right" and "wrong" are relative to differing moral and legal codes, but ethical principles (for instance, versions of the golden rule) cross times and cultures.

When you present the results of your evaluation, you should apply the usual attributes of essay writing with an emphasis on clarifying the analytical process you followed and on giving your interpretation a vigorous emphasis. Instructors commonly refer to critical analytical writing as either "analysis" or "argumentation," since this wide-ranging form really combines analysis, evaluation, and the persuasive component of arguing an interpretation. Regardless of what term is used, instructors are looking to see that you are progressing from "subjective" responses in your thinking to more "objective" (well-rounded, deeply considered) ones.

ASKING A "FRUITFUL QUESTION"

In her book chapter "The Scientific State of Mind" (Reader, p. 398), Jane Jacobs defines science as seeking "to get at truths about how reality works." This quest, she says, is guided by first posing a "fruitful question." Although developing an essay that responds to ideas in another essay is not precisely a science, it does share in the scientist's state of mind, which includes the importance of being informed and methodical as one poses a meaningful question and imagines and assesses possible answers. Here are three questions that might be explored in response to Robertson Davies' "The Pleasures of Love" (Reader, p. 420).

1. Robertson Davies asserts that he will not psychologize about love, suggesting that his argument will not rely on theory. Do you believe he entirely follows through on his stated intention? Why or why not?
2. Robertson Davies claims that "the pleasures of love are not for the very young." Consider other assertions in his essay and decide if he sufficiently supports his dismissal of young love.
3. In what way(s) might Robertson Davies' 1961 essay address social issues of the time when it was written and of the years to follow? Do you believe his view offers a constructive response to those issues? Explain.

Consider how you might go about answering one or more of these questions. We will refer to them again in our following discussion.

CONSIDER STANDARDS OF ASSESSMENT

As the authors of *Essay Writing for Canadian Students* (113–21) point out, critical thinking means considering how we measure values: how subjects are judged to have merit, efficacy, meaning, and the like. To assess a subject, we consider values used in the following categories:

- logic
- applications (practical functionality)
- ethics
- aesthetics

Consider what sorts of criteria your critical question seems to be addressing. Question 1 above seems to be asking whether Davies in any way contradicts himself concerning his declared avoidance of psychological theory. Question 2 also focuses on logic and, again, on the matter of whether Davies' argument (that young love is inferior love) has been soundly demonstrated. But logic usually calls upon practical knowledge of values assigned to premises in an argument. Part of assessing the merit of an argument is assessing whether the writer has arrived at terms (premises) that reflect a true picture of the state of the subject. Practical and ethical criteria (involved in connecting to the world beyond abstract formulations) in addition to logical ones would seem to be likely touchstones for question 3 above. Aesthetic standards, pertaining to concepts of beauty and art, tend to occur in specialized discussions but can certainly enter a wide range of issues across disciplines, especially in literature and film.

The critical process begins as you formulate or review an assigned "fruitful question" and begin to consider what sorts of evaluatory criteria it may imply.

TWO MAIN STAGES OF CRITICAL THINKING

For purposes of helping you to write effective essays in response to a critical topic question, we recommend that, with your critical question in mind, you imagine working through two basic stages:

- analysis (breaking the subject into parts and relationships)
- evaluation (assessment)

Each of these is broken down and illustrated further for you below.

Analysis

As with most steps related to writing, these two critical thinking stages of analysis and evaluation are not mutually exclusive. Nevertheless, to sharpen your own critical thinking, it should prove helpful to concentrate on these two stages one at a time, beginning with **analysis.**

Clarify, Explore, and Focus the Question

The first step in analyzing your subject is to question and refine your assignment. As with any writing assignment, if the initial question seems too vague, your thinking will lack clarity and distinctness. Determine if the topic question is clear and what other important questions may be embedded in it. Decide what type(s) of considerations the question may be addressing—for example, the four broad criteria named above as well as specific fields: political, legal, social, economic, historical, religious, and so on.

Examine the Subject's Context, Parts, Stages, and Processes

Examine your subject (in our example, the Davies essay) in its context, parts, stages, and processes. Research important information surrounding the subject. Cause-effect relationships are especially important to consider. For all three topic questions given above, it is particularly important to analyze Davies' argument, identifying its core parts: controlling idea and reason(s) (premise[s]). You should also identify the rhetorical tools he uses (e.g., literary examples) and his methods of bringing assumptions forward to inform the structure of his argument. You should note features of his writing style as possible elements to examine and question. For question 3 in particular, you should identify any events and trends in the society of the time (the sixties) that might figure in a possible relationship between the essay and that society.

Evaluation (Assessment)

As the word **evaluation** implies, at this stage you propose a tentative answer to your topic question and determine whether it appears sound. You build your answer from possible meanings you find in the elements you have isolated and then considered in various relationships according to what seems to you an appropriate set of criteria. Logic will play a key role in your assessment and in your presentation of it.

As an example of evaluative process, for question 1 above you might look at the premise Davies gives for his conclusion that truly rewarding love takes time and communicative effort. His premise is that meaningful love begins when two people are attracted to each other and sense unconsciously that they will complete each other. Is this assertion a theory, thus contradicting Davies' stated intention not to rely on theory? You could consider definitions and examples of theories. You could look at examples of psychological theories that underlie some of Davies' other writings. From this you might reach an arguable conclusion that Davies seems to contradict himself by basing his argument on a theory. A critic of your response, however, might ask, "So what?" So you would think further and consider possible consequences of this apparent contradiction.

As an example of evaluative process for question 2, you could look carefully at where Davies draws his information about young love. Also look at how he then reaches conclusions based on his assumptions. You might explore whether a Shakespearian play is intended as a generalization about so-called normal psychology. Are young couples all tossed on the seas of ardent abandon like Romeo and Juliet? Is it logical to discuss the creations of a poet's imagination as if they were real people? Why assume that they would not have cared for each other beyond their youth, thus invalidating the integrity of their young love? Your analysis could identify another claim in Davies' essay: the idea that those attracted to each other are responding to an inner wisdom. Why would that same principle of two complementary parts gravitating to each other *not* apply to Romeo and Juliet, who seem so clearly drawn to each other? You could search the essay to see whether Davies concedes to (anticipates) this possible objection and rebuts (answers) it.

As an example of your evaluative process for question 3, you could analyze Davies' argument and methods, of course, but you could also research society at the time, gathering information about music and the birth control pill and various views of how they may have affected changing attitudes. You could note moral, religious, and legal attitudes that opposed premarital sex. You could consider whether Davies' main points are moral or ethical and relate that to an answer that challenges various sides in the growing controversy over sexual relationships as well as gender roles.

From these critical considerations you would form an answer that seems to make sense. You would then test it by considering possible refutations of it. How might you answer the imagined refutations? If your answers represent reliable knowledge and logic, you will have a sound critical position. Your next step is to articulate your newly formed critical view as the thesis of your essay.

Articulating Your Position

From your process of analysis and evaluation, you can shape the controlling idea and reason(s) of your essay, responding to a critical question concerning whatever text (poem, film, song) you are critiquing. Your position may stress some point of agreement or difference between the text and your own thinking. If you agree with the author, you must explain your reasons and not simply re-state his or hers. Your own reasons must somehow add to those of the text. If you disagree with some aspect of an essay, for example, you need to explain precisely in what way and why.

Here are hypothetical thesis statements that you might produce in reply to the three critical questions above, regarding the Robertson Davies essay:

1. Davies contradicts himself when he says he will not psychologize in his essay "The Pleasures of Love," because the central reason supporting his view of love is a psychological theory.
2. Davies' dismissal of young love in his essay "The Pleasures of Love" lacks justification because he contradicts one of his claims about the nature of love and overgeneralizes from a play written from poetic impulses rather than from life.
3. Davies' celebration of long-term relationships with the emphasis on genuine commitment rather than social convention is an interesting, independent position, because people at the time were either entertaining a vision of serial partners or intensifying allegiance to moral and legal codes.

All three statements are worded in a standard way with the controlling idea at the start and the reason(s) following "because." Statement 1 prepares the reader for evidence from the essay to show that Davies himself uses psychological reasoning. Statement 2 prepares the reader for evidence that Davies contradicts himself as well as coming to ill-founded conclusions based on his interpretation of a play. Statement 3 asserts that Davies' essay does respond to issues of the day and does so in an interesting and independent manner by challenging two polarized views common at the time. The reader anticipates explanations of how Davies critiques those two views and provides his own view as a more satisfying solution.

✏ PRACTICE
Critical Response to a Reading

In around 750 words, try to answer the following critical question:

Does Robertson Davies' "The Pleasures of Love" fulfill in all respects the logical elements called for by Stephen Toulmin in his model of argument?

You will find information about Toulmin's model in Chapter 15, "The Summary," p. 155 and in Chapter 18, "Argumentation," p. 205. Davies' essay is in the Reader (p. 420).

Sample Essay Answering a Critical Question about a Reading

"The Pleasures of Love": A Certain Lack of Grounds

Co-Authors Mario Chan and Christine Walker

Identifies Davies'
central argument
Identifies his
subject: the minor
argument
Concedes to value
of Davies' essay

States controlling
idea

Repeats controlling
idea and gives
reasons

Summarizes
Toulmin's model
and the critical
criteria

Davies relies on
warrants attached
to Shakespeare

False analogy
fallacy

Concession

Oversimplified
warrant

Unexamined
assumption

Contradiction

Looking at life
rather than
literature

1   In supporting his major argument that love matures only in the autumn of life,
Robertson Davies presents a minor argument that young love consists of "the riots
of passion" (par. 5), so the joys of love as "marathoner" are therefore denied to the
young. While few would question the value of Davies' main claim that committed,
enduring love will be steeped by the years, the suggestion that young love is therefore
without profound pleasure and integrity needs to be questioned. Despite insisting that
he has nothing to say against young love (par. 14), Davies seems to discount it as
passion only. He reaches this conclusion on the basis of an undemonstrated interpretation of one theatre play. According to Stephen Toulmin's argument model, this
conclusion rests on insufficient "grounds."

2   Toulmin sees three essentials to every argument: the claim (controlling idea);
grounds (data, evidence, proof); and warrants (stated or unstated beliefs that will incline
readers to accept an argument or that must be accounted for before readers will
accept it). Arguments most often fail to persuade readers, says Toulmin, by assuming
a warrant that isn't present or by failing to account for an oppositional warrant that is
present. In other words, arguments may overlook their readers' attitudes. In the case
of Davies' essay, however, the warrant is his strong card: people seem generally to
believe that Shakespeare was a master psychologist (although the term is a
20th-century creation) and that his characters are prototypical "real" people. There is
also a certain elitist warrant: Shakespeare is accepted as great literature studied in
universities and therefore authoritative on many human matters.

3   People familiar with a good portion of Shakespeare's 33 plays will surely agree
that his insight into human behaviour and motivation is remarkable. This, however,
does not make a literary form into a psychology book or a reflection of "real people."
As Robert McKee, a leading authority on story-writing, reminds us, "A character [in
fiction] is no more a human being than the Venus de Milo is a real woman. A
character is a work of art, a metaphor for human nature" (375). A play should not be
taken as grounds for a conclusion about people. If Davies is right that Romeo and
Juliet "are the accepted pattern of youthful passion," then society is suffering from a
seriously unexamined assumption that leads to an oversimplified view of the play, not
to mention of youth—in effect, to a stereotype.

4   Davies himself offers the grounds for accepting that young lovers have every
chance to experience joys deeper than passing passion. "Often, in choosing a mate,
people are unconsciously wise and apprehend what they need to make them greater
than they are" (par. 20). He says "people," not "older people only." When these proposed "soul mates" meet, however young and libidinous, do they experience only lust

and unwise emotions? Romeo and Juliet notwithstanding, we know from life observation and consultation of divorce statistics that many young couples stay together. Even if some of those who stay together are "living in [the] sin" of not really caring for each other or working to express their care (par. 24), some of those young couples are in for the marathon, or else how could Davies refer to those older couples enjoying the rewards of autumnal love? Is there a magic line where youth ends and supposed passionate irresponsibility suddenly gives way to focused, aware love? One has a certain impression from the essay of older people who were never young, all aspects of youth superseded by something more "mature."

A marathon has to start somewhere; it starts with the young, who surely in some cases know they are starting it.

5   After relying on Romeo and Juliet to suggest young love's unreliability, Davies recommends setting Shakespeare aside, since presumably his portrayals of young love are all overly passionate and tragic. But Shakespeare also gave us Katherina and Petruchio of *The Taming of the Shrew* and Beatrice and Benedick of *Much Ado about Nothing,* lovers who while still young at the end of their dramatized journeys have confronted their insecurities and reached the mutual understanding that Davies applauds. Like other young people represented in Shakespeare, they have balanced emotion and passion with reason. They prevail through inner strength, perception, and intelligence. We are left accepting these characters as metaphors of a love unity that endures.

Davies is biased in his selective use of Shakespeare, omitting evidence of intelligent, perceptive youth.

6   Thinking of time as a strictly linear one-way thing and life as a progress (requiring dutiful regular work) from lesser to superior stages raises some problems. So does *not* considering inner experience or knowing—whether we call this psychological or spiritual. There is consequently a certain hierarchy to Davies' way of thinking. While his outlook certainly has merit—recognizing the undeniable special pleasures of mature age—it also results in the oversimplification referred to previously. This linear, external outlook—or theory of time—discounts claims of the poets, mystics, and physicists, that time is relative, even illusional, and that it is indeed conceivable for the present to be one with the future. According to poet William Blake (1757–1827), it is possible

A rigid view of time results in isolating youth as non-participants in their own story. Concession to the merit of Davies' view
Again, the problem is oversimplification
Youth can sense and shape their future

> To see a world in a grain of sand,
> And a heaven in a wild flower,
> Hold infinity in the palm of your hand,
> And eternity in an hour.

7   Blake experienced this insight in relative youth. Real-life examples of young people "wise beyond their years" are legion. Why not, then, with the mate you have discovered by unconscious wisdom, hold the past, present, and future pleasures of love in the knowing of an hour?

Reminder not to stereotype.

Works Cited

Davies, Robertson. "The Pleasures of Love." *Acting on Words: An Integrated Rhetoric, Research Guide, Reader, and Handbook.* 3rd ed. By David Brundage and Michael Lahey. Toronto: Pearson, 2012. 420-24. Print.

McKee, Robert. *Story: Substance, Structure, Style, and the Principles of Screenwriting.*
New York: HarperCollins, 1997. Print.

Toulmin, Stephen. *The Uses of Argument.* Cambridge, UK: Cambridge UP, 1969. Print.

Commentary

Chan and Walker identify Davies' claim concerning young love as an idea lacking argumentative integrity. They thus narrow their focus to one element—a minor argument within Davies' larger argument. Chan and Walker focus on a strong example in reply to the critical question, and this helps circumscribe a discussion that can be handled within the assigned word limit.

Chan states his own controlling idea and reasons at the end of his opening paragraph. With Toulmin's terms at hand, he goes on to discuss how Davies works with certain unexamined warrants about Shakespeare and argues that these warrants, because they contain fallacies, cannot be accepted as legitimate grounds for Davies' assertions about young love. Referring to portions of Shakespeare that Davies overlooks but more importantly advocating for an understanding drawn from life knowledge, Chan suggests an alternative understanding of youth and young love.

From the point of view of successful persuasion, Toulmin is probably right that misjudging a warrant is a writer's biggest problem. If your reader assumes, for example, that blue is noble and you begin with an assertion that it isn't, you have probably lost your reader. But blindly complying with warrants—for instance, agreeing that blue is noble even though you have the latest findings to show that it isn't—can work against the aim of seeking truth, relative as that term may be. Chan upholds a principle of criticism by requiring that grounds for conclusions be solid, researched, and reasoned. A good essay requires the same of its conclusions.

 PRACTICE
Critical Response to a Reading

Read the essay "Saskatchewan's Indian People—Five Generations" by Pat Deiter-McArthur (Reader, p. 379).

    With your instructor and classmates, consider the challenges of responding to that essay. Then read and discuss the two responses that follow by Yellowhead Tribal College students Yolanda Ellis and Ian Kootenay.

All or Nothing Won't Work

Yolanda Ellis

1   Pat Deiter-McArthur's article "Saskatchewan's Indian People—Five Generations" explains the generational loss of Aboriginal identity since contact with European colonialism. The author states that "the fifth generation is faced with choices: assimilation, integration, or separation" (par. 10). For most, the choice cannot be all or nothing: Aboriginals cannot entirely assimilate, nor can they fully integrate or separate.

2   Preventing complete assimilation is the insistence on a separate place for ceremonies such as the Sun Dance. Although with poverty and illness prevalent in Native communities, increasing the toll on the elders, who are main preservers of the traditions, the pass system of the past actually contributed to retaining Aboriginal identity and worldview. Being forced to stay on reserve was difficult for some, but for others it was not. The reserve was viewed as a protective boundary. Legally and politically, Natives will continue to have their treaty lands recognized, thus retaining a base for cultural awareness and practice.

3   Inhibiting separation, however, is a need to fit with global business and communicate in English, the language of international business for the 21st century. Legacy of the British Empire, which dominated the first half of the 20th century, and language of the United States, which dominated the second half, English will remain primary. Some lost their Native languages attending residential schools, but others found their voices by turning the invader's language to their own purposes. Speaking one's Native language is important to preserving culture, but as McArthur points out, "many of this fifth generation are not able to understand a Native language" (11). A certain degree of assimilation cannot be erased. But it is worth noting that documentation of Aboriginal languages exists in many forms; some are in the safekeeping of educational institutions, libraries, and the Web, and can be accessed by those interested, Native and non-Native.

4   Aboriginals must react as individuals in a world where people depend on one another, respect the differences in each other and remember that we are all citizens of this world. Until the sun stops shining or the rivers stop flowing, Aboriginals must learn what other races are doing (assimilate) in order to survive (integrate) so they can have a place to be themselves (separate).

Work Cited

Deiter-McArthur, Pat. "Saskatchewan's Indian People—Five Generations." *Acting on Words: An Integrated Rhetoric, Research Guide, Reader, and Handbook.* 3rd ed. By David Brundage and Michael Lahey. Toronto: Pearson, 2012. 379-81. Print.

The Future for Native People: Only One Choice
Ian C. Kootenay

1   In the essay "Saskatchewan's Indian People—Five Generations," Pat Deiter-McArthur posits that after a damaging history, Native people now have three choices: "assimilation, integration, or separation" (par. 10). I do not agree with her viewpoint, because we Native people have a fourth choice: revolution.

2   We cannot integrate simply because to do so would melt down our culture and destroy what makes us unique. Dominant cultures of the world, from China to the USA, have a tendency to destroy the unique ethnic cultures that try to integrate. This happened even when China was conquered by the Mongolian Khans. After a few generations, the Khan was no longer Mongolian in spirit; he was Chinese. The USA is known worldwide as the "melting pot." Regardless of fluctuations in its economic and political power, its American culture dominates.

3   This leaves us with assimilation and separation. Assimilation is impossible because so many in the mainstream still perceive Aboriginal cultures as worthless. Assimilation assumes acceptance, but acceptance is seldom given by the non-Aboriginal rulers. Examples of this are the conditions of Japan's Aimu peoples, Australia's Aborigines, and America's own Native peoples.

4   So we are left with separation. Yet we cannot separate. The forced dependence of Aboriginal peoples worldwide on the non-Aboriginal conquerors has made it impossible to separate. Separation would be like cutting out the heart that keeps the body moving, because Aboriginals do not have economic independence.

5   The only way to fix this state of affairs would be revolution, a revolution of the way non-Aboriginals view Aboriginal peoples, or a revolution whereby Aboriginals take back what has been stolen from them, as happened in the South African general election in 1994. One can posit that only three choices exist for Aboriginals, but on closer inspection—considering the realities of their situation—only one choice exists, and that is revolution.

Work Cited

Deiter-McArthur, Pat. "Saskatchewan's Indian People—Five Generations." *Acting on Words: An Integrated Rhetoric, Research Guide, Reader, and Handbook.* 3rd. ed. By David Brundage and Michael Lahey. Toronto: Pearson, 2012. 379-81. Print.

PRACTICE
Finding Secondary Sources to Support Critical Response

The previous two essays, "All or Nothing Won't Work" and "The Future for Native People: Only One Choice" were developed as preliminary critical responses to Pat Deiter-McArthur's suggestion that Aboriginal people have three choices in pursuing their political future.

If, as a next step, secondary sources were sought to support these critical positions, what specific points in the essays might benefit from citation, and what types of sources do you think would be suitable?

Discuss research strategies with your classmates and instructor.

Guidelines for Responding to the Ideas in an Article, Essay, or Chapter

- Summarize the author's controlling ideas and reasons (see Chapter 15) and appeals.
- Note your initial responses and formulate questions about the author's ideas.
- Since you are focusing on ideas, pay special attention to logic (see Chapter 3).
- Consider the standard(s) of evaluation you think are best applied to these ideas.
- According to your chosen standards, decide which parts of the arguments you consider sound and which you consider lacking.
- Give reasons for your viewpoints for and against.
- Develop your thesis to express the controlling idea of your response and its reasons.
- Structure your response by summarizing the text you are evaluating (in no more than two or three sentences), then state your thesis and elaborate on your responses. If you agree with some of the essay but mainly take issue with it, recognize the parts you support first, then concentrate on what you consider the shortcomings. If you disagree with some of the thinking but mainly support it, recognize the points that concern you first, then concentrate on explaining what you believe is valid.
- Be careful to avoid the circular trap of simply re-stating the author's ideas as your explanation of why they are or are not worthy.

CRITICAL RESPONSE TO BROADER SUBJECTS

So far we have looked at critical thinking in response to the ideas of a single essay. This is an effective entrance to the nature and methods of critical analysis. But as you can imagine, critical questions are often not restricted to the concerns of a single article. The following essay represents a response to a critical question about a broader subject, the significance of the street artist known as Banksy.

Sample Essay on Broader Subject

Inspired by graffiti, street art may use spray paint, stencils, stickers, posters, art intervention, wheatpasting, and flashmobbing. Although in its broadest sense "street art" refers to art presented in any public place, it usually refers to works not sanctioned by authorities in charge of the spaces concerned.

In her essay, student Erin Cochrane replied to the following critical question: What do you think has been the value of Banksy? Explain your reasons.

Sample Critical Response

This essay was written in 2008 and revised in 2010.

Clever Rat

Erin Cochrane

1 He is known simply as Banksy. Some 15 years after his street art first appeared in and around Bristol, Britain's most celebrated but still anonymous street artist remains the world's number-one art provocateur, continuing to challenge the boundaries of what is considered art while presenting "one giant flip of the finger to authority gone wild" (Reilly). Banksy chooses an illegal method of displaying his witty, anti-establishment messages. In so doing, he outrages certain officials. The Keep Britain Tidy campaign asserts that "we are concerned that Banksy's street art glorifies what is essentially vandalism" (qtd. in Collins). A recent Los Angeles Police Department report claims that graffiti "sets off a vicious cycle that encourages further crime in affected neighborhoods." These attitudes view graffiti as a disease that needs to be cured. Banksy's clever artwork, however, has opened the box in which graffiti and other street art were formerly confined.

2 A recurring theme in Banksy's work is the rat, which is, ironically, an anagram of "art." Banksy's artist persona matches his rat motif, existing underground, dirty, seemingly insignificant. He is the street-rat artist competing against the high-priced and posh world of establishment art. Banksy's rat paintings echo the fantasy of many rebellious anonymous youth: that the powerless will gang up together and make a change. Law forces many citizens to comply with rules they don't necessarily agree with. Banksy says that he began with the idea that anonymous people can make a significant change in society. "They exist without permission. They are hated, hunted and persecuted. They live in quiet desperation amongst the filth. And yet they are capable of bringing entire civilizations to their knees" (Banksy 95). The rats he paints are often depicted breaking into unknown storage places, dressed in upper-class garb, or writing messages on public streets for all to read. His various portrayals of what are seemingly clever rats exhibit the unfair conditions of capitalism.

3   His clever pranks incorporating words and images show great energy and imagination in the cause of political satire. In Disneyland he planted a blow-up doll dressed as a Guantanamo prisoner. In front of the Old Bailey, London, he installed a 20-foot bronze statue of Justice dressed as a prostitute. A plaque with the words "Trust no one" accompanied her. There is the Queen depicted as a monkey, a starving child wearing a Burger King hat, and, upon the Palestinian side of the "security" wall that divides the West Bank, a *trompe l'oeil* illusionary hole revealing paradise on the other side. There can be no denying the political power of these statements.

4   At the same time, his Zorroesque appeal and media savvy (Reilly) have enabled a remarkable rise to fame. *Wall and Piece,* one of his self-published books, was picked up by Random House and has sold well over 250,000 copies. In 2009, the Bristol City Museum and Art Gallery held a twelve-week Banksy UK summer show. There were 300,000 visits. For years Banksy has been represented by a London gallery. Sotheby's auctioned off a Banksy original for $200,000; Bonham's another for $575,000. The five-star Rotten Tomatoes internet rating of his film *Exit Through the Gift Shop,* also heralded by the 2010 Sundance Festival, calls it "an amusing, engross-ing look at underground art [that] entertains as it deflates the myths and hype sur-rounding its subjects." But if the film deflates hype, Banksy has also been accused of manufacturing hype, for instance, of placing seven pieces of art in Toronto locations primarily to coincide with the film's opening in that city.

5   Toronto-based visual art critic Murray Whyte says derisively that Banksy has gone rapidly from street prankster to the "international brand name of subversive street art." Banksy supporters can now buy Banksy T-shirts, stencils, and fake paintings, participating in the very "brandalism" that Banksy denounces. To Whyte, this sort of product-purchasing adulation reflects the street artist's hypocrisy. By gaining such fame and financial success, has Banksy become a sell-out? Is he truly of the world his persona alludes to? Has he turned into his avowed enemy?

6   Hypocrisy is all about the self, and while this rise of fortune has profited the mys-terious artist personally, the wave has gone well beyond Banksy. Whyte himself quotes Simon Cole, owner of Toronto's Show and Tell Gallery, as recognizing "[i]f it wasn't for Banksy, I wouldn't own an art gallery." Whyte explains that Show and Tell represents "a vibrant cross-section of street artists." According to Whyte, "Before Banksy and Shepard Fairey . . . helped build mainstream popularity for the form [street art], it had no place in the art market." San Francisco art consultant and appraiser Alan Bamberger agrees that "Banksy's a major player in terms of advancing the envelope of what art is." Apart from some cynics who continue to see Banksy as an opportunist interested more in what he can take to the "Bank" than in art or political causes, most people who know his work agree that "advancing the envelope of what art is" is primarily what he wants.

7   An important part of this "advancement," as we have seen, is the idea that "art belongs to the people." Whatever world the man behind Banksy is really from, he

wants art to have meaning in the street by speaking a suitable language on relevant topics. His placing that art in the mainstream doesn't necessarily remove it from the street but rather stretches it to more streets. Alistair Briggs comments on the important role of the internet in helping the new movement of art to bypass the traditional elite gatekeepers. Does this mean a loss of quality and standards? Briggs pursues the argument that no, it does not. As he says, internet hubs posting real crap (as opposed to Banksy's talented versions of "crap") do not get much traffic. Quality is its own determiner of appeal, he argues.

8   Commenting on quality, the renowned urban artist Shepard Fairey says that technically Banksy's work is "very strong" and "pleasing to look at"; it is deliberately "not overly complex and intimidating," but that is in the interests of including a wide community. Those who say that all graffiti is simply vandalism need to consider an important message in the fact that the new movement of street art incorporates tributes to many past movements that were also once denounced. Graffiti art mirrors abstract expressionism, Andy Warhol's pop art, conceptual art and new realism. Fairey observes, "Whatever line there is distinguishing art and language, Banksy paints over it to make it disappear." In this he follows in the footsteps of the iconoclast William Blake as well as sharing the current affection for the graphic novel. Those in the conservative art world who dismiss graffiti as mindless colours and shapes are replicating the criticisms that were brought against former artists and movements. It is the nature of art to reach out imaginatively.

9   Despite what some critics may say, more agree that Banksy has talent to equal the museum-piece artists. He places first priority on honesty of intent and substance of message, one that lies beyond himself. From this viewpoint, perhaps the main difference between street art and museum art is the question of permission and who should grant it. The conservatives want it to be the law and the establishment of elite gatekeepers, while Banksy and his host of supporters want it to be the people. Tied in with this question is the one of ownership. By remaining anonymous, by continuing with a method that stresses impermanence, Banksy sends the graffiti artist's message that art should not be about individualism and fame but rather community and political sanity. Yes, there are some in the community, not just in council chambers, who would rather not see graffiti, but when Bristol City Council asked citizens to vote on keeping or removing an illegal Banksy mural, 93 percent supported keeping it.

10   Illegal, unsightly, hypocritical? The controversy remains. Banksy, in fact, may raise as many questions as he answers—deliberately so. He questions motive, ownership, quality, street art, and the future of community and the planet. Breaking through the gatekeepers to ask us these questions without condescension, in a manner that pleases and entertains, is surely Banksy's great achievement on behalf of street art and all of us.

Works Cited

Bamberger, Alan. "Art, Money, Shepard Fairey, Banksy and the Quest for Clarity." ArtBusiness.com. Alan Bamberger, n.d. Web. 10 July 2010.

Banksy. *Wall and Piece*. London: Century, 2006. Print.

Briggs, Alistair. "Banksy: Art Belongs to the People." *Quazen*. Quazen, 5 May 2010. Web. 10 July 2010.

Collins, Lauren. "Banksy Was Here: The Invisible Man of Graffiti." *The New Yorker*. The New Yorker, 14 May 2007. Web. 20 October 2008.

Fairey, Shepard. "Banksy." *Swindle*. Swindle, Summer 2006. Web. 12 July 2010.

Los Angeles Police Department. "What Graffiti Means to a Community." Los Angeles Police Department, 17 Apr. 2008. Web. 10 Oct. 2008.

Reilly, Christopher. "Banksy: Zorro of the Art World." HubPages. YieldBuild, Sept. 2008. Web. 10 July 2010.

Whyte, Murray. "Banksy Street Art Sets Toronto Abuzz." *The Star.com*. Toronto Star, 10 May 2010. Web. 12 July 2010.

For Further Thinking

Clearly, Cochrane's essay deals with a subject surrounded by controversy and polarized views. It thus represents the way in which critical analysis can quickly move into the realm of argumentation, as defined in more detail in Chapter 18. Here are some related critical questions to follow up on Cochrane's essay.

1. Art critic Murray Whyte charges Banksy with hypocrisy because he portrays himself as an outsider when he has really been an insider for years, creating a series of "money-making hype vehicles" while wearing the mask of an angry, disenfranchised young protester. What questions need to be answered to assess Murray's opinion? Identify these and then answer the ones that you consider of primary importance.

2. Street art opposes elitism, but is there a way in which it might erect certain cultural, aesthetic barriers of its own?

3. When asked how long he planned to remain anonymous, Banksy replied that he has "no interest in ever coming out." He says a lot of young people want to be famous without knowing why or caring. He wants his pictures to look good but doesn't care for others to look at him. How are we to make sense of these statements about the hollowness of fame when the speaker has been called "the world's most famous living artist"?

4. When Robertson Davies wrote "The Pleasures of Love," it was illegal in Canada to operate a service offering family planning advice. What were the issues in that matter? What are the issues involving today's laws against graffiti? Would you consider the two cases as more similar or different, and why? Finally, what, if any, action do you think is needed concerning today's laws against graffiti, and why?

FINAL WORD

Critical questions may arise from specific aspects of single essays to multiple aspects of large topics, such as proposed legislation, new technologies, economic policies, global conflicts, historical events, and any number of other concerns. The basic methods we have illustrated with responses to one short essay can be adapted and transferred to all your other critical writing requirements.

Works Consulted

Paul, Richard, and Linda Elder. *Critical and Creative Thinking.* Dillon Beach, CA: Foundation for Critical Thinking, 2004. Print.

Stewart, Kay, Chris Bullock, and Marian Allen. *Essay Writing for Canadian Students.* 4th ed. Toronto: Pearson, 2004. Print.

Chapter 17
Rhetorical Analysis

Rhetorical analysis represents a special form of critical analysis (see Chapter 16). Rhetoric, as defined elsewhere in this text, means the art of using language. Rhetorical analysis therefore involves exploring how certain components of writing interact together, affect the reading process, and contribute to a deeper understanding of a related issue. We suggest that you imagine a piece of writing as an operational system with the ultimate purpose of creating a final meaning. You may picture a car engine, a bridge, a biological system—something based on functioning parts and processes and dedicated to a certain operation. In search of exactly how the process works in a particular text under study, you examine the parts and principles of the text and their process relationships. Your goal is to recognize the writer's intended purpose and answer a critical question dealing with the text *as rhetoric*. To succeed you must first identify the components and interactions that express certain meanings.

Since many students find it difficult to get started on a close study of how language functions in a piece of writing, this chapter provides recommended steps and examples. As you will discover, ability with rhetorical analysis serves students in all subjects that require advanced reading skills.

TWO STAGES OF RHETORICAL ANALYSIS

Rhetorical analysis, like critical analysis in general, comprises two basic stages: analysis and evaluation.

Analysis: Breaking a Text Down into Parts and Relationships (Stage 1 of Critical Thinking)

As defined in Chapter 16, analysis involves breaking a subject down into its parts and relationships. Identifying and describing the important attributes of an essay is an application of Stage 1 critical thinking.

Here is a checklist of basic textual elements, principles, and process relationships to help you perform a preliminary identification of rhetorical components:

1. Who is the author and what biographical information is available on him or her?
2. Where and when was the work published?
3. What type of writing is this (investigative journalism, academic analysis, corporate persuasion, and so forth)?
4. Who is the intended audience?
5. What various public beliefs (warrants) currently exist on the topic?
6. What various public beliefs (warrants) existed on the topic at the time the piece was written?
7. What is the author's purpose?
8. What is the author's controlling idea?
9. What are the author's reasons? (controlling idea + reasons = thesis)
10. What specific methods of inquiry (research) have been used?
11. Where do you think you could find more information about the subject matter discussed?
12. What attitudes to the subject beyond the essay's scope are included or implied?
13. How has the reading been organized and what rhetorical strategies and patterns are featured throughout and in separate parts?
14. What style and therefore tone does the reading use (kinds of words, attitude, lengths of sentences)?

PRACTICE

Select an essay from this textbook. Analyze it according to the above checklist. Fill in all parts of the checklist. Discuss your findings with your instructor and classmates.

A Process Description Consolidates Information from Your Checklist

Once you have considered the reliability of information in your checklist, you may find it helpful to summarize the important parts of that information into one or two paragraphs. You could use full sentences or simply a coherent note-making style. Your description in one or two paragraphs of what you have found in analyzing a selected essay is a form of process description.

Chapter 13, "How-to Instructions, Process Description, and Definition," provides more information on this form (p. 134), closely related to the summary (described in Chapter 15). A close, detailed study of rhetorical elements should come before any intensified attempt to evaluate the significance of the writing. Therefore, you should fill in the above checklist and convert its findings into a short process description before you proceed to the second stage of evaluation.

PRACTICE

Read the essay "College Girl to Call Girl" in the Reader (p. 388). Fill in the checklist of essay attributes and relationships given on p. 184. Convert your checklist into a rough-draft process description. Then turn to p. 191 of this chapter to see Valerie Desjardins' note-form process description of "College Girl." Compare your description to hers. Discuss this comparison with your instructor and classmates.

Evaluating the Significance of Rhetorical Parts and Principles (Stage 2 of Critical Thinking)

After you study a text closely and complete the above checklist, you come to a preliminary idea of what that essay is attempting to say and how it pursues that goal with specific language and patterns of language. Depending on the complexity of the text, you may need to do more examination to test your preliminary ideas and only then consider the significance of what you believe the author is attempting to do with language, patterns, and text organization. This careful consideration of basic components can prove useful in alerting you to your own possibly biased thinking. For example, if the text was written some time ago, certain presumptions may have been different than yours now.

Through careful examination of the writing itself, the student seeks to understand what the author intends as well as what causes or effects the writing presents, and whether these seem intentional or not. First-year rhetorical evaluation generally decides on how well the writer's apparent goals have been met. Critical questions related to rhetoric might be the following: "How effective is Robertson Davies' use of Shakespearean allusions in 'The Pleasures of Love'?"

The standards you use to pursue your evaluation of aspects of style and their significance may be those of proofs (e.g., appeals of pathos, logos, and ethos and their effects upon readers); logic (e.g., premises and their consistency within the essay); aesthetics (e.g., pleasurable designs, patterns, and artistic methods); or ethics (e.g., author's use of language to assert or support a statement of value to others or to obscure possible harmful consequences and changes in relationships and responsibilities to other people). In many cases, two or more of these standards may be examined in your discussion.

We now offer the following three examples. Based on what you have discovered in the first stage of your rhetorical analysis, you may consider that one or more of these approaches will assist you.

THREE EXAMPLES

The following three examples will assist you in adding further detail to your Stage 1 analytical information; these approaches will also guide you into Stage 2 evaluation. Note that in all three cases, the writers have clearly decided on criteria of evaluation, as follows:

- examining for appeals to logos, pathos, and ethos
- examining for implied writer's stance
- improving readability by applying the Gunning Fog Index (see p. 193)

Any approach that applies the reading methods of a particular literary critic or rhetorician participates to some extent in rhetorical analysis. The critical response to "The Pleasures of Love" in Chapter 16, which looks at how Robertson Davies shapes his arguments, illustrates the rhetorical examination that occurs in a great deal of scholarly critique.

The first example that follows analyzes Martin Luther King's "The Ways of Meeting Oppression" (Reader, p. 442). The second example analyzes Sarah Schmidt's "College Girl to Call Girl" (Reader, p. 388). In order to appreciate these examples fully, read the two essays that they discuss and, for each, answer the listed questions concerning an essay's parts and relationships (p. 184). The third example that follows provides a famous readability formula that you may apply to selected passages in essays of your own choosing.

Examining for Appeals to Logos, Pathos, and Ethos

As we learned in Chapter 1, classical rhetoric refers to persuasive attributes as appeals: logos (logical or rational appeal), pathos (emotional appeal), and ethos (ethical appeal or writer credibility). In a classical analysis, you examine the main ways the author has used these appeals and determine how well the appeals have been made.

Sample Essay Analysis 1

A Rhetorical Analysis of "The Ways of Meeting Oppression"
Eugenia Gilbert

1   The excerpt "The Ways of Meeting Oppression" is taken from Martin Luther King, Jr.'s book *Stride Toward Freedom,* published in 1958 by Harper Brothers. The book introduced the man who took the stage as a civil rights leader when he became head of the Montgomery in Action committee, responsible for orchestrating the famous

Montgomery Bus Boycott that lasted over a year and ended with new rights for African-American citizens. This book appealed to black audiences, particularly students and others who were looking for a blueprint to take action against oppressive and unjust laws, and to white audiences, who were curious about this new leader and wanted to know more about the tactics used in nonviolent demonstration, something King would be expanding and expounding on in the years to come. Thus, King's ethos is established as a civil rights leader with some success, and his audiences would be ready to listen to what he had to say, even if they did not completely agree with the aims or methods he describes. In "The Ways of Meeting Oppression," King outlines three methods used to deal with the unjust laws against black American citizens, beginning with the attitude of acceptance he has witnessed (the acceptance of oppression), then the response of defiant force, and finally, something that combines the peacefulness of acceptance with the resistance of violence: nonviolent resistance. Through the rhetorical modes of classification, definition, cause and effect, and illustration, as well as precise and emotive language, King uses logos, pathos, and ethos effectively to persuade his audiences that nonviolent resistance is the path African-Americans must follow to gain equal rights.

2   Although this excerpt does not include research or statistics, there are plenty of examples of logos in the method of development and the use of evidence. From the first sentence, King sets up a logical structure, indicating his argument will be measured and based on reason. First, King organizes his essay by classification, defining and explaining the causes and effects of using the three methods of "meeting oppression." For each method, he provides illustrations that help readers understand how these methods work. For the first method, "acquiescence," he uses the example from the Bible of the Israelite slaves who grumbled at their freedom and preferred whatever security they had in Egypt. King's audiences of the 1950s, both black and white, would be very familiar with the story of Exodus and would certainly not be surprised to see a Baptist minister use it as an example. They might be more surprised to see him go on to refer to a passage from Shakespeare to explain the slaves' reluctance, and this allusion to a literary figure would help establish him as an educated man. To show that he is also in touch with the ordinary black Americans' suffering, he then quotes the guitarist to show "the type of negative freedom and resignation" that characterizes acquiescence. He follows with a logical argument ending with "[a]cquiescence is interpreted as proof of the Negro's inferiority"—a strong call to prove otherwise. For each method that he explains, he shows the effects of choosing this way to deal with the lack of civil rights.

3   King uses the same rhetorical strategies in discussing the second and third methods. In claiming that the second method, a response with violence, "is both impractical and immoral," he once again refers to a passage from the Bible, the one in

which Peter draws a weapon to resist Jesus' capture at Gethsemane and is told to put the weapon aside. This, too, is a strong call to those of Christian faith not to use violence, even against injustice. King also quotes Gandhi, though perhaps his readers would not have recognized it, when he says "an eye for an eye leaves everybody blind." Although he cites no specific examples of the failure of violence as a method, he ends with the easily proven claim that "[h]istory is cluttered with the wreckage of nations" who choose this method of resistance. Finally, he continues to use logos effectively in describing the third method of meeting oppression: "nonviolent resistance." Here he introduces Hegel's dialectic, something that only his educated readers would be familiar with, but explained so that any reader could understand. The third way is explained as the synthesis of the first two, the peace without the violence, the results without the submission. By drawing on Hegel, King emphasizes his educational background and understanding, something that would help establish his ethos as well as showing his ethical character, aiming for the best possible outcome, logically and morally. While his logical thesis can be seen as "[o]ppressed people deal with oppression in three characteristic ways," his persuasive thesis is that nonviolent resistance "[m]ust guide the actions of the Negro in the present crisis in race relations."

4   Since the outcome of his method of resistance is speculative and cannot be proven, King must go beyond logical reasoning and appeal to his readers' sense of justice and hope by using emotional appeals (pathos). While he uses figurative language more sparingly here than in some later famous publications, such as "Letter from Birmingham Jail" and his "I have a dream" speech, there are still plenty of examples of emotionally appealing language throughout the excerpt. He goes beyond merely proving the first two methods to be ineffective by emphasizing that the methods are immoral. Readers may be encouraged to feel guilty if they agree or to feel angry at the "coward[ice]" implied by acquiescence and the aftereffects of violence: "corroding hatred" and "bitterness." In the first way, non-resisters are aligned with "the way of the coward," as "evil as the oppressor," and "willing to sell the future of [their] children." In the second way, those children will "be the recipients of a desolate night of bitterness . . . [and] an endless reign of meaningless chaos." However, in the third way, resisters are aligned with "ris[ing] to the noble height of opposing the unjust system while loving the perpetrators of the system." War metaphors are used further to evoke a rallying cry to "arms": "the Negro can also enlist all men of good will in his struggle for equality," reinforcing his claim that "[t]he problem is not a purely racial one . . . but a tension between justice and injustice." Here the language should especially appeal to his white audience as well. Further, King claims that those involved in this method of resistance "can make a lasting contribution to the moral strength of the nation and set a sublime example of courage for generations yet

unborn." The emotive language sends out a strong call to black readers, which was met by those who took up the call, such as black students involved in SNCC (Student Nonviolent Coordinating Committee; Newfield). While King may be using a bandwagon appeal to some extent, his use of logos balances the use of pathos, and his readers will not be tempted to be swayed by words alone.

5   King's ethos is established by the reason Harper Brothers would publish his ideas: he was a rising civil rights leader who gained nationwide attention during the Montgomery Bus Boycott. In this excerpt, his ethos is increased by his balanced view, apparently careful weighing of options, and support for his observations throughout. He appears to have actually considered the other possibilities, which indicates lack of bias. He is seen to be of an ethical character himself, desiring justice and eschewing hatred, and throughout he emphasizes his connection to Christian belief. It is not surprising that a quotation from Bishop James A. Pike was noted on the book's cover—"May well become a Christian classic"—and certainly this element would not only support King's ethos but have wide appeal for his audiences as well.

6   The response to the book indicates that his appeals were successful in reaching his target audiences. He gained more credibility with white leaders (though not necessarily popularity—he probably showed himself as more dangerous to many) and with blacks who agreed with the methods, especially those who wanted to encourage his leadership and followers who were eager to continue and to try the methods. According to Kerry Taylor, one of the people involved in editing a volume of King's papers for publication by Stanford University, "Stride Toward Freedom essentially became the Bible for many activists following King's footsteps" (Dang). A contemporary reviewer claimed that, in this book, "King throws down a rigorous challenge to American white society and to Negroes. He calls on his fellow Christians to be Christians, his fellow democrats to be democrats, and he asks right-thinking whites and his fellow-Negroes to join him in refusing to cooperate with evil" (Isaacs). While the book may have evoked a variety of responses, it is clear that the excerpt would be persuasive because of King's expert use of logos, pathos, and ethos.

Works Cited

Dang, Jess. "Volume of King Papers Published—Ongoing Stanford Project to Anthologize King's Letters, Talks and Sermons." *Stanford Daily.* Stanford Daily, 9 May 2000. Web. 4 July 2006.

Isaacs, Harold R. "Civil Disobedience in Montgomery." Rev. of *Stride Toward Freedom,* by Martin Luther King, Jr. *New Republic* 6 Oct. 1958: 19-20. *EPSCO.* Web. 4 July 2006.

King, Jr., Martin Luther. *Stride Toward Freedom.* New York: Harper, 1958. Print.

---. "The Ways of Meeting Oppression." *Acting on Words: An Integrated Rhetoric, Research Guide, Reader, and Handbook.* By David Brundage and Michael Lahey. 3rd ed. Toronto: Pearson, 2012. 442-44.

Newfield, Jack. "The Student Left." *The Nation* 10 May 1965: 491–95. Academic Search Premier. EPSCO. Mount Royal College Lib., Calgary, AB. 20 Jul. 2006.

Pike, James A. Cover. *Stride Toward Freedom.* By Martin Luther King, Jr. New York: Harper, 1958. The Martin Luther King, Jr. Research and Education Institute, n.d. Web. 4 July 2006.

Commentary

Much of King's work has been studied in terms of rhetorical analysis. Some analysts use colour-coding, for easy-to-follow visuals of how King balances his appeals. Others use more detailed, sophisticated terms of rhetoric, such as those in the scholarly journal *Rhetoric & Public Affairs*. In your own assessment of the analysis above, does the essayist use every possible example, or only the main ones to make her point? For some students, the Biblical references may seem more aligned with pathos than logos because they would be emotionally evocative of religious belief, but for many of King's followers and audience, the references would be seen as historical, factual, and entirely logical.

PRACTICE

Select an essay from the Reader or some other section of this text and analyze its uses of logos, pathos, and ethos.

Discuss your findings with your classmates and instructor.

Examining for Implicit Clues of Writer's Stance

With various pieces of writing—some more than others—readers cannot seem to agree on the writer's main intention and attitude to the subject. The following analysis came about as student Valerie Desjardins tried to address a disagreement in her university discussion group concerning Sarah Schmidt's intention and attitude in "College Girl to Call Girl" (Reader, p. 388). If you haven't read that essay, do so now and see what you think in response to the critical question that Desjardins decided to answer:

> Behind a stance of journalistic detachment, does Sarah Schmidt actually seem to sympathize with students turning to prostitution to help finance their studies? Demonstrate why or why not.

After reading Schmidt's essay with this question in mind, and reviewing the preliminary questions to consider about any reading (p. 184), read Desjardins' essay for her view and reasons.

Sample Essay Analysis 2 Defining the Writer's Stance

"College Girl to Call Girl": Defining the Writer's Stance
Valerie Desjardins

1 According to at least three people in our discussion group, Sarah Schmidt's article "College Girl to Call Girl" adopts a posture of journalistic detachment but implicitly supports the students who engage in prostitution, shows their actions to be reasonable, and sympathizes with the trials they must go through. One group member objects to an alleged attitude of "political correctness": the students as innocent victims. Certainly the article entices us to conclude that financial need has driven students to the world's so-called oldest profession because fees are said to have risen by 126 percent while "[o]ff-street prostitution has experienced a similar explosion" (par. 8). However, I think that Schmidt simply wishes to report that a certain number of students, concerned about paying high educational fees, suggest that they chose prostitution believing, at least at the time, that it was their most practical option. If we look closely at the article, it seems that Schmidt's main interest is not primarily with the unfairness of the fees for these particular students but rather with what their responses represent.

2   Schmidt herself never says that she thinks university fees have forced students into prostitution. She also never says what she thinks about the unexplained reasons that "led" to the work (par. 20): defaulted loans (par. 10), "financial and personal crisis" (par. 20), and spirit-killing minimum-wage work (par. 27). My group mates argue that a 126 percent increase in fees is so unethical that it must be intended as sufficient evidence of the student prostitutes as innocent victims. Yet these same critics believe that the student prostitutes should work hard at legal jobs and adopt other more acceptable steps toward their goals, such as registering for distance programs part time and adopting patience. They concede that Schmidt does not state an innocent-victims thesis explicitly but challenge me to show where she states explicit refutation. My answer is that although the author does not directly state a personal opinion anywhere in the article, her rhetorical methods suggest her underlying concern, not necessarily at all with the sexual behaviour, but with the social elasticity of redefining morality to keep up with the unquestioned requirements of middle-class status.

Critical question: What is Schmidt's stance?

What some say

Concession to an apparent main idea

Refutation stating what Scmidt's stance and attitude really seem to be

She states a general view anticipating her more focused thesis statement to follow.

A claim to test: Must it be seen this way? Why? Now the focus narrows. This claim represents the others' main reason for their interpretation.

In response, the writer states her controlling idea and reasons.

Investigative approach extends beyond the students and comprises contending viewpoints

3   It is important to recognize that Schmidt's article is a report drawn from investigative journalism. Yes, she interviews one active student prostitute and three former ones. But she also consults a range of other people: two professors, an escort service manager, a police detective, an outreach worker, and a novelist-researcher. Her interviewees all support a perception that more and more students see the increase of middle-class prostitution as a way to cope with the "lean" years while working toward a "respectable" future (par. 5). But otherwise they express differing attitudes toward students in prostitution. The content of Schmidt's discussions with the students deals primarily with what the experience was like for them emotionally and in what ways, if any, it has changed them or could change them. The students themselves describe different feelings and views. Presumably Schmidt consulted this range of people in order to uncover a range of perspectives and thus encourage us to weigh various factors.

4   Is her presentation of her findings impartial?

Organization examined for meaning

Emphasis on Stacy

Contrast of John

5   If we examine her organization, we find that Schmidt has shaped things to the disadvantage of an innocent-victims argument. Openings and closings are powerful positions. The essay opens and closes with Stacy, placing considerable weight on her as the student prostitute representative. Schmidt builds to John, giving him prominence at the end of the line-up of four student interviewees, a location that naturally juxtaposes him with Stacy, who follows him in the cycle back. This intensifies the contrasts in their outlooks, Stacy's "rationalizations" (par. 26), which John calls a "cop-out," versus his frank acceptance that he is a "hustler" and even feels partly drawn to the work (par. 30). Schmidt devotes considerable space to covering John. The article opens with the sorts of troubles Stacy and then Anna face, but builds to John's observation that his father faced "the worst jobs" as a labourer.

John's frankness points to a bigger picture.

Partly through organization, the effect of this contrast qualifies the denials of Stacy with the frankness of John and the bigger picture of misconception that his comments point to.

More organizational impact

6   Paragraph 6 represents another powerful location. Here Schmidt moves from her opening descriptions of Stacy to John Lowman, professor of criminology. His main point on the topic is that contrary to popular belief, we have a "class-based system of prostitution." Far from saying that student prostitutes are innocent, he suggests that they are (perhaps undeservedly) party to privileges denied to others. While Lowman's statement cannot be taken as Schmidt's, the author has chosen to place it right where her own thesis might appear in traditional essay structure. She reinforces Lowman's observation with sociologist Cecilia Benoit's summation: "People think: 'Students? Not students!'" (par. 13).

Where a thesis might be placed

Importance of the warrant

7   "What people think" are other words for a warrant, a common belief that plays with or against the insight of the writer. In this case, from a middle-class perspective, the warrant says that the middle-class doesn't engage in prostitution, something for

"marginal women, women who are down and out" (par. 13). The story that most clashes with this attitude, by most wanting to maintain it while departing from it, is Stacy's. The language used to describe her registers this conflict. She "stumbled" (10) and she "scores" (11) imply a certain criticism. The word "score," drawn from street vocabulary, suggests that Stacy is essentially like any other hooker, although she says there is "a difference" between her and street prostitutes. She admits to not liking the work or her "customers," but feels she is superior to street workers because, "I portray myself with a level of respect." In other words, not what one does but what one "portrays" is what matters. This sounds suspiciously like hypocrisy as defined by John.

Conflict of the warrant and current reality

Language used to describe Stacy reveals attitude

8   This is not to say that Schmidt's intention is to single out Stacy, Anna, and other middle-class students for an old-fashioned reproving of "loose morals." The attitude coming through this structure is less one of reproof than of wry, ironic insight into social pressure experienced as an absolute. In any case, the real subject isn't the sex work but the thinking that accommodates it. As Schmidt puts it in her opening, "For a growing number of middle-class youths . . . prostitution isn't *seen as* a shameful trap, but as a means of making it through . . . to a *respectable* career" (par. 5; emphasis added). The means of coping through the lean years can then be swept away, supposedly. However, a resonating repetition of the word "job" near the end of the article poses a closing sense of what *is* against what is *seen as*: "He's done the worst jobs" (par. 31). Anna says she wishes people "would get over their hang-ups. . . . It's just a job" (34). And very close to the final sentence of the article, "Maybe so, but Stacy would rather land that advertising job." This ironic poetry of job repetition takes us through the labourer's grind of punishing physical work and tedium to the prostitute's detached ministrations to the dream job that one must "land," suggesting through this family progression that in essence the jobs define each other; in essence they are one and the same.

Not reproving individuals but observing middle class in crisis

Prefer adjusting means of social climbing to changing the objects of desire

Entitlement thinking contrasted to street reality

Closing reminds that what is on the street, in the labouring world, and in the dream job may be fundamentally the same

9   Schmidt's tone lacks any note of serious moral accusation, but that's quite a different matter from describing the wonky world of this story as innocent.

Restates controlling idea

Applying the Gunning Fog Index

PhD in mathematics and professor emeritus at UCLA Robert Gunning authored the 1968 text *The Technique of Clear Writing* to promote readability. Gunning is best known, however, for the Fog Index, originally publicized through business publications such as the *Wall Street Journal*. As you will see, his system doesn't presume primarily to help us grasp meaning; its goal is to test and encourage clarity and ease of reading.

How to Use the Gunning Fog Index

1. From the writing you wish to analyze, take a passage of 100 words (or close to 100 words).
2. Count the number of sentences in the passage. You may count as sentences independent clauses that follow one another directly (i.e., after semicolons or colons or coordinating conjunctions followed by a comma).
3. Find the average number of words per sentence by dividing the number of words in your sample by the number of sentences.
4. Count the number of words (excluding proper nouns) of three syllables or more. Don't count verbs that reach three syllables by grammatical endings such as *-es, -ed,* or *-ing.* Exclude simple compounds like "shopkeeper."
5. Calculate the percentage of three-syllable words in the writing sample.
6. Add the average number of words per sentence to the percentage of three-syllable words.
7. Multiple the total by 0.4.
8. The resulting number is an estimate of the years of formal schooling needed to easily read and understand the text from which your sample of writing has been taken.

Example of Applying the Gunning Fog Index

The following reading sample of 123 words occurs in the opening of "Birth of a New Ethnicity," by Matthew Mendelsohn (Reader, p. 382).

Sample for Gunning Fog Index

From "Birth of a New Ethnicity"
Matthew Mendelsohn

Social change is sometimes *difficult* to see. It's like looking at yourself in the mirror every day and not noticing that you're aging. But once in a while it's useful to pull out the high school yearbook and take note of the *transformation.*

The survey we conducted for *The Globe and Mail's* New Canada project asked people what makes them proud of Canada. Over all, things such as the beauty of the land, the country's high ranking by the United Nations and our role in peacekeeping came out at the top of the list. Among young Canadians, those in their 20s, other factors made them proud: *multiculturalism,* the Charter of Rights and Freedoms, *bilingualism,* having people from *different cultural* backgrounds living in peace.

(123 words)

Analysis

The formula may be expressed as follows:

$$\text{Grade level} = 0.4\left(\left(\frac{\text{words}}{\text{sentence}}\right) + 100\left(\frac{\text{complex words}}{\text{words}}\right)\right)$$

The passage includes six sentences. (The words following the colon after "proud" in the last sentence do not constitute an independent clause.)

123 (words) ÷ 6 (sentences) = 20.5 words per sentence

The passage includes six words of three syllables or more (italicized).

Percentage of three-syllable words: 6 ÷ 123 = 0.048 (100), which rounds up to 5

20.5 (average number of words per sentence) + 5 (percentage of three-syllable words) = 25.5

0.4 × 25.5 = 10.2 years of formal education (i.e., up to Grade 10) needed to read the passage with ease

Commentary

As many observers point out, this method lacks fully objective determinations. For example, one three-syllable word may be generally more complex or difficult than

 PRACTICE

Apply the Gunning Fog Index formula to the following two passages:

Passage 1—From "Cuchulain" (Reader, p. 361)

My father is out looking for a job and my mother is at the hospital with Malachy. I wish I had something to eat but there's nothing in the icebox but cabbage leaves floating in the melted ice. My father said never eat anything floating in water for the rot that might be in it. I fall asleep on my parents' bed and when my mother shakes me it's nearly dark. Your little brother is going to sleep a while. Nearly bit his tongue off. Stitches galore. Go into the other room.

My father is in the kitchen sipping black tea from his big white enamel mug. He lifts me to his lap.

Dad, will you tell me the story about Coo Coo? (123 words)

Passage 2—From "The Roots of Continuous Negotiation" (Reader, p. 407)

Renée Dupuis, chief commissioner of the Indian Claims Commission and a leading writer on how Canadian law applies to First Nations questions, puts it that the "Aboriginal roots are mixed into the roots of the two European legal systems." She points out that even in formal lawmaking, Aboriginal customary law has been mixed into the legislation, sometimes unconsciously, sometimes consciously. When we look at this approach toward continuous negotiation, which has come to be the Canadian characteristic, it is hard to find British, French or U.S. origins. It has become what we call federalism. And when we are not sinking into colonial posturing at the international level, it best describes our foreign policy and military approaches. (116 words)

Once you have the result, decide to what extent this formula seems to provide a reliable assessment of the readability of the two longer texts from which the passages have been taken. Is complexity a part of readability, and can a text be complex without scoring a high readability number according to the Fog Index?

another. "Imprecation" might challenge readers more than "transformation," one of the complex or difficult words found in the example above. In fact, many two-syllable words may prove more unfamiliar than certain three-syllable ones. Nevertheless, as we note below, for more than half a century magazine editors have found the Gunning Fog Index to serve quite well as a general measure of how easy or hard a certain reading may prove for a wide general public.

We do not present this formula as a way to analyze literary texts for deeper meaning or as a suggestion that you change your writing to entirely short or long words and sentences. Playing with this formula, however, may encourage you to consider the ways in which you can make your meanings easier to grasp. Even in the academy, clarity is awareness. Although a business tool, this index can measure the degree of verbal simplicity with which one can communicate less than simple ideas.

Popular Uses of the Fog Index

For years, magazine editors have applied the Gunning Fog Index or similar readability measures to establish stylistic parameters for their publications. Writers hoping to place articles with various magazines would do well to study the Fog Index measure of the intended magazine. Without even reading your submission, an editor who uses the Fog Index (and many do) will determine at a glance whether your manuscript deserves further consideration.

FINAL WORD

Rhetorical analysis provides you with a magnifying glass, so often needed to find important clues to meaning that would otherwise go undetected. It also guides you in standing back to see the larger picture again, to appreciate how the newly observed elements relate to each other. You thereby arrive at new and deeper insights. The precise strategies you apply will depend on various needs and your own preferences as a reader and critical thinker. Rhetorical analysis will immensely enrich all your future reading and critical responses.

Chapter 18
Argumentation

Like the words "critical evaluation" (see Chapter 16), the word "argument" as used in rhetoric does not designate what we think when we hear the word in typical daily conversation. When we hear someone say, "They are having an argument," we picture an emotional battle, a desire to get one's way, perhaps at the expense of fairness and consideration. "What's wrong with them?" we ask, noticing that a couple are no longer speaking to each other. "They had an argument," someone says. The word in daily usage suggests something that ends in bitterness and isolation. In rhetoric, however, "argument" refers to presenting one's carefully considered view—a view intended in most cases to be beneficial to all—in a way that considers others. One's goal is the opposite of bitterness and isolation. Rather, the purpose is deepened awareness and possibly new thinking or even desired action taken by your audience or reader.

A SUBCATEGORY OF PERSUASION

Argumentation is a subcategory in the large domain of communication known as persuasion. All forms of **persuasion** attempt to sway an audience to think or act a certain way. In the broadest and most basic sense, *all* writing is persuasive in seeking to convince us of its integrity. All successful authors persuade us of their credibility (see Chapter 1). A good personal essay, for example, persuades us that the writer really knows and in some way understands the place or experience being described. A fictionalized memoir such as "The Hockey Sweater" (Reader, p. 364) may not explicitly appeal to logos, but there is a compelling soundness in the effects—in certain conclusions—that the memoir stirs in the reader. The story appeals to emotions and ethics, but there is a world of logos under its surface. It implies various arguments, counter-arguments, proofs, and the like. If we "believe" the story, even though we know it is partly made up, if we accept its implied thesis or theme, it is persuasive. In the study of communication and writing, however, the term "persuasion" most often refers specifically to appeals made by advocates or exponents seeking, for whatever reasons, in whatever contexts, to change thinking or behaviour related to a particular topic, sometimes one of considerable controversy or choice.

Deciding *How Far* to Try to Influence Your Reader

Most persuasions focus, in general, on one of three possible goals:

- an increase of awareness (which may lead, naturally, to a change of attitude)
- a change of attitude (new way of thinking about a topic)
- a change of behaviour (new action[s] adopted)

These goals are sometimes said to entail differing levels of persuasion, with the first goal aiming for the lowest level of change and the third goal aiming for the highest. Clearly, each goal will incorporate considerable awareness of the other two. These three levels offer choices in answer to the important question "How far should I try to influence my reader in this particular communication?" Remember that persuasion and argumentation are not the same undertaking.

Deciding *How* to Pursue Your Goal

Advertisers often pursue their goal of selling products or services through "card-stacking" (omitting or evading facts, underplaying or overemphasizing issues, and so on). Propagandists seek to influence political decisions by similar marginalizing of logic and fairness. True argumentation, on the other hand, strives to persuade its reader through appeals that respect the full range of reasoning on the debate or controversy. One of the earliest known classical rhetoricians (Gorgias, 483–375 BCE) maintained that an orator (unlike today's advertisers or propagandists) had a duty to refute other arguments explicitly. Although entailing confidence in your viewpoint, argumentation features a moderate, respectful tone that recognizes opposing views. Recognizing those opposing views, argumentation aims to change thinking and often to promote a certain action. Its goal is persuasive, but it "plays fair." When you decide on argumentation over more biased forms, you consider the attributes and benefits that we discuss next.

MAIN ATTRIBUTES OF ARGUMENTATION

We sometimes use the term "formal" to define argumentation for reasons primarily related to the *occasion.* Writing to persuade demands consideration of how the reader will react to how the ideas are expressed as well as what they are. When you write an argument, especially with a goal to change thinking or behaviour, you must imagine a reader opposed to your ideas. How can you change that person's awareness, thinking, or even behaviour? The ways you shape your discussion to introduce your view through well-timed appeals to the reader, as well as your choice of words to avoid or handle fairly "loaded" language are crucial matters of "form."

In addition, argumentation developed from a tradition of oral speeches, often delivered under formal, even ceremonial, circumstances. Protocols (matters of social form) needed to be observed. Issues of social and political importance to many people often figured in these addresses. A formal argument was normally intended for many eyes and levels of officialdom. The style of your formal argument should also consider possible multiple readers in various formalized circumstances. Tone and structure will therefore be formal. Consult the tones chart on the inside back cover of this text and you will find that a formal level "assumes a higher level of education," uses explicit structure, and reflects "complex content organized by clear patterns." Such tones, as the chart further indicates, rely on data and logical formulations.

Benefits of Mastering Argumentation

Your command of argumentative methods will help you as a researcher to analyze your sources by identifying and evaluating the basic elements of the persuasions being made. Command of argumentative methods will also help you as a writer to test and critique your own arguments. Furthermore, many people regard the will and ability to handle even-handed argument to be the lifeblood of political freedom as defined by Western-style democracy. We might further suggest that this will and ability are especially important for Canada, a country of vast geography, pronounced regional differences, and necessary compromise.

How to Be Sure You Meet the Expectations of Argumentation

How do you go about developing an essay that meets the requirements of argumentation? Observe the following guidelines:

- Be sure your topic involves a strong controversy on which opinion is divided or on which the majority support a view opposed to yours.
- Imagine a public occasion for which your essay will be used (instigating circumstances, audience, forum).
- Address readers whose views significantly oppose yours.
- Decide how far you can go in pushing readers to a call for action. Is it wisest simply to promote a new awareness or to take the extra step of specifying action to be taken? Try to push for as strong and specific a reader response as you think you can expect.
- Consult compelling sources on the opposed side of the debate as well as sources that support your view (balance sources for and against in your list of references).
- Construct a tone that is fair-minded, respectful, moderate, and yet firmly persuasive.
- Appeal to ethics, credibility, and logic; however, be sure that logic operates effectively throughout.
- Adapt your voice to the features of formal style noted in the formal column of the tones chart on the inside back cover of this book.

- Follow the steps for analysis and evaluation (Chapter 16) and also apply one of the following four models for formal argumentation or a hybrid model that you and your instructor agree will suit the subject and occasion proposed for your essay.
- Be specific about the circumstances and purpose of your argument. Fill in the following form:

Location of presentation or name of publication:

Nature of audience—size, demographics, attitudes on the topic:

Purpose of presentation or category of publication (e.g., letter to editor, editorial, project pitch, debate, feature article, etc.):

Objective (e.g., "influence at least 25 percent of audience to . . .."):

An important part of defining your objective is deciding whether you should aim for a change of knowledge, a change of thinking, or a change of action. What results do you hope will follow from the change? Be as specific as possible. You may wish to shape your argumentation as an oral address (see Chapter 21). Thinking and writing in terms of oral presentations can be a useful way to remember how you are communicating; this helps you to recognize that the expectations of your readers or listeners is every bit as important to success as the more literary attributes of your work.

MODELS OF ARGUMENTATION

We offer the following four widely used models:

- concession-refutation
- Toulmin's claim, support, and warrant
- Monroe's motivated sequence
- Rogerian conciliation

Concession-Refutation

A major emphasis in what the ancients called rhetoric and dialectic was placed upon recognizing (or conceding) arguments on the opposite side. In her essay "Should Cats Be Allowed to Roam?" (Chapter 5, p. 46), Jayne Schuyler begins, "Many people believe that . . . ." She concedes that there are compelling reasons to allow cats to roam;

however, she goes on to name three undesirable effects of this roaming for the animals themselves. (The critical inquiry demanded of argumentation relies considerably on logical scrutiny of causes and effects, so it would be useful to review Chapter 12, from p. 120, in conjunction with your study of argumentative models.) Opening with what "some people think" represents a concession, but then the writer states her or his controlling idea, a refutation. In different ways, the rest of this sort of essay suggests a continued dialogue with the view conceded, while, of course, the writer argues using reasons for the contending view stated in the thesis. Deductive thesis placement can alienate opposed readers, but you, your classmates, and your instructor might think of occasions in which a concession followed by a deductive thesis and then by arguments supporting the refutation might work well as a persuasive tactic.

In any case, opening with a concession-refutation paragraph assures your reader that you are aware of other views and respect those views. Such an opening illustrates that you have put effort into your inquiry and given fair consideration to opposed views. Your intentions are serious and thoughtful. This alone may not win over readers opposed to your view, but it will help things off to a better start than would an immediate statement of your position. Now, to sharpen your skills in shaping concession-refutation, study the following examples and commentary.

Concession

In reports, research papers, and analytical as well as persuasive essays, you must sometimes concede a valid point or two against your own argument to establish credibility with your reader. Your argument or perspective may well be mostly valid or convincing, but sometimes a strong, indisputable counterpoint still exists and therefore must be recognized—conceded. The ancient rhetorician Gorgias, mentioned above, boasted that a counterpoint always exists and can be made into the strongest argument, if you are clever enough to make it so.

Here are two short examples of concession followed by refutation:

Higher education is certainly helpful in any business career. Textbook learning, however, can never replace common sense, self-confidence, and good judgment, especially in the often rapid world of business developments.

Although the Rolling Stones were originally great innovators in rock 'n' roll, their music over the last three decades has contributed only to their bank accounts, not to new ideas or new musicianship. They are essentially a nostalgia act.

Sometimes a longer concession is necessary. You may need to deal with opposing evidence in more detail. Whether your concession is brief or requires its own paragraph, be fair with these opposing points (never superficially dismissive), but also strategic, to manage your argument effectively. You can fully concede an opposing point or fact, but then minimize its significance so your argument or analysis can develop unobstructed.

Here is a further example of concession followed by refutation:

Although some rap music glorifies violence, mindless materialism, and subjugation of women, these aspects in the genre are not nearly as prevalent as people think.

Furthermore, the rap speaker is often a persona, not meant as a reliable source. Rap's linguistic resourcefulness and representations of the dangers and despair of the urban underclasses offer great social and artistic value. In fact, rap's so-called negative aspects are part of the dangers and despair this music depicts.

By making a concession or two to some valid points that oppose your argument or view, you also avoid falling into some possible logical fallacies: hasty generalizations, false either-or divisions, or bandwagon appeals. (See the section on logical fallacies in Chapter 3.)

Let's say, for example, you want to argue that sports indisputably build strong character. You are ready to discuss numerous examples drawing on high school scenarios, inner-city transcendence, college scholarships, strict coaches as wise mentors, and physical training as a socially admirable form of self-knowledge and self-control. You must nonetheless address, even if only briefly, the far less inspiring fact that many amateur, college, and professional athletes often make headlines for their complete *lack* of character: whether for criminal convictions against professional football, hockey, and basketball players, for proven doping by Olympians and their coaches, or even for sexual assault. Furthermore, if you were to try to argue—by overgeneralizing—that sports "indisputably" build strong character, how can you credibly ignore or blithely dismiss certain well-publicized violent and/or illegal actions by public sports figures?

It would be better to manage your necessary concession as follows:

> Even though, as Brigid O'Shaunessey points out, sports success "sometimes misleads a few athletes (at all levels) into dangerous delusions of vanity, invincibility or unaccountability" (29), the overwhelmingly positive effect of sports on the character of a majority of youths is not in dispute. Sports activity generally generates physical, emotional, and social health.

> Several mediocre, semi-famous, and famous athletes have sometimes made the news for ridiculous, even criminal, activity over the years. Nonetheless, sports still offer proven ways for the average young person to build strong character through effort, responsibility, cooperation, improvisation, and self-reliance.

Once acknowledged, concessions allow you to conduct your argument effectively, fairly, and unobstructed.

Refutation

To "refute" means to disprove someone's analysis, opinion, or findings. An argument, analysis, or report may be refuted with a better, more thorough, or more accurate counter-argument or, just as often, with a valid observation not considered in the original writer's claims.

Here are some examples of refutation:

> Although Mick Shrimpton asserts that technology has "far outpaced our legal system's ability to control it" (82), he has failed to consider that legions of legislators, ethicists, and activists constantly devise new laws and regulations to govern

technology's developments and effects. Though Shrimpton is correct that the law lags behind technology's advancements, the legal system is neither helpless nor static.

If a particular writer has manipulated statistics or offered only partial facts or neglected proper context, such misleading or incomplete aspects can and should be successfully challenged—refuted.

Here is another example along these lines:

Claim   The death penalty lowers the risk of violent crime; every nation should therefore allow such executions.

Refutation 1   According to Jolene Durden, no statistics "have ever reliably established that the death penalty acts as a deterrent for other prospective criminals" (34). Considering the nature of death penalty crimes, which are either psychotically violent, deeply asocial, or catastrophically evident of complete loss of self-control, one quickly sees that the perpetrator may never even consider the concept of such a deterrent. The death penalty, then, may more accurately be defined as society's revenge against a single violent criminal rather than any widespread deterrent.

Refutation 2   In some U.S. cases, according to Eloise Mennier, once a violent perpetrator realizes he is guilty of a death penalty crime, "his crimes continue and even escalate because he knows he can be executed only once" (82).

In these two refutations, critics (secondary sources) help to bolster the counter-argument and prove the original claim wrong, short-sighted, or skewed.

Both concession and refutation will make your essays, research papers, and reports more thorough, mature, and fair. You should also think of concession and refutation as part of your duty as a writer to address the necessity and challenges of accuracy.

Comparison-Contrast Model Blending Concession-Refutation and Critical Analysis

Classical rhetoric essentially advocates a comparison-contrast approach (see Chapter 14), balancing examination and refutation of the opposing side with examination and endorsement of one's own side. Based on his study of classical argumentative texts, composition teacher John Thompson provides the following model for formal argumentation:

1. My opponent says A is true (briefly allude to the potentially credible reasons—concession).
2. A is not or not entirely true; B is more true for these reasons (summarize them—refutation).
3. Elaborate on the reasons for believing A is not or not entirely true (refutation).
4. Elaborate on the reasons for believing B is more true (refutation).
5. State final implications and reflections, perhaps even a call to action.

Depending on the length of your essay, steps 1 and 2 above can be placed in the introductory paragraph. Step 2 is the thesis statement (see Chapter 6) and may be phrased, upon revision, as one complete sentence. Step 3 could be covered in one paragraph. Step 4—representing the essence of your argument—might take two, three, or four paragraphs, leaving a final paragraph for Step 5. Note that steps 3 and 4 as outlined above represent block style in comparison-contrast essays: handling one topic ("Why A is not entirely true" in one paragraph or block and then another topic ("Why B is more true") in another paragraph or block. You could also handle steps 3 and 4 in the alternating point-by-point style, interweaving them into single paragraphs focused on the competing *reasons*. If the reasons given by A and B are essentially opposite views of the same specific issue (French immersion places a person between two languages, which is a good thing, as opposed to French immersion places a person between two languages, which is a bad thing), then you might decide that the alternating structure of point-by-point is the better choice. This choice would help you avoid repetition more effectively than the block approach. Here is a point-by-point arrangement:

Paragraph	Reason 1	A's position
		B's position
Paragraph	Reason 2	A's position
		B's position
Paragraph	Reason 3	A's position
		B's position

Find the comparative pattern that most avoids repetition yet maintains equal consideration of the two sides. Remember to acknowledge any good points and reasoning on the side you are opposing even as you stress the reasons for your final position.

With its deductive thesis coming as the second point (in the first or second paragraph), Professor Thompson's model might suit a number of "hybrid" situations—that is, academic or business occasions requiring considerable attention to critical analysis combined with persuasion.

Toulmin's Model of Argumentation

Modern rhetorician Stephen Toulmin introduced his model of argumentation with his 1958 book *The Uses of Argument*. The webpage "Research and Citation—Toulmin's Analysis," expounding ideas from this book, asks the following interesting question, followed by an astute observation:

> Have you ever noticed that when you research both sides of a question, you find yourself being convinced first by one side, and then by the other? Each argument sounds good—at least while you are reading it. . . . [A]nd soon you may feel completely confused.

Toulmin's model helps you to identify the key parts of an argument so that each can be tested. This model therefore offers great value when it comes to appraising arguments.

Three Parts of Any Argument

Toulmin maintains that every argument contains three essentials: the claim, the grounds, and the warrant. **Claims** present an assertion (e.g., "You should take a writing course"); **grounds**—data or evidence—offer proof (30 percent of people taking such a course were able to spell their names consistently afterwards); **warrants** link the claims and the proof (people want to write well). Warrants may be implicit or explicit (unstated or stated). Toulmin believes that the weakest part of an argument is its weakest warrant (stated or implicit).

Toulmin identifies three other elements: qualifiers, rebuttals, and backing. A **qualifier** may be necessary to limit the claim, if the claim is to be valid. For example, the claim may need to be stated as "Those who wish to pursue university studies in the liberal arts and sciences should take a writing course." Why should *everyone* need to take it? Qualifiers are words such as "most," "usually," "some," and "sometimes."

Rebuttals recognize that despite careful construction of the argument, there may still be strong counter-arguments raised against it. This reality matches the awareness of concession-refutation, in which your concession handles a potential rebuttal against your argument. A rebuttal against the claim that "Those who wish to pursue university studies in the liberal arts and sciences should take a writing course" might be the objection that the course textbook has several chapters printed upside down and a large element of plagiarism. This anticipated counter-argument may be pre-empted by the assurance that "those who attend the course will receive new, improved, correct, and corrected editions of the text."

Backing represents the most important of all ingredients in the Toulmin model by offering support to the warrant. In the above example, the writing course promoters would think of as many solid reasons as possible to support the warrant that people want to write well. This support could be in the form of what Chapter 4 describes as "warm" and "cool" proofs—personal examples, anecdotes, even figurative language on the "warm" side, and various types of rigorously gathered and tested data on the "cool" side.

Monroe's Motivated Sequence

When you wish to stress the element of persuasion over that of inquiry, Monroe's motivated sequence, or some adaptation of it, might serve you well. Professor Alan Monroe introduced his motivated sequence in 1935, as a practical step-by-step approach for speakers wishing to move, in a single speech, from the level of raising awareness to that of inciting action. This model strongly influenced formulas for advertising letters and other types of persuasive written communications. Here are Monroe's five steps:

1. Arouse attention. Offer vivid stories or examples, startling facts, or eloquent statements by admired people.

2. Demonstrate a need. Show that the situation you want to change is urgent. Arrange evidence to build intensity; tap into the motivation of your audience, so that they look forward to your solution to the problem.

3. Satisfy the need. Provide a way, or ways, to solve the problem you have demonstrated. Provide a clear plan of action. Show how this plan agrees with audience principles and desires.

4. Visualize the results. Create vivid images to represent the positive results that will follow. Perhaps create a vivid picture of what may happen if your action plan is not followed.

5. Call for action. Provide a challenge, an appeal, or a statement of personal commitment. "Give listeners something specific that they can do right away" (Osborn and Osborn 458). Taking action to solve a problem is much like putting a canoe in motion—the first paddle strokes are the hardest. This part needs the most encouragement and support on your part as a motivational speaker. When Martin Luther King, Jr., called upon African Americans to register to vote, he had already arranged to have a sign-up table near the door of the assembly.

In Praise of Conciliation: Models That Privilege Ethos and Pathos

The "Golden Rule"—that grand ethical guideline apparent in so many traditions—counsels us to do to others as we would have them do to us. It follows that we *not* do to others what we would *not* want done to us. Most of us do not want our ideas or plans swept aside to be suddenly replaced by someone else's. Aggressive forms of persuasion often fail to respect and convince their audience. Given Canada's history of reaching numerous concessions and compromises, perhaps it's appropriate that we conclude this section on persuasion by considering approaches that place special importance on sympathizing with audiences and recognizing the ethical line in how and how much to entice them toward our own position.

Perhaps the best known persuasive model of this sort today is Rogerian argument. Less concerned with "winning" and "losing" than the classical and Toulmin models, Rogerian argument emphasizes exploring common ground, building bridges, resolving differences, and negotiating and achieving reconciliation. This form places special stress on respecting the audience. As described by the webpage "Rogerian (Common Ground) Argumentation," "This psychological approach encourages people to listen to each other rather than to try to shout each other down."

Psychologist Carl Rogers believed in "empathic listening." He encouraged potential speakers to attend actively to their audience, to enter into reasoning opposed to their own, and to recognize the validity of those views. This discipline he viewed as critical to growth as a person as well as a communicator. Many people from other places, times, and cultures would agree with the strategy of listening rather than confronting, with the effort to build bridges rather than win wars, and with the willingness to accept gradual and partial change.

With its stress on the rights and feelings of the audience, the Rogerian model grants equality to ethos and pathos along with logos. Many people see this as a balancing of the dominance of logos in academic and other institutions. We referred to this concern in Chapter 1, suggesting that complete emphasis on logos can obscure the value of feelings and even ethics. With its stress on reconciliation, Rogers's method seeks to avoid the spectacle of elected members of office shouting insults and gesturing obscenely before TV cameras while another tries to speak. Current disenchantment with oppositional-style party politics, particularly among the young, suggests a growing desire to transcend roadblocks created by stubborn, partisan allegiances. Rogers's approach offers a genuine will to expand the meaning of concession from simply defining a position to be refuted to recognizing the parameters of possible negotiation. Like other empathic approaches, Rogerian argument works with what the audience appears to allow and takes its shape from there.

Speechwriters commonly begin their texts with an anecdote connected to family, since we all come from families, or they may use gentle humour touching on some other universal human situation. Rogerian speech builds from this general sort of starting point by valuing the audience's specific views on the main topic of discussion. Chapter 16 outlines four common standards of assessment: logical, practical, ethical, and aesthetic. If a speaker knows that his audience places utmost importance upon only practical criteria related to the topic, then shifting to ethical or logical criteria could be interpreted as appearing morally superior or out of touch. A Rogerian speaker avoids such appearances by collaborating with the main concerns of the audience, by finding common ground within those.

An example of meeting the evaluative standards of your audience might be if you were on a police service promotion committee that included hardliners who still distrusted that female officers could do the job. Your appeal for promotion of an excellent female candidate would best address not work equity, but the candidate's demonstrated past performance.

According to the Rogerian approach, while you may not care for certain values of your audience, you must see beyond those to the ones you may share—in this case, a common belief in proven performance and the need for the right skills. You must keep those values in mind throughout, demonstrating how they will be respected and perhaps even furthered in certain ways. For instance, you might note that the female candidate led her recruit class in marksmanship and three other disciplines, took no sick days, and has attracted the attention of a larger metropolitan police service interested in sharing her negotiation skills.

Speakers using a Rogerian model delay expounding their theses until they have recognized common ground, explained matters in a way that offers benefits to the audience, and shown continued respect for the audience's way of seeing things. You would not assert your recommendation concerning the promotion until you had reviewed and explained all of the work history and current contexts in terms of performance only. You would concede to your audience's known dislike for equity hiring and promotion. In exchange, you would trust your audience to be prepared to reciprocate with a degree of concession as well.

Here is another simple illustration of the Rogerian approach, adapted from an example by Professor Patricia E. Connors:

- Your company has declared a freeze on office spending until the end of the year, but that is another six months away.
- You state your understanding and agreement with the spirit of this goal of increased savings.
- However, your current printer is slow, needs frequent repairs, and produces poor quality in comparison to that of its competitors.
- You do a cost analysis and find that sharing a superior printer with the other two offices on your floor will result in less expense to the company than if each of you continues with your current equipment. You anticipate increased profits through improved quality, and improved teamwork through cooperative contact. You would not mention the cooperative benefit if you knew your supervisor opposed that attitude toward the two other offices, however.

A persuasive written request to your supervisor would follow the above outline.

Some might object that Rogerian argument pursues "mere compromise," but sometimes convincing others to accept compromise while offering concessions in exchange is an important step forward. After all, Canada achieved and has retained its national standing in large part according to our commitment and ability to negotiate.

Former prime minister Lester B. Pearson (1897–1972), a Canadian famous for his empathic listening and negotiating expertise, faced a truly "tough" audience in 1964 when the Royal Canadian Legion invited him to talk to them, at its national convention in Winnipeg, about plans to replace the Red Ensign with a new Canadian flag. Keeping to his election commitments, Pearson was advocating the new flag (an earlier proposed model of the one we now fly), yet a majority of the Legionnaires felt passionately loyal to the Red Ensign, part of their British heritage and the symbol that they had fought for in the Second World War. Pearson's address demonstrated three main points of Rogerian argument, summarized by Patricia Connors as follows:

- Show the audience that you understand their position.
- Specify the conditions under which you believe the audience's position is correct.
- Convince the audience that you and they share the same moral qualities (honesty, quality, good will, and the desire to solve the problem).

If you watch the recorded segment of Pearson's address to the sometimes rowdy Legionnaires (available at CBC Archives online as well as through the CBC video library), you will see that these three goals are easier to achieve when appealing for a new printer than when trying to change the central symbol of a country. Nevertheless, Pearson demonstrated utmost attention to all three of the above essentials of audience awareness and response. He recognized a strong British history in the flags flown by Canada in the two world wars, the Union Jack in the first and the Red Ensign in the second. When he acknowledged the Red Ensign, the audience rose in a standing ovation. While this moment expressed complete opposition to adopting a new flag, it allowed Pearson to comment on shared ground: a love of country, including a common recognition of the primacy of national symbols. When interrupted by hecklers, Pearson demonstrated good nature and said, "It's all right, Mr. Chairman, this is a *veterans'* meeting." In response, he received a strong round of applause. Wearing his military badges, indications of his own loyal service in the First World War, Pearson demonstrated that he was a veteran, too—that he had fought for the same basic values. He demonstrated that he understood the audience's passion for the Red Ensign and that he shared their emotions of patriotism.

When Pearson stated his thesis—that the time for a new flag had come—he was greeted by hostile booing. He then articulated several points to specify the conditions under which the audience's attachment to the Red Ensign was correct. By mentioning that the Union Jack (not the Red Ensign) had been flown in the First World War, when he had fought, he introduced the idea of time and change. He explained that in 1964, the country had five million or more French descendants and five million or more immigrants from countries other than France or Britain. When interrupted by a heckler who shouted "I don't agree," he replied, "That's good—you have that right." In this way, Pearson reminded his audience of a fundamental common value, fought for in the wars—democracy, the right of free speech followed by majority decisions through the parliamentary process.

Further invoking a fundamental value of good soldiers—courage in the just cause—he read from a letter by a member of Parliament stating that it was the member's duty to vote according to the will of a majority of the people he represented. Pearson implicitly reminded his hostile audience that a condition of the Red Ensign was its representation of courage and freedom. He received grudging applause upon declaring that he was committed to facing the hard, controversial issues upon which the future depended. Although he defended the rights of his hecklers to free speech, Pearson then pointed out his equal right to explain *his* position.

Pearson said that the new model flag consisted of three maple leaves patterned on the Legion badge, to be framed by blue representing not only the two oceans but also the blue of the Legion scroll. He appealed, in his explanation, for his audience to recognize that Canada's future must blend their sense of past heritage with a coming new nationhood embracing multiple cultures and histories as part of a versatile nationhood.

Pearson surely realized that his hostile audience would not likely go away supporting the new flag or planning to vote for him again if they had done so before. His goal was to go as persuasively far as he could—to plant the seeds of new awareness that over time might take root with some. According to Pearson's vision of a democracy of contending positions, he accepted that some would not agree. As we know, Pearson's powers of negotiation and persuasion, which earned him Canada's first-ever Nobel Peace Prize, were not quite equal to achieving the flag of his vision, three joined maples leaves in red framed on either side by two bars of blue. But he did see the adoption of a truly Canadian flag, a colossal achievement in the face of fierce emotional resistance.

CULTURAL CONSIDERATIONS

Canada pre-1960 was a very different place from the country we know today. A great many ideas and patterns assumed to be the only way of doing things have made room—or been made to make room—for other varieties of thought and expression. The same is true, in general, of ideas today concerning argument, rhetoric, and persuasion.

Before leaving this topic of argumentation, we should consider, again, the importance of cultural factors in how we relate to rhetorical traditions. Certain cultures neither engage in nor admire the oppositional, sometimes intensive adversarial approach we discuss in this chapter. However, the oppositional approach is vigorously taught in North American colleges and universities as a test of clarity, research, factuality, and implications.

Works Consulted

Connors, Patricia E. "How to Be Persuasive in Writing." 42nd Annual Conference of the Society for Technical Communication, 23–26 April 1995. Web. 12 July 2010.

Corbett, Edward P. J. "Review: The Contemporary Reception of Classical Rhetoric: Appropriations of Ancient Discourse by Kathleen E. Welch." *Journal of Advanced Composition* 11.1 (1991). Web. 20 Aug. 2006.

Osborn, Suzanne, and Michael Osborn. *Public Speaking.* 7th ed. Boston: Houghton, 2006. Print.

"Research and Citation—Toulmin's Analysis." *The OwLet.* LeTourneau University, 2002. Web. 14 July 2010.

"Rogerian Argumentation." *The Writing Center.* Winthrop University, n.d. Web. 12 July 2010.

Smith, David. "Burying the Hatchet in Language." *Reader's Choice.* Ed. Kim Flachmann, Michael Flachmann, and Alexandra MacLennan. 3rd Can. ed. Scarborough: Prentice Hall, 2000. 540-44. Print.

Soucoup, Charles, and Scott Titsworth. *The Toulmin Project.* University of Nebraska, May 1998. Web. 12 July 2010.

Straker, David. "Toulmin's Argument Model." *Changing Minds.org.* Syque, n.d. Web. 12 July 2010.

Toulmin, Stephen. *The Uses of Argument.* Cambridge: Cambridge U P, 1958. Print.

Zarefsky, David, and Jennifer MacLennan. *Public Speaking Strategies for Success.* Canadian ed. CBC/Prentice Video Library, 1997. Print and Videotape.

Chapter 19
Essays in Exams

Many university courses have exams that require essay writing. The exams are usually significantly weighted into your final grade.

Unlike papers you write at home, exam essays do not allow you a lot of time to develop the strong thesis statement, the clear topic sentences, the satisfactory conclusion, and the perfect grammar and punctuation that you always strive for in essays. Many essay exams are two hours long and require you to write two essays, so therefore require strong organizational skills. The following test-taking tips ought to help you write your exam essays in the allotted time and be reasonably successful at it. Preparing well will help you to structure and organize your time productively during the exam.

KEEP A SENSE OF PROPORTION

Remember that final exams rarely count toward a majority of your final mark for the course. Of course, do your best, but try not to allow worry about the exam to become overly disruptive to you. You must accept that almost no one leaves an exam feeling satisfied that all parts went perfectly, because it is not the nature of exam conditions to promote perfection. By following the tips recommended here, you should certainly be able to demonstrate that you have achieved a high level of knowledge and ability.

PRE-EXAM PLANNING

It should be safe to assume that you have participated in the course as best you were able, and this previous work should give you some assurance.

1. Before you start your actual preparation and studying for the exam, make sure that you know the structure of the exam (check the syllabus/course outline or ask the instructor). Determine whether the exam emphasis will be on particular areas or broad knowledge (ask your instructor if you have any uncertainty).

2. Review the course objectives (check the syllabus/course outline) and the instructor's focus (check your course notes to detect recurrent themes, observations, issues, and so on).

3. Review the exam question key words in the box below.

4. With the exam question key words in mind, review the main topics covered on your course syllabus and recorded in your notes. Focus on any prevailing themes, issues, or periods covered during the course. Anticipate possible essay questions prompted by this content.

5. If the exam will emphasize in-depth knowledge, carefully reread course texts and materials selectively. Carefully choose the texts that are most pertinent to the main themes, periods, or issues covered in the course. As you reread, continue to anticipate possible essay topic questions. Remember the exam question key words in the box below.

6. If the exam will emphasize broad knowledge, quickly or even partially reread course texts and materials widely. Scan the main course texts and take notes with the question key words and possible topics in mind. As you reread, anticipate possible essay topic questions. Jot down key passages and make sure to identify the texts they come from. For help with anticipating the questions, remember the exam question key words in the box below.

7. At the end of this process, you should have several sheets of notes and key passages from the various materials. Reading through these, you can discern the various themes, issues, or periods you previously identified as central to the course (under step 4). If you do not see that relationship, consider the necessity of adjusting your earlier determinations of issues, periods, or themes. However, for a first-year English or writing course, there may be no particular theme, only a smattering of texts. This may make the exam either more "open" or more unpredictable.

8. Go over your notes, reread/scan, and tweak your notes and ideas in the days before the exam. Doing so will help you remain focused and close to the material you covered in the course.

9. You can even go so far as generating possible theses for your different study essays. Using the notes you have made and the quotations or passages you pulled from the texts, write out sample essay plans, including topic sentences.

10. Don't let all this planning prevent you from getting a good sleep on the night before the exam.

Key Words in Essay Questions

Analyze: Discuss, interpret, and closely examine the many components of a single text, concept, or situation. To analyze is to declare significance and implications, not merely to summarize.

Compare: Look at the similarities and, more important, the differences between two or more concepts, situations, or texts. Recognize both similarities and differences, but work toward a thesis emphasizing one or the other.

Contrast: Emphasize the differences between two concepts or texts. Set them in opposition in your discussion. One teacher of analytical writing once said, "A lot of things are like a lot of other things in this world, and that's why distinctions and contrasts are important."

Criticize: Analyze a given number of texts for comparative worth. Make judgments evaluating one against the other.

Define: Provide the meaning of crucial, often complex terms from the course. Be sure to state the exact limits of what is to be defined. Be brief, but articulate a precise meaning. Consider providing an example for pointed clarity.

Describe: Detail a given theme, genre, case, or set of circumstances. List the qualities and characteristics of the account you are rendering.

Discuss: This very broad term invites analysis, or cause-effect, or comparison-contrast to argue or debate an interpretation or set of circumstances. You can define central terms; list pros and cons, complexities, contrasting qualities, unexpected conditions or effects; or analyze meaning and examine effectiveness.

Explain: Clarify by describing logical development, use, and effect. Give examples.

Illustrate: Use examples to explain a concept. Comparisons and contrasts are effective here.

Interpret: Comment on a given text or situation by describing it and its issues. Then analyze it—what might it all mean? Describe comparisons and give examples.

Outline: Describe main themes, interpretations, characteristics, or events.

Relate: Show some broad and many specific connections between themes, ideas, or events. Establish a larger context in which to place your discussion.

Summarize: Briefly discuss or recount an event, text, or discussion, including crucial ideas and facts.

"COLD" READINGS IN THE EXAM

"Cold" readings are those you have not had a chance to see in advance. They come with the exam. It is never easy to read well under time pressure, and the possible added stress of an exam setting is unlikely to make the reading of new material any easier. Below are some suggestions that will help you get the most out of your limited time.

Readings in exams are either part of a question (or contain the question) or require the student to do something with them (summarize, analyze, comment upon, and so on). Make sure you know what you are being asked to do because that will determine what you should focus on as you read.

1. Always start with a quick read through so that you have a sense of the flow and logical (argumentative, narrative) structure of the reading.
2. Read again, with pen in hand. Underline the important points.
3. Contemplate the relationships between the various important points (the glue between the "bits" that hold "everything" together).
4. Once you have the sense of the reading and see the bits and the glue, you are in a good position to do almost anything with the text.
5. Jot down what you consider to be the best approach, in outline form, for what the exam requires you to do.
6. Read the text, quickly, one more time to verify your outline.

These six points should help you to work with exam readings quickly and efficiently. They are unlikely to give you the most in-depth possible analysis or interpretation, but should suffice for a solid response to what the exam requires.

WRITING THE EXAM

Once you are in the exam, plan your time effectively so you can finish the entire test.

1. When you receive the exam, read all the possible topics and questions. Look for topics that are similar to those you considered when you were preparing your study notes. Don't panic if nothing matches exactly. Much of your prepared information is likely flexible enough to work in part or in other combinations to satisfy the exam's essay questions. Remember the special meanings of certain key words used in the language of exam questions. See the "Key Words in Essay Questions" box on pages 212–213.
2. Decide within the first five minutes of the test which one or two topics you will write on. If the examination has other components (multiple-choice, short-answer, definition, fill-in-the-blank), choose your essay topics first and your mind will work on them as you write the other sections.
3. When you begin the essay portion of the test, first note how much time you have. If you have an hour for each essay, divide your time carefully, roughly according to this model:
    • up to 10 minutes for planning by integrating ideas from the notes, topic sentences, and any theses you generated at home
    • up to 45 minutes for writing
    • 5 remaining minutes for looking the paper over for correct syntax, grammar, and clarity

HOW TO HANDLE A DEMANDING EXAM IN ENGLISH COMPOSITION

English exams can be notorious for the amount of reading, summarizing, analyzing, and writing that they demand in what seems like little time. In this section we describe a typical composition exam with four parts. We then use this specific exam as an example of how you need to bring a special approach to bear if you are to complete all sections effectively and within the allotted time.

Sample Exam Questions

Part A Essay—50 percent of exam mark
Choose one of the following topic questions below and write an essay of approximately 500 to 600 words, 4 to 5 paragraphs, 3 to 4 pages double spaced.

[The exam will list a number of topic choices.]

Part B Summary and Critical Response Paragraph—20 percent of exam mark
Read the short essay below entitled. . . . In one short paragraph of 4 to 5 sentences, summarize the essay. In a longer paragraph, write a critical response to the essay. Your response will amplify, modify, or challenge an idea in the essay, or examine some aspect of rhetoric (word choices and patterns of language) and demonstrate its effect.

[The exam will then include a "cold" essay.]

Part C Identifying and Explaining an Excerpt—10 percent of exam mark
Listed below are 6 excerpts from 6 readings on the syllabus of this course. Choose one of the excerpts and (1) identify the title and author of the reading from which the excerpt has been taken and (2) state the relevance of the excerpt to the essay as a whole. Your answer should comprise at least 10 sentences presented in one or two carefully crafted paragraphs.

Part D Correct Common Errors—20 percent of exam mark
1. Most or all of the following 10 lines contain a typical error—no more than one per line. Making as few changes as absolutely necessary, correct the errors.
2. The following paragraph contains 10 of the 15 common errors. Correct these errors, making as few changes as absolutely necessary. Be sure your editing intentions are clear. Be sure to correct documentation style as well.

Time allowed for an exam like this might range from two to three hours. The following suggestions, tips, and advice assume that you have three hours to complete this exam. If that were two and a half hours or even two hours, you would apply the same steps and points of awareness that follow, but reduce the time devoted to each section in proportion to the mark weight for that section.

Strategy for Answering the Above Sample Exam Questions

Be as Rested and Relaxed as You Can

We recommend, above all, that you have a good night's rest and try to relax (though exams make everyone nervous). The exam illustrated above does not throw any curve balls. The examiner simply wants to see your essay-writing, summarizing, critical thinking, and grammar skills in action. The marker likely won't expect your writing to be as fully polished or accomplished as it might be if you had more time. The key to best success is to create thoughtful point-form outlines/rough notes to help you organize and ensure that essentials are included and that the form and organization of your work suits the topic.

Do Not Write Multiple Drafts

Go into the examination planning to write only one draft of your essay (one based on a thesis and topic sentence outline) and any paragraph answers. Double-space your writing; that way, you can go over it afterwards, making corrections between the lines. Your handwriting should be legible (assuming you are not working on a computer), but it is not necessary to aim for a calligraphy award.

Look Over the Whole Examination, Then Begin Planning Part A

Once you have received your examination and filled in any required administrative portions, look the whole exam over once. Decide then on the essay topic you'd like to do for Part A and think about it for a few minutes. In preparing to answer Part A, try to tackle the following questions for yourself—and based on those answers, write a rough outline:

What does the question and implied audience mean for the form of my essay (personal, expository, analytical, argumentation)?
What is my thesis (and conclusion)?
What is the main point (topic sentence) in each of my three or four body paragraphs that will lead me to my final conclusion?
What will I need to mention (evidence) to make my point in each paragraph?

Your essay should have a sufficiently detailed thesis (usually placed at the end of your opening paragraph) and at least three solid body paragraphs of 5 to 10 sentences each. Make sure each paragraph has focus, support, and a clear, effective relationship to your thesis. (Review the material in Chapter 4 on the 4-F Test.)

Double-Space Your Answers for A, B, and C

By double-spacing your writing, you can later insert revisions and make changes. You will also make the writing easier for your reader. Do not worry about writing a second complete draft of any section. Use rough notes and an outline so that you can make do with just one draft. Write legibly.

After Planning Part A, Get Parts B, C, and D Out of the Way

 Once you have outlined Part A, handle Parts B, C, and D to get them out of the way. As you work on those, ideas may come to you for the Part A essay. Add to your rough notes for the essay as you do the other parts (if that method suits you). Alternatively, consider completing Parts B and D and leaving Part C for last, since it has the lowest weight. Exams sometimes require such survivalist thinking.

Match the Time You Spend on Each Part to the Mark Value for That Part

Watch the time and begin on the draft of your essay with at least 80 minutes to go for a three-hour exam. Don't worry about writing a second draft. For revision, go through and make corrections between the lines. This is acceptable revision in exam situations.

Use Your Dictionary Thoughtfully

If your course allows you to use a dictionary during the exam, be careful not to spend too much time with it. First, use your dictionary to check the precise meanings of any key words in assignment instructions. Then, once you reach the essay revision, use your dictionary to check spellings if the time allows.

How to Prepare for Part B

Review Chapter 15, "The Summary," especially "Ten Steps to a Successful Summary" (p. 164). Also review Chapter 16 on critical analysis in general and Chapter 17 on rhetorical response (a specific application of critical response). Follow the guidelines in the section "'Cold' Readings in the Exam" (p. 213) to read the Part B essay and to intensify your comprehension of its main assertions and methods. In writing your summary of four or five sentences, concentrate on expressing the ideas in your own words. Show that you have recognized the controlling idea of the "cold" essay and its supporting reason(s). That is the essence of what the summary requires.

   For the critical response paragraph to the essay, again as briskly as you can, demonstrate knowledge of critical thinking as described in Chapter 16, "Critical Analysis and Evaluation." Decide quickly what should figure in an analysis of the issue raised in the essay, then decide what elements you will focus on in your critique. Choose one or two (and no more) of the evaluative criteria suggested in Chapter 16 (p. 168) to move expeditiously while deciding on a focus. Then work on the topic sentence of your critical response paragraph. Once you have that, the paragraph should flow naturally.

How to Prepare for Part C

See Chapter 20 for how an excerpt relates to the reading from which it is taken. Some instructors who assign this question are often more interested in your understanding of the basic process of an essay than in how many course essays you remember in detail. But many exams require an extensive knowledge and memory of course readings—so be sure to know well in advance how many of the assigned course readings you need to review for the exam.

The sample exam question for Part C above suggests that you need to know only one of the six represented excerpts well. You would simply need to break the one down into its main parts. Chapter 20 gives detailed steps for preparing to write the sort of paragraph(s) required by this exam question.

How to Prepare for Part D

If you have trouble understanding the explanations for the 15 common errors in the Handbook of this text, then you need to brush up on how to identify basic parts of speech and sentence patterns. That basic review information is readily available online, in libraries, and in bookstores. If you have been working with your instructor's notations on your coursework, then you have likely made good progress in correcting the 15 common errors by this stage. Do not spend too long on this section. Answer the questions that you know and leave those that you do not know. Return to the incomplete ones later if you have time.

Be Sure to Return Your "Scrap" or "Rough" Notes

Most, if not all, examination procedures require that you hand in all of your rough notes with the rest of the exam. This requirement may be an important benefit for you in that a marker can quickly see evidence of your thinking and knowledge from your brainstorming and outlines. If you run out of time and fail to complete the essay, and if you have provided an outline similar to those modelled in Chapter 9 (an outline with a clear thesis and topic sentences), you may receive sufficient marks for the incomplete writing. If you severely run out of time, move in the last stage of the essay to note (point) form. This method often earns more marks than students realize. Resist any feeling of despair—make the most of the limited time available, and remember that it is limited for everyone. Providing clear, effective, knowledgeable outlines is one strategy to help you follow plans and, if need be, provide evidence of plans.

Success Does Not Mean Perfection in All Points of the Marking Rubric

Marking schemes or rubrics for English essays generally cover five categories: 1) content, 2) organization and flow, 3) style and tone (adapting to purpose), 4) grammar and spelling, and 5) mechanics (spacing, documentation technique, and so forth). Polishing and perfecting all of these aspects under exam pressures is not realistic. A wise strategy is to provide a strong base of content, structure, and grammar— simply do the best that you can with the other aspects.

Chapter 20
Excerpt Relationships in Exams

A common examination question in composition and literature classes, as well as in other courses in the humanities and social sciences, is to explain how a brief excerpt from an essay, novel, or other text relates to the work as a whole. This question presents a list of excerpts from different course readings. It asks you to pick one (or more) of the excerpts, identify the reading from which it is taken, and then explain the significance of the excerpt to the reading as a whole. In this way the exam tests whether you have familiarized yourself with the reading(s) and also whether you understand how a given text works.

To answer this question successfully, you need to know the assigned readings well. You also need to call upon the skills of summarization and process description as applied to rhetorical analysis. To review the guidelines for these key techniques, see Chapter 15, Chapter 13 (p. 134), and Chapter 17.

DEFINITION OF THE WORD "EXCERPT"

An excerpt is a piece, a portion of a text that is lifted out and reproduced. A short excerpt (less than 30 words) may be presented with quotation marks around it to indicate that it is an exact reproduction of wording from another text—in other words, a quotation. More often, the excerpts will be laid out as block quotations without quotation marks, as shown in the sample question below, which lists excerpts a to e.

SAMPLE EXAMINATION QUESTION

Following is an example of an examination question asking you to explain the relationship of an excerpt to a whole reading. Note that in this example, the excerpts are laid out as block quotations and therefore do not take quotation marks. Also note that in this question, students are asked to select *one* excerpt from among a choice of *five*. Instructors may provide a larger or perhaps smaller number of choices, and they may ask for you to select and discuss more than one excerpt.

Example of excerpt exam question

Listed below are five excerpts from five readings on the syllabus of this course. Choose one of the quotations and (1) identify the title and author of the reading from which the quotation has been taken, and (2) state the relevance of the quotation to the reading as a whole. Your answer should comprise at least 10 to 12 sentences presented in one or two carefully crafted paragraphs.

    a. A second way that oppressed people sometimes deal with oppression is to resort to violence and corroding hatred.

    b. So, our troops remained deployed to (a) guarantee a measure of security while Afghanistan citizens went about the first steps to democracy and the extension of basic rights, (b) assist in building the essential elements—schools, a justice system, infrastructure, roads—that any society must have, and (c) offer humanitarian assistance where possible.

    c. Yes, I let my 10-year-old son and his friend run to the creek and stay there all afternoon. What's more, they were barefoot the whole time.

    d. "You're looking at a very different kind of situation in the year 2000. Most people don't know what prostitution looks like. People have no clue," says sex-trade researcher John Lowman, a professor of criminology at Simon Fraser University in Vancouver.

    e. In Canada, we quit hanging individual criminals in 1962 (and removed capital punishment from the Criminal Code in 1976) because studies showed it was not a deterrent. Whatever reason people kill people, or don't kill them, being hanged, gassed or grilled is not central to the decision. Also, we did not want . . .

Titles of readings from which the excerpts have been taken:

"College Girl to Call Girl," Reader, page 388
"Confessions of the World's Worst Parent," Reader, page 425
"What We Are Fighting For," Reader, page 438
"The Good War: A Propaganda Perennial," Reader, page 440
"The Ways of Meeting Oppression," Reader, page 442

Decide on the excerpt (or excerpts) you feel best able to explain. How you prepare to discuss these readings in relation to the excerpt is laid out in the section "Steps in Preparing to Explain How an Excerpt Relates to the Larger Work" (p. 223). Your preparation must occur *before* you enter the exam.

A Note on Interpreting Quotation Marks

Don't become confused if there is a quotation within the excerpt. Notice in choice d in the example above that the excerpt begins with the author of the essay quoting someone else. If by chance all the excerpts were enclosed by quotation marks, then excerpt d above would look like this:

    d. "'You're looking at a very different kind of situation in the year 2000. Most people don't know what prostitution looks like. People have no clue,' says sex-trade researcher John Lowman, a professor of criminology at Simon Fraser University in Vancouver."

In this case, the double quotation marks around the excerpt indicate what block indentation normally indicates: that the words are an exact transcription from a text. Since the excerpt chosen also begins with an opening quotation mark indicating the exact words of Professor Lowman, quoted by Sarah Schmidt in her article, the exam writer in this case converted the double quotation mark used by Schmidt into a single quotation mark. This quoting of a quotation is sometimes called a triple quote (because it requires three quotation marks). The reader sees the double quotation mark opening the excerpt followed by a single quotation mark and realizes that something has been quoted from somewhere else, and that the material being excerpted begins with a quotation. Normally, however, the exam excerpts will appear as indented blocks without quotation marks.

Make sure you clearly understand what this assignment is asking you to do, and how any quotation marks provide clarity concerning whose words you are reading. Read on to follow our recommended steps for handling this assignment.

PREPARING IN ADVANCE: THREE MAIN STEPS

Most, if not all, examination questions asking you to explain how an excerpt relates to a reading are not "open book." In other words, you have to come to the examination having already worked through the recommended readings, perhaps according to the following three steps:

Three Steps to a Successful Excerpt Relationship

1. Fill in the checklist recommended for Stage 1 rhetorical analysis (Chapter 17, p. 183).
2. Write a process description (or analysis, if fictional text).
3. Write a summary.

The checklist raises pertinent questions to answer and thus prepares you for the next two steps. The process description and summary are short in order to focus you on precise answers as well as to help you remember the outstanding issues. Unless you have a photographic memory, you need to boil the reading down to the key ideas and rhetorical details—the ones most likely to be presented by or required through the excerpt. The discussion immediately following walks you through these three steps in further detail.

Steps in Preparing to Explain How an Excerpt Relates to the Larger Work

Apply these steps for each reading that could be tested on the examination, or at least for a sufficient number of readings to assure your chances of finding an excerpt or excerpts you can knowledgeably explain.

1. In the interests of care and thoroughness, fill in the checklist recommended for Stage 1 rhetorical analysis in Chapter 17 (p. 183), which is the basis for the list below. This list covers the basic textual elements, principles, and relationships, and thereby helps you identify rhetorical parts.

    Who is the author and what biographical information is available?
    Where was the work published?
    What type of writing is it (investigative journalism, academic analysis, poetry, corporate persuasion, etc.)?
    Who is the intended audience?
    What various public beliefs (warrants) exist on the topic?
    What various public beliefs (warrants) existed on the topic at the time the piece was written?
    What is the author's presumed purpose? (See the discussion on models of argumentation in Chapter 18, starting on p. 200.)
    What is the author's controlling idea?
    What are the author's reasons? (Controlling idea + reasons = thesis)
    What specific methods of inquiry (research) have been used?
    Where do you think you could find more information about the subject matter discussed?
    What connections to the subject beyond the essay are included or implied?
    How has the reading been organized and what rhetorical strategies and patterns are featured throughout and in separate parts?
    What style and therefore tone does the reading use (kinds of words, lengths of sentences)?

    Step 2 below is to write a process description of the essay or analysis of its literary devices. Step 3 is to write a summary of the essay or literary work. The process description draws upon the checklist, and the summary draws upon the process description.

2. Write or outline a short process description (or analysis) of the text that the excerpt comes from. Here is a process description written by Valerie Desjardins while preparing her critical analysis. (For the completed essay, see Chapter 17, p. 191.)

    Outline—Process description of "College Girl"

    Investigative journalism; intended for general public audience; omits specific citations; unreferenced statistics—80 percent of prostitution is now off street and college tuition fees have risen 126 percent on average over nine years, both stats juxtaposed toward beginning; uses mostly examples—interviewees, four student prostitutes (three ex), escort service manager, sociologist, outreach worker, police detective, novelist-researcher; main subject at beginning, middle and end is Stacy; Stacy shown by language, actions and comments by others to be in denial; outreach worker Bennett says toward end (impact location) that Stacy uses "rationalization"; John toward end (impact location) suggests the middle-class world is essentially one of imposed prostitution and denials; Lowman, sociology prof, suggests middle class is heavily into prostitution and denial (impact location at beginning where thesis of essay might be, after opening extended anecdote).

The details in your carefully observed process description (analysis of rhetoric) will point you toward the thesis as well as toward supporting arguments, figures of speech, and other rhetorical devices, and the various forms of evidence provided. The process description will assist you to finalize your summary of the main claim and supporting ideas of the reading. You should be able to identify the excerpt as a specific form of rhetoric with a specific purpose related to the main purpose and to the thesis of the reading.

3. Write or outline a short summary of the text that the excerpt comes from. (See Chapter 15 for more on writing a summary.)

Outline summary of "College Girl"

Thesis (main claim): (Controlling idea) Discreet off-street prostitution is significantly on the rise, (reasons) because middle-class students, confronted by rising costs and other pressures on the middle class, have entered the business.

Supporting forms of evidence: Student prostitutes, sociologists, police officers, outreach workers, and other investigators into the issue all confirm the thesis. Statistics show off-street prostitution dominates the trade and college fees have risen by 126 percent.

Assumed public attitude: The middle-class public in general denies or ignores this activity.

Backing for assumed public attitude: Student prostitutes maintain appearances of not being prostitutes and apply rationalizations suggesting they are not doing anything wrong and that middle-class life is fine, as always.

> The summary sketches the main claims and supporting ideas. Your goal is essentially to show how the excerpt serves the purpose and thesis of the reading.

In the Examination: Recognizing the Excerpt and Its Role

Once you have worked through the three preparatory steps at home for the readings concerned, you are ready to be presented with excerpts from them. In the examination, the first thing to ask yourself when you see an excerpt from a reading you intend to discuss is whether the excerpt is the thesis of the reading. Think of the thesis as the tallest tree in the forest. You feel a little lost, so to get your bearings you look for the tallest tree. In preparing for the exam, you have probably written out the thesis (in your own words) and memorized it. If the excerpt from the reading does not appear to be the thesis, ask yourself what relationship it has to the thesis by placing it into one of the following three general categories, which you have identified in your pre-exam preparations:

1. Part of a minor argument in support of the essay's major argument or some idea similarly intended to give support to the controlling idea (e.g., a premise of the major argument)
2. A tool of reasoning, explanation, intensification, or illustration (e.g., an analogy or a figure of speech used to convey a certain conclusion that somehow supports the thesis)
3. Evidence (the words of an authority, an example such as a character description or anecdote, data from some source, other detailed forms of proof)

Once you have chosen one of these three categories for the excerpt, be as specific as you can about the nature of the excerpt within that category and then ask yourself where in the larger work the excerpt occurs. Place it in one of the following areas:

Introduction
Body (be as specific about where in the body as you can)
Conclusion

Chapter 7 of this text provides information on characteristics and functions of openings and conclusions. Chapter 4 covers basic features of paragraphs, and Chapter 11 reviews basic organizational forms used within body sections of readings.

Note that the main point made by the student in the following sample excerpt relationship is how the excerpt relates to the thesis of the reading.

 PRACTICE

Here is a question you might find on an examination:

> Identify which of the following excerpts comes from the reading "College Girl to Call Girl" and explain how the excerpt relates to the essay as a whole.

You might then be given a list of excerpts from different readings, each excerpt identified by a letter. Let's assume that the "College Girl" excerpt is identified by the letter "d," as it is on p. 221:

d. "You're looking at a very different kind of situation in the year 2000. Most people don't know what prostitution looks like. People have no clue," says sex-trade researcher John Lowman, a professor of criminology at Simon Fraser University in Vancouver.

If you haven't already done so, read the essay "College Girl to Call Girl" (Reader, p. 388) and write out your answer in one solid paragraph or two.

Some instructors might give you the choice to come prepared knowing one of several readings and allow you to choose the excerpt from the reading you wish to deal with. Other instructors might want you to be prepared to explain excerpts from several course readings. This question may be presented in various ways, but the underlying skills needed are the same.

Here is how you might answer the question in the previous Practice activity box, drawing upon the information you prepared for yourself in your checklist, process description, and summary preparations. Instructors usually request a short answer to this question (of one or two paragraphs), so you need to identify the relationship as precisely as you can.

Sample student explanation of an excerpt relationship

Excerpt "d" comes from Sarah Schmidt's article of investigative journalism "College Girl to Call Girl," originally published in the Toronto *Globe and Mail*. This excerpt sets up the main claim of the article: that discreet off-street prostitution is significantly on the rise because middle-class students, confronted by rising costs and other pressures on the middle class, have entered the business. Professor Lowman's quoted words appear near the opening, right after a lengthy character description of Stacy. Stacy is depicted as going about her typical moonlighting "business" as an off-street prostitute. Further descriptions of Stacy use words like "scores," suggesting that she is in essence a prostitute like any other, even though she is a middle-class student dressed like a middle-class student.

Relying on interviews with student prostitutes, professors of criminology, and others connected to the field, Schmidt states that tuition fees have risen vastly over nine years and that a large percentage of Canada's sex trade comprises off-street activity. Right after telling Schmidt that "[m]ost people don't know what prostitution looks like," Lowman goes on to say, "What we have is a *class-based* system of prostitution" (my emphasis). This article implicitly argues the thesis (main claim) stated above, supported by the investigative evidence of numerous interview subjects and an understood attitude that the middle-class public in general denies or ignores this activity. This excerpt drives home the actual situation—what is happening and what is denied—and thus prepares us to discover or infer reasons why this is happening and why it is denied. Because Schmidt uses the detached third person, typical of investigative reporting, she does not state her own opinion. That of Professor Lowman, an authority quoted in the essay's beginning therefore carries special weight.

✏ PRACTICE

Reread the preceding sample explanation of an excerpt relationship by student Valerie Desjardins. Answer the following question:

Is there a topic sentence in this paragraph, one sentence that essentially answers the question?

We suggest that the essential answer does appear in one topic sentence. In this case, the topic sentence is the second sentence of the paragraph, not the first, because the writer chose to use the opening sentence to identify where the excerpt appears. Some writers might subordinate the information in the first sentence within a longer opening topic sentence:

> Excerpt "d," which comes from Sarah Schmidt's article of investigative journalism "College Girl to Call Girl," originally published in the Toronto *Globe and Mail,* sets up the main claim of the article: that discreet off-street prostitution is significantly on the rise because middle-class students, confronted by rising costs and other pressures on the middle class, have entered the business.

If Desjardins had written either of these topic sentences and nothing else, she would deserve several marks for this section, as this explanation is so concise and specific. The other parts of her answer are dedicated to expanding on this basic insight, reinforcing why the excerpt is important. The paragraphs are about the excerpt, not about the essay in some general or vague sense. To answer this sort of exam question well, you have to have analyzed the reading with the thorough understanding that an essay is a process involving the operation and cooperation of various parts.

For further practice in this difficult skill, here is one more practice activity.

 PRACTICE

Read the essay "The Ways of Meeting Oppression" (Reader, p. 442). See if you can explain in 250 to 300 words how the following excerpt from this reading relates to the essay as a whole:

a. A second way that oppressed people sometimes deal with oppression is to resort to violence and corroding hatred.

Student Explanation of the Above Excerpt

The following answer to excerpt "a" above was written by student Bernadette Cymbaluk on her mid-term examination at Blue Quills First Nations College in February 2006. Students could not look at the essay; they had to know it well going into the exam, and they had limited time in which to complete the response.

Examination answer by Bernadette Cymbaluk

> Quotation "a" comes from Martin Luther King's essay "The Ways of Meeting Oppression." King argues that resorting to hatred and brutality is only a temporary, ineffective means of responding to mistreatment. He further argues that violence is impractical because it results in destruction for parties on both sides. It is also immoral because it demeans the human race; violence seeks to "annihilate" rather than correct. In using violence as a tool against injustice, African-Americans risk consigning their future generations to a legacy of chaos, loneliness, and bitterness. King argues that this is not the way.

In contrast to hatred and violence, King explains, there are two other means of meeting oppression: consent and peaceful resistance. Living willingly under the veil of injustice serves to wear on the spirit of the oppressed; eventually their lives are engulfed in "negative freedom and resignation." King argues that to consent with an unjust system is as evil as the act of oppression itself. Moreover, the African-American does not gain the respect of people everywhere by acquiescing to the way of the coward. King argues that the other and preferred way of dealing with oppression is peaceful resistance. African-Americans must embrace this method if they are to transcend racial injustice. In taking this path, they will find honour and their rightful opportunity in society. They must meet their oppressor with unbending strength and courage.

King's essay uses classification-division as its structure. Its thesis is there are three ways of meeting oppression: acquiescence, violence and hatred, and peaceful resistance. Excerpt "a" gives strong support to King's main point; it elaborates against the second way, the method of hatred and brutality. The excerpt points to historical evidence, in that section of the essay, that countries engaging in violence have gained nothing but destruction itself.

Commentary on Bernadette Cymbaluk's Answer

Notice that Cymbaluk repeats the verb "argues" in describing the process of this essay. Chapter 15, "The Summary," recommends that you find precise verbs to convey, often in a single word, the rhetorical purpose and strategy of the essay being summarized.

Note that Cymbaluk has memorized and quoted or paraphrased from the essay central words not repeated in the excerpt itself.

Cymbaluk does not give quite as much attention to rhetorical methods in her answer as we find in the previous excerpt relationship dealing with "College Girl." Given that King's essay is more direct and explicit than Schmidt's, however, Cymbaluk's greater attention to summarizing ideas and lessened attention to rhetorical methods make sense.

FINAL WORD

As we have seen, the ability to identify the role of an excerpt in relation to the overall meaning of the larger reading to which it belongs draws on summarization and rhetorical process description. Understanding what is said, especially in more ironic forms, often requires drawing inferences from the figurative meanings of words and images, recognizing how tone contributes to meaning. This interpretation requires you to use your judgment about what the author is really saying—not the same thing as using your judgment to evaluate the reliability or merit of what the author is saying (which is the evaluative stage of critical thinking). Explaining how an excerpt relates to the whole is not an exercise in the evaluation stage of critical thinking. It is an exercise in the summarizing skills and the analyzing skills involved in the first stage of critical thinking—breaking down subjects into their constituent parts and recognizing relationships between those parts.

Section 4 Oral
Presentations

INTRODUCTION

Many of us face the task of writing and delivering oral presentations. These may take the form of student seminars, business meetings, or addresses at community, political, or family gatherings. Speechwriting has much in common with essay writing, but there are some notable differences, because speechwriting must account for oral dynamics. Developing and delivering your presentation includes more than just writing your text or notes. You need to account for audience situation by preparing for oral delivery and practising the skills that ensure a successful presentation. The following chapter helps you with both writing and delivering your oral presentation so that it achieves its purpose as oral communication.

Chapter 21
The Oral Presentation

Presentation audiences have particular expectations, and these place special demands on the speaker. The following chapter outlines five ways in which you, as a speech-writer, can assist your audience. It also provides special tips to deal with the four different modes of presentation. Finally, it provides detailed assistance with how to develop and deliver a presentation using any of the modes.

FIVE WAYS TO ASSIST YOUR AUDIENCE AS SPEECHWRITER

In many ways, writing for public speaking is similar to writing an essay. You still need to know your audience and probably to structure your speech around a direct-list thesis statement containing a manageable number of points. You need an introduction, a conclusion, and smooth transitions. There are, however, important differences between writing for the page and writing for oral presentation.

When you write a speech, always keep in mind that the audience will be listening to the **rhythms** and **enunciations of a voice**, not reading text. Your audience cannot go back and check words or ideas that they have trouble grasping. Although an oral presentation makes special demands on you as an author, you can help your listeners in a number of ways.

1. First, *use informal, conversational language* appropriate to your purpose and to your audience. Use terminology that is familiar to that group. For instance, if you are addressing a group of horse owners, it would be appropriate to use the technical phrase "centre the pommel of the saddle over the withers." A group of novice riders would be confused and eventually alienated by these terms if you continued your speech without explaining them. Use short sentences. Sentence fragments are acceptable in oral speech and can be used to great effect.

2. *Emphasize colourful, concrete language.* Your audience will remember word pictures more easily than extended abstract ideas. Use your word pictures to give vitality to your concepts.

3. *Use previews, repetition, and internal summaries* to present your points clearly and remind the reader of their importance. Make sure that you have included concise internal summaries sufficient for a *listening* audience to make the necessary connections between your main points and between these main points and the overall thesis.

4. In most cases, you will want to *state your thesis clearly* in the introduction and again in the conclusion.

5. A speech has no footnotes, so, for ethical reasons, *cite sources of information and quotations* as you speak. Vary the ways you introduce your quoted material: "One expert, Susan Smith, contends that . . . "; "As Peter Brown points out . . . "; and "According to Melanie Jones . . . . " Such variety will keep your listeners alert to the sometimes multiple sources in your presentation.

Simple, concrete language, internal summaries, and short, uncluttered sentences will give your points impact for the listening audience.

MODES OF ORAL PRESENTATION

The four modes of oral presentation are

- extemporaneous
- manuscript
- memorized
- impromptu

Each of these modes is useful in certain situations, although the extemporaneous approach is generally the most effective.

Extemporaneous Presentations

In the extemporaneous mode, you speak with only key words and phrases written on file cards to remind you of your main points. This approach allows you to maintain eye contact with your audience and move freely as you speak, yet you have cues to keep you from losing your place. Extemporaneous speaking usually sounds the most natural. The section below on "Developing the Oral Presentation" (p. 234) will look at ways you can prepare a speech to be presented extemporaneously.

Reading from Manuscript

In some circumstances, you may wish to read from a full-text manuscript. This mode of delivery is most often used when speeches are televised (usually read off a teleprompter) or in situations where exact wording is crucial. For example, although Pierre Elliott Trudeau was known for his smoothly delivered, colourful extemporaneous speeches, his address to the nation on October 16, 1970, when he announced his decision to invoke martial law in Montreal, was very different. He delivered this televised speech seated at a desk, reading from a carefully worded manuscript that he held in his hand. He used this delivery to signal to viewers that he was in control of the situation and that his plan, like his speech, had been carefully thought through. You can view the speech at <http://archives.cbc.ca/IDCC-1-71-101-618/conflict_war/october_crisis/>.

This sense of careful planning is one of the strengths of using a manuscript when speaking. If you speak confidently, an oral presentation from a prepared manuscript can enhance both your perceived control of the situation and your material. This style does have weaknesses, however. One of these is the loss of eye contact. We have all seen local commercials featuring merchants who are not used to reading from teleprompters. Their eyes look glazed and move from side to side as they read. It takes practice to make yourself appear to be speaking to the viewer. Reading from a paper interferes with eye contact between speaker and audience even more. A class of public-speaking students who viewed the Trudeau speech said his quick glances away from the text and up to the camera made him look "shifty" and as if he were "hiding something." This effect can occur whether the speech is televised or delivered live. A second weakness, one regularly demonstrated by the local commercials mentioned above, is that most people sound stilted or monotonous when they read. Modulate your voice as naturally as possible during manuscript delivery and mark your text ahead of time for words you would like to pronounce more emphatically or more softly. You may also wish to mark the text where natural or even extended pauses occur. Finally, if you lose your place, it can be difficult to find it again. If you choose to deliver a speech with a manuscript, highlight or underline important points and rehearse the speech thoroughly so that you can maintain as much eye contact as possible.

Memorized Presentations

Some professional speakers present speeches from memory. This allows the speaker to maintain eye contact while retaining precise wording. For most people, however, this is a dangerous method. People who are not professional speakers or actors usually use a sing-song voice when they speak material they have memorized. If you forget part of a memorized speech, you risk a long and embarrassing pause while you try to remember your chain of words. Either of these problems may cause your audience to remember the speech in a way you'd rather they didn't. (If you do go blank, improvise—rephrase your last idea and keep talking until your text comes back to you.)

You may wish to memorize parts of an extemporaneous speech. Speakers often like to memorize the introduction, the thesis statement, and the conclusion. This technique gives you the strengths of precise wording and eye contact, but is not so sustained a memory task as to allow problems to present themselves.

Impromptu Presentations

In business meetings or informal gatherings, you may be called upon to "say a few words" unexpectedly or to respond to a point that has been made. In such cases, you need to make an impromptu presentation. Even in these situations, you can and should structure your thoughts. Jot down a few notes if you have time. Decide what your objective is and state it as clearly as possible. That will serve as your thesis statement. Think of one or two points and evidence to support your thesis. Summarize your thesis and your main points as you conclude. Listeners will appreciate your ability to present your thoughts in a simple, concise, structured way.

If you are a member of a community business association, for example, and you are suddenly invited to respond to a concern about liquor laws during a brief meeting, you may be best advised to organize your thoughts around the implications of any changes to or violations of current liquor restrictions. Examples from the community's experience would help illustrate your points. In such an impromptu address, the audience would understand that you are speaking provisionally, offering not shaped conclusions but ideas to be discussed.

Each of these four modes of presenting an oral speech is useful in certain situations. One speech may use several modes: the body of the speech may be delivered extemporaneously while the introduction and conclusion are memorized, quotations and statistics read, and questions answered impromptu. As the extemporaneous mode is the most effective in most situations, the following section will focus on developing that form of speech.

DEVELOPING THE ORAL PRESENTATION

For many people, anxiety is the first obstacle to overcome for a good oral presentation. In fact, a survey conducted by *Psychology Today* (quoted by Lyle W. Mayer in *Fundamentals of Voice and Diction,*10th ed., 1994) found that some people are more afraid of public speaking than they are of death. So if you are nervous, recognize that many people share your feelings. Also realize that "nerves" can help you focus and energize your presentation as you control and channel them rather than allow them to control you. Remember that your **preparation**, your **practice**, and your **focus** are the essential elements in developing a good oral presentation. Whether you are a nervous speaker or not, these three elements are essential for a successful delivery of your carefully written speech, and your attention to them will see you through a case of nervous hesitation.

Preparation

Be absolutely sure you have done your homework, including all the research you would do for any good piece of writing. You may find the following steps helpful:

- Write out a full outline of your speech.
- Highlight the key words and phrases that the audience must hear in order to understand your message.
- Make up cue cards for yourself. Write only the key words and phrases. You may wish to write out the full text of your thesis statement and any quoted material and statistics, but keep these as brief as possible.

Practice

Perhaps the most valuable advice that can be given to a speaker is to practise, practise, practise! Most oral presentations are not rehearsed enough. Speakers who go over their speeches too little in advance undermine their messages as well as themselves. Practise your speech until you can run through it smoothly, using only your cue cards for reference. Practise in front of a mirror to find the best hand gestures to emphasize your points while appearing natural and to eliminate excessive, distracting body language. If you will present while standing, practise standing, making sure your posture is straight but relaxed and that you don't fall into bad habits of fidgeting or shifting from side to side. If you will be seated when you speak, practise a good seated posture that helps you appear confident. Again, try to avoid excessive hand gestures or fidgeting that will advertise any discomfort.

You may wish to make a video of one of your practice runs. Or you may wish to round up a sympathetic audience of friends or family members. Even a child or a pet (other than a goldfish) can help you work at making eye contact and varying your voice.

As well as rehearsing the text of the speech and your presentation of it, prepare for questions the audience may ask you, and practise your answers. Give special consideration to tough questions that may come up so that you will answer them confidently. Even if exact or even similar versions of the questions you have anticipated do *not* arise, you will usually be able to use parts of your prepared answers for other, unanticipated questions.

Focus

There are several techniques you can use to focus on the task at hand rather than on your butterflies as presentation day draws near. The most commonly used techniques are controlled breathing, simple kinetic exercises, and visualization. Whether you are nervous or not, these techniques can help you achieve peak performance.

Breathing

The beauty of breathing exercises is that you can do them lying on your back in a darkened room or seated at a boardroom table surrounded by others. The simple progression described on the next page will help you to concentrate.

First, just notice your breath—is it fast and high in your chest? Begin to slow it down. Breathe deeply into your diaphragm (or belly). Feel your bottom ribs swing out and up slightly as you inhale. Once your breath is low and slow, count silently as you inhale and exhale. Start inhaling, for a count of two, hold for a count of two, and exhale for a count of three. Work up to inhale for a count of eight, hold for a count of eight, and exhale for a count of ten. The count should be slow enough to be relaxing, yet not so slow that you run out of air. If you feel light-headed, return to normal breathing.

Kinetic Exercises

You can use this technique while lying on the floor or discreetly while in a room full of people. Find a relaxed position, seated or lying down. If you are alone, close your eyes. Use the breathing exercises until your breath is relaxed. Starting with your toes and working up to your face, clench and release each muscle group in your body. Hold each set of muscles for a slow count of 10 before relaxing them. Let yourself feel the release for a moment before you move on to the next group of muscles, working your way slowly up your legs, trunk, arms and hands, to neck and head. Pay special attention to places where you hold tension; the shoulders and the jaw are the greatest tension points for many of us.

Visualization

Many professional and top-ranking athletes and executives include visualization in their preparations. Visualization allows you to rehearse your "event" (in this case, your speech) in a relaxed, positive way that reinforces the correct techniques, making errors in your presentation less likely. It is good to try a visualization in the final day or two before you present. You can also do a mini-visualization on the spot if you find yourself losing confidence just before you are to speak. To practise visualization privately, find a relaxed position, seated or lying down. Close your eyes. Run through the breathing exercises and the kinetic sequence. When you feel relaxed, picture yourself in a favourite place where you feel safe and content, perhaps a sandy beach by the ocean. Enjoy the image for a moment. Relax into the sand. Feel the sun's warmth on your face and body. Hold on to the relaxed feeling as you picture yourself preparing to leave. See yourself packing everything you need for the presentation. You remember everything. You arrive at the space where you will present in plenty of time. You check it out and set everything up. It all goes smoothly. Watch your audience arriving. You are relaxed, they are friendly. It is your time to speak. You feel confident and prepared. Visualize yourself delivering your entire speech smoothly. (Do not check your notes or speak out loud—just watch the "movie" of your own polished presentation.) Watch the audience. They are clearly interested. As you finish, they applaud. You smoothly and constructively answer their questions. After you close, they compliment you on the effectiveness of your speech. Open your eyes and hold on to that happy, confident feeling.

If, in the moments before you speak, you start to feel anxious, guide yourself back to your positive visualization. Remember that few problems are beyond your ability to cope with in the context of your presentation. If you forget your speech, you have your cue cards. If you cannot answer a question, replying with an honest "I don't know" can be very effective in sustaining your audience's respect when you follow it with an assurance that you will find the information. Most important of all, see yourself succeeding.

Committed preparation, practice, and focus will help make your presentation an experience that is more pleasant for you and more effective for your listeners. In the longer term, there are many other ways to build your presentation skills.

PRESENTATION SKILLS: VOICE AND BODY

Your voice and body are tremendously important in communicating your presentation. You cannot escape them. They will affect the audience's perception of your message, so use them to fullest advantage. Develop vocal flexibility and physical expressiveness. You can incorporate the following exercises into your rehearsals of one important presentation; you will find they become more effective if you do them over time. If your chosen career involves a lot of public speaking, you may want to consider joining an organization or speaking group where you can hone your skills continually with experienced speakers. If you have speech problems (nasal voice, soft consonants, etc.) or are very inhibited physically, classes in voice, yoga, tai chi, or even kick-boxing can make a big difference in the way your presentations are received.

Voice

Using volume, rate, pitch, and articulation appropriately is as important in public speaking as it is in singing. Speakers who know how to make these vocal qualities work for them deliver many otherwise questionable presentations convincingly. On the other hand, audiences overlook many thoughtful arguments in presentations when the speakers mumble in a monotone or hurriedly spit out their points. In oral presentations the speaker's voice will either contribute to or detract from the spoken content. There is no third alternative.

Volume

As for the volume of your voice, first of all you must be *audible*. Ask the audience if everyone can hear you, especially if you will be speaking without a microphone. Most people speak too softly when addressing a group. Unless you have been told you have a loud voice, always speak at a level that feels slightly too loud without yelling. If you are soft-spoken, speak loudly every time you practise your speech.

A speaker who tries to be loud by straining the throat sounds shrill rather than confident. Learn to support your voice from the diaphragm. Start by breathing deeply. Use your diaphragm (just above your stomach) to push the air out slowly. After you have done this a few times silently, do the same on a hiss, then on an "ahhhh." As you build strength in the muscles between your ribs and your abdomen, start reading your text at a comfortable, fairly loud level. Each time you do the exercise, read further on one breath, always stopping before you start to strain. If you are unsure how to get started, perhaps consult a singing teacher or a voice coach.

Rate

The rate or pace of your speech is also very important. Second to insufficient volume, *racing*—speaking at a rushed rate—is the most common way speakers lose their audiences. If you race because you are nervous, use pauses to force yourself to slow down, even writing "pause here" on your cue cards. If your speech is running long, skip parts. **Do not race.** It is far better for the listeners to get some of your points than none. When you practise, speak more slowly than you normally do. Ask a friend to listen to you run through your speech and signal to you if you are going too fast.

Pitch

Another essential characteristic of speech is your pitch. Most people speak within a very narrow range, seldom using the upper and lower parts of their registers. So think of your presentation as a kind of performance, which it is. Think of pitch as a dramatic instrument that can help establish your presence and your content. Listen to a speaker you find interesting. You will likely notice that he or she uses a slightly wider range of pitch than most of us do in day-to-day conversation. You too can develop this ability through practice.

Articulation

Clear articulation is extremely important when an audience is relying on your oral delivery of information. You can confuse your listeners by phonetically substituting a "d" for a "t" when you are explaining unfamiliar terms. Over the long term, you will find that tongue-twisters featuring consonants can be both enjoyable and useful for sharpening overly casual articulation. Say each tongue-twister several times; the first time, say it slowly to exaggerate each sound, then increasingly speed it up, but don't lose the clear consonants. Follow up by running through your speech, exaggerating the consonants.

Variation of Volume, Rate, and Pitch

Vary your volume, rate, and pitch when you practise your presentation at home. See what effect you create when you slow down and when you speak loudly or softly in making important points. Use the higher and lower parts of your range. Exaggerate. Move from deep down to high and squeaky. Race through some parts, slow to a crawl for others. Whisper a significant point or yell it like an old-time preacher.

Have fun with your whole presentation. After you have done this a few times, run through the speech in a normal speaking voice, holding onto the vocal variations that you found effective.

After you have practised bringing these examples of vocal variety into your speech, record your presentation and check for crisp articulation and interesting, natural-sounding modulation. You will begin to recognize your speaking voice as a responsive instrument, a device valuable in expressing your prepared content and furthering your career.

Body Language

People take in far more information through their eyes than their ears. Body language is therefore an important tool for any presenter. Eye contact and facial expression, posture, and gesture all send important signals to your audience.

Eye Contact

Novice speakers find making eye contact with audience members difficult, but such communication is essential to establishing rapport. Speakers who make eye contact appear friendly, confident, and candid about their messages (even if they are not). If you are nervous about eye contact, practise at home with someone you know. If you present to a small group, make eye contact at some point with each person. If you present to a group of more than 20 people, divide the audience mentally into four parts. If you make eye contact with at least one person in each quadrant, the entire audience will feel included. Choose a sympathetic-looking person to look at if you are nervous, but don't stare at one person too much or you may make him or her more nervous than you are. If there is a bright light on you and the audience area is dim, make "eye contact" where you know someone will be.

Facial Expression

Facial expression also counts for a great deal in public speaking. Smile as soon as you begin your presentation. This will warm the audience to you and make you feel more confident. Smile where appropriate throughout the presentation. It will make a big difference in the listeners' perception of you and your message. In one study customers in a bank were asked to estimate the time they had spent waiting in line for a teller. Those whom the teller had greeted with a smile after their wait in line underestimated their total wait time; the other customers, who received no greeting smile, overestimated their time in line! If you tend not to smile when you are nervous, you may want to add "smile" on your cue cards at strategic spots.

Posture

A good, relaxed posture will also help you appear competent and confident. As you stand, picture your feet sinking into the floor and the crown of your head being gently pulled up by a string hanging from the ceiling above you. You want to avoid a stiff, military posture and at the same time avoid rounded shoulders, slouching, or hunching. You also want to keep track of what your feet are doing—imaginatively sinking them into the floor—comfortably—to anchor you and help you avoid aimless pacing. Note whether you are speaking at a podium that is open at its bottom and allows the audience a full view of your legs and feet. Speakers can often appear purposeful and strong above the podium, while their feet are fidgeting, twisting around each other, and even slipping their shoes on and off! On a raised platform, your busy feet and not your words will become the focal point of your presentation. Change your posture occasionally, of course, but exercise some physical self-discipline to create a minimum of distractions from your presentation.

Feel free to move away from the podium, however. A podium forms a barrier between you and the audience. Leaving it and crossing the stage or floor toward the audience can be a powerful way to emphasize a point, as well as to enact your sense of comfort with your material and the audience itself. By demonstrating this degree of comfort, you will put the audience at ease, and people will be more likely to remember your particular presentation as both enjoyable and convincing.

Gestures

Gestures can greatly enhance a speech by making ideas visible. Keep them simple and natural, to amplify, not compete with, the points you are making in your presentation. For instance, an inclusive gesture on "all of us" visually underlines the meaning. Holding up fingers to count off your main points dramatizes the organization of your presentation. If you are not accustomed to "talking with your hands," decide on a few effective gestures and practise them as you run through your speech. Remember not to overdo gestures, however, since excessively "talking with your hands" can suggest a lack of faith in the power of your words and so undermine your ability to inform and convince through language, logic, analysis, and argument.

Your hands are very influential as you speak. Trembling hands are one of the most common giveaways of nervousness, and one of the most upsetting to speakers. As you speak, your hands shake and the paper rattles. This makes you self-conscious, so the paper rattles more. You cannot stop the trembling, but you can make it irrelevant if you use large file cards rather than paper for your notes. Without the rattling paper, neither the audience nor you will be distracted from your message. Ideally, you will speak from a key-word outline, so all the notes you need should fit on several cards. If you are speaking from a manuscript, place either the whole text or the bottom half flat on your desk or podium to anchor it and keep your hands from shaking. Contact with a steady surface will steady you.

Stretching, breathing, and relaxation exercises will all help you transform the stiffness of your nerves into the fluidity of effective movement, just as vocal exercises will make your voice more flexible and interesting to listen to. You can do these exercises as part of your preparation for a single speech; you will find them more effective if you make them part of your long-term routine.

PRESENTATION AIDS

As you move into final preparations, consider how you have incorporated presentation aids into your speech. These include all visual and audio aids, such as PowerPoint, transparencies, objects, video or audio recordings, and even your own appearance. Visual aids can be especially helpful in keeping your audience with you.

Computer-Generated Aids

Computer-generated aids are effective—*if* you know how to use them. However, many presentations begin late or are delivered with distracting technical difficulties because the speaker is unfamiliar with the program or the room (the outlet, the best place to project, or the best place to stand without blocking the audience's view). Nervous speakers sometimes fidget with a computer mouse, projecting a cursor that wanders distractingly over the image at the front of the room. If you are unfamiliar with the PowerPoint program but must use it, seek a knowledgeable assistant to run the program while you present—and be sure to practise with this person ahead of time. Above all, be prepared to present the speech without the presentation aid if you run into insurmountable technical difficulties. For instance, make a handout of the PowerPoint slides. Your audience will admire your courage and appreciate your consideration of their time.

Ten Tips for Using Visual Presentation Aids

1. Limit the number of aids you use so that they enhance your presentation without overwhelming it.
2. Keep your visual aids simple and uncluttered.
   - Use bulleted lists rather than sentences, with no more than six bullets to a list.
   - Simplify maps so they show only the features relevant to your presentation.
   - Make graphs as simple as possible and use clearly contrasting colours.
   - Use charts that contain the minimum of information you need to get your point across.
3. Ensure all lettering is legible and can be seen from the back of the room.
4. Talk to the audience, not to the aid.
5. Avoid blocking your own aid.
6. Reveal points only as you make them in your speech, or the audience will stop listening to you as they read ahead.

7. Decide on your strategy for distributing a handout; unless you have set up this written material so that the audience uses it to follow you point by point, distribute it when you have finished talking (for the same reason given in point 6). Reproduce photographs large enough that people at the back of the room can see them. Do not pass them around, as this will divide the audience into pockets of people concentrating on them rather than on what you are saying.

8. Do not plan to speak over recorded sound unless it is extremely soft.

9. Keep aids out of sight until you need them.

10. Make sure you have practised with and are in control of the aid. For example, always check that an overhead projector has a spare bulb. Avoid using live animals unless you know you can focus audience attention back on you; a litter of kittens will make a much bigger impact than you do and can quickly get out of control, but a well-trained adult dog may be helpful in a speech about seeing-eye dogs.

Your Appearance

Consider your appearance a powerful presentation aid, too. Dress with your audience in mind. Your T-shirt and jeans would likely alienate a corporate board of directors, while a business suit could have the same effect on an audience of inner-city teens. If you are uncertain of the social atmosphere or your audience's expectations of dress code, seek middle ground: wear dress pants or a simple skirt, dress shoes, and a plain shirt with a blazer you can easily remove or keep on for adding or reducing formality on the spot.

Nine Things to Do on the Day You Present

1. Arrive in plenty of time. Check out the room if it is unfamiliar to you, to make sure it has all the resources you need. Arrange and set up your presentation aids, so you won't keep your audience waiting while you fiddle with them later.

2. Keep your visualizations positive. Breathe.

3. When you begin, smile at the audience and establish eye contact with them individually. Stay in touch with them. If they look puzzled or bored, interact with them if possible: ask if there are any questions, or whether you need to explain anything again. Your honest interaction will keep the audience with you.

4. Speak conversationally. Very few audiences actually want you to fail. In your position, they would be nervous, too. Speaking to them as if they were ordinary people (which they are) will relax both you and them.

5. Find ways to make your presentation interesting as well as informative. Make jokes that illuminate the topic (generic jokes such as "ladies and germs" are rarely effective). Use natural gestures. Vary your voice. Use presentation aids.

6. Rephrase questions aloud as the audience asks them, since people at the back usually cannot hear the people at the front. Answer questions thoroughly, and do not be afraid of admitting you do not have the answer or that you may not have made up your mind on an issue. You may even use the question as an opportunity to strengthen your connection with your listeners by asking if there is anyone else in the audience who could answer.

7. Respect your time limit out of consideration to the audience and any other speakers, and signal clearly when you are drawing to a close. The only thing worse than a speaker who goes on and on is one who repeatedly says "And in conclusion," and then goes on and on.

8. Thank the audience and exit graciously. Save the introspective post-mortem for later.

9. When you do your self-examining post-mortem, look for the strengths, especially if you are usually hard on yourself. Allow yourself to enjoy your strong points and build on them for next time. Audiences enjoy listening to speakers who enjoy speaking!

THE PRESENTATION

In summary, there are many naturally gifted speakers in the world. You may wish to improve your speaking style by emulating one of them, but you need not *be* one of them to be an effective speaker. Respect your audience as you prepare your oral presentations. Carefully word and structure your work to make it effective as spoken text, both in its information and in its argumentation. Develop your ability to use your voice and body to enhance your message. Plan your presentations thoroughly, including your presentation aids. Your listeners will appreciate your respect for them and will receive your message with the warmth it deserves.

FINAL WORD

The principles in this chapter will enrich your writing as well as your speaking; future success may depend at least as much upon the one as upon the other.

Section 5 Completing the
Journey: Revision

INTRODUCTION

Revising contributes far more to a successful essay than many student writers initially realize. Depending on the amount of research required for your paper, the pre-writing and drafting stages will certainly absorb a substantial portion of your time. Nevertheless, you should spend at least 15 percent of your overall writing time on the final phase—revising.

To assist your work as self-editor, the following chapter offers three main steps: sharpening impact at key locations, correcting grammar, and polishing style. For each step, we connect you to the other parts of this textbook that directly support the specific editing principles involved. You should find this an efficient, simple way to gather what you have learned from this text into a final review and polish of your essays. Given all the work involved in pre-writing and drafting, why settle for lowered marks—even failure, or rejection by a publisher—simply because you did not take the final steps to perfect your work? Put in that 15 percent (or more) of revising time that professional writers dedicate to their work.

Chapter 22
Revising

Revising contributes as much to a successful essay as pre-writing and drafting. Think of revising as analogous to delivering an email. You may write the message, but if it sits in your drafts folder, it fails to cross the line from private record to wider communication. "Sending" the message, in this analogy, means executing three main editing steps that, taken together, may require several hours of work, depending on the assignment and your readiness as editor.

THREE STEPS OF REVISION

We recommend revising your essays according to the following three steps:

- Sharpen key locations.
- Correct grammar.
- Polish style.

Sharpen Key Locations

Key locations are introductions and thesis statements, topic sentences, and conclusions. The following sections assist with these topics:

Thesis statements	Chapter 5, Chapter 6
Topic sentences	Chapter 4, Chapter 5, and Chapter 6
Introductions and conclusions	Chapter 7

 PRACTICE
Sharpening Key Locations—Thesis, Topic Sentences, and Conclusion

Review the following version of "Beginning Riders." Consider what you might do to sharpen its thesis and topic sentences. Is there any sharpening touch you can add to the last sentence?

When you are done, see the end of this chapter, p. 253, for our sharpening suggestions and commentary.

Draft Essay for Revision Sharpen Thesis, Topic Sentences, Conclusion

Beginning Riders: The Untold Story

Joyce Miller

1   When a beginning rider mounts a horse for the first time, the rider feels awkward, unbalanced, and unsure of what to do. The horse feels exactly the same way.

2   The horse may adopt the attitude of a middle-aged family pet who belongs to the new rider's neighbour, best friend, or relative. This horse spends its time dreaming in the field, the carefree succession broken only for the odd pleasure ride. The horse doesn't much care what gets on its back, so long as the mounted thing doesn't expect much expenditure of energy. While the new rider tries several times to swing a leg high enough to get on without dislocating a hip, the horse catches a few winks. At an uncertain tap from the rider's heels, the horse ambles a couple of metres, then lowers its head to graze. This process is repeated several times. Thirty minutes later, the ride ends six metres from where it began. The rider is a little frustrated, but no mishaps have occurred and the horse's state of Zen remains undisturbed.

3   A higher level of energy and more experience with beginning riders creates a horse with a foreman mentality. This is usually a lesson or trail horse. The horse knows what needs to be done, quickly senses that the rider doesn't know what needs to be done, and sets out to do it as efficiently as possible. Intelligent new riders realize this and, with great relief, hand over control to the most competent member of the team. This works great until the horse decides it is time to (a) return to its stall, (b) visit with friends, or (c) clear the one-metre jump in the centre of the ring. The rider may come out of this ride embarrassed, but the worst injury is usually to the ego.

4   A third attitude belongs to the horse no beginner should ride, and few do for long. This horse may be the "really calm cutting horse" on Uncle Fred's ranch; the "excellent young prospect" being sold cheap by a dealer; or the high-octane, under-used acreage horse whose owner is sure he's safe to ride, although she's never been on him, because the previous owner was a 13-year-old (never mind that she was a 13-year-old provincial barrel racing champ). Such a horse has lots of energy, a lively imagination, and complete inexperience with beginning riders. The sensation of 100 to 200 pounds of yanking, wobbling weight on his back brings to life a race memory of killer cougars. He makes an instant, life-saving decision which would win him a berth in the Kentucky Derby if only anyone were there with a stopwatch, and if only he still had a rider on his back. This is definitely the most painful introduction to riding, but strangely enough, there are some riders who don't give up.

5   Despite frustration, terror, and/or pain (or perhaps because of them), the stubborn novice rider persists until he or she no longer flops on the horse like a sack of ill-sorted potatoes. The magic day arrives when balance and technique come together. Riding becomes almost effortless; the horse seems to respond to the thought of the rider. Best of all, it is clear that the horse enjoys the experience.

Correct Grammar

Given that many students lack a conscious command of grammar, part of the revising phase should include efforts to learn more about common errors and to find and correct those in the essay. The Handbook in this textbook assists you with grammar.

An efficient method of revising your essays for grammar is to test for the 15 common errors. Finding and correcting these should eliminate 90 percent or more of your grammar concerns. Sections 1 and 2 of the Handbook define and illustrate the terms used in the explanations of the common errors in Section 3 of the Handbook. If you aren't sure what a certain explanatory term means, check its definition in either Section 1 or Section 2. If the principle remains unclear, consult your instructor or someone with sound grammar knowledge. Revision requires that you have sufficient knowledge of grammar to be able to find and correct your deviations from standard usage.

PRACTICE
Correcting the 15 Common Errors

Edit the following two paragraphs making as few changes as necessary to remove the common errors.

Discuss your corrections with your classmates and instructor.

Sample Writing

Paragraph One: Correct for the 15 Common Errors

1 *The Soprano's* have all the features of a Shakespearian history play, as defined by Norrie Epstein; battlefield heroics, familial relationships, feisty characters, power politics and covert scheming (151). Like Prince Harry overcoming Hotspur in Henry IV,

Part 2, Tony prevailed over an attempted assassination (episode 12), as did Chris (episode 21). This is where Chris almost died, so bravery was much on display. Shakespeares use of domestic scenes are paralleled in *The Sopranos* by similar scenes of family relationships involving Tony, Carmela, Meadow, Anthony Junior, and various other members of the extended crime "family." Feisty Shakespearean characters such as Hotspur, Falstaff, and Mistress Quickly find their modern counterparts in *Sopranos* regulars like Chris, Uncle Junior, and Janice. Each has their own feisty manner. In particular, Tony resembled Henry IV in their concealing of private anguish beneath a mask of political action. On the matter of power politics, Shakespeare's histories began with the question of whom will succeed to power, and would there be an answer to the bitter feud which occurred between the houses of Lancaster and York. Similarly, *The Sopranos* begins with the death of the local crime boss, Jackie Aprile, Sr., a consequential power vacuum, and problems of how to gain control according to the old code of honour which only has kept its meaning for Tony. Comparing Shakespeares' language to language in *The Soprano's,* a parallel exists in many visual and linguistic puns and double entendres such as the name of the informant character Pussy (executed at the end of season two). This is little observed, it seems. An essay on the topic, however, is upcoming. Uniting all of these similarities is the strong appeal that both the histories and *The Sopranos* has for their audiences, we envy the rich and the powerful, the vicarious thrill of sin and danger is experienced, in the ruthless main characters the same moral compromise which governs our own lives are recognized. A shared worldview despite the different time periods.

Work Cited

Epstein, Norrie. *Friendly Shakespeare: A Thoroughly Painless Guide to the Best of the Bard.*
    Penguin: New York, 1993. Print.

Sample Writing

Paragraph Two: Correct for the 15 Common Errors,
Misspellings, and Other Errors

1 Eighties music is not as bad or culturally frightening as many people say. Although its hard to defend Duran Duran. One band, Cameo had a great funk song entitled "Word Up" in the early Eighties. Two other band's styles from this decade have defined alot of modern music here and now; U2 and REM. Besides these two examples of writerly talent and innovative musicianship we need to really remember that some of Tom Petty's, AC/DC's, Bananarama's, and, of course Guns n' Roses' best work appeared in the Eighties. However the mysterious problem of all those one-hit or two-hit wonders are a concern to any true connoisseur of this decade's music, for instance: 'Til

Tuesday's "Voices Carry," A-Ha's "Take On Me," Adam Ant's "Goodie Two Shoes," The Bangles' "Walk Like an Egyptian," Fine Young Cannibals' "Good Thing," and Glass Tiger's "Don't Forget Me [When I'm Gone]." Did these artists' managers suddenly run out of ideas, were they abducted by extra-terrestrials or by Lou Reed and Iggy Pop? Considering Elton John's recent work, is it better too burn out then fade away?

Polish Style

To make sure that your style is appropriate and consistent, refer to the following parts of the text:

Tone (word choice, sentence structure)	Chapter 1, Chapter 2, Chapter 16 (persuasive appeals shaped to purpose) Tones chart (inside back cover)
Paragraph craft	Chapter 4
Sentence craft	Handbook, Section 3, Common Errors 1, 5, 11, 12, and 14
Citations	Research Guide, Sections 5–8

As Chapters 1 and 2 explain, you need to establish and maintain your level of language, through careful word choice, in service to the purpose and audience for your essay. You also need to review your sentences to ensure that they are not too informal and that they are contributing through effective rhythm, patterns, and impact points. A particularly important part of revising for style is to improve conciseness. That is the editorial function that we specifically illustrate in the rest of this chapter.

Revise for Conciseness

Conciseness is a form of beauty, yet few people are spontaneously concise writers. Conciseness often defies us in early drafts, and even in subsequent ones. Sometimes you can accomplish this value only after you return to your writing with a strengthened sense of what you are trying to express; economy of expression will match clarity of concept.

Conciseness requires the elimination of unnecessary words and phrases. Delete clunky phrases such as "in terms of," "about the question of," "are indicative of," and "to consider in the context of," which clutter up your sentences and your potentially succinct and crisp expression.

Remember that much redundancy also results from a hasty disregard for logic. Delete unnecessary re-statements of what you have already said or clearly implied.

Draft introduction

Video lottery terminals, available to the public, pose a danger for many of the vulnerable people who are playing them. They are often located in bars, where people tend to drink and lose some of their best judgment about how to spend their money and their time. They sometimes pay out money, but over a year, what would someone who likes to play them, spend annually? Probably a lot more than you would think. The government, bars, and casinos may make money from VLT machines, but not the players, especially those who start to become addicted. Does society have a duty to intervene with new laws and regulations when people's choices harm themselves only and not really anyone else? Should society ban video lottery terminals?

Revision

Video lottery terminals (VLTs) pose a danger for many vulnerable people. The VLTs are often located in bars, where some people tend to lose their best judgment about how to spend their money and time. The machines sometimes pay out money, but over a year, what would a frequent user spend? The amount would probably be a lot more than the winnings. The government, bars, and casinos certainly make money from VLT machines, but the players generally do not, especially those who become addicted. Does society have a duty to intervene with new laws and regulations when people's choices harm themselves only rather than anyone else? Government obligations in relation to video lottery terminals are still dangerously uncertain.

Commentary

The draft introduction's first sentence is a good opening but can be far more concise. Some of this conciseness comes from a stricter logic in expression. Since all video terminal lotteries are "available to the public" (with restrictions only according to age), we can safely delete this qualifier as unnecessary. Similarly, the "vulnerable people" for whom VLTs pose a danger must be those "who are playing them," so we can delete this qualifier as redundant, too. Certainly other people may financially suffer from the VLT user's habit, such as his or her children, but the "vulnerable people" in the paragraph are the gambling participants.

Draft paragraph

In terms of the very many persistent concerns about the question of our ongoing water safety after the frightening scare over health in the Canadian town of Walkerton, Ontario, all Canadians need to start to consider the many facts about all this. The expectations that we have formed that our water will always be safe and hazard-free for us to drink are indicative of how we tend to rely far too much on the bureaucratic assurances that are given to us by people who work in the government agency. Like our other natural resources, water is a valuable resource that we cannot take for granted or fail to consider in the context of supply.

Revised paragraph

After the health crisis in Walkerton, Ontario, all Canadians need to consider the facts about ongoing water safety. Our expectations that water will always be safe to drink indicate how we rely dangerously on bureaucratic, not scientific, assurances. Water, like our other natural resources, cannot be taken for granted as an endless or self-sustaining resource.

Commentary

The revision drops unnecessary words and helps the statements to end with force, placing key terms at the impact points ending the first and third sentences. Since "bureaucratic assurances" are by definition issued by "people who work in a government agency," we can easily eliminate this doubling of meaning. Similarly, if we call water a "valuable resource," then it's understood that "we cannot take for granted or fail to consider" its importance. Calling water a "valuable resource" is fine by itself. We can delete the unnecessary restatement of what that means.

Sample conclusion

To conclude, self-employment is thus far more challenging and riskier than one would think sometimes. The problem of small resources makes competition with corporations tough. A new study claims governments do not take individual small businesses seriously until after five years. Making and maintaining business networks is also difficult, since most of your time is usually spent completing what work or contracts you have already. Even the problems of insurance and benefits are worrisome. Therefore, despite a self-employed person's being his or her own boss and taking lunch breaks whenever, there are reasons why 70 percent of first-year businesses fail and many people falsify tax claims and don't give much time or money to charities anymore.

Revised conclusion

Self-employment is thus far more challenging and riskier than one would think. Small resources make competition with corporations difficult. Making contacts and maintaining business networks are also difficult, since time is usually spent completing work or contracts under way. Even the problems of insurance and benefits are worrisome. Therefore, despite the attractive independence of self-employment, there are reasons that 70 percent of first-year businesses fail. Many of these failures are directly linked to the obstacles of self-employment.

Commentary

Your essay conclusion is a place where conciseness is imperative. As you can see, the revised version compresses the original. The goal of an essay conclusion is to drive home the controlling idea of the essay (presumably the idea that self-employment is riskier and more difficult than one would think) and briskly reinforce the reasons for that view. Many editors consider that the word "reason" contains the word "why," a redundancy similar to "continuing on."

Final Word on Conciseness

All redundancies are a form of illogic. Careful thinking about the nature of the object, person, scene, or concept you wish to describe will eliminate such "doubling" in your writing and, in the process, give you greater clarity and emphasis.

Response to Practice Activity Sharpening Key Locations

Following is a sample of how the sharpening practice on p. 246 might be resolved. The editor has added or made changes to the words in italics. Discuss with your coursemates and instructor what these changes in italics have accomplished.

Sample Revised Essay Sharpened Thesis, Topic Sentences, Conclusion

Beginning Riders: The Untold Story

Joyce Miller

1 When a beginning rider mounts a horse for the first time, the rider feels awkward, unbalanced, and unsure of what to do. The horse feels exactly the same way. *As a result, a horse develops one of three attitudes to beginning riders: playing dead, taking control, and taking off.*

2 *The first attitude* [t]he horse may adopt *is that* of a middle-aged family pet who belongs to the new rider's neighbour, best friend, or relative. This horse spends its days dreaming in the field, the carefree succession broken only for the odd pleasure ride. The horse doesn't much care what gets on its back, so long as the mounted thing doesn't expect much expenditure of energy. While the new rider tries several times to swing a leg high enough to get on without dislocating a hip, the horse catches a few winks. At an uncertain tap from the rider's heels, the horse ambles about a metre, then lowers its head to graze. This process is repeated several times. Thirty minutes later, the ride ends six metres from where it began. The rider is a little frustrated, but no mishaps have occurred and the horse's state of Zen remains undisturbed.

New words clarify cause-effect concern of controlling idea and provide reasons for controlling idea that horses don't take to beginners.

3 A higher level of energy and more experience with beginning riders creates a horse with *the second attitude:* a foreman mentality. This is usually a lesson or trail horse. The horse knows what needs to be done, quickly senses that the rider doesn't know what needs to be done, and sets out to do it as efficiently as possible. Intelligent new riders realize this and, with great relief, hand over control to the most competent member of the team. This works great until the horse decides it is time to (a) return to its stall, (b) visit with friends, or (c) clear the one-metre jump in the centre of the ring. The rider may come out of this ride embarrassed, but the worst injury is usually to the ego.

Words added to create explicit link to thesis statement's reference to "three attitudes."

Changing "A" to "The" adds precision: not just *any* third attitude, but *the* final one of those referred to at the start.

4   The A̶ third attitude belongs to the horse no beginner should ride, and few do for long. This horse may be the "really calm cutting horse" on Uncle Fred's ranch; the "excellent young prospect" being sold cheap by a dealer; or the high-octane, under-used acreage horse whose owner is sure he's safe to ride, although she's never been on him, because the previous owner was a 13-year-old (never mind that she was a 13-year-old provincial barrel racing champ). Such a horse has lots of energy, a lively imagination, and complete inexperience with beginning riders. The sensation of 100 to 200 pounds of yanking, wobbling weight on his back brings to life a race memory of killer cougars. He makes an instant, life-saving decision which would win him a berth in the Kentucky Derby if only anyone were there with a stopwatch, and if only he still had a rider on his back. This is definitely the most painful introduction to riding, but strangely enough, there are some riders who don't give up.

5   Despite frustration, terror, and/or pain (or perhaps because of them), the stubborn novice rider persists until he or she no longer flops on the horse like a sack of ill-sorted potatoes. The magic day arrives when balance and technique come together. Riding becomes almost effortless; the horse seems to respond to the thought of the rider. Best of all, it is clear that the horse enjoys the experience, *no longer feeling the need to play dead, take control, or take off.*

Addition of concluding phrase to reinforce the three reasons.

FINAL WORD

The exercises in this chapter can certainly help you to kick-start your thinking and skills as an editor. Ultimately, however, the best way to improve is to edit your own work carefully. Use past and present revising suggestions from your instructor and peer editors.

Improving as a self-editor takes time, patience, and disciplined time management. As you schedule your pre-writing, drafting, and revising time, allow at least a couple of days between drafting and revising. Time away from the essay provides a fresh eye and increased objectivity. Budget your editing time so that you spend at least an hour on each of the three recommended steps of revision. This professional discipline will begin to pay you back with the pride of more fully achieved writing and improved marks.

Part 2

THE RESEARCH GUIDE

INTRODUCTION

Critical thinking—the core of post-secondary study—requires that you find and respond to reliable, current (or still important), and comprehensive information. Facts should be up to date and correct. Reasoning must be sound. Chapter 18 described the importance of concession-refutation awareness: know the complexity, the multidimensionality of your topic. What different, well-argued, or interestingly supported interpretations are present? How were these derived? Were the methods of investigation and thinking sound or at least in some way promising? Clearly, the research process together with its follow-up essay, report, or presentation is not an isolated strand of scholarly activity: rather, it extends through all scholarly work.

Conducting, Integrating, and Documenting Research: A Five-step Model

In the sciences, conducting research means identifying a "fruitful" question, finding out about other tests of the same or related question that have already been done, and setting up and completing an experiment or study to test certain hypothetical answers that you posit through reason and imagination. Your report of your findings and further speculations may then be referred to as research in the sense of literature reporting research activity.

In the humanities, and for most introductory courses, research typically means searching for information others have contributed to a particular topic. The first steps of this typical undergraduate research process are finding sources, evaluating their usefulness, and selecting information (preparing effective notes to serve your paper or presentation). The three preliminary steps of conducting research may be summed up as **finding, evaluating,** and **selecting.** For teaching purposes we speak of these three as separate and ordered in time as 1-2-3, but in practice all three steps commonly work together. For instance, where you look for something (described as the first step) is based in part on your evaluation of where credible information may be housed (described as the second step). As you skim over various texts to evaluate their apparent quality and suitability, your mind automatically considers portions that stand out (selection).

Once you have found, evaluated, and selected choice information from your sources, you are ready to **integrate** this information into your presentation in the form of summaries, paraphrases, and quotations. As you use these selected portions of content from other sources—ideas and any facts that are not common knowledge—you attribute this content to its source, clearly identifying the author and linking from that attribution to the additional source information your reader needs to find and recover what you have reported. This acknowledging of sources, which must conform to the format directions of the style guide used by the field of study concerned, is called **documenting.** Basic documentation methods of two commonly used style guides—the Modern Language Association (MLA), widely used in the humanities, and the American Psychological Association (APA), used in psychology, medicine, and social sciences—are covered in Sections 5, 6, and 7. Section 8 provides a brief look at the Chicago and American Anthropological Association (AAA) systems, commonly used for history and anthropology.

Steps of the Five-step Model

The following five steps provide a systematic approach to effective and efficient research:

Finding sources
Evaluating sources
Selecting information
Integrating information
Documenting all information taken from sources

For learning purposes we present these steps in linear order, but it is worth repeating that in reality there may be considerable overlap of steps. During evaluation of certain sources, for example, an idea for your essay thesis and outline may flash to mind, and along with that flash you may sense where a certain quotation, summary, or paraphrase should go in your paper. These insights can spur your momentum and should go into the note-keeping you do throughout all the stages. Further questions you may have about points raised in this introduction are covered one step at a time in Sections 1 to 5. Sections 6, 7, and 8 provide additional detailed information related to the common documentation practices of the style guides. Section 9 discusses the basic methods and ethics of conducting interviews, an excellent if sometimes under-appreciated way of generating new information shaped specifically to questions you wish to answer.

At the end of the Research Guide, under "Afterword and Checklists" (Section 10), we provide two checklists for useful reference and reminder: "15 Common Research Errors in First-year Papers" and "10 Steps to a Successful Research Paper."

Finally, while Section 5 on documentation deals with standard ways to acknowledge other people's ideas or statements of generally unknown facts, avoiding plagiarism or any appearance of that misconduct is so important that we end this introduction with a caution.

Although this serious caution may raise anxiety, as long as you credit your sources where credit is due and learn how to do that according to accepted convention, you should not encounter problems in your research. The principles and methods are simpler than they may seem. To ensure that you acknowledge ideas other than your own in the text of your essay, simply be sure that you give the source author's last name with the idea and be sure to list the source at the end of your paper in alphabetical order according to surname of authors. That one practice is all you need as a

foundation. Use the following chapters with diligence, and you will soon have many fine research essays standing on a solid base.

Avoid Even the Appearance of Plagiarism

Any loose or hasty attitude toward full and accurate citation of your sources may lead to charges of plagiarism. (Section 5 of the Research Guide looks at how to ensure that your summaries, paraphrases, and quotations are properly attributed.) When you plagiarize someone else's work, you are presenting his or her ideas or words in your own writing as though they were your own. Academic institutions consider plagiarism a serious offence, one that can result in academic failure or even expulsion. Many students plagiarize without intending to because they haven't learned when and how to document their sources, or because they have developed bad note-taking and composition habits that lead to plagiarism. In fact, some students claim to have gone through high school blissfully unaware that they were plagiarizing virtually in every essay and research assignment they ever wrote.

It is very important to learn the rules and expectations for documenting sources before you find yourself in the unpleasant situation of dealing with an accusation of plagiarism. Make yourself aware of your institution's definition of plagiarism. Treat that definition like a law.

Section 1 Finding Information: Types of Sources

Think of some major purchase you have been involved in, whether it concerned a musical instrument; a bicycle or car; or a house, cottage, or other property. Occasionally, happy fortune leads you promptly to the object of desire—even lands it in your lap. More often, however, the quest for specified quality and suitability takes time. The same principle applies to searching for quality information relevant to your topic: it takes time and care.

SCHEDULING

You cannot pull a research paper together in one afternoon, though many students have tried. Since you have to locate and evaluate several credible sources, you will need to allow several days for preliminary search and probably another several days after that as you narrow your leads. A weak research effort stands out immediately, so *plan ahead.*

Check with your instructor for help with directing your search. Just as your reading for post-secondary purposes needs a critical edge, so your research needs the guidance of active inquiry. What critical questions surround your topic or may surround it? What critical question most interests you? (Chapter 6 of the Rhetoric covered identifying a controlling idea.) Seeking information concerning these questions is a helpful way to direct your initial searches. Remember that all good detectives have days when nothing pans out. Expect dry spells by allowing sufficient time for continued investigation when nothing much immediately emerges. We all know the old saying that if you don't bring a rain coat, it will surely rain. When it comes to research, your rain coat is an allowance of proper time. Get started early, scheduling in several days for preliminary searches, several more for follow-ups, and then at least another week to 10 days for the next stages of integrating and documenting your information.

GETTING STARTED

Where do you look for quality information that is relevant to your topic? Sources may include academic books and journals, historical accounts, government reports, statistics, microfilm, interviews, and legal and medical opinions. Where exactly to look depends in part upon your specific topic, but many of the same general types of sources serve a wide range of research papers. The following is a brief description of the most common ones.

Your College or University Library

Your college or university library is usually the best place to start your search for good, reliable sources. Take advantage of the resources available in your own library. Almost all libraries offer free assistance in the form of information sessions, classes, or individual consultation with reference librarians; these sessions can be extremely helpful to students new to college or university research. Many libraries provide an online library tour as well as tutorials on helpful topics such as Boolean Search Guide, Google Search Scholar, Internet searching, and narrowing search results by adding terms. Most librarians are happy to help you as long as you are polite and patient. Saying "please" and "thank you" is often a productive strategy to ensure assistance with research questions and problems.

Library Catalogues

While library catalogues vary, you will find certain strategies applicable in most situations. You will want to try more than one way of accessing your topic—for example, by various keywords, subject headings, and words in titles. If your searches are pulling up hundreds of sources, narrow your search. Use two keywords instead of one ("vampire and literature" or "vampire and film" instead of just "vampire") or identify a more specific topic ("Dracula" or "Bela Lugosi"). Conversely, if your searches on a topic are pulling up only one or two sources, try synonyms or related words ("pregnancy," "birthing," "midwife," "childbirth," "motherhood," "nursing") or broaden your topic term ("1970s horror film" instead of only "John Carpenter's *Halloween*," or "scientific entrepreneur" instead of only "marketing of lab mice").

Specialized Databases

To find a journal article, you will probably have to use one of your library's specialized electronic databases. Some specialized databases provide abstracts (summaries of articles) or even full articles, while others simply give you a list of articles and their sources. Find out from your library or your instructor which databases are used in your subject area. Some examples are ERIC (for education), MLA (for literature), Medline (for medicine and biosciences), JSTOR (for a wide range of disciplines), and PsychINFO/PsychLIT (for psychology). If the database allows you to limit your search to "peer reviewed" journals, do so, thus ensuring that any article you find has been read, critiqued, checked, and approved by other experts in the field.

Encyclopedias and Dictionaries

Encyclopedias and dictionaries can help introduce you to your subject by defining terms, summarizing facts, and sometimes providing an overview of the main issues associated with your topic. Although these reference works are a good place to start a writing assignment, never stop there; reference books never provide enough depth for a college or university writing assignment. You must be more active in your research efforts.

Encyclopedias can be general or specialized. General encyclopedias cover numerous topics from a wide range of fields. Because of their broad scope, they do not cover subjects in the detail of specialized encyclopedias and dictionaries. Many of the most up-to-date general encyclopedias are now available in electronic form. Encyclopedia

Britannica (available online at www.britannica.com) and the electronic encyclopedia Encarta are just two examples.

You will find specialized encyclopedias and dictionaries useful when beginning your research on a topic. Some of these contain articles of several pages in length, written by experts in the field, while others contain shorter entries with highly specific information on specialized topics. Examples include the *Dictionary of Literary Biography,* *The Encyclopedia of Social Work,* the *International Dictionary of Films and Filmmakers,* and *The Gale Encyclopedia of Native American Tribes.*

Be sure to check the year of publication of any encyclopedia you are using. Some older college and university libraries have reference works dating back several decades. These sources may be extremely well researched and fascinating in their own right, but they can also be catastrophically out of date for your purposes. Research and representation of many subjects (such as mental illness, narrative techniques in fiction, Aboriginal cultures) have changed significantly over the decades, so make sure you examine the most recent sources available in your school library or online.

Books

Scholarly books form a solid basis for most college and university research papers. Often, you will need to read only two or three applicable chapters of the books to gather valuable information. These chapters can provide serious, consistent, current, in-depth information on major ideas and research on your topic. They can help you to find and narrow your issue. Most college and university libraries specialize in scholarly or academic books appropriate for research papers, but not all books on your topic might be good sources for your particular paper. (Our discussion of evaluating sources later in this chapter will help you choose the right books.)

Journals

Articles in peer-reviewed scholarly journals (also called refereed journals) are usually your best source of information for a brief and highly specialized discussion of a topic. However, journal articles are sometimes so specialized that you may find some of the terms difficult to understand. You may have to decide whether you need to understand some of this terminology in order to write about your subject. Often, you can consult a special dictionary on theoretical terms or perhaps another article on the troubling term itself ("first-person confessional narrative," "diegesis," "setting," "isothermic," "historiography," "hip hop," "Tom Jones"). The authors of journal articles engage in specific arguments based on issues particular to their field.

Newspapers and Magazines

Articles in newspapers and magazines are often both more superficial and more accessible than articles in academic journals because they generally address a wider audience. Sometimes you can use these general-interest articles as appropriate sources along with other more specialized sources for a research paper, especially if your topic is very recent and people have not had time to publish on it in longer books and scholarly journals. Reviews and interviews from newspapers and magazines, for instance, can be useful sources of beginning information. On the other hand, if your assignment requires that you draw on scholarly articles from academic journals in a proposed field, do not rely on newspapers or magazines. The journalists who write articles in newspapers and general-interest magazines such as *Maclean's* or *Newsweek* are usually on assignment and have no particular expertise in the areas they cover for those articles, so they are not the most reliable sources when you are investigating serious developments in research or scholarly debates on a given subject. Some specialized magazines, however, such as *The Economist, Atlantic Monthly, New Scientist,* and *Scientific American,* are well researched and well respected by experts in the field and may be good places to begin your research.

Interviews and Personal Experiences

Interviews and personal experiences can add an interesting, surprising, and original dimension to your research paper. For example, one student may gain substantial insights for an essay on contemporary Jewish literature (Mordecai Richler, Philip Roth, Cynthia Ozick, Saul Bellow) by interviewing her grandparents, who may have survived Nazi internment camps, oppression, and/or migration. Another student may successfully incorporate his own Japanese-Canadian experiences in a study of some of the strengths and challenges of Canadian multiculturalism. Interviewing has much to offer (when properly balanced with other sources) yet tends to be underutilized. For more on interviewing, see Section 9 of the Research Guide.

Be aware, however, that personal experiences are not always easy or appropriate to include in research papers, especially if you are very emotional about the experience. Before you include a personal experience in a research paper, ask yourself whether that experience contributes to the paper, provides an illuminating example, or may only distract your reader from your point. Also, some instructors may object to your including personal experiences, while others strongly encourage it. If you are not sure where your instructor stands on the politics of interviews and/or personal comments in a research paper, discuss your ideas with him or her.

The Internet

The World Wide Web can provide vast quantities of information on many subjects, particularly those that are current. Students who are comfortable with the Internet (or who may lack access to conventional libraries) may be tempted to use it as their only source of information. Although more and more authoritative literature is now accessible online, unlike a college or university library, the Internet contains scads of information that is poorly researched, inaccurate, and otherwise misleading. Certain websites, including some that are managed by people with or claiming "PhDs," contain unattributed words from other sources—that is, plagiarism. It is a good idea to seek the advice of your librarian or instructor concerning the sorts of sites that might assist your topic. Your institution's library most likely provides online access to various databases for peer-reviewed material.

Internet Search Engines

If you are looking for information on the World Wide Web, you will use an Internet search engine such as Google, Windows Live, or Yahoo. Review your search engine's help pages on basic and advanced searches, and define the scope of your search as specifically as you can. Bear in mind that your engine likely sorts results according to sites that are most visited or to level of commercial sponsorship. These criteria may offer insights into consumer trends, but they do not provide the best approach to finding what you need for scholarly purposes. Narrow your search by using options such as "all the words" or "the exact phrase." Some search engines can carry out Boolean searches as well. Searching for a site that your library or instructor has recommended is a wise start.

Gateway Sites

Your library or instructor might recommend that you start your search by going to a "metapage": a "gateway" that provides links to other sites related to your field of interest. One such page for the humanities is Voice of the Shuttle (at http://vos.ucsb.edu). Another such site, Intute (at www.intute.ac.uk) provides links for a wide array of scholarly disciplines.

Wikipedia

You are probably used to finding information at Wikipedia. Since its foundation in 2001, Wikipedia has become one of the 10 most visited sites world wide. It represents a major shift in how the Western world thinks about information, scholarship, and learning. At a time of pronounced uncertainty and change, this type of online innovation raises serious questions about authority and intellectual ownership. Attitudes to Wikipedia and other aspects of the Internet appear to have changed considerably in a fairly short time, with more and more academics finding value and benefits in Wikipedia and similar initiatives. However, even the founder of Wikipedia agrees with the following caution.

Do not cite Wikipedia or similar reader-generated encyclopedias. They simply cannot be relied upon to ensure the ethos demanded of an encyclopedia. They may remain current, and, on the whole, they may be accurate, but no assurances of those required qualities exist in the anonymous reader-generated model.

Jimmy Wales, the head of Wikipedia, confirms that he never intended his innovation to provide a definitive research source. He intended it as a quick, friendly way to acquaint readers with amateur knowledge of a topic, and he intended it as a collective exercise relying on trust. In a *Time* magazine interview entitled "Ten Questions," Wales says that he agrees with teachers who advise their students not to cite Wikipedia: "There's always a chance that there's something wrong."

To illustrate this possibility, consider what has been revealed by Virgil Griffith's WikiScanner. Using his tool to trace the IP addresses of anonymous Wikipedia edits, he found that people working from computers operated by corporations, governments (including Canada's), media organizations, and agencies such as the CIA were revising articles, presumably to serve the interests of those organizations. Over 20 percent of Wikipedia edits are performed by anonymous parties.

Many of us go to Wikipedia for a preliminary idea of what threads to trace, but it is important to then trace those threads to clearly identified authoritative sources. A wiki shared and updated by clearly identified experts is one thing; a wiki open to anonymous members of the general public is another.

Saving Material You Find on the Internet

It is often a good idea to download material from a website onto your computer or a disk. You can do this with a simple right-click of your mouse. This step is important because websites may change from day to day, and the material you find today may not be accessible to you tomorrow. Keep a log to document when you referenced specific websites.

To avoid plagiarizing, take "notes" by cutting from a website you visit but pasting in another font, so that you can tell where your words stop and another's words begin. Record important websites among your "Bookmarks" or "Favourites" for easy reference. Always record the date on which you retrieved certain information from the web. Download and keep a copy of the online material you are considering citing.

Primary and Secondary Sources

Post-secondary study makes an important distinction between primary and secondary sources. **Primary sources** are the initial materials you are working with—a work of literature, a philosophical treatise, a historical document, or data you gather directly from an experience. Working directly with these sources allows you to come up with your own interpretation or analysis of them. The primary source or sources are what you are writing about, the topic of the paper.

Secondary sources are other writers' interpretations, analyses, or discussions of an event, an issue, or a primary source. Interpretations of literary or musical works, discussions of film, and political analyses of an international speech are all examples of secondary sources.

If you are writing a term paper on Joseph Boyden's *Maclean's* magazine article on residential schools and Aboriginal suicide, "The Hurting," for example, that text is your main source. Historical and other discussions of issues in that article would be considered secondary sources for the purposes of your assignment. These other discussions would throw light on your primary subject, the Boyden article. A source on rhetoric might serve as a secondary source for this assignment if your purpose were to explore and evaluate Boyden's appeals to pathos, for example.

Sometimes identifying the primary source can be a little tricky. In fact, in some research situations what might usually be a secondary source can become your primary source if you decide to write your paper on that secondary source! If you wish to write a paper or a review on attitudes in literary criticism toward female characters in recent Canadian short stories, for example, the pieces of literary criticism you examine would be your primary sources, since these articles are the texts that your research paper addresses. Similarly, a paper on the 1991 Gulf War would have to rely on a factual account of this event as the primary source, but a paper on one writer's interpretation of this war would use that writer's work as the primary source.

Primary Source/Subject	Secondary Source
Joseph Boyden's "The Hurting"	*From Truth to Reconciliation: Transforming the Legacy of Residential Schools* (Castellano, Archibald, and DeGagné)
Introversion	Academic journals, current textbooks, media reports

SAMPLE STUDENT RESEARCH PAPER

The following essay has been revised from a 2007 paper by student Dean Goodman. Take particular note of the sources he has found. He relies primarily on information from highly regarded peer-reviewed journals, but he extends and enriches the discussion with suitable interviews and two books by well-regarded authors. He also refers to a government report. The range of interesting and relevant information that Goodman has found allows him to interweave an effective blend of cool and warm proofs, discussed in Chapter 4.

Section 6 of the Research Guide covers common practices of MLA style.

Sample Student Research Paper Using 2009 MLA Documentation

Gambling: The New Baseball?

Revised from an essay by Dean Goodman

1   A fly ball loops to deep left, the star fielder lopes under it, the spectators . . . but wait—they've stopped watching. They've turned their gaze to the poker hand on their smartphones. As unlikely as it would have seemed a decade ago, according to Jeffrey Nealon's recent essay in the *South Atlantic Quarterly,* gambling has replaced baseball as the number-one pastime of America (465). In 2003, Nealon observes that some 53.4 million people—26 percent of the entire adult population—gambled in casinos five times or more (465). This total does not include those who participated in lotteries or online gaming (467).

Cites a peer-reviewed article to introduce the critical claim.

2   Here in Canada we have dubiously "evolved" in little more than a decade from government-run lotteries to legalized VLTs and casinos to political visions of online market share. Provincial governments see gambling as one of their latest money-making ventures. Casinos have been springing up from coast to coast while the internet offers endless gaming options under one's own roof. In Alberta, for instance, by 2002, 1400 online gambling sites were operating in 54 jurisdictions; approximately 14 million gamblers had logged in (Alberta Gaming and Liquor Commission 7). With 10 percent of the country's population, Alberta takes in 20 percent of the profits from gambling. In some years VLTs earn more for the government than the oil sands (Saul 199). It therefore appears that gambling is here to stay, but how legalized gaming has affected gamblers in general, people with gambling problems in particular, and our young people remains under-analyzed in this modern gold rush.

3   For gamblers in general our new society has certainly increased their opportunities and no doubt their numbers. In a 1996 satirical essay "Rama-Lama Ding Dong," Drew Hayden Taylor, a writer from the Curve Lake Anishinabe Reserve in Ontario, likened the newly opened Rama Casino to a "new god" near the town of Orillia (55):

> In Eastern religion, the name Rama is a manifestation of the Hindu God Vishnu the Creator, and I'm sure the people who are running the casino at Rama are hoping this new enterprise will "create" lots of money, jobs and various other forms of prosperity for the community. Evidently there are already Gambling Anonymous chapters being set up to assist some of the, shall we say, more enthusiastic followers of the new religion. (56)

4   Although the new enterprise did create lots of money, jobs, and various other forms of prosperity, and not just for locals but for well-paid special guests as wide-ranging as Bill Cosby, Tony Bennett, Reba McEntire, Art Garfunkel, and David Copperfield, the social costs of this sudden prosperity have not been accounted for at all. The aforementioned and many other famous names, including sudden reincarnations of the Beatles (Fab Four Ultimate Beatles Tribute) all appeared at Casino Rama over spring and summer 2007. Just two years after Casino Rama opened, in a report for the American online periodical *Casino Player*, Roger Gros declared that "Casino Rama has proven to be a big success and a significant revenue generator for the province's tribes." According to this cheerful and one-dimensional view, Taylor's observation of future trouble seems needlessly bleak. Defenders of gambling argue that proceeds from the casinos go back into gambling addiction programs, so therefore no one really loses. If some people succumb completely, well, they just didn't make the best use of their free will, like the rest of us. These people—gambling's long-term losers—are the inevitable casualties in the war on economic stagnation.

5   One person less than thrilled, however, by spinning wheels at legalized gaming haunts is singer-songwriter Dennis Lakusta, a Métis of Ukrainian and Blackfoot descent

Connects the claim to a local situation. Common knowledge.

Cites a government source for specific examples.

Cites an established writer.

Suggests three reasons for concern about the legalized rise of gambling.

Cites another author for support.

Concedes benefits.

Summarizes a defence of gambling, citing source.

Cites an Aboriginal folk singer who disagrees with the claimed benefit to Aboriginal peoples.

who tours Canada's folk-music circuits and visits schools with presentations on the policies and effects of the Indian Act. His song "Joy Ride" paints a far different impression of casinos from those in the government financial reports. The following lines come from different sections of the song and are repeated as refrains.

> Joy ride, 7 come 11
> Better get a gettin' while the gettin' is good
>
> . . . .
>
> Sky splits, prairie winds a hissin'
> Spirits running round like they think it's hell
>
> . . . .
>
> Throw another nickel down that slot
> Grab hold the handle pull it down
> The choice you make tonight is all you've got
> And the big wheel keeps going round and round (1–2, 5–6, 20–24)

6   In reply to an e-mail, Lakusta confirms that many Aboriginal people he knows share the spirits' view in this song of casino culture. However, Native consensual values sometimes discourage contentions once decisions are made. Lakusta believes the decisions being made do not come on the basis of having seriously pursued other choices, even though other choices for community development should be and perhaps still could be available. He confirms that the song "Joy Ride" is about the false dreams and moral bankruptcy of institutionalized, big-business gaming, based on what he has seen at various casinos. The word he uses in his song for the purveyors of gaming culture is "bloodsuckers."

Cites a personal interview with the source.

7   Research indicates that much of the supposed "prosperity" flowing in from legalized gambling comes from those with a serious addiction. University of Lethbridge professor Robert Williams has collected data suggesting that 35 percent of gambling revenue in Ontario and 39 percent of gambling revenue in Alberta comes from "problem gamblers" (qtd. in Alberta Gaming and Liquor Commission 5). In a study on internet gambling for *Psychology and Behaviour,* Mark Griffiths suggests that research shows a strong correlation between increased problem gambling and increased access to gambling (559). Two other researchers, Christian Jacques and Robert Ladouceur, agree in a recent study appearing in the *Canadian Journal of Psychology* that pathological gambling increases with availability of gaming activities (764). Mark Griffiths argues that by seeking to generate revenue from non-essential forms of expenditure, and specifically by altering policies to allow for federal and provincial lotteries, casinos, and the like, governments have adversely relaxed controls to create the current climate of private as well as public purveyors (558). Regardless of who, if anyone, is to blame, it seems clear that problem gamblers, to some significant extent, provide the "blood" that Lakusta's song alludes to, and it also seems clear that as access increases, so do personal and social problems.

Cites detailed data from a professor's study.
Cites the source as quoted in another source.

Cites two other studies reported in refereed journals.

Cites related find-
ings reported in
another refereed
journal.

8   The effect of gaming culture on young people is vastly under-investigated despite serious concerns. Researcher Terry Burger reports in *College Student Journal* that internet gambling has increased drastically among university aged students (708). In the last three years, student gambling has increased by 28 percent, he says, with males "leading the way" (708), possibly due to competitiveness that has been linked to both intrinsic and extrinsic motivation (708). In the Alberta Youth Experience Survey 2002, reported in an Alberta Gaming and Liquor Commission proposal (6), 41 percent of Alberta youth said they had gambled at least once in the previous 12 months. Of those who had gambled, 9.5 percent showed addiction "patterns" (6). The usual computer-culture effects on youth—reduced physical activity and remoteness from both relationships and nature—are compounded by the relatively high risk of falling into a destructive personal and social behaviour.

Cites a govern-
ment source.

Cites a second
personal
interview.

9   Mindy Jamieson (not her real name), a recent university graduate and, for the past year and a half, a gambling addictions social worker, believes that governments could be doing much more to prevent and heal the problems. Having grown up in a family-run business of a restaurant and attached lounge, Jamieson observed first-hand the impact of six VLTs on customers young and old. The province recognizes that electronic gaming machines demonstrate higher addiction rates than other forms of gaming but has not acted seriously, she says, on recommendations from a government-funded study. Various recommendations, such as reducing the speed at which the games occur and increasing distance from the nearest bank machine, would help, if implemented. Jamieson notes, however, that annual VLT net profits of $700 million, eclipsing every other government profit category, including even liquor sales, discourage serious corrections and controls. Citing Saskatchewan as the most pro-active province when it comes to discouraging problem gambling, she points out that even there over one-third of profits goes back into highways and similar initiatives while a mere 1.5 percent goes toward problem gambling relief. Returning to the war metaphor, one can fairly say that it seems that the authorities know there will be casualties but have decided to skimp on the medical corps. Unlike Griffiths, however, Jamieson doesn't suggest that government moral abdication is the root of the problem. She suggests that legalized gambling was bound to enter from the USA, where it is not run by government but nevertheless is ubiquitous. If the government is not to blame for social problems, what about those "more enthusiastic followers of the new religion" themselves (to cite Taylor): are these gambling addicts responsible for their "problem"? Are they simply weaker willed than the rest of us?

Works cited in
alphabetical order
by author's
surname. See
Section 6 for more
on MLA style.
An organization as
author.

Works Cited

Alberta Gaming and Liquor Commission. *Problem and Responsible Gambling Strategy: Proposal for Enhancement to Address Increasing Problem Gambling Needs in Alberta.* Alberta Alcohol and Drug Abuse Commission and Alberta Gaming and Liquor Commission, Apr. 2005. Web. 3 Mar. 2007.

Burger, Terry. "College Students and Gambling: An Examination of Gender Differences in Motivation for Participation." *College Student Journal* 40.3 (2006): 704–14. Print.

Griffiths, Mark. "Internet Gambling: Issues, Concerns, and Recommendations." *CyberPsychology and Behavior* 6.6 (2003): 557–68. Print.

Jacques, Christian, and Robert Ladouceur. "A Prospective Study of the Impact of Opening a Casino on Gambling Behaviours: 2- and 4-Year Follow-Ups." *Canadian Journal of Psychology* 51.12 (2006): 764–73. Print.

Jamieson, Mindy. Personal interview. 17 May 2007.

Lakusta, Dennis. Email Interview. 7–8 May 2007.

---. "Joy Ride." *Run with You*. Big Blue Fish Studios, 1997. CD.

Nealon, Jeffrey T. "Take Me Out to the Slot Machine: Reflections on Gambling and Contemporary American Culture." *South Atlantic Quarterly* 105.2 (2006): 465–74. Print.

Saul, John Ralston. *A Fair Country: Telling Truths about Canada*. Toronto: Viking, 2008. Print.

Taylor, Drew Hayden. "Rama–Lama Ding Dong." *Funny, You Don't Look Like One*. Rev. ed. Penticton: Theytus, 1998. 56–57. Print.

Title in quotation marks. Italicize title of journal.

Works Cited

Boyden, Joseph. "The Hurting." *Maclean's.ca*. Maclean's, 1 July 2010. Web. 21 Oct. 2010.

Castellano, Marlene Brant, Linda Archibald, and Mike DeGagné. *From Truth to Reconciliation*. Aboriginal Healing Foundation, 2008. Web. 21 Oct. 2010.

"Ten Questions: Jimmy Wales." *Time Magazine*. Time, 21 Mar. 2007. Web. 21 Oct. 2010.

Section 2 Evaluating
Information

You should always be careful about your sources. There is no need to take home every single book or other publication on your subject, or, on the other hand, to select randomly from the shelf. Good researchers look through a range of sources related to their topics, and use only some of these to write their papers. Evaluating your sources carefully before you use them will save you time on research and make your paper better.

MEASURE RELEVANCE AND USEFULNESS

When you assess a secondary source, you measure its relevance and usefulness to your project. Take into account the secondary source's **date of publication** (are its points and conclusions current or outdated?); its **scope** (is it too general or too special-ized?); and its **Works Cited** page (MLA), **References** page (APA), or **Bibliography** (is it a well-researched discussion or a one-sided "opinion" piece?). You might also be able to find other potential sources listed in a good secondary source's Works Cited or References page. Using such "cross-referencing" is an effective and common research technique.

When you first evaluate a source, "read" quickly—not as an involved reader, but as a research scanner—moving rapidly through the source's main argument to see if you can use it productively. Will it support your paper? Does it provide evidence and facts you can build on? Can you perhaps contend against the source's opinions and findings? Do you suspect errors, gaps, or bias in this source?

Here are five questions to help you evaluate a source:

1. What is the source's main point, claim, or argument?
2. What is the author's perspective and/or tone (for, against, or objective)?
3. Can you summarize the author's evidence?
4. Do you agree or disagree (or a little of both) with the author's point?
5. What questions does the source leave fully or partially unanswered or, equally important, completely unasked—in your opinion?

You should also look carefully at each source's **table of contents** and **index** (if a book), abstract (if an article and if available), introductory chapter or introduc-tory paragraph, and Works Cited or References page. Sometimes these brief sections can help eliminate a useless source or generate new directions and new secondary sources in your research.

One advantage in using a college or university library is that some of the work in evaluating sources has already been done for you. Librarians, professors, and instructors who have a good idea of the sources their students need will have selected these books. If you use only a public library to do your research, you will have to be more careful; many sources there are intended primarily for high school students, hobbyists, or general-interest readers, and they may not be extensive enough for a college or university research paper.

Here are three more questions to help you choose your sources well:

1. *Is the source written for researchers?* Does the book seem to be written for college or university students or for more advanced researchers in the field? Generally, your sources should be pitched just above your own current level of understanding, not a step or two below. You should be learning as you conduct your research. Many students are too easily put off by secondary sources that seem somewhat difficult. If you use a source that simplifies issues too much, you may not gain an understanding of the twists and turns of your subject, or the various debates within it. On the other hand, you need not struggle with a ferociously specialized source way beyond a first- or second-year student's level of comprehension, that is, a source that assumes a large body of knowledge you simply do not have yet. If you are writing a paper on the medical uses of marijuana, for instance, but you do not have a background in biology or medicine, expect to have to deal with some unfamiliar terminology, but don't waste valuable time agonizing over highly specialized scientific articles obviously intended for an audience of MDs and PhDs. Use such articles if you can, but if you feel lost, put them aside for more immediately useful material.

2. *Is the source relevant to my topic?* Always check the introduction, table of contents, and the index to make sure that the source really contains the information you need. If the source has only a couple of pages relevant to your topic, you can photocopy these for a mention in your paper or perhaps a footnote or an endnote, and keep looking.

3. *What is the secondary source's position?* Remember that many published articles are only interpretations of facts and developments rather than completely objective evaluations. The authors of secondary sources offer their expert opinions as persuasively as possible, but remember that the entire secondary source may be only that one person's view, not the whole truth. Be careful as a researcher to distinguish the facts from the perspectives. While using the facts of the primary source or the view of another secondary source, you may be able to argue against or to qualify the perspective presented in any one particular secondary source.

READING AS A RESEARCHER

A great deal of published research (secondary sources) contains aspects of both explicit and implicit interpretation. By definition, all interpretations contain significant aspects of subjective knowledge: personal experience, embedded perspectives, and professional attitudes toward what counts as evidence and toward what counts as a reasonable conclusion. You will come across many disputes between these different authors of secondary sources—all perhaps examining the same primary source—on the basis of the different interpretative strategies they employ. This tension is part of any research territory.

As a junior researcher reading the work of more experienced researchers, you need to be aware of the significant (and even sometimes trivial) ways your sources disagree with each other. Always be prepared to challenge these expert views. Sometimes the "experts" make mistakes in basic facts. Sometimes they draw arguably, or even blatantly, wrong conclusions from ambiguous premises. Sometimes they offer a wildly belligerent opinion or whimsical conclusion with which you have every right to disagree.

If you can "debunk"—that is, successfully challenge, expose, and overturn—a published or established view, you have performed one of the most important and respected functions of a researcher. The larger social function of all research is to locate a true account—a fair, just view.

EVALUATING SOURCES ON THE INTERNET

Many of the strategies for evaluating printed sources apply equally to the World Wide Web. What is the source's authority? What is the source's background research? Does the source have a bias?

The web raises additional concerns:

- *Can you find out who is responsible for the site?* Do the individual organizations responsible for the site tell you anything about themselves? Are they established academics, teachers, or researchers? What if they are only Grade 11 students who harbour deep resentment over the cultural underestimation of the latest young musician? How can you compare the merits of one source and another on the Internet? Wikipedia's open design makes it impossible to know who has written and edited each entry. WikiScan may reveal an editor's IP address, but that does not reveal the individual who performed the edit, nor does it reveal the original author.
- *Is the site connected to a university or college?* Some of the best research sites are based in academic institutions and are entirely sound sources for academic research. However, be cautious about using information posted by other students, who may be designing superficial websites or posting weak drafts of eventually mediocre papers for their own courses. If the document seems to be composed by someone who does not know anything about writing, evidence, essay structure, analysis, or documentation, then steer clear of the site.
- *Is the site trying to sell you something?* If it presents research on something that it also tries to sell, chances are the research is biased in its favour. For example, if a pharmaceutical company posts information about a drug it sells, it will predictably select information that presents the drug in a positive light. Although some of the research may be reliable, look at other sources as well to give you a sense of balance. Some entries at Wikipedia may be trying to sell you something, because they may have been anonymously edited by parties with vested interests.

- *When was the site last updated?* If the site has not been updated for one or two years, its owner might have abandoned it. In any event, a site that has not been updated for some time is usually not a particularly good source of information.
- *Is the site just a cheap collection of flashy graphics?* Remember that you are looking for information in your research, not splashy nonsense. Evaluate the text or substance of the site. In some cases, the graphics may be exactly what you need for your research, yet often they have little or no bearing on the content or substance of the site.

SAMPLE STUDENT RESEARCH PAPER

In writing the essay that follows, Laura Allan guided her search for sources in response to a clear critical question and a hypothetical reply regarding the complexities of legalized gambling. Aware of strong opinion against this activity, she found credible and current sources representing those opinions. Her book source and interviewee both offer grounds for opposition to legalized gambling. Acknowledging those grounds, she then found additional information demonstrating social needs that rely on income from community-sponsored gambling. Allan's use of Hansard records of proceedings of the Northwest Territories legislative assembly demonstrates that certain communities are indeed faced with the loss of essential social services if gambling profits are withdrawn. Allan's firm sense of argumentative purpose contributed to efficient searching and effective evaluations of the various positions. The government sources for data may seem a little compromised in this case because the government sponsors the activity it is reporting; however, the data would be hard if not impossible to find elsewhere, and a critic's main concern here would be more with possible bias of presentation than with the actual numbers reported. On such a hotly debated controversy, the writer does not expect to have "the last say" but to shape a compelling argument for the side she believes makes realistic sense. Like Dean Goodman with his opposed essay in Section 1 of this guide, Allan creates an interweaving of warm and cool proofs through her variety of sources (see Chapter 4).

Section 7 of the Research Guide covers common practices of APA style.

Sample Student Research Paper Using 2010 APA Documentation

Gambling: The Stakes Are What They Are

Laura Jane Allan

Opening uses description drawn from personal interview.

1   Today is Thursday. It is like any other day at the Rolling Thunder Casino in Red Combine. The parking lot is full, the restaurant has patrons, and there is a Greyhound bus from the nearest city in the bus lane. Out-of-town buses stop here nearly every day. Monday the bus comes from the north, and Wednesday brings western buses, says Janet Ishmael (not her real name; personal communication, June 23, 2006), a

full-time cashier at the casino for the last six years. Although the casino is her employer, Janet does not approve of gambling. What she sees every day on her ten-hour shifts at work continues to confirm her suspicions. "Serious gambling causes problems," she says. "When people start using their credit cards for cash, it can only lead to trouble." Gambling has an air of secrecy around it. It stirs up images of free-flowing alcohol and smoke-filled basements. Serious gambling can lead to problems like increased violence and crime in communities; family relationships often suffer the consequences. Difficulties associated with gambling addictions are a sad reality, but not enough to encourage the government to stop legalized forms of gambling and its role in gambling. Can something so ominous have any positive attributes?

2   Gambling profits are a huge revenue generator for all stakeholders. Gambling provides communities with an additional source of tourism, and the local economy also gets a boost. Let us not forget the non-government agencies. Many community-minded groups exist only through funds generated by legalized gambling. Gambling is just one type of legal activity that many people use for entertainment while others think it morally reprehensible. It is all about attitude and choice.

3   Serious gambling can turn into an addiction. Addictions, if not treated, can lead to problems like increased violence and crime in communities and ruined families. Take for example, Patricia Holmes who stole over $100,000 from her employer to feed her VLT habit (Hutchinson, 1999, p. 15). She pocketed money for two years before she was caught. Donald W., an Edmonton Public School senior manager, stole over $70,000 and was fired. His children disowned him, and his wife left him. His shame still holds him captive. Unable to work, Donald needs weekly therapy (Hutchinson, 1999, pp. 47–52). Gambling addictions are a growing concern. According to its casinos and VLTs fact sheets, the Saskatchewan Liquor and Gaming Authority (SLGA, 2006a) is certainly aware of a problem. The *Casinos in Saskatchewan Fact Sheet* reports that the government allotted $4 million for "problem gambling initiatives" (SLGA, 2006a, p. 2). This allotment is 1.53% of annual gaming revenue in Saskatchewan, the highest provincial percentage in Canada as noted in an Alberta Gaming and Liquor Commission report, *Problem and Responsible Gambling Strategy* (2005, p. 4).

4   The Saskatchewan program operates in partnership with the Federation of Saskatchewan Indian Nations: $1.5 million of the $4 million allotment goes to Aboriginal gambling addictions initiatives (SLGA, 2006a, p. 1). The Saskatchewan government pro-motes what it calls "responsible gaming" (SLGA, 2006a, p. 2). One example of this initia-tive, according to the *VLTs in Saskatchewan Fact Sheet* (SLGA, 2006b, p. 2), is changes to VLT machines to show actual dollar amounts wagered (instead of credits) and a machine clock on the screen to help those that lose track of time. Rolling Thunder Casino has clocks in the building but only at the entrance and the banking area, something that surprises the staff as Janet observes with a chuckle (personal communication, June 23, 2006). "People are asking for the time all day long," she says.

Cites Statistics
Canada, a leading
government
service.
Author is named
in the sentence
and appears in the
References list.

5   Gambling profits are a huge cash cow for the federal government. According to Statistics Canada, revenue generated from government-run lotteries, VLTs and casinos went from $2.7 billion in 1992 to over $11.3 billion in 2002; $6 billion of the $11.3 billion was profit (2003, p. 2). The province of Saskatchewan follows the Canadian trend. According to the *Casinos in Saskatchewan Fact Sheet* (SLGA, 2006a, p.1), the Saskatchewan Indian Gaming Authority (SIGA) recorded a net income of $40.2 million in 2005-2006. Profits are divided by formula: 37.5% to the provincial government general revenue fund, 37.5% to the First Nation Trust fund, and the remaining 25% to the Community Development Corporation (SLGA, 2006a, p. 1). Communities are becoming addicted to the revenue gambling provides and are showing signs of dependency, especially when funds are directed to health, education and highways. Voters want to keep the status quo.

Information from
the interviewee is
used to show
benefit.

6   Gaming also provides communities with an additional source of tourism dollars and boosts the local economy. According to Janet (personal communication, June 23, 2006), practically 50% of patrons who frequent the Rolling Thunder are from out of town. Many of the regulars come on the buses or drive in from the region. Since they usually stay all day, she says, casino patrons like to take breaks and go for a walk. Individuals will walk the 400 metres through the parking lot over to the coffee shop or visit Arlington Mall (located between the casino and coffee shop). There are definite spin-offs for communities where casinos are open up to 18 hours a day, seven days a week. More than 81% of staff at SIGA casinos in Saskatchewan is of Aboriginal descent (SGLA, 2006a); for many, steady guaranteed employment has lifted their self-confidence and created an Aboriginal middle class. They can afford meals out, pay off car loans, and serve as role models for First Nations people everywhere.

Transcripts of
legislative sittings

7   What about the volunteer and not-for-profit sector? Many of these groups depend on funds generated through legalized gambling to subsidize their programs and services. Bingos run by churches and their affiliates are still common in spite of the more modern big-box bingo halls. People in Inuvik, NWT, will remember in the late 1980s when a new Catholic bishop was appointed who did not support fund-raising bingos. Suddenly church groups struggled as they searched for a new source of revenue. How to support community services without fund-raising through games of chance remains a problem. On May 27, 2005, in the Northwest Territories Legislative Assembly, MLA Robert McLeod observed that the Inuvik Transition House (a women's shelter) "has to hold bingos on a regular basis to secure . . . necessary funding" (NWT *Hansard,* 2005, p. 8). Despite continued mixed feelings about gambling, without bingos, the Inuvik Diocese would not have been able to maintain essential social supports, and this example is surely representative across the country.

8   Finding a quarter on the sidewalk—what luck. Everyone enjoys lady luck when she smiles, and when she doesn't, it is the topic at coffee time. It is the same for gambling activities. You reach for the smile of lady luck in three gold bars, a good hand of blackjack or the right combination of the 6/49 numbers. You keep playing, hoping for the big win, but losses are more frequent, and patrons at the Rolling Thunder casino will complain to staff when the machines do not pay out. Nevertheless, gambling is all about choice. If you are a responsible adult, surely you can choose your leisure pursuits.

9   I support legalized gambling for two reasons. One, I enjoy games of skill and chance and occasionally purchase lottery and raffle tickets and support contests at my children's schools. I have patronized two casinos and always have a specific limit on what to spend. My winnings have been minuscule, but so have been my losses. Two, I have experienced first-hand the benefits of receiving provincial grants to assist non-profit organizations that provide programming for economically disadvantaged children and families. The volunteer sector in Saskatchewan receives money from Provincial Sport, Recreation, Heritage and Culture Departments through Community Development Corporations, the Community Initiative Fund, and Saskatchewan Lotteries. These programs can help the marginalized leave poverty and become active, independent, and productive members of society. They are a catalyst for change. People who have strong convictions and say no to any and all forms of gambling (school-based raffles, contests in stores, lottery tickets, bingos and casinos) should be admired, as their beliefs are a true guide to behaviour. Every adult has a responsibility to choose.

10   Today is Thursday. The parking lot at Rolling Thunder Casino is full, the restaurant has patrons, and the machines are busy. Will I stop by? I found a quarter on the side-walk. I am feeling lucky. The choice is up to me.

References

Alberta Gaming and Liquor Commission. (2005). Problem and responsible gambling strat-egy 2005–2006. Retrieved from http://www.aglc.gov.ab.ca/being_responsible/problem_and_responsible_gambling_strategy.pdf

Hutchinson, Brian. (1999). *Betting the house: Winners, losers, and the politics of Canada's gambling obsession*. Toronto, ON: Penguin.

Northwest Territories. Legislative Assembly. (2005, May 25). *Hansard*. Retrieved from http://www.assembly.gov.nt.ca/_live/pages/wpPages/hansard.aspx

Saskatchewan Liquor and Gaming Authority. (2006a). *Casinos in Saskatchewan fact sheet*. Retrieved from http://www.slga.gov.sk.ca/x3729.xml

Saskatchewan Liquor and Gaming Authority. (2006b). *VLTs in Saskatchewan fact sheet*. Retrieved from http://www.slga.gov.sk.ca/x3729.xml

Statistics Canada. (2003, March). Perspectives on labour and income: Fact-sheet on gambling. Retrieved from http://www.statcan.ca/english/freepub/75-001-XIE/00403/fs-fi_200304_01_a.pdf

References in alphabetical order by author's surname. See Section 7 for more on APA style. In titles of books, journals, and re-ports, the initial letter of a word following a colon is capitalized. For sources accessed online, the URL is usually provided. APA does not include personal interviews or communications in References; they are cited in the body of the essay.

Section 3 Selecting
Information

Advice in the previous two sections, applied with sound critical thinking, will enable you to find and evaluate highly promising sources. But these will remain only promising without practical organizational skills along with attention to detail. You will not be able to call upon what you find unless you record it, strategically and accurately.

NOTE-TAKING FOR RESEARCH PURPOSES

As you read into your topic area, you need to take exact notes of your findings. Many researchers first make their notes on regular paper and then later condense the most vital information to a small card: a useful quotation, a brief two- or three-sentence summary of an article or chapter, or a paraphrase of a particularly important detailed process or argument. You can easily rearrange and add to these cards later to reflect changes in your essay outline—and your outline will certainly change as you add and delete the information you collect. You will be moving forward to tighten your points and compose topic sentences to represent your revised thesis.

In the note-taking research stage, remember to record all source information *precisely.* The author's name, the source title, publisher, year, city of publication (for books), and page numbers are crucial information. If there are errors in your research paper at this level, you will undermine your credibility as a researcher. All your quotations need to be exact, so be careful when transcribing your initial notes, when condensing your longer notes to points on cards, when incorporating that information into various drafts, and when summarizing or paraphrasing source material. Remember you will have to attribute all summaries and paraphrases to your source by the author's name and either the page or paragraph number. Quotations record the author's exact words and use quotation marks. Summaries and paraphrases capture the author's statements in your own words.

The following is a hypothetical example of a handy research card that you might produce from some of your initial reading and note-taking as you work toward shaping your thesis statement and an outline for your paper. The card contains all the necessary

---

Sample Research Note Card

Tucker, Susan A. *The History of Boxing*. Toronto: McEwan, 1998.

- Chapter Five, "Mike Tyson's Presence," most relevant to my paper, especially the points about "social justification for bad behaviour," p. 134.
- Tucker asserts "only in professional boxing or crime could someone like Tyson flourish financially" (142).
- "Tyson himself seems genuinely confused about why his aggression is tremendously rewarded in the ring, but socially and legally denounced outside the ropes" (149).
- boxing a "circus or art" (151)?

source information (author, title, city of publication, publisher, and date), as well as four exact quotations with their correct page numbers. You may later decide not to use all the quotations in your final draft, but these quotations may help you develop your thinking and initial draft for a research paper tentatively entitled, for example, "Sports Justifications for Bad Behaviour" or "Social Tolerance and Mike Tyson." This brief set of notes with page numbers on the research note card will save you from substantial rereading, since you will be able to relocate useful areas of discussion in the source quickly.

Photocopies from Secondary Sources

Some students photocopy significant articles and book chapters, in whole or part, when collecting their research materials. This may be useful later, when your outline and drafts are underway and expanding. You can later condense the photocopied information in the form of either direct quotations or attributed summaries and paraphrases on your note cards for integration into your drafts. Or you may draw in more detail from the photocopy if you need to expand a certain part of your discussion at a later stage of revision.

Remember Rhetorical Needs

As you take notes, remember the basic strategic needs of an essay. For example, the introduction will require information demonstrating the currency of the topic, the critical question your essay poses, and any essential background to help readers quickly grasp context and main issues. In selecting information, make appropriate notes indicating where certain facts and opinions might fit best in your paper. When you come to drafting the essay, you may add or re-order information in the paper for maximum impact, but these notes to yourself concerning rhetorical (organizational) possibilities can be helpful.

Reflecting Critical Reading in Your Notes

We have already looked at the importance of evaluating your sources. We stressed that when you read your sources and take notes for a research paper, you should approach those sources actively and critically. Look for facts that back your argument, but do not disregard facts that challenge your view. Also try to develop your own ideas. Your notes should reflect (1) helpful information (facts, strong expert views on your selected subject, some useful quotations), (2) perhaps a couple of more provocative quotations (and whether you agree or disagree), and (3) your opinions and analysis. It is important to keep the facts, perspectives, and specific language of your sources separate from your own language and views. Note-keeping should be meticulous to avoid later confusion.

When reading and taking notes as a researcher, be conscious of your own responses to the sources you find and your impression or interpretations of the texts and facts at hand. These are important in pulling together your own thesis and overall research paper.

Here is a summary of the strategies we have discussed to assist you when reading and taking notes from research sources:

- Use the introduction, conclusion, and table of contents to provide an overview of that research source's argument and to point you to the chapters and sections most relevant to your topic. The introduction or first chapter often states the author's thesis and goals, a preview of the argument, and sometimes even a summary of each chapter.
- Distinguish carefully between the author's interpretation and your own interpretation. You are gathering facts and evidence to support your own arguments, while you also assert your interpretation clearly and confidently. Remember that your view may or may not agree with your various sources' interpretations. (See "Fact and Opinion" in Chapter 3, p. 24).
- Keep track of disagreements among your sources. Whether your sources disagree with one another outright or differ only slightly in interpretation of the same events or texts, such discrepancies could lead you toward an interesting topic or thesis. You should also think about which argument you find more convincing and why.
- Keep track of your own impressions and reactions to what you read. Do you agree or disagree with the ideas? Do any facts or assertions seem strange, surprising, or completely wrong? Do you notice a bias in the writer's perspective? Do you object to any particular point or interpretation? Does the author seem to take certain points for granted or overlook certain possibilities?
- Note the source's critical perspective. Some authors will acknowledge that perspective directly within the first few pages; others will leave you to work it out. An awareness of your source's theoretical assumptions or framework—textual, contextual, post-structuralist, environmental, feminist, and conservative are some examples—will help you understand the source's argument and possible limits. You do not have to agree with a source's theoretical perspective in order to use it as part of your paper. In fact, if you strongly disagree with its perspective, reading the source may give you important insight into the other side of the issue and help you sharpen your own argument. (See Chapter 16, "Critical Analysis and Evaluation," and Chapter 18, "Argumentation.")

SAMPLE STUDENT RESEARCH PAPER

In the following paper, notice that Amanda Harrison has used current, pertinent information from credible academic and professional journals. In helping to contextualize her topic, she has also cited an article from the *Los Angeles Times*. Pay attention to how Harrison's opening paragraph uses research findings to fill in an introductory understanding. In selecting her information, she has made note of points that would serve the needs of an effective opening.

Sample Student Research Paper Using 2010 APA Documentation

Multiple Embryo Transfer: At What Cost?

Amanda Harrison

Summarizes
Pence's overview
of the controversy.
APA author-date
style.

Quotes IVF
Canada in
narrowing
discussion.

1   Since the birth of the first "test-tube" baby, Louise Brown, in 1978, artificial reproductive therapy (ART) has become a controversial topic with personal, financial, ethical
and religious implications (Pence, 2004, p. 152). One specific form of ART is in vitro
fertilization (IVF), defined as the "procedure in which an egg is removed from a follicle and fertilized by a sperm cell (outside of the human body) in the laboratory" (IVF
Canada, 2009). The reasons for using such a procedure in order to conceive are multifaceted and may include blocked fallopian tubes, poor sperm quality, or the use of
donor eggs by aging potential mothers. However, one much-debated topic, regardless
of why IVF is used, is the *number* of embryos created by IVF and transferred to the
uterus for implantation. This specific issue has always been debated in the medical
community, but in light of the recent birth of an octuplet "litter" in 2009, embryo
transfer has become a common public debate as well. In the complex debate surrounding reproductive technology, "going too far" includes the transfer of too many
embryos.

2   Couples wanting to conceive but unable to do so are often heartbroken. Their
decisions regarding ART are often based on emotional rather than rational choices. With
this in mind, note that in both Canada and the United States, no laws regulate the
number of embryos to implant in IVF treatment (ARC, 2009). However, there are clinical practice guidelines that the Society of Obstetricians and Gynecologists of Canada
and its American counterpart endorse. These recommendations state that no more
than one or two embryos should be implanted into healthy women of moderate age

Citing more
than one study
or paper.

(Adamson & Ginsburg, 2009, p. 970; Min, Claman, & Hughes, 2006, p. 803). Why
then do situations occur, like the recent octuplet case, where six IVF-created, viable
embryos were transferred? In this specific case, all six embryos successfully implanted,
followed by a splitting of two embryos, resulting in two sets of identical twins, and a
grand total of eight babies (Minkoff & Ecker, 2009, p. 15.e1). The reasons for multiple
embryo transfers can be as diverse as the reasons for using IVF.

3   IVF is not a wholly funded medical treatment. Therefore, individuals must often
pay out of pocket for at least some of the costs, which are significant (Pence, 2004).
Because of the considerable costs, which run into tens of thousands of dollars, those

Quotation
smoothly
integrated in
the writer's own
grammar.
Ellipsis indicates
that Pence's
sentence
continues.

undergoing IVF may opt to transfer more embryos in order to increase their odds of
success. When "the chance of having any baby at all varie[s] directly with the number
of embryos implanted . . ." (Pence, 2004, p. 180), it is no wonder that couples may
decide to implant more to maximize their success. Even without the issue of costs,
couples already in a highly emotional situation, or those facing advanced age, may
want to increase their chance of pregnancy by implanting more embryos.

4   There are also religious and moral considerations. "Some may see in vitro embryos as similar to ex utero children" (Minkoff & Ecker, 2009, p. 15.e1). With this view,
the patient may choose to implant all her available embryos, giving each one a
chance at life, instead of facing a decision to destroy the remainder. Some religions
deem the point of conception the beginning of life, and therefore these individuals
argue that their embryos are living beings (Pence, 2004, p. 178). This may also lead
to the decision to transfer a large number of embryos, because of the belief that they
deserve a chance to live.

5   Since computer communication has become more widespread, families who
have "higher order multiples" (triplets and above) through IVF or other therapies, or
those who face fertility struggles, are increasingly sharing their stories online through
forums and open blogs. Since I am interested in becoming an obstetrician, and find
the topic of multiple births fascinating, I began to follow these blogs a few years ago.
My lay observations based on reading these various sites have led to my position that
embryo transfer should be minimized. The Stansel family in the United States, for example, recently had sextuplets at 22 weeks 6 days gestation. Unfortunately, this
means that the babies were born months early, and of the two surviving babies, both
have suffered brain hemorrhages among many other issues. Even now, at 5 months
of age, they remain in the NICU. The parents, like many others, "decided to move forward with carrying all 6 and leave it up to the Lord" (Stansel & Stansel, 2009). This is
the position of many religious patients, who deem it unethical to reduce the number
of implanted embryos, likening the procedure to abortion.

> Quotation marks indicate special-ized medical term commonly used in the profession.

> No page number given for a quota-tion from an on-line source.

6   Prospective parents who are not aware of the dangers involved may request that
multiple embryos be implanted. However, the risks to a mother carrying multiple babies
are well known to the medical community. She has an increased risk of experiencing
major problems, including hypertension, postpartum bleeding and death. Choosing to
give birth to more than one child also places the babies at risk, as was mentioned
above in the Stansel case. Low birth weight occurs more than half of the time in the
case of twins compared to less than 6 percent of the time with singletons. Mortality
rates are between 5 and 10 times higher for twins than for singletons. Complications
that are more likely to occur include mortality in childhood, congenital anomalies, cerebral palsy, intracranial hemorrhage, blindness, respiratory distress, patent ductus arterio-
sis (meaning the failure of the infant heart pathway to close at birth), infection, and
severe handicaps (Adamson & Baker, 2004, p. 517). For triplets, approximately 90 percent of births are preterm, and each baby is more than 20 times more likely to die in
the first month of life (Adamson & Baker, 2004, p. 518).

7   Unfortunately, these health concerns have an associated cost to society. The
various reasons for this include increased preterm deliveries, more low-birth-weight
infants, longer surveillance time by medical staff, more frequent hospital stays, and
increased caesarean sections. The costs of an average delivery escalate significantly

with multiple infants. As discussed by Adamson & Baker (2004), the cost for a single birth is estimated to be about $9,845 USD, for twins $37,947, while for triplets the delivery would cost $109,765 USD. Furthermore, the expenses in the first year of life associated with low-birth-weight babies are 24 to 44 times higher as compared to normal-birth-weight babies. According to a report published by the Institute of Medicine of the National Academies (2006), the high rate of premature births constitutes a burden of $26.2 billion USD a year.

8   In the past, babies born prematurely would most likely not survive. It was only with the creation of the neonatal intensive care unit (NICU) in the 1960s and 1970s that pre-term babies were given a tangible chance at survival (Pence, 2004, p. 217). Now, physicians justifiably have a duty of care to provide for these tiny humans, despite their poor prognoses and cost to society. Parents undergoing ART are likely thrilled to have a living baby, and are not as focused on the paramount risks and costs of transferring multiple embryos.

9   Embryo transfer is merely one issue in the larger field of assisted reproductive technology. Although I empathize strongly with couples facing fertility issues, I do not believe that the rights of potential children born through IVF should be ignored, and their parents' desire to reproduce should not supersede medical evidence. The fact is that children born in "litters" face developmental disadvantages that their singleton peers do not. It is therefore prudent that the current recommendations for transfer of minimal embryos be heeded, and the quality of life of IVF children should be the foremost concern. Interestingly, the medical community is fighting back against "rogues" who grossly abuse transfer guidelines and submit to patient demands that are clearly harmful. The physician responsible for the transfer of the six embryos resulting in the octuplets of 2009 has very recently been accused of "gross negligence" (Yoshino, 2010), which may lead to the loss of his licence to practise medicine.

References

Give the digital object identifier (DOI), if available, even if the medium consulted is traditional print rather than online (see Section 7 for more about DOIs). No period at the end.

Adamson, D., & Baker, V. (2004). Multiple births from assisted reproductive technologies: A challenge that must be met. *Fertility and Sterility, 81,* 517–522. doi:10.10161j.fertnstert.2003-09.041

Adamson, D., & Ginsburg, E. (2009). The octuplets tragedy. *Obstetrics & Gynecology, 113,* 970–971. doi:10.1097/AOG.0b013e3181a3dfab

ARC (Assisted Reproduction Canada). (2009). *Legislation, regulations and guidelines.* Retrieved from http://www.ahrc-pac.gc.ca/doc.php?sid=44&lang=eng

Institute of Medicine. (2006). *Preterm births cost U.S. $26 billion a year: Multidisciplinary research effort needed to prevent early births.* Retrieved from http://www8. nationalacademies.org/onpinews/newsitem.aspx?RecordID=11622

IVF Canada. (2009). IVF Canada & the life program. Retrieved from http://www.ivfcanada.com/about/index.cfm

Min, J., Claman, P., & Hughes, E. (2006). Guidelines for the number of embryos to transfer following in vitro fertilization. *Journal of Obstetrics and Gynaecology Canada, 28,* 799–813.

Minkoff, H., & Ecker, J. (2009). The California octuplets and the duties of reproductive endocrinologists. *American Journal of Obstetrics & Gynecology* 201(1), 15.e1–e3. http://www.ajog.org/

Pence, G. (2004). *Classic cases in medical ethics* (4th ed.). New York, NY: McGraw-Hill.

Stansel, A., & Stansel, T. (2009). The Stansel journey. 2009. Retrieved from http://www.stanseljourney.com/

Yoshino, K. (2010, January 5). California board accuses octuplets doctor of negligence. *Los Angeles Times.* Retrieved from http://www.latimes.com/news/local/la-me-octuplets5-2010jan05,0,97780.story

Section 4   Integrating
Information

Integrating information refers to how you blend summaries, paraphrases, and direct quotations into your paper. You need to do so in a manner that serves your essay but that also clearly acknowledges your source, accurately relays information, and distinguishes between the source material and your own words and ideas.

SUMMARIZING, PARAPHRASING, AND QUOTING

As you begin to expand your outline into full paragraphs, you will use three main techniques to refer to your sources: summaries, paraphrases, and quotations. These three techniques allow you to provide the supporting detail required in your paragraphs. Knowing when and how to apply these three basic techniques represents a major part of your work as a mediator of research sources. With experience, you will be able to decide in the note-taking stage whether the best way to convey a certain point is to summarize, paraphrase, or quote.

Summarizing

A summary is an extremely compressed representation of a longer text. Compared to a paraphrase, a summary is a far more extensive re-statement. A paraphrase usually includes the fuller meanings and implications, while a summary encapsulates one or two crucial points from the original texts as briefly as possible. We have discussed summarizing in Chapter 15, so here we will look simply at integrating summaries into representative paragraphs.

Sample summary of historical process

The British Conquest of New France on September 8, 1760, ushered in a new era. Now it was Britain's time to pursue its strategy in shaping a British North America. Britain did not always get its way, for the forces within the new colonies also moulded the colonists and their governments—but when the mother country did get its way, it was through metropolitanism.

This is the brisk opening paragraph of student Isaac Paonessa's essay "British North America—Whose Creation?" (p. 331). In three sentences, he sums up the interaction of forces which, in his understanding of the course text, checked against other sources, produced British North America. His summary captures the thesis of the text. From this opening encapsulation, he will go on to look more closely at the forces within the colonies and at metropolitanism, defining each and providing examples of their complex interaction. Openings of essays and of some body paragraphs are often places where brisk summaries work well to set up a topic for further study.

Sample summary of a book's argument

In 1990, historian Page Smith published an indictment of higher education in America, condemning, among other things, the publish-or-perish culture. Now, 14 years later, publish-or-perish at Canadian universities is, if anything, worse than ever. . . .

The essayist here uses his own words to re-state the controlling idea of Smith's book *Killing the Spirit*: American higher education is in a bad way. The essayist includes one of the reasons given by Smith, the publish-or-perish mentality. Although the essayist has not yet named the book here, the reader can refer to the works cited page to see Smith's name and thereby find the source named and listed in complete detail. The essayist's second sentence shows a transition from a cited summary to the essayist's response to the argument—in this case, agreement with it. The essayist will go on to explain his own further reasons.

Sample summary of a writer's view and counter-evidence

After relying on Romeo and Juliet to suggest young love's unreliability, Davies recommends setting Shakespeare aside, since presumably his portrayals of young love are all overly passionate and tragic. But Shakespeare also gave us Katharina and Petruchio of *Taming of the Shrew* and Beatrice and Benedick of *Much Ado about Nothing*, lovers who while still young at the end of their dramatized journeys have grown through trial and error to reach much of the understanding that Davies applauds.

In this example, student Mario Chan summarizes a view he finds in an essay by Robertson Davies as well as a view he interprets in two Shakespeare plays. Chan's interpretation of the love outcomes of *Taming of the Shrew* and *Much Ado about Nothing* opposes the Davies conclusion that Chan has summarized. This use of one summary after another to provide, in this case, a statement and refutation or, in other cases, a concession and a refutation is a staple of critical writing. Chan cites Davies directly by name and cites the two plays by author and title.

Paraphrasing

A paraphrase differs from a summary by representing a concentrated, detailed section of a selected text and by more or less matching the length of the material being represented. Like a summary, however, a paraphrase converts the source's words into those of the researcher. A paraphrase is a close, faithful representation of the original. A good paraphrase always carefully represents the telling details of the original quotation.

Sample text by John Ralston Saul

At the heart of all our talking is the idea that consensus can be reached if positions are laid out fully and enough time is taken to fairly consider what all can see. You will find this idea of consensus in almost every description of Canadian negotiations going back to the seventeenth century. And you will also find that the opposing view—that of complex situations being forced into clear solutions, which are enforced to the letter by contract—undermines our sense that consensus is possible.

Sample paraphrase of Saul's text

Saul maintains that Canada's history of dialogue reveals a persistent belief in achieving mutual agreements when due respect is afforded the process. The record of political discussions dating back to the 1600s demonstrates this belief in possible accord of diverse parties. On the other hand, a contrasting history also emerges in certain cases: simplistic, draconian decisions imposed on nuanced, multidimensional needs. This contrasting history compromises Canadians' faith that solutions can be achieved.

Some writers might be tempted simply to quote Saul's entire passage. Putting another writer's words into your own words, however, helps you to maintain consistent tone and control of the discussion. A summary achieves this, but so does a paraphrase. When the details of the material you wish to report are important, then a paraphrase serves you better than a summary, which must reduce the material to its essence only. Why would one need to convey the entirety of Saul's sample text? One likely reason might be to establish it as a theory or set of criteria to be applied and tested in your own essay. One could explore portions of Canadian history in search of the contrasting spirits Saul posits. One could also explore whether contemporary Canada is conflicted in its view on the possibility of reaching consensus. This passage, in other words, might well define a key concept in a proposed study. It therefore merits the detailed representation of a paraphrase, a method of definition that focuses on the ideas and makes those ideas clear to the writer as well as the reader. Quoting the passage would throw undue attention on Saul's chosen form of expression: it is his theory here that matters more than the precise words he has used to state it.

If you were asked to write an essay testing a certain writer's argument according to Stephen Toulmin's model of argumentation, would you open by summarizing, paraphrasing, or quoting Toulmin? (See Chapter 18, p. 204.)

You would probably paraphrase him, because his model is quite detailed and extensive, and all parts are necessary if one is to apply it as a tool of evaluation.

Quoting

In his writing workshops, writer Clark Blaise used to point out that quotations in a short piece of writing contain enormous force. A quotation, of course, is a word-by-word accurate transcription of someone else's exact words. It is signalled by surrounding quotation marks, "like this." Notice how the quotation marks draw extra attention to the words quoted. Quotations represent high-impact locations; they carry weight. As Blaise used to tell his writing students concerning quotations, in short pieces of writing, less is more—even essays of 20 pages may be considered relatively short pieces of writing. You will gain considerable effect by using quotations, especially if you select them with extreme care. However, if someone has worded something in a clumsy way, why not summarize or paraphrase? If someone you wish to cite has said something in 30 words when 15 would have done, why quote the entire 30 words? Remember Blaise's advice and intersperse quotations in your work with care, using only the choicest, most crucial words.

Look for quotable words that seem to represent the essence of what someone is saying. Copy or retain those words with extreme care for accuracy, noting the author's name and the source (both correctly spelled), as well as the page or paragraph number, if one exists.

Sample quotation

Pat Deiter-McArthur's article "Saskatchewan's Indian People—Five Generations" explains the generational loss of Aboriginal identity since contact with European colonialism. Referring to the fifth generation, the author sees it as confronted with three options: "assimilation, integration, or separation" (par. 10).

Here the writer has chosen to quote three definitive single-word terms. These terms are generally accepted as carrying specific meanings in the ongoing debates concerning future Aboriginal political directions. Using these exact words therefore makes sense: it clearly sets up the discussion to follow. Unlike the earlier passage from Saul, the three terms of reference here are succinct and distinctive, therefore quotable.

Sample quotation

Norrie Epstein describes Shakespeare's history plays as "a wonderful mix of battle-field heroics, familial relationships, feisty characters, power politics, and covert scheming" (159). The same can be said of *The Sopranos,* no longer playing on HBO after a major run but still widely enjoyed on DVD rentals.

This example is similar to the one immediately above. It, too, provides the specific terms used to understand a certain subject. The terms are interesting and colourful. Since the essayist intends to use these descriptive terms to analyze a contemporary organized crime story, using them precisely as given emphasizes the unusual aspect of seeing a modern television story in the light of Shakespeare. Maintaining Epstein's exact wording emphasizes the fun of demonstrating a strict concordance.

Sample quotation

Commenting on quality, the renowned urban artist Shepard Fairey says that technically, Banksy's work is "very strong" and "pleasing to look at"; it is deliberately "not overly complex and intimidating," but that is in the interests of including a wide community.

This quotation follows a discussion of certain skeptical views of Banksy's actual merit as an artist. Including Fairey's exact wording adds something definite and therefore more persuasive to his authority. It shows that Fairey did not simply utter some vague platitudes but truly thought about and articulated what is technically distinguishing and accomplished in Banksy's craft.

Sample quotation

People familiar with a good portion of Shakespeare's 33 plays will surely agree that his insight into human behaviour and motivation is remarkable. This, however, does not make a literary form into a psychology book or a reflection of "real people." As Robert McKee, a leading authority on story-writing, reminds us, "A character [in fiction] is no more a human being than the Venus de Milo is a real woman. A character is a work of art, a metaphor for human nature" (375). A play should not be taken as grounds for a scientific conclusion about people.

The quotation follows a concession. The essayist acknowledges that Shakespeare shows remarkable insight into human nature, but the writer also wants to make the point that this idea becomes excessive when imagining Shakespeare as a twentieth-century psychiatrist and his inventions as flesh-and-blood people. Quoting an authority on storytelling, therefore, represents a striking way to rebut, or correct, the excessive idea. Notice that the essayist has chosen a particularly assured, lively, and vivid quotation. The essayist has inserted the words "in fiction" into the quotation in editor's square brackets to ensure that the sense is clear. The brackets indicate an addition by the writer who is presenting the quotation.

In all four of the above examples, the source is clearly named and can be found listed in the works cited or references list at the end of the essay.

Distinguishing between Quoted Material and Your Own Views

Below the following research note card are hypothetical examples of two pieces of writing that draw from it.

Sample Note Card

Source: "The central question of Michael Ondaatje's poem 'Letters and Other Worlds' is why the turbulent, solitary father could not communicate, at any level, with his family, though he could write so beautifully." (Meghan T. Peters, "Ondaatje's Frightening Family View," *York Experiments* 8:2 (2008): 174. Print.)

The first essayist below falls into inadvertent plagiarism because she borrows language and points from the source without full acknowledgment. The second essayist shows care in separating the secondary source's argument and language from her own views and language.

Incorrect use of quotation

Ondaatje's poem "Letters and Other Worlds" explores how the turbulent, solitary father cannot communicate, at any level, with his diverse family, though, as Peters points out, he "could write so beautifully" (147).

As you can see, most of the language of the secondary source ends up in the student's own sentence, and most of it is not acknowledged. This is plagiarism and can lead to serious consequences.

Correct use of quotation

Although Meghan Peters correctly points out that Ondaatje's poem "Letters and Other Worlds" examines an unpredictable father who cannot communicate with his family, "though he could write so beautifully" (147), Peters overlooks the often complex, painful, and withdrawn relationship many creative people have with the world.

In the preceding example, Peters's language and point are attributed fully to her, and the student takes the opportunity to express her opinions of what Peters's perspective may overlook in an interpretation of Ondaatje's poem.

Such proper handling of your secondary source quotations will contribute to an effective research paper.

Stylistic Considerations

As you move from note-taking and outlining to drafting, one of the challenges you face is how grammatically and formally to integrate the quotations you have gathered. Any quotations you use must fit smoothly into the flow of your own sentences. You need to punctuate carefully when including quotations, as if the quoted words were a natural part of your own sentence. If you use a long quotation (more than four typed lines in MLA style; 40 words or more in APA style), try to precede the quotation with an independent introductory clause followed by a colon. This allows your reader some preparation—a breath—before plunging into the long quotation. Such longer quotations are always set off from the rest of the text by block indentation and do not require quotation marks.

Integrating a long quotation

Despite popular opinion, lemmings are a sturdy, independent species, as Cornelia Zahl observes:

> Investigators are interested in lemmings' seasonal movements, but of even more pressing interest to scientists are the little creatures' population explosions. These significant population increases occur every three or four years, sometimes astounding even the most experienced lemming experts. Lemmings, in fact, are among the most prolific of mammals. Sometimes the weasel population on the tundra starts to soar, since the lemmings, as small rodents, are staples of some carnivore diets. (41)

Note that the period appears before the page citation in parentheses at the end.

If, on the other hand, you want to use only a short part of a quotation, you might begin the sentence with a few words of your own and finish the sentence by incorporating the significant element from your source. Students tend to rely far too much on long quotations—in some cases, because these fill in the word count and get the paper "over with." That is a poor reason for choosing a block quotation. If you use a long quotation, it had better be for a really important reason. A general rule of thumb is to quote only the choicest words and phrases and to handle the remaining ideas through attributed summary or paraphrase.

Integrating short quotations

Franklin is only one of several biochemists who claim that "working with Dr. Kostner was like being in daily contact with an unpredictable force of nature" (274).

Although Lisa-Marie Grierson maintains that society will eventually turn away from the computer, "coming to this point of anti-technological enlightenment will take decades and perhaps a century" (79).

In the second example above, the comma appears before the quotation simply because that is how the sentence would normally be punctuated. This comma separates the introductory dependent clause from the main or independent clause, which is the quotation here. Remember that you should not use any extra punctuation with a quotation when normal grammatical usage would not require that punctuation. In our first example above, no punctuation was required to work the quotation into the sentence's own language and syntax.

Watch for the extremely common mistake of creating a comma splice when introducing the quotation.

Comma splice

Some critics of Wong Kar-Wai's film *Chungking Express* find the camera technique purposefully distracting in order to complicate the representation of the characters, "the shifting and jarring camera work, which sometimes imitates a public area surveillance camera, tries to capture the rushing momentum in daily big city life, as well as the two main characters' emotional isolation" (Bugden 18).

The way to fix this punctuation error is to replace the comma directly before the quotation with a colon (:). This colon will set off the quotation, which is an independent clause, from the writer's own preceding independent clause that introduces it.

Square brackets appearing within a quotation indicate that a capital letter has been either added or removed or that a word or phrase has been added or changed.

Paul Hewson argues that "Big Rock [beer] tastes fresh and crisp . . . [, b]ut satisfying Canadian beer-drinkers is always a challenge" (30).

Here, the essayist has added the word "beer" in square brackets to clarify exactly what the brand name "Big Rock" indicates and has also used square brackets to indicate that a comma has been added and a capital "B" has been changed to a lower-case "b," allowing the essayist to shape the quotation within the syntax of his or her own sentence.

Ellipses

The three dots or "points" after "crisp" in the above example are called an *ellipsis* and indicate that some words have been omitted. Three points form ellipses within a quotation; however, an ellipsis that appears at the end of a sentence still requires the period.

Pamela J. Salzwedel argues that "Heathcliff in Emily Brontë's *Wuthering Heights* experiences a crisis as a boy because of sudden socioeconomic realization, but returns to the scene of his trauma as a wealthy and vengeful man . . ." (69).

As prescribed by MLA (Section 6) and APA style (Section 7), the period follows the parentheses of the page reference. If there are no page references in parentheses, place commas and periods inside your quotation marks. Colons and semicolons should be placed outside your quotation marks, but only if they are not part of the quotation.

E. L. Doctorow's 1971 novel *The Book of Daniel* is "a law-literature classic"; it explores the Rosenberg case during the U.S. Cold War frenzy.

If your quotation runs into another sentence and the quotation does not need to be indented into a block, the quotation marks straddle the two sentences.

Fraser's book *Violence in the Arts* boldly contends that "our attitudes towards violence are deeply confused. The organized violence in the film *The Godfather* seems to have audience support" (19).

Fair Use

In general, small changes using square brackets and ellipses can be made within quotations from your sources, provided these changes do not alter or manipulate the quotation's original meaning. In a quotation, you must represent the author's view fairly.

Original quotation

"The U.S. trade embargo against Cuba stands as a colossal contradiction to the new principles of international free trade. A continuing embargo shows that rather than functioning as a fair and globally open economic plan, free trade is only what the U.S. government says it is at any given moment" (Kostyrenko, *Free Trade and Its Political Contradictions*, 232).

Unfair, misleading use

"The U.S. trade embargo against Cuba . . . function[s] as a fair and globally open economic plan . . ." (232).

Fair use

"The U.S. trade embargo against Cuba [reveals that] . . . free trade is only what the U.S. government says it is at any given moment" (232).

Weak integration of sources (sample paragraph)

Jim Simpson contends that the musical *The Sound of Music* "raises important questions about the fragile triumph of private happiness in the face of turbulent international events" (53). Mary Ciccione seems to disagree: "*The Sound of Music,* as pleasant as the singing is, addresses nothing of any substance, even more blatantly than *Willy Wonka and the Chocolate Factory,* a film musical about chocolate" (178). However, Julie Andrews's optimism, according to Burton Bachman, "allows viewers to believe in the healing-power of music, especially the singing voice as a sign of hope" (22). I guess I agree with some of these points, but not with all of them.

Better integration of sources with essayist's perspective

Critics continue to be divided on the thematic importance of the film musical *The Sound of Music*. Although Mary Ciccione argues that the film "addresses nothing of any substance" (178), Bachman's view is that Julie Andrews's optimism "allows viewers to believe in the healing-power of music, especially the singing voice as a sign of hope" (22). Simpson also agrees that the film has substance, since it raises "important questions of the fragile triumph of private happiness in . . . turbulent international events" (53).

FINAL WORD

Written guidelines can help you to integrate your research sources, but practice and writer's instincts must come into play. Remember your three main choices—summary, paraphrase, and direct quotation—and the special strengths of each.

Section 5 Documenting
Information

Why document sources? *The Chicago Manual of Style* replies: "[e]thics, copyright laws, and courtesy to readers" (594). Kate Turabian, in *A Manual for Writers of Research Papers, Theses, and Dissertations* (see p. 299), lists four good reasons for citing sources: to give credit, to assure readers about the reliability of your information, to share with readers the research tradition with which you are connected, and to offer further directions for pursuing the topics and ideas you have discussed (133–34).

Documentation is therefore taken very seriously in academic writing. When you document your sources, you credit other work that appears in some way in your own essays. You credit all ideas and terms that are not your own and any facts that are not deemed common knowledge. Through citations, proper documentation informs your readers exactly what sources you decided to work with. Citational acknowledgment blended into your careful integrating of summaries, paraphrases, and quotations allows your reader to gather what positions your sources take, and how these sources differ from your own ideas and language. In short, documenting is citing clearly all use of sources in the body of your essay in a manner that keys those usages to complete information about the source (often at the end of your paper or, in some cases, in footnotes at the bottom of the page).

Merely providing a list of your sources at the end of your essay without giving specific citations in the body of your essay, where aspects of those sources have been used, constitutes plagiarism, whether deliberate or not. You must cite on each page where a source's words or ideas appear.

ASSISTING YOUR READER AND AVOIDING THE APPEARANCE OF PLAGIARISM

By clearly acknowledging everything you take from sources and providing complete information on those sources, you give valuable background to your reader and avoid any appearance of plagiarism. See the introduction to this part (p. 257) for an important caution concerning possible perceptions of plagiarism.

LINKING THE AUTHOR'S SURNAME TO YOUR LIST OF SOURCES

The preferred form for citations and bibliographic entries varies among disciplines, but the basic purpose is always the same: to acknowledge sources and make it easy for readers to find them. The basic documentation method shared by MLA, APA, and other systems is also the same: acknowledge your source with a brief citation that keys to more complete information at the end of your paper. Usually this is accomplished by linking the last name of the source author, included with the summary, paraphrase, or quotation in the body of your essay, to the first word of the related bibliographic entry in the alphabetical list at the end of your paper. The following example uses MLA form to illustrate this basic practice, but the principle is the same for other systems.

Example: In your essay you might write the following:

As John Ralston Saul explains, "Anyone whose family arrived before the 1760s is probably part Aboriginal" (8). His point, he says, is not to build a racial argument but to remind us of the fundamental history of intermingling and intercultural exchange . . .

At the end of your essay, in your list of sources, you will present Saul's book, in alphabetical order according to author surnames:

Works Cited

Dickason, Olive. *Canada's First Nations.* Toronto: McClelland & Stewart, 1992. Print.

Moses, Daniel David. *Pursued by a Bear: Talks, Monologues, and Tales.* Toronto: Exile, 2005. Print.

Saul, John Ralston. *A Fair Country: Telling Truths about Canada.* Toronto: Viking, 2008. Print.

Taylor, Drew Hayden. *Funny, You Don't Look Like One.* Penticton, BC: Theytus, 1998. Print.

The reader examining your discussion and encountering the author's surname, "Saul," which you have given with the quotation, will be able to look for "Saul" in your works cited list at the end of the paper. Notice that on a works cited page a paragraph feature called the "hanging indent" helps the reader to find author surnames along the left-hand margin. When source information spills past the right-hand margin, the new line below is indented so that the last name of each author stands out prominently. All the works presented in your works cited list must be explicitly referred to at least once in the body of your essay. That is, in the example above, the writer has somewhere used and acknowledged material from Dickason, Moses, and Taylor, in addition to Saul.

> From the last name of the author in the text to the last name of the same author listed in alphabetical order at the end of the paper is the basic connection in a majority of citations.

After the citation in the body of the essay, the reader notes the page number locating the quotation in the source (in this case, p. 8). By consulting the list of sources, a reader then discovers the title of the text and its important bibliographic details, such as publisher and date of publication. The page number itself provides clear direction to the precise passage that you have used. Your usage in this example involves a quotation, but it might also be a summary or a paraphrase. All three—quotation, summary, and paraphrase—require page or paragraph references in MLA, while APA requires page or paragraph references for quotations and encourages them for summaries and paraphrases.

FORMS OF DOCUMENTATION

Publications in the humanities and arts generally use the Modern Language Association (MLA) style of documentation. Editors in the behavioural and social sciences prefer the American Psychological Association (APA) style. These two styles are regarded as the most widely used forms of documentation, but there are many others, including the University of Chicago style and the American Anthropological Association (AAA) style. In Section 6 we cover some common basics of MLA style and provide a sample essay; in Section 7 we cover some common basics of APA style and provide a sample essay. In Section 8, we provide samples of a history essay using Chicago style and an anthropology essay using AAA style. As you will have noticed, throughout the Rhetoric we have included examples of MLA style as well as some APA style.

The information we provide on this topic should serve as a handy reference and help you get started, but it is your responsibility to find out what form of documentation your instructor requires.

More advanced documentation manuals are available in most college or university bookstores, as well as the reference section of your college or university library. Some of the information can also be found online and, in some cases, downloaded. The most recent versions of APA and MLA documentation guidelines appear in the following publications (listed in MLA style, by the way):

- American Psychological Association. *Publication Manual of the American Psychological Association*. 6th ed. Washington, DC: American Psychological Association, 2010.
- Modern Language Association of America. *MLA Handbook for Writers of Research Papers*. 7th ed. New York: Modern Language Association of America, 2009.
- Modern Language Association of America. *MLA Style Manual and Guide to Scholarly Publishing*. 3rd ed. New York: Modern Language Association of America, 2008.

MLA and APA forms are both based on the use of short *parenthetical* citations within the text. This basic technique is illustrated and explained in Sections 6 and 7. You can also learn more about both styles by visiting their websites:

http://www.mlahandbook.org

http://www.apastyle.org

Also widely used is *The Chicago Manual of Style*. It illustrates two basic systems preferred by Chicago: **notes and bibliography**(demonstrated in Section 8) and **author-date** (similar to aspects of APA and MLA).

- University of Chicago Press. *The Chicago Manual of Style*. 16th ed. Chicago: University of Chicago Press, 2010.
- Turabian, Kate L. *A Manual for Writers of Research Papers, Theses, and Dissertations: Chicago Style for Students and Researchers*. Ed. Wayne C. Booth, Gregory G. Colomb, and Joseph M. Williams. 7th ed. Chicago: University of Chicago Press, 2007.

The American Anthropological Association issues a guide that draws largely on the Chicago author-date system (demonstrated in Section 8).

American Anthropological Association. *AAA Style Guide 2009*. Arlington, VA: AAA Press, 2009.

WHEN TO DOCUMENT

Many students believe they need to acknowledge their sources only when quoting directly from a text. This presumption is very misguided. Any time you use another person's idea or phrasing in an essay, you have to acknowledge your source. This idea or phrasing is someone else's work and someone else's property. (When a work is published, copyright sometimes reverts from the author to someone else.) You must acknowledge sources when you quote directly, summarize, paraphrase, or otherwise use someone else's ideas. Sometimes you also have to acknowledge sources for factual information, not only opinions and interpretations.

You do not, however, need to document sources for factual information that is considered common knowledge either to the public or in your field. Some examples of common public knowledge include Columbus's arrival in North America in 1492, Pierre Trudeau's service as a Canadian prime minister, Alice Walker's authorship of the novel *The Color Purple,* Newfoundland's joining Canada last among the provinces, and Leonard Cohen's creation of sad songs. Sometimes it is difficult to know what would be considered common knowledge, but one indication would be that all the sources you have consulted agree on the facts. If you are doubtful about what counts as common knowledge, be safe and cite your source.

For guidance on how to do that, consult Sections 6, 7, or 8, according to the style guide required by your course or program.

MANUSCRIPT FORMAT

For both MLA and APA, double-space the entire manuscript, including inset block quotations and the works cited or references list. Use $8\frac{1}{2} \times 11$ inch paper, printing on one side only. Observe 1-inch margins, but use ragged style at the right-hand margin, with automatic hyphenation turned off. Indent every paragraph $\frac{1}{2}$ inch ($1\frac{1}{2}$ inches from the left-hand edge of the page). Indent the first line of block quotations 2 inches from the edge of the page and the remaining lines $1\frac{1}{2}$ inch. Use standard font style and size, for example, 12-point Times New Roman. See Section 6 (p. 309) for a sample of an MLA essay first page. See Section 7 (pp. 322–23) for a sample of an APA essay title page and first page. APA also requires a running head for papers that are to be sent for professional external review. Some instructors may therefore want you to learn that feature of presentation. The running head includes the title but not the author's name (so that it can be evaluated without bias by the peer-review committee). The APA-style running head is demonstrated in the sample APA essay (p. 322). See the APA manual or website for guidance on other parts of formal APA papers, such as the abstract.

Remember, again, that your essays should be double-spaced and all new paragraphs should be indented. The sample essays in this text use single spacing; otherwise they replicate the stylistic and formatting features you will be expected to follow.

Section 6   MLA System

Publications in the humanities and arts generally use the Modern Language Association (MLA) style of documentation. Your instructors for courses in the arts and humanities will most likely require that you format your papers and acknowledge your sources according to this system. The following section illustrates some of the basics of MLA, with reference to the most recent MLA updates in the *MLA Handbook for Writers of Research Papers,* 7th edition (2009). If you plan to concentrate on humanities and arts, it would be a good idea to acquire this reference book. A sample essay in MLA style appears toward the end of this section.

PARENTHETICAL CITATIONS WITHIN THE PAPER

MLA style inserts short citations in the body of the essay within parentheses. These brief citations point to full ones listed at the end of your paper, usually by linking the last name of the author in the body of your essay to the same name in the list of works cited. The author's last name is the first word of the related bibliographic entry in the alphabetical list. Some of the most common types of citations are provided below.

Sample Citations within the Paper

The MLA system requires that you provide your citation's page number in parentheses after the reference. You must also provide the author's name if it is not already included in your sentence. If you refer to more than one work by the same author, you should also include in the parentheses a short version of the title, such as one key word.

> Winters argues that *Hamlet* was written by Queen Elizabeth (17).[Here there is no need to repeat the author's name in parentheses, so just include the number of the page on which this information can be found.]

> One critic even suggests that *Hamlet* was written by Queen Elizabeth (Winters 17). [Here the author's name is supplied in parentheses along with the page number because the name does not appear in the sentence.]

> In her most recent article, however, Winters backs away from her earlier claims that *Hamlet* was written by Queen Elizabeth ("Reconsideration" 175-76). [Here a short version of the article's title is given because more works than one by Winters are listed in the works cited list for the essay. The article title takes quotation marks. If the work were a book, then the title would be italicized.]

> Contrary to popular belief, the first underground railroad between the U.S. and Canada existed to free slaves held on Canadian territory (Walker 19). [Here the citation is required to support little-known information.]

> **Tip:** Note that in MLA style, no comma separates author and page number in the parentheses. Note also that MLA style does not use the abbreviation "p." before the page number:
>
> (Winters 17)

More MLA Guidelines: General

The following are more general guidelines for MLA style.

- When first naming an author, general practice is to state the first and last names as they appear in your source (e.g., *Susan Harris*) and only the last name thereafter. Do not include formal titles (*Dr., Ph.D., Mr., Ms.,* etc.).
- Use "qtd. in" (for "quoted in") for quotations taken from an indirect source, that is, when you quote something that is a quotation in your source.

James Bone wrote that London resides in "the appearance of great shadows where there can be no shadows, throwing blackness up and down" (qtd. in Ackroyd 110).

- Use regular numerals to indicate an act and scene in plays (*Lear* 2.2).
- Use Roman numerals (lower case) only for pages from a preface, introduction, or table of contents.
- Use a colon, not a dash, to separate your essay title from its subtitle.
- Use double quotation marks around quotations, and use single quotation marks around quotations within those quotations.

On the street he met Isabel, who said, "My mother told me to tell you, 'Get a life.'"

- Italicize the names of websites and online databases. Place titles of website pages in quotation marks.
- If a work has two or three authors, give all the last names. If the work has more than three authors, you can give either all the authors' names or only the first name followed by "et al."

Some suggest that Canada is more than the sum of its parts (Gold et al. 27).

Use the same form in the works cited entry as you do in the text.

- Be consistent in your formatting throughout your work.
- Download or print off online material that you are using, especially if the site or source appears likely to change or disappear.
- Keep a printout of any paper submitted as well as electronic copies in at least two places.

More MLA Guidelines: Works Cited

Follow these guidelines as you prepare your works cited list:

- For print sources, place that mode of publication, "Print," at the end of the listing.
- For online sources, give the mode of publication "Web" and the date of access (e.g., Web. 28 Sept. 2010.).
- For online sources, give a URL only if the reader will need it to find the source or your instructor requires it. Enclose the URL in angle brackets and end with a period. Place the URL after the date of access. If you must break a URL, do so only after the double slashes or a single slash.
- Shorten publishers' names. Use "Pearson" rather than "Pearson Education."
- If your source is written or edited by two or three people, format the full citation as illustrated here:

Gold, Eleanor, Eli Sky, and James Cedar. *Views of Canada*. Toronto: Maple Leaf, 2000. Print.

MLA FULL CITATION IN THE FINAL WORKS CITED PAGE

Entries in MLA style are listed on a separate page at the end of your essay under the heading "Works Cited" (see the sample research paper in MLA style that follows). All authors are listed alphabetically by surname. The author's last name appears first, followed by a comma, followed by his or her full first name, and then a period. Then the title of the work appears: a book title is italicized; an essay title in a scholarly journal appears in quotations; and the name of the journal, italicized, follows the essay title. For scholarly articles, volume and issue numbers follow the title of the journal, followed by the date in parentheses, a full colon, and the page spread (the article's first and last page). Be sure to include the entire page spread even if you used just a portion of the article. Here are some examples of common MLA works cited listings:

Book

Axelrod, Alan. *Elizabeth I, CEO: Strategic Lessons from the Leader Who Built an Empire*. Englewood Cliffs, NJ: Prentice Hall, 2000. Print.

Article in a journal or magazine

Kelly, Philip F. "The Geographies and Politics of Globalization." *Progress in Human Geography* 135.23 (1999): 379-400. Print. [The number 135 refers to the volume number, and 23 is the issue number. For journals that use only an issue number, the entry would appear as follows.]

Kelly, Philip F. "The Geographies and Politics of Globalization." *Progress in Human Geography* 23 (1999): 379-400. Print.

Article in a scholarly e-journal

Conrad, Dianne. "Cognitive, Instructional, and Social Presence as Factors in Learners' Negotiation of Planned Absences from Online Study." *International Review of Research in Open and Distance Learning* 10.3 (2009): n. pag. Web. 24 July 2010. [Use "n. pag." (for "no pagination") if items are entirely unnumbered or numbered separately rather than continuously across the issue. Date of access follows the mode of publication identifier "Web."]

Scholarly article in an online database

Hashamova, Yana. "(Re)negotiating Identities: Representations of Muslim Minorities in Bulgarian Film." *Film International* 8.3 (2010): 49-61. *Film and Television Literature Index*. Web. 26 July 2010. [The title of the database is in italics as is the name of the journal. Date of access follows the identifier "Web."]

Article in an essay collection (including names of editors)

Partington, Angela. "The Designer Housewife in the 1950s." *A View from the Interior: Feminism, Women and Design*. Ed. Judy Attfield and Pat Kirkham. London: Women's Press, 1989. 206-14. Print.[Include the page span of the reading after the year of publication and before the medium.]

Morrisseau, Norval. "The Indian That Became a Thunderbird." *Canadian Short Fiction: From Myth to Modern*. Ed. W. H. New. Scarborough: Prentice, 1986. 26-29. Print.

Article in a newspaper

Tibbetts, Janice, and Kate Jaimet. "Trudeau Dead at 80." *Edmonton Journal* 29 Sept. 2000: A1. Print. [Abbreviate the names of all months except May, June, and July.]

Article in a newspaper online

Yoshino, Kimi. "California Board Accuses Octuplets Doctor of Negligence." *Los Angeles Times*. Los Angeles Times, 5 Jan. 2010. Web. 5 Jan. 2010 [Los Angeles Times is given twice, once as the name of the publication and once as the publisher of the publication. Often the name of a website publication differs from that of the publisher. The article does not have page numbers or refer to the location of the article in the print issue. The works cited listing therefore omits reference to page location.]

Article in a magazine

Boyden, Joseph. "The Hurting." *Maclean's* 5 July 2010: 20-23. Print. [Abbreviate the names of all months except May, June, and July.]

Article in a magazine online

Fairey, Shepard. "Banksy." *Swindle.* Swindle Summer 2006. Web. 12 July 2010.
[Swindle is given twice, once as the name of the publication and once as the publisher of the publication. As already noted, often the name of a website publication differs from that of the publisher. The article does not have page numbers. The works cited listing therefore omits reference to page location.]

Book by a group or corporate author

American Psychological Association. *Publication Manual of the American Psychological Association.* 6th ed. Washington, DC: APA, 2010. Print.

Book or film review

Ebert, Roger. Rev. of *Jesus of Montreal,* dir. Denys Arcand. *Chicago Sun-Times* 18 July 1990: E4. Print.

Website

Walker, Alice. "Letter from Alice Walker to President Clinton." Cuba Solidarity, 13 Mar. 1996. Web. 26 Oct. 2000 <http://www.igc.apc.org/cubasoli/awalker.html>. [The writer provides the URL to assist the reader in finding the document.]

Blog

Astyk, Sharon. "So You Want to Cut Your Resource Usage?" Archives. Going Green. *Casaubon's Book.* Sharon Astyk, 21 Jan. 2010. Web. 12 July 2010. [Astyk recently joined the hub ScienceBlogs, but this works cited listing treats her long-standing blog *Casaubon's Book,* rather than the hub, as the larger work under which her article-posting resides. The listing treats her as publisher since she created *Casaubon's Book* and continues to write and post to it, though under a hub agreement she could receive modest monthly remuneration for her work. No URL is given as *Casaubon's Book* may well be more permanent than its Internet location. The words "Archives" and "Going Green" assist visitors with a pathway of links to the article from the blog landing page.]

The Hanging Indent

Note that all lines subsequent to the first line of each works cited entry are indented half an inch, a format known as a "hanging indent." Also double-space both within and between all your entries on the works cited page.

FOOTNOTES AND ENDNOTES

A handy device for providing extra information briefly in your essays, especially research papers, is the footnote or endnote. Footnotes appear at the foot (or bottom) of the relevant essay page, three line spaces below your last line of text.

Endnotes appear at the end of the essay, on a separate page entitled "Notes" or "Endnotes." This page appears just before your last page, where you alphabetically list your sources.

In an MLA-style essay, you can use either footnotes or endnotes, but not both. The first line of each footnote is indented half an inch, and any remaining lines in the footnote are flush against the left-hand margin. The footnote is single-spaced, but double-space between each footnote if you are including more than one on a single page. The notes or endnotes (in contrast to the footnotes) are double-spaced.

Designate a footnote or endnote using a superscript number:

Elephant herds in Kenya are fluctuating because of uneven government protections and surges of poaching.[3]

The footnote related to this point then appears with its corresponding number at the bottom of the page or, if you are using endnotes, at the end of the essay—but before your works cited page, if you have quoted sources.

Footnotes and endnotes usually function in three ways:

1. provide other references
2. supply further factual content
3. advance related observations to bolster argument

Footnotes and endnotes can supplement your discussion effectively and economically.

Footnote and endnote usage (hypothetical examples)

Britain's Royal Family continues to face damaging public exposure. The Duchess of York, Sarah Ferguson, seems prepared to become a spokesperson for almost anything to fend off her financial troubles,[1] while the young Royal Princes, William and Harry, continue to be ejected from London nightclubs for unruly behaviour. Furthermore, a former assistant to one of the chauffeurs for the late Diana, Princess of Wales, has recently given a controversial interview about Diana's alleged belief in intergalactic abductions.[2] Meanwhile, many senior members of British Parliament are raising legal questions about abolishing the Queen's traditional immunity to prosecution because of decades of unpaid parking tickets accrued by her carriage and horses during various royal processions.[3]

Footnote or endnote #1 (other references, in MLA style)

1. For a detailed discussion of the Duchess of York's previous financial troubles, see Theodore E. Bear's "Sarah's Creditors in a New Royal Age," *Monarchy Quarterly* 3.2 (1998): 114-27; and Ja-Yoon Kim's *Duchess for Hire* (Toronto: Pentium Press, 2001).

Footnote or endnote #2 (further content)

2. This account has been vigorously denied by spokespeople for Buckingham Palace. As well, the chauffeur's former assistant has recently told BBC News that he was misquoted, claiming that he said "ablutions," not "abductions."

Footnote or endnote #3 (further observations or argument)

3. I believe, along with several constitutional law experts, that the Queen's complete legal immunity, as well as the Royal Family's blanket immunity, from ever being

called to testify in court has no place in a modern England. Legal immunity actually damages their credibility rather than protecting it in the eyes of the public.

For more information on how to document sources in MLA style, see the MLA website at www.mla.org/style as well as the *MLA Handbook,* 7th edition.

SAMPLE STUDENT RESEARCH PAPER USING MLA DOCUMENTATION

Student Melanie Klingbeil's English 101 research essay on two poems by William Butler Yeats and two poems by Emily Dickinson offers an example of textual analysis drawing upon helpful secondary-source quotations. MLA style has been revised to reflect the latest (2009) MLA style updates.

Sample Student Research Paper Using 2009 MLA Documentation

Klingbeil 1

Melanie Klingbeil
Professor Lahey
English 101
24 March 2002

Selected Poems of Emily Dickinson and W. B. Yeats:
Beyond the Answers

1   Only without the universal questions of this world, without the mysteries that baffle great minds, and without the existence of contradictions, would the world be able to exist without philosophy. Mesmerized by their shared belief that there is more to understand than they already do, the poets Emily Dickinson (American) and W. B. Yeats (Irish) tried to walk through a door of understanding that could lead them into the realm of philosophy. Their contemplation and their philosophies emerged as poetry. Examples of their poetry prove that they were both capable philosophers, that they both vigorously contemplated realities beyond the fundamental world of material reality. Consider some titles of their works: Dickinson's "I know that He exists" (160) and "This world is not conclusion" (501); Yeats's "Byzantium" (1323) and "The Second Coming" (1320). Interpretations of these works can establish the differences between their two philosophies: where Dickinson questions religion, Yeats creates his own; where Dickinson considers the effects of the belief on the believer, Yeats puzzles over what shapes all human consciousness. What significance does this difference between the two poets truly bear? How does the distinction work? Interpreting these poems can lead to answers to these questions. I will consider what is at stake for both poets, and what, in their lives, accounts for their philosophical inclinations in order to explain what truly matters about the differences between Dickinson and Yeats.

2   The church was a part of Dickinson's early life. She understood the doctrines of Christianity and the practices of traditional religion. This understanding brought her to question, then reject the church. When the church claimed to have all the answers, Dickinson came up with new questions. How was Christianity an issue for Emily Dickinson? What would Christianity have taken from her were it not for her philosophy? Dickinson could not live as though she had the answers to the transcendental questions that troubled her, nor could she live as though she would ever attain them. Her poetry nourished her: with sanity, her contentment, her peace. As a critic has noted, "Dickinson lived with doubt without ever despairing" (Ferlazzo 31).

3   Dickinson's poem "I know that He exists" affirms not only her spiritual beliefs, but also the persistent disbeliefs that consume her. Her affirmation of her disbeliefs held her to an unconventional integrity—that all strong faith requires an ingredient of uncertainty in order for it to exist. Faith, by definition, must struggle with doubt.

No separate title page for MLA. Student name, instructor, course, and date are at top of page, flush left.

First letters of major words capitalized.

No underline or italics.

Usual MLA style is "I Know That He Exists," with major words capitalized. Instead, Klingbeil respects Dickinson's way of writing her titles.

Numbers in parentheses refer to pages in primary sources, listed under authors' names in Works Cited.

Biographical information common knowledge— no citation.

Quotation marks close sentence, then parenthetical citation appears, followed by period.

Author name cited, then page of quotation. Period follows final parenthesis

Quotation from primary source, and poem already identified.

Sentence identifies words of first line.

3   This uncertainty the church often ignores. The poem's first line, however, obviously makes a statement of faith. Dickinson acknowledges the separation God has from man by describing how He hides his "rare life / From our gross eyes." She thus affirms her belief in a supernatural being; she endorses a deity that seems no different than conventional Christianity's. Kimpel points out that other distinctions, however, between Dickinson's spiritual view and that of organized religion eventually resulted in her social rejection:

Quotation of more than four lines set off. No quotation marks. Period *before* parentheses.

> What she rejected, on the other hand, was their version of religion with
> its smug certainties. . . . Her disparagement of their self-satisfied attitude
> about their own understanding of the nature of God was, consequently,
> their provocation for ostracizing her from the "converted" and the
> "saved." (209)

4   Dickinson's faith emerges in her poetry not from what she knows about God, but from what she does not know about Him. Once her faith is affirmed in her poetry, Dickinson then suddenly expresses a profound perplexity over the possibility that this God plays a cruel game with his believers by offering salvation as nothing more than a joke:

More than three lines of poetry should be set off from the text.

> Would not the fun
> Look too expensive?
> Would not the jest
> Have crawled too far?

5   To deny this cosmic possibility would be to deny the spiritual uncertainties that engulf the human condition. For Dickinson, denying the uncertainties and anxieties of the human condition would be blasphemous, more so than questioning God's existence or God's intentions.

6   While Dickinson examines the personal uncertainties of spiritual beliefs, Yeats seeks broader answers to the metaphysical questions of the universe. Yeats pursues a life of fascination with metaphysics and the occult. Studying his philosophical poetry is much like taking a journey through a luminous spirit world. This is Yeats's non-institutional religion—a deep philosophy influenced by the realm of metaphysics. As one critic puts it, "Everywhere, he felt, was incontrovertible evidence of an invisible but eminently active spirit world" (Unterecker 19). But what was the value of this fascination to Yeats? Beckson, quoting Symons, one of Yeats's colleagues, points out that Yeats pursued the mysterious instinct to become an artist: "'he discovers immortal moods in mortal desires'" (128). These "mortal desires" underlie the purposes of Yeats's poetry. These desires reveal what was at stake for Yeats in his passion for metaphysics.

Following academic style, writer introduces quotation.

Smooth handling of Symons reference.

7   "Byzantium," for example, says more about the poet than most readers may real-ize. Yeats connects the flesh-and-blood reality of the twentieth century to the reality

Klingbeil 3

(that he believed) of the supernatural. The first stanza concludes with the clashing of two contradictions, but only through their clash do they truly become distinct:

> A starlit or a moonlit dome disdains
> All that man is,
> All mere complexities,
> The fury and the mire of human veins.

8   Yeats describes one of his major symbols, the full moon, which represents full and complete consciousness: all that the mind can become. For the human mind to attain such a supernatural feat, it must escape the constraints of this material world—reality as we know it. This elevation was Yeats's aim, his ambition, his necessity to become a great metaphysician and poet. This ambition is what the poem tells us about the poet. The contradiction between this world and the one beyond, Yeats points out, clashes as the "moonlit dome disdains." Only when the potential transcendental consciousness looks down upon its current, lesser state does either become truly defined. This potential consciousness Yeats longed for. His belief that he could in fact attain it was what was at stake for Yeats. According to Unterecker, "[o]nly, Yeats believed, if he could discover the design of the world of spirit would the pattern of the world of matter in which he felt himself to be trapped make sense" (23). Yeats's only way to preserve the spirituality he felt at stake was to manifest his intellectual escape from the confines of material reality into his philosophy and his poetry.

Square brackets used to change capital letter to lower case.

9   Dickinson's unusually solitary life accounts for her deep introspection and her heightened state of self-awareness. Dickinson might have been considered a recluse, yet as Richard Sewall observes, "she kept in vital touch throughout her life with all the people she loved and with many who just interested her" (521). This private yet expressive life allowed Dickinson to think philosophically about the internalized world of faith. By ceaselessly pondering and challenging herself over the nature and existence of the supernatural, Dickinson explored the concept of the sublime. She considered such transcendental concepts with amazement, only because she realized her own minute existence relative to it. Her poem "This world is not conclusion" describes the struggle of a believer trying to reconcile daily experience with the conception of a higher, divine, more perfect reality. This is the human struggle of knowing of the existence of a spiritual world, but perhaps lacking the ability to absorb it: "A sequel stands beyond, / Invisible, as music" (lines 2-3). Dickinson by no means claims that the sublime is simple: "The poet admirably characterizes the inaccessibility of this reality which is transcendent of the physical world and transcendent alike to the sensory experiences of which the human being is capable. It is, in other words, 'invisible'" (Kimpel 229).

The Kimpel quotation comes to less than five lines, so it is run into the text rather than being set off as a block quotation.

Single quotation marks around a quotation within a quotation.

10   Dickinson's words pose another dimension to this struggle. By comparing the "invisible" to music, she speculates that perhaps internalizing the sublime is no more

difficult than engaging with the presence of invisible, yet real music. The poem contin-ues with a firm statement that logic and faith are not to be confused. When it comes to believing in something that is invisible, "Sagacity must go" (8). This ambiguous statement could have two meanings.

11   "Sagacity" is defined as shrewdness, or keen perception. One could interpret the poet's statement as one of disdain for those who believe in something that is invisi-ble. In this view, to have faith means to throw aside all rational thought. The opposing but equally valid interpretation of this line would commend those who do not require logic in order to have faith—those people who can successfully internalize the sub-lime. Dickinson's poem strongly suggests that the human spirit does indeed possess the capacity to embrace more than a material world. The capacity to spiritually em-brace the unknown, however, does not require keen perceptive skills. In fact, "sagac-ity" is irrelevant; it fails to offer human beings any guarantees about spirituality. The last two lines of the poem describe the irony of the nature of human existence: we have an immense ability to sense a connection between ourselves and a "divine" force but, at the same time, we have no sure means of defining that force: "Narcotics cannot still the Tooth/That nibbles at the soul" (19-20). Neither timeless doctrines and intellectual theologies, nor structured religions (the "Narcotics") are capable of soothing or distracting us from the continual uncertainties (the "Tooth") that press upon the human soul. Narcotics are numbing; they induce sleep. Dickinson suggests that a rigid system of belief actually destroys and undermines, rather than nourishes, our spirituality and our philosophical sensibilities. Dickinson's introspective, yet socially aware life accounts for her philosophy that focuses on the hope for the human condi-tion in reality. Her poetry offers a brief meditation on the effects of the possibilities of an unknown world, the sublime, on a soul that exists in a material world.

12   As Dickinson contemplates the cosmos from her human standpoint, Yeats attempts to imagine the opposite. Yeats contemplates the fate of the human condition from the position of the cosmos. Yeats's intricate poetry never directly acknowledges the human soul—the soul of the individual. Instead, his poem "The Second Coming" vividly and intensely describes the onset of the new millennium—the chaotic onset of the second antithetical period. The entire poem penetrates into the horror that Yeats prophesies. Where does this horror come from? The *Spiritus Mundi,* a predominant concept of Yeats's philosophy, accounts for his fear. It releases the antithetical beast: "The Second Coming! Hardly are those words out / When a vast image out of Spiritus Mundi / Troubles my sight" (11-13). The *Spiritus Mundi* represents the soul of the world, the spirit of all human consciousness. Yeats no longer separates the supernatu-ral world from this one. The two realities become one. The soul of the world is, in fact, the source of the release of the beast. Yeats's apocalyptic images in the begin-ning of the poem do not centre on any physical details that appeal to our senses.

Lines are from primary-source poem, which reader can find under Works Cited.

Rather, the events he describes are conceptual and abstract, suggesting that what the speaker "sees" is the product of a mental world: "The ceremony of innocence is drowned; / The best lack all conviction, while the worst / Are full of passionate intensity" (6-8). Although the title of the poem alludes to the biblical prophesy of the return of the Saviour, Yeats's vision emerges not from an all-powerful deity, but from a source that is embedded in the human mind. Yeats designates humans as the source of their own chaos. Perhaps our minds and imagination have far more power than we are apt to realize. Yeats obviously believed just that.

13   At this point, considering the meaning of Yeats's philosophy is meaningless without considering Yeats's life and work. What could possibly account for his complicated and horrific vision? Yeats's world was full of political chaos and upheaval. An Irish nationalistic movement was taking place, but Yeats's class and personal beliefs prevented him from ever completely participating in it. Perhaps he never felt as though he belonged to his own social reality because of this personal exclusion.

14   MacGloin criticizes Yeats for not being more accountable to the social conditions around him: "William Butler Yeats's world was devastated, doomed, and unredeemable. His work is, in part, the marvel of a long personal anguish in its loss—a threnody—that by its obsessive and particularized nature allowed little compassion for the living" (484).

15   The beauty of philosophy lies in the combination of discipline and creativity it conceives. Logic, science, and even religion, in contrast, attempt to bear evidence for the separate proofs these areas of thought require to progress. Unfortunately, this sort of evidence might also terminate the seeking of spiritual development. Dickinson and Yeats, although very different, travelled this philosophical road through their poetry. While Dickinson expresses what spiritual change happens with her as a human being, Yeats theorizes about the effects that human consciousness has on the universe as a whole. Their philosophical searches exemplified how aspects of their lives accounted for their specific thoughts about their existence. Dickinson acknowledges in her poetry her belief that evidence for faith does not exist. In life, her refusal to join the church represented her refusal to diminish the concept of faith. For Yeats, his philosophy was his only means of coping with the politically unstable world around him. He was mesmerized by the possibilities of a spiritual world, simply because he was horrified by the material world around him. He does not look at the world of beyond from an individualistic point of view. It is almost as though Yeats tries to write to us from beyond that spirit world; his poetry gives him a place in that world—a claim to a part of it. Another beauty of philosophy.

Works Cited

Beckson, Karl. "'The Tumbler of Water and the Cup of Wine': Symons, Yeats and the Symbolist Movement." *Victorian Poetry* 28.1 (1990): 125-33. Print.

> For articles in academic journals, first author's name, then article title in quotation marks; next title of journal, underlined or in italics. Volume number is "28"; issue number is "1." Year of publication follows in parentheses, then colon introduces pages.

Dickinson, Emily. "I know that He exists." *The Complete Poems of Emily Dickinson*. Ed. Thomas H. Johnson. Boston: Back Bay, 1976. 160. Print.

> Copies of these poems available in many books and accessible online, yet best to provide source used. Textual and pagination differences occur from edition to edition, so listing primary-source edition ensures accuracy. Above, "160" refers to page of poem.

---. "This world is not conclusion." *The Complete Poems of Emily Dickinson.* Ed. Thomas H. Johnson. Boston: Back Bay, 1976. 501. Print.

> When author listed for two or more entries, MLA uses three hyphens.

Ferlazzo, Paul J. *Emily Dickinson.* Boston: Twayne Publishers, 1976. Print.

Kimpel, Ben. *Emily Dickinson as Philosopher*. Lewston: Edwin Mellen, 1994. Print.

MacGloin, T. P. "Yeats's Faltering World." *Sewanee Review* 95.1 (1996): 470-84. Print.

Sewall, Richard B. "In Search of Emily Dickinson." *Michigan Quarterly Review* 23.1 (1984): 514-27. Print.

Unterecker, John. *A Reader's Guide to William Butler Yeats*. London: Billing & Sons, 1959. Print.

Yeats, W. B. "Byzantium." *The Norton Introduction to Literature.* Ed. Jerome Beatty and J. Paul Hunter. 7th ed. New York: Norton, 1998. 1323. Print.

---. "The Second Coming." *The Norton Introduction to Literature.* Ed. Jerome Beatty and J. Paul Hunter. 7th ed. New York: Norton, 1998. 1319. Print.

Connections: Strong Points in Klingbeil's Use of Sources

1. *Awareness of time:* Different topics experience different rates of academic activity and change. Computer programming and fields related to science and technology, for example, tend to change on a weekly, even daily basis; research and development drives these disciplines. Contemplation of spiritual and philosophical ideas in poets of the past, however, tends to move at a much slower rate, with fewer new titles "hitting the presses." Thus when you note that Klingbeil's most recent source is 1994 (she wrote her paper in 2003), this does not necessarily indicate a lack of research, as it might if the subject had been technological change or English as the official language of the

United States. In fact, Klingbeil researched current information on her topic in journals and academic presses, but she did not neglect earlier publications that she found worthwhile. Ignoring the past is particularly inappropriate in humanities areas that often focus on the importance of history.

2. *Awareness of the need for credibility:* All of Klingbeil's sources are written by recognized professional scholars whose findings have been published by credible presses or peer-reviewed academic journals.

3. *Awareness of the need for recoverability:* All of Klingbeil's sources are in books and journals, and therefore recoverable by any reader.

4. *Awareness of balance and variety:* Within the parameters of her topic, Klingbeil reflects balance and variety by considering a number of different views and interpretations.

5. *Awareness of documentation norms:* Klingbeil closely follows all the guidelines in the *MLA Handbook for Writers of Research Papers*, 6th edition. For purposes of representing the latest MLA practices, we have updated her MLA form to the standard of the 7th edition.

FINAL WORD

Diligence, discipline, and patience are required for you to become familiar with academic research and documentation. More special situations occur in practice than we can possibly cover in this relatively short space. What we have covered here should serve most of your needs at the first-year level, but if you are serious about future scholarly work, you will obtain the *MLA Handbook for Writers of Research Papers,* 7th edition, and refer to it on a regular basis.

Section 7 APA System

Publications in the behavioural and social sciences generally use the American Psychological Association (APA) style of documentation to format papers and acknowledge sources. The following section illustrates some of the basics of APA, with reference to the most recent APA updates in the *Publication Manual of the American Psychological Association,* sixth edition (2010). If you plan to concentrate on the behavioural and social sciences, it would be a good idea to acquire this reference book. A sample essay in APA style appears toward the end of this section.

PARENTHETICAL CITATIONS WITHIN THE PAPER

APA style inserts short citations in the body of the essay within parentheses. These brief citations point to full ones listed at the end of your paper, usually by linking the last name of the source author in the body of your essay to the first word of the related entry in the alphabetical reference list. Some of the most common types of citations are provided below.

Sample Citations within the Paper—Emphasis on the Date

The APA system requires that you provide not only the author's name and a page number or numbers if you are referring to a specific part of a work, but also the date of the work in the body of your paper. Supply information in parentheses when it is not already part of your sentence. In the APA system these parentheses are placed within the sentence, right after the reference to the article or study:

In 1996, Hintz studied the intellect of mice. [There is no need for a page number here because there is no direct quotation, and the summary is very general.]

A recent study of the "previously underestimated intellect of mice" (Hintz, 1996, p. 56) proved that mice are smarter than seagulls. [Both author and date must be included in parentheses with the page number if the author and date do not appear in the sentence.]

Hintz (1996) argued that mice are not as large as they seem close up. [The author is part of the sentence, so only the date must be provided in parentheses. Note that this date appears right after the author's name.]

Three recent studies of the intellect of mice (Hintz, 1996; Lamb, 1994, 1997) have shown that mice have not yet discovered electricity or television. [Here is an example of how you would cite more than one study in parentheses. In this case, you are referring to one study by Hintz and to two studies by Lamb, conducted in different years. The sources are placed in alphabetical order.]

APA FULL CITATION IN THE FINAL REFERENCES LIST

References in APA style are listed on a separate page at the end of the essay under the heading "References." (See the sample research paper in APA style later in this section.) Like MLA style, APA uses the hanging indent format, with the first line of an entry flush left and all subsequent lines of that entry indented half an inch. Again like MLA, double-spacing is used between and within entries in APA. The author's last name appears first, followed by his or her initials, rather than the full first name. Then the date of publication follows in parentheses. The entries on this References page should appear in alphabetical order according to author surname. Print and electronic sources are mixed together. Many of the items will be journal articles that can be consulted through either medium. The APA style for the References page is a highly detailed format and requires these additional rules:

- Italicize titles and subtitles of books and journals.
- Do not place titles of articles in quotation marks.
- Capitalize only the first word of a book or article title [this does not apply for book or article titles within the body of the essay].
- For works with two authors, cite both names every time the citation occurs. For works with three to five authors, list all authors' names the first time the article is cited, then list only the first author followed by "et al." for subsequent citations. For works with six or more authors, give the first author's last name plus "et al." for all citations.
- Separate two or more authors' names with an ampersand (&), not the word "and."
- Italicize volume numbers of journals.
- Use the abbreviation "p." (or "pp." for plural) before page numbers of newspaper articles and works in anthologies, but not before page numbers of either scholarly journal articles or magazine articles.
- For reference list entries of articles in a journal that begins each issue in a volume at page 1, include the issue number after the volume number.
- For reference list entries of articles in a journal that pages upwards through all issues of a single volume, do not include the issue number.
- Include the digital object identifier (DOI) number for any journal article that has one assigned.
- For online sources, do not include date of access/retrieval unless you suspect the material may change over time, as in the case of wikis.
- If you access an online item that lacks a DOI, include the home page URL of the journal, book, or publisher (even for articles you retrieved from a database).
- In general it is not necessary to include database information, but if the item may be available only on a certain database (e.g., JSTOR), give the home or entry page URL for the online archive.

- Do not enclose URLs in angle brackets, and do not place a period at the end of URLs or DOIs.
- Use the words "available from" to denote a URL that leads to information about accessing an article or resource rather than to the item itself.

> **Tip:** Whenever possible, copy DOIs and URLs electronically, to avoid errors in transcribing them.

Here are some common examples of APA style:

Book

Axelrod, A. (2000). *Elizabeth I, CEO: Strategic lessons from the leader who built an empire.* Eaglewood Cliffs, NJ: Prentice Hall.

Italicize the title of the book, but capitalize only the title's first letter, the first letter after a colon, and any proper names. Next, list the place of your publication. Name the city of publication, plus the state or province, abbreviated (if published in North America), or the name of the country. Follow the location with a colon, then give the publisher's name. Close the citation with a period.

Reprint of an older book

Lampman, A. (1978). *Lyrics of the earth.* Ottawa, ON: Tecumseh Press. (Original work published 1895)

Check the copyright page for information about earlier publication. The in-text citation for this work would be (Lampman, 1895/1978).

Article in a journal

Kelly, P. F. (1999). The geographies and politics of globalization. *Progress in Human Geography, 23,* 379–400.

Article titles appear in much the same form as book titles in APA style. Only the first letters, the first letter after a colon, and the proper nouns are capitalized. Each important word is capitalized in the title of the journal, however. The page numbers of the article are listed from first to last page. No abbreviation for "page" or "pages" is included with journal articles. The volume number, as well as the title of the journal, is italicized in this style. The issue number is not given in this case because the journal pages through all issues in a volume.

Article in a journal with issue number

Kramer, T., Keindorfer, K., & Colarelli-Beatty, K. (1994). Who is the client: A replication and extension. *Consulting Psychology Journal: Practice and Research, 46*(3), 11–18.

Journal article with DOI

Adamson, D., & Ginsburg, E (2009). The octuplets tragedy. *Obstetrics & Gynecology, 113,* 970–971. doi:10.1097/A06.0b013e3181a3dfab

Do not include a space after the colon when providing the DOI.

Journal article without DOI, online

Min, J., Claman, P., and Hughes, E. (1999). Guidelines for the number of embryos to transfer following in vitro fertilization. *Journal of Obstetrics and Gynaecology Canada, 28,* 799–813. Retrieved from http://www.sogc.org/jogc/archive_e.aspx

Article in an essay collection

Partington, A. (1989). The designer housewife in the 1950s. In J. Attfield & P. Kirkham (Eds.), *A view from the interior: Feminism, women and design* (pp. 206–214). London, UK: Women's Press.

Morrisseau, N. (1986). The Indian that became a thunderbird. In W. H. New (Ed.), *Canadian short fiction: From myth to modern* (pp. 26–29). Scarborough, ON: Prentice Hall.

In the References list, APA style does not require quotation marks to enclose the titles of articles or chapters. Capitalize only the first words and proper nouns. To identify the book, supply the names of the editors, the book title, and the publication information after the title of the article. Note that it is important to identify any editors by including "(Ed.)" for "editor" and "(Eds.)" for "editors" after those editors' names. APA style requires the symbol "&" rather than "and" when the work has more than one author or editor. If the articles are contained in a book rather than in a journal, use the abbreviation "pp." for "pages" and place the listing of inclusive pages in parentheses after the book title, as in our example. Remember that the appropriate abbreviation for a single "page" is simply "p." For plural "pages" it is "pp."

Article in a newspaper

Tibbetts, J., & Jaimet, K. (2000, September 29). Trudeau dead at 80. *Edmonton Journal,* p. A1.

A newspaper article requires the year and the day of publication after the author's or authors' names. List the information in parentheses, with the year first. If you can find no author for the article, begin with its title and then give the date and other information. Note that the name of the newspaper is italicized to indicate that it is a publication. The page number follows after a comma with the abbreviation "p." for "page."

Reports and unpublished online material

Walker, A. (1996, March 13). Letter from Alice Walker to President Clinton. Retrieved from http://www.igc.apc.org/cubasoli/awalker.html

Unpublished work and material such as reports retrieved from a website is cited in a manner similar to that of a book. Begin with the author's name, if available. Follow this by the date in parentheses, then the title. As with most items on the References page, separate each item with a period. After the title, provide the information to enable the reader to find the article online, including your date of retrieval if the information may change.

Name the host if the document is in a large and complicated website, such as a university site (note that APA style breaks URLs *before* most punctuation):

Means, B., Toyama, Y., Murphy, R., Bakia, M., & Jones, K. (2010). *Evaluation of evidence-based practices in online learning: A meta-analysis of online learning studies.* Retrieved from Canadian Virtual University website: http://www.cvu-uvc.ca /Studentlearnbetteronline.htm

Online magazine article

Fairey, S. (2006). Banksy. *Swindle* 8. Retrieved from http://swindlemagazine.com /issue08/banksy/

Blog posting

Astyk, S. (2010, January 22). Going green: So you want to cut your resource usage? [Web log post]. Retrieved from http://scienceblogs.com/casaubonsbook/2010/01 /so_you_want_to_cut_your_energy.php?id=143441

For more information on how to document sources in APA style, go to http://www .apastyle.org/apa-style-help.aspx

SAMPLE STUDENT RESEARCH PAPER USING APA DOCUMENTATION

The following paper by Colleen McCaffery, written for her first-year composition course in 2006, demonstrates APA style. Form has been revised to reflect the latest (2010) APA style updates.

Sample Student Research Paper Using 2010 APA Documentation

APA requires paginated title page. Abbreviated and capitalized title appears as header on the left side of the page, preceded by "Running head:" (which appears on the title page only).

Full title of essay appears in upper and lower case with no underlining or other marks, on upper half of page. Follow it with your name, course information, instructor's name, and submission date, each on a separate line. Centre and double-space everything.

Introversion: The Dreaded Other

Colleen McCaffery

English 1112

Professor Jill Deschamps

March 12, 2006

INTROVERSION   2

1   When five-year-old Adam gets into the car after school dismissal, his parents
know to wait until later to ask him about his day. They have discovered that he prefers
simply to listen to music during the drive home. Once home, he usually unpacks his
latest library book and then escapes to the privacy of the family room to play with
some toys and unwind. After some time playing alone, he then becomes vocal and
social with his family for the rest of the evening. Since this is Adam's first year at
school, his parents were worried at first when he was uncommunicative and would
resist their efforts to get him to "open up" and talk about his day.

Quotation marks around "open up" signal colloquialism.

2   "Could there be something wrong at school?" they wondered. They decided to
observe him at school and noticed that he tends to prefer to be invited to join a
group rather than just jump in. He also seemed to prefer interacting with small groups
of children. Adam's teacher reported that the boy was doing well in all respects and
appeared to enjoy school. After reading a couple of books recommended by the
school guidance counsellor, the parents came to understand that there was nothing
"wrong" with Adam; he was simply introverted.

Quotation marks enclose parents' thought—a direct question.

3   The terms "introversion" and "extroversion" became known in psychology largely
due to Carl Jung's theory of psychological types (1921), and define two "complementary orientations to life" (Myers & Briggs Foundation, n.d., p. 7). Jung believed that
people had innate tendencies toward either the "inner world of concepts and ideas"—
introverts, or the "outer world of people and things"—extroverts (Briggs Myers & Myers,
1980, p. 7). Scientific studies and findings now show that Jung's theory may have
been accurate; people do seem to be born with innate preferences. For example, in
The Introvert Advantage (2002), psychotherapist M. O. Laney highlights the findings
of a twin study by N. Segal, a researcher, which reveal remarkable similarities in the
personality traits of adult twins raised in completely different environments and
without contact with each other. Other studies reported in the *American Journal of
Psychiatry* (as cited in Garcia, 1999) have shown, through brain scanning, that introverts and extroverts have blood flow differences in the brain. In addition to the biological findings supporting the idea of different inborn temperaments, the Myers-Briggs
Type Indicator (MBTI), a personality inventory tool based on Jung's "type" theory, has
been in widespread use for many years and is widely acclaimed by educators and
human resources officers to have merit. If, however, the concepts of introversion and
extroversion are generally recognized as innate and natural orientations, then why is it
that introversion seems to be considered the less desirable orientation—and more like
an affliction—in North America?

Note date right after source, in parentheses.

Note page or paragraph number with author(s) and date right after quotation from source.

Author first identified by initials and surname

Mentioning place of publication increases ethos of studies.

4   It is likely that some of the feeling that extroversion is a "more healthy" orientation is due to the significant influence of Sigmund Freud. In spite of a period of collab-
oration, Jung and Freud parted ways over a disagreement, after which Freud referred

Disagreement is common knowl-edge.

Date of Laney's book before page, since date not cited earlier in paragraph. Note Laney quotes from Freud.

to introversion only in relation to mental disorders. For example, Laney (2002) refers to Freud's writings on narcissism, where he emphasized the narcissist "turning inward away from the world" (p. 26), and also Freud's belief that the success of psychological development was to "find gratification in the world of external reality" (p. 26). Conversely, Jung felt that both extroversion and introversion were normal and natural points on a continuum, and not pathological unless these orientations were all-pervasive. It would appear that Freud's outlook on introversion is still more prevalent than Jung's, as evidenced in our language. In *The Introvert Advantage,* Laney provides

McCaffery clarifies that she quotes from Laney, who quotes from dictionary.

some of the following examples: the *Dictionary of Psychology* (as cited in Laney, 2002) defines introversion as "orientation inward toward the self. The introvert is pre-occupied with his own thoughts, avoids social contact and tends to turn away from reality" (p. 49). The same dictionary defines extroversion as "a tendency to direct the personality outward, the extrovert is social, a man of action, and one whose motives are conditioned by external events" (p. 50). Many other dictionaries use similarly neg-ative definitions for introversion. One particularly striking example is by *Webster's New World Thesaurus,* which defines an introvert as "a brooder, self-observer, egoist, nar-cissist, solitary lone wolf and loner" (as cited in Laney, 2002, pp. 50–51).

5   It is not hard to imagine why introversion might be considered the less desirable of the two orientations, if using the definitions above, and especially in North American culture where the ideal qualities are those associated with extroverts (loves

Quotation marks around "people person" signal professional and popular jargon.

to chitchat, likes to be the centre of attention, a "people person," feels energized and eager from social interactions, talks a lot, enjoys knowing a lot of people). The need for reflection and solitude, a reserved attitude, enjoyment of ideas more than people, and a small circle of deep friends are not traits we hear praised or valued much, and in some cases they can be mistaken for pathological tendencies. For instance, there is confusion around normal introverted traits and somewhat similar traits that are exhib-

No page numbers cited because refers to entire study.

ited by people with anxiety and personality disorders. Shyness is often thought to be the same thing as introversion, but it is not, though certainly introverts can be shy. Studies have differentiated shyness from introversion (Crozier,1990.) Shy people have social anxiety, which is a fear of social activities, but introverts prefer solitary activities for reasons other than fear. It is possible to be a shy extrovert. People with schizoid disorders also avoid contact with people and tend to isolate themselves; however, as with shyness, this is due to fear. When introverts prefer solitude, it is generally to reflect and restore their energy, which becomes drained from too much social interaction.

Cites article in *Atlantic Monthly* but also online. Online pages cited in References.

6   It is estimated that around 75 percent of North Americans are extroverts and 25 percent are introverts (Rauch, 2003, p. 2), and so it is possible that part of the bias against introversion may simply be due to percentages. In other words, the qualities of extroversion are considered more "normal" because that is the way most people are

INTROVERSION   4

in our culture, and therefore extroverts set many of the benchmarks of "normal" traits. As Laney (2002) points out, "America was built on rugged individualism and the importance of citizens speaking their minds. We value action, speed, competition, and drive" (p. 5). Does this, then, call the basic definition of introversion as an innate and complementary orientation into question? The Myers & Briggs Foundation webpage (n.d.) reports that "distribution" of the standard personality types, which feature introversion and extroversion, shows different yet similar patterns across cultures. The foundation reports research suggesting that the expression of introversion in different cultures may vary. Perhaps there is room to consider an interaction between innate and culturally conditioned traits, a pull toward the norm that could, over time, repress if not erase certain innate traits that do not affirm the culture's norms. Perhaps some introverts, rather than deal with a self-image of being deviant, reply to personality typology with the answers they have grown to feel are most acceptable?

7   This possibility seems arguable when considering a final factor contributing to the negative perception of introversion: certain studies have reported that extroverts are "happier" than introverts (as cited in Laney, 2002). Surely this idea could have an influence on attitudes in society in general and on the self-image of introverts. Whether this idea is actually true, however, is another question. Laney (2002) argues that these studies are flawed because the types of questions used to measure happiness are not suitable for both introverts and extroverts. For example, in response to a question asking a participant to rate the importance of a statement such as "I like to be with others," an introvert may choose "not important" to happiness. Extroverts might interpret this response to mean that an introvert must be unhappy, because to an extrovert "not wanting to be with others" would be a sign of depression. But to introverts, not being with others does not imply that they are depressed but simply that they enjoy solitude. It seems that different things make introverts and extroverts happy, so questionnaires would have to be devised accordingly in order to gauge accurately which group is "happiest."

8   In March 2003, Jonathan Rauch published "Caring for Your Introvert" in the *Atlantic Monthly*. As a result of that article, media went on to dub Rauch the figurehead of the so-called new introverts' rights movement. On February 14, 2006, Sage Stossel of the *Atlantic* reported that "Rauch has received more mail in response to his [2003 *Atlantic*] article than for anything else he has written" (p. 1). In addition, Rauch's 2003 article on introversion, now on the *Atlantic* website, continues to draw "more traffic than any other piece [the magazine] has posted" (Stossel, 2006, p. 1). As Stossel notes in an interview with Rauch (2006), which her above comments introduce, there continue to be a number of misconceptions that contribute to the reputation that introverts have in North America. In Rauch's words, introverts are "one

Webpage does not give date, so "n.d."

Since Laney is paraphrased, not directly quoted, page number optional

Common knowledge from media

Square brackets signal minor change to quotation.

INTROVERSION   5

of the most misunderstood and aggrieved groups in America, possibly the world"
(Stossel, 2006, p. 1). These misconceptions, together with a society where the majority are extroverts, have led to a bias that can be damaging to the self-esteem of introverts. This prejudice also requires introverts to "develop extra coping skills in life
because there will be an inordinate amount of pressure on them to 'shape up,' and
act like the rest of the world" (Laney, 2002, p. 6). If these misconceptions are not
challenged, then extroverts lose as well, because it seems that introverts also have a
great deal of value to offer to society. For example, it is interesting to note that though
extroverts tend to dominate in many spheres, according to several studies and
observers, introverts comprise the majority of the gifted population (Gallagher, 1990;
Hoehn & Birely, 1988; Stossel, 2006, p. 2). While this reverse claim may no doubt do
much for the self-esteem of beleaguered introverts, it seems most reasonable to
conclude that both introverts and extroverts have their own sets of innate gifts and
contributions to offer. Whether introverts should truly be considered as more gifted
than others, in the words of Rauch, they should be seen simply as "a different kind of
normal" (Stossel, 2006, p. 1).

Single quotation
marks around a
quotation within a
quotation. The
comma falls
inside.

List multiple
sources if fact or
claim supported
by more than one.

INTROVERSION   6

References

Briggs Myers, I., & Myers, P. B. (1980). *Gifts differing*. Palo Alto, CA: Consulting Psychologists Press.

> No quotation marks for titles of essays and articles. Italicize book titles. Capitalize only first word of title and subtitle, plus proper nouns.

Crozier, W. R. (Ed.). (1990). Introduction. *Shyness and embarrassment: Perspectives from social psychology* (pp. 1–17). New York, NY: Cambridge University Press.

> No specific essay in collection identified because in-text citation is to introductory remarks by Crozier. When citing a specific essay, use author's name and include pages.

Myers & Briggs Foundation. (n.d.). Multicultural use of the MBTI instrument. Retrieved from http://www.myersbriggs.org/more-about-personality-type/international-use /multicultural-use-of-the-mbti.asp

> Use essay-title style for web page title. Give date information was retrieved; download and archive material cited.

Gallagher, S. A. (1990). Personality patterns of the gifted. *Understanding Our Gifted, 3*(1), 11–13.

> Article title first, then journal title. Volume number is "3," followed by issue number "(1)." Symbols "pp." do not precede academic journal pages.

Garcia, T. (1999). Brain activity indicates introverts or extroverts. *News in Science.* Retrieved from the Australia Broadcasting website http://www.abc.net.au/science /news/stories/s21104.htm

> Treat name of web feature as journal title. List hosting corporation, ABC, as publisher.

Hoehn, L., & Birely, M. K. (1988). Mental process preferences of gifted children. *Illinois Council for the Gifted Journal, 7,* 28–31.

> No issue number here—journal is continuously paginated ("7" is volume number); "28–31" refers to pages in volume of journal.

Laney, M. O. (2002). *The introvert advantage*. New York, NY: Workman.

Rauch, J. (2003, March). Caring for your introvert: The habits and needs of a little-understood group. *The Atlantic Monthly*, 291(2), 1–4. Retrieved from http://www .theatlantic.com/doc/200202/rauch

> Pages here refer to online article. Better to obtain print version and supply those page numbers.

Stossel, S. (2006). Introverts of the world, unite! A conversation with Jonathan Rauch. *The Atlantic Online*. Retrieved from http://www.theatlantic.com/doc/200602u /introverts

Connections: Strong Points in McCaffery's Use of Sources

1. *Awareness of time:* McCaffery has found that her central theme traces back to Carl Jung's work in 1921 and remains, in 2006, a media topic as well as a subject of ongoing scientific study. McCaffery gives prominence to the 2002 book of researcher Dr. Marti Olsen Laney as well as to the even more current *Atlantic* articles by Rauch and Stossel.

2. *Awareness of the need for credibility:* Four of McCaffery's sources are by recognized professional researchers whose findings have been published by credible presses or recognized academic journals.

3. *Awareness of the need for recoverability:* Only one of McCaffery's sources (the item in *News in Science*) seems likely to disappear from its website, and that source does refer to an academic journal where the cited studies were published. A reader could track down the studies. *The Atlantic* online interview, not published in printed form, is likely to remain available for some time through the Atlantic online archive. *The Atlantic Monthly* citation refers to a text that was also published in the print magazine, and the month, year, volume, and number of the print publication have been provided, though the page numbers refer to the online version.

4. *Awareness of balance and variety:* McCaffery refers to the Myers & Briggs Foundation's print publication as well as to the foundation's website. While this source certainly has "something to sell," it also represents a long-standing commercial and professional instrument based on Jung's original formulation. While this source alone would be entirely insufficient, including it together with other disinterested sources adds an important awareness.

5. *Awareness of documentation norms:* McCaffery closely followed all the guidelines in the *Publication Manual of the American Psychological Association*, fifth edition. For purposes of representing the latest APA practices, we have updated her APA form to the 2010 standard. We have not been able to provide DOIs, but see Amanda Harrison's essay in Section 3, p. 282, for examples of DOI citation.

FINAL WORD

Diligence, discipline, and patience are indeed required for you to become familiar with academic research and documentation. More special situations occur in practice than we can possibly cover in this relatively short space. What we have covered here should serve most if not all of your needs at the first-year level, but if you are serious about future scholarly work, you should obtain the *Publication Manual of the American Psychological Association*, sixth edition, and refer to it on a regular basis.

Section 8

Chicago and AAA Systems

The purpose of this section is simply to offer examples of the *Chicago Manual of Style* notes and bibliography system, used in post-secondary departments of history, and the American Anthropology Association author-date system, used in anthropology. Student Isaac Paonessa's essay on cultural and political forces that shaped British North America demonstrates a carefully considered response to a typical assignment question for introductory history: to review assigned core texts and course readings in search of a challenging definition and to provide a response. Student Ryganas Ple Čkaitis's essay on the research complexities and problems involved in relating to cultural spaces demonstrates the nature of scholarly work within anthropology.

If you are already working in either of these fields or have an interest in them, you may wish to obtain their respective style manuals:

University of Chicago Press. *The Chicago Manual of Style*. 16th ed. Chicago: University of Chicago Press, 2010.

Turabian, Kate L. *A Manual for Writers of Research Papers, Theses, and Dissertations: Chicago Style for Students and Researchers*. Ed. Wayne C. Booth, Gregory G. Colomb, and Joseph M. Williams. 7th. rev. ed. Chicago: University of Chicago Press, 2007.

American Anthropological Association. *AAA Style Guide 2009*. Arlington, VA: American Anthropological Association Press, 2009.

Shortened Citations

The Chicago Manual of Style offers a shortened citation system "[t]o reduce the bulk of documentation in scholarly works" (667). In the sample essay that follows, notice how footnoted references are shortened in repeated citations following an initial citation that provides the complete information. "Ibid." (from *ibidem*, "in the same place") "refers to a single work cited in the note immediately preceding" (669). "Ibid." should never be used if the preceding note included more than one source. If the preceding source is the same but the page reference is different, then the new page reference follows "Ibid."

Sample Student History Paper: Chicago Style Notes and Bibliography

British North America—

Whose Creation?

Isaac Paonessa

History 224

November 30, 2010

1   The British Conquest of New France on September 8, 1760, ushered in a new era. Now it was Britain's time to pursue its strategy in shaping a British North America. Britain did not always get its way, for the forces within the new colonies also moulded the colonists and their governments—but when the mother country did get its way, it was through metropolitanism.

2   Metropolitanism stresses that the ideas and decisions of the mother country determine a colony's character and institutions.[1] An example of near-total metropolitanism is the unusual land "lottery" in 1767 on St. John's Island (now Prince Edward Island). The British government gave away 64 of the possible 67 townships to the king's favourites. There were two main reasons for this: maintaining power and wealth in the hands of a few who would be loyal to Great Britain and having private initiative bear the cost of attracting Protestant settlers.[2] This design rankled Prince Edward Island's social structure and politics for over a century.

3   Metropolitanism also left its mark in the west via the Hudson's Bay Company (hereafter HBC). From its inception in 1670, the HBC was part commercial venture and part de facto government agency. Heavily involved in the fur trade, the HBC helped Great Britain acquire huge swaths of land and forestall the expansion of the

---

1. Alvin Finkel, *History of Canada to 1867: Study Guide 1* (Athabasca, AB: Athabasca University, 2005), 34.

2. Margaret Conrad and Alvin Finkel, *Beginnings to 1867,* vol. 1 of *History of the Canadian Peoples* (Toronto: Pearson Longman, 2009), 170.

United States. An HBC policy under governor Sir George Simpson was to overtrap in the areas that are now British Columbia, Washington, and Oregon. The aim was to create a "fur desert" to discourage American fur traders who were mistakenly thought to be the precursors of agricultural settlement. This dispatch from Simpson reflects the thinking behind the policy:

> The greatest and best protection we can have from opposition is keeping the country closely hunted[,] as the first step that the American Government will take towards Colonization is through their Indian Traders[,] and if the country becomes exhausted in the Fur bearing animals[,] they can have no inducement to proceed thither.[3]

4   Evidently the political value of extirpated beaver was even higher than its market price.[4] Here the HBC was serving the broader political strategy of the metropolis: Great Britain.[5]

5   By the 1840s, however, it was becoming apparent that the policy of overtrapping was not working, for the American westward push continued at an alarming rate. And because Britain's Pacific territories were thinly populated, they remained vulnerable to seizure by the United States. To remedy this, in 1846, Britain reached a landmark agreement with the United States—the Oregon Treaty—which established the present-day border along the forty-ninth parallel. More measures were taken to open the door to settlement when Britain cancelled the HBC's lease on Vancouver Island and made the Pacific mainland a Crown colony. Furthermore, in 1866, to reduce administrative costs, Britain combined the colonies of Vancouver Island and British Columbia without consulting the settlers—a metropolitan stroke, indeed.

6   The mother country also profoundly influenced Newfoundland's development. In order to build Newfoundland into a colony that would want British sovereignty, in 1841, the British colonial office appointed Sir John Harvey as governor. Harvey sought to produce a native-born outlook and culture among Newfoundlanders. So he "invented tradition." He did this in two main ways: working with the Natives' Society and emphasizing public spectacle. The Natives' Society, ironically, produced British outlooks and perceptions by ostensibly promoting the interests of average, white, colonial-born Newfoundlanders. It "fused nativism, patriotism, and a respect for social order into a political creed."[6] Its philosophy resonated with both Catholics and

---

3. Lorne Hammond, "Marketing Wildlife: The Hudson's Bay Company and the Pacific Northwest, 1821–1849," in *The Invention of Canada: Readings in Pre-Confederation History*, ed. Chad Gaffield (Toronto: Copp Clark Longman, 1994), 384.

4. Ibid.

5. Conrad and Finkel, *Beginnings to 1867,* 321.

6. Phillip McCann, "Culture, State Formation, and the Invention of Tradition: Newfoundland, 1832–1855," in Gaffield, *Invention of Canada* 278.

Protestants, which neutralized religious animosity and achieved the imperial goal of fostering allegiance to the British sovereign. Furthermore, Harvey understood the power of grand public ceremony and used it to fan the flames of nativist sentiment. He turned ornate Society banquets into fixtures of culture where patriotic toasts and tributes to Queen Victoria became the norm. Harvey's horse races, boat races, and potato-sack races were "calculated occasions of popular patronage," for they brought the different classes together to revel on a platform of equality.[7] By 1860, the metropolis had succeeded: Newfoundland possessed a strong colonial-born identity and yet remained proud of its place in the imperial orbit.

7　　Other instances of metropolitanism came in the heady wake of conquest. In 1763, the British Crown issued a royal proclamation that imposed English criminal and civil law on what is now Ontario and Quebec. It also barred Catholics from public office, made tithing voluntary, and legally established Britain's freehold land tenure system.[8] This provoked grievances among Francophones who were accustomed to French law and the seigneurial landholding system.[9] In time, cognizant of colonial disaffection and its drift into war with the Thirteen Colonies, Britain made more of an effort to adapt to colonial realities. So, with the Quebec Act of 1774, Parliament sought to mollify Francophones by restoring French civil law, making tithing compulsory again for Catholics, allowing Catholics to run for public office, and legally upholding a modified version of the seigneurial system.[10] The concessions in this legislation favoured landlords and the Catholic clergy who Britain thought would loyally support it in the event of war with the Thirteen Colonies.[11] But more concessions were forthcoming. After losing the Thirteen Colonies, Parliament sought to prevent more revolutions of the American kind. Therefore, the Constitutional Act of 1791 split the colony of Quebec to address the serious language and cultural differences in the population. The mostly Anglophone western section became Upper Canada (now Ontario), and the mostly Francophone eastern section became Lower Canada (now Quebec). Lower Canada kept all the concessions of the Quebec Act, while Upper Canada received British civil and criminal law. The Crown reserved one-seventh of the land for itself and granted another seventh to the Anglican clergy in an attempt to establish one church that would support State interests.[12] In this series of legislation, Britain's imperial strategy increasingly made allowances for frontier pressures.

---

7. Ibid., 279.

8. Alvin Finkel, *History of Canada to 1867: Study Guide 2* (Athabasca, AB: Athabasca University, 2005), 11.

9. Ibid., 12.

10. Ibid.

11. Ibid., 20.

12. Ibid., 18–19.

8   The theory of frontierism emphasizes the frontier environment and pioneer experience as the shapers of a colony's personality and institutions.[13] In British North America, frontierism played an important role in affecting the location and viability of settlement. For example, in the prairie settlement of Lord Selkirk at Red River, pioneers had a difficult time establishing themselves because of crop failures, locust plagues, and drought. These conditions racked the fledgling village for years, and settlers avoided starvation only by purchasing a Native foodstuff made of dried Buffalo and berries.[14]

9   In Newfoundland, the main driver and pillar of development was the fact that its waters were teeming with cod.[15] Moreover, it seems reasonable to conclude that Newfoundland's long, harsh winters along with little to do provided an environment for inordinate alcohol consumption to increase to an alarming degree (over 20 litres annually per person, not including beer and wine)—and, consequently, gave momentum to the temperance movement, which, in turn, exerted reformist pressure on the government.[16] These features of the pioneer environment generally dictated the economic opportunities and social classes that arose in a colony.

10   Many times, though, a mix of metropolitanism and frontierism left a mark on British North America. Instances of British ivory-tower syndrome such as the Royal Proclamation, Quebec Act, Sugar Act, and Stamp Act (to name a few) provoked the American Revolutionary War.[17] Yet an unexpected by-product of the war was the great migration northward. From 1775 to the early 1800s, many who had fought on the British side or disliked the United States moved to the Canadas and the Maritimes. They called themselves Loyalists and were from every class of the societies in the Thirteen Colonies.[18] About 35,000 emigrated to the colony of Nova Scotia and about 15,000 moved to the colony of Quebec.[19] They brought with them a craving for land ownership and had grown fond of their franchise in the quasi-democratic assemblies of the Thirteen Colonies. This wave of immigration spread the innovations of Anglo-American culture to Upper Canada and the Eastern Townships, bestowing a measure of identity on English-speaking Canadians.[20]

11   Near the end of this migrational period, another war of both frontier and metropolitan character shaped the British colonies unexpectedly—the War of 1812. A

---

13. Alvin Finkel, *History of Canada to 1867: Study Guide 1*, 32.
14. Conrad and Finkel, *Beginnings to 1867*, 308–309.
15. Ibid., 246.
16. McCann, "Culture, State Formation, and the Invention of Tradition," 280.
17. Conrad and Finkel, *Beginnings to 1867,* 172.
18. Finkel, *History of Canada to 1867: Study Guide 2*, 16.
19. Conrad and Finkel, *Beginnings to 1867,* 182.
20. Ibid., 203.

jingoistic common enemy united many in a patriotic defence of British North America, which included radical evangelical churches and conservative Anglican elements.[21] Britain seized this opportunity by establishing the British Wesleyan Methodist Society. The Society encouraged acceptance of traditionalism while still holding to many evangelical precepts, thus fostering a passive spirit in the evangelicals. The War of 1812 enabled Britain to rein in some of the republicanism that was sweeping across its colonies and furthered its goal of moulding a loyal ruling class. Moreover, the issues that led to conflict, military strategy during the war, and the war's resolution were handled by British authorities in England.[22] So, the above-mentioned wars were actually mother-country influences with a veneer of frontierism.

12   Frontierism, however, took on a greater role when joining metropolitanism in the religious context. Between 1760 and 1860, British North Americans were steadily influenced by a tapas buffet of evangelical religions. In many of these, metropolitan and frontier values co-existed and synergized. The evangelical movement hatched in Great Britain under John Wesley, but Wesley's approach was more passive when compared to the emotionally charged methods that North American preachers used. For example, Henry Alline's New Light movement in Nova Scotia rejected a clergy class and promoted a personal connection with God. Alline preached that a person's emotional religious experience took precedence over the laws and doctrines of the Holy Scriptures. Consequently, his speeches inspired social and political ferment in the Maritimes.[23]

13   Though evangelicalism was an idea born in Britain, one can identify in it frontier innovations, especially in its emphasis on the rights of the "free individual" and equality of opportunity, which were burning issues in the Thirteen Colonies. Evangelicalism eventually became a "mass social movement" that shaped many peoples' values, changed the way they viewed authority, and provided a cultural alternative to the prim civility of the British gentry. Moreover, in the late 1700s and early 1800s, Upper and Lower Canada formed part of the New York Methodist preaching circuit, and many of the travelling ministers were American-born. Consequently, according to Nancy Christie, evangelicals unwittingly used Methodism as a vehicle for transplanting the reformist spirit of the United States into Upper Canada.[24] The widespread appeal of evangelicalism nurtured liberal political sentiments among British North Americans.

14   While many other forces shaped British North America between 1760 and 1860, the above examples offer a sense of proportion. To properly evaluate what created British North America, one must consider the weight that metropolitan and frontier

21. Nancy Christie, "'In These Times of Democratic Rage and Delusion': Popular Religion and the Challenge to the Established Order, 1760–1815," in Gaffield, *Invention of Canada,* 268.
22. Conrad and Finkel, *Beginnings to 1867,* 193–94.
23. Christie, "'In These Times of Democratic Rage and Delusion,'" 262.
24. Ibid., 245.

influences deserve. To illustrate, imagine a creek in a valley that is fed by an underground spring and runoff from the surrounding hills. The construction of a hydroelectric dam begins, and a large river in a nearby valley is diverted toward the creek. As a result, the creek grows into a giant lake. What forces created the lake? While it is true that the spring and runoff contributed, the construction of the dam and diversion of the river were more influential. Like the giant lake, British North America embodied a hodgepodge of metropolitan and frontier influences that held sway in turns, but with metropolitanism dominating in something of a 60:40 ratio. Britain's strategic cultivation of elitist institutions, provocations of war, allowance for Quebec's distinction, and commercial policies left a slightly deeper and more lasting impression than frontier evangelical beliefs and the challenges of agriculture. All these forces teamed up and laid the corner stones for a pluralistic Canada, but British North America grew into a hybrid creature of metropolitan and frontier character, with metropolitanism playing the dominant role.

Bibliography

Christie, Nancy. "'In These Times of Democratic Rage and Delusion': Popular Religion and the Challenge to the Established Order, 1760–1815." In *The Invention of Canada: Readings in Pre-Confederation History*, edited by Chad Gaffield, 240–70. Toronto: Copp Clark Longman, 1994.

Conrad, Margaret, and Alvin Finkel. *Beginnings to 1867.* Vol.1 of *History of the Canadian Peoples*. 5th ed. Toronto: Pearson Longman, 2009.

Finkel, Alvin. *History of Canada to 1867: Study Guide 1*. Athabasca, AB: Athabasca University, 2005.

Finkel, Alvin. *History of Canada to 1867: Study Guide 2.* Athabasca, AB: Athabasca University, 2005.

Hammond, Lorne. "Marketing Wildlife: The Hudson's Bay Company and the Pacific Northwest, 1821–1849." In *The Invention of Canada: Readings in Pre-Confederation History*, edited by Chad Gaffield, 379–401. Toronto: Copp Clark Longman, 1994.

McCann, Phillip. "Culture, State Formation, and the Invention of Tradition: Newfoundland, 1832–1855." In *The Invention of Canada: Readings in Pre-Confederation History*, edited by Chad Gaffield, 271–89. Toronto: Copp Clark Longman, 1994.

Sample Student Paper Using AAA Documentation

The Ethics of Conservation and Politics of Ownership:

Contesting and Controlling Cultural Spaces

Ryganas Ple čkaitis

Anthropology 100

15 December 2010

Introduction

It is for this that they hate us. And I am tired of it. . . . Because we have given
them their symbols . . . We have built them a museum. . . . We have given them
the element so that they can have culture, man, culture! Do you understand? And
for this, they hate us more.

—*Jesus Gonzalez (Executive Director, Sinchi Sacha, 2003)*

1   When students, tourists, travel writers and government officials think about collapsed
civilizations, they should keep in mind that the remnants of fragmented material culture and subtler aspects of a more figurative ethos always permeate descendant communities. These cultural artifacts can be actively studied and worked on and
intentionally perpetuated, or they may be discarded and obscured—in both literal and
metaphoric senses—until later unearthed, rediscovered.

2   While civilizations may change drastically in material form, culture, identity and
heritage prove very difficult to wipe out completely, even under direct action (as with
the residential schools in Canada). Cultural and legal debates between Indigenous
groups, government and non-governmental organizations are particularly complex because control over lands and resources comes down to proprietary rights. The very
idea of ownership, which forms the basis of Western law, is virtually absent in Native

tradition (insofar as Western definitions are concerned). This conflict of definitions brings us to fundamental questions about what constitutes cultural property, who owns it, who represents it and who may sell it.

Territorial Property

3 Although pre-colonial North American Indigenous tribes had notions of territory, they did not in any sense believe that the land within these territories belonged to them, in the sense of physical ownership as we understand the term. For instance, Paul Nadasdy (2002:250) points out in the scholarly journal *American Anthropologist*, "a pack of wolves, too, has a fairly well-defined hunting range, but it makes little sense to talk about the wolves owning it as 'property.'" Likening Indigenous peoples to wild animals (in even a loose metaphor) is unfortunate given North American colonial history, but the point that a territorial range is different philosophically and socially from private ownership is valid. This territorial perspective is amplified through an anecdote of the then elected chief of the Kluane First Nation (KFN) in Canada's Yukon Territory in the 1970s. Chief Joe Johnson was in the process of land claim negotiations and attempted to explain them to his grandmother:

> She became upset when she learned that he was trying to figure out which land belonged to Indians and which to the white men. She told him that was a crazy thing to do, for no one can own the land—neither white men nor Indians. The land is there; we move around; we die. How can anyone own it? (Nadasdy 2002:247)

4 Nevertheless, the entire land-claim process and the basis of drafted treaties enacted in the 18th, 19th and 20th centuries were predicated on European definitions of ownership completely foreign to Indigenous populations. Many people agree that the validity of such agreements is questionable. However, I seek to explore how, by imposing British definitions on property, white "civilizers" pushed land negotiations into colonial arenas of control. Significantly, this imposition of colonial power continues today, often in subtle ways.

5 This colonizing attitude is perpetuated through the entire free-world court system, the arbiters of law and legitimacy. The language of the courts is in a very real sense the only cultural language these legal systems speak and understand:

> Anthropologists who participate in the land claims process, like aboriginal people themselves, are forced to speak in the language of property if they wish to be taken seriously. (Nadasdy 2002:253)

Both intended and unintended consequences of this incorporation of legal language must be considered.

6 Some immediately identifiable consequences emerge through recent disputes among Native groups on how to manage territory and resources. The problem, it seems, with translating "First Nation people's relationship with land and animals into the language of property (ie: hunting rights)" is that "along with the idea of 'rights'

comes a sense of entitlement" (Nadasdy 2002:257). Hunting, once regarded as an earned responsibility and obligation, is now increasingly being seen by younger generations as a "right" that must be exercised. This illustrates an important shift in perception and action. Identity politics has possibly shifted from interpreting hunting as a cultural expression (and necessity) to a legal exercise—the rhetoric of rights. New attitudes and behaviours aren't limited to territory and animal hunting rights, however.

Physical and Intellectual Property

7   A pressing question bearing on physical and intellectual property remains: "Who controls and has the authority to sell culture and reap its benefits?" If anything, the digital age, which has so quickly and smoothly engulfed the entire planet, has mired these debates of ownership and control in emerging legalities in uncertain jurisdictions. Intellectual and physical property intersect most often in ethnographic museums. While physical remains of ancestors and materials may be the most widely and publically contested, there are more subtle ethical issues as well. For instance, anthropologist A. M. Tozzer worked with the Navaho in the early part of the 20th century, and he made several sketches that replicated Navaho ceremonial sand paintings. Typically, Navaho paintings are destroyed at the end of each ceremony, but Tozzer's sketches are on display at Harvard's Peabody Museum. According to one scholar writing in the journal *Current Anthropology*, the museum staff in 1994 wondered whether the drawings' continued presence was disrespectful or even stood in violation of contemporary privacy norms (Brown 1998:193). I agree with this view, because while Tozzer might have been acting in a way he thought was ethical, he fundamentally transgressed the spirit of the Navaho rituals.

8   The Apache tribes have taken this dilemma of spiritual integrity and notions of property and attempted to co-opt the law to exploit it in their favour. As Michael Brown (1998) observes, in 1995 the Apache declared that they and they alone had exclusive control over Apache "cultural property." They defined cultural property "as 'all images, text, ceremonies, music, songs, stories, symbols, beliefs, customs, ideas and other physical and spiritual objects and concepts' relating to the Apache" (Brown 1998:194). But how these abstract ideas are to be protected and copyrighted—especially once information and images have been copied, reprinted and disseminated through books and over the internet—is absolutely unclear. Furthermore, with the New Age movement and its continued trendy and superficial appropriation of Native religion (Brown 1998), at what point can the rituals and beliefs now taken out of their original context be reclaimed? How can such poaching be stopped through assertion of cultural copyright?

Conservation, Ownership and Selling Culture

9   Conflicting notions of ownership and property rights often intersect at ethnographic museums. It is here that "cultural forms are consciously selected, appropriated, and displayed with the goal of conveying particular images of the ethnic or cultural groups

in question" (Wilson 2003:162). This control, even creation, of images in ethnographic museums can also be observed in heritage tourism sites. The difference between museums and heritage tourist sites is that artifacts are removed from their original context and transported to museums, whereas heritage tourist sites are typically built on (or next to) traditional sacred or ceremonial land.

10   For instance, Writing-on-Stone Provincial Park in Alberta may soon qualify for UNESCO status as a world heritage site due to the spiritual, historical, and cultural significance inscribed upon it by the Blackfoot people. The politicization of sacred space can be witnessed here. By what mysterious right does UNESCO (United Nations Educational, Scientific and Cultural Organization) have the authority to "recognize" this site? Since this site has been recognized for centuries by the Blackfoot, UNESCO's endorsement seems unintentionally patronizing, even oddly imperialistic despite its best hopes. Nevertheless, gaining official status grants certain protection of the land.

11   Heritage tourism sites that are built upon inscribed space, such as at Writing-on-Stone Provincial Park, are faced with the dilemma of eroding petroglyphs and pictographs. Often the material culture that is left over serves as the claim to space. This material culture draws visitors, and therefore money, to the surrounding communities. However, the issue of what percentage of the proceeds goes to descendants and how much goes to the government/officials/managers of the land remains controversial. Also, with regard to the material culture, debate rages as to whether the pictographs and petroglyphs should be conserved and preserved using modern techniques. Because I do not belong to the Blackfoot community, I feel as though I cannot give an opinion as to whether or not the sacred pictures should be conserved and preserved, or allowed to vanish from the environment. Other than allowing Blackfoot descendants, themselves, to decide what happens to their landscape, any action I suggest is, by definition, colonizing. It must be remembered that even if spiritual symbols may disappear from the physical environment, they live on, according to various Native beliefs, in the spiritual landscape of a place itself. The simultaneous existence of multiple landscapes is what Margaret Rodman (1992) refers to as the multivocality and multilocality of space.

Selling Ethically

12 Bearing the multivocality of space in mind, we must recognize that even well-intentioned NGOs can be guilty of the co-optation of culture. Consider, for instance, the case of the Sinchi Sacha, a Central American NGO that received funding from the Canadian government through the Canadian Fund for Ecuadorian Development to start a museum project in a small rainforest town (Wilson 2003:164). The museum's centrepiece is a massive petroglyph boulder thought to date to 2000 YBP (Wilson 2003:164). *Sinchi Sacha* means "powerful forest" in Quichua, and indeed this NGO's mandate is to provide "support for indigenous peoples of the continent in their

development efforts" and participate in a worldwide movement of environmental defence (Wilson 2003:164). Well-intentioned and "progressive," Sinchi Sacha, in a stunning moment of cultural blindness, has seen fit to appropriate one of the petroglyph
images as their corporate logo (Wilson 2003:163–164).

References

Brown, Michael F.
  1998   Can Culture Be Copyrighted? Current Anthropology 39(2):193–222.
Deacon, Janette
  2006   Rock Art Conservation and Tourism. Journal of Archaeological Method and
     Theory 13(4):379–399.
Nadasdy, Paul
  2002   "Property" and Aboriginal Land Claims in the Canadian Subarctic: Some
     Theoretical Considerations. American Anthropologist 104(1):247–261.
Rodman, Margaret C.
  1992   Empowering Place: Multilocality and Multivocality. American Anthropologist
     94(3):640–656.
Wilson, Patrick C.
  2003   Ethnographic Museums and Cultural Commodification: Indigenous
     Organizations, NGO's and Culture as a Resource in Amazonian Ecuador. Latin
     American Perspectives 30(1):162–180.

FINAL WORD

Diligence, discipline, and patience are indeed required for you to become familiar with
academic research and documentation. More special situations occur in practice
than we can possibly cover in this relatively short space. What we have covered here
should serve most if not all of your needs at the first-year level, but if you are serious
about future scholarly work, you should obtain the *Chicago Manual of Style*, 16th
edition, or the *AAA Style Guide*, and refer to the relevant one on a regular basis.

Section 9

Interviewing: Ethics and Methods

In our attention to researching and documenting secondary sources, we sometimes overlook the considerable benefits to be gained from creating a new source: an interview with someone who offers expertise and/or a distinctive angle related to our topic. Interviewees might include teachers, professors, doctors, lawyers, journalists, businesspeople, sledge-hammer operators, or the Rolling Stones, to suggest only a few possibilities.

In some cases, your interview subject may even be your primary focus. More often, that person will serve as a secondary source, throwing additional light on your primary subject of study. An interview that you conduct with someone you perceive as having potential to inform your topic serves like a "mini" survey (one lacking statistical significance, of course). Because you can ask your subject questions, you exert more control over the research process than you do simply by searching existing information. You place yourself and thus your reader closer to the discussion.

Interviews, however, must be set up and conducted in accordance with professional and ethical standards. The following tips should assist you in conducting a personal interview.

TIPS FOR CONDUCTING A PERSONAL INTERVIEW

1. Be professional in your request. Think about an angle that might appeal to the subject (e.g., an opportunity to share his or her expertise with a class of first-year students and possibly a broader audience), but do not exert any pressure. If the person declines, express cordial understanding and, if you can, approach another possible subject.
2. Explain precisely what you intend to use the interview for and clarify any re-use intentions.
3. If the person asks for confidentiality, you are ethically bound to honour the request should you decide to proceed with the interview.
4. If you have any reason to suspect an interview could result in harm or embarrassment to the potential interviewee, seek the advice of your instructor, your institution's research ethics board (REB), or your institution's normal advisor on such matters.
5. You do not have to begin your initial discussion with the prospective interviewee by referring to a signed agreement, but if the person wants a written agreement concerning what you intend to do with the interview and how you intend to treat the information afterwards, we have provided a template (following) from which you can adapt terms and wording to suit both of you. See if your college or university has its own preferred or recommended form for such purposes.
6. Suggest an interview method and location that you believe will be conducive to a successful interview, but also one that respects the convenience, safety, and general well-being of your interviewee. Face-to-face interviewing allows

visual cues that sometimes help you to time and phrase questions effectively. Email and telephone interviews, however, may also be effective.

7. Taping your interview provides you with an opportunity to double-check for completeness and accuracy; it also liberates you to a certain extent from note-taking, allowing you added opportunity to listen carefully and consider your questions. Be sure to inform your interviewee that you would like to tape the discussion (whether in person or by phone), and be sure to receive permission before taping. If you do tape your interview, it is still a good idea to take notes, in case the tape system malfunctions. Be sure to test your taping system before the interview, and try not to draw too much attention to the recording process. The less you fuss with equipment of any kind, the more relaxed your subject should feel. Many people tend to draw back from microphones, so it is important to proceed with reassurance and confidence, perhaps using some humour or personal discussion to provide a diversion from commencement of the taping. For longer interviews, it is a good idea to transcribe the discussion (or arrange to have it transcribed for you). Looking over a written text of the interview can often help you to decide what parts to choose and how best to use them.

8. Strive to ask unbiased questions and let your interviewee say the things that she or he would naturally say, not things that you want to hear; for example, ask "What do you think of legalized gambling?" not "What do you think is wrong with legalized gambling?"

9. Have several clear questions ready, but be open to improvising other questions that follow naturally from answers given. For example, if you ask, "What do you think of legalized gambling?" and the interviewee says, "I was against it till last week when someone gave me a lotto ticket that won a million dollars," you might want to ask for the story of that event before pushing ahead to the next question you had planned.

10. Guide the discussion but do not be so concerned with moving to the next planned question that you cut your interviewee off or suppress a potential naturally flowing dynamic. It may be that your interviewee wishes to wind to the topic more indirectly than you do initially, but if you establish trust and good will as the discussion proceeds, you may find more value in even the indirect sections than you had initially believed was present.

11. A little social interaction and relaxing before the interview proper can be most helpful, but as with any business meeting, do not run longer than you had initially stipulated, unless your interviewee clearly offers to extend the time.

12. Unless your interviewee asks you not to, send him or her a copy of the essay you have written and include a thank you for his or her time and contribution.

13. If your interviewee asks to see your essay draft to review how you have used his or her information before you submit or present the final draft, you should agree (this increases good will and offers you a further critical eye), but as author of the work you can insist on final say over using content if it conforms *accurately* with the interview transcript. If you misunderstood what the interviewee intended to say, however (regardless of whether that person used misleading words), you

have an obligation to fairness to gain clarification. There is seldom much bene-fit to proceeding with a work that represents someone else's words or ideas in a way that that person questions or even denies intending.

14. Whenever you use material from the interview in your essay, whether as a summary, paraphrase, or quotation, acknowledge your usage according to the complete documentation procedures of the style manual you are following.

Interview Request Agreements

It is most important to confirm ahead of time that your interviewee clearly under-stands how you propose using the material, whether that understanding is oral or writ-ten. A written confirmation signed by the interviewee is always best to avoid future confusion or dispute. Following up on a preliminary oral agreement, even through a sim-ple email restating your understanding of what has been agreed, can also be a useful con-firmation. If you decide to proceed with a more formal written agreement with your interviewee, the following generic letter may be of assistance. Your intent, somewhat like that of a psychologist entering into an agreement with research participants, is to clar-ify the nature and purpose of your research and the responsibilities of the parties involved.

Template for Interview Request Agreement

Dear _____:

To assist my research into_____, I am hoping you will agree to a brief interview with me. This research is toward a university essay for my _____ class; I do not have immediate plans to publish this work but might consider adapting it for that purpose at some future date.

If you agree to the interview but wish to be treated as a confidential source, or if you have any other special requests, questions, or concerns, could you please note them here:

On condition:

Permission to Cite Personal Interview Granted: _____
Signed:_____
Please specify how you wish to be named: _____
Date:_____
Signature of requester:_____   Witness: _____
Date: _____   Date: _____

PREPARING INTERVIEW QUESTIONS AND INTEGRATING AND CITING RESPONSES

You should be prepared before your interview. Read in the field and be aware of what your interviewee has already contributed to the topic. Prepare questions based on critical inquiry into your background reading and research. Organize your questions in a manner that seems likely to encourage a natural flow, perhaps moving from broader starting points to more specific concerns. If you were interviewing a senior who had witnessed the early days of a certain community or organization, for example, you might start by asking for first impressions of what it was like in those days—what stood out.

Documenting a Personal Interview

APA style does not include personal interviews in its References list, on grounds that the interview transcripts are not recoverable. If you were to publish the interview in some audiovisual media or as text, then you could list it as a recoverable piece of information. Within the body of your essay, you would cite a personal interview, telephone discussion, email, or similar exchange as a "personal communication," for example, "D. Lakusta (personal communication, May 7, 2007)" or "(D. Lakusta, personal communication, May 7, 2007)."

With MLA style, you are requested to provide personal interviews in your works cited list, using the interviewee's surname to begin the entry. This may be a subtle sign that MLA covers arts and humanities areas that often give particular importance to personal experience. APA style pertains to areas based on a historical model of detached observation, a preference for minimizing personal components. In any case, using MLA style, your citations within your essay will link your reader to the works cited entry by using the interviewee's surname, in the same way you use an author's surname to establish a connection between your in-text citation and the works cited entry. The three main works cited forms of personal interviews in MLA are as follows:

Lakusta, Dennis. Personal interview. 7 May 2007.

Lakusta, Dennis. Telephone interview. 7 May 2007.

Lakusta, Dennis. Email interview. 8-12 May 2007.

STUDENT WRITER'S COMMENTS ON INTERVIEWS

Laura Allen used a personal interview to support her argumentative essay "Gambling: The Stakes Are What They Are" (p. 274). You can see how she used her interview material by reading the essay in Section 2, Research Guide. In the following discussion, "In Praise of the Personal Interview," she offers her thoughts on this particular method of inquiry.

Student Comment on Interviewing

In Praise of the Personal Interview
Laura Allan

1   Searching for suitable sources and writing an essay can be a daunting task. One way to alleviate some of the stress associated with sourcing is to use the personal interview. A personal interview in itself suggests that a relationship exists between the interviewer and interviewee, and that can be a catalyst for a lively and frank discussion. Interviews are a valuable tool for data gathering as they are available, intimate and personal. For some distance education students, particularly in rural areas, traditional sources for data gathering (the public library) may not be close by or may not provide the material required in the student's time frame. This has changed somewhat with the use of computers; however, an interview with a person who has firsthand knowledge and current information and know-how cannot be compared to what is available in textbooks or journals. Students often find themselves struggling to get a grasp of the information, so it comes as a welcome relief to get that first-hand account in the common language of everyday conversation. It also helps to have the "expert" right there to answer further questions about various points.

2   In my opinion, the interview can be considered to have three parts: the preparation or pre-interview, the actual interview, and the evaluation or review. Preparing for the interview is more than asking the right questions. Students need to understand their topic and what kind of information they are looking for. This understanding provides the basis for the questions. Questions need to be specific and clearly worded. Always leave room for added comments at the end to allow for flexibility and for your interviewee to add any extras that he or she may want to share. Arranging the interview ahead of time is essential as it shows commitment to the project and your professional conduct. Be sure to inform the person about the essay topic and course information. Receive oral and even written consent. It is important to be sensitive to the interviewee's needs as he or she may be nervous or reluctant at first. Inform your source as to why you feel he or she is the best choice for your project—be honest. I sought out women for my interview subjects as I was looking for a female perspective. Be flexible and considerate of the interviewee's needs.

3   The actual interview takes a short while, but know that the intimacy of the relationship is directly proportional to the length of the interview as chitchat can creep in and take up valuable interview time. While informal visiting may put everyone at ease, be aware that it can take away from the importance of the interview. It is the responsibility of the interviewer to stay on track. Allow a short period for those involved to get comfortable, and then move on to the interview. Another caution is to cover the questions as prepared, and allow the source to answer without any bias from you. Try to record exactly what you have heard, and repeat key statements, to be sure you have understood correctly. When the interview is complete, thank your source for his or her time.

4   As an evaluation, review and examine all the statements and data. Ask yourself how the information you received during the interview will be useful to your topic. Getting things right at the writing stage can be daunting. Go back to your notes. If something still doesn't make sense, as a last resort, check back with your source to clarify the uncertain point. The information likely includes your source's opinion, and you should make an effort to present that accurately.

5   Interviews are only one option for data gathering, but one that should not be overlooked. They can contribute valuable insight and individuality to practically any topic.

FINAL WORD

Interviews help you to balance the forms of appeals and proofs that you weave into your writing. One interviewee tends to function as a "warm" proof (see Chapter 4, p. 37), adding an element of personal appeal, although interviewees may often furnish "cool" data and other non-personal types of appeals and proofs. An essay or speech that relies solely on one interview will usually lack balance, as will any writing that leans too much on one source. As the samples in this chapter demonstrate, however, interviews often place you and your reader closer to the actualities of a topic than many secondary sources are able to do; interviews inject locality and specificity. They almost always make the writing more textured, more interesting.

Designing thoughtful interview questions is good preparation for learning to develop, administer, and evaluate surveys (which, though beyond the scope of *Acting on Words*, are nonetheless important forms of primary research and of "cool" proofs). When possible, try to conduct an interview or two during the research for your essay assignments. What you can learn from the experience may well transcend the information gained in response to your questions.

Section 10 Afterword and
Checklists

You may ask yourself how anyone can possibly cope with all the points of form that pertain to documentation of sources. Take heart in knowing that even the most seasoned professional scholars do not know or remember all the guidelines for formal matters. However, they know what they do not know or remember and therefore keep the latest edition of the style manual for their field close to hand. They use it whenever they have uncertainty regarding a point of documentation or other stylistic matter (e.g., accepted abbreviations, form for numbers). Meticulous attention to points of form helps you make a careful, professional impression, while disciplined attention to consistent and correct form encourages you to apply that same discipline to all levels and stages of your work. At the same time, it's always a good idea to maintain a sense of proportion, to not lose sight of the bigger picture in all the fine points, as discussed further under the next two headings.

LETTER OF THE LAW SHOULD NOT OBSCURE SPIRIT OF THE LAW

Some students enter their field of study having heard how important it will be to "master the style manual." Yes, that is important. In some cases, however, students tend to imagine that mastering formal procedures of the style manual is *primarily* what will be expected. They place most of their concern on how to document sources. Students are not the only ones who slide into this imbalance. Authors of reference texts, style manual committees, and instructors, as well, can sometimes become overly preoccupied with forms and the discipline of documentation to the detriment of substance. Of course, correct form in itself is no assurance of reliable results or constructive thinking. Form, while important, exists ultimately to serve the stages of research and critical thinking that precede one's final draft.

As a relatively neophyte scholar, you succeed as you attend to primary principles and do your best to meet those. The five steps outlined in this Research Guide are intended to help those principles stand out. Keep up-to-date with the latest forms but remember the essence of what you are doing.

CULTURAL BIAS

In a recent issue of *Academic Matters,* UBC Professor William Rees makes the following observation: "People generally believe that modern nations are no longer the slaves and dupes of myth—humanity has long moved beyond the groundless fears, falsehoods and unscientific beliefs that distorted reality and shaped the lives of earlier cultures" (9). He then adds,

But for all the achievements of modernity, it is time that we acknowledged an increasingly evident paradox. This may well be the age of science, but this fact has not prevented us from being as myth-bound as any preceding culture. . . . The assertion that ours is a myth-free culture may actually be one of our most important cultural myths! (9)

Today's academic style manuals, even those pertaining to humanities and liberal arts, very much reflect the priorities and assumptions of an "age of science." They cast an authoritative presence, an implied belief in objective truth. This is not to advocate disregarding the manuals but simply to keep in mind that they are cultural expressions and, as such, can conceal biases that may, at times, run counter to the professed spirit of open-minded inquiry. In an excerpt from "Understanding People on Their Own Terms: A Rationale for an Aboriginal Style Guide," writer Greg Young-Ing expresses a familiar concern of many Aboriginal observers of Western research guides, which is that their rules and procedures have done little to prevent serious mistreatment of Aboriginal intellectual and cultural content or to avoid general harmful misunderstanding. To some observers, at least, having a set of written commitments to ethics and believing one is applying them is not the same thing as truly applying them. The basic reason for documentation procedures, after all, is consideration: giving credit, respecting others—ethics.

15 COMMON RESEARCH ERRORS IN FIRST-YEAR PAPERS

1. A list of sources appears on the last page, but the paper lacks in-text attributions of any sort. The reader therefore has no idea how the listed material has been integrated. Although such papers may not reflect deliberate cheating, they can be classified as plagiarism.
2. In-text attributions appear, but there is no final list of sources.
3. The paper makes references to Wikipedia and other online sources that lack reliable ethos (no cited author, no reliable author[s], no identified host organization or contact person, no reliable host organization, or no critical judgment of sources that "have something to sell").
4. The paper presents an idea from another source as its own (plagiarism).
5. Facts have been stated as common knowledge, when they are not, and therefore require citation (could also constitute plagiarism).
6. When integrating material, the paper fails to make the most appropriate choices among summarizing, paraphrasing, or quoting.
7. Names of the authors or works referred to are misspelled (which reflects lack of focus, intention, or interest).

8. Quotation marks are omitted around short quotations or they are incorrectly inserted around longer quotes (five lines for MLA style or 40 words for APA style) that should be set off from the text as block quotes.

9. The paper uses a documentation style system that is not preferred or accepted by the field addressed by the topic of the paper.

10. The paper fails to acknowledge that words have been quoted from an indirect source.

11. The paper fails to represent sources offering a balance of different points of view on the topic.

12. Too many sources have been used (perhaps including some of dubious value).

13. The paper does not reflect any current information on the topic.

14. The writer has misunderstood the ideas in the sources.

15. The writer has handed control to the research sources while remaining on autopilot. It is therefore difficult, even impossible, to distinguish the writer's voice and views from those of the sources.

10 Steps to a Successful Research Paper

1. Make a realistic schedule that considers not only reading and rereading your sources, but also drafting and rewriting your paper.

2. Select, then narrow, your topic; define your point of interest, your specific research context.

3. Define crucial terms in your instructor's assignment, your selected research topic, and your subsequent research. You may have to research your terms to pursue your project.

4. Gather preliminary research and resume narrowing your topic and angle of inquiry.

5. Evaluate secondary sources.

6. Take notes: ideas, issues, authors, titles, dates, summaries of arguments, paraphrases, quotations (with page numbers).

7. Create your outline on paper: main points, your position, provisional topic sentences, and paragraphs.

8. Refine your working thesis, then adjust topic sentences and parts of your paragraphs accordingly.

9. Combine your analysis and opinion with your material, solidifying your own position on the research. Keep your position distinct from those of your sources.

10. Draft, document, revise, proofread—be sure you have avoided the 15 common errors listed in section 3 of the Handbook.

Works Cited

Rees, William. "Science, Cognition, and Public Policy." *Academic Matters* (April-May 2008): 9-12. Print.

Young-Ing, Greg. "Understanding People on Their Own Terms: A Rationale for an Aboriginal Style Guide." *Crisp Blue Edges: Indigenous Creative Non-fiction*. Ed. Rasunah Marsden. Penticton, Theytus, 2000. 51-53. Print.

Part 3

THE
READER

INTRODUCTION

In the following three Reader sections, you will find personal and critical writing that deals with connections between self-identity and place, times, family, and many other aspects of life and thought. Literary work, popular books and magazine pieces, student essays, and other forms of writing are represented. None of the following pieces perfectly demonstrate the five-paragraph short academic essay form that we have modelled in the Rhetoric, but part of your work as a student is learning to negotiate your way through a wide range of forms and ideas. Regardless of the specific form of writing, all of the pieces in this Reader illustrate to greater or lesser degrees the basics of good writing. These basics have much in common with those of good driving: a sense of purpose, careful respect of distance and relationships, and a concern to signal to others where one is going. See if that isn't true throughout the selections that follow. Take note of places where you believe this isn't always true, and try to define why.

You will find topics and themes of relevance to university students as well as to anyone interested in what it means to be Canadian and human. We believe you should find much to admire and emulate in the following works. For each reading we have provided a short introduction of background information as well as follow-up questions, intended to help you make useful connections among these pieces, rhetorical information elsewhere in the text, and your own growth as a reader and writer. We have organized the three Reader sections according to a general curve: from primarily evocative works to pieces more intent on changing what readers know, to still others intent on changing how readers think (and perhaps what they will do as a consequence). None of these purposes is necessarily separate from the others: what we consider the fundamental purpose of a piece of writing is a matter of its relative and immediate emphasis. However, we offer this basic layout—from personal to overtly critical—as a reminder, once again, that writing is about choices related to communication, about shaping information and ideas in the interests of some new state of being in one's self, one's reader, and one's world.

Review Summarizing and Rhetorical Analysis

To help you benefit from these selections to the fullest, read Chapter 15, "The Summary," and Chapter 17, "Rhetorical Analysis," in the Rhetoric. These chapters describe the importance of active reading, with detailed guidance on how to write a summary and a rhetorical process description. You will probably be asked to write at least one summary as part of your writing assignments, but it is also a good idea to write a brief summary of any selection that particularly interests you or that has been selected for class or group discussion. Check with your instructor and classmates to see how successfully you are capturing the main intents, strategies, and ideas of the different selections. The first step to becoming a stronger reader and thinker is learning how to write a successful summary.

If writing may be likened to breathing out, then reading is breathing in. All good writers realize it is not possible to do one without the other. We hope our selections help to make your reading as valuable as it can be, by gaining your interest as well as furthering your personal, academic, and community growth.

Section 1

Storytelling: Narration and Description

In college or university, you will be expected for the most part to produce analytical and persuasive writing. In style, it will likely resemble various models presented in Sections 2 and 3 of the Reader as well as in the Research Guide. On first impression, then, the selections that follow in Section 1 may seem to have minimal relevance to scholarly work. Nevertheless, deepening your appreciation of personal, expressive, and evocative forms will enrich all your thinking and writing in important ways.

First, these samples illustrate a command of narration and description, techniques examined in Chapter 10 and Chapter 11 of the Rhetoric. These methods, suitably adapted, help to carry all types of writing. Notice how precisely a fictionalized memoir such as "The Hockey Sweater" describes its setting, and how, using just the right balance of slower and swifter sections, it propels us forward in anticipation of what will happen next.

Whether or not you have room for personal writing in your current English or communications course, you will gain by recognizing the unity of voice, tone, mood, and purpose that informs these samples. You will no doubt recognize the writer's underlying commitment to the topic and theme: no one else but the particular writer in question could have handled the material in quite the same way. Like good researchers adding to communal knowledge, personal writers add their original voices to the communal story.

A second value to be gained from engaging with the following selections is the reminder that authors are always present in their writing, that ultimately they are accountable. You may not submit personal essays as course work, but you can benefit by keeping a journal of responses to readings and research. By recording your personal thoughts about what you read, you explore the relevance of the author's ideas. You take ownership of issues, recognize meaningful connections, and increase awareness of personal responsibility. The essential skill of putting ideas into one's own words is valuably practised in personal writing. We think you will find that the models in this section provide excellent examples of that essential skill in the service of reflection and response.

A closely related third value of the following personal reflections may well be the meaningful topics and critical questions they suggest to spur your own essays. We have aimed to present quality but also timeliness, timelessness, and a wide range of voices and experiences. In their different ways, all seven selections in this section explore the idea of a heroic or at least special person, place, or occupation: What is the connection of this idea to the self? What is the relationship between what is imagined and what remains to be reconciled in some way?

Finally, you may be called upon to use first person in course assignments or future professional work, either to inform parts of your analysis and research or to produce full-fledged personal reflections. In that case, you should find directly relevant inspiration and ideas in the models that follow.

Richard Wagamese Richard Wagamese has said that his goal is to bridge the divide between Native and non-Native peoples. His writing is both honest and healing, and he often deals with the moments of happiness that came during his own unhappy childhood in the Child Welfare system during the 1960s. The foster care and adoption program of that era is often called the "Sixties Scoop" because of the vast number of Native children who were seized from their homes and placed with white families; Wagamese was one of them.

Lemon Pie with Muhammad Ali

1   It was February 25, 1964, deep winter in northern Ontario. At that time of year the nights descended like judgements, dark and deliberate. I shared a room with my foster brother, Bill Tacknyk, and my bed was the lower of the two bunks. When bedtime came I always fell asleep to the sound of his radio playing softly in the darkness.

2   That night he was listening to a boxing match. Cassius Clay was fighting Sonny Liston in a place called Miami. You could hear the crowd behind the announcer's voice. It was like a sea, roaring, then murmuring, then crashing into silence. The announcer was excited, and his words came out of the darkness like the jabs and combinations of the fight itself.

3   Clay was lightning quick as he pounded the lumbering Liston. He opened a cut over Liston's eye and the announcer yelled that there was blood everywhere. The crowd noise was enormous. It filled the corners of our dark room, and when Bill's legs draped over the edge of his bunk, I sat up too. We were galvanized by the details of that fight.

4   I swear I could smell the sweat of it. I could feel the thud of blows landing, and in my mind's eye I could see the younger, faster Clay wheeling around the ring taunting Liston, hitting him at will. I began to cheer for him when Clay was blinded by something and Liston started to win.

5   Clay recovered, and as I rocked in my bunk, arms wrapped around my knees, I clenched my fists and willed him on. In the end, a battered Liston refused to come out and fight again. The crowd cheered and booed and raged, and Bill and I celebrated the new heavyweight champion of the world. My foster mother had to come in and tell us to get to sleep.

6   Cassius Clay changed his name about the same time I did. In my new adopted home I got to see some of his fights on television. He was beautiful. He was outrageous. He was a warrior poet, and when he crashed over refusal to fight in Vietnam I hurt for him. In my mind he was a giant.

7   But my adopted home was a fiasco from day one. No one had told my new family about the history of abuse I came from. No one had told them about the terror I'd faced as a kid and the horrific physical abuse I'd suffered. No one knew then that post-traumatic stress disorder wasn't just a soldier's pain; it could happen to a kid, too.

8   Physical punishment was the rule in that home, and it was the last thing I needed. When I was strapped and beaten, it only exacerbated the trauma in me.

When I was banished to my room, it only embedded the isolation I felt. I found it difficult to fit in and become the kid they wanted me to be, and there were always clashes.

9   I ran away a few times and then, when I was fifteen, I emptied my bank account of paper-route money and found my way to Miami Beach. It was February and I wanted to be somewhere warm. More than anything I just wanted to be away.

10   I got a job in a cafeteria as a busboy and moved in with a pair of old hippies I met. We smoked weed and hung out on the beach, hitting up tourists and swiping drinks from tables. But when I couldn't produce a social security number, the cafeteria let me go. I wandered Miami Beach, lost and hurt and hopeless.

11   One day I went into a lunch counter at Fifth Street and Washington Avenue. They served lemon meringue pie, and I ordered a piece in hopes that a childhood favourite might make me feel better. It was marvellous. When a man came and sat beside me, I bent my head out of shyness. He ordered a piece of pie like mine, and the waitress asked him if he was allowed to have it. He laughed and said he could eat whatever he wanted; he was the Champ, after all. I looked up and saw Muhammad Ali beside me. His training gym was right above that lunch counter, it turned out, and he came in often.

12   He bought me a piece of pie when he ordered another, along with a chocolate shake. We ate together and he smiled at me and rubbed my head like a brother. When he was leaving, I asked him for an autograph and he signed my napkin. Muhammad Ali. A giant. A warrior poet. I was honoured. Watching him walk away I felt healed, like I could bear up. When the police found me eventually and shipped me back to my adopted home, I held onto the sight of him.

13   I left for good soon after, and my life became the road. Thirty-seven years later, I still remember the feel of his big hand on my head and the taste of that lemon pie. Finding Ali saved me, gave me the strength to carry on. I guess that's what heroes do—imbue us with the gold dust of their courage. Ali made me a fighter, and I've come out for every round since then.

For Further Thinking

1. Have you ever had a chance to meet a personal hero? How did the encounter turn out?

Looking Back and Ahead

1. Compare the ways that Wagamese in "Lemon Pie" and Frank McCourt in "Cuchulain" (p. 361) indicate the importance of one act of kindness to a neglected young person.
2. What other similarities do you see between the purpose and the style of Wagamese and McCourt?
3. Read "Canada's 'Genocide': Thousands Taken from Their Homes Need Help" (p. 445). How does Wagamese's essay deepen your understanding of Downey's, and vice versa?

Frank McCourt Frank McCourt was a retired high school English teacher who gained fame at age 67 when his first book, *Angela's Ashes*, won the Pulitzer Prize. *Angela's Ashes* is his memoir of a childhood filled with poverty and neglect, but also with love. The following two excerpts, both from the opening pages of McCourt's book, take place in New York, where the parents have settled in search of a better life than the hardship they faced in their native Ireland. McCourt recalls learning at an early age the nature of both stories and kindness.

Cuchulain

1   The apartment is empty and I wander between the two rooms, the bedroom and the kitchen. My father is out looking for a job and my mother is at the hospital with Malachy. I wish I had something to eat but there's nothing in the icebox but cabbage leaves floating in the melted ice. My father said never eat anything floating in water for the rot that might be in it. I fall asleep on my parents' bed and when my mother shakes me it's nearly dark. Your little brother is going to sleep a while. Nearly bit his tongue off. Stitches galore. Go into the other room.

2   My father is in the kitchen sipping black tea from his big white enamel mug. He lifts me to his lap.

3   Dad, will you tell me the story about Coo Coo?

4   Cuchulain. Say it after me, Coo-hoo-lin. I'll tell you the story when you say the name right. Coo-hoo-lin.

5   I say it right and he tells me the story of Cuchulain, who had a different name when he was a boy, Setanta. He grew up in Ireland where Dad lived when he was a boy in County Antrim. Setanta had a stick and ball and one day he hit the ball and it went into the mouth of a big dog that belonged to Culain and choked him. Oh, Culain was angry and he said, What am I to do now without my big dog to guard my house and my wife and my ten small children as well as numerous pigs, hens, sheep?

6   Setanta said, I'm sorry. I'll guard your house with my stick and ball and I'll change my name to Cuchulain, the hound of Culain. He did. He guarded the house and regions beyond and became a great hero, the Hound of Ulster itself. Dad said he was a greater hero than Hercules or Achilles that the Greeks were always bragging about and he could take on King Arthur and all his knights in a fair fight which, of course, you could never get with an Englishman anyway.

7   That's my story. Dad can't tell that story to Malachy or any other children down the hall.

8   He finishes the story and lets me sip his tea. It's bitter, but I'm happy there on his lap. . . .

9   The twins are able to stand and walk and they have accidents all the time. Their bottoms are sore because they're always wet and shitty. They put dirty things in their mouths, bits of paper, feathers, shoelaces, and they get sick. Mam says we're all driving her crazy. She dresses the twins, puts them in the pram, and

Malachy and I take them to the playground. The cold weather is gone and the trees have green leaves up and down Classon Avenue.

10   We race the pram around the playground and the twins laugh and make goo-goo sounds till they get hungry and start to cry. There are two bottles in the pram filled with water and sugar and that keeps them quiet for awhile till they're hungry again and they cry so hard I don't know what to do because they're so small and I wish I could give them all kinds of food so that they'd laugh and make the baby sounds. They love the mushy food Mam makes in a pot, bread mashed up in milk and water and sugar. Mam calls it bread and goody.

11   If I take the twins home now Mam will yell at me for giving her no rest or for waking Margaret. We are to stay in the playground till she sticks her head out the window and calls for us. I make funny faces for the twins to stop their crying. I put a piece of paper on my head and let it fall and they laugh and laugh. I push the pram over to Malachy playing on the swings with Freddie Leibowitz. Malachy is trying to tell Freddie all about the way Setanta became Cuchulain. I tell him stop telling that story, it's my story. He won't stop. I push him and he cries, Waah, waah, I'll tell Mam. Freddie pushes me and everything turns dark in my head and I run at him with fists and knees and feet till he yells, Hey, stop, stop, and I won't because I can't, I don't know how, and if I stop Malachy will go on taking my story from me. Freddie pushes me away and runs off, yelling, Frankie tried to kill me, Frankie tried to kill me. I don't know what to do because I never tried to kill anyone before and now Malachy, on the swing, cries, Don't kill me, Frankie, and he looks so helpless I put my arms around him and help him off the swing. He hugs me. I won't tell your story anymore. I won't tell Freddie about Coo Coo. I want to laugh but I can't because the twins are crying in the pram and it's dark in the playground and what's the use of trying to make funny faces and letting things fall off your head when they can't see you in the dark?

12   The Italian grocery shop is across the street and I see bananas, apples, oranges. I know the twins can eat bananas. Malachy loves bananas and I like them myself. But you need money, Italians are not known for giving away bananas, especially to the McCourts, who owe them money already for groceries.

13   My mother tells me all the time, Never, never leave that playground except to come home. But what am I to do with the twins bawling with the hunger in the pram? I tell Malachy I'll be back in a minute. I make sure no one is looking, grab a bunch of bananas outside the Italian grocery shop and run down Myrtle Avenue, away from the playground, around the block and back to the other end where there's a hole in the fence. We push the pram to a dark corner and peel the bananas for the twins. There are five bananas in the bunch and we feast on them in the dark corner. The twins slobber and chew and spread banana over their faces, their hair, their clothes. I realize then that questions will be asked. Mam will want to know why the twins are smothered in bananas, where did you get them? I can't tell her about the Italian shop on the corner. I will have to say, A man.

14   That's what I'll say. A man.

15 Then the strange thing happens. There's a man at the gate of the playground. He's calling me. Oh, God, it's the Italian. Hey, sonny, come 'ere. Hey, talkin' to ya. Come 'ere.

16 I go to him.

17 You the kid wid the little bruddas, right? Twins?

18 Yes, sir.

19 Heah. Gotta bag o' fruit. I don' give it to you I trow id out. Right? So, heah, take the bag. Ya got apples, oranges, bananas. Ya like bananas, right? I think ya like bananas, eh? Ha, ha. I know ya like the bananas. Heah, take the bag. Ya gotta nice mother there. Ya father? Well, ya know, he's got the problem, the Irish thing. Give them twins a banana. Shud 'em up. I hear 'em all the way cross the street.

20 Thank you, sir.

21 Jeez. Polite kid, eh? Where ja loin dat?

22 My father told me to say thanks, sir.

23 Your father? Oh, well.

For Further Thinking

1. Is it fair to say that McCourt's youthful possessiveness of the story of Cuchulain is reflective of the uneasiness people have when someone from another culture "appropriates" one of their stories? Is Frankie's fear childish and unfounded, or is there a real danger when the stories of one culture move into the possession of people from another?

Looking Back and Ahead

1. McCourt deals with a theme of keeping yet sharing one's cultural identity. Contrast this with Carrier's treatment of this theme in the next essay, "The Hockey Sweater."
2. How does this essay support or contradict the claims of Morris Berman in "The American Character" (p. 401)?
3. What themes does this essay share with "Lemon Pie with Muhammad Ali" (p. 359)?

Roch Carrier One of Quebec's foremost writers, Roch Carrier (b. 1937) has achieved success in a remarkable range of forms: novels, short stories, children's fiction, plays, screenplays, and poetry. In the late 1960s and early 1970s, Quebec nationalism was at a peak. The CBC commissioned Carrier to write something that would explain to English Canadians "What does Quebec want?" "The Hockey Sweater" was the result. The story accurately reflects 1950s Quebec. One man, Maurice "Rocket" Richard (1921–2000), number 9 of the Montreal Canadiens, symbolized the pride and aspirations of French-speaking Quebecers. In March 1955, Clarence Campbell, president of the National Hockey League, suspended Richard for striking a referee; his decision provoked the "Richard Riot," identified by some historians as the beginning of Quebec's nationalist movement. However, the story does so much more than simply explain what Quebec wants that its opening lines are featured on Canada's five-dollar bill.

The Hockey Sweater

1   The winters of my childhood were long, long seasons. We lived in three places—the school, the church and the skating-rink—but our real life was on the skating-rink. Real battles were won on the skating-rink. Real strength appeared on the skating-rink. The real leaders showed themselves on the skating-rink. School was a sort of punishment. Parents always want to punish children and school is their most natural way of punishing us. However, school was also a quiet place where we could prepare for the next hockey game, lay out our next strategies. As for church, we found there the tranquility of God: there we forgot school and dreamed about the next hockey game. Through our daydreams it might happen that we would recite a prayer: we would ask God to help us play as well as Maurice Richard.

2   We all wore the same uniform as he, the red, white and blue uniform of the Montreal Canadiens, the best hockey team in the world; we all combed our hair in the same style as Maurice Richard, and to keep it in place we used a sort of glue—a great deal of glue. We laced our skates like Maurice Richard, we taped our sticks like Maurice Richard. We cut all his pictures out of the papers. Truly, we knew everything about him.

3   On the ice, when the referee blew his whistle the two teams would rush at the puck; we were five Maurice Richards taking it away from five other Maurice Richards; we were ten players, all of us wearing with the same blazing enthusiasm the uniform of the Montreal Canadiens. On our backs, we all wore the famous number 9.

4   One day, my Montreal Canadiens sweater had become too small; then it got torn and had holes in it. My mother said: "If you wear that old sweater people are going to think we're poor!" Then she did what she did whenever we needed new clothes. She started to leaf through the catalogue the Eaton company sent us in the mail every year. My mother was proud. She didn't want to buy our clothes at the general store; the only things that were good enough for us were the latest styles from Eaton's catalogue. My mother didn't like the order forms included with the catalogue; they were written in English and she didn't understand a word of it. To order my hockey sweater, she did as she usually did; she took out her writing paper and wrote in her gentle schoolteacher's hand: "Cher Monsieur Eaton, Would you be kind enough to send me a Canadiens' sweater for my son who is ten years old and a little too tall for his age and Docteur Robitaille thinks he's a little too thin? I'm sending you three dollars and please send me what's left if there's anything left. I hope your wrapping will be better than last time."

5   Monsieur Eaton was quick to answer my mother's letter. Two weeks later we received the sweater. That day I had one of the greatest disappointments of my life! I would even say that on that day I experienced a very great sorrow. Instead of the red, white and blue Montreal Canadiens sweater, Monsieur Eaton had sent us a blue and white sweater with a maple leaf on the front—the sweater

of the Toronto Maple Leafs. I'd always worn the red, white and blue Montreal Canadiens sweater; all my friends wore the red, white and blue sweater; never had anyone in my village ever worn the Toronto sweater, never had we even seen a Toronto Maple Leafs sweater. Besides, the Toronto team was regularly trounced by the triumphant Canadiens. With tears in my eyes, I found the strength to say:

6   "I'll never wear that uniform."

7   "My boy, first you're going to try it on! If you make up your mind about things before you try, my boy, you won't go very far in this life."

8   My mother had pulled the blue and white Toronto Maple Leafs sweater over my shoulders and already my arms were inside the sleeves. She pulled the sweater down and carefully smoothed all the creases in the abominable maple leaf on which, right in the middle of my chest, were written the words "Toronto Maple Leafs." I wept.

9   "I'll never wear it."

10   "Why not? This sweater fits you . . . like a glove."

11   "Maurice Richard would never put it on his back."

12   "You aren't Maurice Richard. Anyway, it isn't what's on your back that counts, it's what you've got inside your head."

13   "You'll never put it in my head to wear a Toronto Maple Leafs sweater."

14   My mother sighed in despair and explained to me:

15   "If you don't keep this sweater which fits you perfectly I'll have to write to Monsieur Eaton and explain that you don't want to wear the Toronto sweater. Monsieur Eaton's an Anglais; he'll be insulted because he likes the Maple Leafs. And if he's insulted do you think he'll be in a hurry to answer us? Spring will be here and you won't have played a single game, just because you didn't want to wear that perfectly nice blue sweater."

16   So I was obliged to wear the Maple Leafs sweater. When I arrived on the rink, all the Maurice Richards in red, white and blue came up, one by one, to take a look. When the referee blew his whistle I went to take my usual position. The captain came and warned me I'd be better to stay on the forward line. A few minutes later the second line was called; I jumped onto the ice. The Maple Leafs sweater weighed on my shoulders like a mountain. The captain came and told me to wait; he'd need me later, on defense. By the third period I still hadn't played; one of the defensemen was hit in the nose with a stick and it was bleeding. I jumped on the ice: my moment had come! The referee blew his whistle; he gave me a penalty. He claimed I'd jumped on the ice when there were already five players. That was too much! It was unfair! It was persecution! It was because of my blue sweater! I struck my stick against the ice so hard it broke. Relieved, I bent down to pick up the debris. As I straightened up I saw the young vicar, on skates, before me.

17   "My child," he said, "just because you're wearing a new Toronto Maple Leafs sweater unlike the others, it doesn't mean you're going to make the laws around

here. A proper young man doesn't lose his temper. Now take off your skates and go to the church and ask God to forgive you."

18 Wearing my Maple Leafs sweater I went to the church, where I prayed to God; I asked him to send, as quickly as possible, moths that would eat up my Toronto Maple Leafs sweater.

For Further Thinking

1. Make an outline of the narrative structure of this story. Does it have specific parts and connections between the parts? How do these work? After you have given some thought to these questions, see our analysis of this story in Chapter 10 of the Rhetoric.
2. What would you state as the theme of this story?
3. What are your own connections with the narrator of the story? Is his childhood significantly different from yours? Explain.
4. Discuss the commingling of hockey and religion in this story.

Looking Back and Ahead

1. Although the story deals with barriers between French and English, hockey is often said to be "in the blood of all Canadians." After reading "I Was a Teenage Hijabi Hockey Player" (p. 368), do you think the shared experience of hockey could help Canadians from different backgrounds understand each other better? How?

Kerry Li In this personal essay written for an exam, Kerry Li reflects on the sometimes-amusing interplay between the cultural expectations of Canada and Hong Kong as they are expressed by her father.

My Father the Hero

1 In order to seek out a "character" in my family, one is confronted by a plethora of choice. I have distant relatives in Guangdong, China, who can barely speak their own language properly and who ride their steers home from work. On the other side of the world, I also have family residing in the projects of Glasgow, who carry their Irish roots stoutly in their souls and maniacally rant about assassinating the Queen. For the purposes of this essay, however, I will choose to focus on a "character" who is close to my heart and yet far from my comprehension: my father. My dad never ceases to baffle, surprise, and amuse both me and the people who know him. He accomplishes this simply by being a product of his own culture, which is manifested in the way he dresses, communicates and behaves.

2 To begin with, my dad's fashion sense has never strayed very far from his Hong Kong roots. I remember the dread I used to feel every Christmas when

my mama would send a huge box filled with fluorescent colored pants and shirts with "Kelvin Cloin" proudly displayed on the front. Although my sister and I were forced to wear the garments, my father always seemed to enjoy putting them on, much to our chagrin. In retrospect, it is funny to recall the reactions of my friends to his garments; they were unable to tear their gaze away from the kaleidoscope of color in front of them. It would be no exaggeration to say that we used to tell strangers he was colorblind in order to prevent stares! To this day, my dad maintains his unique approach to clothing. Just the other week, at my cousin's wedding, he wore brown sandals with his three-piece suit. He made the valid point that they were more comfortable.

3   Another endearing facet of my dad's personality is the means by which he does (or doesn't) communicate. Over the years I have had a series of mates and boyfriends who have elicited nothing more than a grunt or mumble from the man. I am sure that some of them would be surprised to learn that he can actually have a conversation. He can, of course, speak. I have witnessed him babble on inanely with his friends, most of whom are Chinese, of course. For this reason, my dad has always struck me as a "selective conversationalist."

4   The funniest aspect of my father's character is, by far, his behaviorisms. Although I was mortified as a child, I actually get great amusement now at seeing people's reactions to my father use a toothpick and how he folds his legs up into a pretzel.

5   Over the years I have learnt to embrace these—shall I say—"special" attributes of my father. This is essentially what multiculturalism is all about. One way that his "character" has benefited me is exemplified in my lack of surprise or culture shock in what I encounter during travel. When taking this into consideration, as well as the amount of entertainment I have had throughout my life, my father's fashion sense, my father's communication skills, and my father's behaviorisms have culminated into one satisfactory label: my father, the hero.

For Further Thinking

1. Have you had an experience where someone (perhaps you) seemed eccentric or odd because of carrying a set of cultural values into a situation where they were not shared? This could refer to the values of a generation, as well as those of a place.

Looking Back and Ahead

1. In "I Was a Teenage Hijabi Hockey Player" (p. 368), Shema Khan, like Li in this essay, uses humour to deal with the tension of finding that one's behaviour doesn't always fit the culturally biased assumptions of others. Why is humour a good technique to deal with this subject?
2. Examine the differences between the way Li sees things and the way her dad does. How does each person reflect his or her generation as it is described in "Birth of a New Ethnicity" (p. 382)? How does Li herself personify the "new ethnicity"?

Shema Khan Holder of a PhD in chemical physics from Harvard University, Khan writes a weekly column for the *Globe and Mail* on issues that relate to Muslims and have important connections for all Canadians. The following piece comes from her book *Of Hockey and Hijab: Memoirs of a Muslim Canadian Woman.* In this essay, she pokes gentle fun at colleagues who are surprised that a hijab-wearing Muslim woman can also be a hockey fanatic.

I Was a Teenage Hijabi Hockey Player

1 "When I used to play hockey," I began telling my co-workers over lunch. All of a sudden, eyes looked up in disbelief. "You played hockey?" asked a friend incredulously. "Yes," I replied with a smile, thinking, "Doesn't every Canadian play hockey at some point in their life?" And then it hit me. Muslim women, especially hijabis, aren't expected to be interested in sports, let alone play. Perhaps a calming sport like croquet. But hockey?

2 Come on! I grew up cheering the Montreal Canadiens. My allegiance to the Habs was minted during their phenomenal upset Stanley Cup win in 1971 that featured a law student/goalie named Ken Dryden (I still have his rookie card). My love of the game reached its zenith during that magical September of 1972. I still remember cheering passionately with the rest of my school when Paul Henderson scored in Game 8.

3 During the '70s, I, like many Montrealers, became spoiled by the Canadiens. Every May, my friends and I would line up on Ste-Catherine Street to see the "annual" Stanley Cup parade. One year, we lingered near City Hall, and were rewarded with meeting Bob Gainey, Yvan Cournoyer and Ken Dryden. My seven-year-old brother refused to wash his hands for days.

4 I grew up playing street hockey, driveway hockey and table hockey. I was both Danny Gallivan and Yvan Cournoyer, describing the play-by-play of an electrifying rush leading to a goal with seconds left to play. At the time, there was no organized hockey for girls—only ringette. Later in high school I found a recreational league and laced up every week. In one game, I had a breakaway from the blue line. I was Guy Lafleur, ready to swoop in on the hapless goalie. As I lunged toward the puck, I tripped over the pick of my figure skates, falling flat on my face. Goodbye, figure skates.

5 Once I bought my prized hockey skates, I had to learn to skate all over again. (I kept falling over the front edges of my pick-less hockey skates.) At McGill, I didn't have the talent to make the varsity women's team. So I played intramural hockey, joining a women's engineering team called the Tachyons (named after a subatomic particle by the lone physicist on the team). Some didn't know how to skate. But that never mattered. We just enjoyed the thrill of hockey. I still remember one pre-game warm-up with a player from the other team. We had both been skating at full speed in opposite directions, passing a puck the length of the rink to our respective teammates—heads down. You get the picture. Good thing we were playing the med-school team that night.

6   After moving to Boston for graduate school, I inquired about intramural hockey. There was a league for men, but not for women.

7   Why not start one? And so, a teetotalling Muslim Canuck introduced women's intramural hockey at Harvard. I was one of the few who could lift the puck off the ice. My friends from California and Florida seemed to have the most fun, even though few knew how to skate. It was the sheer thrill of playing hockey that brought out the smiles.

8   Now middle-aged, three pregnancies later, I look back wistfully at my hockey-playing days. I am not yet a hockey parent. If I do go down that road, I will look to the example of Daniele Sauvageau—the legendary coach of the Canadian women's Olympic hockey team that won gold in 2002—for maintaining grace and poise under pressure.

9   I have found other Muslim women who share a passion for hockey, including one friend who recently played for a varsity team in Alberta. On the ice, there was no problem. Hockey equipment lends itself to maintaining modesty in attire, as opposed to say, swimming. It was off the ice where negotiations were made in good faith. Teammates understood when she excused herself from beer outings and the "girls' night out." They went out of their way to help her find a place to pray on road trips. But perhaps the most awkward issue she faced—and one that many observant Muslim women still face—was the casual nudity of the locker room. Modesty is prescribed in Islam, not merely between men and women, but between members of the same gender as well. Locker rooms, showers, open-concept washrooms—all pose challenges to Muslims. Those of us who play sports often dash in and out of dressing rooms, usually with our eyes glued to the floor.

10   Having completed a season of pond hockey, my kids and I are now ready to play a few weeks of street hockey. The only difference from my childhood days is that now I imagine myself as Hayley Wickenheiser, scoring with only seconds left to play.

For Further Thinking

1. Has anyone ever made incorrect assumptions about your abilities or interests based on your appearance or background? Have you ever found yourself making an assumption about someone else based on their appearance or background?

2. What does "I Was a Teenage Hijabi Hockey Player" have to say about being a Canadian in America, a woman in Canada, or a Muslim in a predominantly non-Muslim society?

Looking Back and Ahead

1. Like Nelofer Pazira in "The Pilgrimage" (p. 374), Khan uses the memoir form to challenge stereotypes. How effective is this form for this purpose?

2. "The American Character" (p. 401) claims that there is an American character that influ-ences the way Americans think and behave regardless of their ethnic background. "The Roots of Continuous Negotiation: In Praise of the Courts" (p. 407) argues that the interac-tion of Aboriginals and Europeans early in Canada's history still influences Canadians today, resulting in what one might call a Canadian character. How does "I Was a Teenage Hijabi Hockey Player" relate to one or both of these essays?

3. Like "I Was a Teenage Hijabi Hockey Player," "Lemon Pie with Muhammad Ali" (p. 359) originally appeared as a newspaper column. What stylistic elements do the essays share?

Melisa-Maurice P. Janse van Rensburg Melisa-Maurice P. Janse van Rensburg's "Not Like the Movie" is a personal essay that contrasts a student writer's girlish expectations with her real-life experiences as a young nurse. The violence of the St. James Church massacre in Cape Town on July 25, 1993, had a profound impact on the writer as well as on the national psyche of South Africa. From the point of view of a rescue worker, Janse van Rensburg describes the grue-some aftermath of the attack on a Sunday-evening Christian church service of approximately 1400 white South Africans by the Azanian People's Liberation Army (APLA) who burst through the church doors and opened fire on the congregation with automatic weapons. The APLA attributed the assault to an act of a war against apartheid. The perpetrators have since been granted amnesty by the Truth and Reconciliation Commission, a court-like body assembled after the fall of apartheid in South Africa.

This essay is an example of creative non-fiction, a genre that has gained considerable popularity in contemporary literary communities.

Not Like the Movie

1 Her hair blew in the wind, surrounding her like a thick, black mane. The cam-era zoomed in, focusing on the single tear in her eye as she cried for her true love, lying beside her—dead. She had been a nurse in the Second World War; he was a pilot, shot down over enemy soil but rescued and brought back into her care to be nursed back from near death. That old black and white film is where my love first breathed. My love for men in uniform and my love for nursing flourished in such romantic and such dramatic scenes.

2   As a child I dreamt of being a nurse. I would serve man on the front lines of war, marry a dashing young pilot and, after the war, return as a heroine. I would save many lives while at war, without regard for my own safety. Then we would have two kids, a dog and a white picket fence. Did I mention my dad's bosom swollen with pride as he pinned the Purple Heart on my chest? I imagined a parade in my honour, perhaps even a holiday or a street named after me. I would be the best nurse ever; move over Florence.

3   Years later I remembered this fantasy. The smell of the ocean cut the air, the sun burned my back, and a gentle breeze cooled me as I walked home from nursing school. At the time, terrorism and violence were all around us. Our patients included 13-year-old boys shot after killing two policemen, and the man in Forensic Psychiatry who had murdered and eaten a small child. I stood

at the top of the hill, overlooking the Atlantic ocean, and I wept. An old cliché boomed through my mind: "Be careful what you wish for." Dramatic? Yes. Romantic? Not at all.

4   I started nursing school in January 1993. I had returned to Cape Town after living in the Transvaal for a number of years. I started nursing school because my mother told me to. I had no idea where I wanted to be or which career path to follow. Going to school full time while doing practicums in the hospitals gave me a great balance of academic and hands-on experience. It also gave me a home away from home. All the nursing students lived in "res." The independence and liberty were great. We partied all night, and we slept through lectures all day. It was pretty unremarkable as far as student life goes.

5   One particular Sunday evening, life changed. My reality shifted. A couple of the girls and I had made our way along the Pipe Trail. This trail ran along the sunny side of Chapman's Peak, an extension of Cape Town's world-renowned Table Mountain, where two oceans collide with one another. It's about a four-hour hike, not too strenuous, and surrounded by magnificent trees that date back centuries. We flirted with the boys along the trail and giggled like sixth-graders when they flirted back. We were about a half hour from the end of the trail when dense towers of cumulonimbus clouds thundered and roared in off of the ocean with an ominous fury. I remember looking out of the window on the drive home. I gazed at the black sea feeling small, insignificant and yet, calm and peaceful. Life was perfect. Then we neared the hospital where we lived.

6   Ambulances raced past us, and crowds of people stopped in the streets. There was panic in the air. I was frantic as I tried to find a radio station that might tell us what was happening. Then we heard. There had been a massacre at St. James Church, just two blocks from where we were. They were asking all staff from Victoria Hospital to report for duty immediately. "Mass casualty . . . AK-47s . . . Hand grenades . . ." These were the only words I heard. Conny and I looked at each other in horror, and she turned her beat-up, little Golf in the direction of St. James Church.

7   We were among the first to respond to the call. People staggered around crying, sobbing, and screaming. Dads searched frantically for their kids; sisters searched frantically for their brothers, and everywhere there was chaos. Fear enveloped me. Fear forced me to breathe through the layers of silence that had grabbed hold of my mind. It demanded that I extract courage from the depth of my now-wounded soul. The air was heavy with the smell of gunpowder and burning flesh. As if God himself was responding to this tragedy, lightning strobed across the sky; it illuminated church-goers as they made their way out of the building. A deluge of rain poured from the sky, adding to the assault. We were cold, wet and terrified. The Fire Department had arrived but the firemen just stood around whispering to one another. I hadn't noticed myself run toward the church entrance until a police officer tried holding me back.

8   "I'm a nurse," I screamed at him. "I work at Victoria Hospital: let me through." He waved us on, instructing us to help where we could. "Oh, dear God," I heard myself whisper as we ran inside.

9   I knelt beside a young man who had been killed instantly—a single bullet hole through his head. I moved on to the next victim, then the next, and the next. I was in a daze. I was on autopilot. A mother, Marita, who had twice survived cancer, now lay dead. She had been shot in the chest at close range. She would be buried on her birthday. Gerard had thrown himself on a hand grenade immediately before it exploded and ripped apart his husky, 21-year-old body. That is how July 25th, 1993, ended for me; for others, it simply ended. There were 11 dead and 50 more wounded.

10   The following day brought about a new reality that felt contrived. It was a reality where people were safe to worship and meet with friends. Children were free to ride their bicycles around the neighbourhood, and voiceless screams were absent from my dreams. The all-night parties resumed and the nightmares returned while I slept through lectures. The Pipe Trail saw more of us and we continued to flirt with the boys along the way. I went on to complete my nursing diploma. I never spoke of that night.

11   Hoping to escape those memories, I packed a small bag, boarded an aeroplane, and crossed the African continent arriving at London's Heathrow Airport. The air was palatable and smelled different. It smelled of sweet peas and fresh, crisp watercress, and it smelled like liberty. I remember disembarking after my overnight flight, and feeling determined to find an escape from the hatred and the imprisoning politics in South Africa. I spent two years in London, England. A year of that was spent taking care of the elderly in their homes, which allowed them to maintain some independence. The second year I spent caring for two young boys as a live-in nanny. All this time I studied different fields related to psychiatry. In retrospect, I think that I was trying to understand the workings of the evil that has destroyed, and continues to destroy, so many lives. I had decided that Canada was the perfect country to live in and focused on finding a way to immigrate. When I left London for Canada, it was with a few letters of the alphabet behind my name and a fluffy little white feather in my hat.

12   Nearly eight years have passed since I arrived in Canada. I have been institutionalized by Tim Horton's, and although I don't skate very well, I proudly support the Calgary Flames. Two years ago, I stood before God and more than 100 witnesses and humbly pledged allegiance to the Queen. I spent a year studying to become a Licensed Practical Nurse and now I work at Foothills Hospital in Calgary. It's a hard job physically, emotionally and mentally. Our Health Region suffers from poor staffing and an ever-growing geriatric population. Still, peace and sleep continue to elude me at times, and I lie awake, listening to my husband's peaceful breathing. Geography cannot replace that part of me that died back in 1993.

13   Being a nurse has defined me in many ways. The experience has taken me to many places where I have seen many things. I hope it will remain a large part of my life. I never did marry a pilot, and my husband and I are struggling to maintain our second pregnancy. We don't yet have a dog, nor do we have a white picket fence around our home. There has been no parade in my honour,

and no street named after me. My hair tangles in the wind and the only thing purple on my chest is blueberry jam stains left by my little boy. My dad is proud of me, and sometimes I feel proud of myself, too. I am proud that I have found the strength to forge forward over all the hurdles in life and that I continue reaching for my dream—to serve our fellow man.

For Further Thinking

1. How many different tones can you pick out in this essay? Where does the tone of the essay change and why?
2. The writer contrasts her expectations of what a nursing career would be like with her real-life experience. Can you think of a similar encounter in your life whereby your experience of something did not match your expectations of it? Would a similar essay format be an appropriate form in which to write about it?

Looking Back and Ahead

1. Roch Carrier writes nostalgically about "the winters of [his] childhood" spent on the hockey rink. How does Janse van Rensburg use nostalgia in "Not Like the Movie"? What effect does it have on the reader?
2. Is Janse van Rensburg's relationship to Canada in "Not Like the Movie" similar to Shema Kahn's relationship to Canada as described in her essay "I Was a Teenage Hijabi Hockey Player" (p. 368)? How and how not?
3. How do we define violence? Read "Saskatchewan's Indian People—Five Generations" (p. 379) and "Canada's 'Genocide'" (p. 445). Is there a possibility that Janse van Rensburg's essay leaves an impression of Canada as too much like the official movie most of us have been raised to believe in (tolerant, non-racist, peaceful)? Must we see blood flowing in our own communities in order to judge whether violence is occurring?

Nelofer Pazira On December 24, 1979, the Soviet Union invaded Afghanistan to prop up a weak Marxist government that had enjoyed friendly relations with Moscow. In the minds of most Soviets, the occupation was a mission to help modernize and stabilize a poor, strife-ridden country. In fact, the occupation quickly turned into a full-scale military crisis, which lasted 10 years and led to the deaths of 15 000 Soviet soldiers ("1989") and as many as 670 000 Afghanis (Zucchino). It is considered one of the major factors in the collapse of the Soviet Union.

In *A Bed of Red Flowers*, which has been made into the movie *Kandahar*, Afghan-Canadian journalist Nelofer Pazira describes what it was like to grow up in Afghanistan during the Afghan-Soviet war. When she was 16, her family fled Afghanistan and came to Canada as refugees. In this excerpt, about a pre-war vacation taken by her family and their friends early in her childhood, she describes an Afghanistan very different from the one that appears in media coverage.

The Pilgrimage

1   The Baghlan Mazar-e-Sherif Highway is a road of great beauty, and we are not in a hurry. We stop from time to time to buy fruit from farmers' stands at the side of the road, to take pictures of sheep grazing in the valleys and to fill our flasks with cold water from a stream. Our caravan of four families is driving north for a three-day holiday. Uncle Sultani is leading the way in his long black Chevrolet. We are following him in our orange Passat, behind us is Uncle Hatiq in his pale blue Beetle, and the last car is Uncle Bokhtari's navy blue hatchback.

2   Uncle Sultani pulls over. "Should we go straight to the port?" My father nods. In a short time we arrive at Sher Khan Bander—the Afghan-Soviet border. We children run as fast as we can into the open fields, arms stretched on each side of us like an airplane's wings. My father and his friends, all of whom we call "uncle," pull the picnic carpet from the car.

3   All doctors from Kabul, my father and my uncles have been posted to Baghlan to work in the city's only hospital. The wives of Uncle Hatiq and Uncle Sultani are also doctors; Uncle Bokhtari's wife stays at home.

4   Other than the three sons of Uncle Bokhtari and Uncle Hatiq, who are in their teens, we are between four and six years old. While the older children have to help set up the picnic, we dance in circles, holding hands. We pick yellow flowers that are scattered around the field like tiny stars and bring them to our mothers.

5   My father takes me to a precipice and helps me hold on to an iron balustrade from which we can peer far down into the gorge at the great river. My father tells me that we are looking at the Amu Darya, a silver, moving line that separates Afghanistan from the Soviet Union. At this side of the border, a diminutive ship is being loaded by a crane. My father points far down into the valley at the little boat, holding me from behind. Matchstick men are tying a net over the cargo. I watch the ship move slowly, cutting across the flow of the water. "Habib!" I hear my mother calling. "Habib! Don't let her go farther." I hold tighter to the iron bars, worried that the wind might throw me into the river. "The river is the border," my father carefully explains. "And that"—here his hand points to the other shore—"is the Soviet Union."

6   We stood and looked across into the Soviet Union on New Year's Eve of 1978. No one could have imagined that in just a year's time, the people on that other shore would invade our country; nor could we have foreseen that in four years' time a bridge called Pole Dostee—Friendship Bridge—would be built across the Amu River. And when the Soviets built the bridge, they could not have imagined that their soldiers would one day retreat across it in humiliation. The last Soviet soldier crossed the Friendship Bridge, which by then had become the enemy bridge, in 1989.

7   When I watched that cargo ship with such excitement as it crossed the waterway frontier, the river looked so gentle, and the surrounding world was at peace.

8 We play in a restaurant garden, the Amu River behind us with its ships crossing. My father and uncles have gone fishing. When they return, each carrying several fish, they brag about their catch. The frying pans and oil stoves are brought from the car. I run to the corner of the garden, where the women are stretching their legs over the picnic carpet. They're cooking fish, I tell my mother. "Good!" says Uncle Sultani's wife. "Tell them to hurry—we're hungry." Soon, we're settled around the tablecloth, eating the freshly fried fish. I cover the fish head and skin with a piece of flat bread. Fish heads always look scary: the ever-open eyes, the dry mouths, the gills pressed against the plate; the skin is greasy and wrinkled from burns. Uncle Sultani complains that he has to force his daughter and son to eat. "This is the time of their growth; they should eat well," he says. Uncle Bokhtari, who is very skinny, lifts each of us up by the shoulders, telling us we are so light that the strong border wind could blow us to the other side of the river. What would it be like to land suddenly in the Soviet Union?

9 Before we leave, we wave across the frontier. There is no one we can see from our Afghan cliff, but we say goodbye anyway. We throw the remains of the fish into the river, watching them as they dive and tumble through the air currents towards the water. Their clan may be relieved to have their bones, skulls and skins back, albeit broken, crooked and burned. We drive away slowly through a small shabby town, leaving the river, the dead fish and the frontier behind.

10 The next day, March 21, 1978, is Now Rouz, our New Year. We stop in the city of Mazar-e-Sherif. It is crowded with hundreds of visitors from across Afghanistan, all wanting to watch the raising of the flag at the famous Ali shrine. We take pictures in front of a fountain that splashes water over a large rectangular pond. For my parents, this is one of the best times of their lives. They have their wishes and plans for the New Year: buying a new car, visiting family and relatives in Kabul. They even talk of going to another province once my father's three-year term in Baghlan is over.

11 As we drive on, we pass through hills that look like mountains of green velvet. Thousands of red flowers called *gule dokhtaran* (girls' flowers) stand across the landscape like an impressionist masterpiece, a mass of red dots. This is *meli guli sourkh,* the red flower picnic everyone comes to Mazar to see. We stop to pick a few of the flowers, but they soon wither.

For Further Thinking

1. Taking into account all that has happened in Afghanistan since Pazira's family vacation, what effect does she achieve by describing Afghanistan from the point of view of a child?
2. During the Afghan-Soviet war, the United States supplied the Mujahideen with weapons, including Stinger missiles, and educational materials that included children's textbooks with instructions on how to make hand grenades ("Back to School"). When Soviet troops withdrew,

the United States ended its support of Afghanistan, and in the chaos that followed the Taliban rose to power.

Does this history support or refute an argument for American military involvement in Afghanistan today? Write an argumentative essay that supports one of these views.

3. Although this is a work of non-fiction, how does Pazira use literary devices to foreshadow the coming war?

Looking Back and Ahead

1. Read "What We Are Fighting For," by Rex Murphy (p. 438) and "The Good War: A Propaganda Perennial," by Fred Stenson (p. 440). Are there assumptions in either of those essays that seem inconsistent with the picture Pazira presents of Afghanistan in 1978?

2. Read "The Hockey Sweater" (p. 364). What strategies are shared by the writers of these two accounts of volatile political situations?

Works Cited

"1989: Soviet Troops Pull Out of Afghanistan." *On This Day 1950–2005. BBC News.* BBC, 15 Feb. 2008. Web. 24 July 2010.

"Back to School in Afghanistan." *CBC News Online.* CBC, 27 Jan. 2004. Web. 24 July 2010.

Zucchino, David. "The Untold War." *Los Angeles Times.* Los Angeles Times, 2 June 2002. Web. 17 Nov. 2010.

Section 2 Exploring
Subjects

All of the entries in the previous section of this Reader use the first person. In Section 2, only one entry uses the first person ("Newfoundlandese, If You Please"), and only to a very limited extent. The purpose of work in the following pieces has shifted from the expressive and evocative purpose of Section 1 to a primary concern with exposition. The following pieces, unlike personal essays or short stories, identify their topics explicitly and use more formal means than those in Section 1 to pursue the discussion. Chapters 11 to 15 in the Rhetoric are particularly relevant to the following readings.

Like the readings in Section 1, however, those in Section 2 deal in their own ways with related issues of identity; generational, social, and cultural experience; as well as relations to nationhood and learning. As in Section 1, questions for further thinking and for comparison to other essays in the Reader are listed after the readings.

Pat Deiter-McArthur (Day Woman) The following piece of written history by an Aboriginal writer represents something new, as Aboriginal history was traditionally handed down orally. In 1992, Métis historian Olive Dickason published the country's first book of Aboriginal history by an Aboriginal writer: *Canada's First Nations*.

In his book *A Fair Country,* John Ralston Saul refers to a 95 percent reduction in Aboriginal population that occurred in what is now North America from the late 15th century to the end of the 19th century (23). As Deiter-McArthur's essay suggests, that trend has reversed, particularly in Saskatchewan where over 13 percent of the population now identifies as Aboriginal and a quarter of the province's children are Aboriginal (Mitchell 152). Within foreseeable decades, the "flip" could occur, resulting in a majority of the province being Aboriginal. For Canada as a whole, the Aboriginal population is around 3.3 percent of the total.

The Vision Quest

I am an Indian and a member of the Fifth Generation.

I have choice, strength, and freedom.

I have an obligation to my Treaty-Signers, and others who knew no freedom,

and to my future—to be the best I can be.

What I dream, I am. The fulfillment of my dream is my Vision Quest.

Saskatchewan's Indian People—Five Generations

1   It has been about five generations since Saskatchewan Indian people have had significant contact with European settlers. The First Generation strongly influenced by Europeans were the treaty-signers. The key characteristic of this generation was their ability to have some input into their future. They retained their tribal cultures but realized that they had to negotiate with the Europeans for the betterment of future generations. They did not give up their language or religion or the political structures of nationhood. They were perceived by government as an "alien" nation to be dealt with by treaty.

2   The Second Generation (1867–1910) of Indian people was the object of legal oppression by the government. This generation lived under the absolute rule of an Indian agent, a government employee. Through the Indian Act, this generation was denied their religion, political rights, and freedom to travel off their reserves. A pass and permit system was strictly adhered to on the prairies; every Indian person required a pass to leave the reserve and a permit to sell any agricultural produce. All children were required to attend residential schools run by the churches. The goals of their schools were, first, to make Christians out of their students and to rid them of their pagan lifestyles and, second, to provide a vocational education.

3   Tuberculosis was a major killer of Indian people during this time and contributed to decimating their population in Saskatchewan to a low of five thousand in 1910. This generation was treated as wards and aliens of Canada.

4   The laws which served to oppress the second generation were in place until the early 1950s. The Third Generation (1910–1945) was greatly affected by

these laws and schooling. This generation can be described as the lost generation. These people were psychologically oppressed. They rejected their Indianness but found that because of the laws for treaty Indians they could not enjoy the privileges accorded to whites. This third generation was our grandfathers' generation. Many Indians at this time could speak their language but would not because of shame of their Indianness. They were still required by law to send their children to residential schools, to send their sick to Indian hospitals, and to abide by the Indian agent. They rarely had a sense of control over their own lives. This generation was considered wards of the government and denied citizenship.

5   Our fathers' time, the Fourth Generation since treaty-signing, can be best described as the generation of an Indian rebirth. This generation (1945–1980) is characterized by a movement of growing awareness—awareness that being Indian is okay and that Indian people from all tribes are united through their aboriginality, historical development, and special status.

6   This generation saw the rise of Indian and Native organizations across Canada, the return of traditional ceremonies, and an acknowledgement of the need to retain traditional languages and cultural ways.

7   Indian people of this generation were given the right to vote in 1960. The pass and permit system was abandoned in the late 1930s. In 1956, Indian children could attend either residential schools or the local public schools. However, the effects of this generation being raised within an institution and their parents being raised in the same way had a severe impact on these individuals. The residential school not only taught them to suppress their language but also to suppress their feelings and sense of individualism. The continued attack on Indian languages by residential schools left this generation with an ability only to understand their language, but many were not sufficiently fluent to call their Native language their first language.

8   During the sixties, there was a rise in Indian urbanization, a trend that continues today. This generation also contributed to an Indian baby boom that is estimated to be eight to ten years behind the non-Indian baby boomers. The federal and provincial vote allowed Indian people to legally consume alcohol. Alcoholism, suicides, and violent deaths were on the rise for this generation.

9   This was a period of experimentation by both the Indian communities and the government. Unfortunately, neither side was ready for each other. The intended government goal of assimilation was besieged with problems of racism, poverty, maladjustment, and cultural shock.

10   Today's Indian people are part of the Fifth Generation. The fifth generation is faced with choices: assimilation, integration, or separation. Indian people are now able to intermarry or assimilate with non-Indian without the loss of their Indian status. Indian leaders across Canada are seeking a separate and constitutionally recognized Indian government. Indian government is to provide its own services within Indian reserves. Integration allows Indian people to retain a sense of their cultural background while working and living within the larger society.

11   The fifth generation people are the first children since treaty-signing to be raised by their parents. Many of this fifth generation are not able to understand a Native language. Their first and only language is English. This generation is generally comfortable about their Indianness without strong prejudicial feelings to others. However, this generation is challenged to retain the meaning of Indian identity for their children.

For Further Thinking

1. Is the history reported in this article new information for you, or do you feel it has already been satisfactorily covered in previous school curricula? Have you had direct experience of Aboriginal history?
2. If you have direct knowledge of Aboriginal cultures, do you think they have elements that would benefit our wider society? If so, explain.
3. Comment on Deiter-McArthur's basic methods of exposition in this essay. Does she leave interpretation to us? Explain.

Looking Back and Ahead

1. As Deiter-McArthur's essay points out, government policies inflicted on one generation of Aboriginal people often carried on through future generations. The first missionary-operated schools, dedicated to assimilation through education, began in 1620. Government-supported, Church-run residential schools and industrial schools followed in the 1800s. Forced apprehensions of Aboriginal children began with the residential schools. Beginning in the 1950s, in McArthur's Fourth Generation, there began a wave of forced adoptions in which Aboriginal children were placed in white homes. The provincial governments had been newly assigned responsibility for Aboriginal health, welfare, and education by the federal government and received payment for each child apprehended. Thousands of Aboriginal children, some but by no means all in situations of neglect, became subjects of this campaign of assimilation, sometimes known as the "Sixties Scoop." According to Michael Downey, forced adoptions during this time "skyrocketed." Author Richard Wagamese, whose mother had attended residential school, was caught in the "scoop." Read "Lemon Pie With Muhammad Ali" (p. 359), and discuss how, as a member of the Fourth Generation, Wagamese experienced the particular challenges of that generation, with perhaps some impacts from the Third Generation and some anticipation of the Fifth Generation to follow. His novel *Keeper 'N Me* adds to the picture presented in his essay.
2. Discuss Deiter-McArthur's essay in connection with "The Fear of the Unknown" (p. 419) and "Canada's 'Genocide'" (p. 445). Based on evidence in these two essays, how rigid are the generational definitions that Deiter-McArthur describes?

Matthew Mendelsohn In the summer of 2003, the *Globe and Mail* published a series of articles by a number of writers profiling young Canadian adults in pictures, stories, and statistics. In 2004, these stories were revised, updated, and published as *The New Canada: A Globe and Mail Report on the Next Generation*. Matthew Mendelsohn's article comes from that collection.

Birth of a New Ethnicity

1 Social change is sometimes difficult to see. It's like looking at yourself in the mirror every day and not noticing that you're aging. But once in a while it's useful to pull out the high school yearbook and take note of the transformation.

2 The survey we conducted for *The Globe and Mail's* New Canada project asked people what makes them proud of Canada. Over all, things such as the beauty of the land, the country's high ranking by the United Nations and our role in peacekeeping came out at the top of the list. Among young Canadians, those in their 20s, other factors made them proud: multiculturalism, the Charter of Rights and Freedoms, bilingualism, having people from different cultural backgrounds living in peace.

3 These are the elements of the new Canadian mythology, one created in the period between the late 1960s and the early 1980s and codified as official in the Charter of Rights and Freedoms. Perhaps it is not surprising that these are sources of pride. After all, this is the only Canada that young people have ever known, and one quite different from that of their grandparents.

4 One of the biggest changes in Canada over the past twenty years has been the emergence of a more deeply entrenched pan-Canadian national identity. It was once thought that attachment to Canada was quite weak, with local attachments being more important. This is no longer the case. Waves of new immigrants from non-European countries chose to come to Canada, not to any particular province. Young Canadians, at least outside Quebec, are far more likely than older Canadians to define themselves as Canadian first, rather than in terms of their province.

5 The "I am Canadian" marketing phenomenon tapped into something real: Canadians are very proud of their national identity. With no trace of irony, they proudly yell about how modest they are, and patriotically proclaim that they have no patriotism. Despite our claim to a modest and deferential nationalism, our nationalism has become as emotional and assertive as anyone's. The introduction of the Charter of Rights was explicitly designed to unite all citizens in a pan-Canadian community, and it worked. Outside Quebec, a real national consciousness has been created—this despite simmering regional resentments and disaffection from the federal government.

6 The result has been the emergence over the past 20 years of a new ethnicity—simply Canadian. As more young people consider themselves ethnically fractioned—half of this and a quarter of that—fewer will have a strong connection to an ethnic group other than Canadian. In the 2001 census, when asked about the ethnic origins of our ancestors, fully 39 per cent of us said "just Canadian," and this number grows higher every year. The very term "ethnicity" is an awkward one, but it fits: We are creating a new multiracial, multicultural boundary-free ethnic group called "Canadian."

7 These are large and significant changes. Take immigration, for example. In 1946, almost half of all Canadians (46 per cent) said our immigration policy should ensure that Jews do not come to Canada. In 1961, 40 per cent of Canadians

said that we should prevent the immigration of non-whites. Today, almost no one holds such views.

8   And, although many of us still consider our ethnic background important to us, virtually no one under the age of 30 thinks that a similar ethnic background is important when choosing a spouse or friends. Canadians date, marry, work and hang out with people from all kinds of backgrounds. What you believe, not where you come from, matters. For most Canadians, their ethnicity is a mark of personal identity, but in no way grounds for exclusion.

9   In surveys in France, Britain, Italy, the United States and other countries, anywhere from 30 to 50 per cent of people say that relations between different ethnic groups are a big problem; in Canada, just 12 per cent say this. In Canada, 81 per cent of those under 30 say immigrants are having a positive effect on our country, which is a significantly higher number than found among older Canadians, and significantly higher than young people in other countries, according to a major international study conducted for the Pew Research Center for People and the Press, an independent group based in Washington, D.C. In the United States, about one in three Americans say blacks and whites should not marry each other. In Canada, fewer than one in 10 hold that belief, and almost no one under 30 does. It is not merely starry-eyed back-patting to highlight these very real differences between Canada and other countries. They are real facts that define our national identity.

10   Canada integrates immigrants better than any other country in the world today. You might think we would rejoice in this, but instead some among us still choose to worry about multiculturalism, about "ethnic ghettos," and about whether immigrants retain too much attachment to their country of origin. Some—the Fraser Institute in its report *Canada's Immigration Policy: The Need for Major Reform*, for example—seek out an anti-immigrant backlash, fail to find it, but still warn ominously that it could come any day now. They seek out an anti-immigrant backlash that never materializes and refuse to acknowledge the reality of the country: People from different backgrounds are getting along better every year, not worse. While some remain uncomfortable with the changing face of Canada and project their own insecurities onto the country, young Canadians are simply not concerned.

11   Many Canadians do worry that immigrants are not adopting Canadian values quickly enough. However, immigrants come to share the same values as other Canadians relatively quickly. Our survey showed that within one generation, the children of immigrants have virtually identical values as other young Canadians. Moreover, even first-generation Canadians take pride in Canada for the same reasons as non-immigrant Canadians.

12   That's the good news. However, although Canadians' attitudes toward diversity have changed, this does not mean that we live in a colour-blind society. Most Canadians, regardless of ethnic background, continue to believe that racism exists, and this belief is higher among immigrants. For example, about 65 per cent of young visible-minority immigrants believe the police show bias in their treatment of blacks and aboriginals. This experience of lived racism is a reality. In

particular, new immigrants are not doing as well economically as they used to. In 1980, after being in Canada for 10 years, immigrants were earning as much as native-born Canadians. Today, those who've been here 10 years only earn about 83 per cent as much as native-born Canadians. Some groups, particularly some visible-minority groups, are threatened with social exclusion. In our survey, 61 per cent of Canadians agreed that success depends more on "who you know" than on how hard you work. This sense that many opportunities may be closed to new immigrants is a potential source of tension in the new Canada.

13   Moreover, the issues of Quebec and aboriginal peoples have not been addressed in the New Canadian nation. The claims of these groups, to different rather than simply equal status, do not fit easily with the official ideology of individual rights articulated in the Charter. Non-aboriginal Canadians outside Quebec continue to ignore the fact that almost half of francophone Quebeckers would like to secede from Canada and that aboriginal peoples have outstanding land claims and treaty rights. English-speaking Canadians express great affinity with and solidarity for aboriginal peoples and francophone Quebec, but appear to be unwilling to make any sacrifices to do anything about this.

14   One of the most important changes in Canada over the past decade has been Canadians' embrace of trade and globalization as part of the New Canadian national identity. Canadians are more engaged with the world than every before, more prepared to work abroad, and see this international engagement as key to Canadian prosperity. "Internationalism" has now been incorporated into Canadians' identity. Consistent with our multicultural nature, Canadians believe we have a moral obligation to other countries, we would like to encourage the adoption of Canadian values abroad, and we believe these can be furthered by trade and engagement with the world.

15   Comparing who we once were to who we are today can be startling. It is not so long ago in Canada that aboriginals on reserves couldn't vote, non-whites could not immigrate, and there were quotas to make sure there weren't too many Jews at Canadian universities. When your kids get hold of the old yearbook, they no doubt laugh at your funny hair and strange clothes. In much the same way, the beliefs of Old Canada are equally anachronistic.

16   The New Canada is the Canada that we hoped to create in the 1970s. The values in the Charter of 1981 may not have reflected who we were as a country then, but it is those values which have created who we are as a country today. This is exactly what we'd hoped for.

For Further Thinking

1. Does the description of a "new ethnicity" reflect your own experience? Do you find that young Canadians tend to see themselves as Canadian first? In your experience, is it true that few young people consider ethnicity when choosing a life partner?

2. What are your own ethnicities? If they are mixed, how do you balance cultural demands, if any? Do you think of yourself as Canadian first, as your ethnic group first, or by some other designation first?

3. This essay dwells on the positive aspects of the assimilation of children of immigrants into the Canadian mainstream. However, in *The Wayfinders,* a published collection of 2009 Massey Lectures at the University of Toronto, noted anthropologist Wade Davis says, "Of the 7,000 languages spoken today, fully half are not being taught to children. Effectively, unless something changes, they will disappear within our lifetimes . . . . What this really means is that within a generation or two, we will be witnessing the loss of fully half of humanity's social, cultural and intellectual legacy" (3).

    What is gained and what is lost as the children of different backgrounds are assimilated into the "new ethnicity"? Do the losses outweigh the gains, or vice versa?

Looking Back and Ahead

1. "Birth of a New Ethnicity" relies primarily on statistics to illustrate and prove its points. Look at the chapters on persuasive appeals and logic. Although this essay is primarily expository, does it also have a persuasive purpose? Is this purpose best served by statistics? Are there other effective ways to support its thesis?

2. As Kerry Li describes with humour in "My Father the Hero" (p. 366), although young Canadians see themselves as Canadian first, often their parents or grandparents do not. How do Li and her father (and perhaps you and your parents) fit into the patterns described in "The New Ethnicity"?

Diane Mooney As Canada's youngest province (it entered Confederation in 1949), Newfoundland is this country's oldest point of European contact. The population resides mainly on the island of Newfoundland, principally on the Avalon Peninsula. By contrast, Labrador, on the mainland, is sparsely populated.

In the following essay, marine biology student Diane Mooney takes us on a tour of major linguistic regions, combining classification-division, spatial process, and descriptive process to celebrate the range of cultures and languages in her home province. A trained environmental technician, Mooney grew up along the rugged shores of Newfoundland. She calls herself "an avid tourist of the island . . . where there is always a new culture and dialect to discover." If you have never visited Newfoundland, talk to some of your classmates who have been there, to prepare you for reading this essay.

Newfoundlandese, If You Please

1   I learned recently that people who visit Newfoundland become fascinated with our unique dialect. If they travel to different areas of the island, they quickly realize that every little nook and cranny, of which there are many, has its own specific sound. Not too long ago I travelled to the Port au Port peninsula on the province's West Coast. Here, the inhabitants are French descendants and speak with an odd

accent, Newfoundland French, I guess. Being from an Irish settlement on the East Coast, I had difficulty understanding their speech as they did mine. All the different descendants in Newfoundland play a major role in our dialect. It seems as though our ancestors, who came from many different areas, never quite lost their own speech: they all just adapted to the lives they settled into. There were many settlements all along the coast and inland across the island, all with a different adaptation of English. As Baldwin says in his essay "If Black English Isn't a Language, Then Tell Me, What Is?" "people evolve a language." He was referring to the African Americans of the United States. The same can be said for the Irish, English, British, and French of Newfoundland. The difference is that they didn't just evolve into one, they evolved into one with many different variations.

2   Starting with the Avalon Peninsula of the East Coast of Newfoundland, with which I am most familiar, it is easy to tell who first settled in what area simply by their speech. The Southern Shore of the island is Irish, and to this day you can hear an Irish accent in their voices. People on the Southern Shore refer to their fathers as "daa." Whether this is an Irish thing or just a Southern Shore thing, you won't hear it anywhere else in the province. You may look even deeper into each individual community. Some are all Catholics and came from one area of Ireland with their own dialect; others are all Anglican coming from a different area of Ireland with another dialect. However, there are very few Anglicans on the Southern Shore; the Catholics drove out most.

3   Not too far away in the Trinity-Conception area, again they are mainly Irish—Anglican Irish. The dialect here can be quite difficult to understand. A number of areas drop their "h's" and this is one of them. For example, "I'm goin' 'ome to clean me 'ouse de once." Translation: "I am going home to clean my house now." "De once" means it is going to be done immediately—at once. To a visitor from outside the province or even to someone from within the province this can also be very difficult to understand, especially with the speed of Newfoundland speech. All Newfoundlanders talk fast; this is just a given.

4   Moving off the Avalon into Central Newfoundland we have moved out of the fishing communities into logging and mining towns; mainly fishermen who moved inland in winter to hunt and log when they couldn't fish settled in these areas. The settlements there today are pretty mixed with dialects coming from all over. One area in particular always uses "we" and "I" when making references to themselves instead of "us" and "we." For example, "Be careful or they'll come after we or I." Translation: "Be careful or they will come after us." Again something that can be very confusing and interesting to the non-native.

5   Most of Newfoundland believes that the West Coast of the island is trying to sound like mainlanders. They say "eh" a lot and have a slight twang in their speech. In reality though, it probably goes back to when the French settled, which is still so strong on the Port au Port peninsula.

6   The Northern Peninsula, which is very large and stretched out but not heavily populated, seems to be in a world of its own. Some communities drop their "h's"

while others add extra "h's." For example, "First you put your happles in the hoven and you bake 'em on 'igh." Translation: "First you put your apples in the oven and you bake them on high." Some others on the tip of the Northern Peninsula, which is so close to Quebec, have a tendency to slip into some French dialect as well.

7　　Taking in only major sections of the province, any tourist can see clearly that Newfoundland has many different descendants and therefore many different dialects. As Baldwin suggests, when so many different languages are put together, they have to come up with a way to communicate that everyone can understand. Because Newfoundland is so spread out, a language evolved and each little cove and inlet adapted its own version.

For Further Thinking

1. Would you say that you speak English fast or slowly? Is your accent difficult for others? How have your ancestry and region shaped your style of English?
2. In your own words, express Mooney's thesis as completely and precisely as you can.
3. From what you know of Newfoundland—and you could always add to that knowledge with a little further research—how important do you think its forms of English have been to its cultural life?

Looking Back and Ahead

1. Think of someone you know who emigrated to your community from a country that speaks little or no English or that speaks a different form of English from yours. Would this person's language difficulties be heightened or lessened in Newfoundland? Why or why not?
2. Read "Birth of a New Ethnicity" (p. 382). Do you think Canada is headed toward a single culture, perhaps a global culture, where the distinctions of a Newfoundland dialect will have all but disappeared?

Sarah Schmidt Observing that tuition fees over nine years have risen on average by 126 percent—far more rapidly than inflation or the minimum wage—Schmidt finds "a growing number of middle-class youths" who are turning to that oldest of professions to make it through their school years. Drawing upon interviews, Schmidt describes students working in all forms of Canada's off-street prostitution trade, which now accounts for 80 percent of the country's sex trade. Consulting a number of sources, including police detectives, escort service managers, sociologists, and other researchers, she ends by asking whether this practice is unavoidable, as some of her subjects claim.

This article originally appeared in 2000 in the *Globe and Mail*. Since Schmidt presented this problem, educational fees have continued to escalate, if not at the same astronomical rate as obtained at the time of writing.

College Girl to Call Girl

1   Stacy is dealing with all the typical end-of-term pressures of university: term-paper angst, exam anxiety, career stress. And by day, she is indeed a typical, perhaps model student, working at her co-op job placement and visiting the library at York University in Toronto to prepare for a career in advertising.

2   But at around eight, most evenings, Stacy heads out to pay the bills.

3   And this 25-year-old, from an upper-middle-class Oakville, Ont., home, doesn't serve up coffee at Starbucks. Though she grew up much like any suburban child of a chartered accountant and a homemaker—bedtime stories, piano lessons, cottage weekends, trips to Disneyland—Stacy now goes out on "calls," as many as six times a night, condoms in hand, to pleasure clients as a prostitute.

4   Most men expect intercourse. A few are satisfied with oral sex. The odd one—either "really drunk or really lonely," she says—just wants to talk. But she doesn't call herself a hooker, and she doesn't wear high heels, fishnet stockings or short skirts. As a student "escort," Stacy dresses like any college girl going out to the movies or a bar. That's the way the men like it.

5   For a growing number of middle-class youths graduating this spring, prostitution isn't seen as a shameful trap, but as a means of making it through the lean student years on the way to a respectable career. Escorts like Stacy are dispatched by agencies to upscale hotel rooms, private homes and even offices. She may turn tricks, but in her own mind she is far away from the streets and alleys and whores desperate for $20 for a fix. She serves mostly professionals, who can afford the house call.

6   "You're looking at a very different kind of situation in the year 2000. Most people don't know what prostitution looks like. People have no clue," says sex-trade researcher John Lowman, a professor of criminology at Simon Fraser University in Vancouver. "What we have is a class-based system of prostitution. Just like you have a hierarchy of food services, you have a hierarchy of sex services."

7   Over the last nine years, tuition fees in Canada have risen on average by 126 per cent, far more rapidly than inflation and the minimum wage. About half of the student population graduates with an average debt load of $25,000, up from $8,000 in 1990.

8   Off-street prostitution has experienced a similar explosion, and many Canadian cities have cashed in by charging annual licensing fees to "massage parlours," "escort agencies" and "encounter counsellors." Researchers estimate that off-street prostitution now comprises approximately 80 percent of Canada's sex trade. And students work in every part of it, from phone sex and stripping up to turning tricks. Ads in weekly newspapers promote "College Cuties," "Adorable Students," "University Girls," and "Hot College Hard Bodies."

9   Fifteen years ago, such ads were unheard of. This year alone, escort ads in the *Montreal Mirror*, for example, have increased by 50 per cent. Since 1995,

they've increased five-fold in Victoria's *Monday Magazine*. Even NBC's new megahit, *The West Wing*, has featured a subplot about a Washington, D.C., law student who doubles as a high-priced call girl.

10   For her part, Stacy stumbled into the business three years ago. She knew someone else who was doing it. She was ineligible for student loans because she had defaulted on a previous one, and her stepfather did not want to pitch in. "There's no way a $7-an-hour job is going to pay my rent and tuition. It's not possible."

11   Escort work is far more lucrative: Stacy scores $170 for a one-hour call, $130 for a half-hour (the agency keeps $80 and $70 in each case). On the other hand, it's also a lot more demanding than steaming up a latte while wearing a funny hat.

12   "I remember the first time, I felt sick," recalls Stacy. And it has not gotten much easier with time. "It's not something I want to be doing. I hate it."

13   "People think, 'Students? Not students!'" says sociologist Cecilia Benoit. "They think of sex workers as marginal women, women who are down and out. It ain't like that."

14   The University of Victoria professor, in partnership with the Prostitution Empowerment and Education Society of Victoria, is undertaking a study on the health conditions of the city's off-street sex-trade workers. Findings so far show that some come from troubled backgrounds, but many don't, and their control over working conditions also varies. The danger of assault or murder is certainly lower than it is for street prostitutes.

15   Stacy's boyfriend knows how she pays her bills. "He doesn't like it, but he doesn't make me feel bad about it." Otherwise, she doesn't discuss it with family or friends.

16   Still, Detective Bert O'Hara of the Sexual Exploitation Squad of the Toronto Police Services observes that off-street sex work has "become more socially acceptable." In the past, it occurred in cheap motels; now, it's in private homes and commercial establishments. When Det. O'Hara and his colleagues take a peek inside, they find a range of participants: housewives earning extra cash, students covering their bills, single moms making grocery money.

17   Police continue to focus on the more visible, and cheaper, blue-collar street prostitution, Lowman says, while "men with money can buy sex with impunity." And at this end of the sex trade, both sides get to pretend they're just having a normal social interaction, at least to a degree.

18   Louis, manager of a Montreal escort service, knows students sell well to a particular class of men. His Baby Boomers' Playground serves up "young female students for your utmost fantasy," according to the ad. It's a perfect match: The clients, middle-aged professionals, prefer to mix sex with intelligent talk, not just idle chatter, Louis says.

19   Harvard grad Bennett Singer came to the same conclusion when he investigated the sex industry to research a novel he co-authored about his alma mater. *The Student Body,* to be released in paperback next month, is based on a real-life prostitution scandal that rocked the prestigious Brown College in 1986. "They

enjoy an intelligent conversation with a young, refined person with an active mind," says Singer, executive editor of *Time Magazine*'s education program.

20   Anna, the daughter of a businesswoman and an academic, was recruited a few years ago to pursue graduate work at one of Canada's leading research institutions, but a financial and personal crisis led her to work as a "high-end call girl." Her clients' educations matched her own.

21   And you can see why they would fall for Anna's quick wit, wholesome face, welcoming eyes and a warm smile. As an escort, she dressed business-casual, "so we could get past the front desk." Her first client, "a virgin who didn't want to be a virgin anymore," made it easier for her to break into the business.

22   "I still felt cold, though," she says, and she never got over that feeling. She just "put on a happy face," even on the night she had seven calls. "I was in total shock. That night was a bit stunning."

23   Still, she says she actually met one man, a broker, whom under different circumstances she would have dated. "My God, you're like a girlfriend," Anna remembers him saying. Unlike most, he "needed a full connection. He was so nice."

24   University of Toronto student and former escort Alicia Maund has heard similar coping strategies from Toronto's sex-trade workers. "They say, 'He's a banker. It's at the King Eddie [a high-class hotel], so it's okay.'"

25   Stacy is a case in point. "To me, there's a difference," she says. "It's not prostitution. I realize in essence everybody's doing the same thing, but I portray myself with a level of respect." That doesn't mean she's all that fond of her regulars, though. "They like to think we have something. I just fake it. I don't want these people to know me. I don't want to be friends with them."

26   Carolyn Bennett shakes her head at Stacy's rationalizations. "Whatever way you look at it, it's prostitution. You still get paid for sex," says the outreach worker for the Halifax-based Stepping Stone Association, a drop-in centre for street prostitutes.

27   John, a general-studies college student and former sex worker in Vancouver, agrees completely. "It's a cop-out," he says. "I don't mind being called a hustler." Before he started hustling, minimum-wage work was "killing my spirit," he says, and his parents, a nurse and labourer, couldn't really help out. He was saddled with a growing student loan when his girlfriend, also a student, introduced him to the idea of escort work.

28   "It really freaked me out initially. It was unimaginable for me. It seemed horrible, but I was totally desperate for money."

29   John has floated in and out of the massage business since 1996. There, the rules were clear: the rub-down always includes a hand job, but nothing else. But he had more flexibility as an independent. On outcalls, "I charged what I could get away with," he says, which sometimes exceeded $150 an hour.

30   Though he was raised with "traditional values" in the suburbs, John, like many young, educated sex workers, is also a bit of an adventurist. "To have

someone project a fantasy onto you, for the purposes of the hour, to see you as the fantasy, that's powerful. I think there's something that draws me in."

31   Nonetheless, at first he didn't tell anyone. "I didn't want to deal with them trying to comfort me, or seeing me differently." Today, most of his friends know, but not his parents. "It would kill my mom. It would kill them both." They're still wrestling with his bisexuality, he says, though he feels like his father should understand. "He's done the worst jobs."

32   John is facing a more immediate decision, though. He's been out of the business for a while, but a friend at the University of British Columbia has a regular client that would like to add John to the equation. "I have to figure that out for myself and my partner. But I could sure use the money."

33   His caution makes sense. For many students, it seems, the real stigma in sex work is tied to how long you do it. Anna only lasted six weeks—her parents intervened when they found out, and gave her "total freedom, total choice and support." She still sounds a bit stunned by the experience. "It was a very healthy choice in a bizarre situation. Had I stayed longer, it would have hurt me," says Anna, now a high-tech professional.

34   Another reason to get out quickly is to minimize the risk of running into former clients in later life. Anna says she would pretend not to recognize them. "People don't deal with the issue well." But she also wishes people would "get over their hang-ups," she says. "It's just a job."

35   Maybe so, but Stacy would rather land that advertising job after graduation and put this kind of work behind her for good. "I don't want to be doing this," she says. "I want to do something for myself. I know I'm an intelligent person."

For Further Thinking

1. Review our section on examples in Chapter 12 of the Rhetoric. Does "College Girl to Call Girl" use this kind of organizational approach effectively? Explain.
2. What is your opinion of Schmidt's implication that the students she spoke with reveal self-delusion, as well as a form of snobbery?
3. What is your opinion of Schmidt's research on this article? Is there any point she could or should have pursued more thoroughly?

Looking Back and Ahead

1. Read "Enough Already, It's Time We Decriminalize Prostitution" (p. 436). How does Patty Kelly's thesis differ from Schmidt's? What are some other points of comparison and contrast between the two essays?
2. For student Valerie Desjardins' rhetorical analysis of Schmidt's essay, see Chapter 17 (p. 191). Before reviewing this response by Desjardins, however, try to summarize Schmidt's essay and shape your own critical thesis in response to it. Your thesis should contain your controlling

idea and your reason(s) for that idea. You may compare your summary to that of Desjardins, Chapter 20, pages 223–24. Desjardins wrote her rhetorical response (in Chapter 17) after working out her summary/process description.

Robert Penner A fellow of the Royal College of Physicians of Canada, Dr. Penner practises gastro-enterology at Kelowna General Hospital and is assistant clinical professor with the University of British Columbia and the University of Alberta.

Elementary Observations: The Special Skill of Sherlock Holmes (Adapted from a longer essay)

1 "You have been in Afghanistan, I perceive," Sherlock Holmes says to Dr. Watson, MD, upon meeting the physician who is to become his junior partner (Doyle 7). Watson thereafter credits Holmes with a power of reasoning unattainable by lesser mortals. These words of greeting, from Arthur Conan Doyle's first Holmes novel, *A Study in Scarlet,* provide a foretaste of many remarkable, yet as Holmes would say, "elementary," observations to follow. Watson, a physician like his creator, might be expected to recognize that reasoning is rarely the step whereby Holmes surpasses those around him. Rather he employs a skill most often associated with physicians: that of looking in the correct direction when all around is distraction.

2 To appreciate the significance of Holmes' first words to Watson, some brief story background is helpful. It is the 1880s. Watson, an army surgeon, has recently returned to London from the British campaign in Afghanistan, weakened from a gunshot wound, the hardships of escape, and a subsequent fever. Pressed for money, he has met up with an acquaintance, Stamford, who suggests meeting with "a fellow who is working at the chemical laboratory up at the hospital" (3), someone interested in shared lodging. Of course, the "fellow" in the chemical lab is Sherlock Holmes, still a complete stranger to Watson. Surrounded by "retorts, test-tubes, and little Bunsen lamps, with their blue flickering flames" (7), Holmes sees Stamford approaching, informs him of an exciting new discovery, then sees Watson and observes, "You have been in Afghanistan . . . "

3 In explaining *how* he knew that Watson had been in Afghanistan, Holmes states the following:

4   [My] train of reasoning ran, "Here is a gentleman of a medical type, but with the air of a military man. Clearly an army doctor, then. He has just come from the tropics, for his face is dark, and that is not the natural tint of his skin, for his wrists are fair. He has undergone hardship and sickness, as his haggard face says clearly. His left arm has been injured. He holds it in a stiff and unnatural manner. Where in the tropics could an English army doctor have seen much hardship and got his arm wounded? Clearly in Afghanistan." (13)

5 Though this particular example may not seem as remarkable as others involving key plot disclosures, it prepares us for Holmes' famous technique of

looking in *unusual* directions (the fair wrists), then drawing confident conclusions. Holmes rarely makes impressive leaps of logic from that which is obvious to all. At the moment of a spectacular revelation, he invariably confides that he has simply been looking in a different direction than have Dr. Watson and the reader. To the disdainful Holmes, all of so-called everyday life is a cheap, transparent card trick able to fool only inferior observers. Ironically, Holmes impresses the physician with a physician's skill of observation that routinely mystifies patients.

6   To better appreciate how this manner of observing is a "physician's skill," one might consider the standard method used to detect endocarditis, an infection of the heart valves. A man suffering from shortness of breath can reason that a physician is applying physical senses towards a diagnosis when the stethoscope is used. The patient does not know exactly for what the doctor is listening, but will draw the conclusion that the sounds of heart and lungs convey information. Imagine the patient's surprise, however, when he goes to the doctor due to shortness of breath and the doctor gives special attention to examining the patient's eyes and fingernails. When the doctor then suspects a diagnosis of endocarditis, the patient might be tempted to suspect magic. It is not unusual, in fact, for patients to credit physicians with supernatural powers of observation. A clean bill of health at an annual physical exam is seen as a promising look into the future. A diagnosis of cancer yields the inevitable question of "How long?" as though the doctor has one's lifeline from birth to death printed out in advance on a mystical chart. What is magic, on the other hand, if not the ability to reach conclusions by observing that which others do not know they can see? To a doctor who knows that an infected heart valve launches microscopic blood clots into the periphery of the body, there detectable through magnification as tiny spots in the eyes and as hemorrhages under the fingernails, no impressive degree of reasoning is required. The doctor simply applies a specialized—or more focused—awareness to direct his eyes.

7   While it is likely no accident that Doyle selected a physician for Holmes' perennially impressed sidekick, given that Doyle himself was a medical doctor, as previously suggested, it does seem ironic, or at the least "interesting," that a physician should be so surprised by Holmes' powers of observation. Is this a weakness—a lack of verisimilitude—or a strength, a way of conveying the extraordinary powers of Holmes? Certainly Doyle intended to endow Holmes with extraordinary powers. The discovery that Holmes announces in *A Study in Scarlet* before greeting Dr. Watson for the first time is, in fact, within or near the border of science fiction. Practising chemistry, Holmes has found an "infallible test for blood stains" (7), a procedure to replace the guaiac test. The guaiac test, disdained and fictitiously replaced by Holmes, is still used in the twenty-first century on stool as a screening test for colon cancer. Unfortunately its results are no more reliable today than they were a century ago. If only Doyle had elaborated further on his character's discovery, Holmes might have had a chance to mystify a much greater number of doctors, at a benefit far surpassing the several crimes he so brilliantly solved.

Work Cited

Doyle, Arthur Conan. *A Study in Scarlet*. First published 1887. New York: The Modern
    Library, 2003. Print.

Michael Lahey and Ari Sarantis In the following essay of critical analysis and evaluation, Michael Lahey and Ari Sarantis respond to the famous poem "Richard Cory" by E. A. Robinson. Robinson published this work in 1897. Paul Simon and Art Garfunkel brought it back to public awareness with their song adaptation in the 1960s.

Edwin Arlington Robinson was born in 1869 in Head Tide, Maine; he is a distant descendant of the famous British writer Anne Bradstreet. He established himself as one of the United States' most important poets, winning the Pulitzer Prize for poetry three times. *Children of the Night* is generally considered Robinson's best-known book of poems. Also well known are the poems in his Arthurian trilogy, *Merlin, Lancelot*, and *Tristram*. Despite his accomplishments, Robinson's success was not easily made. He and his family suffered a series of emotional, physical, and financial misfortunes; it is Robinson's own brushes with tragedy that give him his keen insight and sympathy for many of his poetic characters. Robinson died in 1935.

While reading Robinson's poem, take note of the form, its use of conventional poetic structure, and the way in which its content challenges conventionality (for its time) by addressing subject matter not generally considered worthy of poetry. Then think about what the poem means to you before you read the essay.

Richard Cory

Whenever Richard Cory went down town,
We people on the pavement looked at him:
He was a gentleman from sole to crown,
Clean favored, and imperially slim.

And he was always quietly arrayed,
And he was always human when he talked;
But still he fluttered pulses when he said,
"Good-morning," and he glittered when he walked.

And he was rich—yes, richer than a king—
And admirably schooled in every grace;
In fine, we thought that he was everything
To make us wish that we were in his place.

So on we worked, and waited for the light,
And went without the meat, and cursed the bread;
And Richard Cory, one calm summer night,
Went home and put a bullet through his head.

Words and Bullets: A Rhetorical Analysis of E. A. Robinson's "Richard Cory"

1   Edwin Arlington Robinson's poem "Richard Cory" could be mistaken for an easy text. It seems structurally unremarkable, almost like a small-town conversation, and thematically commonplace: the painful truth of despair underlying the superficial appearance of fulfillment, a presumed completeness. Yet the poem, on closer scrutiny, offers structural and linguistic opportunities for considerable analysis and interpretation. This poem is at once highly accessible and deceptively complex. It uses specific language choices and language patterns to reveal the sad, fantasy relationship between Richard Cory and the townspeople.

2   Although a student usually focuses most of his or her analysis on a poem's (or a song's) content, a rhetorical analysis more closely examines the strategies of the language. A rhetorical analysis explores how meaning can be created so subtly, even slyly, by word choices that it seems to spring wholesale, "naturally," from the page. A rhetorical analysis examines how such meaning derives from or is construed by virtue of the words themselves, either through specific word choice (**diction**), through relationships to other words (**rhythm, alliteration, conceptual sameness, contradiction, rhyme**) or through types of meaning (whether **denotative**—direct—or **connotative**—implied, emotional, political). A poem's rhetorical structure relies partly on the literary devices the poet uses to generate, even complicate, the poem's content. An insightful rhetorical analysis would thereby reveal how the structure and the reader's sense of content are by no means mutually exclusive, but that the structure generates and deepens content. Often, however, it is difficult to isolate one from the other. A poet's calculated repetition of a word, synonym, or even rhythm at certain points in the poem likely has structural and substantive significance. Rhetorical analysis, therefore, can reveal, sometimes unsettlingly, exactly how much of what a reader might consider as the transparent, indisputable content is really the effect of the rhetoric, of language strategies.

3   Robinson's "Richard Cory," composed uniformly of four stanzas of four lines, changes its pacing from stanza to stanza to reflect the speaker's awe of, then investment in, then baffled disappointment with Richard Cory. The first four lines establish a public scene and mood with Richard Cory as a revered communal figure, almost valuable public property. He is "down town," where "we people," apparently the entire community, "looked at him." The poet's language here starkly sets Richard Cory apart from, rather than as part of, the group—on a stage, whether he wants to be or not. As with a stage, the curtain rises on the poem, so to speak, and the rapt audience (both townspeople and reader) watches a person who is treated like a spectacle.

4   With the second stanza, however, the poem starts to flow faster. This sense of slightly urgent movement occurs in part through Robinson's skilful uses of **anaphora** (repetition of a word or words at the beginning of successive clauses

or sentences) and of **epistrophe** (repetition of a word or words at the end of successive clauses or sentences). These language devices, whether noticed by the reader or not, nonetheless create a rhythmic effect that paces the language, quickening it in this second stanza to reflect the town's excitement that someone like Richard Cory would ever be in their midst.

5   This beginning (anaphoric) repetition initiates the second stanza, creating a chanting, hymnal effect. Consider the first two lines: "*And he was always* quietly arrayed, / *And he was always* human when he talked." Then note how seamlessly Robinson follows this chanting effect with three instances of epistrophe, an ending repetition, which appears here as a recurrent phrasing: ". . . was always human *when he talked*; / But still he fluttered pulses *when he said*, / 'Good-morning,' and he glittered *when he walked*." This chanting pattern—repetitive language—suggests the townspeople's accelerated, nearly breathless worship of Richard Cory. Then the poet returns to his established beginning repetition (anaphora) with "*And he was* rich . . . / *And* admirably schooled." This return to the anaphora deliberately coincides with the reader's visual return to the left side of the page upon finishing the second stanza and beginning the third, essentially locking the reader into a language pattern that mirrors the way the town is locked into a pattern of static perception regarding Mr. Cory. These many repeated "ands," appearing in succession in stanza two, three and four, also contribute to the poem's casual, conversational, familiar tone. The "ands" represent the informality of spontaneous conversation, a democratic notion through language of "the people," but here also represent inferiority, not equality, increasing their sense of unbridgeable social distance from this rich, aristocratic citizen, who, unlike the townsfolk, is "admirably schooled in every grace." In fact, this democratic phrasing of "we people" ironically excludes Richard Cory from the community. So E. A. Robinson's subtle language choices—from "we people" and the informal, folky repetition of "and" to Richard Cory's initial presentation as spectacle—quietly perform the deep tensions of inclusion and exclusion that the poem explores.

6   The anaphoric (beginning) repetitions, which give the poem its subtle, chanting hymnal quality, in turn define and articulate that collective, communal "voice" in the poem. This is an instance where a rhetorical analysis—how the poem is specifically built by selected words—now shades into a substantive analysis of what the meaning may be. While only one direct speaker articulates the poem, that person is speaking on behalf of a collective, further developing the point of Cory's exclusion from that collective, the impoverished townspeople: "*We people* on the pavement looked at him"; "[i]n fine, *we thought* that he was everything"; [s]o on *we worked*." This repetitive phrasing further establishes the two oppositional social identities in the poem: the anonymous collective and the glorious Richard Cory. Interestingly, these phrasings seem to empty democracy of its potential for strong personal identity.

7   So, the question arises, why do the people invest so much intense speculation about happiness and personal completeness in this one person? The poem's

speaker even uses distinct emblems of royalty—"crown," "imperial," "glittering"— and then takes this regality one explicit step further: "[a]nd he was rich—yes, richer than a king." In this particular line, Robinson's word choice and especially word patterning actually seem to dramatize a quick verbal exchange *outside* the written poem, a *paratextual* conversational moment. The speaker's slightly but suddenly interrupted utterance, signalled by the poem's only use of dashes and then followed by the insistent word "yes" suggest the speaker suddenly takes a cue from someone else in a group of listeners to be more accurate about the degree of Cory's wealth.

8   Robinson begins the final stanza by bringing the reader out of the collective speaker's communal reverie to harsher facts. The pleasant current of praise for Cory carrying the reader through the almost breezy second and third stanza suddenly fades. As hard times resume their full, immediate emphasis, the statement "[s]o on we worked"—in its succinct phrasing yet ceremonial rhythm—summarizes both the burden of physical toil and its accepted continuity over the course of their lives. This "light" they passively wait for may be a metaphor for hope or change, but, significantly, one only helplessly invoked externally, from beyond them and their own resources. More grimly, the light may be the peaceful compensation of death, a cessation at last of life's struggles. The "light" may even indicate Richard Cory, who comes down town and flutters pulses when he says "Good-morning." As the townspeople go without the "meat," a traditional metaphor for feasting, and curse the "bread," a traditional metaphor for the crude necessities, they articulate unsatisfied lives, wanting what they believe they cannot have, having only what they do not appreciate, but need. Robinson's rhetorical strategy here hinges on a beautiful series of compressions, where three instances of single words—"light," "meat," "bread"—manage to represent poignantly much larger, even universal ideas of social, economic, and emotional longing.

9   As the thought of Richard Cory enters the final stanza in the third line, the serenity of "one calm summer night" seems to represent if not life's potential fullness, then perhaps a fulfilling balance quietly achieved in quiet lives. The reference to the summer night's calmness, a soothing moment of potential hope, also disarms the reader as Richard Cory's suicide suddenly occurs, an outcome all the more unexpected for the poem's previous word choices.

For Further Thinking

1. How does the town presume it knows certain facts about Richard Cory? How does E. A. Robinson's poem examine not just Richard Cory, but also the gap between our knowledge and our presumptions about most people with whom we interact (or think we interact)?
2. How does Robinson use Richard Cory as an unknowable presence? How is the poem an irresolvable mystery?

Looking Back and Ahead

1. "Lemon Pie with Muhammad Ali" (p. 359) could be called creative non-fiction. Is it possible to critique the techniques in that essay the way Lahey and Sarantis have done with this poem?

Jane Jacobs The writings and activism of Jane Jacobs (1916–2006) were highly influential in moving North American cities away from the car-dependent vision of the 1950s and 1960s, and toward the ideal of "walkable cities." Jacobs was instrumental in the cancellation of the proposed Lower Manhattan Expressway in New York City and the Spadina Expressway in Toronto. She received the Order of Canada in 1996 for her influential writings on urban development. Although she was most known for her critiques of urban policy, she also investigated why societies fail. In this excerpt from *Dark Ages Ahead,* she defines the scientific state of mind in order to demonstrate that our society is in danger of failing due to its loss of rigorous scientific method.

The Scientific State of Mind

1   In North America, science is admired almost to the point of worship. It is easy to understand why. Science and its offspring, science-based technology, have lengthened and lightened the human life span. Science has enriched our acquaintance with our planet: revealed its geological history, instructed us in the life the planet supports, cautioned us about its vulnerabilities and the protection we owe it, and clarified the interdependence of its parts.

2   To be sure, science is also mistrusted by those who don't like its discoveries for religious, political, ethical, or even esthetic reasons. Some thoughtful people complain that science has erased enchantment from the world. They have a point. Miracles, magic, and other fascinating impossibilities are no longer much encountered except in movies. But in the light shed by the best science and scientists, everything is fascinating, and the more so the more that is known of its reality. To science, not even the bark of a tree or a drop of pond water is dull or a handful of dirt banal. They all arouse awe and wonder.

3   Science doesn't supply happiness; but neither does its lack. The same can be said of social utopias: they aren't created by science, but neither does lack of science provide them. Science has cast up dangerous and cruel knowledge, which has been exploited for warfare and dictatorial power; but so have cultures so little gifted with scientists that they either make do with imported weapons or rely on clubs, axes, and daggers. Scientific information about our mistakes—for instance, that deforestation invites mud slides and deserts, that overfishing depletes fish stocks—doesn't guarantee we will avoid such mistakes or correct them, but that is owing to failure to heed what science uncovers.

4   Despite all of science's shortcomings as a source of perfection, it still remains that the wealth, well-being, and creative power of our culture, and increasingly of South and East Asia as well, depend heavily on science and technology.

5   What is this valuable thing? It isn't a thing but a state of mind. Its aim is to get at truths about how reality works. However, that aim in itself does not distinguish science from spying, guessing, and using analogies, which also, with less success than science, aim at discovering truths. The scientific pursuit of truth uses no end of tools, ranging from sensitive scales able to register the weight of a hair to observatories of the heavens.

6   Science is distinguished from other pursuits by the precise and limited intellectual means that it employs and the integrity with which it uses its limited means. The standard description of the scientific state of mind outlines four steps or stages, beginning with a fruitful question.

7   Science constantly builds further upon truths it has already bagged. Each further discovery starts anew with its own fruitful question. "Fruitful" means that the question must take into account, as far as possible, everything already known about the object, event, or process under scrutiny and, amid this richness of information, must single out a salient mystery or obscurity. This is harder than it sounds, because salient mysteries are apt to be overlooked or taken for granted. Examples from the past could be: "How does water get up into clouds?" and "How does blood from the feet get up to the heart?" Each of these questions, in its own context, was splendidly fruitful. I have mischievously coupled them here to suggest how misleading analogies can be.

8   After fruitful questions are answered, the answers themselves dispose of false analogies: for instance, what an absurdity to suppose that evaporation does the work of leg veins' valves, or vice versa. Yet as we shall see, slovenly use of analogies is one pitfall of some North American science.

9   Equipped with a fruitful question, the scientist frames a hypothetical answer, accounting as elegantly and economically as possible—"parsimoniously" is the word favored—for the truth that he or she suspects is hiding behind the question. The question, and the hypothetical answer, together constitute two closely linked stages that require insight, imagination, and courage, qualities possessed by all creative scientists, and in high degree by scientific geniuses.

10   In the third stage, the hypothesis is tested, by both its creator and others. Ultimately, the real world tests all hypotheses, and usually quickly. When answers from the real world seem to come slowly, it is seldom the evidence itself that is slow to appear; rather, observers are blind to evidence or emotionally can't bear to credit it. This is why the crashing of the Berlin Wall finally was required as an exclamation point, after unheeded evidence of many decades reported that Marxism was untruthful as an economic theory. An example from medicine is the discovery that peptic ulcers are caused by bacteria, not psychological stress; for years, the evidence assembled by an Australian doctor was ignored by other specialists.

11   Deliberate tests of a hypothesis can often be contrived experimentally. Tests contrived in the laboratory, like those coming in unsought from life, are useless in the absence of observers alert to evidence, or in the presence of observers

who lack respect for evidence. Wishful thinking absolutely does not do. If a hypothesis stands up well to assault by testing, it is eventually accepted as theory or even law, as in "the law of gravity" or "the laws of perspective."

12   In its fourth and final stage, a successful hypothesis opens up questions previously not even known to exist. For instance, a theory that cholera epidemics spread from contaminated drinking water—a startling finding by John Snow, a nineteenth-century London physician who noticed a correspondence between incidence of cases and a district in the city that was served by a specific well—opened up the sequel question, "How does drinking water become contaminated by cholera as an infectious agent?" The answer, "Sewage," opened up still further questions. Copernicus's stupendous theory that the earth revolves around the sun opened up many other questions, such as "What holds the earth to its course?"

13   This fourth stage, the question chain, sustains science as a coherent process, erecting continuous, coherent bodies of knowledge. Thus science itself, rather than the will of scientists or the judgments of patrons and grant givers, directs its own organization, along with providing automatic and continual self-renewal. New questions turning up in the question chain, especially if they are a surprise, return the entire process to its first stage: again, the time is ripe to pose a salient and fruitful question.

For Further Thinking

1. Jacobs proceeds from her definition of the scientific state of mind to a criticism that much of North America today is crippled by the inability of scientists and others to surrender accepted paradigms in order to ask fruitful questions. She states: "The combination of the appearance of professional respect for scientific rigor coupled with professional contempt for scientifically rigorous behaviour is toxic . . . It cripples foreign aid programs, pedagogy, and illegal drug policies, and it promotes dubious and harmful medical treatment fads, nutrition and other lifestyle advice, and agricultural recommendations" (99). Find a current issue that you feel is hampered by bad science or reliance on a false or outdated paradigm, and use Jacobs' definition of the scientific state of mind to show where the science in question falls short.

2. Analyze the expository pattern and techniques of this essay. What strategies does Jacobs use to make a complex subject accessible to a broad audience?

Looking Back and Ahead

1. In "The Environmental Crisis: The Devil Is in the Generalities" (p. 430), Ross McKitrick argues that much public perception, policy, and academic study of environmental issues is hampered by overgeneralization. Read his article and decide whether the problems he identifies are caused by misapplication of the "scientific state of mind."

2. Using "The Scientific State of Mind" as a guide, discuss how public relations trump science in "Put It on Ice?" (p. 428).

Morris Berman A cultural historian and social critic, Morris Berman has taught at a number of universities in the United States and Europe, and from 1982 to 1986 was the Lansdowne Professor of the History of Science at the University of Victoria. He is the author of a number of books on the evolution of human consciousness and on social criticism.

In this excerpt from *Dark Ages America,* published in 2006, Berman argues that despite differences between individuals and between cultural groups, there is an American character that is distinct from that of other countries and that defines the attitudes and behaviour of most Americans.

The American Character

1   The concept of national character is very much out of fashion these days, violating as it does the much more popular notion of multiculturalism. Surely in a land as diverse as ours, containing large percentages of blacks, Hispanics, and Asians, for example, it makes no sense to speak of a central set of traits that characterize "the American people." There are, so the argument goes, many Americas, not just a single (let alone unified) one. And yet, once we get past the tedious rhetoric of political correctness and identity politics, what do we see? Blacks and Hispanics, for all their community and family and (often) religious orientations, essentially want a larger share of the economic pie. That is their "vision" for America, and for themselves in America. A few disaffected white liberals aside, the only people in the United States who view the American Dream as a nightmare are Native Americans, and then only some of them.[4] In fact, any group or individual that rejects the dominant ethos in this country and sees it as a species of illness is going to pay a very high price. Regardless of race, religion, historical background, or country of origin, everybody in the United States is effectively a Protestant capitalist individualist whose life is grounded in the ideology of an expanding market economy. When it comes down to the basics, America is about as diverse as a one-string guitar.

2   The scholar who (to my knowledge) first argued this from a behavioralist and social science perspective was the historian David Potter, in his *People of Plenty* (1954). Despite certain problems with it half a century later, it is impressive to see how well his argument has held up. Wittingly or not, writes Potter, all historians employ the concept of national character because history shapes culture and culture molds the national character. Americans are not an arbitrary conglomerate united by nothing more than geography or location; rather, they possess "distinctive traits and social adaptations which characterize them as a group." One can certainly appeal to things such as the influence of corporations or the presence of a frontier or any other causal factors, in order to argue that this national character is not genetic—some sort of "racial" property, as it were—but

what's the difference? Regardless of the forces that have shaped the American character, the bottom line is that there *is* one: the forces involved generated a modal personality, a dominant psychology, and a mainstream way of behaving. This configuration, asserts Potter, is based on the expectation of material abundance, of inexhaustible plenty—of living in a nation whose streets will (and should) be paved with gold, if they aren't already. The error of the eminent American historian, Frederick Jackson Turner, according to Potter, was to see the frontier strictly in terms of geographical territory, which is far too narrow a framework. Turner ignored the *psychological* frontier, which in America is based on the interaction of technology with the environment. The promised expansion, as a result, is endless. Historically, the promise of abundance and the social mobility attendant on that created a social flux that deprived Americans of the psychic comfort of having a place in an organic social order. This means that the individual has very weak ties to the community (such as it is), and that the American idea of social justice is not to redistribute wealth but just to make more of it (the specious trickle-down theory). Ultimately, as some scholars have argued, this vision of plenty led to the relentless commodification of life, to consumption as literally a mode of perception. And if a few Native Americans and white middle-class "greens" or "reds" view this as a collective pathology, well, the collective definitely does not.[5]

3   Fifty years after the publication of Potter's book, Walter McDougall, who is a Pulitzer Prize–winning historian at the University of Pennsylvania, came to much the same conclusion, expressed in somewhat starker terms. There certainly is an American character, says McDougall in *Freedom Just Around the Corner*; it's called "hustling." We are a nation of people on the make, he argues, and this certainly antedated Enron and Halliburton. To be sure, he says, this hustling has a sunny, upbeat face to it, the Yankee "can do" mentality. But the dark side is no minor aspect, and it was present from Day One: nearly everyone in early America, he suggests, had little interest in what was good for the colony or the nation, and a very great interest in "what's in it for me?" The overall picture is that of a scramble for profit, and the result has been a nation that is not only endlessly competitive, but remarkably violent.[6]

4   The "infancy" of a nation may have some similarities with human infancy, in an individual sense, because in both cases we can recognize the formative power of the early years. The Jesuits were fond of saying, "Give us the child for the first seven years; after that, nothing much matters." Or, as Heraclitus put it nearly 2600 years ago, character is destiny; once the tramlines of personality are laid down, modifications will occur in the course of a person's growth, but there is no avoiding the fact that "the child is father to the man." After a certain point, changes are at most variations on a theme; nothing is going to be terribly different. The same may be true of civilizations. Thus in his discussion of the history of the "counterculture" in American history—which he defines as the attempt to subordinate the material to the ideal, or the spiritual—historian David Shi, in *The Simple Life,*

does a good job of tracing the dominant culture back to the early seventeenth century. In 1616, he notes, Captain John Smith observed that most of the Virginia colonists, religious sentiments notwithstanding, were in the New World for material gain. "I am not so simple to think," wrote Smith, "that ever any other motive than wealth will erect there a commonweal." Of course, this was not quite correct: religion was a very strong current in colonial America, with Quakers, Puritans and other groups playing a significant role. Yet none of this managed to derail the individualistic and commercial ethic of American society, and the two aspects probably went hand in hand. The early Puritan merchants, for example, often wrote "in the name of God and profit" at the top of their ledgers. John Winthrop, the first governor of Massachusetts Bay Colony, kept warning his followers that they would have to be vigilant to ensure that the "good of the public oversway all private interests." But by the time he died, in 1649, it was reported that "men were generally failing in their duty to the community, seeking their own aggrandizement" instead. A communitarian outlook never seemed to really take root in the culture at large. "The pristine vision of the [Massachusetts Bay] colony's founders," writes Shi, "continued to be dashed upon the rock of selfish individualism." This was the pattern set in America's formative years, and it has been repeated again and again down to the present time. Deviations from it— whether we are talking about the Shakers, the Amish, the arts and crafts movement of the late nineteenth century, the progressives, Lewis Mumford, Jimmy Carter, Marxism, Buddhism, whatever—were easily suppressed, co-opted, or brushed aside. Even the Depression did little to alter the basic commercial outlook and individualistic way of life, and ultimately wound up strengthening them. Sokei-an, America's first Zen master (who died in 1945), once wrote that introducing Buddhism to the United States was "like holding a lotus to a rock and hoping it will take root." Like all of the alternatives discussed in Shi's book, Buddhism took root to some tiny extent, but ultimately the rock remained the rock, and has so to this day. The "Coca-donald Society" is ultimately where all of us live.[7]

Notes

4.   For a poignant example of two Native American tribes taking very different paths, see Debbie S. Miller, "Clinging to an Arctic Homeland," in *Arctic National Wildlife Refuge: Seasons of Life and Land,* ed. Subhankar Banerjee (Seattle: Mountaineers Books, 2003), pp. 132–41. The ANWR is the homeland of the Inupiats as well as the Gwich'in Athabascans. For the latter, the coastal plain is sacred ground, the home of the porcupine caribou, which they wish to see left undisturbed. Meanwhile, the corporate world has convinced the Inupiat that if they opt for "development," a storehouse of oil beneath the tundra will bring them jobs and millions of dollars. While the salary of Inupiat maintenance workers is now $41 an hour as a result, that of maintenance workers in the Gwich'in villages—who refused the deal (they formed a steering committee in 1988 to protect their land and way of life from corporate development)—is at most $19 an hour. The Inupiat have entered the world of an oil-rich economy, watching the industrial development of the coastal plain, whereas the Gwich'in own title to 1.8 million acres of tribal lands, call themselves the "caribou people," and continue to make clothing from hides and perform caribou songs and dances. They refer to the coastal plain as "the sacred place where life begins."

5.   David M. Potter, *People of Plenty* (1954; repr., Chicago: Phoenix Books, 1958). See also reviews by Geoffrey Gorer in *American Quarterly* 7, no. 2 (Summer 1955), 182 and 184–86; and Robert M. Collins in *Reviews of American History* 16, no. 2 (June 1988), 321–35.

6.   Walter M. McDougall, *Freedom Just Around the Corner* (New York: HarperCollins, 2004). See also the review by Gordon Wood in the *NYT Book Review,* 28 March 2004, p. 7.

7.   David E. Shi, *The Simple Life* (New York: Oxford University Press, 1985), pp. 4, 8, 12, and 15–17; William Grimes, review of John Steele Gordon, *The Empire of Wealth,* in *IHT,* 14 December 2004, p. 12; and Michael Hotz, ed., *Holding the Lotus to the Rock* (New York: Four Walls Eight Windows, 2003), p. 1. Classic studies of the Puritans include Perry Miller, *The New England Mind: The Seventeenth Century* (New York: Macmillan, 1939); and Edmund Morgan, *Visible Saints: The History of a Puritan Idea* (New York: New York University Press, 1963).

For Further Thinking

1.   Do you agree that there is an "American character"? Describe a person or group of people who, in your opinion, either illustrate or refute Berman's thesis.
2.   Is there a "Canadian character"? If so, what is it, and why does it exist? Does it, as Berman argues in the case of America, supersede multiculturalism and cultural differences?

Looking Back and Ahead

1.   Compare Berman's concept of an American character to John Ralston Saul's idea of Canada as a Métis nation (p. 407). What do the two concepts share? How do they differ?
2.   Compare and contrast Berman's "American character" with Mendelsohn's "new ethnicity" (p. 382). If it is true, as Berman claims, that the American character has not changed in 400 years, how can the Canadian character have changed so quickly, given that both countries have experienced waves of immigration and economic changes?

Karen Armstrong   Historian of monotheistic religions, Armstrong explains how Muslims both moderate and radical have throughout the history of Islam viewed and continue to view suicide attackers with complete disapproval. She claims that violent extremists for Islam are motivated by politics and not by their religion.

Murderous Martyrdom: Religion or Politics?

1   Critics of Islam believe that the cult of murderous martyrdom is endemic in the religion itself. This is not the case. Apart from the brief incident of the so-called assassin movement at the time of the Crusades—for which the Ismaili sect responsible was universally reviled in the Muslim world—it has not been a feature of Islamic history until modern times. The American scholar Robert Pape has made a careful study of suicide attacks between 1980 and 2004, including the al-Qaeda atrocities of September 11, 2001, and concluded:

2   Overwhelmingly suicide-terrorist attacks are not driven by religion as much as they are by a clear strategic objective: to compel modern democracies to withdraw military forces from the territory that the terrorists view as their homeland. From Lebanon to Sri Lanka, to Chechnya to Kashmir, to the West Bank, every major suicide-terrorist campaign—more than 95 percent of all the incidents—has had as its major objective to compel a democratic state to withdraw.[15]

3   Osama Bin Laden, for example, cited the presence of American troops in his native Saudi Arabia and the Israeli occupation of Palestinian land high on his list of complaints against the West.

4   Terrorism undoubtedly threatens our global security, but we need accurate intelligence that takes all the evidence into account. It will not help to utter sweeping and ill-founded condemnations of "Islam." In a recent Gallup poll, only 7 percent of the Muslims interviewed in thirty-five countries believed that the 9/11 attacks were justified. They had no intention of committing such an atrocity themselves, but they believed that Western foreign policy had been largely responsible for these heinous actions. Their reasoning was entirely political: they cited such ongoing problems as Palestine, Kashmir, Chechnya, and Western interference in the internal affairs of Muslim countries. But the majority of Muslims who condemned the attacks all gave religious reasons, quoting, for example, the Qur'anic verse that states that the taking of a single life is equivalent to the destruction of the entire world.[16]

5   Since 9/11, Western politicians have assumed that Muslims hate "our way of life, our democracy, freedom, and success." But when asked what they most admired about the West, the politically radicalized and the moderates both listed Western technology; the Western ethic of hard work, personal responsibility, and the rule of law; as well as Western democracy, respect for human rights, freedom of speech, and gender equality. And, interestingly, a significantly higher percentage of the politically radicalized (50 percent versus 35 percent of moderates) replied that "moving toward greater governmental democracy would foster progress in the Arab/Muslim world."[17] Finally, when asked what they resented most about the West, its "disrespect for Islam" ranked high on the list of both the politically radicalized and the moderates. Most see the West as inherently intolerant: only 12 percent of the radicals and 17 percent of the moderates associated "respecting Islamic values" with Western nations. What could Muslims do to improve relations with the West? Again, among the top responses from both radicals and the moderates was "improve the presentation of Islam to the West, present Islamic values in a positive manner."[18] There are 1.3 billion Muslims in the world today; if the 7 percent (91 million) of the politically radicalized continue to feel politically dominated, occupied, and culturally and religiously disrespected, the West will have little chance of changing their hearts and minds.[19] Blaming Islam is a simple but counterproductive answer; it is far less challenging than examining the political issues and grievances that resonate in so much of the Muslim world.

Notes

15. Interview with Scott McConnell, "The Logic of Suicide Terrorism," *The American Conservative*, 18 July 2005; John L. Esposito and Dalia Mogahed, *Who Speaks for Islam? What a Billion Muslims Really Think* (New York, 2007), p. 77.

16. Qur'an 5:32.

17. Esposito and Mogahed, *Who Speaks for Islam?*, p. 80.

18. Ibid., pp. 86–87.

19. Ibid., p. 97.

Selected Bibliography

Esposito, John L., and Dalia Mogahed. *Who Speaks for Islam? What a Billion Muslims Really Think, Based on the Gallup World Poll.* New York, 2007.

For Further Thinking

1. How does Armstrong support her argument? Does she rely most on logos, pathos, or ethos?
2. Are there religions other than Islam where the actions of certain groups overwhelm public perception of the actual tenets of the faith?

Looking Back and Ahead

1. Does Armstrong's essay change or reinforce your thoughts about Canada's involvement in Afghanistan? Can you use it to support the arguments made by either Fred Stenson (p. 440) or Rex Murphy (p. 438)?
2. Read Martin Luther King, Jr.'s essay "The Ways of Meeting Oppression" (p. 442). Are there similarities between the approach he recommends and that favoured by most Muslims? What are the reasons for the similarities? What are the reasons for the differing tactics favoured by some radicals?

John Ralston Saul   Author of three philosophical works, five novels, and numerous essays on political matters, John Ralston Saul was born in Ottawa and studied at McGill University. He holds a PhD from King's College, London.

In *A Fair Country,* Saul argues that Canada is a "Métis nation." By this he means that Canada has been influenced as much by Aboriginal ideas as by European ones, and that Canada will not reach its potential unless this reality is recognized and embraced.

In this excerpt, Saul demonstrates that the Canadian judicial system, equalization payments, single-tier health care, and public education all have their roots in two great meetings between Aboriginal and European leaders that took place in the eighteenth century. Partly as a result of those meetings, Canadian policy has been shaped by the Aboriginal concept of consensus as "an interrelated place for continuing differences inside the great circle." Saul argues that recent Supreme

Court decisions based on this concept have made it possible for Canadians to "shove back the delusion that our society is merely a provincial descendant of European concepts."

The Roots of Continuous Negotiation: In Praise of the Courts

1   Renée Dupuis, chief commissioner of the Indian Claims Commission and a leading writer on how Canadian law applies to First Nations questions, puts it that the "Aboriginal roots are mixed into the roots of the two European legal systems." She points out that even in formal lawmaking, Aboriginal customary law has been mixed into the legislation, sometimes unconsciously, sometimes consciously. When we look at this approach toward continuous negotiation, which has come to be *the* Canadian characteristic, it is hard to find British, French or U.S. origins. It has become what we call federalism. And when we are not sinking into colonial posturing at the international level, it best describes our foreign policy and military approaches. Over four centuries, these sorts of federal negotiations have been tough and aggressive. They fall apart only when one party takes advantage of its strength to undermine the balance or when one party defines itself as permanently aggrieved, never taking into consideration whether it is actually doing better or doing well, or how *the other* is doing. Both of these positions—the perception of the fixed overdog versus that of the fixed underdog—are profoundly nineteenth-century European. They make this country seem ungovernable because they undermine the idea of equilibrium built into our way of negotiating.

2   At the heart of all our talking is the idea that consensus can be reached if positions are laid out fully and enough time is taken to fairly consider what all can see. You will find this idea of consensus in almost every description of Canadian negotiations going back to the seventeenth century. And you will also find that the opposing view—that of complex situations being forced into clear solutions, which are enforced to the letter by contract—undermines our sense that consensus is possible. During the Mackenzie Pipeline debate thirty years ago, Chief Alexis Arrowmaker of the Dogrib Dene reflected that initially the southerners "had talked to us, but now they only give us pieces of paper. [So] we were forced to have our own paper people." The Aboriginals began to hire good lawyers and to encourage their young to become lawyers. In this way, the Dene were able to out-negotiate the governmental and oil company lawyers. But their concern and a more general concern for the country is that this Europeanization of our approach to negotiation gradually makes the existence of a place such as Canada more problematic. Curiously enough it has been the Supreme Courts, both federal and provincial—institutions traditionally associated here and elsewhere in the world with the pedantically written word—that have consistently ruled in ways that reinforce the ideas of consensus and of the oral.

3   The normal description of Canadian history highlights key moments such as 1763—the Royal Proclamation; 1774—the Quebec Act; 1840—the Lord Durham version of how to unite Upper and Lower Canada; 1848—the Canadian reaction through Responsible Government, democracy and a version of federalism; 1867—Confederation. But the other way to read our civilization is to look for deeper foundations. It could be argued that the key moment in the creation of the idea of Canada was the gathering of thirteen hundred Aboriginal ambassadors from forty nations with the leaders of New France in 1701. The result was the Great Peace of Montreal. It was here that the indigenous Aboriginal ways of dealing with *the other* were consciously and broadly adopted as more appropriate than the European. Here the idea of future treaties was born. Here an approach was developed that would evolve into federalism. Sir William Johnson's great gathering of two thousand chiefs at Niagara in 1764 had been organized in order to cement the Royal Proclamation. In many ways, this was the second act in the creation of the idea of Canada—a continuation of the Great Peace of Montreal.

4   The idea of both was to establish a continuous equilibrium, shared interests and shared welfare. The phrase in the Great Peace was that they would all "Eat from a Common Bowl." Which is to say that relationships were about looking after one another. This is the shared foundation for equalization payments and single-tier health care and public education. What I am describing here is not the technical footnoting of particular policies, but the origins of the mindset that made them possible. I am making an argument about culture, not about mere instrumentalism.

5   This profound current began to re-emerge as a conscious, that is to say intentional, approach in the late quarter of the twentieth century. You can see it happening in three pivotal Supreme Court judgments—*Guerin, Delgamuukw* and *Oakes.*

6   In 1984, in *Guerin,* the Supreme Court reasserted a very old idea—the Honour of the Crown. This has nothing to do with someone wearing a crown. The Crown is not a person, it is a concept. The Crown is legitimacy. With the arrival of responsible government, the Crown could no longer be presented as the legitimate will of any individual, even if ministers were doing the talking. It could no longer be represented as an expression of power, legitimate or not. Instead, it gradually became an expression of legitimate authority built upon an abstract representation of the land, the place, the people and the obligation of those in authority to the land, place and people. So the Honour of the Crown is not simply the obligation to respect formal commitments. It is the responsibility of the civilization to respect its reality. In other words, the underlying idea of the Crown has nothing to do with monarchy, any more than it does with contract and ownership. The Honour of the Crown exists whether or not there is a monarchy and it overrides both contract and ownership. At its core, it is about responsibility.

7   As a court case, *Guerin* was all about a low level bit of misrepresentation by public officials to Aboriginals over some land in the Vancouver area that was to be sold off for a golf course. The civil servants were, if you like, doing things

by the letter of the law. They were taking a pure contractual approach. In its judgment, the Supreme Court reprimanded the Crown for trying to "hide behind the language of its own document" and condemned it for breaching its fiduciary duty. The court held the Crown to standards that rose far above written contract, far beyond the letter or even the language of the law. "The issue was not one of contract, but rather conduct."

8   And just as the Supreme Court made it clear that its judgment was shaped by relationships predating the Royal Proclamation of 1763, so the primacy the court gave to conduct over contract has implications far beyond differences between the Crown and the First Nations. It defines the general responsibility of the state to the country and to the people. The maintenance of the Honour of the Crown is meant to prevent particular politicians of a particular day from using a panic or a fashion to override the broad public good. To put this another way, the Honour of the Crown is our tiller and it is intended to maintain an equilibrium in society.

9   With the *Guerin* decision, the court brought together two of the strategic elements in our society—the roles of consensus and of the oral. Consensus in the U.S. and European tradition is used to mean agreement. If you look at statements by Thomas Jefferson or James Madison or by a wide variety of French leaders, consensus is used as an evocation of loyalty to the nation. The implication is that fractious minorities—whether ethnic groups or those with different opinions—must find ways to fall into line with the majority for the good of the whole. It's a question of loyalty. Consensus is used to describe the healthy functioning of a monolithic society.

10   The Aboriginal idea of consensus is quite different. Being a spatial rather than a linear concept, it has to do with there being an interrelated place for continuing differences inside the great circle. It is, if you like, the Honour of the Crown or the conduct of the Crown that makes this possible. And because the oral is also spatial and not goal-oriented in a linear way, it does not readily narrow relationships and exclude differences. Rather, it gives people the time and the space to work out how to maintain or develop relationships.

11   And so the Maher Arar case, in which a Canadian was sent to prison and tortured in Syria by U.S. authorities with the cooperation of Canadian authorities on the basis of incorrect information that the Canadians had not bothered to verify, was all about the Honour of the Crown. There are still security *experts* in Ottawa whispering off the record about damning information too sensitive to be revealed, but they are not and never were capable of meeting the standards of the shared public good in a democracy.

12   Decades before, Justices Jack Sisson and William Morrow in a series of rulings refused "to place the law in a strait-jacket" in the Arctic. They believed in the Honour of the Crown. In the process, they invented new approaches to justice that are now common in the south. Their judgments withstood appeals or the threat of appeal because they reflected conduct, not contract.

13   The continued existence of homelessness and widespread poverty in Canada is all about selfishness and public laziness hiding behind contract—that is, defining public instrumentalism in such a way that homelessness and poverty are said to be beyond action by the state. This is the single greatest Dishonour to the Crown today—a failure of our civilization.

14   It is a particularly deep failure because it can be seen as such even if contextualized back through our history to those early conversations between the First Nations and the French, when the former were shocked by the acceptance of poverty in European class-based societies.

15   *Delgamuukw* in 1997 was the second judgment. Here, the Supreme Court gave oral evidence an equal weight to the written. There was no philosophical discussion about the broader implications of this decision for Canada, but the justices had in effect swept away the European concepts of progress. Why? Because the idea of *the written* is intimately linked to the idea of societies passing from an oral hunting society to a partly oral agrarian society to a dominantly written urban society. Suddenly Canada was representing itself—through that most written of things, a Supreme Court judgment—as a non-linear society, one that could contain the reality of those three stages, not as stages but as stable elements in a complicated civilization within a great circle. The justices explained that oral evidence could have the same weight as written or even greater. Why? Because it had been endlessly repeated in public and in that way constituted a form of group memory—and therefore was capable both of exactitude and of expressing broader purpose. In saying so, they noted that oral history is not linear, not human centred. It is "tangential to the ultimate purpose of the fact-finding process at trial—the determination of the historical truth"—because it sees history and truth in a very different context. In part the Court said we must be "sensitive to the Aboriginal perspective" and that this could only be accomplished by accepting the oral.

16   But something much more profound was happening here. With *Delgamuukw*, we opened ourselves up to the full import of our history, so much of which was built upon oral agreements and an oral idea of how to organize and run society. Suddenly, the four centuries of intertwined relationships with indigenous philosophy at its core was visible to us, if we wished to see. Suddenly, we had set ourselves up for the possible return of an historic perspective that makes sense of our society. Suddenly, it was possible through the most official of mechanisms to imagine that we could shove back the delusion that our society is merely a provincial descendant of European concepts.

For Further Thinking

1. Saul argues that the belief that "homelessness and poverty are . . . beyond action by the state . . . is the single greatest Dishonour to the Crown today—a failure of our civilization." How has he supported this claim? Has he provided sufficient evidence? Do you agree?

2. How significant is it that the Supreme Court of Canada has chosen to value oral evidence as at least equal to written evidence? What implications can you see in that decision?

Looking Back and Ahead

1. How do the essays "Saskatchewan's Indian People—Five Generations" (p. 379) and "Canada's 'Genocide': Thousands Taken from Their Homes Need Help" (p. 445) support Saul's argument that inequities in Canadian society come about when contract is valued over conduct?
2. Does "Birth of a New Ethnicity" (p. 382) demonstrate that Canada's comfort with multiculturalism is due to the Aboriginal concept of consensus as "an interrelated place for continuing differences inside the great circle"?

Katherine Gibson British-born artist Ted Harrison is a member of the prestigious Royal College of Art and a holder of the Order of Canada, the Order of British Columbia, and four honourary doctorate degrees. His brightly coloured depictions of Yukon life are known internationally. Despite this, his work has yet to be exhibited at the National Gallery of Canada. In fact, no work by a Yukon-based artist has been exhibited as of this writing. This may change, however, as his latest champion in the cause is Laureen Harper, wife of Prime Minister Stephen Harper.

In these excerpts from *Painting Paradise,* a biography of Ted Harrison, Gibson describes the long process Harrison underwent to shed his art school training and adopt the style he says was demanded by the land itself.

Finding His Style

1   The West Hartlepool College of Art's mission to "provide systematic instruction for the Artist and the Teacher of Art" and to "give students training on practical lines in whatever branch of art they may desire to study" did little to motivate Ted. "But we were made to work, I tell you. Our principal, whom we called Old George, made Hitler look like a Sunday school teacher," recalled Ted, who often commiserated with other students over lunches of horsemeat pies. During one lesson, students were instructed to make a drawing of Venus using a plaster cast for a model. To check whether they had placed the navel in the correct position, they were to use a plumb line from nipple to navel. "Old George would come by with a T-square and a thick pencil. After what seemed like hours of drawing, he would take our work to his desk and scratch and scrape and leave a great mess," said Ted. "It was that sort of thing that stifled my creativity. Every artist needs academic training, but it left me all buttoned up. I could never really get past it until I went to the Yukon." But he did have some light moments. In life drawing class, he remembers an aging model who rouged her nipples like miniature stop lights in hopes of attracting the attention of the instructor.

2   If drawing class was a disaster, painting class was just as dismal. "I learned to paint academically—my mountains sort of looked like mountains, a head

sort of like a head. We copied Degas and Cezanne, even using the same size brushes they had used. It was really something to see our results, which were nothing more than poor imitations of those great painters." An oil-on-canvas self-portrait Ted painted during that time was just such an imitation. The painting replicates Cezanne's self-portrait of 1875. In both, we see subjects dressed in sombre-coloured clothing, positioned on the diagonal, eyes averted, with stern, serious expressions. "I was shut in," remembers Ted. "I didn't know how to express anything and just did as I was told." Copying, copying, copying but never disturbing the surface to see what beauty might lie beneath. Honest work, but unemotional. The essence—the spark—in a subject was stamped out in the rendering of subjects made stale by the brush of others. . . .

[*During a break from art college in the spring of 1946, Harrison was conscripted for military duty. As the Second World War had recently ended, much of his military experience was enjoyable, especially for an adventurous young man from a family of humble means. However, his stint in India nearly ended his life.*]

3   [T]here were other thoughts and events he didn't share with his sister or his parents. India's hot, humid environment was more than many English soldiers could bear. His men, used to Britain's temperate climate, sweltered under the persistent heat, often breaking out in skin rashes. Sandstorms struck without notice, shredding unprotected flesh in minutes. After one wild episode, Ted developed a facial rash. The attending doctor passed him off for treatment to the local RAF hospital. "I arrived with a simple skin rash. Any competent doctor might have cured it with medication of some sort, but I was ordered to stay overnight, assigned to a ward with seventeen other men."

4   That evening, the patients ate a dinner of chicken curry and dhal. Within hours, they were groaning with abdominal cramps. Spiking fevers and bloody diarrhea followed. A few days later, the ward was a nightmare of men tormented by amoebic dysentery. Ted became critically ill. Men began to die.

5   Ted's roommate, Roy Wallace, a merry, red-headed Scot they called Jock, learned of Ted's condition and raced by bicycle six miles from the garrison to his friend's bedside. "I must have been very close to the end because I sensed I was passing into another dimension," said Ted. "All worry vanished along with my hellish pain." He recalled feeling sad for his family, knowing they would miss him. Then an infinite peace flooded through him as he felt himself rise toward the ceiling. Looking down, Ted saw his decimated figure on the bed. A nurse stood over him, shaking her head. Then she left to arrange a coffin.

6   As Ted hung suspended between heaven and earth, he heard his friend talking to him in his broad Scottish accent. "Harrison, dunna ya be so idle lying aboot while ya comrades slave away in camp!" Wallace's words drew Ted back. He recovered slowly. By the time he was discharged, ten of the eighteen men on his ward had died. Ted was almost the eleventh. He later learned an infected kitchen worker had spread the disease.

7   Although that illness was a most horrible experience, Ted had found the actual transition between this life and the next, gentle, even pleasant. Through it, he lost his fear of death and gained a perspective on life that guided him from that day forward. "I should have died in India. But somehow I survived. It got me thinking. Why did Fate take the others but let me live? What was I really meant to do with my life? What is the point of life, anyway? I had been given the 'peace which passeth all understanding.' I lost all ambition for greatness, or to be rich, famous, or any of those things. I realized joy is ours when we summon the courage to express who we are meant to be." . . .

[Harrison continued his tour of military duty in Uganda and Kenya, then returned to West Hartlepool to complete his art program. From there he went to teachers' college, and then took a post in Malaysia where he met his equally adventurous Scottish wife, Nicky. Back in England in 1966, Harrison spotted an ad placed in a local newspaper by the government of Alberta that challenged teachers to "teach in the land of the moose" and contained the warning "no weaklings need apply." In short order, the Harrison family was on its way, first to northern Alberta, and then to the Yukon.]

8   Even as the Group of Seven was discovering Ontario's wilderness, and Emily Carr her magical trees, the Canadian art establishment of their day had dismissed Canada's wild regions as places to travel *through*, not as subjects to paint. With time that changed—except in the North—which was regarded as a frozen wasteland in winter and a mosquito-plagued backwater in the summer. But Ted Harrison saw a raw beauty in the land and a resilient exoticism in the people.

9   When he arrived in Canada, he had known nothing of The Group, or of Carr. But he did know the Yukon commanded a form of expression that defied how he had been taught. "My art school experience left me unable to enjoy painting. My head was full of rules and prescriptions as to what I should and shouldn't do. My brush became a hesitant tool and my spirit was choking with all I had learned in school."

10   Carr made peace with her trees by surrendering to their strength, their spirit. In that way, she found her métier and her greatness. Like her, Ted *sensed* the land. But where Carr embraced forests of cedar and fir, Ted fell under the spell of the Yukon's open spaces, Native settlements, grand horizons, and glorious sunsets. He brought all of this inside of himself where lived his boyhood curiosity, a profound sense of humanity, and the vibrancy of India, Kenya, Uganda, and Malaysia.

11   On a clear autumn morning in 1968, Ted gathered up his easel and paints and drove to a spot overlooking Bennett Lake. He planted his sketching stool on the gravel surface and anchored the easel with a stone to steady it against the breeze. Beside it, he placed his satchel of oil paints and a tin pie plate, his makeshift palette. Then he gazed up into the stunning spectacle of Montana

Mountain, its forested sides aflutter in reds, amber, and vivid greens. Marshmallow clouds floated in the sky above. The memory of northeast England's smoggy colliery towns dissipated in the invigorating spectacle of lake, mountains, and sky. "The air was so bracing it would make even a dead man sit up," he quipped.

12   "I fixed my eyes on an area, mixed the medium on the palette, and applied the brush with some vigour to the canvas. Everything seemed to be going well until I became aware of a subtle force emanating from the land itself. There were so many colours! Trees, bushes, rocks, and mountains were conspiring to force me to paint in *their* colours and in *their* particular forms. I was literally trembling with frustration. How do I paint this sky and these mountains? How can I capture the movement, the music of this land? Deep inside of me, I felt a streak of rebellion fanning into flame. I knew then that my method and style were useless in this northern world. I packed up the paint tubes and brushes and drove home." When Ted arrived, he shared his exasperation with Nicky. "I'm going to paint *my* Yukon," he declared. And he would no longer paint *en plein air* but inside the house on the kitchen table.

13   Ted wondered if it was possible to change his painting technique after years of academic training. "By a process of retrogression and simplification I threw out all the academic bric-a-brac which had stratified my thoughts. From there, my personal view of the Yukon began to emerge, leading to greater freedom of line and colour. The whole experience of painting became a wonderland whose doors opened as soon as I picked up the brush."

14   He made other changes, adopting the new, quicker-drying acrylic paints with their clear, fresh tones. Like Alice tumbling into the rabbit hole, Ted let himself fall, relishing the exhilaration of the unknown. "For the first time in my life, I actually felt the thrill of creating a new vision on canvas," he recalled. He experimented with contradictions in style and expression. He stripped away all but the barest suggestion of subject and place. Like a baby learning to walk, he took small steps, testing each one before moving forward. His work now resembled that of a primitive painter, devoid of any art school training whatsoever. "It must be understood that I had been trained as an academic painter in the old tradition, drawing from the casts of ancient Greek sculptures . . . repeating intricate exercises in linear perspective, mathematically precise and accuracy to a fraction of an inch," he said. Ted stayed with his new direction, gradually integrating certain elements of his art school training. . . .

15   Ted's knack of noticing what others may overlook accounts for the appearance of ravens in his work, which he elevates to iconic proportions. Despite the extreme cold, ravens do not migrate. Their ubiquitous shaggy forms pepper the North as they feed on carrion; scavenge for seeds, berries, and insects; and, in their role as consummate recyclers, wreak havoc on garbage dumps and unfastened trash cans. Ted devoted a charming undated essay to glorifying these hardy tenacious creatures, considered in Native mythology to represent the Trickster. His essay reads in part:

16   "At first I did not see the ravens. Oh yes, they were around all right, all through the short winter days. The funny thing was that they were so much a part of everyday life that one took them for granted. You understand, of course, that my eyes *saw* their large black-feathered forms, but I was not then aware what made them such interesting neighbours. That was, of course, until my first New Year's Day in the North.

17   "How cold it was. So cold that the thermometer dipped below minus fifty degrees Fahrenheit. So cold that the smoke from the wood stoves flowed upwards from the cabins in straight columns. So cold that no human was to be seen through the frosted panes of glass. However, there they were—those bulky black ravens—squatting down to allow their feathers to form a warm protective covering for their skinny legs." With those observations, ravens became a Harrison signature element.

For Further Thinking

1. Do you think there is a connection between Harrison's near-death experience and his willingness to break away from his training? Do you know anyone (including yourself) who changed their views after a brush with death or other traumatic experience?

2. As this excerpt relates, Harrison worked so rigorously to jettison the rigidity of his training that his work looks like that of someone with no formal training. As a result, it was many years before he was invited to join the Royal Academy of Art. Do you think this apparent primitivism is why the National Gallery has chosen not to display his work? Is it right for bodies that represent art to do their best to uphold standards? Can standards go too far, and stifle creativity?

3. The last part of this essay deals with Harrison's sudden ability to "see" ravens that had been there the whole time, and his consequent decision to put them in almost all of his paintings. Have you had an experience where you suddenly became aware of something important that had been there all along?

Looking Back and Ahead

1. How does this essay relate to "The Scientific State of Mind" (p. 398)? Is there a similarity between the scientific technique of the "fruitful question" and Harrison's frustrated attempt to impose onto a new landscape the technique he had been taught in England?

2. In "My Father the Hero" (p. 366), Kerry Li discusses with loving humour what her Hong Kong–born father brings to Canadian culture and the nuances he seems oblivious to. What does Ted Harrison, with his experiences in England and other countries, bring to his Canadian-based art? Is it likely that, like Li's father, there are things about Canada that he doesn't see that would be obvious to someone native-born? Might his "outsider's vision" help him to see things a Canadian wouldn't?

Works Cited

Davis, Wade. *The Wayfinders: Why Ancient Wisdom Matters in the Modern World*. Toronto: Anansi, 2009. Print.

Downey, Michael. "Canada's 'Genocide': Thousands Taken from their Homes Need Help." *Maclean's* 26 April 1999. Print.

Mitchell, Alanna. "The Time of Crossing Over." *The New Canada: A Globe and Mail Report on the Next Generation*. Toronto: McLelland & Stewart, 2004. 150–160. Print.

Saul, John Ralston. *A Fair Country: Telling Truths about Canada*. Toronto: Viking, 2008. Print.

Section 3 Problems,
Proposals,
and Opinions

As a post-secondary student, you are vitally engaged in preparing for your future—most obviously, for your career, but surely no less for your role as a person and citizen. Many of us, young and old, would agree that today's younger generation, on the whole, has encountered different challenges and complexities than those who graduated in the 1960s and 1970s. A Southam News feature of February 2001 consulted a panel of philosophers, ethicists, and religious studies professors for their views of the most pressing issues facing humanity in the next 10 years (Todd). The panel identified major concerns related to the environment, computers, genetic engineering, nuclear arms, and nationalism, along with rising social dilemmas—an increasing gap between rich and poor, immoderate work patterns, and a perceived increase in callousness. They all pointed, as well, to colliding values and beliefs: "With globalism and immigration bringing cultures closer together, whose ethical system will we follow?" (Todd).

With the third edition of *Acting on Words* heading to press 10 years after Todd's news feature on future problems was written, the question arises: Do these same major problems spill forward to the next decade? Are new ones entering the mix? If so, what do you think they are?

In the following section, which deals again with the main themes we have visited in Reader Sections 1 and 2, you will find writers using language specifically to outline problems, to weigh choices, to assert their own values, and in some cases to propose solutions. Rhe-torically, the following selections relate to the aims and methods discussed under "Critical Analysis and Evaluation" (Chapter 16) and, to some extent, under "Argumentation" (Chapter 18), so it would be a good idea to review those parts of the Rhetoric. Again, you will not find simple or incontestable answers—but you will, most likely, come to appreciate the importance of analytical and argumentative skills in preparing for a future of complexity and challenge.

In this section of the Reader, the expository purpose of Section 2 has intensified to a greater insistence on arguing an analytical position. In other words, the argumentative edge of Section 3 is somewhat more pronounced. This will be evidenced in part by a return to considerable use of the first person, as a number of the writers have chosen to identify their views directly with their individual thinking, shaped in part by personal experience. Whether you follow a similar style as you respond to these views in your own writing or adopt the more formal academic approaches illustrated in Chapters 16 and 18 and other parts of the Rhetoric and Research Guide will depend on the nature of your assignment. In any case, we believe you will find much in the following section to raise important critical questions for your consideration.

Work Cited

Todd, Douglas. "Our Top 10 Moral Issues." *Edmonton Journal* 11 Feb. 2001: E5. Print.

Susan Aglukark Susan Aglukark is an Inuk singer/songwriter. She describes her songwriting as mostly inspired by her culture and her people. It addresses many of the issues facing Canada's Aboriginal Peoples. In 2005, she was named an Officer of the Order of Canada for her contributions to Canadian culture, both musically and as a workshop facilitator and mentor in the Aboriginal community. She is currently Distinguished Scholar in Residence in the Native Studies Faculty at the University of Alberta.

The Fear of the Unknown

1   Ever feel like you are on the outside looking in? Like life is going on all around you and you are standing still, not moving along with the rest? I felt that way when I first left home. I knew I had to leave home (for personal reasons) but I was not prepared for what was to come. I was not prepared for how fast life was happening in the "big city." I'm not referring to the life I now have as a celebrity, just life in general and life as a first time city dweller. It was all so frightening.

2   So I asked myself, why am I (are we) so frightened, or intimidated by it all? And is it this fear that keeps me (us, Inuit) from "belonging" to it (idea that is Canada). What prevents us from feeling like true citizens of Canada? No matter where we come from or where we live or what our history is or has been, we should feel like we belong, but we don't. I believe the biggest obstacle is the fear of the unknown.

3   This is what I had to ask myself back in 1998, what am I afraid of and why am I afraid? What is keeping me from engaging?

4   I needed to answer these two questions before I could fully engage in my life. I needed to understand what I was dealing with and on that journey to better understanding I came to the realization that all these troubles are:

a. not exclusive to Inuit (youth)

b. not insurmountable

c. and in most cases, part of a natural process

5   Upon identifying the key factor in my inability to engage one of the first things I did was to read. I read everything from fiction novels to self help books to books on Inuit culture. I ate up whatever I could to better understand this fear and to get over it.

6   Through all of this reading, one of the key things I've come to appreciate is that fear is not a bad thing, it is a healthy thing, it can be used to our advantage. Fear is a trigger for instinct and we need our instincts intact in order to function in this day and age.

7   I believe that once we develop a healthy understanding of our fear in terms of engaging in the mainstream, we will not feel so intimidated by its prospect. We will reach a place where we know with absolute certainty that we belong to all of it and once we reach this point the next thing that will happen is that we will want to contribute, to engage. I.e., our wants and desires will become clearer, we will want to set goals, secondary education, etc.

8   . . . but it all begins with overcoming/understanding the fear, all aspects of fear.

For Further Thinking

1. If you are not from a northern territory, do you picture northerners when you think of Canadians? How can Canadians of the south help Canadians of the north overcome Aglukark's experience of feeling excluded?

Looking Back and Ahead

1. How does "Lemon Pie with Muhammad Ali" (p. 359) function as an example of the process Aglukark describes?
2. Ted Harrison, the Yukon artist whose artistic journey is described in "Finding His Style" (p. 411), says that one reason no work of his hangs in the National Gallery of Canada is that the Yukon is entirely ignored, both by the gallery and by the establishment in general. Do you agree that Canada as a whole tends to overlook its citizens of the North, leaving them feeling on the outside?

Robertson Davies Novelist, playwright, raconteur, and essayist Robertson Davies (1913–95) grew up in Thamesville, Ontario, the son of a journalist. He was educated at Upper Canada College, Queen's University, and Oxford. After a spell as a professional actor, he edited *Saturday Night* magazine in Toronto and then the Peterborough *Examiner*. In 1961 he was appointed Master at Massey College, University of Toronto, where he remained until retirement. He died at the age of 82 on December 12, 1995.

In 1971, the *Penguin Companion to English Literature*, edited in England, pronounced that Davies' "urbanity and elegance are unique in [English] Canadian fiction." But the qualities Canadian readers appreciate in his work are also those of his journalistic background—a sharp eye for the detail and spirit of small-town Ontario. His best-known work remains *Fifth Business,* a finely crafted and graceful novel. Raised a Protestant, Davies nevertheless had an abiding interest in the more mysterious side of religious experience and in explorers of the psyche like the Swiss psychotherapist Carl Jung (1875–1961).

The Pleasures of Love

1 Let us understand one another at once: I have been asked to discuss the pleasures of love, not its epiphanies, its ecstasies, its disillusionments, its duties, its burdens or its martyrdom—and therefore the sexual aspect of it will get scant attention here. So if you have begun this piece in hope of fanning the flames of your lubricity, be warned in time.

2   Nor is it my intention to be psychological. I am heartily sick of most of the psychologizing about love that has been going on for the past six hundred years. Everybody wants to say something clever, or profound, about it, and almost everybody has done so. Only look under "Love" in any book of quotations to see how various the opinions are.

3   Alas, most of this comment is wide of the mark; love, like music and paint-ing, resists analysis in words. It may be described, and some poets and novelists have described it movingly and well; but it does not yield to the theorist. Love is the personal experience of lovers. It must be felt directly.

4   My own opinion is that it is felt most completely in marriage, or some com-parable attachment of long duration. Love takes time. What are called "love affairs" may afford a wide, and in retrospect, illuminating variety of emotions; not only fierce satisfactions and swooning delights, but the horrors of jealousy and the desperation of parting attend them; the hangover from one of these emo-tional riots may be long and dreadful.

5   But rarely have the pleasures of love an opportunity to manifest themselves in such riots of passion. Love affairs are for emotional sprinters; the pleasures of love are for the emotional marathoners.

6   Clearly, then, the pleasures of love are not for the very young. Romeo and Juliet are the accepted pattern of youthful passion. Our hearts go out to their furious abandonment; we are moved to pity by their early death. We do not, unless we are of a saturnine disposition, give a thought to what might have hap-pened if they had been spared for fifty or sixty years together.

7   Would Juliet have become a worldly nonentity, like her mother? Or would she, egged on by that intolerable old bawd, her Nurse, have planted a thicket of horns on the brow of her Romeo?

8   And he—well, so much would have depended on whether Mercutio had lived; quarrelsome, dashing and detrimental, Mercutio was a man destined to out-live his wit and spend his old age as the Club Bore. No, no; all that Verona crowd were much better off to die young and beautiful.

9   Passion, so splendid in the young, wants watching as the years wear on. Othello had it, and in middle life he married a young and beautiful girl. What happened? He believed the first scoundrel who hinted that she was unfaithful, and never once took the elementary step of asking her a direct question about the matter.

10   Passion is a noble thing; I have no use for a man or woman who lacks it; but if we seek the pleasures of love, passion should be occasional, and common sense continual.

11   Let us get away from Shakespeare. He is the wrong guide in the exploration we have begun. If we talk of the pleasures of love, the best marriage he affords is that of Macbeth and his Lady. Theirs is not the prettiest, nor the highest-hearted, nor the wittiest match in Shakespeare, but unquestionably they knew the pleasures of love.

12   "My dearest partner of greatness," writes the Thane of Cawdor to his spouse. That is the clue to their relationship. That explains why Macbeth's noblest and most desolate speech follows the news that his Queen is dead.

13   But who wants to live a modern equivalent of the life of the Macbeths—continuous scheming to reach the Executive Suite enlivened, one presumes, by

an occasional Burns Nicht dinner-party, with the ghosts of discredited vice-presidents as uninvited guests.

14   The pleasures of love are certainly not for the very young, who find a bittersweet pleasure in trying to reconcile two flowering egotisms, nor yet for those who find satisfaction in "affairs." Not that I say a word against young love, or the questings of uncommitted middle-age; but these notions of love correspond to brandy, and we are concerned with something much more like wine.

15   The pleasures of love are for those who are hopelessly addicted to another living creature. The reasons for such addiction are so many that I suspect they are never the same in any two cases.

16   It includes passion but does not survive by passion; it has its whiffs of the agreeable vertigo of young love, but it is stable more often than dizzy; it is a growing, changing thing, and it is tactful enough to give the addicted parties occasional rests from strong and exhausting feeling of any kind.

17   "Perfect love sometimes does not come until the first grandchild," says a Welsh proverb. Better [by] far if perfect love does not come at all, but hovers just out of reach. Happy are those who never experience the all-dressed-up-and-no-place-to-go sensation of perfection in love.

18   What do we seek in love? From my own observation among a group of friends and acquaintances that includes a high proportion of happy marriages, most people are seeking a completion of themselves. Each party to the match has several qualities the other cherishes; the marriage as a whole is decidedly more than the sum of its parts.

19   Nor are these cherished qualities simply the obvious ones; the reclusive man who marries the gregarious woman, the timid woman who marries the courageous man, the idealist who marries the realist—we can all see these unions: the marriages in which tenderness meets loyalty, where generosity sweetens moroseness, where a sense of beauty eases some aridity of the spirit, are not so easy for outsiders to recognize; the parties themselves may not be fully aware of such elements in a good match.

20   Often, in choosing a mate, people are unconsciously wise and apprehend what they need to make them greater than they are.

21   Of course the original disposition of the partners to the marriage points the direction it will take. When Robert Browning married Elizabeth Barrett, the odds were strongly on the side of optimism, in spite of superficial difficulties; when Macbeth and his Lady stepped to the altar, surely some second-sighted Highlander must have shuddered.

22   If the parties to a marriage have chosen one another unconsciously, knowing only that they will be happier united than apart, they had better set to work as soon as possible to discover why they have married, and to nourish the feeling which has drawn them together.

23   I am constantly astonished by the people, otherwise intelligent, who think that anything so complex and delicate as a marriage can be left to take care of itself.

One sees them fussing about all sorts of lesser concerns, apparently unaware that side by side with them—often in the same bed—a human creature is perishing from lack of affection, of emotional malnutrition.

24   Such people are living in sin far more truly than the loving but unwedded couples whose unions they sometimes scorn. What pleasures are there in these neglected marriages? What pleasure can there be in ramshackle, jerrybuilt, uncultivated love?

25   A great part of all the pleasure of love begins, continues and sometimes ends with conversation. A real, enduring love-affair, in marriage and out of it, is an extremely exclusive club of which the entire membership is two co-equal Perpetual Presidents.

26   In French drama there used to be a character, usually a man, who was the intimate friend of husband and wife, capable of resolving quarrels and keeping the union in repair. I do not believe in such a creature anywhere except behind the footlights. Lovers who need a third party to discuss matters with are in a bad way.

27   Of course there are marriages that are kept in some sort of rickety shape by a psychiatrist—occasionally by two psychiatrists. But I question if pleasure of the sort I am writing about can exist in such circumstances. The club has become too big.

28   I do not insist on a union of chatter-boxes, but as you can see I do not believe that still waters run deep; too often I have found that still waters are foul and have mud bottoms. People who love each other should talk to each other; they should confide their real thoughts, their honest emotions, their deepest wishes. How else are they to keep their union in repair?

29   How else, indeed, are they to discover that they are growing older and enjoying it, which is a very great discovery indeed? How else are they to discover that their union is stronger and richer, not simply because they have shared experience (couples who are professionally at odds, like a Prime Minister and a Leader of the Opposition, also share experience, but they are not lovers) but because they are waxing in spirit?

30   During the last war a cruel epigram was current that Ottawa was full of brilliant men, and the women they had married when they were very young. If the brilliant men had talked more to those women, and the women had replied, the joint impression they made in middle-age might not have been so dismal. It is often asserted that sexual compatibility is the foundation of a good marriage, but this pleasure is doomed to wane, whereas a daily affectionate awareness and a ready tongue last as long as life itself.

31   It always surprises me, when Prayer Book revision is discussed, that something is not put into the marriage service along these lines—"for the mutual society, help, comfort and unrestricted conversation that one ought to have of the other, both in prosperity and adversity."

32   Am I then advocating marriages founded on talk? I can hear the puritans, who mistrust conversation as they mistrust all subtle pleasures, tutting their disapproving tuts.

33   Do I assert that the pleasures of love are no more than the pleasures of conversation? Not at all: I am saying that where the talk is good and copious, love is less likely to wither, or to get out of repair, or to be outgrown, than among the uncommunicative.

34   For, after all, even lovers live alone much more than we are ready to admit. To keep in constant, sensitive rapport with those we love most, we must open our hearts and our minds. Do this, and the rarest, most delicate pleasures of love will reveal themselves.

35   Finally, it promotes longevity. Nobody quits a club where the conversation is fascinating, revealing, amusing, various and unexpected until the last possible minute. Love may be snubbed to death: talked to death, never!

For Further Thinking

1. What do you think of the statement that love cannot be analyzed, that it "is the personal experience of lovers. It must be felt directly"?
2. "Love takes time"—is this true? With age, are people prepared to settle for less in love or, conversely, do they expect more?
3. Davies introduces a striking metaphoric comparison to emphasize his thesis. What is that comparison?
4. What is Davies's major recommendation for achieving the pleasure of love?
5. How would you define the style of this essay? What are its features?

Looking Back and Ahead

1. Contrast the style and rhetorical methods of this essay to those of "Enough Already, It's Time We Decriminalize Prostitution," by Patty Kelly (p. 436). Consider both purpose and the period of publication; while Davies' essay was published in 1961, Kelly's article appeared in 2008.
2. Compare the style and rhetorical methods of this essay, published in 1961, with "The Ways of Meeting Oppression" (p. 442), which was published in 1958.
3. Compare the way this essay challenges accepted notions of love to the way "Confessions of the World's Worst Parent" (p. 425) challenges accepted notions of parenting.

Jerri Cook Jerri Cook is a staff writer for *Countryside Magazine,* an American magazine that "reflects and supports the simple life, and calls its practitioners homesteaders." In this essay, she uses Lenore Skenazy's book *Free Range Kids: Giving Our Children the Freedom We Had Without Going Nuts with Worry* to reflect on how she raised her son, and how she wishes she had raised him.

Confessions of the World's Worst Parent

1   "Just run away, Josh! She can't catch you!" With that, the nine-year-old whom I was roundly chastising for drop-kicking my watermelons bolted, disappearing into the corn field. My son, then 10, stood on the other side of the field, his head barely visible above the canopy, prodding his friend to hurry. When Josh reached the other side, the two of them, along with Duke the black Lab, took off towards the creek. They didn't come back to get fed and scolded until dusk. They were scolded first. And, they had to pick up the demolished melons before they got fed. I know. I should be locked up. At the very least publicly whipped.

2   Yes, I let my 10-year-old son and his friend run to the creek and stay there all afternoon. What's more, they were barefoot the whole time. When I asked them what they had been up to, they relayed how they climbed the trees that lined the creek and then jumped in. When they got tired of that, they threw rocks at some beavers (big gasp here) and squirrels. They skipped rocks across the creek, and talked to a couple of "old guys" fishing on the opposite bank. They spit on stones to see who could let it fly further.

3   All was well. Until Josh told a classmate about throwing rocks at some beavers, and a teacher overheard. The school called his mom and me. They were concerned that the children were 1) being made to work too hard in the garden and 2) that they weren't being properly supervised. Josh's mom and I were both dumbfounded. We had let the pair roam our farms and countryside around us since they were in second grade. And how is drop-kicking watermelons forced child-labor?

4   We learned, quickly, that allowing kids to be on their own, even if we thought they were quite capable and quite safe, was a definite no-no. Good parents never let their kids out of their sight. Why didn't I get in the car and go get them? What if something happened?

5   I spent the next two decades being a "good" mom. From that point on, my kids could count on mom being constantly at their side. It was hell for all of us. But, I didn't want to be the "bad" parent—you know, one of those parents who lets their kids ride their bikes around the block alone, or lets them walk to the park with their friends, or worse yet—one of those parents who lets their nine-year-old go trick-or-treating with friends, after dark. What horrible parents. What if something happened?

6   Without a doubt, one of the worst parents in the world is Lenore Skenazy. She let her nine-year-old son ride the New York subway alone. Lenore reasoned that since her son had lived in the area all his life, had ridden the subway hundreds of times, knew the route, and was responsible, he could handle the trip alone. So she let him. But what if something happened?

7   Well, something did happen, but not to her kid. He made it home just fine and two years later, continues to ride the subway alone. But she was nearly devoured by the media and other parents. Lenore, a well-known New York

writer, wrote about her son's solo adventure on the subway in a column for the *New York Sun.* The night the column appeared, Skenazy received calls from MSNBC, Fox News, CNN and a myriad of local TV and radio stations. All wanted her to come on their shows and talk about why she would do such a thing. She admits being slightly taken aback by all the immediate attention; she hadn't expected it. She also didn't expect the attacks on her character launched at her by talking heads on the morning news shows.

8   Skenazy was criticized by every child safety "expert" you've ever heard of, and a few no one had any idea existed. The decision was final. Lenore Skenazy was either hopelessly naive or profoundly flippant about her child's safety. Either way, to a person, the experts agreed that what she did was out-and-out neglect, probably criminal. Someone should investigate.

9   Someone did investigate. Lenore Skenazy wanted to understand the reaction she received from the media and public. Why was everyone so worried that something would happen? She went looking for answers and found them. In her book *Free-Range Kids: Giving Our Children the Freedom We Had Without Going Nuts with Worry*, she points out the horrifying truth: the chances that "something" will happen are extraordinarily slim. The perception that "something" could happen, according to Skenazy, is out of proportion with reality. If you believe her, we've been duped by crafty marketers. Lenore Skenazy found out just how profitable fear is. Fear sells. Better yet, fear sells safety equipment for children, anti-depressants for parents, and all those books by child safety experts.

10   Skenazy talked with Dr. F. Sessions Cole, chief medical officer at the St. Louis Children's Hospital. Dr. Cole told her that today's media contributes greatly to the culture of fear because "[. . .] the public assumes that any risk to any individual is a 100 percent risk to them." When we hear about a child being snatched from a park, it's our nature to assume that there is a huge risk that our child will be snatched at any moment. Not only is the fear irrational, according to the statisticians Skenazy interviewed, it's based solely on perception. The actual chances of a child being abducted and killed by a stranger in the United States is .0007 percent, so infinitesimally small argues Skenazy that it is impossible to fully guard against it. "Just like it's almost impossible to guard against the possibility of being hit by an asteroid." Yes, teach your children the basics of personal safety, but don't terrify them or yourself. (And don't make them wear a hard hat just in case of the asteroid thing.)

11   She also addresses the issue of parent peer pressure. According to Lenore Skenazy, "Hell hath no fury like a self-righteous parent." As bad as she was vilified in the press, it was the reaction of parents who tried to shame her into admitting she was wrong that caused her the most stress. It was here that I think she showed the most character, writing "Blamers thrive on shame. Take away their power. Do not be ashamed of making parenting choices based on who your kid is, rather than on what the neighbors will say. Why are they talking about you anyway?"

12   Skenazy has single handedly slain the fear mongers who want all children supervised at all times. These helicopter parents are wasting their time, responding to threats that don't exist. For instance, how many cases have there been of children being injured or killed by tainted Halloween candy? Take a wild guess. Ready? None. Ever.

13   After interviewing dozens of seasoned law enforcement officers and crime experts across the country, Lenore Skenazy discovered the truth: there has never been a case of a child injured or killed from eating their hard-earned trick-or-treat bounty. Once, a child got into a relative's stash of heroin and died. The relatives, in an attempt to save their sorry selves, sprinkled some of the drug on the dead child's candy. It was the morning after Halloween. An urban legend was born. Today, trick-or-treating is seen as running the gauntlet in a crack-infested ghetto with needled-up sleaze balls just waiting to stuff wads of hardcore drugs into little Johnny's trick-or-treat bag.

14   *Free-Range Kids* is a humorous look at a serious problem: helicopter parents who micro-manage their kid's childhood. It's an easy read, and even though my kids are grown, I wouldn't give my copy away for anything. I will, however, buy a copy for my son and daughter-in-law. I want my grandson to climb a tree and splash in the creek without constant safety warnings from his parents. My only criticism is that this book was written 20 years too late.

15   If you're a free-range kid who grew up to be a free-range parent, this book will lift your spirits and wipe away all the condemnation heaped on you by helicopter parents. If you are one of those helicopter parents, this book will make you laugh at yourself and help you to discover that the world is only as scary as we make it out to be. *Free-Range Kids: Giving Our Children the Freedom We Had Without Going Nuts with Worry* is available on Lenore Skenazy's website www.freerangekids.com.

For Further Thinking

1. This essay is a critical response to Lenore Skenazy's book *Free-Range Kids: Giving Our Children the Freedom We Had Without Going Nuts with Worry*. Use Chapter 16 as a guide to determine how successful it is as a critical response.
2. Were you a "free-range kid" or did you have "helicopter parents"? What is your own parenting style, or what would it be if you had children?
3. Although this article focuses on children, it raises the question, how much security is too much? Can the debate in this essay be seen as an analogy for the greater debate about democracy and individual freedom over national security?

Looking Back and Ahead

1. Can you use evidence from "The American Character" (p. 401) to account for either or both of the extreme views of childrearing expressed in this article?

2. Is Skenazy correct that parents' fear is based on bad science, or is her own research an example of bad science? Read "The Scientific State of Mind" (p. 398) and compare Skenazy's investigative methods to the process outlined in that essay.

James Hoggan   James Hoggan is president of the public relations firm Hoggan and Associates, as well as chair of the David Suzuki Foundation and the Canadian chapter of Al Gore's Climate Project.

This excerpt is taken from Hoggan's book *Climate Cover-up: The Crusade to Deny Global Warming.* Earlier in the book, he describes how, in the United States in 1991, the Western Fuels Association joined with the National Coal Association and the Edison Electric Institute to form an organization called I.C.E. with stated goals to "reposition global warming as theory (not fact)" and "supply alternative facts to support the suggestion that global warming will be good." In this essay, he describes in more detail the process used by the Western Fuels Association to form the organization and to reach their goals. Throughout the book, he uses the term "Astroturf" to refer to false grassroots organizations that in fact have been formed by corporations or professional associations.

Put It on Ice?

1   Many corporations, trade associations, and politicians employ pollsters and analysts to run focus groups and test words, phrases, and key messages. Until you do so, it is sometimes very difficult to know whether your target audience is hearing and understanding what you *think* you are saying. But there is a presumption that what you are saying is either objectively true or fairly represents a legitimate opinion.

2   That presumption may have been too optimistic when the Western Fuels Association was working the ICE file, a process that also involved a significant front-end investment in testing words and messages. As Naomi Oreskes writes in a chapter titled "My Facts Are Better than Your Facts: Spreading Good News about Global Warming," the Western Fuels Association even tested the name of their new Astroturf group. They thought ICE was a good acronym, but couldn't decide whether to call their organization the "Information Council for the Environment," "Informed Citizens for the Environment," "Intelligent Concern for the Environment," or "Informed Choices for the Environment," Oreskes writes. "The focus groups indicated that American citizens trusted scientists more than politicians or political activists—and industry spokesmen least—so Western Fuels settled on *Information Council for the Environment,* because it positioned ICE as a 'technical' source rather than an industry group."[3]

3   As I mentioned in Chapter 4, some of the Western Fuels Association's messages were aimed primarily at making the notion of climate change sound silly ("Some say the Earth is warming. Some also said the Earth was flat."), but they also tested others that were "fact" specific. For example, they tried out, "If the Earth is getting warmer, why is Minneapolis getting colder?" and they tested, "If the Earth is getting warmer, why is the frost line moving south?"

4   Again, the first test for these messages should have been whether they were true. Minneapolis was *not* getting colder. The frost line was *not* moving south. And all but the scientists whom the Western Fuels Association was paying to say otherwise seem to have agreed, even then, that the Earth was getting warmer and that people were to blame. But the Western Fuels Association was not testing for facts. It was testing the tolerance and responsiveness of its target audience. It was also clear in its agenda, which it summed up in three points:

1. to demonstrate that a "consumer-based awareness program can positively change the opinions of a selected population regarding the validity of global warming";
2. to "begin to develop a message and strategy for shaping public opinion on a national scale"; and
3. to "lay the groundwork for a unified national electric industry voice on global warming."

5   The target audience in question was nested in four cities: Chattanooga, Tennessee; Champaign, Illinois; Flagstaff, Arizona; and Fargo, North Dakota. These were chosen because they got most of their electricity from coal, they each were home to a member of the U.S. House of Representatives Energy and Commerce or Ways and Means Committees, and they had low media costs, which meant that it was going to be cheap to test the national campaign.

6   These were all wonderful details. They show a real degree of thoughtfulness, even professionalism, on the part of the people who designed the program. As with the Luntz analysis, you can see the intelligence, even tactical brilliance, that went into the campaign. What you cannot see is any evidence that anyone, at any time, asked whether what they were doing was right—whether, for example, the messages they were testing could have been incorrect and ultimately harmful.

7   Luntz, in the previously quoted radio conversation with the National Public Radio's Terry Gross, continued throughout the interview to defend his use of language—even to suggest that what he was doing was a good and necessary thing. He said, "Corporations, trade associations, and politicians have a responsibility to communicate in a way that makes it most likely that the public will support where they stand."

8   Really? Don't corporations, trade associations, and politicians have a responsibility to communicate in a way that is fair, honest, and in the public interest? Do we assume that because it proved effective in the Western Fuels Association focus group testing, presenting incorrect information to the public about the actual details of climate change is a *responsible* option?

Note

3. Naomi Oreskes, "My Facts Are Better than Your Facts: Spreading Good News about Global Warming," in *How Do Facts Travel?* (Cambridge University Press, Fall 2009).

For Further Thinking

1. Do you agree with Hoggan that organizations running consumer focus groups have a responsibility to let participants know if the statements they are presented with are true, or do you agree with the organizations that if all they are testing is reaction to a slogan, it doesn't matter whether the participants know if it is true or not?
2. Have you ever participated in a consumer focus group, or done an online or telephone consumer survey? Did you assume the information you were given was true, or did you assume the organization was test-marketing an idea? Did anyone explain this to you? Do you think they should have?

Looking Back and Ahead

1. How does the information in this essay affect your reading of "The Environmental Crisis: The Devil Is in the Generalities" (p. 430) or vice versa? Are some of the problems Hoggan describes caused by thinking in generalities rather than specifics?
2. How does this essay relate to "The Scientific State of Mind" by Jane Jacobs (p. 398)? Is the climate change discussion being shaped more by science or by public relations and politics?

Ross McKitrick is a professor of economics at the University of Guelph; his specializations are environmental economics and policy analysis. He is a senior fellow of the Fraser Institute, the co-author of *Taken by Storm: The Troubled Science, Policy and Politics of Global Warming* (2003), and author of *Economic Analysis of Environmental Policy* (2010).

The Environmental Crisis: The Devil Is in the Generalities

1 I've started encouraging my students not to use the word "environment." Taken literally, it includes everything between your skin and outer space, and as such it covers too much to be meaningful. I can understand being "pro-environment," since this amounts to being in favour of the world's existence. The difficulty is trying to picture someone being against it.

2　But these days when people say they are "pro-environment" they typically have something more specific in mind. With so much anxiety on the subject, and so many public policy decisions influenced by that anxiety, it is important to try to clarify those specifics. In this respect, common usage of the term "environment" seems to me to create two problems.

3　First, using the general word "environment," instead of more specific terms, tends to detach any ensuing discussion from the prospect of measurement with real data. We can measure specific types of pollution, biological conditions, resource scarcity, etc. But there is no way to measure the "environment" as a whole.

4　At a minimum, we ought to distinguish between air, water and land-related issues. But even within these categories the sub-distinctions are large and important. Consider air pollution, for example. If we start with the question of whether air quality in your region is getting better or worse, we soon run into the complexity that it is not one thing, but many different things. There are hundreds of air pollutants addressed by contemporary regulation. Some are gases, some are particles, some are aerosols. Some are emitted, some are formed by chemical reactions involving ambient levels of precursor compounds. Some are toxic, some are not. Some are more prevalent in cities, some in rural areas. Some are affected by meteorological conditions, some are not. All these distinctions matter when trying to characterize the issue.

5   Each year, my students' first assignment is to get long term air pollution data from Environment Canada for the city (or, if available, the neighborhood) in which they grew up, and write a report on how air quality, as represented by the major contaminant species, has changed since they were born. Most are surprised to see how much it has improved (and if I had asked them to go back to 1970s data they would have seen even larger improvements). In the mid-1960s, sulphur dioxide levels in downtown Toronto averaged over 100 parts per billion. Today they average less than five parts per billion. The effective disappearance of sulphur from urban air is a common pattern in Canadian data. But not all contaminants have gone down. Compared to the early 1980s, ground-level ozone has risen, though the number and intensity of summertime peaks has tended to diminish in some places.

6   If we ask whether air pollution has gotten worse, the answer is "it depends." Many air pollutants have been reduced. If we focus on ozone and ask how it should be reduced further, the distinction between emitted and precursor-based pollutants comes into play. Ground-level ozone is not emitted, it is the result of complex chemical reactions between nitrogen oxides and volatile organic compounds, each of which comes from both human and natural sources. Depending on meteorological conditions and the current concentrations of these precursor gases, a decrease in, say, nitrogen dioxide, might lower the ambient ozone level, but it might also raise it. Or it might lower it locally but cause it to increase in a downwind region.

7   I saw a vivid example of the disconnect between perception and measurement last year, when I heard a well-known Canadian newspaper columnist give a keynote address to a conference of economists. He expressed his hope that the federal government would soon move to regulate air pollution. He grew up in rural Ontario, he said, in a place where there never used to be smog warnings. But in recent years, air quality in Ontario had become intolerable. There have been smog warnings even in his home town, he said, and there was even one in winter a few years ago. He was dismayed that governments had allowed air pollution to be unregulated for so long, and he called on the federal government to take action.

8   I introduced myself to him after his talk. I explained that he did not recall any so-called "smog warnings" (actually Air Quality Advisories) from his youth because the system did not exist back then, but smog certainly did. The Air Quality Index was only introduced in 1992, and in late 2002 the formula was revised so that it is

triggered under broader conditions. That is why we recently had our "first ever" winter smog warning. But actually air pollution levels have gone down across Ontario, even in Toronto. If the current smog warning system had existed in the 1960s, there would have been alerts all year round; they would seem remarkably infrequent today, by comparison. I also explained that air pollution has been subject to provincial regulation for decades, and is not under federal jurisdiction.

9   He was taken aback by all this, and said he would like to write a column about it. Later I emailed some information sources to him, but by then he had moved to a new assignment and wasn't able to write further on this issue. What struck me at the time was that this was a well-educated national journalist, whose job requires him to be informed about major policy issues, who was giving a prepared speech on a topic of obvious personal concern to him, before a conference of professionals, and yet when he stood up to speak, what he had to say was completely wrong on points that are easy, with minimal effort, to look up.

10   That is, in a nutshell, my first concern about the word "environment." Academics tell their students to "look it up." But this requires a habit of thinking about specifics. You can't "look up" the state of the environment. You can look up specific aspects of it: air pollution, water pollution, forest cover, land use patterns, resource stocks, species populations, and so forth. But if the conversation treats the environment as a single, abstract whole, we lose the ability to guide our thinking with the tools of measurement, experimentation, modeling and hypothesis testing.

11   My second concern about the E-word follows from the first. In the absence of specific measurement, or even agreement on what we ought to be measuring, the discussion too readily seems to get framed in the language of crisis. I grew up hearing about the environmental crisis. Twenty years ago I decided to specialize in environmental economics after hearing more and more about the environmental crisis. But in the intervening years I have found that the perception of crisis is often inversely proportional to the specificity of the discussion. . . .

12   One year an environmental science student challenged me over the data I was showing. He was convinced that I was cherry-picking. So I invited him to go to the library and find all the data he could, and I promised to show anything he wanted to the class. He arrived in my office the next day convinced that he had found data refuting the general pattern that wealthy countries were cleaner. When he showed me the graph, I pointed out that the axis measured water *quality*, not pollution, and the implication was the opposite of what he thought.

13   At this point he slumped in the chair with a mystified look. He said that on his first day of class four years earlier, the professor had told them: "The environment is in worse shape now than it was ten minutes ago, and ten minutes from now it will be even worse. It is up to you to stop this." Since then he had been filled with a great sense of purpose and excitement but somehow he hadn't actually looked at much data. Now that he was, for the first time, seeing measurements of the things he had been talking about for years, the picture was not what he expected it to be.

For Further Thinking

1. Have you ever had an experience like the one McKitrick's student had, where you discovered flaws in a fundamental personal belief? What changes did you have to make? Was the outcome good, bad, or both?

2. Environmentalists argue that the reason pollution has improved in North America since the 1960s is simply that wealthy countries have exported their polluting industries and by-products to the Third World, resulting in a cleaner North America, but a more polluted planet. In the article "Effects of Consumerism" (http://www.globalissues.org/article/238/effects-of-consumerism#ExportingPollutionandWastefromRichCountriestoPoorCountries), Anif Shah uses as evidence an internal memo leaked to *The Economist* written in 1991 by Larry Summers, then Chief Economist for the World Bank, which reads:

   > Just between you and me, shouldn't the World Bank be encouraging more migration of dirty industries to the LDCs [less-developed countries]? . . . The economic logic behind dumping a load of toxic waste in the lowest wage country is impeccable, and we should face up to that . . . Under-populated countries in Africa are vastly under-polluted; their air quality is probably vastly inefficiently low compared to Los Angeles or Mexico City . . . The concern over an agent that causes a one in a million change in the odds of prostate cancer is obviously going to be much higher in a country where people survive to get prostate cancer than in a country where under-five mortality is 200 per thousand.

   What is the relationship between pollution levels and economic levels? What political and economic forces come into play, and what are the implications for overall planetary health?

Looking Back and Ahead

1. In Jane Jacobs's book *Dark Ages Ahead*, she proceeds from her definition of "The Scientific State of Mind" (Reader, p. 398) to a criticism that much North American policy today is crippled by the inability of scientists and others to surrender accepted paradigms in order to ask fruitful questions. McKitrick implies that the perception of an environmental crisis is due to the inability of the parties involved, including scientists, to surrender an accepted paradigm that there is an environmental crisis. Do you agree? Are we at risk of implementing wrong policies because we haven't asked the right questions?

James Hansen In 1988, NASA planetary climatology researcher Dr. James Hansen was one of the first scientists to publicly announce that human activity was causing a rise in the level of carbon dioxide in the earth's atmosphere, which in turn was introducing a period of long-term warming.

Since then, Hansen has appeared before several senate hearings and committees as he continued his study of the earth's changing atmosphere. By 2009, he had become frustrated by what he sees as the failure of governments and corporations to respond in any meaningful way to the findings of scientists, so he wrote his first book for a popular audience, *Storms of My Grandchildren: The Truth about the Coming Climate Catastrophe and Our Last Chance to Save Humanity*. In it, he attempts to explain climate science in layperson's terms, since he has come to believe that the best hope for change is through the actions of individuals. In this excerpt, he presents a possible solution to the climate problem followed by a call to action.

A Solution to the Climate Problem

1   Today we are faced with the need to achieve rapid reductions in global fossil fuel emissions and to nearly phase out fossil fuel emissions by the middle of the century. Most governments are saying that they recognize these imperatives. And they say that they will meet these objectives with a Kyoto-like approach. Ladies and gentlemen, your governments are lying through their teeth. You may wish to use softer language, but the truth is that they know that their planned approach will not come anywhere near achieving the intended global objectives. Moreover, they are now taking actions that, if we do not stop them, will lock in guaranteed failure to achieve the targets that they have nominally accepted.

2   How can we say that about our governments? How can we be so sure? We just have to open our eyes. First, they are allowing construction of new coal-fired power plants. Second, they are allowing construction of coal-to-liquids plants that will produce oil from coal. Third, they are allowing development of unconventional fossil fuels such as tar sands. Fourth, they are leasing public lands and remote areas for oil and gas exploration to search for the last drop of hydrocarbons. Fifth, they are allowing companies to lease land for hydraulic fracturing, an environmentally destructive mining technique to extract every last bit of gas by injecting large amounts of water deep underground to shatter rocks and release trapped gas. Sixth, they are allowing highly destructive mountaintop-removal and long-wall coal mining, both of which cause extensive environmental damage for the sake of getting as much coal as possible. In long-wall mining, a giant machine chews out a coal seam underground—subsequent effects include groundwater pollution and subsidence of the terrain, which can damage surface structures. And on and on. . . .

3   The problem is that our governments, under the heavy thumb of special interests, are not pursuing policies that would restrict our fossil fuel use to conventional oil and gas and move the world rapidly toward a post-fossil-fuel economy. Quite the contrary, they are pursuing policies to get every last drop of fossil fuel, including coal, by whatever means necessary, regardless of environmental damage. With the policies governments are pursuing, fossil fuel emissions will be . . . possibly larger than emissions today. . . .

4   The backbone of a solution to the climate problem is a flat carbon emissions price applied across all fossil fuels at the source. This carbon price (fee, tax) must rise continually, at a rate that is economically sound. The funds must be distributed back to the citizens (not to special interests)—otherwise the tax rate will never be high enough to lead to a clean energy future. If your government comes back and tells you that it is going to have a "goal" or "target" for carbon emission reductions, even a "mandatory" one, you know that it is lying to you, and that it doesn't give a damn about your children or grandchildren. For the moment, let's assume that our governments will see the light.

5   Once the necessity of a backbone flat carbon price across all fossil fuel sources is recognized, the required elements for a framework agreement become clear. The principal requirement will be to define how this tax rate will vary between nations. Recalcitrance of any nations to agree to the carbon price can be handled via import duties, which are permissible under existing international agreements. The framework must also define how proceeds of carbon duties will be used to assure fairness, encourage practices that improve women's rights and education, and help control population. A procedure should be defined for a regular adjustment of funds' distribution for fairness and to reward best performance. . . .

6   The picture has become clear. Our planet, with its remarkable array of life, is in imminent danger of crashing. Yet our politicians are not dashing forward. They hesitate; they hang back.

7   Therefore it is up to you. You will need to be a protector of your children and grandchildren on this matter. I am sorry to say that your job will be difficult— special interests have been able to subvert our democratic system. But we should not give up on the democratic system—quite the contrary. We must fight for the principle of equal justice.

8   One suggestion I have for now: Support Bill McKibben and his organization 350.org. It has the most effective and responsible leadership in the public struggle for climate justice. McKibben has done a remarkable job of helping young people get organized.

9   But as in other struggles for justice against powerful forces, it may be necessary to take to the streets to draw attention to injustice. There are places where action has begun to have some effect. The government in the United Kingdom, for example, may be turning against coal plants that do not capture carbon emission—strong activism there is surely playing a role. There have been some locally effective actions in the United States as well. But overall, results are small in comparison to what is needed. The international community seems to be headed down a path toward inadequate agreements at best. Civil resistance may be our best hope.

10   It is crucial for all of us, especially young people, to get involved. . . . This will be the most urgent fight of our lives.

11   It is our last chance.

For Further Thinking

1. Do you agree with Hansen that a carbon tax is the solution to climate change? What are the strengths and weaknesses of this approach?

2. Hansen says, "We should not give up on the democratic system." However, has democracy caused some of the roadblocks to action on climate change?

Looking Back and Ahead

1. Which model (or models) of argumentation does Hansen use? (Models of argumentation are described in Chapter 18.)
2. How does Hansen narrow his topic to avoid being guilty of dealing in generalities, as described by Ross McKitrick in "The Environmental Crisis: The Devil Is in the Generalities" (p. 430)? Is Hansen specific enough?

Patty Kelly In 2008, a scandal broke out when it was revealed that New York Senator Eliot Spitzer, who had campaigned on an "ethics and integrity" platform and who in his career as a lawyer had prosecuted several prostitution rings, had spent more than $80,000 over a period of several years on high-priced prostitutes. Spitzer was forced to resign or face impeachment. When she wrote this essay, Patty Kelly was an assistant professor of anthropology at Washington State University who had just completed a study of the place of commercial sex in the modern world. This essay is Kelly's response to the scandal.

Enough Already, It's Time We Decriminalize Prostitution

1 Eliot Spitzer paid a woman for sex. And got caught. Depending on whose statistics you choose to believe, more than one in every 10 American adult males have paid for sex at some point.

2 What's more, in 2005 about 84,000 people were arrested on prostitution-related offences.

3 In other words, it's not terribly uncommon. It's a part of our culture, and it's not going away any time soon.

4 Perhaps Spitzer's resignation will help convince Americans that it is finally time to decriminalize prostitution across the country.

5 Recently, I spent a year working at a legal, state-regulated brothel in Mexico, a nation in which commercial sex is common, visible and, in one-third of the states, legal. I was not working as a prostitute but as an anthropologist, to study and analyze the place of commercial sex in the modern world.

6 I spent my days and nights in close contact with the women who sold sexual services, with their clients and with government bureaucrats who ran the brothel.

7 Here's what I learned: Most of the workers made some rational choice to be there, sometimes after a divorce, a breakup or an economic crisis, acute or chronic. Of the 140 women who worked at the Galactic Zone, as the brothel was called, only five had a pimp (and in each of those cases, they insisted the man was their boyfriend).

8 The women made their own hours, set their own rates and decided for themselves what sex acts they would perform.

9 Some were happy with the job. (As Gabriela once told me: "You should have seen me before I started working here. I was so depressed.")

10   Others would have preferred to be doing other work, although the employment available to these women in Mexico (servants, factory workers) pays far less for longer hours.

11   At the Galactic Zone, good-looking clients were appreciated and sometimes resulted in boyfriends; the cheap, miserly and miserable ones were avoided, if possible.

12   To be sure, the brothel had its dangers: Sexually transmitted diseases and violence were occasionally a part of the picture. But overall, it was safer than the streets, in part because of police protection and condom distribution by government authorities.

13   Legalizing and regulating prostitution has its own problems—it stigmatizes sex workers (mostly by requiring them to register with the authorities), subjects them to mandatory medical testing that is not always effective and gives clients and workers a false sense of security (with respect to sexual health and otherwise).

14   But criminalization is worse.

15   Sweden's 1998 criminalization of commercial sex—a measure titled "The Protection of Women"—appears not to protect them at all.

16   A 2004 report by the Swedish Ministry of Justice and the police found that after it went into effect, prostitution, of course, continued.

17   Meanwhile, prices for sexual services dropped, clients were fewer but more often violent, more wanted to pay for sex and not use a condom—and sex workers had less time to assess the mental state of their clients because of the fear of getting caught.

18   New Zealand's 2003 Prostitution Reform Act is perhaps the most progressive response to the complex issue of prostitution. The act not only decriminalizes the practice but seeks to "safeguard the human rights of sex workers and protects them from exploitation, promotes the welfare and occupational health and safety of sex workers, is conducive to public health, (and) prohibits the use in prostitution of persons under 18 years of age."

19   Furthermore, clients, sex workers and brothel owners bear equal responsibility for minimizing the risks of STD transmission. In 2005, a client was convicted of violating the act by slipping his condom off during sex.

20   And this brings me to the clients. I have met hundreds of men who have paid for sex. Some seek any kind of sex; others want certain kinds of sex; a few look for comfort and conversation.

21   Saying that all sex workers are victims and all clients are demons is the easy way out. Perhaps it's time to face this like adults (or at least like Mexico)—with a little less moralizing and a good deal more honesty.

22   As for Spitzer, if he had walked into the Galactic Zone, my questions would have been these: Was he respectful? Was he safe? Did he pay well? If the answer to all three was yes, then, well, I voted for him once, and I would vote for him again.

For Further Thinking

1. Does Kelly present compelling arguments for decriminalizing prostitution in North America, or does the fact that her research was done in one of the poorest parts of Mexico make her points invalid?
2. Do you agree with Kelly that North American societies maintain a hypocritical attitude to prostitution? What are some examples of inconsistent laws and attitudes?

Looking Back and Ahead

1. "College Girl to Call Girl" (p. 388) describes university students who work as prostitutes to pay their educational expenses. In a world where middle-class students earn money this way, is it time to re-examine Canada's prostitution laws? How would legalization of prostitution make the situation better or worse?

Rex Murphy   Many Canadians feel frustrated that the government has failed to clearly define why Canadian troops are in Afghanistan. In this essay, first published in the *Globe and Mail* on 23 May 2006, veteran journalist Rex Murphy outlines what he sees as the most compelling reasons.

What We Are Fighting For

1   After last week's Commons vote, I wonder how many people are much clearer in their understanding of our mission in Afghanistan. We have made commitments to Afghanistan. We were part of the operation that rid that country of the Taliban government and pursued al-Qaeda after 9/11. We did that, not only as an ally of the United States after the attack on the Twin Towers and the Pentagon, but also because there were Canadians killed in those attacks. Canada agreed that eliminating a government that had sheltered and nursed the terrorist organization that committed the atrocity of 9/11 was both right and in our own self-interest, that not pursuing the Taliban and al-Qaeda would only leave Afghanistan as a potential site of similar designs in the future.

2   That mission had UN approval, was composed of a concert of forces, of which our country's was one. But protection against future terrorism meant more than just displacing the Taliban government. It meant offering, insofar as an international force could offer, the citizens of Afghanistan the opportunity to build a new kind of government, one elected, one less hospitable to hijacking by sinister forces and more open to the basic civil liberties that people in the democracies take for granted. It was to assist in that effort that Canadian troops remained.

3   It is not possible merely to wish benevolent government on a nation whose history, both recent and of old, has been a field of war, invasion and lawlessness. So, our troops remained deployed to (a) guarantee a measure of security

while Afghanistan citizens went about the first steps to democracy and the extension of basic rights, (b) assist in building the essential elements—schools, a justice system, infrastructure, roads—that any society must have, and (c) offer humanitarian assistance where possible.

4   Four years after the Taliban were deposed, even after Afghanistan made the first steps to building a democracy, that country is still under threat from forces, both Taliban and others, who do not wish to see that result and who are on a campaign to demoralize Afghans, destabilize their government, intimidate their citizens and drive from Afghanistan all those who are assisting its democratic growth.

5   Those forces must be fought. The first principle of establishing a representative government in Afghanistan is to fight those who would deny it: the Taliban, remnants of al-Qaeda and the so-called insurgents. There is no other way that the secondary parts of the mission, the more benign or peacekeeping operations, can be performed.

6   So, we are at war. We are at war because we acknowledge our own interest in Afghanistan and because, as Canadians, we see the value of extending, if we can, some measure of liberty and democracy to a people who have not tasted those virtues. The campaign in Afghanistan can be seen as harmonious with the liberation efforts that Canadian forces, to their honour, were associated with in the far more enormous campaigns of the First and Second World Wars. That, as I see it, is the rationale of our mission in Afghanistan. To the extent that a majority of Canadians accept these goals and fully appreciate and understand them, the mission will have the kind of support outside Parliament that is necessary to maintain it.

7   Achieving that appreciation and understanding will take far more, however, than the very mixed effort in Parliament last week.

For Further Thinking

1. On 30 March 2010, CBC radio broadcast an interview with Colonel Sergey Goncharov, a veteran of the former Soviet Union's Alpha Unit during the Soviet war in Afghanistan in the 1980s. He said that Western forces, including Canadian troops, were making many of the same mistakes that Soviet forces did and wouldn't be able to avoid a similar disastrous fate unless they rethought their approach. You can access the interview at www.cbc.ca/thecurrent/2010/03/march-30-2010.html

    Do you agree or disagree with the colonel? How does his analysis compare to those by Fred Stenson ("The Good War," p. 440) and Rex Murphy?

2. If Afghanistan is likely to become a morass, as predicted by Stenson and Goncharov, was Canada's decision to pull out by a specific date a good one, or, given Murphy's argument, is it necessary to keep troops in Afghanistan until the job is done?

Looking Back and Ahead

1. Read Chapter 18. What persuasive techniques does Murphy use? Are they convincing? Why or why not? What are the weaknesses and strengths of his argument?

Fred Stenson Fred Stenson writes a regular column for *Alberta Views* magazine. In this article from April 2007, he compares the wars in Iraq and Afghanistan to the Second World War and the Boer War, which he researched for his novel *The Great Karoo,* short-listed for the Governor General's Award.

The Good War: A Propaganda Perennial

1   I have been thinking about war. Actually, I have been obsessing about war for two years, while I try to write a war novel. Whether it's the Anglo-Boer War of 1900 or the Iraqi and Afghan conflicts of today, the subject of war always seems to boil down to one question: why are humans so determined to do battle?

2   In Canada, we quit hanging individual criminals in 1962 (and removed capital punishment from the Criminal Code in 1976) because studies showed it was not a deterrent. Whatever reason people kill people, or don't kill them, being hanged, gassed or grilled is not central to the decision. Also, we did not want to be the kind of nation that officially kills its citizens, however loathsome those citizens might be.

3   If you apply the same reasoning to war, our nation's desire to partake in wars should have stopped as well. If history proves one thing, it is that war does not prevent war. If Canadians did not want to be people who kill criminals as national policy, how can we be any more at ease about killing international criminals (insurgents, terrorists)—to say nothing of the innocent bystanders who inevitably get "collaterally damaged" to death?

4   One reason modern Canadians are able to do this cerebral double Axel is, I contend, the fact of World War II. Was there ever a cause so just or an enemy so evil? Like most Canadians, I am grateful to every person who gave their life or youth to fight Hitler's Nazis. When, by accident, I was in Ottawa for the opening of the National War Museum, I stood along the parade route and watched our nation's living veterans pass (marching, riding tanks, sitting in buses) for two hours. Afterwards, I needed salt pills and wringing out.

5   At the same time, I wish there was a way of banning the mention of World War II from political rhetoric. This is because of the countless times I have listened to some weak weasel of a politician pitch his war-of-the-week by comparing it to the war on Hitler. When Bonsai Bush wanted to declare war on Iraq, move number one was to compare Saddam Hussein to Adolf Hitler. Any political leader in the West who was reluctant to join in the war on Iraq was a Neville Chamberlain, looking for a Sudetenland to sacrifice and a führer to appease. This sort of thing should not work but it does. Because our feelings about the war

that stopped Hitler are so strong and positive, a comparison to it, no matter how spurious, can make any damn fool's political ratings go up.

6   The special status of World War II can be proven by the exercise of momentarily subtracting that war from history. If World War II disappears, it is suddenly much more difficult to compare one war to another in a rousing fashion. To illustrate, I'm going to write a sentence and leave some blanks. I want you to fill those blanks with reference to any other war than World War II. Here goes.

7   "Just as we did in (YEAR) to defeat (ENEMY NATION) and rid the world of (EVIL IDEOLOGY), we should arm ourselves today and bring the power of our collective might and will to bear against (TAKE YOUR PICK)."

8   I tried the following:

1965–1975: North Vietnam: communism.
1950–1953: North Korea: communism.
1914–1918: Germany: my imperialism is better than your imperialism.
1899–1902: Boer Republics; Dutch stubbornness.

9   I don't think you could get anyone today to risk young lives or spend billions for any of those causes. But say you want to beat up some jerk just like we did the Nazis in 1945, and all hands are on deck.

10   If it were not for World War II, we would probably be comparing the war in Iraq to the Boer War. An imperial power makes war on a distant nation, allegedly to bring democracy to that nation. The anti-democratic enemy just happens to have resources that the attacking nation wants (gold and diamonds in the Boer Republics; oil in Iraq).

11   There are also aspects of the Boer War in Canada's conflict against the Taliban in Afghanistan. Just as Canada got involved in Afghanistan to show support for the US after 9/11, Canada got involved in the Boer War to show support for Britain after it was trashed several times in one week by the Boers. In both wars, we started with very little emotional involvement, but became more and more emotionally aroused as our soldiers came home dead and missing limbs. To say anything against the war became an insult to the dead and an insult to the men still fighting—even though, at the start of those wars, a lot of Canadians could not have won a quiz show by pointing to the enemy nation on a map.

12   For the record, the Boer War led to World War I, a much bigger, bloodier and longer conflict.

For Further Thinking

1. Stenson implies that politicians draw a false analogy between the Second World War and the current wars in Afghanistan and Iraq to get Canadians to approve of them. Do you agree with Stenson that this is a false analogy, or is he ignoring important similarities between the older and present wars? Are there any problems or fallacies in his own argument?

2. Stenson begins the essay by drawing an analogy between capital punishment and war.
   a. Do you believe this is a good analogy? If so, discuss some parallels between war and capital punishment that demonstrate this.
   b. Do you believe it is a false analogy? If so, discuss some differences between war and capital punishment that prove it is inaccurate.

Looking Back and Ahead

1. While Fred Stenson believes the war in Afghanistan is not a "good war," Rex Murphy believes it is. Murphy closes his essay by citing the analogy to the Second World War that Stenson refutes. How has each writer supported his argument? Which is more convincing? Why?

Martin Luther King, Jr. In 1954, Dr. Martin Luther King, Jr., was pastor of the Dexter Avenue Baptist Church in Montgomery, Alabama, when he became leader of the Montgomery Bus Boycott; thousands of black citizens refused to travel on the city's buses for 382 days until the Supreme Court of the United States declared unconstitutional the city's requirement that black riders sit only at the backs of buses. From then until 1968, King led numerous peaceful protests for the civil rights of African Americans. He delivered more than 2,500 speeches and wrote five books, as well as numerous articles. He based the ideals of the civil rights movement on those of Christianity and the techniques on those used by Mahatma Gandhi in India's successful passive resistance to British rule. He was arrested twenty times and assaulted four times, and his home was bombed once. He also became a world figure, and at age 35, he was awarded the Nobel Peace Prize. On 4 April 1968, he was assassinated. The following is an excerpt from a speech in which he recounts the story of the Montgomery Bus Boycott and details the principles on which it was based.

The Ways of Meeting Oppression

1 Oppressed people deal with their oppression in three characteristic ways. One way is acquiescence: the oppressed resign themselves to their doom. They tacitly adjust themselves to oppression and thereby become conditioned to it. In every movement toward freedom some of the oppressed prefer to remain oppressed. Almost 2800 years ago Moses set out to lead the children of Israel from the slavery of Egypt to the freedom of the Promised Land. He soon discovered that slaves do not always welcome their deliverers. They become accustomed to being slaves. They would rather bear those ills they have, as Shakespeare pointed out, than flee to others that they know not of. They prefer the "fleshpots of Egypt" to the ordeals of emancipation.

2 There is such a thing as the freedom of exhaustion. Some people are so worn down by the yoke of oppression that they give up. A few years ago in the slum areas of Atlanta, a Negro guitarist used to sing almost daily: "Been down so long that down don't bother me." This is the type of negative freedom and resignation that often engulfs the life of the oppressed.

3   But this is not the way out. To accept passively an unjust system is to cooperate with that system; thereby the oppressed become as evil as the oppressor. Non-cooperation with evil is as much a moral obligation as is cooperation with good. The oppressed must never allow the conscience of the oppressor to slumber. Religion reminds every man that he is his brother's keeper. To accept injustice or segregation passively is to say to the oppressor that his actions are morally right. It is a way of allowing his conscience to fall asleep. At this moment the oppressed fails to be his brother's keeper. So acquiescence—while often the easier way—is not the moral way. It is the way of the coward. The Negro cannot win the respect of his oppressor by acquiescing; he merely increases the oppressor's arrogance and contempt. Acquiescence is interpreted as proof of the Negro's inferiority. The Negro cannot win the respect of the white people of the South or the peoples of the world if he is willing to sell the future of his children for his personal and immediate comfort and safety.

4   A second way that oppressed people sometimes deal with oppression is to resort to physical violence and corroding hatred. Violence often brings about momentary results. Nations have frequently won their independence in battle. But in spite of temporary victories, violence never brings permanent peace. It solves no social problem; it merely creates new and more complicated ones.

5   Violence as a way of achieving racial justice is both impractical and immoral. It is impractical because it is a descending spiral ending in destruction for all. The old law of an eye for an eye leaves everybody blind. It is immoral because it seeks to humiliate the opponent rather than win his understanding; it seeks to annihilate rather than to convert. Violence is immoral because it thrives on hatred rather than love. It destroys community and makes brotherhood impossible. It leaves society in monologue rather than dialogue. Violence ends by defeating itself. It creates bitterness in the survivors and brutality in the destroyers. A voice echoes through time saying to every potential Peter, "Put up your sword." History is cluttered with the wreckage of nations that failed to follow this command.

6   If the American Negro and other victims of oppression succumb to the temptation of using violence in the struggle for freedom, future generations will be the recipients of a desolate night of bitterness, and our chief legacy to them will be an endless reign of meaningless chaos. Violence is not the way.

7   The third way open to oppressed people in their quest for freedom is the way of nonviolent resistance. Like the synthesis in Hegelian philosophy, the principle of nonviolent resistance seeks to reconcile the truths of two opposites, acquiescence and violence, while avoiding the extremes and immoralities of both. The nonviolent resister agrees with the person who acquiesces that one should not be physically aggressive toward his opponent; but he balances the equation by agreeing with the person of violence that evil must be resisted. He avoids the nonresistance of the former and the violent resistance of the latter. With nonviolent resistance, no individual or group need submit to any wrong, nor need anyone resort to violence in order to right a wrong.

8   It seems to me that this is the method that must guide the actions of the Negro in the present crisis in race relations. Through nonviolent resistance the Negro will be able to rise to the noble height of opposing the unjust system while loving the perpetrators of the system. The Negro must work passionately and unrelentingly for full stature as a citizen, but he must not use inferior methods to gain it. He must never come to terms with falsehood, malice, hate, or destruction.

9   Nonviolent resistance makes it possible for the Negro to remain in the South and struggle for his rights. The Negro's problem will not be solved by running away. He cannot listen to the glib suggestion of those who would urge him to migrate en masse to other sections of the country. By grasping his great opportunity in the South he can make a lasting contribution to the moral strength of the nation and set a sublime example of courage for generations yet unborn.

10   By nonviolent resistance, the Negro can also enlist all men of good will in his struggle for equality. The problem is not a purely racial one, with Negroes set against whites. In the end, it is not a struggle between people at all, but a tension between justice and injustice. Nonviolent resistance is not aimed against oppressors but against oppression. Under its banner consciences, not racial groups, are enlisted.

For Further Thinking

1. Where is King's thesis statement? Comment on the effect of its location.
2. What pattern of organization has been used, and how are links to the thesis statement established?
3. How does King balance personal connection with research and knowledge about the topic?
4. King's recommendations suggest the philosophy of Mahatma (Great Soul) Gandhi (1869–1948) and the ideal of "passive civil resistance." What percentage of humanity do you think is liable to understand and act upon this philosophy? Does your answer have implications for social policy here and elsewhere? Explain.

Looking Back and Ahead

1. See Eugenia Gilbert's rhetorical analysis of King's essay in Chapter 17, "Rhetorical Analysis" (p. 186). Has the analysis helped you to a further understanding of King's essay? Explain why or why not.
2. Read "Murderous Martyrdom" by Karen Armstrong (p. 404). Would most Muslims be sympathetic to King's recommendations, according to the results of the surveys she cites? Why are some people unwilling to restrict themselves to peaceful protest? Is there a time when violence is necessary?

Michael Downey "Canada's 'Genocide,'" which originally appeared 26 April 1999 in *Maclean's* magazine, chronicles the Sixties Scoop adoptions in which thousands of Aboriginal children were removed from their biological homes and relocated into white families by the provincial authorities under a federally funded program. While the Canadian government has offered an official apology for the infamous abuses suffered in residential schools and dedicated funds toward healing strategies for individuals and communities, no such apology or action plan has been proffered to the children, families, and communities of the Sixties Scoop. Canada's First Nations people still experience disproportionately high rates of adoption.

Canada's "Genocide": Thousands Taken from Their Homes Need Help

1   Carla Williams was 4 when the authorities knocked on the door and took the terrified Manitoba native youngster away from her parents forever. It was 1968, and Williams was thrust into a white society where nobody spoke her native tongue. Three years of cultural confusion later, she was adopted by a family that then moved to Holland. There the young girl was permitted no contact with her grieving parents back in Canada. Subjected to emotional and sexual abuse, she had three babies by the age of 16—two of them, she says, by her adoptive father, and one was given up for adoption. Finally, after her descent into alcohol, drugs and prostitution, the Dutch government received an official request from Canada to have her returned. Williams left Amsterdam in 1989 at the age of 25, shouting, "I'm going home!" She arrived back in Canada too late to meet the parents she had barely known: after the removal of three of their children, her native mother and father committed suicide.

2   Williams, now a saleswoman in Winnipeg, has had considerable success in turning her life around. But a new study being prepared for release next week sheds light on a tragically disruptive program that saw thousands of young natives removed from their families for three decades starting in the 1950s. Children from native communities in British Columbia, Alberta and Ontario as well as Manitoba were routinely shipped to non-native foster homes or adoptive families far from their homes. Most of the 3,000 from Manitoba alone and many from the other provinces went to the United States, where placement agencies often received fees in the $15,000 to $20,000 range from the adoptive parents. One Manitoba judge has branded the child seizures "cultural genocide," and they do seem to fall well within the United Nations post–Second World War definition of genocide, which includes "forcibly transferring children of [one] group to another group."

3   Now, after almost a year of hearings, a report will be delivered this week to the funding body, a joint committee of aboriginal groups and a unique partnership of four Ontario government ministries. Prepared by an aboriginal social agency, Native Child and Family Services of Toronto, and Toronto-based consultants Stevenato and Associates and Janet Budgell, the report is expected to

examine the history of what authorities called the "apprehensions" of native children, which continued into the early 1980s. The practice is sometimes referred to as the Sixties Scoop because the numbers peaked during that decade.

4   The seizures were carried out by child welfare agencies that insisted they were acting in the children's best interest—simply moving them into a better environment than they were getting in their native parents' home. Forced apprehensions of native children in fact began up to five generations earlier with the creation of residential schools, which functioned more as alternative parenting institutions than educational facilities. Those strict boarding schools effectively incarcerated native children for 10 months of the year.

5   Unfortunately, many of the students returned from residential schools as distant, angry aliens, lacking emotional bonds with their own families. Having missed out on nurturing family environments, they were ill prepared to show affection or relate to their own children when they became parents—as most did at an early age. Then, in the 1950s and 1960s, the federal government delegated responsibility for First Nations health, welfare and educational services to the provinces, while retaining financial responsibility for natives. With guaranteed payments from Ottawa for each child apprehended, the number of First Nations children made wards of the state skyrocketed. In 1959, only one per cent of Canadian children in custody were native; a decade later the number had risen to 40 per cent, while aboriginals made up less than four per cent of the population.

6   Ultimately, it became clear that the seizures were doing terrible damage to uncounted numbers of young natives. "It was perhaps—perhaps—done with the best of intentions," says David Langtry, current assistant deputy minister of Manitoba's child and family services. "But once it became recognized that it was the wrong thing to do, changes were made to legislation." A process introduced in 1988, he says, assures that an aboriginal child removed from a family will be placed in a new home according to strict priorities, turning to a non-native placement only as a last resort.

7   As previous investigations in other provinces have shown, the Sixties Scoop adoptions were rarely successful and many ended with children committing suicide. The new Ontario report will undoubtedly refer to formal repatriation programs already in place in Manitoba and British Columbia—as well as Australia, where there was a similar seizure of aboriginals—with a view to helping others return to Canada, find their roots and locate their families. The study will also set the stage for new programs aimed at healing the collective native pain and perhaps, in time, the deep-rooted anger.

8   Individual stories of the Sixties Scoop paint a heart-wrenching picture. Sometimes, whole families of status and nonstatus Indian or Metis children were separated from each other, never to meet again. Names were changed, often several times. They were shipped thousands of kilometres from their people and denied contact with their parents, siblings or communities or information about their heritage or culture. Some were enslaved, abused and raped. And no Canadian body has ever officially taken responsibility, or apologized, for the policies.

9   *Maclean's* has learned that the new report will be soft on blame but frank about the extent of the tragedy still gripping native parents and plaguing the thousands of survivors who lost their names, language, families, childhood and, above all, their identities. It will seek faster access to adoption records to speed repatriation. However, Sylvia Maracle, a member of the committee of the umbrella group that funded the study, says repatriations are only a partial remedy. "We need to bring them back into the native circle," she says, "in a way that is comfortable for them." The decision to commission the study recognized the bitterness felt by all native people, says Maracle, who is Mohawk. "We are grieving," she says, "we are angry and we must do something to at least start the healing and in a holistic way."

10   Joan Muir would agree. "I was taken away from my family because my grandparents were alcoholics," says the Vancouver resident, now 33, "and placed with adoptive parents who were—as social workers had noted on my records prior to adoption—known alcoholics and racists." Muir says she was raised to be ashamed of her native status. "It just hit me a couple of years ago, that it's OK not to hide it anymore," she says. "Now that I'm away from my adoptive parents, I'm allowed to be native."

11   The report will also refer to the tragic story of Richard Cardinal, a northern Alberta Metis forcibly removed from his family at age 4. Over the next 13 years, he was placed in 28 homes and institutions. In one, he was beaten with a stick for wetting the bed. Another provided a bed just two feet wide in a flooded basement. One entire Christmas Day, while his adoptive family celebrated the holiday, Cardinal was kept outside in the cold, staring in. His suicide attempts began when he was 9. At his 16th foster home, aged 17, he nailed a board between two trees and hanged himself.

12   Toronto social worker Kenn Richard, a coauthor of the report, says it outlines the history of the seizures through the words of people who experienced them firsthand. But he feels strongly that the practice was only one part of a long history of wrongheaded and disastrous policies towards Canada's native population. "It's the legacy of child welfare in this country," says Richard, "that we have dysfunctional families and a deep anger among aboriginals."

13   In the late '70s, Manitoba's native leaders rebelled against the permanent loss of their children. "This was cultural genocide," concluded Manitoba family court Judge Edwin Kimelman, called on to investigate the seizures in 1982. "You took a child from his or her specific culture and you placed him into a foreign culture without any [counselling] assistance to the family which had the child. There's something drastically and basically wrong with that." That year, Manitoba banned out-of-province adoptions of native children and overhauled its child welfare system. Native child welfare authorities were established across Canada.

14   The task of repairing the damage is still under way. Lizabeth Hall, who grew up in a native family and now heads the B.C. repatriation program, was shocked at the loss of identity among those removed from their native community. "People have called and asked, 'Can you just tell me what kind of Indian I am?'" says Hall.

"It made me cry. I'd like Canadians to know what happened and why. Non-natives always 'justify' their protection of natives; they don't realize the racism in that."

15 At a 1992 B.C. government hearing into the Sixties Scoop seizures, a First Nations elder addressed Canada's history of "protecting" aboriginals. "For 30 years," said the elder, "generations of our children, the very future of our communities, have been taken away from us. Will they come home as our leaders, knowing the power and tradition of their people? Or will they come home broken and in pain, not knowing who they are, looking for the family that died of a broken heart?" Those are questions that new repatriation and education programs could help answer.

For Further Thinking

1. Is the title of this article apt? How does the use of the word "genocide" inform your expectations of the article? What effect do the quotation marks around the word "genocide" produce? Does "Canada's 'Genocide'" (the title and the article) suggest that the removal of Aboriginal children from Aboriginal homes during the second half of the twentieth century is a rare blight in Canada's history?

2. A few years ago in a Canadian newspaper, a young Aboriginal man wrote that he had been adopted by a white family that was kind and loving. He wanted to protest the popular idea—repugnant to him—that every adoption of an Aboriginal person by non-Aboriginals is genocide. In her one-woman play *Moonlodge*, Blackfoot writer-actor Margot Kane portrays with deep affection the Ukrainian woman who adopted her. Some adoptions occur with full consent of the biological parents who remain welcome to visit their child. Is there a danger of all adoption of Aboriginal children being painted with the same brush? From your own experience or from research, decide what you think about coming to generalized judgments on this question.

3. The second part of the title of this essay is "Thousands Taken from Their Homes Need Help." Downey looks toward future "programs aimed at healing the collective native pain." Have the adoptees received help in the years that have passed since this article was written? What sources would you use to do a follow-up on Downey's article?

Looking Back and Ahead

1. Richard Wagamese, author of "Lemon Pie with Muhammad Ali" (p. 359), was a child caught up in the Sixties Scoop. Although he acknowledges that he had to be removed from his biological home, he has said in *One Native Life* and elsewhere that at least some of the difficulty he experienced was as a result of the policy described by Judge Edwin Kimelman: "You took a child from his or her specific culture and you placed him into a foreign culture without any [counselling] assistance to the family which had the child." How does "Lemon Pie with Muhammad Ali" deal with these painful issues and yet achieve a sense of healing?

2. Read "Saskatchewan's Indian People—Five Generations" (p. 379). How does the timing of the "scoop" described in Downey's article tie in with the historical stages of Aboriginal experience reported by Pat Deiter-McArthur?

Part 4

THE HANDBOOK

INTRODUCTION

THE HANDBOOK covers the most common mechanical problems that arise in student writing. To be sure, it is simply a brief primer, reminder, and reference. You and your instructor will want to supplement this section with further exercises and examples. Our immediate goal is to introduce you to the principles and terminology that will help you understand an instructor's advice and identify grammatical functions. For ease of understanding, we have used the same terminology in the Rhetoric. With these condensed basics, you should begin to edit your own work more thoroughly and confidently.

The following three sections define principles that every writer works with daily.

1. Forms (Including Nine Parts of Speech)
2. Punctuation Terms
3. Fifteen Common Errors

We explain the terms and provide examples for each grammar principle. With a little attention to the rationale of these principles and terms, you should find them fairly easy to grasp. Remember, however, that almost everyone seems to feel embarrassed about his or her lack of knowledge on this subject, and therefore hesitates to ask questions. The most useful thing you can do after exploring your instructor's references to various terms in this handbook is to ask questions and clarify the principles.

Section 1

Forms

(Including Nine Parts of Speech)

Words are like actors: they have their own identities but they also play roles, and some words may change their function, their relationship to other words, and the sentence as a whole. Sometimes words change "parts" or "roles" without taking on any altered form whatsoever. Sometimes words add or lose endings and thereby change their ability to play different functions. The following types of words and players will be briefly defined and illustrated in this section: nouns, verbs, adjectives, adverbs, pronouns, phrases, clauses, modifiers, conjunctions, articles, subjects, predicates, objects, participles, gerunds, infinitives, prepositions, subject and object complements, comparatives and superlatives, and interjections.

1. NOUNS

Nouns are naming words. They name persons, places, things, and concepts. Often nouns end in the suffixes *–ence, –ance, –ism,* or *–ity.* Nouns may be made possessive by adding an apostrophe and usually *–s.*

Plural or Singular

Many nouns may be either *plural* (more than one thing indicated) or *singular* (one thing indicated).

> **Examples**   bands, band

In the case of *collective* nouns, a single unit (treated as a singular subject) contains more than one thing.

> **Example**   The <u>team</u> prepares for the big game.

Some other collective nouns are *union, group, tribe, family,* and *herd.*
Count nouns name things that can be counted and therefore expressed in singular or plural form.

> **Examples**   one woman, three women, 20 cities, six trees

Non-count nouns or *mass nouns* name things that cannot be counted and seldom have plural forms. These are often abstract nouns, grouped items, food and drink, or natural elements.

> **Examples**   hopelessness, traffic, flour, air

Articles (or Determiners) and Nouns

The article (also called a *determiner*) *a* is used before a singular count noun when your reader or you do not know its specific identity, and when no other noun marker, such as a possessive pronoun, precedes the noun. The article *the* (also a determiner) is used before a noun when your reader knows its specific identity, except for plural or non-count nouns meaning "in general" or "all" or proper nouns.

Examples   The shopkeeper spoke to <u>a</u> customer on the telephone.

Fires can result from <u>the</u> smallest of sparks.

Four Main Types of Nouns

Nouns can be classified as one of four types: *proper, common, concrete,* and *abstract.*

A) *Proper nouns*, unlike all other nouns, are indicated by an initial capital letter. These "capital letter" nouns are the names of people, places, and some things.

Examples   Katrina, Salmon Arm, Charter of Rights and Freedoms

B) *Common nouns* name general groups, places, people, or things.

Examples   vegetables, cities, witness, instrument

King Arthur was an early <u>king</u> of England.

C) *Concrete nouns* name things perceived by the five senses.

Examples   muffin, sandpaper, perfume, sky, thunder

D) *Abstract nouns* refer to intangible concepts or values (things not perceived by the five senses).

Examples   love, truth, indecisiveness, pity

There is some overlap between categories: persons and proper nouns (Lisa), places and proper nouns (Cape Breton), and concrete and abstract nouns (tomorrow).

2. VERBS

Verbs are action words (*jump, realize, write*). Verbs also express states of being (Peter Gabriel is here). A transitive verb is followed by an object that completes its meaning (They *found* the keys). Intransitive verbs do not require objects (We *listened*).

Verb Tense

Verbs have different tenses: present, past, future. Each one of these categories has subcategories. *Uninflected* verbs (the infinitive) are expressed this way: *to think, to feel, to understand.* In order to express the time of action (tense) as well as to connect with the subject, verbs take on various regular or irregular endings and, in some forms of tense, helping or auxiliary words. A helping or auxiliary word (*am, had, could, would have*, etc.) together with some form of the root verb creates a new verb tense. For example, *is* + *talking* creates *is talking* (present progressive tense).

Examples	I <u>think.</u>
	She <u>thinks.</u>
	I <u>thought.</u> [irregular verb form to express past tense]
	She <u>calls</u> the meeting to order. [regular verb ending]
	She <u>called</u> the meeting to order. [regular verb ending to express past tense]
Present tense	They <u>run.</u> [simple present—a conjugated verb expressing actions or conditions happening now]
	Helen <u>has decided to exercise</u> better judgment. [present perfect—actions or conditions that began in the past but continue in the present]
	Lisa <u>is rowing.</u> [present progressive—an auxiliary verb and participle expressing ongoing actions or conditions]
Past tense	Anthony <u>fell</u> on the sidewalk. [simple past—actions or conditions that occurred in the past]
	We <u>had left</u> the movie theatre before Melanie and Kirsten realized they had forgotten to call Mr. Salinger. [past perfect—actions or conditions that occurred in the past but were completed before some other past actions or conditions occurred.]
	The happy couple <u>was dancing</u> to swing music. [past progressive—ongoing actions or conditions that occurred in the past]
Future tense	Jim and Tammy <u>will sell</u> their Nashville house. [simple future—actions or conditions that have yet to occur]
	Cirque du Soleil <u>will have given</u> countless performances in Las Vegas over the next two years. [future perfect—current actions or conditions that will be completed by some definite time in the future]
	Batman and Robin <u>will be waiting</u> for the Riddler to send another clue by next week. [future progressive—actions or conditions that will occur in the future]

Verb Mood

The form a verb takes can also show (besides a time period) the **mood** of the verb: how the action is viewed by the speaker. The *indicative* mood states a fact or asks a question (e.g., *I am going to the lake. Are you coming to the reunion?*). Some grammar texts consider the asking of a question as a separate mood: the *interrogative*. The *imperative* mood expresses a command (e.g., *Submit your assignment by Wednesday.*). The *subjunctive* mood expresses doubt, wish, or conditionality (e.g., *I don't think you should* *go to the party. She wishes she were older. If she were 16, she could go. Her brother talks as if he were in charge of the house.*). For several decades, however, the convention of altering forms of the verb "to be" for subjunctive mood has been weakening (e.g., *I wish I was rich* is now often written instead of the more formal *I wish I were rich*).

Verb Voice

The form a verb takes can also indicate voice: whether the doer of the action is presented as the doer of the action (*active voice*) or simply implied (*passive voice*). *She filed the complaint* is written in the active voice, whereas *A complaint was filed* is in the passive voice. In the latter example, the noun "complaint" functions as the grammatical subject of the sentence, even though the real doer is she or someone else not named. Passive and active voice can operate in any time and tense (e.g., *She files the report. A report will be filed. A report will have been filed.*).

Transitive and Intransitive Verbs

Some verbs (*transitive*) require an object for a complete thought to be expressed (e.g., *She threw a strike.*). Other verbs (*intransitive*) do not require an object to express a complete thought (e.g., *She celebrated.*). Your dictionary uses the abbreviation "tr." to denote transitive verbs and "intr." to denote intransitive verbs. Some verbs may be transitive or intransitive, depending on how they are being used (e.g., *She celebrated her perfect game.*).

For more detailed information on verbs, see the appendixes at the end of this section, "Appendix A: Twelve Verb Tenses" (p. 466) and "Appendix B: Irregular Verbs" (p. 469).

3. ADJECTIVES

Adjectives modify nouns or pronouns. Adjectives tell the reader *what kind* and *what quantity*. Adjectives may be identified by various suffixes, including *–able, –ible, –ile, –ive, –ous, –ar, –ic, –ent, –ant,* and *–ful.*

Example   The <u>busy</u> accountant checked her <u>various</u> forms to determine which of the <u>five corporate</u> files needed <u>careful</u> review in the <u>busy</u> days <u>ahead</u>.

In the *positive, comparative,* and *superlative,* adjectives change.

Examples	**Positive**	**Comparative**	**Superlative**
	hot stove	hotter stove	hottest stove
	reasonable idea	more reasonable idea	most reasonable idea
	good student	better student	best student

Tip: Most academic and business writers use adjectives only sparingly to maintain a formal tone. Personal and creative writers of fiction and non-fiction may use adjectives more frequently to intensify expression and effects. Advertising overuses adjectives to the point of meaninglessness: "colossal blowout bonanza sale."

Tip: Adjectives created by the past participle form of a verb take an –ed ending.

Incorrect	She was bias.
Correct	She was biased.
Explanation	If you rely on how statements sound in conversation, you may not hear certain syllables being pronounced, or sometimes speakers leave off syllables that are meant to be used. We would not say, "The car was stole." We would say, "The car was stolen." *Stolen,* like *biased,* is the past participle of the verb functioning as an adjective.

4. ADVERBS

Adverbs modify verbs, adjectives, other adverbs, and entire clauses. Adverbs tell the reader *how.* Adverbs may be identified by the suffix *–ly,* though not all adverbs end in *–ly,* and not all words ending in *–ly* are adverbs.

Example   Unexpectedly, the musician resourcefully sampled some Sly and the Family Stone, subtly but insistently, in her new song in a very bold way.

Like adjectives, many adverbs change form from the *positive* degree to express the *comparative* and *superlative* degrees.

Example   intelligently, more intelligently, most intelligently

Tip: As with adjectives, adverbs should be used sparingly in formal writing (academic and business composition), but can appear more frequently in personal and creative writing.

5. PRONOUNS

Pronouns take the place of nouns. When the pronoun stands in for a noun, that noun is then called the *antecedent* or *referent.*

The eight categories of pronouns are personal, demonstrative, relative, reflexive, intensive, interrogative, indefinite, and reciprocal. We cover only personal and relative pronouns here.

Personal pronouns refer to specific persons or things. They agree in number and gender with the nouns they represent. Personal pronouns have three *cases,* including subjective and objective. *Case* refers to the inflectional form taken by pronouns (or the possessive form of nouns) to indicate their function in a group of words.

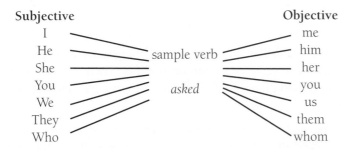

Pronoun case is determined by whether the pronoun functions as a subject or an object. Decide this according to the pronoun's relation to a verb or a preposition.

Examples
(verb)

subj verb   obj   infin   obj
<u>I</u> *asked* <u>them</u> *to visit* <u>her</u> at her new job.

subj   verb   obj
<u>They</u> *drove* <u>him</u> to Vancouver for ice cream.

Examples
(preposition)

prep obj
The sale of the car will be left up *to* <u>her</u>.

prep   obj
The study group consisted *of* Dionna, Xiu, and me.

The possessive case of pronouns occurs when the pronoun is used as an adjective (e.g., *her* dog, the dog is *hers*).

Relative pronouns (*who, which, whose, whom, that*) introduce adjective clauses. They refer to the noun or pronoun that the clause modifies.

Examples   The runner, <u>who</u> had an early burst, has dropped back in the last two kilometres.

The physics principle <u>that</u> we reviewed last week will be on the exam.

Tip: *That* and *which* differ because *that* introduces restrictive clauses, while *which* introduces non-restrictive clauses.

Example   The Clint Eastwood movie <u>that</u> needs more scholarly attention is 1971's *Dirty Harry.* This film, <u>which</u> is set in San Francisco, explores violence and urban alienation.

Some writers, however, occasionally use "which" with restrictive clauses.

(Please note that in the above example an apostrophe is used to indicate possession. The term "1971" is used as an adjective to describe the film; that is, *Dirty Harry* is a film *of* or *belonging to* 1971. Note, however, that the plural form to indicate an entire decade simply adds an "s" but no apostrophe: the 1970s. This is the same as adding an "s" to the singular word "book" in order to indicate additional "books.")

6. PHRASES

Phrases are groups of words that do not contain a conjugated verb and that function in some way as a unit to serve as a noun or modifier. There are various types of phrases, including gerund phrases, infinitive phrases, participial phrases, appositive phrases, and prepositional phrases.

As a noun	<u>Becoming a lifeguard</u> takes many hours in the pool. [This is a gerund phrase: the present participle here (verb ending in *–ing*) functions as a noun and, in this case, as the subject of the sentence.]
As a noun	<u>To err</u> is human. [This is an infinitive phrase, and the infinitive here functions as the sentence's subject.]
As a modifier	<u>Linked by prison handcuffs,</u> Sydney Poitier and Tony Curtis were fugitives in the film *The Defiant Ones*. [In this participial phrase, "linked" is the participle. Participial phrases always function as modifiers.]
As a modifier	Emily Brontë's novel, <u>known as *Wuthering Heights,*</u> was her only published novel. [This is an appositive phrase, which names the noun preceding it.]
As a modifier	The bowl <u>of fresh kiwi and grapes</u> looks refreshing. [This is a prepositional phrase, which modifies the noun "bowl" (a bowl of what?). A prepositional phrase begins with a preposition and ends with a noun or pronoun. The subject of the sentence is "bowl," not the prepositional phrase that modifies it.]

7. CLAUSES

A clause is a group of words containing a subject and a verb or predicate. There are two types of clauses: *independent* (which have subjects and predicates and can stand alone as sentences) and *dependent* (which have subjects and predicates but cannot stand alone as sentences). Dependent clauses function as adverbs, adjectives, or nouns.

Independent clause	subj verb A <u>cigar smells</u>. [subject + conjugated verb]
	The blues <u>singer,</u> an experienced Chicago musician, <u>looked</u> above the crowd while she performed a famous Lightning Hopkins song. [subject + conjugated verb]
Dependent clause	The teachers, <u>since they were undecided about the strike action,</u> asked for more information.

8. MODIFIERS

A modifier qualifies other words, providing extra information. Modifiers may be adjectives (*tall, inexpensive, startled*), adverbs (*very, quickly, tightly*), articles (*the, a*), phrases (*of the valley*), or clauses (*which frightens Uncle Jim*).

Example   Soaked in rain, the young postal worker walked steadily toward the tall building, which had been built in 1965.

Tip: Watch out for misplaced modifiers, which do not clearly refer to the words they seek to modify. You will produce meanings you do not intend!

Examples   Last year, Sigourney only smoked two packs of cigarettes. [Is that *all* she did all year? Or, more likely, did she smoke *only* two packs last year?]

Tasha presumed in Seattle that everyone liked playing Crazy Eights. [Did "Tasha presume *in Seattle*" or did she presume that "everyone *in Seattle*" liked this card game?]

9. CONJUNCTIONS

Conjunctions are joining words. They link words or word groups, expressing the relations between these elements. There are three types of conjunctions: coordinate, subordinate, and correlative.

A)   There are seven *coordinate conjunctions* (*for, and, nor, but, or, yet, so*). They can be remembered as the acronym "FANBOYS." These conjunctions may be used to combine two independent clauses into one sentence (known as a compound sentence). A comma falls before the coordinating conjunction, in order to clarify for the reader that a new clause is about to begin.

Examples   Moby is an interesting musician, but he is not as interesting as Miles Davis.

The gifted photographer Yousuf Karsh created portraits of many famous people, yet he did not photograph Pat Benatar or Barbara Carter.

B)   *Subordinate conjunctions* introduce dependent clauses and express relations between dependent clauses and independent clauses. The type of sentence represented by the following example (*independent clause + subordinating conjunction and subordinate clause*) is called a complex sentence.

Example   We didn't realize Elvis Presley was a truck driver before he became a recording artist, although we thought we knew a lot about him.

Some subordinate conjunctions are *after, although, as, because, before, even though, if, once, rather, than, since, that, though, unless, when, whenever, where, whereas,* and *while.*

C)   *Correlative conjunctions* appear as pairs of conjunctions that join word groups. Some correlative conjunctions include *both . . . and, either . . . or, neither . . . nor, not . . . but, not only . . . but also,* and *whether . . . or.*

Example   Both porpoises and chimpanzees are very intelligent creatures.

Tip: The words or word groups joined by correlative conjunctions must be grammatically parallel.

D) *Adverbial conjunctions* (or *conjunctive adverbs*) are used to add information (*furthermore, moreover, likewise*), provide contrast (*however, nevertheless*), show results (*consequently, therefore*), or show an alternative (*otherwise*). An adverbial conjunction may occur as a non-restrictive modifier set off by commas in the midst of a statement (*She is the smallest student in the school. She is, however, the fastest runner.*). These may also follow a semicolon in compound sentences that combine two independent clauses using a semicolon (*She is the smallest student in the school; however, she is the fastest runner.*).

Tip: When used following a semicolon to introduce a second independent clause, the adverbial conjunction is followed by a comma, indicating that it is an introductory element.

Tip: Grammarians of yore used to forbid starting a sentence with a coordinating or adverbial conjunction. Even when that rule was imposed (and some people still abide by it), accomplished writers "broke" it frequently. A better rule is to exercise stylistic discretion in when and why you start a sentence with either of these types of conjunctions.

10. ARTICLES (DETERMINERS)

An article is a modifier appearing before a noun, adjective, or adverb. The three articles are *a*, *an*, and *the*. *A* and *an* are general, while *the* is specific.

Examples <u>An</u> enzyme may be <u>the</u> source of this scientific mystery. [general (*an*) and specific (*the*)]

<u>The</u> old piano needs tuning. [specific]

Tip: *An* should appear before words beginning with vowel sounds or a silent "h." *A* should appear before words beginning with consonant sounds or a sounded "h" (<u>a</u> history lesson, <u>an</u> hour).

11. SUBJECTS

A subject is one of two main parts of a sentence, the other being the predicate. There are simple subjects, complete subjects, and compound subjects.

A) A *simple subject* is a noun or pronoun that performs an action or is acted upon.

Examples   The <u>movie</u> *was filmed* in black and white. [subject acted upon]

The <u>car</u> *turns* right on the red light. [subject performing action]

> **Tip:** To find the simple subject of a sentence when it is part of a noun phrase, imagine a line scoring out the preposition and the words following it (e.g., *The Night of the Long Knives was a nuisance to Pierre Trudeau.*). The noun phrase in this example is *Night of the Long Knives,* but the simple subject is *Night.* The preposition is *of.* See section 17 (p. 463) for more on prepositions. This point on how to recognize the simple subject as opposed to the complete subject is necessary, because the verb of the subject agrees with the simple subject only. One would not inflect the verb to agree in number with the nearest noun. It would be incorrect to write *The Night of the Long Knives were a nuisance to Pierre Trudeau.*

B)   A *complete subject* includes the simple subject and any words that modify it.

Example   <u>The tall mechanic with the beard</u> fixed the Volkswagen van.

C)   A *compound subject* consists of two (or more) simple subjects joined by a coordinate conjunction or correlative conjunction.

Example   <u>Alfred Hitchcock and Ridley Scott</u> have made interesting movies.

> **Tip:** In some sentence constructions, the subject may not appear at the beginning of your sentence, nor appear in subject-verb sequence.

Examples   Where *does* <u>Lionel</u> find all those novels? [question]

verb

Don't *call* Patricia! [command—"you" is implied subject]

verb

Here *are* some <u>Torontonians.</u> ["there" and "here" reverse subject-verb order to verb-object]

verb

It *is* a rainy <u>day.</u>

Writers sometimes use the expletives—also called *dummy words*—*there* or *it* combined with forms of the verb *to be* in order to control pace and emphasis in certain sentences. In the last example above, the actual subject *day* comes at the end of the sentence. Avoid expletives unless they seem the natural choice.

12. PREDICATES

A sentence consists of a subject and a predicate (which contains the verb). There are three types of predicate: *simple predicate* (which is the main verb), *complete predicate* (the main verb and its auxiliaries, including objects or complements and their modifiers), and *compound predicate* (two or more verbs that have the same subject and are linked by a coordinating conjunction or a correlative conjunction).

A) Simple predicate

   Example   The runner <u>stumbles</u>.

B) Complete predicate

   Example   Lydia <u>will have represented her client to the best of her limited ability</u>.

> **Tip:** In this example of a complete predicate, those words that indicate action, tense, and mood (*will have represented*) are followed by the direct object (*client, the word that is the answer to the question *Whom did she represent?*) and two adverbial modifying phrases (*to the best, of her limited ability*). Being able to subdivide complete predicates helps you to remain alert to specific functions within the combinations that a complete predicate may comprise.

C) Compound predicate

   Example   The Halifax driver <u>signalled a left turn</u>, <u>slowed the school bus</u>, and <u>turned on the flashing green traffic light</u>.

> **Tip:** The inflected form taken by verbs and auxiliaries in a predicate may express tense, mood, and voice. These matters are explained under Verbs (p. 453).

13. OBJECTS

There are two types of objects: *direct* and *indirect*.

A direct object (DO) is a word or word group that names the person or thing acted upon by the subject. A direct object can answer the questions *what?* or *whom?* about the verb.

   Examples   Lisa laced <u>her figure skates</u>.

   Russell Crowe pushed <u>another bar patron.</u>

An indirect object (IO) is a noun or pronoun that can answer the question *for whom? to whom? to what?* or *for what?* about the verb.

   Examples   Stephanie lent <u>her classmate</u> her notes.

   Marc sold <u>the highest bidder</u> his drum set.

14. PARTICIPLES

A participle is a verb form with either *–ing* or *–ed* on the end. Participles function as adjectives and appear as either *present* participles or *past* participles.

Examples   The <u>oncoming</u> ocean liner parted the cold waves. [present participle]

Now <u>stalled,</u> the car slowed the traffic on Sherbrooke Street. [past participle]

15. GERUNDS

A gerund is a verbal form that ends in *–ing* and functions as a noun. A gerund can be a subject or an object.

Subject   <u>Napping</u> is sometimes necessary.

Object   I love <u>swimming.</u>

> **Tip:** Gerunds appear in the same form as present participles, but present participles function as *adjectives*, while gerunds operate as *nouns*.

Examples   <u>Hoping for more peace</u>, the neighbour went on a <u>fishing</u> trip. [participle phrase and present participle (adjectives)]

<u>Fishing</u> takes more skill than bingo. [gerund (noun)]

16. INFINITIVES

An infinitive consists of the form of the verb preceded by "to" (*to* lift, *to* photograph, *to* kiss). We conjugate infinitives to derive specific verb forms (I lift, she photographs, they kiss).

Infinitives may function as subjects or objects of verbs.

Examples   <u>To dream</u> is courageous. [subject]

The cook wants <u>to relax.</u> [object]

The doctors hope <u>to find</u> the problem soon. [object]

> **Tip:** In efforts to treat English as Latin, grammarians of yore used to forbid the splitting of an infinitive (e.g., Don't say, *I am going to sweetly sing.* Say, *I am going to sing sweetly.*). The *Oxford English Dictionary* now recognizes that there are times when writers legitimately break this old rule.

17. PREPOSITIONS

Prepositions are connectors that express relationships between nouns or pronouns (or verbs or adjectives serving as nouns) and the other words in a sentence. They are primarily function words. Prepositions include the following words: *about, above, across, after, among, around, as, at, before, behind, below, beside, between, beyond, down, for, from, in, into, near, of, off, on, onto, over, toward, under,* and *within.*

A prepositional phrase begins with a preposition and ends with a noun or pronoun.

Examples   The agreement <u>between the accountants</u> has been signed.

The bowl <u>of fruit</u> sits on the kitchen table.

> **Tip:** Remember to make your verb agree with your simple subject (*bowl*), not any noun in the prepositional phrase.

<dl>
<dd>
<pre>
                           subj   prep phrase   verb
</pre>
</dd>
</dl>

Example   This *collection* <u>of fishing rods, old comic books, and toys</u> *has* sentimental value.

> **Tip:** In efforts to treat English as Latin, grammarians of yore used to forbid ending a sentence with a preposition (e.g., Do not say, *Whom are you singing to?* Say, *To whom are you singing?*). This rule still makes basic sense in that it recognizes the end of a sentence as an impact location. Why place a small connective word in a point of importance? A more useful rule for today, however, is that you should avoid ending sentences with a preposition except when it seems natural to do so.

> **Tip:** One of the trickiest aspects of English is mastering the correct preposition to use with various words in order to express one of two or more meanings that could be conveyed by that word.

Examples   Contending *with* rude customers is part of being a food server.

Contending *for* improved quality is part of the new manager's agenda.

This movie was adapted *from* the book.

The script was adapted *by* a new writer.

She has not yet adapted *to* life in Hollywood.

There are many prepositions and many different meanings conveyed by the same words if followed by different prepositions. Consult other, more comprehensive usage references if you have problems deciding which preposition expresses your intended meaning.

18. SUBJECT AND OBJECT COMPLEMENTS

A subject complement is a word or word group that follows a *linking verb* and identifies or describes the subject. Linking verbs are forms of being and include the verbs *be, seem, appear, stay, look, become, sound, taste, feel,* and *smell.*

<pre>
                        linking verb   subj compl
</pre>
Examples   This flower *smells* <u>like a mixture of talcum powder and fresh rain.</u>

<pre>
                        linking verb
</pre>
This milk *seems* sour.

An object complement is a word or word group that follows a *direct object* and identifies or describes that object.

Example The CBC reporter called the author's *work* <u>self-centred.</u>

19. COMPARATIVES AND SUPERLATIVES

Comparatives are forms of adjectives and adverbs that describe a relation between *two* items or concepts.

Example Irvine Welsh, who wrote *Trainspotting,* is a <u>better</u> writer than Jane Owen, who wrote *Camden Girls,* in describing the modern urban dance club in the United Kingdom.

A superlative is the form of an adjective or adverb that describes the relationship between *more* than two items or concepts.

Examples Muhammad Ali is still the <u>most</u> spiritual and influential of all heavyweight champion boxers.

Barbara Frum was the <u>best</u> of all CBC interviewers in the 1970s and 1980s.

> **Tip:** Usually, the comparative of one-syllable adjectives is formed by adding *–er* (small, smaller), while the superlative of many one-syllable adjectives can be formed by adding *–est* (kind, kindest). Adjectives with two or more syllables can often be handled by adding *more* for the comparative and *most* for the superlative (*more* frightening, *most* frightening).

> **Tip:** Be alert that there are many irregular comparatives and superlatives (little, less, least).

> **Tip:** In formal writing, try to include both parts of your comparison in your sentence. [not *Canada is the best* but *Canada is the best country <u>of those I have experienced</u>*]

20. INTERJECTIONS

Isolated words or phrases expressing emotion are interjections, and although they are not independent clauses, usually they are permitted to stand alone as complete utterances.

Examples *Alas*, poor Yorick! (*Hamlet* 5.1.171)

O, brave new world. . . . (*Tempest* 5.1.186)

Holy hole in a doughnut, Batman!

Appendix A
Twelve Verb Tenses

There are 12 verb tenses in English. The verb action can take place in the past, the present, or the future. There are usually word clues that indicate when the verb action occurs. Within each of these times there are four different situations.

1. *Simple tenses* occur at a particular point in time, or on a repeated or habitual basis.
2. A *progressive* or *continuous tense* indicates that the action takes place over time, and these tenses always use part of the verb "be" as the first part of the verb phrase and end with the main verb + *ing*.
3. A *perfect tense* indicates an action that ends before another action, always uses part of "have" as the first part of the verb phrase, and ends with the past participle of the main verb.
4. A *perfect progressive tense* indicates an action that happened over time and ends before another action. A perfect progressive tense starts with the relevant part of the verb "have" followed by "been" and ends with the main verb + *ing*.

If you remember these basic rules, you can always identify the verb tense being used, or use the verb tense you need without having to continually refer to a textbook or a table. Meanwhile, a chart like the one shown here can provide a quick and easy reference until you feel comfortable using the various verb tenses.

Also pay attention to the time clues in the following chart; while some of them can be used with more than one verb tense, they do restrict the number of possibilities and help you to understand which verb tense is being used, or which verb tense you should use.

Some examples:

simple past	yesterday
simple present	every day
simple future	tomorrow
past progressive	while
present progressive	now

Note: This appendix was prepared by Veronica Baig and is reprinted with the permission of Athabasca University.

Active Verb Tenses

	Past	Present	Future
Simple	*an action that ended at a point in the past*	*an action that exists, is usual, or is repeated*	*a plan for future action*
	cooked	**cook/cooks**	**will cook**
(time clue)*	He cooked yesterday.	He cooks dinner every Friday.	He will cook tomorrow.
Progressive be + main verb + ing	*an action was happening (past progressive) when another action happened (simple past)*	*an action that is happening now*	*an action that will be happening over time, in the future, when something else happens*
	was/were cooking	**am/is/are cooking**	**will be cooking**
(time clue)*	He was cooking when the phone rang.	He is cooking now.	He will be cooking when you come.
Perfect have + main verb	*an action that ended before another action or time in the past*	*an action occurring over time that started in the past and continues into the present*	*an action that will end before another action or time in the future*
	had cooked	**has/have cooked**	**will have cooked**
(time clue)*	He had cooked the dinner when the phone rang.	He has cooked many meals.	He will have cooked dinner by the time you come.
Perfect progressive have + be + main verb + ing	*an action that happened over time, in the past, before another time or action in the past*	*an action occurring over time that started in the past and continues into the present*	*an action occurring over time, in the future, before another action or time in the future*
	had been cooking	**has/have been cooking**	**will have been cooking**
(time clue)*	He had been cooking for a long time before he took lessons.	He has been cooking for over an hour.	He will have been cooking all day by the time she gets home.

*Time clues: These are words that give some information about when an action occurs. Many words are time clues; some can be used to indicate a number of tenses.

If you learn to recognize these time clues, you will find them very helpful. Note that some time clues can be used with more than one verb tense and also that this table is not a complete list of all the time clues that can be used with all of the tenses.

Time Clues and Verb Tenses

Simple	Simple past	Simple present	Simple future
	yesterday	every morning/day/etc.	tomorrow
	last year/month/etc.	always	tonight
	before	usually	next week/month/etc.
	for five weeks/days/etc.	frequently	soon
	one year/month ago	sometimes	in the future
Progressive	**Past progressive**	**Present progressive**	**Future progressive**
	while	now	when
	when	right now	after
		this week/minute/etc.	as soon as
			before
Perfect	**Past perfect**	**Present perfect**	**Future perfect**
	before	until now	by the time you go
	already	since	(somewhere)
	by the time	ever	by the time you do
	until then/last week/etc.	never	(something)
	after	many times/weeks/years/etc.	already
		for three hours/minutes/etc.	
Perfect progressive	**Past perfect progressive**	**Present perfect progressive**	**Future perfect progressive**
	before	for the past year/month/etc.	by the time
	for one week/hour/etc.	for the last two	for 10 days/weeks/etc.
	since	months/weeks/etc.	by
		up to now	
		for six weeks/hours/etc.	
		since	

Irregular Verbs

There are a number of irregular verbs in English; they are irregular in the simple past form and/or the past participle. Rather than learning each verb separately, you can put many of the verbs into a group of verbs that change their forms in similar ways. If you are in any doubt about a verb—about whether it is irregular or not, or about the exact form that an irregular verb takes—refer to your dictionary. Many dictionaries contain a supplement listing a large number of irregular verbs alphabetically; they all indicate in the main listing whether a verb is irregular and, if so, the form(s) it takes.

Group I Verbs

- The verb name, the simple past, and the past participle forms are all different.
- The past participle forms end in **n**.
- The vowel changes in the simple past and the past participle.

Note: V = vowel, C = consonant

	Change	Verb name		Simple past		Past participle
I A	$i \rightarrow a \rightarrow u$	begin	⟹	began	⟹	begun
I B	$o/a \rightarrow e$	blow	⟹	blew	⟹	blown
I C	double vowel $\rightarrow o$	break	⟹	broke	⟹	broken
I D	vowel $\rightarrow o$ (past)	drive	⟹	drove	⟹	driven
I E	$a \rightarrow oo$ (past)	take	⟹	took	⟹	taken

Group I Verbs

I A	I B	I C	I D	I E
i ➡ a ➡ u	*o/a ➡ e*	VV ➡ *o*	V ➡ *o* (past)	*a ➡ oo* (past)
begin	blow	bear	arise	forsake
drink	draw	break	drive	mistake
ring	grow	choose	ride*	shake
shrink	know	freeze	rise	take/undertake
sing	throw	speak	stride*	
sink		steal	tread*	
spring		swear	write*	
stink		tear		
swim		wear		
		weave		

*The spelling of these past participle are, respectively, "ridden," "stridden," "trodden," and "written."

Other Group I Verbs

Verb name		Simple past		Past participle
be	➡	was/were	➡	been
bite	➡	bit	➡	bitten
do	➡	did	➡	done
eat	➡	ate	➡	eaten
fall	➡	fell	➡	fallen
fly	➡	flew	➡	flown
get/forget	➡	got/forgot	➡	gotten/forgotten
give/forgive	➡	gave/forgave	➡	given/forgiven

(continued)

Other Group I Verbs (continued)

Verb name		Simple past		Past participle
go	⇒	went	⇒	gone
hide	⇒	hid	⇒	hidden
lie	⇒	lay	⇒	lain
see	⇒	saw	⇒	seen
swell	⇒	swelled	⇒	swollen
wake	⇒	woke	⇒	woken

Group II Verbs

The simple past and past participle forms are the same.

	Change	Verb name		Simple past/Past participle
II A	*ee/ea* ⇒ *e/ea** + d	feed	⇒	fed
II B	*e* ⇒ *o* + *ld*	sell	⇒	sold
	ay ⇒ *ai* + *d*	say	⇒	said
	i ⇒ *ou* + *nd*	find	⇒	found
II C	*ee/ea* ⇒ *e* + (C) + *t*	keep	⇒	kept
II D	*i/a* ⇒ *u* + (*n*) + *g/k*	sting	⇒	stung
II E	final *d* ⇒ *t*	send	⇒	sent

*Spelling may not change but vowel sound does change.

Group II Verbs

II A		II B			II C	II D	II E
ee/ea ➡ e/ea* + d		e ➡ o + ld	ay ➡ ai + d	i ➡ ou + nd	ee/ea ➡ e + (C) + t	i/a ➡ u + (n) + g/k	final d ➡ t
flee		sell	lay	bind	creep	cling	bend
bleed		tell	pay	find	feel	dig	
breed			say	grind	keep	fling	lend
feed				wind	kneel	hang**	send
hear					leave***	stick	spend
lead					meet	sting	
read*					sleep	strike	
speed					sweep	string	
					weep	swing	
						wring	

*Spelling may not change but vowel sound does change
**"Hang" means "to fasten or attach from above." In the other meaning of "hang," "to hang a person," it is a regular verb.
***Spelling changes, "leave" to "left."

Other Group II Verbs

Verb name	➡VV + ght	Past/Past participle*	Verb name	➡ d	Past/past participle	Verb name	➡o/u	Past/Past participle
bring	➡	brought	have	➡	had	shine	➡	shone
buy	➡	bought	hold	➡	held	spin	➡	spun
catch	➡	caught	make	➡	made	win	➡	won
fight	➡	fought	prove	➡	proved**			
seek	➡	sought	slide	➡	slid			
teach	➡	taught	stand	➡	stood			
think	➡	thought						

(continued)

Other Group II Verbs (continued)

Other Verbs		
deal	➡	dealt
light	➡	lit
lose	➡	lost
mean	➡	meant
shoot	➡	shot
sit	➡	sat

*Spelling is *au/ou* but pronunciation remains the same.
**"Proven" is also acceptable for the past participle.

Group III Verbs

The simple past is different from the other verb forms; the past participle is the same as the infinitive.

Verb name		Simple past		Past participle
become	➡	became	➡	become
come	➡	came	➡	come
run	➡	ran	➡	run

Group IV Verbs

The verb form stays the same in the infinitive, the simple past, and the past participle.

Verb name		Simple past		Past participle
bet	➡	bet	➡	bet

Other Group IV Verbs

bid	cut	let	set	split
burst	fit	put	shed	spread
cast	hit	quit	shut	thrust
cost	hurt	rid	slit	upset

Group V Verbs

The simple past is the same as the verb name; the past participle is different.

Verb name	Simple past	Past participle
beat	beat	beaten

THE
HANDBOOK

Section 2 Punctuation
Terms

There are few punctuation marks available to writers. However, by varying your patterns of punctuation, you can keep your writing fresh and vital.

The forms of punctuation are the period, comma, semicolon, colon, apostrophe, quotation marks, parentheses, dash, slash, brackets, ellipses, question mark, and exclamation mark.

1. PERIOD [.]

The period provides the full stop at the end of sentences. A period brings order to writing, letting readers know when your sentence has ended. Pico Iyer, a travel writer, refers to the period as the dot that brought the world of writing to its senses. Correct use of the period shows that you recognize independent clauses.

Examples   Wayne Gretzky works on behalf of several charities. He is still an energetic, enthusiastic person.

Office flirting, a delicate matter, raises professional and ethical questions. Consequences and power relations must be considered.

2. COMMA [,]

The comma has many uses and may be considered the all-around utility player of punctuation. Commas can simply *separate* elements in your writing, or commas can also *set off* elements in your writing.

A) Commas separate elements in a *list* (three or more items).

Examples   Pope John Paul II was the first pope to preach in a Lutheran church, visit England since before the time of King Henry VIII, address a Muslim audience of 80,000 people, re-establish diplomatic relations between Israel and the Vatican, and ask other religions and peoples to forgive the Catholic Church for its historical sins against them.

Pizza ingredients may include pepperoni, tomatoes, feta cheese, black olives, mushrooms, or onions.

> **Tip:** Some people place a comma before the *and* or *or* as the list draws to a close, and some people don't. Whether you do or not, be consistent through your paper or report.

However, there is sometimes a reason of clarity to use the comma before *and* or *or* in a list of items. Consider these:

Examples   The theatre conference featured well-known artists including Linda Griffiths, Ann-Marie MacDonald, and Mump and Smoot.

The theatre conference drew well-known artists including Linda Griffiths, Ann-Marie MacDonald, Tomson Highway, and Drew Hayden Taylor.

Explanation: Mump and Smoot are a team and therefore may be considered as a single entity, such as Laurel and Hardy or Gilbert and Sullivan. Highway and Taylor are individual artists, not a team. Placing the comma before the *and* allows the writer to clarify that the final item is not considered united with the one before it. Leaving out the comma clarifies that the last two items are considered part of one item in the list. This code will not work if you choose never to use the comma before the *and* or *or.*

B)   Commas separate *independent clauses* that are joined by *coordinate conjunctions (for, and, nor, but, or, yet, so)*. The comma is placed before the coordinate conjunction.

Examples   Some doctors and nutritionists claim vitamin supplements are necessary for a healthy diet, but other experts claim bottled vitamins enrich only manufacturers and urine.

Parenting deeply changes most people, so it is not surprising that watching children grow compels parents to grow as well.

C)   Commas separate *parts of dates and addresses.*

Examples   On March 10, 1978, a beagle named Barney ran away.

All fan mail for Donny Osmond for his Halifax and Toronto performances in *Joseph and the Amazing Technicolor Dreamcoat* may be sent to his Canadian agent at 2602 Agnes Street, Toronto ON M2A R9A.

Tip: No comma appears either before the provincial abbreviation or before postal code.

D)   Commas set off a sentence's introductory qualifier (whether word, phrase, or clause). The comma separates this introductory element from the independent (or main) clause to help the reader recognize these two parts of the sentence.

Examples   When the government clerk Igor Gouzenko defected from Russia to Canada in 1945, he brought with him 109 secret documents that revealed a highly developed spy ring operating effectively out of Canada.

Named the Gouzenko Affair, this unexpected international revelation forced Canada to confront Cold War espionage as both a global and a domestic activity.

E)   Commas set off *non-restrictive qualifiers.* These are qualifiers that add extra, but not essential, information to the sentence.

Examples   Herb Alpert and the Tijuana Brass, a world-famous horn band, recorded the songs "A Taste of Honey" and "Tijuana Taxi" in the late 1960s.

Retro fashions, which have somehow managed to compress the forties, fifties, sixties, seventies, and eighties into one strangely layered moment of expression, present beautiful opportunities of expression and discovery through comparison and contrast.

F) Commas also set off *transitional expressions, parenthetical expressions, direct address,* and *interrogatives.*

Examples   Dr. Schaeffer is, thirdly, a fine poet. [transitional]

He was, of course, overlooked. [parenthetical]

Daphne, it's my round for beer, isn't it? [direct address and interrogative]

> **Tip:** Watch out for mistaking *restrictive qualifiers* for non-restrictive qualifiers. You cannot remove a restrictive qualifier from a sentence without changing the meaning of the subject or noun being qualified.

Example   The car insurance that we discussed provides full coverage for our van.

3. SEMICOLON [;]

Semicolons join related independent clauses.

Examples   In some parts of South Korea, spicy dog soup remains a popular delicacy; this is mostly among the older generations.

David Bowie issued his own investment bonds several years ago; they were financially backed by the future royalties on his music.

Sometimes, a semicolon can be used to separate complex items in a list where each item in that list already features a comma or commas for qualification. This use of the comma is called internal qualification.

Example   The judges include Chief Justice Beverley McLachlin, who is from Pincher Creek, Alberta; Justice Claire L' Heureux-Dubé, who was the second woman to be appointed to the Supreme Court of Canada; and Justice Andrew MacKay, who used to be president of Dalhousie University in Halifax, Nova Scotia.

4. COLON [:]

A colon is used after an independent clause to introduce a list, clause, phrase, or single word. An independent clause must precede the full colon, however.

Examples   We worried about one thing all year: money.

The following cartoon characters will appear at the charity event: Tweety Bird, Sylvester the Cat, Space Ghost, Kamandi, Betty and Veronica, and Lex Luther.

Full colons are also used in memo headings, titles, bibliographical entries, and time notations.

Examples   The Vulnerable Self: State Power in Kafka's *The Trial* [essay title]

                 To: Jon Bon Jovi [memo]

                 From: Melanie Moustafa [memo]

5. APOSTROPHE [']

Apostrophes signal the possessive case and also act as substitutes for letters in contractions. There are two types of possessive case: the singular ('s) and the plural (s').

Examples   The carjacker's attempt was thwarted by a passerby. [singular possessive]

                 The two biology teachers' attempts to coach the volleyball team were welcomed. [plural possessive]

                 They don't charge HST here. [contraction]

Tip: Individual possession by two or more owners requires an apostrophe for each noun.

Example   Both Susan's and Nancy's parties went late into the night.

Tip: Joint possession requires one apostrophe.

Example   Sid and Nancy's party went late into the night.

Tip: Most style guides now recommend against an apostrophe to form the plural of numbers.

Incorrect   Grammar went out in the 1960's.

Correct   Grammar went out in the 1960s.

6. QUOTATION MARKS [" "]

Quotation marks are used for direct speech, textual quotations, and some titles (stories, newspaper articles and scholarly articles, songs, poems, speeches, chapters of books, radio programs). Sometimes quotation marks also set off certain words as ironic or as special terms.

Examples   Michael Ondaatje's poem "Letters and Other Worlds" examines emotional distances. [title]

                 Kofi Annan, the former United Nations secretary-general, said, "The use of child soldiers in Sierra Leone continues to concern all nations." [direct speech]

                 Faulkner wrote that "between grief and nothing, I'll take grief." [textual quotation]

> **Tip:** Quotations of more than four lines require block quotation format, which is indented from the left margin and requires no quotation marks.

> **Tip:** Punctuation with quotation marks can be a little tricky. Put semicolons and colons outside closing quotation marks. Put commas and periods inside your closing quotation marks, unless you include a line or page reference in parentheses after the quotation. With such a reference, place the punctuation after the closing parenthesis.

Examples   "Oh, don't deceive me," goes the old song.

Some deep-water divers experience "shallow water blackout"; that is, sudden unconsciousness in the final moments of ascent.

The "belief in life elsewhere in the universe is widely held" (173), according to Davis Marble and Mavis Darby in their article "Life Elsewhere."

7. PARENTHESES [( )]

Parentheses are rounded enclosing marks, sometimes mistakenly referred to as brackets (which are actually square and look like this: [ ]). Parentheses are sometimes used to enclose non-essential (non-restrictive) information.

Example   Britney Spears (whose website was once visited more than any other) championed virginity while taking sexually suggestive appearance to a new extreme.

Parentheses are also used to provide abbreviated terms for items.

Example   We attended the fourteenth annual Canadian Information Technology Security Symposium (CITSS).

Terms to be replaced by abbreviations should be used in full the first time they occur in a piece of writing, followed as above by the abbreviation in parentheses. Thereafter the short form is used.

8. DASH [−]

The dash is the Evel Knievel of punctuation marks—a freewheeling, daredevil, expressive stretch. The dash can substitute for many other punctuation marks, but should be used sparingly in formal writing. The dash can set off non-restrictive and parenthetical elements (as commas can); can introduce a list, phrase, clause, or single word (as a colon can); can join two independent clauses (as a semicolon can); and can signal an interruption (usually in creative writing).

Examples   The white T-shirt worn by itself—popularized initially by Marlon Brando and James Dean—has become widespread rather than a rebellious or anti-establishment statement. [setting off a non-restrictive]

Etiquette lessons can become quite detailed—when to bring a gift, when to write a thank-you card, how formal to be on a first date, what shoes are suitable for a wedding. [introducing a list]

The African famine continues—the G8 must take steps to avoid human catastrophe. [joining two independent clauses]

9. SLASH [/]

The slash or solidus is seldom used in formal writing. It usually separates lines of poetry and song lyrics in quotations, numbers in abbreviated dates, overlapping calendar years, and sometimes paired terms.

Examples   Be shrewd my eyes / Lest you shall reveal / The sadness of my nature / And the truth of what I feel. [separating lines of poetry]

Every voter should be familiar with his/her candidate's political beliefs. [paired terms: note that use of *his/her* is usually awkward]

10. BRACKETS [ ]

Brackets are not used often, but they are very important in research papers when you have to insert a word or phrase to help the quoted syntax; to identify people, events, or action; to make connections within quotations after you have omitted some elements for the sake of brevity; or to clarify references.

Examples   "When he [Peter Parker] says that he knows now that a radioactive spider gave him unusual powers, he realizes his life has changed forever."

"It [consumer culture] manipulatively forces children and youth to make identity choices based on commodities before developing a full sense of identity" (47), according to a recent report conducted at the University of Western Ontario.

You may occasionally see the Latin word *sic* enclosed in editorial brackets within a quotation.

Example   "She was always so tired that she would just lay [*sic*] on the couch all day."

The speaker has confused the verbs "to lie" and "to lay" (meaning to place an object). Correct usage would be "she would just lie on the couch all day." The inserted word *sic*, Latin for "thus," indicates that the quoted wording, though incorrect, remains faithful to the original source.

Brackets may occasionally also be used to enclose further parenthetical elements that occur within existing parentheses.

Example   She told him that her mother (a mysterious woman with complex motives [some of which were even now under investigation] and boundless energy) was returning from Europe that very evening.

Such awkward constructions are best avoided.

11. ELLIPSES [. . .]

When words are omitted from a quotation, three spaced ellipsis dots (referred to as *points*) express this change—this gap—in the original material.

Original   "Doctors and nutritionists have cited the influence of the long Canadian winter, a geographical aspect, as a major contributing factor in the steady depletion that amounts to a shortage of vitamin D in Canadians."

Revised with ellipses   "Doctors and nutritionists . . . cit[e] . . . the long Canadian winter . . . as a major contributing factor in the . . . shortage of vitamin D. . . ."

Tip: If an ellipsis occurs at the end of a sentence, the three spaced dots follow the period, as in the example above, amounting to four dots.

12. QUESTION MARK [?]

The question mark appears after a question.

Examples   Who disagrees that golf knickers are foolish?

Why wasn't Rachel the academic valedictorian?

Sometimes a declarative statement can seem like a question, but it isn't.

Example   The controversy focuses on whether or not Christina Aguilera is a responsible female role model.

13. EXCLAMATION MARK [!]

Exclamation marks or points supposedly emphasize strong expression. The problem, however, is that so many young writers are tempted to use exclamation points to emphasize almost anything (!!) that this punctuation mark has been rendered meaningless!

Example   Some doctors claim that drinking eight glasses of water a day may not be enough!

Tip: Keep exclamation points to a bare minimum and try to express strength or urgency through your language and your ideas.

Section 3   Fifteen Common
Errors

FIFTEEN COMMON ERRORS

Most usage errors in first-year essays fall into one of the following 15 common categories. Removing these 15 errors from your work will significantly improve your writing in all its forms.

We encourage your instructor to indicate occurrences of these errors in your writing by using the "CE" abbreviation and adding the pertinent number. CE 8 includes six sub-categories represented by the letters *a, b, c, d, e,* and *f.* When you find one of the common errors pointed out, first read the brief explanation of that error. Then, if necessary for clarification, refer to background terms and principles presented in Sections 1 and 2 of this Handbook. For example, the explanation of a comma splice refers to two independent clauses. Look in Section 1 for a definition of the terms *clause* and *independent clause.* The more familiar you become with Sections 1 and 2 of this Handbook, the more efficiently you will be able to find supporting explanations of terms used in the following discussions. We do not use terms simply for the sake of using them; in order to understand various basic principles, you need to know something about the following basic parts of speech and parts of the sentence: *noun, pronoun, subject, verb, clause, phrase,* and *modifier (adjective, adverb,* or *phrase behaving as an adjective or adverb).* Finally, keep asking questions until the principle is clear and you can begin to apply it in editing your work.

A Word about Spell-Checks and Grammar-Checks

You cannot rely totally on computer spell-checks or grammar-checks. They might be compared to an inflated inner tube for the young person who is learning to swim. Too much reliance on a tool that supposedly does the activity for you can prevent you from internalizing the skills you need to handle the activity on your own. That, in turn, reduces your thinking—and post-secondary education is all about thinking, isn't it?

1. SENTENCE FRAGMENT

A *sentence fragment* is a group of words that is not a sentence. At its minimum, every sentence must form an independent clause; that is, it must have a subject and a predicate.

Example   Marissa misunderstands.

With a subject ("Marissa") and a conjugated verb ("misunderstands"), we have an independent clause, a complete sentence. Although most sentences will contain more than just a subject and verb, these two elements represent the simplest form of sentence. A sentence fragment is mistakenly missing one or both of these two elements.

Sentence fragment (missing subject and verb)   Not for a while.

Corrected   The *bus* <u>will</u> not <u>stop</u> for a while.

Sentence fragment (missing subject)   Agrees, however, that some changes are necessary and should be made soon.

Corrected   *Jennifer* agrees, however, that some changes are necessary and should be made soon.

Sentence fragment (missing conjugated verb)   John, hoping for a better job in the accounting field in either Nova Scotia or Ontario.

Corrected   John *hopes* for a better job in the accounting field in either Nova Scotia or Ontario.

Sentence fragment (dependent clause)   Although U2 have often altered their musical style by introducing more futuristic technotronic sounds into some songs.

Corrected   U2 have often altered their musical style by introducing more futuristic technotronic sounds into some songs.

2. COMMA SPLICE AND FUSED SENTENCE

A comma splice is a frequent writing error committed by using a comma to join two independent clauses, "splicing" them together. The comma by itself is not considered a strong enough piece of punctuation to join or coordinate two independent clauses.

Comma splice   Cathy likes to read *People* magazine, Helen likes to read stock reports.

Corrected #1   *While* Cathy likes to read *People* magazine, Helen likes to read stock reports.

Corrected #2   Cathy likes to read *People* magazine, *but* Helen likes to read stock reports.

Tip: Here are the four most common ways to correct a comma splice:

1. Add one of the seven coordinate conjunctions (mnemonic device FANBOYS) after the comma joining the two independent clauses.
2. Keep the comma but change one of the independent clauses into a dependent clause.
3. Delete the comma and separate the independent clauses with a semicolon instead.
4. Delete the comma and use a period instead to make the two independent clauses into two sentences.

A fused (or run-on) sentence occurs when two or more grammatically complete thoughts follow one another with no punctuation. As the following example indicates, this problem may be thought of as the comma splice without the comma:

Fused sentence	Cathy likes to read *People* magazine Helen likes to read stock reports.
Corrected #1	*While* Cathy likes to read *People* magazine, Helen likes to read stock reports.
Corrected #2	Cathy likes to read *People* magazine, *but* Helen likes to read stock reports.
Corrected #3	Cathy likes to read *People* magazine; Helen likes to read stock reports.

3. SUBJECT-VERB AGREEMENT PROBLEM

In English, subjects and their verbs agree in number. If your subject is singular, then your verb form should be singular. If your subject is plural, then your verb form should be plural.

Subject-verb error	The lawyer for the nurses, doctors, technicians, and medical students involved in the series of medical errors are prepared to admit guilt on behalf of his clients.
Corrected	The *lawyer* for the nurses, doctors, technicians, and medical students involved in the series of medical errors <u>is</u> prepared to admit guilt on behalf of his clients.
Subject-verb error	The long Canadian winter, including snowstorms, ice storms, short days, nearly Arctic temperatures, and unpredictable wind chills, require great endurance and patience.
Corrected	The long Canadian *winter* . . . <u>requires</u> great endurance and patience.

Tip: Watch out for collective nouns that function grammatically as singular nouns but represent more than one person or unit (e.g., *government*).

Subject-verb error	The group of electricians, welders, and carpenters vote tonight for a change in negotiations.
Corrected	The *group* of electricians, welders, and carpenters <u>votes</u> tonight for a change in negotiations.

Remember, since there is only *one* group here, "group" is a singular subject, although it may represent many people.

4. PRONOUN PROBLEMS—AGREEMENT, REFERENCE, OR UNWARRANTED SHIFT WITHIN PARAGRAPH

Pronouns need to *agree* in number and gender with the nouns they represent, sometimes called their referents or antecedents.

Incorrect pronoun	Since the candles are not on sale, it is too expensive.
Corrected	Since the <u>candles</u> are not on sale, *they* are too expensive.

"They," a plural pronoun, refers correctly in number to the plural noun "candles."
    The most typical pronoun-agreement error is misuse of *their.*

Incorrect pronoun	Everyone in the class used *their* textbook.
Corrected #1	All the students in the class used their textbook.
Corrected #2	Everyone in the class used *his or her* textbook.

> **Tip**: Indefinite pronouns such as *person, one, any, each, either, neither,* and words ending in *–one, –body,* and *–thing* require singular pronouns such as *she* or *he.* When possible, replace the indefinite singular pronoun with a plural noun, as illustrated above: *All the students* in the class, instead of *everyone.* This avoids the exclusionist choice (of using *he* rather than *she* or *she* rather than *he*) as well as the clumsy choice of *he or she.* Use of *their* with indefinite pronouns is beginning to be sanctioned, but many readers still object to it. You are best to avoid this usage in your academic writing.

Pronouns should also refer clearly to their intended referents so that a reader has no confusion over what that particular pronoun represents. If you have more than one choice, consider that pronoun unclear or sometimes even incorrect.

Unclear pronoun reference	The difference between these corporate and government deductions in the three financial reports, prepared by rival accounting firms, raises a troubling question about the senator's travel expenses and a possibly illegal discount. <u>This</u> is very suspicious. ["This" = ?]

You have several options in clarifying the unclear pronoun reference, "This," depending on your intended meaning.

Corrected #1	This <u>difference</u> is very suspicious.
Corrected #2	This <u>corporate and government discrepancy</u> is very suspicious.
Corrected #3	This <u>rivalry between accounting firms</u> is very suspicious.
Corrected #4	This <u>possible illegal discount</u> is very suspicious.

> **Tip:** "This" is a relative pronoun and may refer to a condition or state rather than specifically to a noun.

Example   It's raining today. This is good for the crops.

Unclear pronoun reference   Helen told Viola that *her* purse had gone missing.

Clarify whose purse has gone missing. Is it Helen's or Viola's? It is better to repeat words, if necessary, than to allow serious ambiguity caused by unclear pronoun reference.

Corrected   Helen told Viola that Viola's purse had gone missing.

Use "who," "whom," and "whose" when the referent/antecedent is human.

Example   I spoke to the man that took the tickets.

Corrected   I spoke to the man who took the tickets.

Some grammar-checks mistakenly recommend *that* instead of *who* when the antecedent is human. Don't rely on grammar-checks!

Finally, pronouns should not shift in person or number within a paragraph, except for justified reasons. Such changes tend to disrupt tone (using *I* and *you* is more informal than using the third person) and perspective (are we looking at the matter from a first-person viewpoint, a third-person viewpoint?). In conversation, speakers typically use "you" or "they" to mean *everyone, people,* and so on. In writing, more care and consistency are needed. See "Watch Your Point of View: Avoid *Confusing* Shift in Person," in Chapter 4 (p. 35).

5. DANGLING PARTICIPLE

Dangling participles do not match the subjects or nouns they intend to qualify. A participle is a verb form ending in *–ing* or *–ed.* Participles and participle phrases modify nouns. When a participle or participle phrase appears at the beginning of a sentence, it functions as an introductory qualifier for the subject that should follow it directly.

Dangling participle   Skating hard, the open net loomed up ahead of the hockey player.

Corrected   Skating hard, *the hockey player* saw the open net loom up ahead.

Dangling participle   Flipping through the magazine, the recent articles on new bands seemed irrelevant to David Bowie.

Corrected   Flipping through the magazine, *David Bowie* thought the recent articles on new bands seemed irrelevant.

> **Tip:** Ask yourself who or what is performing or experiencing that participle and then check to see if an appropriate subject or noun directly follows the participle or participle phrase.

6. MISPLACED MODIFIER

Be alert to what your modifiers are qualifying. Be sure they modify what you intend to qualify rather than modifying any noun or concept haphazardly.

Misplaced modifier   The Diabetes Foundation, a quiet killer, needs donations for further research.

Corrected   The Diabetes Foundation needs donations to fight the disease, a quiet killer.

Misplaced modifier   If mowed regularly by highway crews, many more elk and deer might be visible from the Trans-Canada Highway through the field grass.

Corrected   Many more elk and deer might be visible from the Trans-Canada Highway if the field grass were mowed regularly.

7. PRONOUN CASE PROBLEMS

Case refers to the different forms that personal pronouns take to indicate their function in a group of words. Many people use the incorrect form of personal pronouns, especially when trying to sound formal. Personal pronouns have three cases: *subjective, objective,* and *possessive.* Problems usually arise, however, in deciding simply between the subjective and objective forms.

Determining whether the case of a personal pronoun should be subjective or objective depends on the pronoun's relation to either (a) the relevant verb or (b) the relevant preposition. The relevant verb determines whether the pronoun is a subject or an object, depending on how the pronoun functions with that verb. A subject pronoun takes the subjective form (*I, she, he, they*), while an object pronoun takes the objective form (*me, her, him, them*).

Pronoun Case with Verb

Examples   Ian asked Tim, Cliff, and *me* for some fitness advice.

Tracy Q. kissed Tina and *him* on their cheeks.

"Me" is the objective form of the pronoun because it is the object of the verb "asked" in the first example. "Tina and him" are the objects of the verb "kissed" in the second example, so "him" appears as an objective pronoun. Pronoun case with a preposition follows a simple rule: the objective form of pronoun follows any preposition unless that pronoun is simultaneously the subject of a verb.

Pronoun Case with Preposition

Example   Stephen left a lot of the research up <u>to</u> Ravi, Tasha, and *me*.

"Me" takes the objective form because it follows the preposition "to." Often, you have to deal with pronoun case in relation to both verbs and prepositions.

Example   *She* <u>told</u> *him* <u>to ask</u> *them* to leave the choice of gifts up <u>to</u> Steve Miller, Peter Frampton, and *me*.

"She" is the subject, performing the verb "told," and so appears in the subjective form of the pronoun. "Him" and "them" are objects of the verb "told" and of the infinitive "to ask," respectively, so appear as objective pronouns. "Me" appears as an objective pronoun because it follows the preposition "to" in a list.

> **Tip:** The objective form of a pronoun appears after a preposition, despite an intervening list.

An increasingly common error is the use of a reflexive pronoun in the objective case.

Example   The coach gave the award to myself.

Corrected   The coach gave the award to me.

The reflexive form should be used to express an action done to oneself.

Example   He taught himself grammar.

The same form is also used as an *intensive* pronoun, simply to express emphasis.

Example   Although in favour of a clean-shaven look, the chief himself recognized that beards were not a sign of social rebellion.

The correct use of *who* or *whom* (forms of a relative pronoun) also causes confusion. The solution uses the same strategy as given above to decide between using *I* or *me, he* or *him, she* or *her, they* or *them*.

Example   She asked me to find out whom was coming to the reception.

Corrected   She asked me to find out who was coming to the reception.

Explanation   The pronoun stands in relation to the verb "was coming" as the subject of that verb. Therefore the subjective form *who* is correct.

Example   To who are you sending the invitations?

Corrected   To whom are you sending the invitations?

Explanation   The pronoun stands in relation to the preposition "to" as its object. The pronoun here is also the indirect object of the sentence (which stated another way is, *You* [subject of the sentence] *are sending the invitations to whom?*). Therefore, the objective form of the pronoun is required.

8. MISSING OR UNNECESSARY COMMA

Comma errors are common in first-year, undergraduate, graduate, and even profes-sional writing. Often, bad advice circulates regarding the comma; this misinformation amounts to the claim that one should insert a comma wherever you would pause to draw breath if you were speaking. This bad advice, which is sometimes called "rhetorical punctuation," will mislead you. It whimsically bases itself on fluctuating vocal patterns. For example, since people from New Jersey have speech rhythms that differ from those of people from Saskatchewan, you need to rely on defined, logical, and mechanical rules to sort out the proper locations of commas rather than on inconsistent chit-chat from around the globe.

There are some distinct grammatical rules for use of the comma:

A) Comma after introductory phrase or clause

Examples   Though she usually disagreed with Mike and Rebecca, Aimée finally conceded that Bryan Adams has an interesting voice.

Although beautiful, the long Canadian winter depletes our bodies of vitamin D.

B) Two commas to set off a non-restrictive qualifier

Examples   The loonie, our dollar, has gained strength against the U.S. dollar.

Tommy Hunter, a Canadian musician, is considered the quiet gentleman of country music.

C) Comma to separate initial independent clauses from subsequent dependent clauses

Examples   Legal decisions at the Appeal Court are seldom unanimous, partly be-cause judges represent opposing legal, social, and philosophical views.

Mr. Simpson now likes golf and bingo, although he still enjoys the *New York Times* and some of the quieter musicals.

D) Comma before a qualifying phrase

Examples   Vancouver residents receive the best health care, according to recent surveys.

Tanya always liked to listen to the sounds of the New Brunswick night, especially ocean waves, crickets, freight trains, and wind in thick grass.

E) Comma before a coordinating conjunction

Example   Tasha trekked 20 kilometres from the disaster site to the heights, but still she had the stamina to scale the bluff and to build a large signal fire.

F) No single comma between a subject and its verb

Example   Gertrude O'Grady enjoys Toronto.

Incorrect Example	Members of the control group representing the four territories involved in the study, were later interviewed individually.
Corrected #1	Members of the control group representing the four territories involved in the study were later interviewed individually.
Explanation	The writer reviewed the sentence and decided that surely a comma must be required after such a longish preamble. But the incorrect comma in this case creates a blockage, so to speak, between subject ("members") and verb ("were interviewed"). Remember that the basic English sentence structure is a direct movement from subject to verb. If anything of a parenthetical (nice-to-know but not essential) nature stands between the subject and verb, then a pause in flow is acknowledged by surrounding commas (e.g., *The members, who represented four regions, were later interviewed.*). In the example above, the words "of the control group representing the four territories" are all essential to defining the members in question. These words are therefore restrictive (see CE 15); that is, they must be there to clarify the subject. They may be thought of as a part of the subject (see the Handbook, Section 1, p. 461 for discussion of a "complete subject," i.e., the main subject and its qualifying terms).
	From the point of view of style, note that the example above is in the passive voice (discussed under CE 14). Using the active voice and perhaps breaking the information into two sentences would help avoid the sense of extending the sentence for too long without a pause.
Corrected #2	Members of the control group represented the four territories involved in the study. Following the first stage of the experiment, a researcher interviewed each control group member individually.

Two rules of thumb for mastering commas are (1) if in doubt, leave it out, and (2) remove doubt by learning the advice offered on page 491 (A–F). Also see "B" on page 477, in Section 2 of this Handbook.

9. MISUSED COLON OR SEMICOLON

These two pieces of punctuation are neither mystical nor inscrutable. The colon and semicolon are distinct units of punctuation and are governed by simple, definite rules.

The Colon

The colon allows several choices following it: that is to say, on the right side of the colon, you have options. However, the colon requires that an independent clause precede it: on its left side. The colon, sometimes called the full colon to distinguish it from the semicolon, can introduce a range of grammatical elements: a list, an independent or dependent clause, a phrase, or even a single word. Remember, however, that the colon must be preceded by an independent clause.

Incorrect use of colon	Some of the kind and interesting students from the SJHS Class of 2008 are: Tanya, Louise Mennier, Tzigane, Mike Moore, Peggy Grimmer, and Sue Logan.
Corrected #1	There are many kind and interesting students from the SJHS Class of 2008: Tanya, Louise Mennier, Tzigane, Mike Moore, Peggy Grimmer, and Sue Logan.
Corrected #2	Some kind and interesting students from the SJHS class of 2008 include the following: Tanya, Louise Mennier, Tzigane, Mike Moore, Peggy Grimmer, and Sue Logan.

Other uses of the colon include these options:

List	Many common household pets are quite small: poodles, cats, gold-fish, and iguanas.
Phrase or dependent clause	Montreal has long been considered the Paris of North America: a city that offers francophone style and the second-largest number of French speakers in the world.
Single word	Barbara teaches at one of Canada's best universities: Dalhousie.

The Semicolon

The semicolon joins independent clauses. The semicolon, however, is often misused as a comma (perhaps a comma with a hat). To use the semicolon correctly, you must be able to recognize an independent clause (a subject with conjugated verb).

Incorrect use of semicolon	Yellow golf pants are silly; especially for Mr. and Mrs. Almond.
Corrected	Yellow golf pants are silly; this is especially true for Mr. and Mrs. Almond.

10. TENSE PROBLEMS

Knowing when to use the various tenses in English can be a challenge; however, a number of tense errors occur simply because the writer is unfamiliar with the correct form of the verb called for in certain contexts.

Examples	Yesterday, he seen her skip class.
	That evening she come back from the rock concert with a big poster and new T-shirt.
	She was so tired today that she laid on the couch.

The correct form of the simple past of "see" is "saw," not "seen." "Seen" is a past participle, as in "She had seen the cougar in the ravine on several occasions before it was reported in the paper." In the second example, the correct word should be "came," the simple past of "come." The third example commits a common confusion between the verbs "to lie" and "to lay" (meaning to put down an object). The simple past of "lie" is "lay." The simple past of "lay" is "laid."

More detailed help with verb tenses is provided in the Handbook, Section 1, Appendix B, "Irregular Verbs" (p. 469).

> **Tip**: When summarizing and analyzing an essay or other form of writing, use present tense (sometimes called "literary" or "historical" present), even if the reading itself uses past tense and even if the work was written some time ago.

Example   In her essay "Canadians: What Do They Want?" Margaret Atwood suggests that many Canadians resent the United States.

11. MIXED CONSTRUCTION

Because English has alternative syntactical ways to express the same idea, writers sometimes find themselves stuck between two approaches.

Example   By endorsing the candidate at today's meeting means having to support him next month as well.

The writer has become caught between two possible statements:

Corrected #1   Endorsing the candidate at today's meeting means having to support him next month.

Corrected #2   By endorsing the candidate at today's meeting, you [or possibly "we"] will have to support him next month.

Mixed constructions often involve clauses joined incorrectly by coordinating and subordinating conjunctions or conjunctive adverbs.

Example   *Because* you are such a good writer, *so* you should begin to outline a book.

Corrected #1   You are such a good writer that you should outline a book.

Corrected #2   Because you are such a good writer, you should outline a book.

Corrected #3   You are a remarkably good writer, so you should outline a book.

Be careful not to use subordinate adverbial clauses as subject complements.

Example   Another difficult situation in Scrabble is *when* your opponent has a blank and an "S."

Corrected   Another difficult situation arises when your opponent has a blank and an "S."

Be careful not to use subordinate clauses beginning with "where" to describe conditions.

Example   Envy is *where* you wish you had someone else's possessions.

Explanation	Envy, a quality or state of being, is not a place, so the modifying word "where" (normally used to refer to places) is inappropriate. Similarly, envy is not a unit of time, so you should not use "when" in the above example.
Corrected	Envy involves wishing you had someone else's possessions or achievements.

12. PARALLEL STRUCTURE REQUIRED

Some sentence structures require a writer to complete—by making parallel—a grammatical structure that he or she has already begun earlier in the sentence. Parallelism requires this completion of a language pattern. This is really a matter of word order, which is also called *syntax*. Your sentence construction will be parallel if it expresses equivalent elements in equivalent syntactical divisions.

Be alert to the need for parallelism in sentence structures with the following:

A) lists
B) verbs
C) prepositions
D) a "not only . . . but also" construction
E) an "either . . . or" construction

A) Lists

Faulty parallelism	Canada has become famous for its defence of human rights, democratic health care, *for* the interspace Canadarm, and when SCTV produced all those good comedians.
Corrected	Canada has become famous *for its* human rights, health care, Canadarm, and SCTV comedians.

After "for its," the list now runs parallel to a series of nouns.

B) Verbs

Faulty parallelism	Recent biotechnology developments *have sparked* fierce health debates, consumer rights, outcries, and <u>have raised</u> general concern about "Frankenfoods" in everyone's grocery order.
Corrected	Recent biotechnological developments *have sparked* fierce health debates, consumer rights outcries, and general concern about "Frankenfoods" in everyone's grocery order.

By deleting "have raised," we make the sentence parallel as a list whose different items all hang on "have sparked" (have sparked a, b, and c).

C) Prepositions

Faulty parallelism	We asked for more popcorn, extra chocolates, and <u>for more</u> peanuts.
Corrected #1	We asked *for* more popcorn, chocolates, and peanuts.
Corrected #2	We asked *for* more popcorn, *for* extra chocolates, and *for* more peanuts.

Though both versions are grammatically parallel, #1 is more concise.

D) "Not only . . . but also" constructions

Faulty parallelism   John F. Kennedy cared *not only* for civil rights, *but also* cared about increased education.

Corrected #1   John F. Kennedy cared *not only* for civil rights *but also* for education.

Corrected #2   John F. Kennedy *not only* cared for civil rights *but also* advocated education.

Though both versions are parallel, #1 is more concise. In #1, "not only . . . but also . . ." are followed by nouns introduced by the same preposition. In #2, "not only . . . but also" are followed by the operative verbs.

E) "Either . . . or" constructions

Faulty parallelism   We either take the bus or a taxi.

Corrected #1   We *either* take the bus *or* call a taxi.

Corrected #2   We take *either* the bus *or* a taxi.

13. APOSTROPHE PROBLEMS

The apostrophe signals possession or contraction.

Possession

The possessive case signals that one noun possesses another. "The hat that belongs to Samantha" becomes "Samantha's hat." "The trouble in Denmark" is "Denmark's trouble."

There are two types of the possessive case: singular and plural. You can determine which one you require by asking yourself what number (how many) is or are *possessing*, not how many *are possessed*.

Singular possessive   The International Space Station's problems are serious.

Since there is only *one* space station here, you use the *singular* possessive case ('s).

Plural possessive   These various students' concerns are serious.

Since there is *more than one* student here ("various"), you would use the *plural* possessive case (s's or s').

> **Tip:** Watch out for collective nouns, which usually operate as singular nouns, though they refer to more than one person or thing.

Example   The committee's representatives asked for a meeting with the reporter.

Contraction

A contraction uses an apostrophe to note the omission of a character in a word. Do not confuse a contraction with the possessive case.

Example   The car wouldn't start this morning.

Do not use the apostrophe to express the plural of numbers or dates.

Example   Those who wish to get nine's, put up your hands.

Corrected   Those who wish to get *nines*, put up your hands.

Example   Neglect of grammar began with well-meaning ideas of the 1960's.

Corrected   Neglect of grammar began with well-meaning ideas of the *1960s*.

14. OVERUSE OF PASSIVE VOICE

"Voice" is conveyed partly by the form of the verb and its helpers (the predicate); however, be careful to distinguish between the concepts of tense (when a thing is taking place) and voice (whether the subject of the action is stated as the grammatical subject of the sentence). Passive voice can operate in any tense.

Examples   That bridge will be crossed by me when it is gotten to by me.

That bridge is crossed by me when it is gotten to by me.

That bridge was crossed by me when it was gotten to by me.

Passive voice adds unnecessary words and often results in awkward indirectness. Note that the person doing the action in the examples above is relegated to serving as the complement of the verb "will be crossed." It is even possible to express a complete sentence in the passive voice without including the doer of the action at all.

Example   That bridge will be crossed when it is gotten to.

Grammatically, this sentence is considered complete, because "bridge" functions as the subject. As you can see, passive voice tends to be wordy, indirect, and vague. Someone will cross the bridge, but who? In certain cases, you and your reader do not need to be concerned with the identity of the doer of the action; sometimes the passive voice is preferred as a way to deflect accountability. (Example: "A problem was introduced during the processing stage." The writer may well be attempting to cover up for the culprit: who caused the problem.) Sometimes the doers of the action are less important to the idea and purpose than what they have done or said ("Smoking is prohibited," "*Basic Instinct* will be shown at midnight"). For most occasions, however, active voice is the better choice: it gives more complete information and communicates energy.

Some handbooks and instructors consider all forms of "being" or "to be" to constitute passive voice, since a state of being may be thought of as inert.

Example   She was doubtful of her chances.

The same idea can be expressed more vigorously as "She doubted her chances." To constitute true passive voice as we are defining the concept, the above sentence would have to read, "Her chances were doubted [by her]." Regardless of the line between definitions, a good general rule is to make the *doer of the action* in any sentence you write the grammatical subject of your sentence—and when you can, try to add vigour by replacing verbs of being with more energetic alternatives.

15. CONFUSION OVER RESTRICTIVE AND NON-RESTRICTIVE QUALIFIERS

Some qualifiers require two commas to set them off from the rest of the sentence, while other qualifiers do not. Qualifiers that require commas are called non-essential or non-restrictive. They are not structurally necessary for the sentence in which they appear. Qualifiers that do not require commas are called restrictive and are essential for meaning in their sentences.

Restrictive   No commas, since qualifier is *essential* to meaning

Non-restrictive   Qualifier that is *not* essential to meaning

Two commas if appearing within a sentence

One comma if appearing at the beginning or end of a sentence

Example (non-restrictive)   Violence in the Middle East, an ongoing problem, has disrupted the lives of all citizens in the region.

The qualifier "an ongoing problem" is extra, not essential to this sentence. Since the sentence's grammatical structure and meaning can work without this qualifier, it is non-restrictive: this qualifier does not restrict the meaning of what it qualifies. By placing two commas around the qualifier, you show that it is non-restrictive.

> **Tip:** Often, students will forget the second comma, therefore forgetting to close off the non-restrictive qualifier from the rest of the sentence. If you open the qualifier, remember to close it: "Our Irish friend, Ulton, likes funk music."

Example (restrictive)   The Tragically Hip song "Cordelia" explores the attitude of a self-destructive man who takes the generous concern of others for granted.

Restrictive qualifiers are sometimes tricky. If you *cannot* "pop" the qualifier out of the sentence without changing or blocking the meaning of the sentence, then it is an essential or restrictive qualifier (and so requires no commas). In our example above, if you placed commas around "Cordelia," you would mistakenly turn it into a non-restrictive qualifier and just as mistakenly convey that it is optional, or non-essential, to the sentence's meaning. If "Cordelia" were not in the sentence as it is, what song would the sentence refer to? Since the Tragically Hip have several songs, the sentence's meaning would be unclear, so "Cordelia" is necessary, essential, and restrictive—and therefore appears without commas.

Example   People who live in glass houses should not throw rocks.

If you can "pop" the qualifier out of the sentence, then it is non-restrictive (or non-essential) and requires two framing commas. A non-restrictive qualifier provides extra, not essential information.

Example   Toronto and Vancouver, our largest cities, have high costs of living.

OTHER COMMON MISUSES FROM A–Z

If an instructor marks three short essays in one evening, chances are good that one of the following misused words or terms will appear at least once in the writing.

Incorrect   <u>Alot</u> of students say that grammar isn't important.

Correct
but informal   <u>A lot</u> of students say that grammar isn't important.

Correct in
scholarly writing Many students say that grammar isn't important.

Explanation   *A lot* is two words, generally considered to express a colloquial tone.

Incorrect   She tested her ankle and said that it was <u>alright</u>.

Correct   She tested her ankle and said that is was <u>all right</u>.

Explanation   According to most sources, the only accepted spelling is *all right*.

Incorrect   The counsellor divided the 20 cookies <u>between</u> the 10 camp

Correct   The counsellor divided the 20 cookies <u>among</u> the 10 ca

Explanation   *Among* is used for three or more parties; *between* i
                     parties.

Exception   If an idea of reciprocity is involved, betwee
                     was discussed between the three leaders.)

Incorrect   The candidate shook hands with

Correct   The candidate shook hands

Explanation   *Amount* refers to quanti
                     to countable items.

Incorrect   Don't forget t

Correct	Don't forget to <u>take</u> your coat to the picnic.
Explanation	*Bring* is used only for movement from a farther to a nearer location.
Incorrect	The instructor was cross because I had <u>sited</u> Wikipedia.
Correct	The instructor was cross because I had <u>cited</u> Wikipedia.
Explanation	*Site* is a noun meaning a particular place (*a camp site*).
Incorrect	As the crowd roared, the winger <u>come</u> out of nowhere and deflected the loose puck.
Correct	As the crowd roared, the winger <u>came</u> out of nowhere and deflected the loose puck.
Explanation	The verb form "come" is sometimes used in conversation as the simple past of "to come," but the standard simple past of the verb is "came."
Incorrect	He is the <u>craziest</u> of my two brothers.
Correct	He is the <u>crazier</u> of my two brothers.
Explanation	Adjectives may be changed to show degrees of quality or intensity. Three degrees occur (*big, bigger, biggest; interesting, more interesting, most interesting*). The first degree is called the positive form. Next is the comparative. The comparative (*crazier*) is used to compare two things, as in the case of two brothers. *Craziest*, the superlative form, is used to compare one of three or more things to the others.
	On a related note, in formal writing avoid using comparatives or superlatives in statements that do not explicitly provide the thing(s) being contrasted. [Not recommended: *By second term, I found English more helpful.* Better: *By second term, I found English more helpful than it had seemed at first,* or *By second term, I found English more helpful than my other courses.*] Completing your comparison explicitly ensures that the reader knows exactly what things are being contrasted. Sometimes the surrounding context of what you have just said or will say provides the needed clarity, but in formal writing, sentences containing comparatives usually need to state both sides of the comparison.
Incorrect	I'm tired of these <u>continuous</u> sales calls.
Correct	I'm tired of these <u>continual</u> sales calls.
Explanation	Unless the calls occur one immediately after the other, without a gap, the term should be *continual*, meaning *repeated*. *Continuous* means ongoing.
	Despite the problems I have been having, I plan to <u>continue on</u> with my studies.
	problems I have been having, I plan to <u>continue</u> with my

Explanation	The preposition is redundant, since the meaning of *continue* includes the concept of something ongoing.
Incorrect	My textbook this year is extremely <u>different than</u> the one we used last year.
Correct	My textbook this year is extremely <u>different from</u> the one we used last year.
Explanation	*Different than* is used only colloquially, and only when the object of the preposition (the following words) is a clause. [Formal: *The house looked different from what he had remembered.* Informal: *The house looked different than he had remembered it.*]
Incorrect	I am <u>dis</u>interested in grammar.
Correct	I am <u>un</u>interested in grammar.
Explanation	Being *disinterested* means being without bias. The two words are increasingly used interchangeably, but any blurring of separate distinctions needs to be questioned, because it causes a loss of precision and choice.
Incorrect	My essay was returned unmarked <u>due to</u> my lack of in-text citations.
Correct	My essay was returned unmarked <u>because of</u> my lack of in-text citations.
Explanation	Many editors dislike this use of *due to* as a preposition to mean *as a result of*. It would be acceptable to use *due to* when introducing a subject complement. (*My low mark was due to lack of citations.*)
Incorrect	The <u>affects of</u> stress seem to be hurting society more every year.
Correct	The <u>effects of</u> stress seem to be hurting society more every year.
Explanation	*Affects* is a verb meaning to influence or impact something: for example, "This problem *affects* the whole community." *Effects* is usually a noun (meaning results), though it can sometimes be used as a verb to mean cause: for example, "She hopes to *effect* a change in voter behaviour with her new campaign." In "Politics and the English Language" (http://mla.stanford.edu/Politics_&_English_language.pdf), George Orwell would call "effect a change" a "verbal false limb," because to effect a change simply means to change.
Incorrect	We hope to have <u>less</u> losses over the second half of the season.
Correct	We hope to have <u>fewer</u> losses over the second half of the season.
Explanation	*Less* refers to degrees, or values; *fewer* refers to numbers, to discrete items that can be counted.
Incorrect	The cat licked <u>it's</u> tail.
Correct	The cat licked <u>its</u> tail.
Explanation	*It's* is a contraction of "it is." The possessive pronoun for *it* is *its*.

Incorrect	These <u>kind</u> of errors should be corrected.
Correct	These <u>kinds</u> of errors should be corrected.
Explanation	Plural is preferred throughout the construction. If one error is referred to, then use singular throughout the construction (*This kind of error*).

Incorrect	<u>Hopefully</u>, we will lose less often in the second half of the season.
Correct	<u>We hope</u> to lose less often in the second half of the season.
Explanation	Used in the incorrect example, "hopefully" is meant to mean "we hope" or "it is hoped that." However, what it really says, grammatically, is "in a hopeful manner." This misuse may be considered akin to CE 5 and CE 6, because the modifier does not make the connection it is intended to. This error is also related to CE 1, in that the writer intends a fragment (one word) to express a complete thought. Many instructors and editors resist this informal usage.

Not recommended	She told me my essay had some problems <u>in terms of wordiness</u>.
Recommended	She told me my essay <u>was wordy</u>.
Explanation	We use the categories *not recommended* and *recommended* in this case because the concern is a matter of style rather than grammar. Expressions such as *in terms of, with respect to, with regard to,* and the like are almost always replaceable with more concise and more precise alternatives.

Incorrect	It was so hot yesterday that my dog <u>laid</u> on the floor all day.
Correct	It was so hot yesterday that my dog <u>lay</u> on the floor all day.
Explanation	*Lay* is the simple past form of "to lie." *Laid* is the simple past of "to lay," meaning to place (*She laid her books on the kitchen table.*). Consult your dictionary to clarify the correct verb forms between "to lie" and "to lay."

Incorrect	<u>Much</u> of these advances are the result of hard work.
Correct	<u>Many</u> of these advances are the result of hard work.
Explanation	The noun *advances* is countable, unlike a mass (like *sugar, ink,* or *honesty*), so the modifying term should be *many*. *Much* would be used for a noun that expresses a single amount rather than discrete units: for example, "*Much* of this essay seems plagiarized." Note that words defined by *much* take the singular form of the verb, while those defined by *many* take the plural form of the verb.

Incorrect	No one can write a better essay <u>then</u> I.
Correct	No one can write a better essay <u>than</u> I.
Explanation	The writer has confused the adverb *then* with the preposition *than*. This likely happened because some of us pronounce the word *than* as if it were the word *then*. In formal English, using the subjective form of the

pronoun (*I*) following the preposition is correct, because of the implied or elliptical verb that follows the pronoun (*No one can write a better essay than I* [*can*].). Informal English would likely use the objective form of the pronoun (*No one can write a better essay than me.*).

Incorrect	She said she had <u>to</u> many assignments to get done this week.
Correct	She said she had <u>too</u> many assignments to get done this week.
Explanation	The adverb *too,* meaning excessively, is not spelled *to* (which is the preposition) or *two* (which is the number).

Incorrect	My friend has a <u>very unique</u> ability to drink water and snort it out his nose.
Correct	My friend has a <u>unique</u> ability to drink water and snort it out his nose.
Explanation	A number of adjectives, such as *unique, perfect, ideal, absolute,* and *straight,* refer to qualities that do not vary in degree. They are absolutes. They are what they are, and cannot be more than that.

Incorrect	I <u>would of</u> told you that the dog ate my essay, but I forgot.
Correct	I <u>would have</u> told you that the dog ate my essay, but I forgot.
Explanation	Substituting the preposition *of* for the auxiliary *have* is non-standard.

Incorrect	A <u>women</u> called to ask if I would donate to the university.
Correct	A <u>woman</u> called to ask if I would donate to the university.
Explanation	*Woman* is the singular word to designate one female person; *women* is the plural form to designate two or more female persons. Perhaps this error has become ubiquitous because people are starting to pronounce *–an* syllables as if they were *–en* syllables.

USING NUMBERS

Different professions and disciplines represent numbers differently. Scientific and technical writing almost always represents numbers as numerals. (*There are 27.3 metres of electromagnetic activity stretching between our 5-metre observation post and the location of the reported outbreak of ectoplasm.*)

Non-technical writing, such as arts, humanities, and social sciences essays, usually represents numbers as written words. (*The thirty-year-old police sketch artist produced four slightly differing portraits of the alleged offender.*)

Use numerals (1, 2, 3, 4 . . .) in the following instances:

- numbers that cannot be spelled out in only one or two words (*Carolyn has more than 1350 different pictures of Diana, Princess of Wales.*)

- dates (*Duran Duran slightly altered their musically significant hairstyles on 5 May 1985.*)
- page, act, scene, and line numbers (*In Jolene Armstrong's most recent play,* Tear It Down in the Heatwave, *a minor crisis on the work site occurs in Act 2, Scene 3 when the sledgehammer spontaneously combusts.*)
- decimals, fractions, ratios, and percentages (*There is a 90% probability that ¾ of all Jon Bon Jovi concerts have a 3:1 female-to-male ratio.*)
- amounts of money (*Press baron Conrad Black was sentenced to 6.5 years and fined $125,000 after being found guilty of mail fraud and obstruction in Chicago in 2007.*)
- addresses (*The Canadian prime minister lives at 24 Sussex Drive in Ottawa, while Dr. Lisa Schaefer-Ausman lives at 25 Arlington Road in Camden, England.*)
- temperatures (*While the Edmonton, Alberta, heat record is still 36 degrees Celsius, in the summer of 2007, temperatures hit 31 degrees Celsius, forcing some wine aficionados to switch to ice-cold beer.*)

Use written words, however, to express numbers in the following instances:

- numbers that can be spelled out in only one or two words (*At least seventy million music fans watched the 2007 Live Earth Concerts, simultaneously staged around the world on all five continents and closing with all three members of The Police performing four songs, including "Walking on the Moon" with surprise guests Kanye West and John Mayer.*)
- numbers that begin a sentence (*Two hundred and fifty-eight optimistic young people recently auditioned for* Canadian Idol *in Halifax, Nova Scotia.*)

  Note: It is less awkward to rearrange your sentences so that a large number does not appear at the beginning (*In Halifax, Nova Scotia, 258 people believe they can sing.*).

- Round dollar or cent amounts of one or two words are usually spelled out (*forty cents, five dollars*).

Other Helpful Notes

- If using more than one number to modify a noun, spell out the first number or the shorter of the two numbers to avoid confusion (*Jesse James, the famous outlaw, stood in the hot noon sun as the deputies pointed 100 six-shooters at him from various windows, doorways, and rooftops.*).
- With days as dates, use ordinal numbers expressed as numerals (*July 2nd, Dec. 7th*). For dates without the years, the ordinal numbers may also be expressed in words when the year does not follow (*April second*).
- When using "o'clock" to express time, spell the number (*two o'clock*).

Some Correct Examples of Usage (Non-technical Writing)

Although Leiann thought the sushi cost only $1.50 a piece, it was much more, almost four dollars. Nonetheless, we ordered sixteen pieces to eat while we watched some of the second season of *The Sopranos* at 7:30 p.m. Leiann's good friend Jenna, who will meet us at eleven o'clock in front of the Sudbury Regional Library, built in 1952, always enjoys dancing later in the evening. Jenna once toured through twenty cities with the musical *Grease* and danced before audiences of three hundred people or more. At 11:15 p.m., our taxi, which cost twelve dollars, took us to a club that featured 1970s funk music. We decided that for Leiann's upcoming birthday, Dec. 12th, we would call into the local radio show at 640 FM to request two full hours of jazz, so that even if it's –20 degrees Celsius outside, it will be hot where we are dancing.

APA Rules for Numbers

These rules come from the *Publication Manual of the American Psychological Association,* Sixth Edition.

General Rule

The APA *Publication Manual* states, "The general rule governing APA Style on the use of numbers is to use figures to express numbers 10 and above and words to express numbers below 10" (111). Sections 4.31 to 4.33 of the Manual expand on this rule as well as giving exceptions and special usages.

Exceptions to the General Rule

- In the 2nd and 11th grades . . . the 2nd grade students
- 15 traits on each of four checklists [different categories of items that are not being compared]
- a 5-mg dose [immediately precedes a unit of measurement]
- multiplied by 5 [numbers that represent statistical or mathematical functions]
- in about three years [approximations of time]
- 1 hr 34 min [time]
- at 12:30 a.m. [time]
- January 10, 1952 [dates]
- the 2-year-old [ages]
- 7 participants and 7 subjects [but seven raters, six observers]
- scored 5 on a 7-point scale [scores and points on a scale]
- won $7 [sums of money]
- my essay was given a 6 [numerals as numerals]
- Chapter 5 [numbers that denote a specific place in a numbered series]

- Seventy-five percent of the sample was reviewed. [numbers that start sentences]
- one-fifth of the class [common fractions]
- the Twelve Apostles [universally accepted usage]
- 2 two-way interactions [back-to-back modifiers]
- Step 1 [not Step I—use Arabic numbers for routine seriation]
- 1,000,000 [commas between groups of three digits in most cases of figures of 1,000 or more]
- sevens and eights [plural]
- 10s and 20s [plural]
- 1950s [plural]

MLA Rules for Numbers

The *MLA Handbook for Writers of Research Papers,* Seventh Edition, says the following:

> If you are writing about literature or another subject that involves infrequent use of numbers, you may spell out numbers written in one or two words and represent other numbers by numerals . . . (81)

You would write *two thousand* but *2½.*

If, however, your paper calls for frequent use of numbers, then the guidelines are mostly the same as those for APA, but possibly with less use of abbreviations.

- Use numerals for all numbers that precede technical units of measure (*5 mL*).
- Use numerals for numbers that are presented together and that refer to similar things (*5 absences over 12 days in group 4; 6 absences over the same time in group 6*).
- Spell out numbers if they can be written in one or two words, if they do not precede units of measure, and if they are not presented with related figures. The following example comes from page 82 of the *MLA Handbook:* "In the ten years covered by the study, the number of participating institutions in the United States doubled, reaching 90, and membership in the six-state region rose from 4 to 15."
- Do not begin a sentence with a numeral.
- Use numerals with abbreviations and symbols (*6 lbs, 8 KB, 2"*).
- Use numerals in addresses (*4401 13th Avenue*).
- Use numerals in dates (*24 July 2007* or *July 24, 2007*).
- Use numerals in decimal fractions (*4.6*).
- Use numerals in page references (*page 7*).
- Express related numbers in the same style (*7 of the 340 delegates*).
- For large numbers, you may use a combination of numerals and words (*7.3 million*).

A Final Word: Use a Guide and Be Consistent

As this section has suggested, different professions and publications may observe somewhat differing rules governing when to use words or numerals for numbers, as well as when and how to abbreviate for technical units. For comprehensive, reliable guidance, you should refer to the pertinent style guide, whether it be the *MLA Handbook,* the *Publication Manual of the American Psychological Association,* the *Canadian Press Stylebook,* or some other reference produced by a publishing body (including in-house systems for internal readership). The rules and examples reproduced in *Acting on Words* will likely suffice for your first-year essays (especially for those in a non-numeric-based discipline). For advanced papers relying on statistics, however, you will need more guidelines than we can provide in this text.

The most important principle of all is this: be mindful of how you present numbers in various circumstances, and be consistent.

Literary Credits

Dr. Susan Aglukark, OC. "The Fear of the Unknown." From www.susanaglukark.com/blog (September 6, 2007). Reprinted by permission of the author.

Laura Allan, "Gambling: The Stakes Are What They Are." Student essay, 2010. Reprinted by permission of the author.

Karen Armstrong, Excerpt from *The Case for God*. Copyright © 2009 Karen Armstrong. Reprinted by permission of Knopf Canada.

Morris Berman, Excerpt from *DARK AGES AMERICA*. Copyright © 2006 by Morris Berman. Used by permission of W. W. Norton & Company, Inc.

Roch Carrier, "The Hockey Sweater." From *The Hockey Sweater and Other Stories* by Roch Carrier copyright © 1979 by House of Anansi Press. Reprinted with permission from House of Anansi Press.

Jerri Cook, "Confessions of the World's Worst Parent." From *Countryside & Small Stock Journal,* Vol. 93, No. 6 (Nov/Dec 2009), 90–91. Reprinted with permission of the publisher.

Robertson Davies, "The Pleasures of Love." First published in *Saturday Night Magazine,* December 23, 1962. Used by permission of the Estate of Robertson Davies.

Pat Deiter-McArthur, "Saskatchewan's Indian People—Five Generations." From *Writing the Circle: Native Women of Western Canada,* edited by Jeanne Perrault and Sylvia Vance (Edmonton: NeWest Press, 1990). Reprinted by permission.

Michael Downey, "Canada's 'Genocide': Thousands Taken from Their Homes Need Help." Reprinted with permission of the author.

Katherine Gibson, Excerpt from *Ted Harrison: Painting Paradise* (Crown Publications, Queen's Printer of British Columbia), 2009.

Dean Goodman, "Gambling: The New Baseball?" Reprinted by permission from a revised essay by Dean Goodman.

James Hansen, Excerpt from *Storms of My Grandchildren.* Copyright © 2009 James Hansen. Reprinted by permission of Bloomsbury USA.

Amanda Harrison, "Multiple Embryo Transfer: At What Cost?" Student essay, 2010. Reprinted by permission of the author.

James Hoggan and Richard Littlemore, Excerpt from *Climate Cover-Up*, published 2009 by Greystone Books, an imprint of D&M Publishers Inc. Reprinted with permission from the publisher.

Jane Jacobs, Excerpt from *Dark Age Ahead.* Copyright © 2004 Jane Jacobs. Reprinted by permission of Random House Canada.

Patty Kelly, "Enough already, it's time we decriminalize prostitution." From *LA Times* (13 March 2008). Reprinted by permission of the author.

Sheema Khan, "I Was a Teenage Hijabi Hockey Player." From *Of Hockey and Hijab: Reflections of a Canadian Muslim Woman.* © 2009 TSAR Publications. Reprinted by permission of the publisher.

Index